P9-DXR-378

ADVANCED DELPHI DEVELOPER'S GUIDE TO ADO

ALEX FEDOROV AND NATALIA ELMANOVA

Wordware Publishing, Inc.

Library of Congress Cataloging-in-Publication Data

Fedorov, Alex.
    Advanced Delphi developer's guide to ADO/ by Alex Fedorov and Natalia Elmanova.
      p. cm.
    Includes index.
    ISBN 1-55622-758-2 (pbk.)
    1. Computer software—Development. 2. Delphi (Computer file) I. Elmanova,
Natalia. II. Title.
    QA76.76.D47F42   2000
    005.75'8—dc21   00-033394
                                         CIP

© 2000, Wordware Publishing, Inc.

All Rights Reserved

2320 Los Rios Boulevard
Plano, Texas 75074

No part of this book may be reproduced in any form or by any means
without permission in writing from Wordware Publishing, Inc.

Printed in the United States of America

ISBN 1-55622-758-2

10 9 8 7 6 5 4 3 2

0005

Product names mentioned are used for identification purposes only and may be trademarks of their respective companies.

All inquiries for volume purchases of this book should be addressed to Wordware Publishing, Inc., at the above address. Telephone inquiries may be made by calling:

(972) 423-0090

Contents

Chapter 8
More Delphi ADO Components

Contents

About the Authors

Alex Fedorov

Alex Fedorov is an executive editor for *ComputerPress* magazine, a monthly software and hardware magazine, published in Moscow, Russia. During his work in magazine, Alex authored more that 200 articles on various programming topics, including Delphi programming, Internet programming, COM/OLE and other technologies. Alex was one of the co-authors of *Professional Active Server Pages 2.0* and *ASP 2.0 Programmer's Reference* published by Wrox, and has written several books published in Russian.

Alex holds a MS in systems engineering from the Moscow Institute of Electronic Machinery (MIEM).

Natalia Elmanova

Natalia Elmanova is an associated professor of the Sechenov's Moscow Medical Academy, and a freelance Delphi/C++ Builder programmer, trainer, and consultant. Natalia authored more that 50 articles on various programming topics, including Delphi/C++Builder programming, CASE tools, distributed computing, COM/OLE, and other technologies for the *ComputerPress* magazine, published in Moscow, Russia. Natalia was a speaker at the 10th Annual Inprise and borland.com Conference. She has also authored several books on programming technologies published in Russian.

Natalia holds a Ph. D. in physics and mathematics from the Moscow Engineering Physics Institute (MEPhI).

Acknowledgments

The authors would like to thank the following people, in no particular order, for their help during the work on this book:

Charlie Calvert at Borland, who has known us for a long time and who was the first to suggest that we should try to write a book for English-speaking readers. It was Charlie who pointed us to Wordware Publishing and helped us during the work on this book to get some insights on the current and even the future versions of Delphi. Thank you, Charlie; we owe you a lot.

Jim Hill at Wordware Publishing, who gave us a chance to write this book. A big thank you also to all the people at Wordware Publishing who proofread the manuscript and corrected our grammar and spelling errors.

Dan Miser who was our technical reviewer. He suggested a lot of improvements and corrections that really helped to make this book better. Dan also helped us to solve a couple of tough cases and provided us with several code solutions.

We also would like to thank the Delphi R&D people at Borland for such a wonderful product, as well as all of the people who asked the questions and provided the answers at `borland.delphi.database.ado` newsgroup—you gave us the idea to write a book about Delphi and ADO, and the topics discussed there indirectly influenced the contents of our book.

And last, we would like to thank our families for their support and patience during the writing of this book.

Foreword

This is a hardcore technical book full of the kind of information needed by serious database developers. Both Natalia and Alex are hard-working experts with the skills to deliver to the reader the fruits of their experience and insight.

Before this book came out, ADO development in Delphi was an area where there was a real scarcity of good information. Over the years, I've gotten any number of desperate sounding letters from developers who had a real need for information about ADO, ODBC, or OLE DB issues. "I've looked everywhere," they would say with a note of desperation, "and other than a few sparse articles on the web, there is nothing available!"

That was the way it was, but now everything has changed. Natalia and Alex take you through the entire process of developing ADO applications, starting with a conceptual overview, and then digging in, one layer at a time, to uncover all the esoteric technical details that we need to master before we can feel comfortable with this complex subject.

This is a book for people who are serious about databases. It is not always an easy book to read, but it is one that delivers on the promise given by its title. If you want deep, rich information on ADO databases, then you've come to the right place. The presentation is always logical and well thought out, and you can expect to find plenty of technical material of the kind needed by database professionals.

When reading through these chapters, I kept stumbling across routines that I wanted to add to my own database libraries. I was reading a pre-publication copy of the book in manuscript form, working with binary files. After a bit I decided to keep a copy of Delphi open in one Window and copy of the manuscript in another. That way it was easy to test routines that caught my eye. A quick cut and paste put them into my database archive of routines, and then a moment later I was testing them out. More often than not, I was thinking: "Excellent! I've always wanted a routine that does just exactly that!" You, of course, won't have the manuscript in binary form, but you do have the CD, and you can get quick access to all the routines that intrigued me.

Let me close this preface by saying a few words about Natalia and Alex. I first ran across Natalia when she submitted a database article to the Borland Advisory Board, which decides which speakers will come to the annual Borland conference. The members of the board are, if they'll forgive my saying so, a difficult group of people to impress. When at work for the board, they sit in a brightly lit room with no windows, going through a stack of four or five hundred papers or outlines for papers, and generally their reaction to the average submission is less than enthusiastic. They've seen it all, and it takes something exceptional to catch their eye.

In the midst of one of these exhausting afternoons, one of the brighter lights in the Delphi programming world raised his head from his pile of papers and said: "Hey, this one is really good. It's from some woman in Russia, and she really knows her stuff."

A few minutes later I was reading the paper on distributed computing, and then we all passed it around, commenting on its depth of detail, and orderly, well thought out presentation. Here was a real find, an expert on a difficult subject who knew all about the dark little nooks and crannies that trip up developers who are working on tough projects.

I had the honor of meeting both Natalia and Alex a few months later when I was giving a technical talk in Moscow. There is no more serious or enthusiastic Delphi community than the one in Moscow, and both Natalia and Alex were right at the heart of it. They both gave well-received and well-attended presentations at the conference, and they were courteous and helpful to everyone who needed their expertise.

This book provides the same level of expert guidance and never-say-die perseverance that I saw from Natalia and Alex when I was in Moscow. These two programmers know databases inside out, and they know Delphi from top to bottom. Take a ride with these experts as they show you how to become a master of ADO arcana! Here you can find all those impossible-to-discover details that you've been looking for since you first became intrigued by this powerful technology. Best of all, this information comes to you from two professionals who know and love the world's greatest programming environment: Borland Delphi!

Charles Calvert
Borland Developers Relations Manager

If you're getting ready to read this book, then you most likely know the difficulties of accessing databases from a development environment. Things have gotten easier over the years, but there is still a wealth of knowledge that you must accumulate in order to produce an efficient and well-written database application.

In the beginning, accessing databases required writing code to a native API that would tie your application to a specific database. Porting to another application would require extensive rework and recoding in order to make your application access a new database.

As a result, abstraction layers such as Microsoft's Open Database Connectivity (ODBC) and Borland's Borland Database Engine (BDE) became popular. By programming to this common data access layer, as opposed to coding directly to the API, a programmer could seamlessly switch from one database to another with little or no code rewriting required—at least in theory. ODBC has become an industry standard, and every major vendor has written an ODBC driver to allow communication to their database via ODBC. In addition, some independent companies have been created that provide highly optimized ODBC drivers for various databases.

Borland has integrated access to the BDE into their RAD development tools, like Delphi, to let programmers easily read and write to a database without having to write thousands of lines of code. While this solution is still preferable when accessing databases like Paradox and dBase, there were some problems in using the BDE. Namely, Borland took on the responsibility of writing the database drivers to access various databases. Historically, this has meant there would be a delay between the time a new version of a database was released, and when the features would be usable from the BDE. In addition, Borland has only provided database drivers for the more popular databases.

Microsoft finally introduced the Universal Data Access strategy to solve some of the problems that had plagued solutions such as ODBC and BDE. Namely, the ability to access both relational and non-relational datasources from a simplified API. OLE DB and ActiveX Data Objects (ADO) are the central pieces of this strategy. As we move forward in time, vendors will provide high performance OLE DB drivers to access their datasource, much as ODBC drivers were written earlier. In addition, the ability to use these datasources will be the same by accessing them through ADO. Lastly, ADO is designed to provide excellent scalability for applications such as web-based data servers.

This book will give you a solid foundation for using ADO with Delphi—both native ADO and ADOExpress. Not only is this book unique because it is the first such book of its kind, but it is also unique due to the quality and depth of coverage provided. The authors have done a commendable job of introducing the basics and following that up by providing examples to cement that knowledge. I hope your journey into using ADO with Delphi can be made more pleasant by reading this book.

Dan Miser
Co-founder, DistribuCon

Introduction

This book is about Delphi and ADO—the two topics that lead us to database programming in Microsoft Universal Data Access architecture using Microsoft ActiveX Objects for the family of Windows operating systems. It is not a secret that database development is one of the most interesting areas to all programmers, and that's why we have decided to write a book for the serious Delphi database programmers and developers that contains in-depth information of how to use ActiveX Data Objects and Extensions in Delphi applications.

Here we focus on practical aspects of using ADO in Delphi database applications, while providing a lot of reference materials and additional information that will help our readers to better understand the topics covered in the book. Besides the topics covered here, there is a comprehensive chapter dedicated to ADOExpress components, several chapters about ADO Extension libraries, as well as materials discussing building OLAP and multi-tier applications with ADO.

The Featured Chapters

Chapter 1: Data Access Basics

This chapter introduces the reader to Data Access Technologies. It covers the basic terms and concepts of data design and data access, the basics of relational model, normalization, and various database objects, and explains what database management systems (DBMS) are, what types of them are used now, and which data access mechanisms are used to work with them.

Chapter 2: Microsoft Data Access Components

The Microsoft Data Access Components (MDAC) is a set of key technologies that enable Universal Data Access. This chapter covers the role of Open Database Connectivity (ODBC), OLE DB, and Microsoft ActiveX Data Objects (ADO).

Chapter 3: Standard OLE DB Providers

To successfully create Delphi ADO applications, we need to understand the role the OLE DB providers play in the whole Microsoft data access architecture called

Universal Data Access. In this chapter, we will give you more details for every standard OLE DB provider available in MDAC, as well as show you where to get additional OLE DB providers, what tools can be used to build your own OLE DB providers, and, at the end of this chapter, we will create a Providers List (ProvList) utility, that will give us details on every provider installed on the computer.

Chapter 4: Delphi Database Architecture

The material presented in this chapter is necessary for those readers who are new to database programming. The ADO support implemented in Delphi 5 takes a lot from the basic Delphi data access architecture, bringing some features that are not available in the native ADO objects, and makes the ADO components more "BDE-compatible." That means that, in most cases, we can migrate from one data access technology (Borland Database Engine, BDE) to another (Microsoft ActiveX Data Objects, ADO). That's why, to fully understand the mechanisms that lay behind the Delphi ADO components, we need to understand the basics of Delphi data access architecture.

Chapter 5: The TADOConnection Component

In this chapter, we will start to look at the Delphi ADO components. Here we will meet the TADOConnection component that is the Delphi version of ADO Connection object. This component is used to connect to various ADO data sources. First, we will discuss the properties, methods and events of the TADOConnection component, and then we will give you several examples of how to use it.

Chapter 6: The TADOCommand Component

The topic of this chapter is the TADOCommand component that is the direct Delphi implementation of the ADO Command object. It is used in Delphi applications to provide an ability to execute commands, such as SQL Data Definition Language statements, or stored procedures that do not return results.

Chapter 7: The TADODataSet Component

In this chapter, we will introduce the TADODataSet component—the direct descendant of the TCustomADODataSet class that can be used to retrieve data from one or more tables in a data source, accessible through ADO. Using this component, we can get all data from the table, set some filters to retrieve only partial data that meets some criteria, perform SQL queries, run user-defined and system stored procedures, save record sets into a file, and load them from a file.

Chapter 8: More Delphi ADO Components

Here we will take a look at the three more TCustomADODataSet component descendants, that, contrary to the TADODataSet component, are used for more specific tasks. The TADOTable component can be used to extract data from a single table, the TADOQuery component is used to execute various SQL queries, and the TADOStoredProc component is the best suited one to run user-defined and system stored procedures.

Chapter 9: Introduction to Structured Query Language

In this chapter, we will take a look at the SQL language and learn its major features. Here we will learn the role of the SQL, its purpose and major statements, and will have several examples for the following operations on data: retrieving data, summarizing data, adding data, deleting data, updating the database, protecting data and creating a database.

Chapter 10: Working with Database Objects

Here we will give you more details on several database objects that may be found in databases. The objects covered in this chapter are stored procedures, views, and triggers. We will start with the views, then discuss the stored procedures, and will end this chapter with the general overview of triggers.

Chapter 11: Building Delphi ADO Applications

In this chapter, we will discuss several topics related to creation of Delphi database applications using ADO data sources. We will start with the TDataSource component and Delphi data aware controls that can be used to show, edit, and navigate data, and we will show how to use and customize grids, how to use components for editing a single field, and how to select which component is better to use to represent a particular field.

Then we will discuss how the descendants of TField object are used in applications. We will show how to create calculated and lookup fields using these objects. After that, we will show how to create and use nested datasets using Microsoft Data Shaping and the TDataSetField object.

Then, we will spend some time discussing data validation techniques and database error trapping in Delphi applications. And, at the end of this chapter, we will discuss how to edit and use data modules.

Chapter 12: Business Graphics with ADO

Here we will discuss the charting component that is used to add various charting capabilities and business graphics to our Delphi ADO applications—the TDBChart component.

We will start with the brief discussion of the TeeChart library itself, then move to the more detailed explanations of the TDBChart component and the objects it uses. Then we will talk about creating Delphi ADO applications that use charts, and provide you with examples of creating a simple pie chart, using several series, using the Gantt series and standard functions.

Chapter 13: Creating Reports with ADO Components

In this chapter, we will discuss how to create and use database reports with ADO components. We will cover the basics of QuickReport components usage and show how to create list, label, master-detail reports, as well as reports with calculated expressions, charts, memos, and images from BLOB fields in Microsoft databases.

We will also show how to save reports in files of different formats, and how to preview reports in custom preview windows.

Chapter 14: OLAP Basics

In this chapter, we will start to talk about using ADO for On-Line Analytical Processing (OLAP)—the data management techniques that are widely used in decision support systems and data warehousing. Here we will also discuss the two ways of implementing OLAP with ADO and Delphi. One way is to use client-side OLAP with the help of the Decision Cube components in Delphi VCL, while the other way is the server-side OLAP, based on the MS SQL Server 7.0 OLAP services.

Chapter 15: OLAP and ADO Multidimensional

The topic of this chapter is another way to create server-side OLAP applications. It is based on using ADO Multidimensional Extensions (ADO MD), that are Automation objects designed to retrieve OLAP cube metadata and related data. In this chapter, we will discuss these objects, and will show you how to use them in Delphi ADO applications.

Chapter 16: Using ADOX in Delphi Applications

In this chapter, we will look at the ADO Extensions for DDL and Security (ADOX) library, its object model and features, and give you some examples of how to use them. Note that all this functionality comes with a single installation file—MDAC_TYP.EXE, and available without requiring some extra installation.

Chapter 17: Working with JRO Objects

In this chapter, we will look at the last extension library available for ActiveX Data Objects—the Microsoft Jet and Replication Objects (JRO) library. The JRO library provides some features that are specific to the Microsoft Jet Database

Engine, and since then, its functionality is mostly applicable to the Microsoft Access databases.

Using the Microsoft Jet and Replication Objects library, you can add the following functionality to your applications: create database replicas and synchronize them, compact databases, set passwords on databases, set encryption on databases, write pending data changes to the database, and retrieve the most recent data from the database.

Chapter 18: Deploying Delphi ADO Applications

To create a Delphi ADO application that uses data from some data source and provides the ways to manipulate it, is only the first part of the job. The other part is to be able to successfully deploy this application to the user's computer. In this chapter, we will talk about how we can deploy Delphi ADO applications, what tools can be used for this, and what should be concerned.

Chapter 19: Introduction to Distributed Computing

Here we will start to discuss three-tiered database applications that are also called distributed applications. In this chapter, we will learn the fundamentals of distributed computing, and the general concepts of Windows DNA—Distributed interNet Applications that is the application development model for the Windows platform. We will also provide a brief description of some particular implementations of the Delphi ADO distributed applications and show how they comply with the Windows DNA concepts.

Chapter 20: Creating RDS-based Applications

This chapter will be devoted to one of these particular technologies—Remote Data Service (RDS) that comes as part of Microsoft Data Access Objects, and enable applications to access OLE DB providers, that are running on remote machines. With RDS, we can use remote business objects that can access databases available on computers where these objects are instantiated, and supply other applications with the results of querying them. Such business objects are called data access servers. These servers could send recordsets obtained from databases that are available for them, to the client applications, where they can be manipulated, edited and sent back. In this chapter, we will show how to create RDS applications that use standard business object, how to customize their behavior, and how to create and use custom business objects.

Chapter 21: Distributed MIDAS ADO Applications

This chapter is devoted to another technology used to create distributed applications—Borland Multi-tier Distributed Application Service Suite (MIDAS) that is a technology of creating data access servers and "thin" clients such as Automation servers and Automation controllers correspondingly, that exchanges data packets containing dataset data between each other. This technology is implemented in Delphi classes and components, and, also, in some separate services.

Chapter 22: ADO Applications and Microsoft Transaction Server

In this chapter, we have discussed creating transactional ADO applications with MTS. The principles of creating MTS objects and implementing in them distributed transactions that affect tables in several database servers of different types were studied. This chapter contains a set of examples of how to create different types of data access MTS objects using ADO data sources, including objects that implement distributed transactions affect Microsoft SQL Server and Oracle databases simultaneously.

Chapter 23: Using ADO 2.5

In this chapter, we will look at the future of ADO—the version 2.5 of ActiveX Data Objects that comes as integrated part of Windows 2000 operating system, and is available as a separate set of components to be used under Windows 9.x and Windows NT operating systems. Here we will briefly discuss what is really new in ADO 2.5, and then we will take a more detailed look at the new objects that appeared in the ADO object model, and will create several examples that show how we can use them in Delphi applications.

Appendix A: BDE to ADO Migration Issues

This appendix contains an overview of the most popular desktop and client/server database types from the point of view of data access mechanisms. Recommendations of which of these two technologies is preferable to use for different data sources are provided, along with some tips of how to replace some BDE features that have no direct analog in ADO (such as the TUpdateSQL and the TBatchMove components, as well as some BDE-specific properties of the TTable, TQuery and TStoredProc components).

Appendix B: ADO Express Quick Reference

This appendix contains a chart listing properties, methods, and events of all components that comes with Delphi ADO Express. This appendix can be found on the companion CD.

Appendix C: ADO, ADOX, ADOMD and JRO Constants

This appendix contains a chart listing constants used in ADO, ADOX, ADOMD, and JRO. This appendix can be found on the companion CD.

Appendix D: Data Types

This appendix contains a chart listing how ADO and OLE DB data types corresponds to the Delphi data types and the data type in Microsoft Access, Microsoft SQL Server, and Oracle databases. This appendix can be found on the companion CD.

Appendix E: Properties Collections

This appendix lists properties of the ADO Connection and Recordset objects—its purposes, read/write accessibility, data types, and whether they are implemented for Jet, ODBC, SQL Server, or Oracle OLE DB Providers. This appendix can be found on the companion CD.

Appendix F: Schema Information

This appendix contains a chart listing schemas used with the OpenSchema method of the TADOConnection component to extract various metadata from the connected data source. This appendix can be found on the companion CD.

Appendix G: Who is Who in MDAC

This appendix contains a chart listing the major components of MDAC, a brief description, and its location. This appendix can be found on the companion CD.

Appendix H: Web Resources

A set of Web links to additional resources that can be used to get more information on the topics covered in this book as well as to the products that can be used during Delphi ADO application development. This appendix can be found on the companion CD.

Appendix I: Glossary

This appendix contains a list of the most important terms that are used through-out the book. This appendix can be found on the companion CD.

The CD-ROM

The companion CD-ROM contains all of the source code from the book and appendixes B through I.

Please note that all connection strings used in the examples provided on the CD-ROM are tuned for the authors' computers and must be replaced with the connection strings that reflect the data sources on your computer or LAN. The best way to do so is to open the source code and to change the value of the ConnectionString property of the ADOConnection component or any other ADO Express component that has this property already set. In some examples, we have used hard-coded connection strings. In this case, you need to locate such a string in the source code and modify its contents manually.

All source code corrections, as well as errata, additional materials, and related information can be found on the book support site:

`http://d5ado.homepage.com`

Who This Book is For

This book is designed for Delphi programmers who are already familiar with Delphi, but are novices in using ADO. This book is not a replacement for manuals or help files but rather a supplement to them. The purpose of it is to help you solve problems that can arise when you develop Delphi ADO applications, as well as to acquaint you with a wide range of possibilities provided by Microsoft Universal Data Access technologies, that are beyond the help files and Delphi documentation.

DATA ACCESS BASICS

In this opening chapter, we will talk about data access technologies, and discuss the basic terms and concepts of data design and data access. We will cover the basics of the relational model, normalization, and various database objects. Then we will talk about what database management systems (DBMSs) are, what types are used today, and which data access mechanisms are used to work with them.

General Concepts of Relational Databases

In this section, we will start with the general concepts of relational databases and provide you with related terms and definitions. After that, we will give an overview of the Northwind database that will be used in most of the examples in this book and will talk about database normalization and its first three forms.

The Relational Model

Throughout this book, we will deal primarily with relational databases. Therefore, we need to explain in brief what relational databases are. If you are familiar with them, you can skip this section.

The relational model was introduced by database researcher Dr. E.F. Codd of IBM (see his classic work "A Relational Model of Data for Large Shared Data Banks," *CACM 13(6)*, 1970). The relational model provides a simple concept of logical data design, and represents data in the form of two-dimensional tables.

Therefore, a relational database is data storage containing a collection of two-dimensional tables. Tools for managing such storage are called *relational database management systems* (RDBMSs). Along with tables, RDBMSs can contain services, applications, utilities, and so on.

Any table in a relational database contains one or more *rows* (also called *records*) and *columns* (also called *fields*). Note that in this book, we will use both pairs of terms.

The columns of a table contain information about the table structure. The rows of a table represent occurrences of the facts (or documents, or things) represented by the table. A data value is stored at the intersection of a row and column.

Data in tables satisfies the following principles:

- Each row-column entry in the table must have a single "atomic" value.
- Data values in a column are of the same type (for example, numeric, string, date, time, Binary Large Objects (BLOB), etc.), which can be selected from a list of possible data types. This list is specific for each DBMS, but there are several common types.
- Each record is unique; that is, no two records may have an identical set of values.
- Each field must be uniquely named.
- The sequence of fields is insignificant.
- The sequence of records is also insignificant.
- Therefore we can say that in relational tables, fields and records are not well ordered.

In spite of the fact that rows of tables are not well ordered, any DBMS provides service for ordering data in the way user desire. Columns can also be retrieved in any order and in various sequences. Since the sequence of columns is insignificant, columns must be referenced by their names, and these names must be unique within a table (but not in the database).

So far, we have learned that the relational database consists of one or more tables. Now we need to have a sample database containing several tables to illustrate several theoretical issues and to be able to provide some examples. In order to not have to re-invent the wheel, we will use a sample database that comes with Microsoft Access and Microsoft SQL Server. In the next section, we will provide a brief description of this sample database that we will use to create most examples in this book.

The Northwind Database

The database we will use throughout this book is the Northwind database that comes with Microsoft Access 97, Microsoft Access 2000, and Microsoft SQL Server 7.0. This sample database contains sales data for an imaginary company called Northwind Traders, which specializes in exporting and importing food from around the world.

The implementations of this database are slightly different for different DBMSs because of differences in these DBMSs themselves, but all of them contain similar tables with similar data.

To obtain one of these databases, you can install Microsoft SQL Server 7.0 with its sample databases and client software. Or you can use the evaluation version of Microsoft SQL Server 7.0 (it can be ordered on the Microsoft Web site), which is sufficient to build Delphi examples. If you have only one computer, you can install the Desktop Edition of Microsoft SQL Server. If you have Microsoft Office 2000, you can install Microsoft Access 2000 with the same sample databases.

If you are using Microsoft SQL Server, start its engine and run Microsoft SQL Server Enterprise Manager. You can use its tree to find a set of sample databases. Among them is the Northwind database that we will use.

If you are using Microsoft Access, open the Northwind sample database and select the Tables item from the Objects list; you will receive almost the same list of tables:

The Northwind database consists of eight tables with several columns in each. These are shown in the table below.

Table Name	Field List	Description
Customers	CustomerID CompanyName ContactName ContactTitle Address City Region PostalCode Country PhoneFax	Information about customers of Northwind Traders (company name, address, phone, fax, etc.)

Table Name	Field List	Description
Categories	CategoryID CategoryName Description Picture	List of product categories
Employees	EmployeeID LastName FirstName Title CourtesyTitle BirthDate HireDate Address City Region PostalCode Country Home PhoneExtension Photo Notes ReportsTo	Information about employees of Northwind Traders (name, address, title, to whom this employee reports, etc.)
Order Details	OrderID ProductID UnitPrice Quantity Discount	Information about ordered items (name of the product, ordered quantity, etc.)
Orders	OrderID CustomerID EmployeeID OrderDate RequiredDate Shipped Date ShipVia FreightShip NameShip AddressShip CityShip RegionShip PostalCodeShip Country	Information about orders (the customer, and when the order was received, shipped, and required)

Table Name	Field List	Description
Products	ProductID ProductName SupplierID CategoryID QuantityPerUnit UnitPrice UnitsInStock UnitsOnOrder ReorderLevel Discontinued	Information about products available to order (product category and name, supplier, unit price, quantity per unit, units in stock, units ordered, whether it is discontinued, etc.)
Shippers	ShipperID CompanyName Phone	List of companies responsible for shipping
Suppliers	SupplierID CompanyName ContactName Contact Title Address City Region PostalCode Country Phone Fax HomePage	List of product suppliers (company name, address, phone, fax, etc.)

Now that you have the sample database, we are able to illustrate how tables in databases can be related with each other. Now we will talk about relationships between tables.

Keys and Relationships

Let's look at the following "light version" of the Customers table in the Northwind database. Notice that we have removed several fields that are not significant in order to illustrate how tables are related.

CustomerID	CompanyName	City	Country
ALFKI	Alfreds Futterkiste	Berlin	Germany
ANATR	Ana Trujillo Emparedados y helados	México D.F.	Mexico
ANTON	Antonio Moreno Taquería	México D.F.	Mexico
AROUT	Around the Horn	London	UK
BERGS	Berglunds snabbköp	Luleå	Sweden
BLAUS	Blauer See Delikatessen	Mannheim	Germany
BLONP	Blondesddsl père et fils	Strasbourg	France
BOLID	Bólido Comidas preparadas	Madrid	Spain
BONAP	Bon app'	Marseille	France
BOTTM	Bottom-Dollar Markets	Tsawassen	Canada

CustomerID	CompanyName	City	Country
BSBEV	B's Beverages	London	UK
CACTU	Cactus Comidas para llevar	Buenos Aires	Argentina
CENTC	Centro comercial Moctezuma	México D.F.	Mexico
...	...	...	...

According to relational model principles, rows in a table are not well ordered. Thus, we need a column (or a set of columns) that uniquely identifies each row. Such a column (or set of columns) is called a primary key. The *primary key* of any table must contain unique, non-null values for each row. If a primary key consists of more than one column, we can say that this key is a *composite key*.

A typical database may contain more than one table and these tables can be linked. Let's look at the following simplified version of the Orders table:

OrderID	CustomerID	OrderDate	Freight	ShipAddress
10254	CHOPS	11.07.96	22.98	Hauptstr. 31
10259	CENTC	18.07.96	3.25	Sierras de Granada 9993
10265	BLONP	25.07.96	55.28	24, place Kléber
10278	BERGS	12.08.96	92.69	Berguvsvägen 8
10280	BERGS	14.08.96	8.98	Berguvsvägen 8
10289	BSBEV	26.08.96	22.77	Fauntleroy Circus
10290	COMMI	27.08.96	79.7	Av. dos Lusíadas, 23
10297	BLONP	04.09.96	5.74	24, place Kléber
10308	ANATR	18.09.96	1.61	Avda. de la Constitución 2222
10326	BOLID	10.10.96	77.92	C/ Araquil, 67
10331	BONAP	16.10.96	10.19	12, rue des Bouchers
10340	BONAP	29.10.96	166.31	12, rue des Bouchers
10355	AROUT	15.11.96	41.95	Brook Farm Stratford St. Mary
10360	BLONP	22.11.96	131.7	24, place Kléber
10362	BONAP	25.11.96	96.04	12, rue des Bouchers
10365	ANTON	27.11.96	22	Mataderos 2312
10370	CHOPS	03.12.96	1.17	Hauptstr. 31
10383	AROUT	16.12.96	34.24	Brook Farm Stratford St. Mary
10384	BERGS	16.12.96	168.64	Berguvsvägen 8
10389	BOTTM	20.12.96	47.42	23 Tsawassen Blvd.
10410	BOTTM	10.01.97	2.4	23 Tsawassen Blvd.
10411	BOTTM	10.01.97	23.65	23 Tsawassen Blvd.
10431	BOTTM	30.01.97	44.17	23 Tsawassen Blvd.
10435	CONSH	04.02.97	9.21	Berkeley Gardens 12 Brewery
10436	BLONP	05.02.97	156.66	24, place Kléber
...	...	...	...	...

In the CustomerID field of this table, we can see the identifier of the customer that placed an order. If we need to know the name of the company that placed the order, we need to look for the appropriate CustomerID value in the Customers table, and read the CompanyName value in the row found. In the case of the Orders table, such a column that indicates the linked record in another table is called a foreign key. This is shown below.

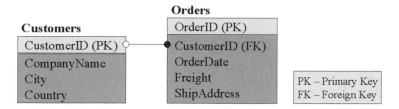

A *foreign key* is a column or a set of columns whose values are the same as the primary key of another table. Think of a foreign key as a copy of another table's primary key.

Such an association between two or more tables is called a relationship. A *relationship* is made between two tables by matching the values of the foreign key in one table with the values of the primary key in another. The table containing a foreign key is called a *detail table*, and the table containing the primary key that defines values in this foreign key is called the *master table*.

Now look again at the above figure. If any customer from the Customers table can place only one order, we can say that it is a *one-to-one relationship*. If any customer from the Customers table can place none, one, or many orders, we can say that it is a *one-to-many* (or *master-detail*) *relationship*. This type of relationship is the most common in databases. Along with one-to-many relationships, many-to-one relationships are also used. We could say that the Orders table is related to the Customers table in a *many-to-one* (or *lookup*) *relationship*.

It is also possible to have *many-to-many relationships*. For example, the Northwind database contains the Orders table and the Products table. Any one product can be contained in several orders, and any order can contain several products. Such a relationship must be resolved before creating physical database tables, however. In the case of the Northwind database, such a relationship is transferred to two one-to-many relationships by means of creating the OrderDetails table (in this case, it is called an *associative table*). Note that an associative table usually has a composite primary key (ProductID, OrderID), which consists of the primary key values of the Products table and Orders Table. Other fields of this associative table describe details of the particular product in the particular order (for example, how many units were ordered).

A group of linked tables is called a *database schema*. Information about their columns (such as the column name, length, and data type), primary and foreign keys, and other database objects (which will be discussed later in this chapter) is called *metadata*.

Any manipulation of data in databases (both relational or non-relational), such as inserting, deleting, updating, or retrieving data, or retrieving or changing metadata—for example, creating or deleting tables or adding and deleting fields—is called querying a database. Usually, queries can be formulated in terms of query languages that can be either standard or DBMS-specific.

We also need to say a few words about surrogate keys. A *surrogate key* is a unique identifier for a record within a database table. Every relational table has at least one surrogate key, and, in this case, it becomes the primary key for this table. If the table has more than one surrogate key, the primary key could be selected from these surrogate keys. All surrogate keys that have not become the primary key are called *alternate keys*.

Referential Integrity

We have already said that the primary key of any table must contain unique, non-null values for each row. This rule is one of the possible referential integrity rules. Some DBMSs can force this column value to be unique, but some cannot. If the uniqueness of the column is not controlled by the DBMS, it is possible that the primary key referential integrity can be violated. For example, if this column contains the same values in two different records, we could say that the primary key referential integrity is violated.

If two tables are linked by a master-detail relationship, the foreign key of the detail table must contain only values that already exist in the primary key value set of the master table. As in the previous case, some DBMSs can control this column value, but some cannot. If this column, existing in the set of primary key values of the master table, is not controlled by the DBMS, it is possible that the foreign key referential integrity can be violated. For example, if we delete a record from the Customers table that has at least one corresponding record in the Orders table, this results in the Orders table containing orders that no longer have a customer. In other words, the foreign key referential integrity is violated.

Most modern DBMSs are able to control their data following the referential integrity rules, provided the rules are described in the DBMS. To do this, such DBMSs use different database objects, discussed later in this chapter. Any attempts to violate these rules generate appropriate error messages or exceptions.

Introduction to Normalization

The process of data design consists of defining the metadata of the database in accordance with specific requirements and tasks of the information system. The details of how to provide system analysis and create entity-relationship diagrams and data models are out of the scope of this book. There are many other books where you can find such details of data design and useful recommendations (see, for example: Date, C.J. *An Introduction to Database Systems, 6th Ed.* Addison-Wesley Longman, Inc., 1995).

Here we will discuss only one of the basic principles of data design—data normalization, which allows us to avoid data redundancy and violation.

Normalization is a widely used data design technique. It can be defined as a process of reorganizing data by removing repeating groups of data and other data inconsistencies so that tables can be modified consistently and correctly.

The theory of normalization is based on the concepts of *normal forms*. We say that a table is in a particular normal form if it satisfies a certain set of requirements. In theory, we can use five normal forms, but in practice, only the first three are widely used. Moreover, the first two normal forms are intermediate steps to achieve the goal of having all tables in third normal form.

The First Normal Form

We will illustrate the process of normalization with the following example using data from the Northwind database. Assume we enter all ordered products in the following table:

OrderID	ProductID	CustomerID	Address	Quantity	OrderDate
10265	17	BLONP	24, place Kléber	30	07.25.96
10265	70	BLONP	24, place Kléber	20	07.25.96
10278	44	BERGS	Berguvsvägen 8	16	08.12.96
10278	59	BERGS	Berguvsvägen 8	15	08.12.96
10278	63	BERGS	Berguvsvägen 8	8	08.12.96
10278	73	BERGS	Berguvsvägen 8	25	08.12.96
10280	24	BERGS	Berguvsvägen 8	12	08.14.96
10280	55	BERGS	Berguvsvägen 8	20	08.14.96
10280	75	BERGS	Berguvsvägen 8	30	08.14.96
10289	3	BSBEV	Fauntleroy Circus	30	08.26.96
10289	64	BSBEV	Fauntleroy Circus	9	08.26.96
10297	39	BLONP	24, place Kléber	60	09.04.96
10297	72	BLONP	24, place Kléber	20	09.04.96
10308	69	ANATR	Avda. de la Constitución 22	1	09.18.96
10308	70	ANATR	Avda. de la Constitución 22	5	09.18.96
10326	4	BOLID	C/ Araquil, 67	24	10.10.96
10326	57	BOLID	C/ Araquil, 67	16	10.10.96
10326	75	BOLID	C/ Araquil, 67	50	10.10.96
10331	54	BONAP	12, rue des Bouchers	15	10.16.96

The figure at right shows the appropriate table structure.

Any relational table, by definition, is in the *first normal form*. Being in the first normal form means that all values of the columns are atomic, and all rows are different. Thus, the OrderedProducts table is in the first normal form.

OrderedProducts

OrderID (PK)
ProductID (PK)

CustomerID
Address
OrderDate
Quantity

PK – Primary Key
FK – Foreign Key

However, this table contains redundant data. As we can see from the figure above, information about the customer and the order date has to be repeated for every ordered product. Redundancy results in *update anomalies*, which are problems that arise when information is inserted, deleted, or updated. For example, the following anomalies could occur in the OrderedProducts table:

- The fact that a certain customer has a particular address cannot be added until this customer places at least one order.

- If a row is deleted, not only the information about the ordered product is deleted but also information about the order itself (the customer and when this order was placed).

- If a customer's address changes, then many rows must be updated with this new information.

Some of these anomalies can be solved by converting this table to the second normal form.

The Second Normal Form

To avoid some of the anomalies outlined above, we need to move our data model to the *second normal form*. A relational table is in the second normal form if it is in the first normal form and every non-key column is fully dependent upon the primary key.

The OrderedProducts table is in the first normal form but not in the second normal form, because the CustomerID, Address, and OrderDate columns are dependent upon the OrderID of the composite key (OrderID, ProductID).

The process for transforming the first normal form table to the second normal form is:

- Identify all determining columns (or sets of columns) that are parts of the composite key and the columns they determine.

- Create and name a new table for each determining column and the unique columns it determines.

- Move the determined columns from the original table to the newly created table. The determining column (or a set of columns) becomes the primary key of the new table.

- Delete the columns you just moved from the original table, except columns that will play the role of foreign keys.

Let's see how we can transfer the OrderedProducts table into second normal form. To do this, we move the CustomerID, Address, and OrderDate columns to a new table called OrdersInfo. The OrderID column becomes the primary key of this new table. The appropriate data diagram is shown here.

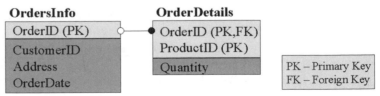

The results of transforming both tables are shown on the following page.

The OrdersInfo table

OrderID	CustomerID	Address	OrderDate
10265	BLONP	24, place Kléber	07.25.96
10278	BERGS	Berguvsvägen 8	08.12.96
10280	BERGS	Berguvsvägen 8	08.14.96
10289	BSBEV	Fauntleroy Circus	08.26.96
10297	BLONP	24, place Kléber	09.04.96
10308	ANATR	Avda. de la Constitución 2222	09.18.96
10326	BOLID	C/ Araquil, 67	10.10.96
10331	BONAP	12, rue des Bouchers	10.16.96

The OrderDetails table

OrderID	ProductID	Quantity
10265	17	30
10265	70	20
10278	44	16
10278	59	15
10278	63	8
10278	73	25
10280	24	12
10280	55	20
10280	75	30
10289	3	30
10289	64	9
10297	39	60
10297	72	20
10308	69	1
10308	70	5
10326	4	24
10326	57	16
10326	75	50
10331	54	15

As you can see, if we now delete a row from the OrderDetails table, this does not result in the deletion of the information about the order inself.

Tables that are in the second normal form but not in the third normal form still contain anomalies. In the case of the OrdersInfo table, they are:

- The fact that a certain customer has a particular address still cannot be added until this customer places at least one order.
- Deleting any row in the OrdersInfo table destroys all information about the customer.
- If a customer's address changes, then many rows must be updated with this new information (though less than in the previous case).

These anomalies can be removed by transferring this table to the third normal form.

The Third Normal Form

A relational table is in the *third normal form* if it is already in the second normal form and all non-key attributes are functionally dependent only upon the primary key.

The OrderDetails table is already in the third normal form. The non-key Quantity column is fully dependent upon the primary key (OrderID, ProductID). However, the OrdersInfo table is in the second normal form but not in the third normal form because it contains a dependency between the non-key columns. As we can see from the content of the OrderInfo table shown above, the Address column is dependent upon the CustomerID column.

In order to transform a table into the third normal form, we need to:

- Identify all determining columns (or sets of columns), other than the primary key, and the columns they determine.
- Create and name a new table for each determining column and the unique columns it determines.
- Move the determined columns from the original table to the new table. The determining column (or a set of columns) becomes the primary key of the new table.
- Delete the columns you just moved from the original table, except columns that will serve as foreign keys.

To transform the OrdersInfo table into the third normal form, we create a new table called Customers and move the CustomerID and Address fields into it. Then, the Address field is deleted from the original table, but the CustomerID field is left because it will serve as a foreign key. The appropriate data diagram is shown below.

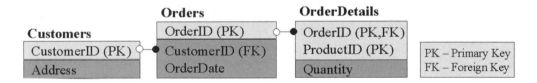

Thus, putting the original OrderedProducts table into the third normal form results in creating three tables—Customers, Orders, and OrderDetails.

The advantages to having relational tables in the third normal form is that it eliminates redundant data, resulting in saving space and reducing update anomalies. The improvements to our sample database after we have transferred it to the third normal form are:

- Information about the customer address can be added even if this customer has not placed an order.
- Information about ordered products can be deleted without destroying information about an order or a customer.

- Changing the address of a customer or a date of the order requires modifying only one row.

Orders table

OrderID	CustomerID	OrderDate
10265	BLONP	07.25.96
	10278	08.12.96
10280	BERGS	08.14.96
10289	BSBEV	08.26.96
10297	BLONP	09.04.96
10308	ANATR	09.18.96
10326	BOLID	10.10.96
10331	BONAP	10.16.96

Customers table

CustomerID	Address
ANATR	Avda. de la Constitución 2222
BERGS	Berguvsvägen 8
BLONP	24, place Kléber
BOLID	C/ Araquil, 67
BONAP	12, rue des Bouchers
BSBEV	Fauntleroy Circus

Implementing the Relational Model in Databases

Now we will see how the ideas of keys, relationships, and normalization are implemented in the Northwind database. If you look at the database diagram by selecting an appropriate item in the Microsoft SQL Server Enterprise Manager, you can see that all these tables are linked to others by master-detail relationships.

For instance, the Customers table is the master table for the Orders table. It contains the CustomerID primary key that is a foreign key for the Orders table.

Foreign key — Orders / Customers — Primary key

We can look at the properties of this relationship and see what keys are used to create it. To do so in Microsoft SQL Server, right-click on the relationship in the database schema and select the Properties item from the pop-up menu:

The Employees table illustrates how to store hierarchical data in relational tables. In this case, the master and detail tables are the same. The EmployeeID field is the primary key for this table, and the ReportsTo field is the foreign key referencing the EmployeeID field of the same table.

We can also see that this database is in the third normal form, as every non-key column fully depends upon the entire primary key (especially since all primary keys consist of a single column). Therefore, these tables are in the second normal form. In addition, all non-key attributes of all tables are functionally dependent only upon appropriate primary keys; thus, all tables are in the third normal form.

Designing Databases

How do you create tables and keys inside a database? There are different ways to accomplish this. Some DBMSs, including Microsoft Access and Microsoft SQL Server, contain tools for designing tables, their fields, keys, and relationships between them. The table designer of Microsoft SQL Server Enterprise Manager is shown below.

Column Name	Datatype	Length	Precision	Scale	Allow Nulls	Default Value	Identity	Identity Seed
CustomerID	nchar	5	0	0				
CompanyName	nvarchar	40	0	0				
ContactName	nvarchar	30	0	0	✓			
ContactTitle	nvarchar	30	0	0	✓			
Address	nvarchar	60	0	0	✓			
City	nvarchar	15	0	0	✓			
Region	nvarchar	15	0	0	✓			
PostalCode	nvarchar	10	0	0	✓			
Country	nvarchar	15	0	0	✓			
Phone	nvarchar	24	0	0	✓			
Fax	nvarchar	24	0	0	✓			

Another way to create tables, keys, and relationships is to write Data Definition Language script for creating them. This can be done either manually, if you are experienced enough in the SQL language, or with the help of some appropriate tools. This is discussed more thoroughly in Chapter 9.

A third way that has become very popular is to use computer-aided software engineering (CASE) tools. There are several types of CASE tools, but tools for creating entity-relationship (E/R) diagrams are the main instruments for database design.

With these tools we can design the logical model of the facts and objects, which will be registered in the new database. In logical data models, table prototypes are called *entities*, and field prototypes are called *attributes*. After defining attributes and relationships between entities, and providing the normalization of this model, the physical model for a specific DBMS is generated and can then be edited. At this step, all tables, fields, and other database objects are defined. After the physical model is finished, the database can be generated with all appropriate objects (or an appropriate Data Definition Language script to create them).

Discussing CASE tools in more detail is outside the scope of this book. If you are interested in using them, here is a list of the most popular CASE tools vendors:

CASE Tool	Vendor	Site
ERwin	Computer Associates	http://www.cai.com
System Architect	Popkin Software	http://www.popkin.com
PowerDesigner	Sybase	http://www.powersoft.com
EasyCASE	Visible Systems	http://www.visible.com
EasyER	Visible Systems	http://www.visible.com
ER/Studio	Embarcadero	http://www.embarcadero.com
Designer 2000	Oracle	http://www.oracle.com

Special Types of Databases

Beside the "ordinal" databases such as the Northwind database, there are several other specific types of databases that have become very popular in the last few years.

Object-Oriented Databases

Most relational databases contain a restricted set of field types. As a rule, they can be strings, integer and float numbers, memos (i.e., long text), currency, and, in some cases, BLOBs, pictures, and other documents.

No model can adequately describe reality, and this applies to the relational model too. There are many tasks that require more complicated data than strings, numbers, etc., in the fields. For example, we may need other data types such as arrays, tables, structures, or objects. Databases that support such complex data types as arrays, structures, and nested tables are called *object-oriented databases*.

Oracle 8 is an example of an object-oriented database, and its complex data types are supported by Oracle 8 BDE (Borland Database Engine) driver. However, discussing the features of such databases in more detail is out of the scope of this book, because current OLE DB providers (as we will learn later, OLE DB is a data access mechanism underlying for ADO) do not support them directly. Nevertheless, we will deal with complex data types when we work with data shaping and distributed data sets. We will return to this topic later in this book; see Chapters 11 and 21.

Multidimensional Databases

As we already know, relational databases store data in two-dimensional tables. However, in principle, it is possible to store data in three-dimensional or multidimensional "cubes." Such databases are not relational, but they are becoming widely used. Some of them are accessible through OLE DB providers, but none of them are available through BDE.

The details of organizing data in such databases, and the ways of using them from Delphi applications are discussed in Chapter 15.

Technical Implementations of Databases

In this section, we will discuss the types of databases now in use and what file-server and client/server databases are.

History in Brief: Databases on Host Computers

Let's forget about modern technologies for a moment, and recall how we processed data 20 or 30 years ago. The most popular computers then were mainframes such as IBM-360/370 and minicomputers such as DEC PDP-11. As a rule, the most popular device for providing user interface was a "dumb" terminal that was operated by this mainframe or minicomputer.

This way of processing data has some advantages, including:

■ The possibility of sharing resources and devices, such as CPUs, random access memory, and peripheral equipment (i.e., printers, plotters, tape devices, and other data storages)

■ Centralization of data storage

The serious disadvantage of this way of processing data was the fact that in most cases users could not install the software they needed and could not modify system files. The ability to personalize the environment was very limited. One of the reasons for this was that all software (including text processors, compilers, DBMSs, and so on) was also centralized.

Desktop and File-Server Databases

This disadvantage was one of the reasons for the very rapid growth of the personal computer industry. Along with simple maintenance and cost benefits, the possibility of workspace personalization attracted many users. Now any user could buy software that satisfied his or her needs. At that time, 10 to 15 years ago, desktop databases were very popular (including dBase, FoxBASE, Paradox, and several others). These database management systems contained no engines. They operated the database storages using the file access services of the operating system. Sometimes such software included, along with the database management system itself, some development tools oriented, as a rule, to the specific database management system data formats. All data processing was performed only in user applications.

The next step of desktop database management systems development was the network versions of them (they are also called *file-server databases*). Such versions allowed multiuser processing of shared data stored somewhere on a local area network.

Disadvantages of these multiuser database management systems are not very obvious, because they become apparent only during database growth and when there are numerous users. At some point, the data processing performance decreases and database failure may occur. The reason for this is the desktop database management system's basic concept of processing data in user applications itself.

Let's look at a simple example. Imagine you have 10,000 records in a table, and you need to select five of them (for example, orders placed during the last hour). If this table is indexed by a particular field, the application gets the entire index, finds the position of the necessary records in a database file, and then gets the appropriate parts of these files. If the table is not indexed by this field, the application must get all 10,000 records and look through them to find the five that we are looking for. Therefore, if the amount of data and the number of users increase, the network traffic increases too, and this reduces the performance of applications.

Another problem of some desktop databases is the possibility of reference integrity violations. The only way to maintain integrity in such databases is with a client application. So, the code to maintain it must be in all client applications, and any access to the database files, except via these applications, must be prevented.

Client/Server Databases

To avoid the problems described above, we can move to the client/server architecture. The client/server architecture is, to a certain extent, a return to the old model of centralization of processing data on a host computer. The core of such database management systems is a database server that can be an application or an operation system service. The database server is responsible for storing data in its files, creating backups, maintaining referential integrity, providing user access and data security, writing to the database log, and, of course, executing user queries for modifying, creating, or deleting data. User applications can be executed on personal computers.

The advantages of the client/server architecture are:

- Network traffic while querying the database does not increase. When using database servers, selecting the last five orders from 10,000 results in sending these five records through the network. All operations of selecting them are done by the database server. The time of processing such a query, of course, depends on whether an appropriate index exists, but in all cases, only five resulting records are sent to the client application.

- Business and referential integrity rules can be stored on the server. They are implemented in different database objects stored inside a database and specially designed for this purpose. It allows us to avoid duplicating the code for them in different client applications. It also forces us to obey these rules while editing data with tools different from client applications.

- Any server DBMS provides data security based on storing the user list and granting different privileges to users for using database objects. We will discuss this later in this chapter.

Multitier and Distributed Information Systems

The next step of database development is creating distributed applications. These are applicable for huge enterprises with several international subsidiaries or when there are a large number of users. The different architectures of distributed information systems and the ranges of their application are discussed in Chapter 19.

So far, we have learned the basics of the relational data model and now we understand the logical structure of a typical database. Now is a good time to move to the physical objects that implement this logical structure.

An Overview of Database Objects

Most databases consist of several types of database objects. Among them are tables to store data, indexes for sorting data and implementing keys, constraints to support referential integrity and restrict data values, and triggers and stored procedures to execute code. Different database management systems support different sets of them, but in this section we will look at the most common database objects that can be found in most modern databases.

Tables and Fields

We have already discussed that relational databases consist of tables, and tables contain a set of columns (or fields). Tables exist both in desktop and in client/server databases. Typical data types in columns are:

- **Strings**. There can be different types of strings, for example, with byte and 2-byte characters, or with different maximum lengths. The particular data types are different for different database management systems.

- **Numbers**. There can also be different types of them, for example, integer or float. This is tied to the particular hardware platform.

- **Currency**. This is a special kind of number field. Sometimes it has a fixed decimal or is used to represent the "money" data in a special accounting form in client applications, or/and to use special rules for rounding up.

- **Dates**. Any valid data can correspond to an integer number, for example, the number of days from Christmas. Often the number of days from 12/30/1899 is used. Sometimes, dates are stored in databases as integer values. If date and time values are stored in a database, float numbers are mostly used.

- **Memos**. This kind of field is used to store long text. In some desktop database management systems, the length of such text is restricted by some specific value (for example, 32 Kbytes).

- **BLOBs**. A Binary Large Object is a set of bytes that can contain any data (text, graphics, multimedia, OLE objects, documents, etc.). Some DBMSs support special types of BLOBs, for example, fields for storing bitmaps, OLE objects, formatted text, and so on).

This is not a complete list of possible data types. For example, object-oriented database management systems may support special data types for storing nested tables and arrays.

If we return to the Northwind database, we will see that its tables contain all of the above-mentioned types of fields, including a special BLOB type field to represent graphics. Take a look at the Employees table structure shown below.

We see that it contains:

- Several string fields (called nvarchar fields in SQL Server), for example, the LastName, FirstName, and Title fields.

- Several numeric fields (int fields in SQL Server and in this table), for example, the EmployeeID and ReportsTo fields.

- Two date fields (datetime fields in SQL Server), for example, the BirthDate and HireDate fields.

- The Notes memo field (ntext field in SQL Server).

- The Photo BLOB field of special type for storing images (an image field in SQL Server).

In Chapter 4, we will see the field types that are supported in Delphi database applications.

Indexes

We have already discussed the role of primary and foreign keys. In most relational databases, implementing keys requires creating special database objects called indexes.

An *index* is a list of record positions that shows how to order them. We already know that the records in a relational table may not be well ordered. Nevertheless, any record has, of course, a physical position in a database file. This position can be changed by the database management system during data processing, but, at a particular point in time, it is unique for any record. For example, let's consider that, at some point in time, the records in the Customers table are stored in the following order:

Physical Position	CustomerID	Address
1	ANATR	Avda. de la Constitución 2222
2	BOLID	C/ Araquil, 67
3	BSBEV	Fauntleroy Circus
4	BLONP	24, place Kléber
5	BONAP	12, rue des Bouchers
6	BERGS	Berguvsvägen 8

Now we want to retrieve these data ordered by the CustomerID field values:

Physical Position	CustomerID	Address
1	ANATR	Avda. de la Constitución 2222
6	BERGS	Berguvsvägen 8
4	BLONP	24, place Kléber
2	BOLID	C/ Araquil, 67
5	BONAP	12, rue des Bouchers
3	BSBEV	Fauntleroy Circus

Without going into the details of the technical implementation, we can say that an index on the CustomerID field is the sequence of the position numbers: 1,6,4,2,5,3.

We can also say that an index on the Address field is the sequence of the position numbers: 5,4,1,6,2,3.

Storing such indexes requires significantly less space than storing the differently sorted versions of the table itself.

If we need to retrieve data about customers who have a CustomerID beginning with "BO" using the CustomerID field as the index, we can find the positions of these records in an index (in this case, 2 and 5), and then retrieve those parts of the database file instead of looking through the entire table. Thus, using indexes reduces the time needed to retrieve data.

We have already mentioned that the physical positions of records can be changed when inserting, updating, or deleting data, and during some manipulations performed by a database server (such as compressing the database files). In some desktop database management systems (for example, dBase II and dBase III+), indexes were non-maintained. This means that the client application had to call a special reindex procedure to adjust indexes with the current positions of records and their field values. However, most modern desktop database management systems and all client/server database management systems support *maintained indexes*. This means that these indexes are changed along with changing positions of records and field values. In this case, any inserting, updating, or deleting of records results writing not only to the table itself but also to all the indexes associated with this table. This increases the time needed for data modifications. Thus, to optimize the performance of the database application, you need to decide what kinds of queries are used most often, and create only the necessary indexes.

Some database management systems (such as dBase III+, FoxBase, and Clipper) support *expression indexes*. These indexes are used to order data by the value, which is the result of a calculated expression based on some fields of the table. Now such indexes are used very rarely.

It should be mentioned that some kinds of fields, for example, Memo and BLOB fields, cannot be indexed.

If we look at the indexes for the Customers table of the Northwind database (by selecting the All Tasks | Manage Indexes item from the Orders table pop-up menu in the Enterprise Manager), we could find several indexes there:

Some of them are used to support primary keys (for example, the PK_Orders index); others are used for sorting data and to support the foreign keys.

Constraints

Most server database management systems support special kinds of objects called constraints. A *constraint* is a restriction on a possible value that can be stored in the field. For example, if you set the maximum or minimum values for a field, the database management system will not allow saving a record if it does not satisfy the specified restrictions.

One type of constraint is the *referential constraint*. For example, the master-detail relationship can be implemented in a constraint that requires that values of the CustomerId field (foreign key) in the Orders table can only be one of the values of the CustomerId field of the Customers table.

Note that there are database management systems that do not support constraints (including dBase III, Clipper, and FoxPro). When using such databases, you need to place a code implementing your custom constraints into the client applications, or use other database objects (for example, triggers that will be discussed later in this chapter) to provide the same functionality.

Views

Almost all database management systems support views. A *view* is a virtual table, usually created as a subset of columns from one or more tables. A view is only a description; it does not contain any records itself. Most client/server database management systems provide special visual tools for creating a view that can define what tables are involved in this view, how they are linked, what columns must be presented, and what restrictions (filters) there are on their values.

Views can be used as a security mechanism, by allowing users to access data through the view without granting the users permission to directly access the underlying tables. Views also allow users to focus on specific data that interests them without retrieving all of the data. For example, if we want to get a list of customers in Canada, we can create a view that filters the data according to this restriction. The view can determine which data to retrieve using the user name or the name of the group to which the user belongs—sales manager, human resources department, and so on.

Very often, views are used to store complex queries inside a database. In other words, a view is just a stored query. To receive the list of views, select the appropriate item in the SQL Server Enterprise Manager.

An example of creating and executing a view on two tables with Microsoft SQL Server 7.0 is shown at right:

Triggers and Stored Procedures

We have already mentioned that databases can store business rules. Most client/server database management systems support special objects to implement them. These objects are called triggers and stored procedures.

A *stored procedure* is a special kind of procedure stored inside a database. Stored procedures must be written with a procedural language specific for each database management system. They can read or change database data during execution. Stored procedures can call each other and can be called from a client application. Stored procedures are usually used to perform common tasks (for example, calculating an account balance, etc.). They can return parameters, error codes, or a set of rows and columns (usually called the *data set*). There can also be a set of system stored procedures to implement some specific tasks. For example, in Microsoft SQL Server there is a set of such system stored procedures that have names started with SP_ and XP_.

Triggers also contain code written with the same procedural language. However, they cannot be called directly from a client application or from a stored procedure. They are executed if a predefined event of the specific table occurs, for example, inserting, updating, or deleting a record. From this point of view, triggers work the same way as Delphi event handlers, but are executed in a database server address space instead of a client application.

A trigger, unlike a stored procedure, is associated with a specific table, and is fired only if an inserting, deleting, or updating operation occurs in this specific table. In most database management systems, there can be several triggers defined for the same event; in this case, the order of their execution must be set.

Using triggers and stored procedures in Delphi ADO applications is discussed in Chapter 10.

To obtain the list of stored procedures, select the Stored Procedures item from the SQL Server Enterprise Manager.

We can also look at the source code of the selected stored procedure and edit it if necessary, as shown at right.

Objects for Generating Primary Keys

Very often, primary keys are generated by a database management system. This is preferable to inserting them with a client application, because we can avoid duplication of possible keys and use a continuous set of key values.

Objects for generating keys vary for different database management systems. Some of them support objects that store an integer value and rules for generating the next one. Inserting a record into a specific table results in, for example, executing a trigger that selects this value and puts it into the key column of a new record (after that, the current value in this object changes according to the defined rules of change). Such objects are supported, for example, by Oracle (where they are called *sequences*) and by InterBase (where they are called *generators*).

Another way to generate primary keys by a database management system is to have special fields that are primary keys by definition. When inserting a record, this field is filled automatically with the next value by the database management system itself. Such a mechanism is supported, for example, in Microsoft Access and Microsoft SQL Server (where they are called *Identity fields*) and Corel Paradox (where they are called *Autoincrement fields*).

In the Northwind database, the OrderID field of the Orders table is an Identity field.

An example of using such fields is provided in Chapter 22.

Users and Roles

Data security, particularly preventing access to data for those who do not have rights for this access, is a serious issue. Different database management systems address this in different ways. The simplest way is by using password protection for tables or specific columns in a table (such a mechanism is supported, for example, by Corel Paradox).

A more advanced means, supported by all client/server database management systems and by several desktop database management systems (such as Microsoft Access), is to create a list of users with their own user names and passwords. Thus, any database object belongs to a specific user, and this user can give permission to (or grant) another user permission to read or modify data contained in this object or to modify the object itself.

You can see the list of database users by selecting the Users item in the SQL Server Enterprise Manager.

Some client/server database management systems also support roles. A *role* is a set of grants and privileges. If a role is granted to a specific user, he automatically receives all permissions defined in this role.

You can obtain the list of database roles by selecting the Roles item in the Enterprise Manager.

An example of granting roles to the user of the Northwind database in Microsoft SQL Server 7.0 is shown at right:

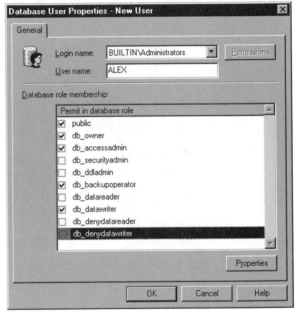

The System Catalog

Any relational database that supports such objects as users and roles must store lists of them. It is also desirable to store the list of tables, indexes, triggers, procedures, and other objects. In many cases, such information is stored in special tables called *system tables* (and the appropriate part of a database storage is called the *system catalog*).

You can find details about the system catalog in the documentation accompanying your database management system.

Note that some database management systems do not have the system catalog, such as dBase and Paradox. To obtain the list of tables for such database management systems, you can use operation system services to retrieve the names of files. Data about indexes can be stored either in index files themselves or inside the file containing the appropriate table (this depends on the version number of the database management system).

Queries

Data and metadata manipulation in databases is performed with queries. A *query* is a request to modify or retrieve data. Most modern database management systems and some development tools come with tools for generating queries.

One of the popular ways of manipulating data is to create *queries by example* (QBE). QBE consists of linking tables visually and then selecting fields that must be retrieved by this query. In most database management systems (except some desktop databases), QBE results in generating a query in a special language called structured query language (SQL). In addition, you can create SQL queries directly without using QBE and visual tools by entering SQL statements.

Very often, querying databases results in a set of rows. To work with them, we need to use cursors.

Cursors

When data is retrieved from a database, we can say that an application receives a set of rows, often called a *row set*. Very often, this row set is similar to a table; like a table it contains rows and columns. However, unlike fields and records in a database table, the rows and columns in such a set are well ordered. The way in which they are ordered is usually defined by a query the row set results from, and, sometimes, by existing indexes.

As these rows are well ordered, we can define a current position in this row set. The pointer to a current position is called a *cursor*.

Most modern database management systems support bidirectional cursors, allowing us to move back and forth in the resulting row set. However, some older database management systems support only "firehose" cursors that allow moving only from the beginning to the end of the resulting row set.

As we have already learned, we need to use a query language to obtain a row set. The most popular of them is structured query language (SQL), which is briefly discussed below.

SQL Language

Structured query language (SQL) is a non-procedural language that is used to manipulate data in the relational database system. It is a set of commands used to access and manipulate data stored in a database. It is also an industry standard used for querying most database management systems.

The word *non-procedural* means that with SQL, you can ask a database management system to do something, but you cannot describe an algorithm for how to do it. Any algorithms must be generated by the database management system itself.

SQL statements can be divided into several categories. Among them are:

- **Data Definition Language** statements, which allow us to create, alter, and drop databases and objects within them.

- **Data Manipulation Language** statements, which allow us to query and manipulate data in existing database objects.

- **Data Control Language** statements, sometimes called Access Control statements, which are used to perform administrative functions that grant and revoke privileges to use the database, a set of tables within the database, or specific SQL commands.

- **Transaction Control Language** statements, which are used to manage changes made by the group of data manipulation language statements.

- **Cursor Control Language** statements, which are used to define a cursor and to prepare SQL statements for execution and in other operations.

A detailed description of the SQL language, its standards, and the basic set of statements are covered in Chapter 9.

SQL Extensions

We have already mentioned that triggers and stored procedures are written in a procedural language specific to the particular database management system. In most database management systems, this language is just a procedural SQL extension, i.e., SQL plus some algorithmic operators such as Begin..End, If..Then..Else, etc.

Unlike the SQL language itself, which satisfies ANSI standards, SQL extensions are not standardized. Any database management system vendor can invent its own extended SQL dialect (in Oracle it is called PL/SQL, in Microsoft SQL Server it is called Transact-SQL, and in Microsoft Access it is called Jet SQL). If you want to write triggers and stored procedures, you should refer to the documentation on SQL extensions for your database management system.

Some SQL extensions are also designed to access non-relational and object-oriented databases. One of these extensions, called Multidimensional Extensions (MDX), is discussed in Chapter 15.

User-Defined Functions

Some database management systems allow the use of user-defined functions (UDFs). As a rule, these functions are stored in the external libraries or COM servers and are to be registered in the database. After registering the UDF, it can be used in queries, triggers, and stored procedures.

As parts of external libraries, UDFs can be written with any development tool that allows creating libraries for the particular platform where the database server is executed. For example, you can use Delphi to write UDFs for database servers executed in 32-bit Windows. For other platforms (e.g., different versions of UNIX), the C language is used most often.

Transactions

Transaction is a basic term for client/server database management systems. A *transaction* is a group of database operations combined into a logical unit of work that is either wholly committed or wholly rolled back. There is also a more extended non-database definition: a transaction is a set of operations that must be either executed altogether or not executed at all.

Committing a transaction means that all operations are done and fixed in a database, and *rolling back* a transaction means that all operations that are completed are reversed, and all database objects involved in this set of operations are returned to their initial state.

To allow for the possibility of rolling back transactions, client/server database management systems write to a special transaction log. This allows for the restoration of changed data in the case of a rollback.

A transaction must satisfy four requirements, called the ACID properties:

- **Atomicity** means that a transaction must be an atomic unit of work; either all of its data modifications are performed or none of them are performed.

- **Consistency** means that a transaction must leave all data in a consistent state after its completion. For example, in a relational database, all referential integrity rules must be applied to the transaction's modifications.

- **Isolation** means that modifications made by concurrent transactions must be isolated from the modifications made by any other concurrent transactions. So, a transaction must not "see" data that arises from transactions that are uncommitted.

- **Durability** means that after a transaction has completed, its effects are permanent even in the case of a system failure.

Note that a transaction can consist of several other nested transactions. Some database management systems support a two-phase commit, which is a process that ensures transactions that apply to several servers of the same database management system are completed either on all servers or on none of them.

As for transactions that apply to several servers of different database management systems, using them requires special tools called *transaction managers*. Using one of them, the Microsoft Transaction Server (MTS), with Delphi ADO applications is discussed in Chapter 22.

Data Access Mechanisms

In the previous section, we discussed processes that take place mainly inside the database. Now it is time to discuss processes outside the database, i.e., in client applications used to provide a user interface to a database.

A common problem in creating database applications is to find how to provide access to the database objects for a client application. There are different ways to do this.

Most database management systems provide libraries that contain a special *application programming interface* (API), which is a set of functions to manipulate its data. For desktop database management systems, this API just reads or writes to database files. For client/server database management systems, this API (in this case, it is also called the database management system client software) initiates sending queries to the database server through the network and obtaining query results or error codes that are interpreted by a client application.

The most common way to access data is to use this API directly. However, this means that your application will be database management system-specific. In this case, moving to another database management system (for example, for extending data storage or for moving from desktop to client/server database) means rewriting most of the code of such a client application. So, the next step of providing data access to the client application is to create some universal data access mechanism that provides a standard set of common functions, classes, or services to use in client applications for different types of database management systems. These standard functions (or classes or services) must be placed into libraries (called *database drivers* or *providers*). Each such library implements a set of standard functions, classes, or services in terms of API calls for the specific database management system.

An Overview of Universal Data Access

Here we will briefly discuss the most popular Universal Data Access (UDA) mechanisms, and which of them can be used for providing access to the most popular database management systems.

Universal Data Access Mechanisms

The Universal Data Access mechanisms that can be used in Delphi applications are:

- ODBC
- OLE DB
- ADO
- BDE

ODBC, OLE DB, and ADO are, in fact, industry standards. BDE is mentioned here because it was the only data access mechanism in Delphi for many years, and thus influenced the ADO support implementation in Delphi. It should be clear that it is a proprietary mechanism developed by Borland for its own products. The different data access mechanisms, including direct client database management system API calls, are schematically shown below:

ODBC

ODBC (Open Database Connectivity) is a widely used API that satisfies the ANSI and ISO standards for a database call level interface (CLI). To access a relational database through ODBC, we need to have the ODBC Administrator and an appropriate ODBC driver installed. An ODBC driver is a dynamic-link library (DLL) that a client application can use to access an ODBC data source. Each ODBC driver is specific to a DBMS, because it uses API calls of the DBMS client software.

ODBC supports access to any database (and even to some non-database files such as spreadsheets) for which an ODBC driver is available. You can use both ODBC API calls directly and some overlying data access mechanism (e.g., OLE DB and ADO) that implements standard functions, classes, or services in the terms of ODBC API calls.

Details of using ODBC and creating ODBC data sources are described in Chapter 3.

OLE DB and ADO

OLE DB and ADO are parts of the Microsoft Universal Data Access. Its purpose is to provide access to all data sources, including non-relational ones, such as file systems, e-mails, and multidimensional databases.

Microsoft ActiveX Data Objects (ADO) is an application-level programming interface to such data. We will talk about ADO throughout this book. We will also discuss some ADO extensions, such as ADOX (ADO Extensions for DDL and security), JRO (Jet Replication Objects), and ADO MD (ADO Multidimensional).

OLE DB provides the low-level interface to data. ADO uses OLE DB, but it is also possible to use OLE DB directly. OLE DB is designed to provide access to all types of data in the Component Object Model (COM) environment through the COM interfaces.

To access a specific data source through OLE DB, you need to have an appropriate OLE DB provider installed. OLE DB provider is a dynamic-link library (DLL) that a client application can use to access a specific OLE DB data source. Each OLE DB provider is specific to a database management system, because it uses API calls of the client software of this particular database management system.

Among OLE DB providers, there is the Microsoft OLE DB provider for ODBC drivers. This provider is written in terms of ODBC API and we can use it with an appropriate ODBC driver.

ADO itself contains a set of libraries (DLLs), which implements the ADO object model that can be used in client applications. Delphi ADO components—ADOExpress—are built on top of these objects, but they are available for direct manipulation through COM interfaces and type libraries.

ADO has become very popular for data access, as it comes with popular tools such as Microsoft Office 2000 and Microsoft Internet Explorer 5.0. In addition, ADO is an integrated part of Windows 2000. Thus, after moving to this generation of operation systems, we may no longer worry about installing and deploying ADO. Nevertheless, for those who create solutions for Windows 9.x and Windows NT, we devote all of Chapter 18 to a discussion of the possible ways to deploy ADO applications.

Other Data Access Mechanisms

Among other data access mechanisms, we need to mention BDE (Borland Database Engine). This data access mechanism is often used in applications created with Borland development tools (e.g., Delphi and C++Builder). You can think of it is as some kind of universal data access mechanism. It is a descendant of the Paradox Engine library written for Borland Pascal and Borland C++ to provide access to Paradox tables.

To access a database through BDE, you need to have an appropriate BDE driver installed. In the case of client/server database management systems, such drivers are called SQL Links. These drivers provide a set of functions called BDE API, and are written in terms of the DBMS client API calls. Among BDE drivers, there is a driver written in terms of ODBC API; it is called ODBC Link and can be used only with an appropriate ODBC driver.

The number of existing BDE drivers is restricted by several popular database servers, several desktop database formats, and the InterBase server that comes with Delphi. All other databases are accessible only through an appropriate ODBC driver and ODBC Link.

Accessing the Popular Databases

In this section, we will give you some idea of the types of Universal Data Access that are available for the most popular databases. We will start with the desktop databases and then briefly discuss the client/server databases. The following table shows the major database management systems:

DBMS	Vendor	URL
Paradox	Corel	http://www.corel.com
Visual dBase	dBase, Inc	http://www.dbase2000.com
Microsoft Access 2000	Microsoft	http://www.microsoft.com
Microsoft FoxPro	Microsoft	http://www.microsoft.com
Microsoft Visual FoxPro	Microsoft	http://www.microsoft.com
Microsoft SQL Server	Microsoft	http://www.microsoft.com
Microsoft Data Engine	Microsoft	http://www.microsoft.com
Oracle Workgroup Server/Oracle Enterprise Server	Oracle	http://www.oracle.com
Adaptive Server Enterprise/Adaptive Server Anywhere	Sybase	http://www.sybase.com
Informix Dynamic Server.2000	Informix	http://www.informix.com
IBM DB2	IBM	http://www-4.ibm.com/ software
InterBase	InterBase	http://www.interbase.com

Paradox, dBase, and Text Files

To access Paradox, dBase, and text files we can use an appropriate ODBC drivers (they come, for example, with Microsoft Office 2000) and OLE DB Provider for ODBC drivers. Details of using them are discussed in Chapter 3.

It is also possible to access these databases through BDE using dBase, Paradox, and ASCII BDE drivers that implement writing to appropriate files directly. We can also use ODBC Link and appropriate ODBC drivers, but the performance of such a system is, as a rule, worse than direct usage of the BDE drivers.

Microsoft Access

To work with Access 2000 databases, we use the special OLE DB provider called the Microsoft Jet 4.0 OLE DB Provider. The previous version of this OLE DB provider (Microsoft Jet 3.51 OLE DB Provider) can be used to access the older versions of Access databases. This is the preferable way to work with Access databases. Details of using this OLE DB provider are discussed in Chapter 3.

We can also use an appropriate ODBC driver (it comes with Microsoft Office 2000) and OLE DB provider for ODBC drivers (or BDE ODBC Link).

An appropriate BDE driver is available for Access 95 and Access 97. They require an appropriate version (3.0 or 3.5) of the Microsoft Jet Engine (which comes with Microsoft Access and Microsoft Visual FoxPro) installed. These BDE drivers do not work with Access 2000 databases.

Microsoft FoxPro and Visual FoxPro

To work with Visual FoxPro databases, we can use the Visual FoxPro ODBC Driver (it comes as part of Microsoft Data Access Components) and OLE DB Provider for ODBC drivers. Details of using them are discussed in Chapter 3.

Accessing FoxPro databases through BDE is also possible when we use the native BDE driver that implements writing to FoxPro files directly. We can also use ODBC Link and appropriate ODBC driver.

When moving to the client/server database management system side, we encounter the Microsoft SQL Server, Microsoft Data Engine, Oracle, Sybase, IBM DB2, Informix, InterBase, and several other client/server DBMSs.

Microsoft SQL Server

To work with Microsoft SQL Server 7.0 databases, we need to use the Microsoft OLE DB Provider for SQL Server. This is the preferable way to work with Microsoft SQL Server 7.0. Details of using this OLE DB provider are discussed in Chapter 3.

We can also use an appropriate ODBC driver (which comes with Microsoft SQL Server itself) and OLE DB Provider for ODBC drivers (or BDE ODBC Link).

The BDE driver is available for Microsoft SQL server 4.x and 6.x. It does not work with Microsoft SQL Server 7.0.

Microsoft Data Engine

Microsoft Data Engine (MSDE) is a data store based on Microsoft SQL Server technology, but it is designed and optimized for use on smaller computer systems, such as a workstation or small workgroup server. It has a 2 GB database size limit.

To access the MSDE databases, you can use the same data access mechanisms as for Microsoft SQL Server.

Note: MSDE is available as part of Microsoft Office 2000 Premium or Developer editions or can be downloaded for free by any licensed user of Microsoft Visual Studio 6.0 Professional or Enterprise editions or any Professional or Enterprise edition of any Visual Studio 6.0 language tool.

Applications built on MSDE with any of these Visual Studio 6.0 products (or with Office 2000 Developer) can be freely redistributed to customers and end users.

Oracle, Sybase, IBM DB2, Informix, and InterBase

To access these client/server databases, we can use the appropriate ODBC drivers (they come, for example, with Microsoft Office 2000) and OLE DB Provider for ODBC drivers.

In addition, we can use OLE DB providers for these servers. The Microsoft OLE DB Provider for Oracle comes with the Microsoft Data Access Components (MDAC). Details of using this OLE DB provider are discussed in Chapter 3.

Other OLE DB providers can be obtained from appropriate DBMS vendors or third-party vendors. Details of where to get them are also discussed in Chapter 3. All these DBMSs are also accessible through BDE drivers. For Oracle 8, using BDE is more preferable because of its object-oriented facilities; the appropriate BDE driver, unlike the Microsoft OLE DB provider, supports object-oriented facilities provided by Oracle 8.

Thus, we can summarize all available data access mechanisms for the widely used databases:

DBMS	Native OLE DB Provider in MDAC 2.1	ODBC Driver	BDE Driver
Paradox	No	Yes	Yes
dBase	No	Yes	Yes
Microsoft Access 97	Yes	Yes	Yes
Microsoft Access 2000	Yes	Yes	Yes
Microsoft FoxPro	No	Yes	Yes
Microsoft Visual FoxPro	No	Yes	No
Microsoft SQL Server 6.5	Yes	Yes	Yes
Microsoft SQL Server 7.0	Yes	Yes	No
Microsoft Data Engine	Yes	Yes	No
Oracle	Yes	Yes	Yes
Sybase	No	Yes	Yes
Informix	No	Yes	Yes
IBM DB2	No	Yes	Yes
InterBase	No	Yes	Yes

Conclusion

Let's outline some major points of this chapter. We have learned that:

- Each relational database consists of one or more tables that contain rows (records) and columns (fields), with the sequence of these rows and columns being insignificant.

- Primary keys are used to identify the rows of a table. They must be unique and can contain no null values.

- Tables in relational databases can be related with each other. Foreign keys are used to define relationships between tables.

- Normalization is used to eliminate redundant data and to reduce update anomalies.

We have also learned how the relational model and principles of normalization are implemented in the sample Northwind database.

In this chapter, we have also seen how these logical principles are implemented in real databases. We have learned that:

- There are desktop, file-server, and client/server databases, with these last ones being advantageous from the point of view of network traffic, security, and storing business and referential integrity rules.

- Besides tables and fields, most databases contain indexes to implement keys and to allow sorting data.

- Most server databases can contain constraints to provide referential integrity and to restrict field values.

- Most databases can contain views to provide users with data from one or several tables that satisfy some conditions or filters.

- Most server databases can contain stored procedures that contain code and can be executed in order to manipulate data.

- Most server databases can contain triggers that contain code and are executed when inserting, deleting, or updating operations are performed.

- Most databases can contain special objects or special field types for generating primary key values.

- Many databases contain a list of database users, and any database object belongs to one of them. Some databases also contain a list of roles, which are a set of grants to database objects. A role can be granted to a user.

- Most modern databases include the system catalog, which contains tables that store information about database objects.

- Querying databases can be performed with the structured query language.

We have also seen which of these database objects are available in the sample Northwind database.

Also, we have discussed the most popular Universal Data Access mechanisms used. These include:

- Open Database Connectivity (ODBC), used to access relational databases.

- OLE DB and ADO, which are part of Microsoft Universal Data Access, and are used to access both relational and non-relational databases.

- The Borland Database Engine used only by Borland development tools.

And finally, we have discussed the most popular databases and what data access mechanisms can be used with them. Among desktop databases, there are:

- Paradox and dBase, accessible through OLE DB provider for ODBC drivers, and BDE.

- Microsoft Access, accessible through native OLE DB provider, OLE DB provider for ODBC drivers, and, sometimes, BDE.

- Microsoft FoxPro and Visual FoxPro, accessible through OLE DB provider for ODBC drivers, and, sometimes, BDE.

Among server databases, there are:

- Microsoft SQL Server and Microsoft Data Engine, accessible through native OLE DB provider, OLE DB provider for ODBC drivers, and, sometimes, BDE.

- Oracle, Sybase, IBM DB2, Informix, and InterBase, accessible through OLE DB provider for ODBC drivers and BDE.

Now you are ready to start studying ADO database programming in more detail. The next chapter is devoted to Microsoft Data Access Components, which are a key part of the Microsoft data access mechanisms.

MICROSOFT DATA ACCESS COMPONENTS

In this chapter, we discuss Microsoft Data Access Components (MDAC)—a set of key technologies that enable Universal Data Access. These technologies include Open Database Connectivity (ODBC), OLE DB, and Microsoft ActiveX Data Objects (ADO). We will start with a brief discussion of the Microsoft data access strategy called Universal Data Access.

Microsoft Universal Data Access

According to Microsoft, Universal Data Access is the "strategy for providing access to all types of information across the enterprise. It provides high-performance access to a variety of information sources (including relational data and non-relational data), including mainframe ISAM/VSAM and hierarchical databases; e-mail and file system storage; text, graphical, and geographical data; and more."

Developers building today's database solutions are trying to integrate data spread across various sources. This data can be stored in DBMS sources like IBM DB2 mainframe databases, Oracle and Microsoft SQL Server server databases, Microsoft Access, Microsoft FoxPro, and Paradox or on desktop or in non-DBMS sources like file systems on multiple platforms, indexed-sequential files, e-mail, spreadsheets, project management tool, and any other types of data. In addition, the database solution should be able to have interfaces to all of these sources. Moreover, as data storage continues to evolve, new data formats appear and should be considered in the application. Therefore, we really need a universal data access method to give us an interface to both present and future data formats.

The main goal of Microsoft Universal Data Access is to provide access to all of the above-mentioned types of data through a single data access model. If you are familiar with ODBC, you can think of Universal Data Access as "ODBC for all types of data, both relational and non-relational."

Today, Universal Data Access works with all the major database platforms, which were listed in the previous chapter, as well as with several other non-DBMS data sources, giving us the ability to create database solutions more easily, using a set of common interfaces. In the next chapter, we will see what types of standard OLE DB providers are available.

The Universal Data Access architecture is composed of the following elements:

- **Microsoft ActiveX Data Objects (ADO)** is an application-level programming interface to data in its various sources and information. We will talk about ADO and several of its additional libraries, such as ADOX, ADO MD, and JRO throughout the book. From the programmer's point of view, ADO and its extensions are a simplified, high-level, object-oriented interface to OLE DB.

- **OLE DB** provides the low-level interface to data across the enterprise. ADO works with OLE DB behind the scenes, but we can use OLE DB directly if needed.

- **Open Database Connectivity (ODBC)** is the Microsoft standard for working with relational data. This component is provided for backward compatibility, as in modern solutions its role is played by the native OLE DB providers.

The architecture of Microsoft Universal Data Access is illustrated below.

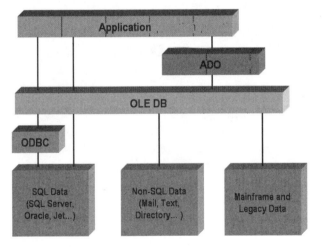

OLE DB is Microsoft's strategic low-level interface that enables Universal Data Access. So, let's start our discussion of data access components with it.

Here we will look at the OLE DB architecture and interfaces, and then we will show you how it interacts with the main topic of our book—Microsoft ActiveX Data Objects. Let's start with a definition of OLE DB.

OLE DB

OLE DB is a system-level programming interface to various data sources, such as traditional relational data and non-relational data, including text, graphical, and geographical data, electronic mail stores, file system stores, and custom business objects. OLE DB specifies a set of Component Object Model (COM) interfaces that encapsulate various database management system services to provide uniform access to the data. Using these interfaces programmers can implement additional database services.

The Components of OLE DB

At a very high level, we can indicate the three major components of OLE DB. They are *consumers*, *data providers*, and *service providers*.

Any software component that uses or consumes an OLE DB interfaces is an OLE DB *consumer*. This can be a business application, a software development tool like Borland Delphi, sophisticated applications, or even the ActiveX Data Objects object model that uses the OLE DB interfaces. Consumers use either ActiveX Data Objects that are the application-level interface to OLE DB to indirectly access data or OLE DB itself to directly access data using the OLE DB provider. All demo programs that we will create in this book are good examples of OLE DB consumers.

A *provider* is a piece of software that implements and exposes a set of core OLE DB interfaces. From the OLE DB point of view, there can be two kinds of OLE DB providers—*data providers* and *service providers*.

The *data provider* is a software component that owns data. It resides between a consumer and the actual data store. In OLE DB, all providers expose data in tabular format (which we already know from relational database systems and spreadsheets) through virtual tables. The data provider performs the following tasks:

- It accepts requests for data, issued from the consumer.
- It retrieves or updates the data from the data store.
- It returns the data to the consumer.

One example of a data provider is Microsoft Jet 4.0 OLE DB Provider, which is used to work with the Microsoft Jet database engine to access data in Microsoft Access databases, as well as to provide database access to installable Indexed Sequential Access Method (I-ISAM) data supported by Jet: tabular data stored in Excel workbooks, Outlook, and Microsoft Exchange mail stores, dBase and Paradox tables, text and HTML files, and so on. Another OLE DB provider is the Microsoft OLE DB Provider for SQL Server that is used to work with databases stored on Microsoft SQL Server 6.5 and 7.0.

The *service provider* (recently Microsoft changed the name to *service component*) implements extended functionality (service) that is not supported by ordinary data providers and does not own the data. For example, it provides sorting, filtering, transaction handling, SQL query processing, cursor functions, and so on. A service provider can work with the data store directly or through an appropriate data store provider; in this case, the service provider acts as a consumer and a provider. For example, OLE DB service providers like Microsoft Cursor Service for OLE DB and Microsoft Data Shaping Service for OLE DB can integrate with the basic OLE DB data providers to extend their functionality.

The following diagram shows the interaction between the three OLE DB components and how consumers can access data.

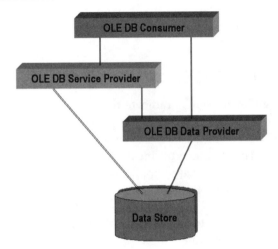

As we can see from this diagram, the consumer can either access data directly through a data provider or use the services of the service provider. In the next chapter, we will look in detail at the data and service providers available as part of the Microsoft Data Access Components pack and with several other Microsoft products. Following is a list of available OLE DB providers:

Provider	Description
Microsoft OLE DB Provider for ODBC Drivers	Allows us to connect to any ODBC data source
Microsoft Jet 4.0 OLE DB Provider	Used to connect to Microsoft Access databases, as well as several other datasources
Microsoft OLE DB Provider for SQL Server	Used to connect to Microsoft SQL Server databases
Microsoft OLE DB Provider for Oracle	Used to access Oracle databases
Microsoft OLE DB Provider for Internet Publishing	Used to connect to Web servers and access resources served by Microsoft FrontPage or Microsoft Internet Information Server
OLE DB Provider for Microsoft Directory Services	Used to connect to heterogeneous directory services through Microsoft Active Directory Service Interfaces (ADSI)
Microsoft OLE DB Provider for Microsoft Index Server	Provides programmatic read-only access to file system and Web data indexed by Microsoft Indexing Service
Microsoft OLE DB Simple Provider	Used to connect to simple text files
Cursor Service for OLE DB	Enhances cursor functionality

Provider	Description
Data Shaping Service for OLE DB	Used to create relationships between keys, fields, and rowsets, and to construct hierarchical rowset objects from the data provider
OLE DB Persistence Provider	Used to save rowset data in Advanced Data Table Gram (ADTG) format or the eXtensible Markup Language (XML) format
OLE DB Remoting Provider	Allows us to invoke data providers on a remote machine
Microsoft OLE DB Provider for OLAP Services	Used with the ADO Multidimensional (ADO MD) extensions to access the services of the OLAP Server for SQL Server 7.0

As we have mentioned earlier, OLE DB is a set of Component Object Model (COM) interfaces. The following figure shows the four main COM objects and interfaces it exposes, as well as various methods to access one object from another. Note that every OLE DB provider must implement the Data Source, Session, and Rowset objects. There may be a number of additional objects exposed by some OLE DB provider, but these three are the most important.

Let's look at these and other OLE DB objects in more detail.

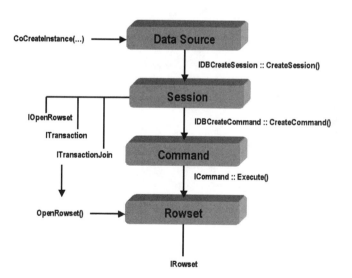

OLE DB Objects

Four basic OLE DB objects form the core object model of OLE DB. They are:

- The Data Source object
- The Session object
- The Command object
- The Rowset object

The Data Source Object

The Data Source object is used by an OLE DB data consumer to connect to a data provider. This object can be created in several ways, including calling the OLE function CoCreateInstance with the class identifier (CLSID) of an OLE DB provider, using an enumerator (see the Enumerator object section), or binding a file moniker or other data source moniker. Each OLE DB provider defines its own data source object class identifier. In Chapter 3, we will see how to programmatically find the CLSID of the OLE DB provider. The Data Source object encapsulates the environment and connection information, including a user name and password. The main goal of the Data Source object is to provide the data from the data store to the consumer. To create a new session (the Session object) consumers call the IDBCreateSession.CreateSession method of a Data Source object.

The Session Object

The Session object provides a context for transactions, and can generate rowsets from the data source and commands that can query and manipulate the data source. The Session object acts like a factory for Command and Rowset objects (described later) and Transaction objects that can be used to control nested transactions (ITransaction and ITransactionJoin interfaces). The Command and Rowset objects can be used to create and modify tables and indexes. The IOpenRowset interface is used by consumers to open and work directly with individual tables or indexes in a data store. There can be one or multiple Session objects created by the Data Source object. To create a new command (the Command object) the IDBCreateCommand.CreateCommand method is used.

The Command Object

The Command object is used to process commands, which are strings that are passed from a consumer to a provider Data Source object for execution. In most cases, the command is a SQL SELECT statement, but it can contain other data manipulation and data definition statements as well. There also can be commands with parameters; in this case, the ICommandWithParameters interface is used. A single session can have multiple commands associated with it. The result of the command execution (the ICommand.Execute method) is a new Rowset object.

The Rowset Object

The Rowset object enables OLE DB data providers to expose data from a data source in tabular format. A row set is a set of rows, in which each row has one or more columns of data. This object can be created as the result of command execution or generated directly from the data provider if the data provider does not support commands. All data providers must be able to create row sets directly. The Rowset object can also be used to update, insert, and delete rows, although this depends on the data provider's functionality.

By accessing the IRowset interface, exposed by the Rowset object, consumers can traverse rows in the rowset forward and, if the rowset supports it, backward as well. Some providers may expose additional functions such as direct access and approximate positioning.

A special case of the Rowset object is the Index object, which represents a row set that uses an associated index to provide ordered access to a data source row set.

There also can be *schema rowsets*, which contain metadata (structural information) about a database, and *view rowsets*, which define a subset of the rows and columns from a rowset.

Besides the four basic objects listed above, there are other OLE DB objects also defined in OLE DB. They can be used for data source enumeration, transaction control, error retrieval, and so on. Some of these are discussed below.

The Enumerator Object

The Enumerator object is used to list available data source objects (OLE DB providers) and other enumerators available on the system. This object can be used by the consumer to search an appropriate data source object to use. In most cases, the information the Enumerator object returns is extracted from the System Registry. The Enumerator object exposes the ISourceRowset interface, and returns a Rowset object with descriptions of all data sources and enumerators visible to this particular enumerator. This can be done through the GetSourcesRowset method of the ISourceRowset interface. There is a root Enumerator object that returns the top-level data sources and other enumerators. Other enumerators can be used to extract provider-specific information.

The Transaction Object

The Transaction object supports transactions with a data source. Transactions, as we already know from the previous chapter, enable consumers to define units of work within a provider. These units have the atomicity, concurrency, isolation, and durability properties. There can be local and distributed transactions.

Local transactions are transactions that run in the context of a local data provider. A data provider that supports local transactions exposes ITransactionLocal interface through the Session object. The transaction begins with the StartTransaction method, is committed with the Commit method, and is rolled back (aborted) with the Abort method. The transaction capabilities of a provider can be obtained through the IDBProperties interface.

To perform transactions over multiple distributed data providers, consumers use the ITransactionJoin interface. This interface is available only if the data provider supports distributed transactions. The consumer calls the JoinTransaction method to enlist the session in a distributed transaction. After joining the distributed transaction, the consumer uses the ITransaction interface to commit or abort the transaction.

The Error Object

In addition to the return codes and status information indicating the success or failure of each OLE DB method call, OLE DB providers can expose extended error information through the Error object. Consumers can use ISupportErrorInfo to determine whether an object can return OLE DB Error objects and, if so, the interfaces that return these objects.

In the next chapter, we will spend some time looking at the standard OLE DB providers that are available as part of the Microsoft Data Access Components pack and several other Microsoft products. Later in that chapter, you will learn where to get additional OLE DB providers and what tools are available to create your own OLE DB providers.

Note: For more information on OLE DB, refer to Microsoft's Web site at:
        `http://www.microsoft.com/data/oledb`
or to the following newsgroups at `nntp://msnews.microsoft.com`:
        `microsoft.public.oledb`
        `microsoft.public.oledb.sdk`

Now let's look at Microsoft ActiveX Data Objects, and see how these objects interact with the OLE DB objects we are now familiar with.

Microsoft ActiveX Data Objects

As we have already mentioned, ADO is an application-level programming interface to low-level OLE DB interfaces. It enables us to access and manipulate data through any OLE DB provider—either standard providers that come as part of the Microsoft Data Access Components, which are discussed in the next chapter, providers that are available with other Microsoft products, or even third-party OLE DB providers. ADO contains a set of objects used to connect to a data source and read, add, update, and delete data.

The ADO Connection object is used to establish a link to a data source. It represents a unique session with it. We use this object to start working with a database; it allows us to customize connection options and start and end transactions. Using the Connection object, we can execute commands—queries and SQL statements—through the Execute method. If the command returns rows, a default Recordset object is automatically created and returned.

The Error object is used to extract details about errors that occurred during the operation.

The Command object represents a command that can be executed against the data source. Commands can be simple SQL statements or calls to stored procedures. In the latter case, the Parameters collection of the Command object is used to specify the individual parameter information—its size, data type, direction, and value.

The Recordset object represents a set of records retrieved from a data source. This object can be used to add, update, delete, and scroll through records in the recordset. The Recordset object can be either opened directly or created from the Connection or Command object.

The Field object represents a column in a recordset and can be used to obtain values, modify values, and extract column metadata, such as its name and type.

The following figure shows the ADO object model:

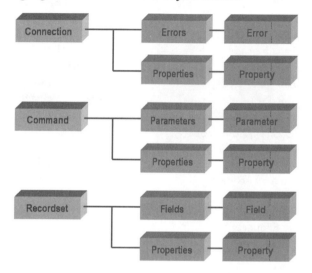

The ADO 2.5 library that is now a standard part of the Windows 2000 operating system contains two new objects—the Record object and the Stream object.

The Record object represents a single record within a Recordset object and can be used to work with heterogenous and hierarchical data.

The Stream object represents binary data associated with a Record object. For example, if a Record object represents a file, its Stream object would contain the data within that file.

Record and Stream objects are discussed in more detail in Chapter 23.

OLE DB and ADO

Earlier in this chapter, we discussed several basic objects that comprise the OLE DB object model. These objects are used by ADO objects in the following way:

- The ADO Connection object uses OLE DB DataSource and Session objects. The transactions are supported by the ITransaction and ITransactionLocal interfaces, the Execute method though the ICommand.Execute or IOpenRowset.OpenRowset methods, and most of the properties through the IDBProperties interface. The

Error object is supported through the IErrorRecords interface. This is shown in the following table.

ADO Connection Object	Uses OLE DB Interfaces and Methods
Open Method	IDBInitialize.Initialize
	IDBCreateSession.CreateSession
Close Method	-
Execute Method	ICommand.Execute
	IOpenRowset.OpenRowset
OpenSchema Method	IDBSchemaRowset.GetRowset
BeginTrans Method	ITransactionLocal.StartTransaction
CommitTrans Method	ITransaction.Commit
RollBack Method	ITransaction.Abort
Attributes Property	ITransactionLocal.StartTransaction
CommandTimeout Property	ICommandProperties.SetProperties
ConnectionTimeout Property	IDBProperties.SetProperties
DefaultDatabase Property	IDBProperties.GetProperties
	IDBProperties.SetProperties
IsolationLevel Property	ITransactionLocal.StartTransaction
Mode Property	IDBProperties.GetProperties
	IDBProperties.SetProperties
Provider Property	ISOurceRowset.GetSourceRowset
Errors Collection	IErrorRecords

- The ADO Command object uses the OLE DB Command object and ICommand interface. For example, its Execute method maps directly to the OLE DB Command object methods. Its CommandText property is available through the ICommandText.GetCommandText property and ICommandText.SetCommandText methods, and the Parameters collection is supported by the ICommandWithParameters interface. The following table shows how the methods of the ADO Command object are mapped to OLE DB interfaces and methods.

ADO Command Object	Uses OLE DB Interfaces and Methods
Execute Method	ICommand.Execute
CommandText Property	ICommandText.GetCommandText
	ICommandText.SetCommandText
CommandTimeout Property	ICommandProperties.SetProperties
Prepared Property	ICommandPrepare.Prepare
	ICommandPrepare.Unprepare
Parameters Collection	ICommandWithParameters.GetParameterInfo
	ICommandWithParameters.SetParameterInfo
Properties	IDBProperties.GetPropertyInfo
	ICommandProperties.GetProperties
	ICommandProperties.SetProperties

- The ADO Recordset object maps to the OLE DB Rowset object. It uses the IRowset, IrowsetLocate, and IRowsetInfo interfaces to implement most of its methods, properties, and collections. The Field object maps to the IColumnsInfo interface. This is shown in the table below.

ADO Recordset Object	Uses OLE DB Interfaces and Methods
Open Method	IOpenRowset.OpenRowset ICommand.Execute
Close Method	IAccessor.ReleaseAccessor IRowset.ReleaseRows
Move Method	IRowsetLocate.GetRowsAt IRowset.GetNextRows
Requery Method	IOpenRowset.OpenRowset ICommand.Execute
Update Method	IRowsetChange.SetData IRowsetUpdate.Update
UpdateBatch Method	IRowsetUpdate.Update
AbsolutePage Property	IRowsetScroll.GetApproximatePosition
ActiveConnection Property	IDBInitialize.Initialize IDBCreateSession.CreateSession
Filter Property	IRowsetUpdate.GetPendingRows IRowsetLocate.GetRowsByBookmark IViewFilter.SetFilter
Fields Collection	IColumnsInfo.GetColumnInfo
Properties Collection	IDBProperties.GetPropertyInfo IRowsetInfo.GetProperties IRowsetInfo.SetProperties

For more information, refer to *Microsoft OLE DB Programmer's Reference*, which is included with the Platform SDK.

ADO Library Extensions

Starting with version 2.1 (the version currently available for Windows 9.x and Windows NT computers), ADO includes several extensions that we will briefly cover below. Note that each of these extensions—ADOX, ADO MD, and JRO—is covered in separate chapters later in this book.

ADO Extensions for Data Definition and Security (ADOX)

The ADO Extensions for Data Definition and Security (ADOX) is a set of objects that allows us to manipulate the schema of a database (this is the data definition part of the ADOX) and to control the security objects within this database. ADOX adds several objects to the ADO object model described earlier in this chapter. These objects are shown in the following table.

Object	Purpose
Catalog	Represents the entire schema of a database
Table	Represents a single table within a database
Column	Represents a single column within a table, index, or key
Index	Represents a single index within a table
Key	Represents a primary or foreign key
Group	Represents a group of users
User	Represents an individual database user within a group
Procedure	Represents a single stored procedure within a database
View	Represents a single view within a database

The following figures show the ADOX object hierarchy.

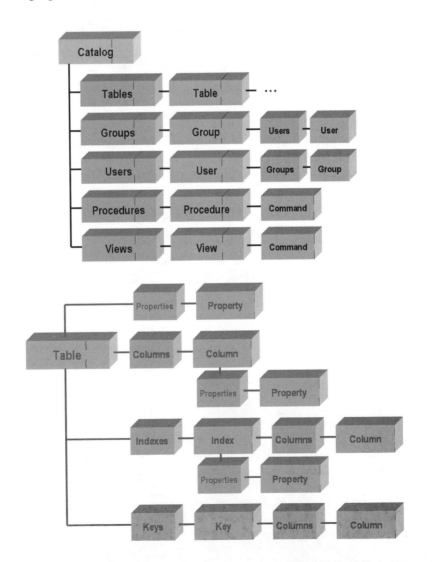

As we can see from these figures, the Table, Column, and Index objects have a standard ADO Properties collection. The ADOX objects represent most basic objects in a typical relational database, and their properties and methods can be used to create and manipulate these objects.

We will learn more about ADOX objects in Chapter 16.

ADO Multidimensional Extensions (ADO MD)

The ADO Multidimensional Extensions (ADO MD) provides a set of additional objects that allow us to use the multidimensional data from ADO application. Such data comes from an online analytical processing (OLAP) server such as Microsoft OLAP Server that ships with Microsoft SQL Server 7.0. OLAP servers are widely used in decision-support applications where you need to get a summary of large amounts of data, obtain statistics, and so on. The following table shows ADO MD objects that are part of the library.

Object	Purpose
Catalog	Represents schema information for a single OLAP database
CubeDef	Represents a cube from an OLAP Server
Dimension	Represents a dimension within a cube
Hierarchy	Represents a relationship of items within a dimension
Level	Represents a single level of hierarchy
Cellset	Represents the results of a single multidimensional query
Cell	Represents the partial result of a single multidimensional query
Axis	Represents filter for a single multidimensional query
Position	Specifies additional information for Cell and Axis objects
Member	Represents a unit of information for the Level object

The following figure shows the ADO MD object hierarchy.

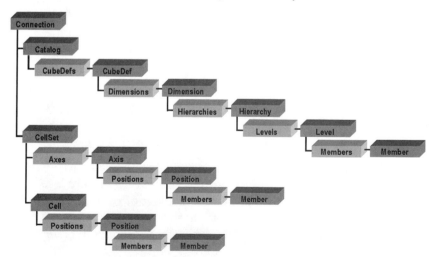

We will learn more about the ADO MD objects in Chapter 15.

Jet and Replication Objects (JRO)

Jet and Replication objects are a set of objects designed specifically for use with the Microsoft Jet OLE DB Provider. Its properties and methods allow us to create, modify, and synchronize replicas. A *replica* is a copy of a database in which changes are synchronized with the master database.

The Replica object is used to create new replicas, modify the properties of the existing replicas, and synchronize changes with other replicas.

The JetEngine object compacts the database and refreshes data from the memory cache.

The following figure shows the JRO object model.

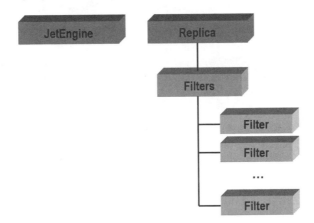

We will learn more about the JRO objects in Chapter 17.

> **Note:** For more information on ADO, refer to Microsoft's Web site at:
>   `http://www.microsoft.com/data/ado`
> or to the following newsgroups at `nntp://msnews.newsgroups.com`:
>   `microsoft.public.data.ado`
>   `microsoft.public.data.ado.rds`

Where to Get MDAC

The Microsoft Data Access Components are available to download from the Microsoft Web site at `http://www.microsoft.com/data`. They are also part of Delphi 5 Enterprise (the mdac_typ.exe file in the MDAC folder of your CD-ROM), Microsoft Office 2000, and Internet Explorer 5.0. Note that you should check the Microsoft site to get the most current version of MDAC; this will guarantee the latest bug fixes and the most recent versions of all components.

ADO 2.5 is a system component of Windows 2000 and does not require additional installations; everything is set during the operating system setup. The MDAC Software

Development Kit—a must-have for serious ADO developers—is available as part of the Microsoft Platform SDK. It is available on a CD-ROM or from Microsoft's Web site.

Conclusion

In this chapter, we have looked at the major parts of Microsoft Data Access Components (MDAC)—a set of key technologies that enable Universal Data Access. We have seen the purpose of OLE DB, which is the low-level interface that enables Universal Data Access, explored the objects that comprise the ADO object model and its extensions, and discussed how the methods of these objects are mapped to low-level OLE DB interfaces. This chapter gave us a lot of background to understand the material presented in following chapters.

In the next chapter, we will look at all the OLE DB providers available in MDAC, along with their properties, connection strings, and other information.

STANDARD OLE DB PROVIDERS

In the previous chapter, we explored the role that OLE DB providers play in the Microsoft data access architecture called Universal Data Access. We listed OLE DB providers that come as part of Microsoft Data Access Components (MDAC) and briefly described their purpose.

Here we will give you more details about the standard OLE DB providers available in MDAC, as well as show you where to get additional OLE DB providers and what tools can be used to build your own OLE DB providers. At the end of this chapter, we will create a Providers List (ProvList) utility that will give us details on every provider installed on the computer.

OLE DB Providers

This part of the chapter is organized in the following way. For each provider, we show its full name, short name, default path, and classID. Then we describe its purpose, connection string, and properties.

OLE DB Provider for ODBC

Full Name	Microsoft OLE DB Provider for ODBC Drivers
Short Name	MSDASQL
Path	\PROGRAM FILES\COMMON FILES\SYSTEM\OLE DB\MSDASQL.DLL
CLSID	{c8b522cb-5cf3-11ce-ade5-00aa0044773d}

The Microsoft OLE DB Provider for ODBC Drivers allows us to connect to any ODBC data source.

Connection String

To use this provider, specify the name of the provider in the connection string:

```
'Provider=MSDASQL; DSN=dsnName; UID=UserName; PWD=Password'
```

where:

Provider=MSDASQL	Specifies the OLE DB Provider for ODBC Drivers
DSN=dsnName	Specifies the Data Source Name
UID=UserName	Specifies the user name
PWD=Password	Specifies the password

If you are using a non-secured connection, the UID and PWD arguments of the connection string can be omitted:

```
'Provider=MSDASQL; DSN=dsnName'
```

In the example above, we have assumed that we use the Data Source Name, which is created with the help of ODBC Data Source Administrator. If you don't know where to get one, see the section below.

Creating an ODBC Data Source Name

Data Source Name (DSN) is the mechanism provided by ODBC for creating a package of connection information instead of you having to supply it every time you need to connect to a data source. In most cases, the DSN contains the name of the ODBC driver in use, the name of the database, the user name, and password.

To create an ODBC Data Source Name, perform the following steps:

1. Open the Control Panel window (**Start | Settings | Control Panel**) and double-click on the **ODBC Data Sources (32bit)** icon.

2. This will open the ODBC Data Source Administrator.

ODBC Data
Sources (32bit)

Note: In Windows 2000, the ODBC Administrator can be found under **Administrative Tools**.

ODBC Data Source Administrator   ? ☒

| User DSN | System DSN | File DSN | Drivers | Tracing | Connection Pooling | About |

User Data Sources:

Name	Driver	
dBASE Files	Microsoft dBase Driver (*.dbf)	**Add...**
dBase Files - Word	Microsoft dBase VFP Driver (*.dbf)	
demo	Microsoft Access Driver (*.mdb)	**Remove**
DEVELOP	Microsoft Access Driver (*.mdb)	
DevRes	Microsoft Access Driver (*.mdb)	**Configure...**
Excel Files	Microsoft Excel Driver (*.xls)	
FoxPro Files	Microsoft FoxPro Driver (*.dbf)	
FoxPro Files - Word	Microsoft FoxPro VFP Driver (*.dbf)	
GALLERY	Microsoft Access Driver (*.mdb)	
GAMES	Microsoft Access Driver (*.mdb)	
hardinfo	Microsoft Access Driver (*.mdb)	

An ODBC User data source stores information about how to connect to the indicated data provider. A User data source is only visible to you, and can only be used on the current machine.

| OK | Cancel | Apply | Help |

Note that the list of data sources shown in the above figure may differ from what is on your computer.

To run this applet programmatically, use the following code:

```
//
// OpenDSNSetup — calls the
// ODBC Data Source Administrator Applet
//
procedure TForm1.OpenDSNSetup(Sender: TObject);
var
 SysDir : Array[0..255] of Char;
 Path   : String;
begin
 GetSystemDirectory(SysDir, 255);
 Path := StrPas(SysDir) + '\odbcad32.exe';
 ShellExecute(Handle, 'Open', PChar(Path), '', '',
  SW_SHOWNORMAL);
end;
```

 Note: This procedure uses the `ShellAPI` unit, which must be included in the Uses clause.

Now you can create three types of Data Source Names: User DSN, System DSN, and File DSN.

■ The *User DSN* is the Data Source Name that is local to a computer, and can be used only by the current user.

■ The *System DSN* is also local to a computer but is not dedicated to the current user. The System DSN can be used by the system or any user with the appropriate privileges.

■ The *File DSN* is a file-based data source that is not dedicated to a user of a computer and can be shared among all users that have the same drivers installed.

Let's create a System DSN to show you the steps required.

1. First, select the **System DSN** tab, and click the **Add** button. This will activate the Create New Data Source dialog box with a list of ODBC drivers currently installed on the computer.

2. For this example, let's select **Microsoft Access Driver**, and then click on the **Finish** button. This will open the ODBC Microsoft Access Setup dialog box, where we supply the name and an optional description of the data, select a database or create a new one, and set some additional options.

3. After supplying the information required, press the **OK** button; the newly created System DSN will appear in the list.

4. Note that on the Tracing tab, we can start ODBC Tracing, which allows us to create logs of the calls to ODBC drivers. This is mostly needed during debugging.

5. Press the **OK** button to finish working with the ODBC Data Source Administrator.

The OLE DB Provider for ODBC Drivers also allows us to specify the DSN-less connection string and ODBC File DSN.

For DSN-less connections we specify the name of the provider and the name of the ODBC driver we will use:

```
'Provider=MSDASQL; Driver=DriverName'
```

Additional parameters here can be: `Server=`, `Database=`, as well as security information: `UID=UserName` and `PWD=Password`.

The driver name can be obtained from ODBC Data Source Administrator. See the Drivers tab for a list of ODBC drivers available on your computer.

To programmatically obtain a list of ODBC drivers installed on your computer, use the code below:

```
//
// GetODBCDriversList — Returns a list of ODBC Drivers
// installed on a computer
//
procedure GetODBCDriversList(List : TStrings);
var
 Reg     : TRegistry;
 TmpList : TStringList;
 I       : Integer;
begin
 try
  Reg := TRegistry.Create;
  TmpList := TStringList.Create;
  with Reg do
   begin
    RootKey := HKEY_LOCAL_MACHINE;
    OpenKey('\SOFTWARE\ODBC\ODBCINST.INI\ODBC Drivers', False);
    GetValueNames(TmpList);
    CloseKey;
    For I := 0 to TmpList.Count-1 do
     begin
      OpenKey('\SOFTWARE\ODBC\ODBCINST.INI\'+TmpList[I], False);
      List.Add(TmpList[I]);
     end;
 finally
  TmpList.Free;
  Reg.Free;
 end;
end;
```

Note: This procedure uses the Registry unit, which must be included in the Uses clause.

The driver name should be enclosed in curly braces. For example:

```
'Provider=MSDASQL; Driver={Microsoft Access Driver (*.mdb)}'
```

If we use the File DSN, we specify it with the FileDSN parameter. For example:

```
'Provider=MSDASQL; FileDSN=MyNorth'
```

Using Different Data Sources

As we indicated at the start of this section, the OLE DB Provider for ODBC Drivers allows us to connect to any ODBC data source. Following are some examples of the connection strings for several popular data sources.

Microsoft Access

To connect to a Microsoft Access database, use the following syntax:

```
'Provider=MSDASQL; Driver={Microsoft Access Driver (*.mdb)};
DBQ=c:\data\northwind.mdb'
```

Microsoft SQL Server

To connect to a Microsoft SQL Server database, use the following syntax:

```
'Provider=MSDASQL; Driver={SQL Server}; Server=main; Database=pubs;
UID=sa; PWD='
```

Microsoft Excel

To connect to a Microsoft Excel file, use the following syntax:

```
'Provider=MSDASQL; Driver={Microsoft Excel Driver (*.xls)};
DBQ=c:\data\customers.xls'
```

Note that the range should be specified in Excel before you will be able to extract data. To do so, select the data required in your spreadsheet and set the name of the range.

Text Files

To connect to a text file, use the following syntax:

```
'Provider=MSDASQL; Driver={Microsoft Text Driver (*.txt; *.csv)};
DBQ=c:\data\'
```

Note that in this example we have not specified the name of the text file. This is done when we open a connection or recordset.

Properties

The OLE DB Provider for ODBC Drivers supports some initial properties that can be set either through the Data Link Properties dialog box or programmatically.

Property	Meaning
Connect Timeout	How much time to wait for the connection to complete
Data Source	Indicates the name of the database to connect to
Extended Properties	Indicates provider-specific properties
Initial Catalog	Indicates the name of the default catalog used to connect to the data source
Locale Identifier	Indicates the locale ID for the consumer
Location	Indicates the location of the database to connect to

Property	Meaning
Mode	Specifies the access permissions
Password	Specifies the password
Persist Security Info	Indicates whether the data source can save authentication information
User ID	Specifies the user name that is used along with the password

To programmatically set one of the properties, use the following syntax:

```
ADOConnection1.Properties['Locale Identifier'].Value := 1033;
```

Note that some of the properties will become read-only after you open the connection. We will discuss this in Chapter 5.

OLE DB Provider for Microsoft Jet

Full Name	Microsoft Jet 4.0 OLE DB Provider
Short Name	Microsoft.Jet.OLEDB.4.0
Path	WINDOWS\SYSTEM\MSJET40.DLL
CLSID	{dee35070-506b-11cf-b1aa-00aa00b8de95}

The Microsoft Jet 4.0 OLE DB Provider is used to connect to Microsoft Access databases, as well as several other data sources.

Connection String

Use the following connection string to use this provider:

```
'Provider=Microsoft.Jet.OLEDB.4.0; Data Source = c:\data\northwind.mdb'
```

If we use the system database, then we need to specify it in the connection string:

```
'Provider=Microsoft.Jet.OLEDB.4.0; Data Source = c:\data\northwind.mdb;
Jet OLEDB:System Database=d:\Program Files\Microsoft
Office\Office\system.mdw'
```

Using Different Data Sources

Besides the Microsoft Access database, we can use other data sources with the Microsoft Jet 4.0 OLE DB Provider. To get a list of supported formats (called ISAM drivers in Jet terms), use the following code:

```
//
// GetISAMFormats - returns a list of ISAM drivers
// supported by the Jet OLE DB Provider
//
procedure GetISAMFormats(List : TStrings);
var
 R : TRegistry;
begin
 try
  R := TRegistry.Create;
```

```
  With R do
   begin
    RootKey := HKEY_LOCAL_MACHINE;
    OpenKey('Software\Microsoft\Jet\4.0\ISAM Formats\', False);
    GetKeyNames(List);
    CloseKey;
   end;
 finally
  R.Free;
 end;
end;
```

Note: This procedure uses the Registry unit, which must be included in the Uses clause.

Examples of connection strings follow:

dBase

To connect to a dBase database, use the following syntax:

```
'Provider=Microsoft.Jet.OLEDB.4.0; Data Source = c:\data\;
Extended Properties="dBase 5.0;"'
```

Depending on the version of your dBase database, you can also specify dBase III or dBase IV in the Extended Properties parameter.

HTML File

To connect to an HTML file, use the following syntax:

```
'Provider=Microsoft.Jet.OLEDB.4.0; Data Source = c:\data\customers.htm;
Extended Properties="HTML Import;"'
```

Microsoft Excel

To connect to a Microsoft Excel file, use the following syntax:

```
'Provider=Microsoft.Jet.OLEDB.4.0; Data Source = c:\data\customers.xls;
Extended Properties="Excel 8.0;"'
```

Depending on the version of your Excel file you can also specify Excel 3.0, Excel 4.0 or Excel 5.0 in the Extended Properties parameter.

Paradox

To connect to a Paradox database, use the following syntax:

```
'Provider=Microsoft.Jet.OLEDB.4.0; Data Source = c:\data\; Extended
Properties="Paradox 7.X;"'
```

Depending on the version of your Paradox database you can also specify Paradox 3.X, Paradox 4.X, or Paradox 5.X in the Extended Properties parameter.

Text File

To connect to a text file, use the following syntax:

```
'Provider=Microsoft.Jet.OLEDB.4.0; Data Source = c:\data\; Extended
Properties="Text;"'
```

To connect to a text file in which values are separated with characters, such as comma separated values text files, you should create a SCHEMA.INI file that contains information about your text file. For example, if your data is tab delimited, the SCHEMA.INI file may look like this:

```
[mytext.txt]
Format=TabDelimited
```

Properties

The Microsoft Jet 4.0 OLE DB Provider supports some initial properties that can be set either through the Data Link Properties dialog box or programmatically.

Property	Meaning
Extended Properties	Indicates provider-specific properties
Jet OLEDB:Compact Reclaimed Space Amount	Indicates the amount of space reclaimed during a compaction
Jet OLEDB:Compact Without Replica Repair	Specifies whether to repair damaged replicas
Jet OLEDB:Create System Database	Indicates whether to create a system database
Jet OLEDB:Database Locking Mode	Specifies the mode to use when locking the database
Jet OLEDB:Database Password	Specifies the database password
Jet OLEDB:Don't Copy Locale on Compact	Indicates what sort order to use when compacting
Jet OLEDB:Encrypt Database	Specifies whether to encrypt the database
Jet OLEDB:Engine Type	Indicates the version of the database engine used to open or create the database
Jet OLEDB:Global Bulk Transactions	Indicates transactional bulk operations
Jet OLEDB:Global Partial Bulk Ops	Indicates whether it is possible to use the partial values in the bulk operations
Jet OLEDB:New Database Password	Sets the new password for the database
Jet OLEDB:Registry Path	Sets the path to the registry settings for the Jet engine
Jet OLEDB:SFP	Undocumented
Jet OLEDB:System database	Indicates the system database to use
Locale Identifier	Indicates the locale ID for the consumer
Mode	Specifies the access permissions
OLE DB Services	Specifies the OLE DB services to enable
Persist Security Info	Indicates whether the data source can save authentication information
Prompt	Specifies whether to prompt the user during initialization
Window Handle	Indicates the window handle that can be used to prompt for extra information

OLE DB Provider for SQL Server

Full Name	Microsoft OLE DB Provider for SQL Server
Short Name	SQLOLEDB
Path	PROGRAM FILES\COMMON FILES\SYSTEM\OLE DB\SQLOLEDB.DLL
CLSID	{0C7FF16C-38E3-11d0-97AB-00C04FC2AD98}

The Microsoft OLE DB Provider for SQL Server is used to connect to Microsoft SQL Server databases.

Connection String

Use the following connection string to use this provider:

```
'Provider=SQLOLEDB; DataSource=main; Initial Catalog=pubs; User ID=sa;
Password='
```

You specify the name of the server in the DataSource parameter and the name of the database on this server in the Initial Catalog parameter. The last two parameters, User ID and Password, are used for SQL Server authentication.

Properties

The Microsoft OLE DB Provider for SQL Server supports some initial properties that can be set either through the Data Link Properties dialog box or programmatically.

Property	Meaning
Application Name	Specifies the name of the client application
Auto Translate	Indicates whether to use OEM/ANSI character conversion
Connect Timeout	How much time to wait for the connection to complete
Current Language	Specifies the language for system messages
Data Source	Indicates the name of the database to connect to
Extended Properties	Indicates provider-specific properties
Initial Catalog	Indicates the name of the default catalog used to connect to the data source
Initial File Name	Indicates the filename of a database
Integrated Security	Specifies the name of the authentication service
Locale Identifier	Indicates the locale ID for the consumer
Network Address	Indicates the network address of the SQL Server
Network Library	Indicates the name of the network library used to communicate with the SQL Server
OLE DB Services	Specifies the OLE DB services to enable
Packet Size	Indicates a network packet size in bytes, which must be between 512 and 32767; the default value is 4096
Password	Specifies the password
Persist Security Info	Indicates whether the data source can save authentication information
Prompt	Specifies whether to prompt the user during initialization
Use Procedure for Prepare	Determines whether SQL Server creates temporary stored procedures when commands are prepared

Property	Meaning
User ID	Specifies the User ID used to connect to the database
Window Handle	Indicates the window handle that can be used to prompt for extra information
Workstation ID	Specifies the workstation

OLE DB Provider for Oracle

Full Name	Microsoft OLE DB Provider for Oracle
Short Name	MSDAORA
Path	PROGRAM FILES\COMMON FILES\SYSTEM\OLE DB\MSDAORA.DLL
CLSID	{e8cc4cbe-fdff-11d0-b865-00a0c9081c1d}

The Microsoft OLE DB Provider for Oracle is used to access Oracle databases.

Connection String

Specify the following connection string to use this provider:

```
'Provider=MSDAORA; Data Source=oramain; User ID=admin; Password=;'
```

The Data Source parameter specifies the name of a server.

Properties

The Microsoft OLE DB Provider for Oracle supports some initial properties that can be set either through the Data Link Properties dialog box or programmatically.

Property	Meaning
Data Source	Specifies the name of a server
Extended Properties	Indicates provider-specific properties
Locale Identifier	Indicates the locale ID for the consumer
OLE DB Services	Specifies the OLE DB services to enable
Password	Specifies the password
Persist Security Info	Indicates whether the data source can save authentication information
Prompt	Specifies whether to prompt the user during initialization
User ID	Specifies the user ID used to connect to the database
Window Handle	Indicates the window handle that can be used to prompt for extra information

OLE DB Provider for Internet Publishing

Full Name	Microsoft OLE DB Provider for Internet Publishing
Short Name	MSDAIPP.DSO
Path	PROGRAM FILES\COMMON FILES \SYSTEM\OLE DB \MSDAIPP.DLL
CLSID	{AF320921-9381-11d1-9C3C-0000F875AC61}

Using this provider, you can connect to Web servers and access resources served by Microsoft FrontPage or Microsoft Internet Information Server. Such resources include

HTML files and Windows 2000 Web folders. Web servers should support either the Microsoft FrontPage Server Extensions or the Distributed Authoring and Versioning Protocol.

Connection String

To connect to the OLE DB Provider for Internet Publishing, specify the following connection string:

```
"Provider=MSDAIPP.DSO; Data Source=ResourceURL; User ID=UserName;
Password=UserPassword"
```

where:

Provider=MSDAIPP.DSO	Specifies the OLE DB Provider for Internet Publishing
Data Source	Specifies the URL for file or directory on a Web server
User ID	Specifies the user name
Password	Specifies the user password

Instead of using the `Provider` and `Data Source` keywords, we can use an alternate form of the connection string:

```
"URL=ResourceURL; User ID=UserName; Password=UserPassword"
```

where:

URL	Specifies the URL for file or directory on a Web server
User ID	Specifies the user name
Password	Specifies the user password

In this case, we should not explicitly specify the provider name, either with the `Provider` keyword, or with the Provider property.

Property	Meaning
Bind Flags	Specifies the binding behavior for resources
Cache Aggressively	Indicates whether provider will download and cache all properties
Connect Timeout	How much time to wait for the connection to complete
Data Source	Specifies the URL for file or directory on a Web server
Ignore Cached Data	Specifies whether to ignore any cached data
Locale Identifier	Indicates the locale ID for the consumer
Lock Owner	Indicates the string that will be shown when other users attempt to access the locked resource
Mark For Offline	Indicates whether the URL can be marked for offline use
Mode	Specifies the access permissions
Password	Specifies the password
Prompt	Specifies whether to prompt the user during initialization
Protocol Provider	Specifies the protocol to connect; can be either WEC or DAV
Treat As Offline	Specifies whether the resource can be treated as an offline resource

Properties

Property	Meaning
User ID	Specifies the user ID used to connect to the database
Window Handle	Indicates the window handle that can be used to prompt for extra information

OLE DB Provider for Microsoft Active Directory Service

Full Name	OLE DB Provider for Microsoft Directory Services
Short Name	ADsDSOObject
Path	WINDOWS\SYSTEM\ACTIVEDS.DLL
CLSID	{549365d0-ec26-11cf-8310-00aa00b505db}

The OLE DB Provider for Microsoft Directory Services can be used to connect to heterogeneous directory services through Microsoft Active Directory Service Interfaces (ADSI). This gives read-only access to Windows NT and Windows 2000 directory services as well as to any LDAP-compliant directory services such as Novell Directory Services.

Connection String

Specify the following connection string to use this provider:

```
'Provider=ADSDSOBJECT; User ID=userName; Password=userPassword'
```

OLE DB Provider for Microsoft Index Server

Full Name	Microsoft OLE DB Provider for Microsoft Index Server
Short Name	MSIDXS
Path	SYSTEM32\MSIDXS.DLL
CLSID	{F9AE8980-7E52-11d0-8964-00C04FD611D7}

The Microsoft OLE DB Provider for Microsoft Indexing Service provides programmatic read-only access to file system and Web data indexed by Microsoft Indexing Service. ADO applications can issue SQL queries to retrieve content and file property information.

Note: This provider comes with the Microsoft Index Server.

Connection String

Specify the following connection string to use this provider:

```
'Provider=MSIDXS; Data Source=Catalog; Locale Identifier=xxxx'
```

where:

- The Data Source parameter specifies the Indexing Service catalog name. If this keyword is not specified, the default system catalog is used.

■ The Locale Identifier parameter specifies the language preferences.

OLE DB Simple Provider

Full Name	Microsoft OLE DB Simple Provider
Short Name	MSDAOSP
Path	PROGRAM FILES\COMMON FILES\SYSTEM\OLE DB\MSDAOSP.DLL
CLSID	{dfc8bdc0-e378-11d0-9b30-0080c7e9fe95}

The Microsoft OLE DB Simple Provider is created with the Microsoft OLE DB Simple Provider Toolkit. It allows us to connect to simple text files.

Connection String

To use this provider, specify the following connection string:

```
'Provider=MSDAOSP; Data Source = dataSource'
```

Properties

Property	Meaning
Asynchronous Processing	Specifies the asynchronous processing performed on the rowset
Data Source	Specifies the data source to use
OLE DB Services	Specifies the OLE DB services to enable
Persist Security Info	Indicates whether the data source can save authentication information

In the sections above, we have looked at several features available for the OLE DB providers, which allow us to connect to the data sources—various databases, stored locally or on the remote computers, and database servers. A second group of OLE DB providers is called *service providers*. This name implies that they provide services rather than data. In most cases, service providers are used in conjunction with data providers.

Service Providers

In this section we will take a brief look at several of the available service providers, including the following:

■ Cursor Service for OLE DB

■ Data Shaping Service for OLE DB

■ OLE DB Persistence Provider

■ OLE DB Remoting Provider

■ OLE DB Provider for OLAP Services

There may be more OLE DB service providers installed on your computer. Use the ProvList utility described later in this chapter to get a list of the installed OLE DB providers.

Cursor Service for OLE DB

Full Name	Cursor Service for OLE DB
Path	PROGRAM FILES\COMMON FILES\SYSTEM\MSADC\MSADCE.DLL

This service provider enhances cursor functionality but is not used directly. Its services are invoked by setting the `adUseClient` value of the `CursorLocation` property of the ADO Recordset or Connection objects.

 Note: In Delphi, the CursorLocation property is available for the TADOConnection and TCustomADODataSet components.

Data Shaping Service for OLE DB

Full Name	MSDataShape
Short Name	MSDataShape
Path	PROGRAM FILES\COMMON FILES\SYSTEM\MSADC\MSADDS.DLL
CLSID	{3449A1C8-C56C-11D0-AD72-00C04FC29863}

The Data Shaping Service for OLE DB can be used to create relationships between keys, fields, and rowsets, and to construct hierarchical rowset objects from the data provider.

Connection String

To use the Data Shaping Service for OLE DB, specify the name of the provider in the connection string. For example:

```
'Provider=MSDataShape; Data Provider=MSDASQL; Driver={SQL Server};
Server=main; Database=pubs; UID=sa; PWD=;'
```

Before you can use the Data Shaping Service for OLE DB, the Cursor Service for OLE DB must be installed. Make sure that both service providers come from the same set of MDAC components.

OLE DB Persistence Provider

Full Name	OLE DB Persistence Provider
Short Name	MSPersist
Path	PROGRAM FILES\COMMON FILES\SYSTEM\MSADC\MSDAPRT.DLL

With the help of the OLE DB Persistence Provider it is possible to save rowset data in Advanced Data Table Gram (ADTG) format or eXtensible Markup Language (XML) format.

The services of the OLE DB Persistence Provider are invoked when you call the Save method of the ADO Recordset object. As we will learn later in this book, the Save method allows us to save recordsets in XML and Microsoft's own ADTG format and use such saved recordsets in disconnected mode.

OLE DB Remoting Provider

Full Name	MS Remote
Short Name	MS Remote
Path	PROGRAM FILES\COMMON FILES\SYSTEM\MSADC\MSDAREM.DLL
CLSID	{27016870-8E02-11D1-924E-00C04FBBBFB3}

The OLE DB Remoting Provider allows us to invoke data providers on a remote machine. There are two ways to use this service provider. The simplest one is to use the RDS (Remote Data Services) objects (such as RDSConnection) that are designed to work within the Microsoft Internet Explorer browser. The other way is to specify the name of this provider in the connection string as shown below:

```
'Provider=MS Remote; Remote Server=http://localhost; Remote
 Provider=SQLServer; Data Source=pubs; User ID=sa; Password='
```

In this example, we use the OLE DB Remoting Provider to invoke the OLE DB Provider for SQL Server on the remote computer and to access the Pubs database.

OLE DB Provider for OLAP Services

Full Name	Microsoft OLE DB Provider for OLAP Services
Short Name	MSOLAP
Path	PROGRAM FILES\COMMON FILES\SYSTEM\OLE DB\MSOLAP.DLL
CLSID	{a07ccd00-8148-11d0-87bb-00c04fc33942}

The Microsoft OLE DB Provider for OLAP Services is used with the ADO Multidimensional (ADO MD) extensions to access the services of the OLAP Server for SQL Server 7.0. For more information, see Chapter 15.

Several other Microsoft products come with a set of OLE DB providers that exposes its services. As we have already mentioned, one of them is Microsoft Index Server. Another good example is Microsoft Site Server, which comes with the following providers: Content Index DSO, Net Library DSO, and Net Library Collator. Consult your product documentation to see whether the product exposes its services via an OLE DB provider.

Where to Get OLE DB Providers

In the section above, we looked at the OLE DB providers that come with Microsoft Data Access Components (MDAC), as well as the providers installed with Microsoft SQL Server 7.0.

Some database vendors provide OLE DB providers with their products. The following table lists several popular database vendors:

Vendor	Providers	URL
Computer Associates, Inc.	Jasmine OLE DB Provider	http://www.cai.com/
Informix Software, Inc.	INFORMIX OLE DB Provider	http://www.informix.com
Object Design, Inc.	ObjectStore OLE DB Provider	http://www.odi.com
SAS Institute	SAS/MDDB	http://www.sas.com
Sequiter Software Inc.	CodeBase OLE DB Provider	http://www.sequiter.com

In addition, there are companies that implement OLE DB providers for various data sources. They are listed in the table below:

Vendor	Providers	URL
Applied Information Services – UniAccess	AIS UniAccess	http://www.uniaccess.com
ASNA	Acceler8-DB and DataGate/400	http://www.asna.com/
B2 Systems – SQL Integrator	Oracle, Sybase, Informix, Microsoft SQL Server, RDB, DB2, Flat files	http://www.b2systems.com/
HiT Software, Inc.	HiT OLE DB Server/400	http://www.hit.com/
ISG – ISG Navigator	C-ISAM, DB2, IMS, INFORMIX, Jasmine, OpenIngres, Oracle, SQL Server, Sybase, ADABAS, Rdb, RMS, VSAM	http://www.isgsoft.com/
MERANT plc – CONNECT OLE DB	INFORMIX 7.x and 9.x, Lotus Notes v 4.11a, 4.5, Microsoft SQL Server 6.5, 7.x, Oracle 7.x, 8.0.x, Sybase System 10,11, Adaptive Server 11.x	http://www.merant.com
MERANT plc – Reflector	Query processor for SQL and non-SQL data sources	http://www.merant.com
MERANT plc – SequeLink OLE DB Edition	CA-Open Ingres, IBM DB2/MVS, DB2/400, DB2 UDB, MVS/VSAM via CICS 4.1, INFORMIX Dynamic Server, Online, SE, Microsoft SQL Server 6.5, 7.x, Oracle 7.x, 8.x, Sybase System 10.x, 11.x, Sybase Adaptive Server, ODBC Socket	http://www.merant.com
MetaWise Computing	AS/400, MVS/VSAM	http://www.metawise.com/
Microsoft Corp.	LDAP, NetWare, NT directories, text, HTML, Offices documents, SQL,VSAM, AS/400, SQL Server, ODBC data sources	http://www.microsoft.com/data /oledb
NCR Corporation – Teradata OLE DB Provider	Teradata	http://www.ncr.com
Novell, Inc. – Database Manager for NetWare (ODBX-OLE-DB)	Flat files, INFORMIX, Ingres, Oracle, Microsoft SQL Server, Sybase	http://developer.novell.com
Sagent Technology, Inc. – Sagent Data Mart Server	Flat files, INFORMIX, Oracle, Red Brick, Sybase, Microsoft SQL Server, ODBC data sources (including DB2)	http://www.sagenttech.com
X-Tension Projects Ltd. – OLE DB for OLAP MDX Parser	ProGnosis Data Explorer, other providers	http://www.xdb.com

Note: Up-to-date information on available OLE DB providers can be found at the Microsoft Universal Data Access site:

        http://www.microsoft.com/data/partners/products.htm

In rare cases, when you need to build your own OLE DB provider, there are several tools available on the market:

Vendor	Tool	URL
Simba Technologies	SimbaProvider SimbaProvider for OLAP SDK	http://www.simba.com/
Automation Technology Company	OpenAccess OLE DB SDK	http://www.odbcsdk.com/
Geppetto's Workshop	AntMDX	http://www.geppetto.com/
X-Tension	MDX Parser for OLE DB for OLAP	http://www.x-tension.com/
IBM	Client Access for Windows 9x/NT SDK	http://www.as400.ibm.com/

Note: At least one tool for Delphi programmers was still in the development stage when we wrote this book. It is called the OLE DB Provider Toolkit for Delphi 5 and was developed by Binh Ly. For more information, check the following Web site:

        http://www.techvanguards.com

Getting a List of Installed Providers

We end this chapter by implementing the ProvList utility, which will allow you to find providers installed on your computer. For simplicity, this is the console utility, i.e., without any graphical user interface with output directly on the screen. To save its output you need to redirect it to file, as shown below:

    C:\>provlist.exe >provlist.txt

Most of the information it provides is taken from the System Registry. The first step is to obtain a list of OLE DB provider names. There are several ways to do so, but we will use the handy GetProviderNames procedure from the ADODB unit. It calls low-level OLE DB API functions and fills the list, supplied as an argument with the names of the OLE DB providers, available on the computer. Here is what we can get from it:

```
ADsDSOObject
MSDataShape
MS Remote
SQL65Prv
Microsoft.Jet.OLEDB.3.51
DTSPackageDSO
```

```
DTSFlatFile
MSOLAP
MSDAIPP.DSO
MSDASQL
MSDAOSP
SQLOLEDB
MSDAORA
Microsoft.Jet.OLEDB.4.0
```

Not very impressive at first look. To get more information on each provider, for example, its readable name, version, and even a CLSID, we need to dig into the System Registry. This task is simple once we have a list at hand. We iterate through the `HKEY_CLASSES_ROOT\CLSID` branch looking for one of the names from the providers list. If we find one, we read its `\InProcServer32` and `\OLE DB Provider` subkeys to obtain the full filename and description and then extract the file version information from the file. For the list of providers above, the information returned by the `ProvList` utility may look like this:

```
Name    : OLE DB Provider for Microsoft Directory Services
          (ADsDSOObject)
CLSID   : {549365d0-ec26-11cf-8310-00aa00b505db}
Path    : activeds.dll
Version : 4.01.110.1

Name    : MSDataShape (MSDataShape)
CLSID   : {3449A1C8-C56C-11D0-AD72-00C04FC29863}
Path    : D:\PROGRAM FILES\COMMON FILES\SYSTEM\MSADC\MSADDS.DLL
Version : 2.10.4202.1

Name    : MS Remote (MS Remote)
CLSID   : {27016870-8E02-11D1-924E-00C04FBBBFB3}
Path    : D:\PROGRAM FILES\COMMON FILES\SYSTEM\MSADC\MSDAREM.DLL
Version : 2.10.4202.1

Name    : Microsoft SQLServer 6.5 To 7.0 conversion
          OLE DB Provider (SQL65Prv)
CLSID   : {871E9159-18A4-11d0-913B-00AA00B4DFEA}
Path    : D:\MSSQL7\UPGRADE\CNV6X70.DLL
Version : Not found

Name    : Microsoft Jet 3.51 OLE DB Provider
          (Microsoft.Jet.OLEDB.3.51)
CLSID   : {dee35060-506b-11cf-b1aa-00aa00b8de95}
Path    : D:\PROGRAM FILES\COMMON FILES\SYSTEM\OLE
          DB\MSJTOR35.DLL
Version : 3.52.1527.4
```

```
Name     : Microsoft OLE DB Provider for DTS Packages
           (DTSPackageDSO)
CLSID    : {10010031-EB1C-11CF-AE6E-00AA004A34D5}
Path     : D:\MSSQL7\BINN\DTSPKG.DLL
Version  : 7.00.623


Name     : SQL Server DTS Flat File OLE DB Provider (DTSFlatFile)
CLSID    : {10010100-0224-11D1-B7B8-00C04FB6EFD5}
Path     : D:\MSSQL7\BINN\DTSFFILE.DLL
Version  : 7.00.623


Name     : Microsoft OLE DB Provider for OLAP Services (MSOLAP)
CLSID    : {a07ccd00-8148-11d0-87bb-00c04fc33942}
Path     : D:\PROGRAM FILES\COMMON FILES\SYSTEM\OLE DB\MSOLAP.DLL
Version  : 7.0.1073.1114


Name     : Microsoft OLE DB Provider for Internet Publishing
           (MSDAIPP.DSO)
CLSID    : {AF320921-9381-11d1-9C3C-0000F875AC61}
Path     : D:\PROGRA~1\COMMON~1\SYSTEM\OLEDB~1\MSDAIPP.DLL
Version  : 8.102.1403.0


Name     : Microsoft OLE DB Provider for ODBC Drivers (MSDASQL)
CLSID    : {c8b522cb-5cf3-11ce-ade5-00aa0044773d}
Path     : D:\PROGRAM FILES\COMMON FILES\SYSTEM\OLE
           DB\MSDASQL.DLL
Version  : 02.10.4202.0


Name     : Microsoft OLE DB Simple Provider (MSDAOSP)
CLSID    : {dfc8bdc0-e378-11d0-9b30-0080c7e9fe95}
Path     : D:\PROGRAM FILES\COMMON FILES\SYSTEM\OLE
           DB\MSDAOSP.DLL
Version  : 2.10.4202.1


Name     : Microsoft OLE DB Provider for SQL Server (SQLOLEDB)
CLSID    : {0C7FF16C-38E3-11d0-97AB-00C04FC2AD98}
Path     : D:\PROGRAM FILES\COMMON FILES\SYSTEM\OLE
           DB\SQLOLEDB.DLL
Version  : 07.01.0690


Name     : Microsoft OLE DB Provider for Oracle (MSDAORA)
CLSID    : {e8cc4cbe-fdff-11d0-b865-00a0c9081c1d}
Path     : D:\PROGRAM FILES\COMMON FILES\SYSTEM\OLE
           DB\MSDAORA.DLL
Version  : 02.10.4202.0
```

```
Name     : Microsoft Jet 4.0 OLE DB Provider
           (Microsoft.Jet.OLEDB.4.0)
CLSID    : {dee35070-506b-11cf-b1aa-00aa00b8de95}
Path     : D:\WINDOWS\SYSTEM\MSJETOLEDB40.DLL
Version  : 4.00.2927.2
```

The same information can be obtained from OLE DB functions using the root enumerator. This is left as a reader exercise.

As you can see, now it is easier to understand what providers you have, their purpose, where are they stored, and the current version of a particular one. The full source code for the ProvList utility is shown below.

```
{-------------------------------------------------------

 ProvList - Command line utility that shows the list
 of OLE DB Providers installed on the computer along
 with its names, descriptions, CLSIDs and paths

 -------------------------------------------------------}
program ProvList;
{$APPTYPE CONSOLE}
uses
  SysUtils,
  ADODB,
  Classes,
  Registry,
  Windows,
  ComObj,
  ActiveX;

var
 List      : TStringList;
 ClassList : TStringList;
 OutList   : TStringList;

function GetFileVer(FileName : String) : String;
var
 VerSize : DWORD;
 Zero    : THandle;
 PBlock  : Pointer;
 PS      : Pointer;
 Size    : UINT;
begin
{** Get size of Version resource **}
 VerSize := GetFileVersionInfoSize(PChar(FileName), Zero);
 If VerSize = 0 Then
  Begin
   GetFileVer := 'Not found';
```

```
   Exit;
  End;
{** Allocate memory **}
 GetMem(PBlock, VerSize);
{** Get Version resource **}
 GetFileVersionInfo(PChar(FileName), 0, VerSize, PBlock);
 If VerQueryValue(PBlock,
   '\\StringFileInfo\\000004E4\\ProductVersion',PS, Size)
  Then
   GetFileVer := StrPas(PS)
 Else
  If VerQueryValue(PBlock,
   '\\StringFileInfo\\040904E4\\ProductVersion',PS, Size)
   Then
    GetFileVer := StrPas(PS)
 Else
  If VerQueryValue(PBlock,
   '\\StringFileInfo\\000004B0\\ProductVersion',PS, Size)
   Then
    GetFileVer := StrPas(PS)
 Else
  If VerQueryValue(PBlock,
   '\\StringFileInfo\\040904B0\\ProductVersion',PS, Size)
   Then
    GetFileVer := StrPas(PS)
 Else
  GetFileVer := '';
 FreeMem(PBlock, VerSize);
end;

procedure Init;
begin
 ClassList := TStringList.Create;
 List      := TStringList.Create;
 OutList   := TStringList.Create;
 Writeln('ProvList 1.0'^M^J);
end;

procedure Run;
var
 Reg      : TRegistry;
 I,J      : Integer;
 Path     : String;
 Desc     : String;
 Item     : String;
begin
// Initialize COM Kernel
 CoInitialize(Nil);
```

```
try
  Reg := TRegistry.Create;
// ---------------- OLE DB Info ----------------- //
// Get a list of Providers from OLEDB
  Writeln(^M^J'[OLE DB Providers]'^M^J);
  GetProviderNames(List);
  With Reg do
    begin
      RootKey := HKEY_CLASSES_ROOT;
      OpenKey('\CLSID\', False);
// Load all CLSIDs found in the Registry
      GetKeyNames(ClassList);
      For I := 0 to ClassList.Count-1 do
        begin
// Open one key
        OpenKey('\CLSID\'+ClassList[I], False);
// Read ID
        Item := ReadString('');
        For J := 0 to List.Count-1 do
          begin
// If this is one of the Provider IDs
          If List[J] = Item Then
            begin
            CloseKey;
// Read its path
            OpenKey('\CLSID\' + ClassList[I] + '\InProcServer32',
              False);
            Path := ReadString('');
            CloseKey;
// Read its Description
            OpenKey('\CLSID\' + ClassList[I] + '\OLE DB Provider',
              False);
            Desc := ReadString('');
            CloseKey;
// Store in the list
            OutList.Add('Name    : ' + Desc +
              ' (' + List[J] + ')');
            OutList.Add('CLSID   : ' + ClassList[I]);
            OutList.Add('Path    : ' + Path);
            OutList.Add('Version : ' + GetFileVer(Path));
            OutList.Add('');
            end;
          end;
        end;
    end;
finally
  Reg.Free;
end;
```

```
// Finally, show
 For I := 0 to OutList.Count-1 do
  Writeln(OutList[I]);
end;

procedure Done;
begin
 ClassList.Free;
 List.Free;
 OutList.Free;
end;

begin
 Init;
 Run;
 Done;
end.
```

The source code for the ProvList utility is available on the CD-ROM in the SOURCE\CH03 folder.

Conclusion

In this chapter, we provided information about the standard OLE DB providers that come with the Microsoft Data Access Components (MDAC) pack. We have learned the purpose of each provider, have seen its connection string and properties, and now know where to look when we need an OLE DB provider for additional data sources. We also learned what tools are available to create our own OLE DB providers. At the end of this chapter, we implemented a small utility that outputs a list of providers installed on the computer along with its name, version, path, and CLSID.

In the next chapter, we begin to talk about Delphi and discuss the Delphi database architecture—the database related part of VCL and the architecture behind the Delphi ADO components.

DELPHI DATABASE ARCHITECTURE

In this chapter, we will provide a brief overview of the Delphi database architecture, as we believe this material is necessary for readers who are new to database programming. The ADO support implemented in Delphi 5 takes a lot from the basic Delphi data access architecture, providing some features that are not available in the native ADO objects and making the ADO components more "BDE-compatible." That means that in most cases we can migrate from one data access technology (Borland Database Engine, BDE) to another (Microsoft ActiveX Data Objects, ADO). Note that the migration from BDE to ADO is not as seamless as it may look. For example, there is no easy way to port code that uses the TUpdateSQL component or cached updates. We should also take into account differences between parameters and other problems that we may encounter during migration.

That's why to fully understand the mechanism behind the Delphi ADO components, we need to understand the basics of Delphi data access architecture.

It should be clear that one chapter cannot cover all the components and objects, as well as their methods, properties, and events, that comprise the Delphi data access architecture. Here we will cover just the basics that you need to know to successfully create Delphi ADO applications.

Back in Chapter 1, we discussed the main data access mechanisms that can be used in Delphi applications. Now it is time to look at how these mechanisms are implemented on the components level—in Delphi Visual Component Library (VCL).

In this chapter, we will cover Delphi's data access mechanisms, a brief history of data access in Delphi, the main parts of a Delphi database application, Delphi data access components, classes, and events, and ADO components and data-aware controls.

Before discussing Delphi data access architecture in detail, let's recall the data access mechanisms that can be used in Delphi applications.

Delphi Data Access Mechanisms

Delphi supports several ways to access data from user applications. All of the methods listed below have advantages and disadvantages, but we do not intend to discuss them in detail here, since the main topic of this book is data access through Microsoft ActiveX Data Objects.

There are the following ways to access data from Delphi applications:

■ *Using BDE*—This is the "native" Delphi method of data access that is supported on the components level. Only relational data sources are supported. BDE receives great support from third-party developers, and now there are hundreds of components that extend its functionality. One of the alternatives to BDE is ADO, which is the main topic of this book. There are several others; see the BDE Alternatives Guide (http://www.kylecordes.com/) for more information.

■ *Direct use of OLE DB interfaces*—This involves the direct manipulation of low-level COM interfaces without any support on the components level, and is recommended in cases where there is no other way to access the data. As we already know, OLE DB is the low-level interface to various data sources, both relational and non-relational, that makes the Microsoft Universal Data Access strategy possible. For more information on OLE DB and UDA, see Chapter 2.

■ *Using ADO components*—The Delphi ADO components provide direct access to ADO objects, thus giving your applications access to multiple relational and non-relational data sources. ADO works with OLE DB behind the scenes. Note that there are several third-party ADO components that can be used in Delphi applications, which give us, for example, the ability to use previous versions of Delphi.

■ *Using ODBC API calls*—This is a rarely used method of data access, as in many cases, there is no need to call ODBC API directly. Instead, we can use either BDE or ADO components. ODBC provides data access only to relational data sources. There is also at least one third-party tool called ODBCExpress (http://www.odbcexpress.com), which encapsulates ODBC API calls and allows ODBC to be used on the component level.

■ *Using BDE + BDE/ODBC Link +ODBC*—Using ODBC Link, we can connect our BDE applications to ODBC-compatible relational data sources that do not have proper direct BDE drivers. Few BDE drivers are currently available, and there is no indication that this number will grow in the future. As an alternative, we can use the ADO + OLE DB Provider for ODBC drivers + ODBC combination outlined below.

The list gives the ODBC drivers that are certified for use with Delphi 5 and BDE.

ODBC certification for using with BDE	ODBC Driver Manager Version	DBMS	ODBC driver vendor	ODBC driver version
Fully certified drivers	3.5	Access 95, 97	Microsoft	3.40
		Foxpro	Microsoft	3.40
		Microsoft SQL Server 6.5	Microsoft	3.00
		Microsoft SQL Server 6.5	Intersolv	3.01
		Oracle 7.3	Intersolv	3.01
	3.51	Access 95,97	Microsoft	3.51
		Foxpro	Microsoft	3.51
		Microsoft SQL Server 6.5	Microsoft	3.6
		Microsoft SQL Server 6.5, 7.0	Intersolv	3.11
		Oracle 7.3	Intersolv	3.11
Drivers certified for basic functionality	3.5	Informix 7.20 and 9.11	Intersolv	3.01
		DB2 (IBMv5 client 6/98); tested against 2.12 and 5.0 (UDB) server	No driver version info available	
		Sybase 11.02	Intersolv	3.01
	3.51	DB2 (IBMv5 client 6/98); tested against 2.12 and 5.0 (UDB) server	No driver version info available	
		Sybase 11.02	Intersolv	3.11
		Oracle 7.3 and 8.04	Intersolv	3.11

■ ***Using ADO + OLE DB Provider for ODBC drivers + ODBC***—This is the way to access various ODBC-compatible relational data sources that have no direct OLE DB provider for them. This method can be used as an alternative to the BDE + BDE/ODBC Link +ODBC method outlined above. Note that in this case, you are dependent on the ODBC drivers vendors; there may be no way to access some new versions of DBMSs since there is no proper ODBC driver for this.

■ ***Using DBMS client API calls (or DBMS client objects)***—In some cases, using the specific DBMS client API calls makes our application work faster; here we skip the universal data access mechanisms and "talk" with the DBMS directly. Note that this also "ties" it to some particular DBMS. One example of such direct DBMS access is Delphi InterBase components that come with Delphi and can be found at the InterBase page of the Components Palette. We should mention here that not all DBMSs support client API calls and there are not many components for this, so pure visual programming is not available.

Now that we have discussed the various ways that Delphi programmers can access data from myriad sources, we will provide a short historical overview of data access in Delphi and then introduce the main parts of the Delphi database application.

Data Access in Delphi: History in Brief

The Borland Database Engine was, in fact, the only universal data access mechanism widely supported on the Visual Components Library level until the Delphi 5 release.

BDE is a data access library that contains several universal functions for retrieving, navigating, and editing data that is exposed to the application code. BDE functions, in turn, call DBMS API functions (Oracle, InterBase), ODBC API functions (Access 2000, Microsoft SQL Server 7.0, and any other ODBC data source), or some functions for direct access to the data files (dBase, Paradox); this depends on the data type we are trying to access.

The BDE was built on the foundation of the Paradox Engine library, which was designed to provide the Paradox API to Pascal and C++ users. Later, several additional libraries called SQL Links were developed. These libraries extended BDE's ability to use the same set of functions to access data in dBase files, ODBC data sources, and SQL servers from major vendors. Some time later, the Access and FoxPro Links were added to this set. And thus, the Borland Database Engine was born. It was widely used to create data access solutions with Borland Pascal 7.0 and Borland C++ 4.5 and 5. Then Borland's development tools were re-created with the Rapid Application Development (RAD) paradigm in mind, and most of the API calls were moved to the components level implemented in the Visual Components Library.

In earlier Delphi versions, all data access VCL components and all other components primarily used in database applications (e.g., data-aware controls, reporting components, and so on) were able to access data only through BDE.

There were also several database utilities included with Delphi:

- SQL Builder for visually creating database queries to extract data
- Database Desktop for creating and managing tables in databases
- SQL Explorer for managing database objects
- BDE Administrator for managing database connections
- SQL Monitor for tracing calls to various SQL servers

All these tools were able to work only with BDE-accessible data sources. This is true for all the utilities listed above that are part of the Delphi 5 toolkit; they are useless if you are trying to work with ADO data sources. This situation may change in future releases of Delphi.

It was possible to use Microsoft ActiveX Data Objects in all 32-bit versions of Delphi prior to Delphi 5, since these versions come with the solid support of COM technologies. To access ADO data sources from your Delphi code you needed to either use the ADO object model directly or purchase some third-party VCL components. Some of these components are listed in the following table.

Name	Developer	Delphi Version	URL
Adonis Component Suite	Cybermagic Productions	3+	http://www.cybermagic.co.nz/adonis/
AdoSolutio	Lectum Information Technology	3+	http://www.lectum.com/
Diamond ADO	Timur Islamov	3+	http://www.islamov.com/diamondado/
Free ADO DataSet	Larry Nezar	4+	http://www.agric.za/freeway/
GM-Components	GM-Software	3+	http://www.gm-software.de/
Kamiak ADO	Kamiak	3+	http://www.kamiak.com/

The major changes to the database part of VCL started in Delphi 3, when the TDataSet abstraction was first introduced. By allowing for TDataSet descendants that were not tied to the BDE, Borland gave developers the opportunity to create their own TDataSet classes that did not require the BDE but still allowed them to use data-aware controls.

In Delphi 5, the VCL database classes was redesigned once again. Now we can extend these high-level classes to support custom data access mechanisms besides the BDE, ADO, and InterBase client API support that comes straight from the box.

The Main Parts of the Delphi Database Application

Earlier in this book, we learned what databases are and saw the popular types of data access, paying some attention to OLE DB and ADO. Now it is time to talk about how these data access mechanisms are used in Delphi applications.

The typical Delphi database application is shown below.

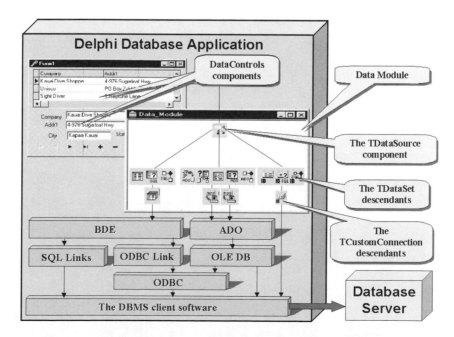

There are three major parts that work together to make the Delphi database application:

- Visual data-aware components that reside on the main form or any other forms within the application. These components are used to show, edit, and navigate database data. The visual data-aware components can be found at the Data Controls page of the Component Palette.

- Nonvisual objects and components, such as data modules and data access components that are responsible for supplying the visual components with database data. These components interact with data access libraries implementing one of the data access mechanisms. As we have already mentioned, in Delphi 5 VCL there are three different sets of data access components for different data access mechanisms:

  - Data Access components for providing data access via BDE. These components reside on the Data Access page of the Component Palette.

  - ADO components for providing data access via ADO (they are also called ADOExpress). You can find these components on the ADO page of the Component Palette.

  - InterBase components for providing direct access to InterBase. These components can be found on the InterBase page of the Component Palette.

- Various data access mechanisms that do the real job. This can be BDE, ADO, direct DBMS client API calls, and various combinations outlined earlier in this chapter.

Most of the visual data-aware components are implemented as custom versions of the standard Windows controls. For example, the TDBText component used to represent read-only data is a descendant of TCustomLabel, while the TDBMemo component is built on the TCustomMemo base. These components have the ability to be connected to the nonvisual data access objects and components through the DataSource and DataField properties. We will talk about this later in this chapter.

The nonvisual objects and components in the three sets contain components responsible for setting connections to databases. To access database objects such as tables, stored procedures, and views, the TDataSet component descendants are used. These components provide data to the visual components through the TDataSource component for editing and browsing. The table below shows data access components for BDE, ADO, and InterBase.

BDE Components	ADO Components	InterBase Components
TTable	TADODataSet	TIBDataSet
TQuery	TADOTable	TIBTable
stright TStoredProc	TADOQuery	TIBQuery
TNestedTable	TADOStoredProc	TIBStoredProc

The following diagram shows the database part of the VCL class hierarchy.

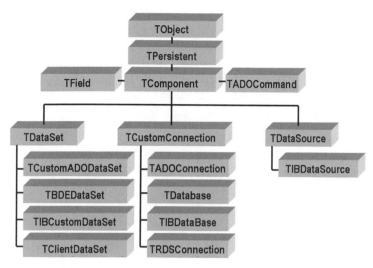

Note that besides BDE, ADO, or InterBase, we can use client datasets (TClientDataSet) that don't require a database engine and rely on a single DLL (MIDAS.DLL) and some custom datasets, built as descendants of TDataSet class.

All nonvisual components can be placed both on forms and on data modules, which are special containers for them.

That was a very high-level overview of the three major parts of a Delphi database application. Now we will look in more detail at Delphi data access components and classes.

Delphi Data Access Components and Classes

In the introduction to this chapter, we said that the ADO support implemented in Delphi 5 takes a lot from the basic Delphi data access architecture, bringing some features that are not available in the native ADO objects and makes the ADO components more "BDE-compatible." Here we will take a look at Delphi data access components and classes and will learn what Delphi ADO components inherit from them.

The following diagram shows where Delphi ADO components fit into the VCL object hierarchy.

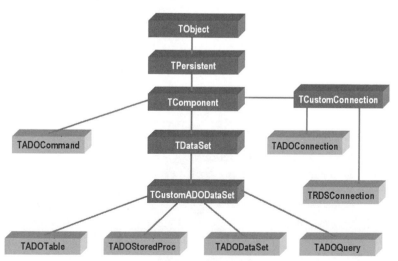

Each of the TADOxxx components shown above is covered in a separate chapter later in this book, but here we will map these components to their higher level counterparts as well as discuss some issues of database access architecture in Delphi.

To understand how ADO components fits into the Visual Components Library architecture, first we should discuss its major ancestors. We will start with the TCustomConnection component, then we will discuss the concept of the dataset, implemented through TDataSet and its descendants, and finally we will discuss other VCL components, including DataControls components, directly and indirectly used by the ADO components.

Connection Components

All Delphi data access components contain one of the TCustomConnection class descendants. This class is the base class for all connection components that represent the source of the data contained in a dataset.

- For BDE access, there is the TDatabase component that allows us to connect to BDE-based databases.

- For ADO we use the TADOConnection component or TRDSConnection component, depending on how we are planning to access the data.

- The TIBDatabase component is used for InterBase.

The TCustomConnection class and its descendants have methods for connecting and disconnecting from the data source to provide user access verification (the user name and password) when establishing a connection and several properties for keeping track of the connected datasets.

The TDatabase, TADOConnection, TRDSConnection, and the TIBDatabase components are responsible for database connections, They implement all appropriate calls to the underlying libraries (BDE API, ADO Objects, InterBase, and client API).

Later in this book, we will discuss the TADOConnection component (see Chapter 5) and the TRDSConnection component (see Chapter 20).

The VCL library contains several other TCustomConnection descendants. They are used in client applications for data access servers. Some of the components—TSocketConnection, TDCOMConnection, and TwebConnection—are discussed in Chapter 21.

As we have mentioned in this section, all connection components represent the source of the data contained in a dataset. Therefore, the next topic in our overview of Delphi data access components and classes is the concept of dataset.

Datasets

A *dataset* is an in-memory "table" with data. This data can reside in a table in the database, or can be created as the result of query or stored procedure execution against the database. Delphi VCL contains the abstract dataset object—TDataSet, which serves as the "template" to provide database-engine independent properties, methods, and events for its descendants. There are several of them already implemented in Delphi VCL, such as TBDEDataSet and TDBDataSet for BDE-based applications, TCustomADODataSet for ADO-based applications, and TClientDataSet for flat-file applications. Appropriate descendants, such as TTable, TQuery, and TStoredProc in the case of BDE-applications or TADOTable, TADOQuery, and TADOStoredProc, are used to work with database objects such as tables, stored procedures, views, and queries.

The ADO components, as we already mentioned, have some duality. On one hand, these components provide access to the underlying ADO Command and Recordset objects. On the other hand, they were written to be similar to the appropriate BDE components; some of the methods specific for BDE data access were implemented in terms of underlying ADO methods. This is convenient for experienced BDE users, but may puzzle novices.

Note that the TADOCommand component provides a direct interface to the ADO Command object. It is not the TDataset descendant, because it does not return datasets. That's why its direct ancestor is the TComponent class.

Data Modules

All Delphi data access components are nonvisual. We can use them on either the main form of our Delphi application or any other form within the application. Sometimes such components can be placed in a data module, which is a container of data access and other components that is the descendant of the TDataModule class.

Data modules are discussed in Chapter 11.

Other Classes Used in Database Applications

In this section, we will look at some VCL components that are used directly and indirectly by the ADO Components. They are the TFields collection of TField objects, TFieldList, TFieldDefs and TFieldDef, TFieldDefList, TIndexDefs and TindexDef, and TIndexOptions and TIndexOption.

The TFields Collection

TFields is a class that stores a collection of TField objects. Each of the TFields collection items represents the physical field in a dataset. This class is used to manage these objects and contains properties and methods for accessing a specific field, add or delete fields from the list, and to find out how many fields there are.

The TField Class

The TField class represents one field in a dataset. It encapsulates the common behavior of all specific field components and introduces the properties, methods, and events for changing values of a field, converting values from one data type to another, validating data input, calculating the value of a field and looking up the field's value from another dataset.

The real fields in datasets are represented by several TField descendants. These descendants are created automatically when a dataset is activated. They can be both dynamic, created at run time based on current dataset columns, and persistent (i.e., created at design time to define some specific behavior, for example, field order in grids or display labels). We will discuss how to create them in Chapter 11.

There are the following TField descendants in Delphi 5:

TField descendant	Direct ancestor	Description
TNumericField	TField	An abstract class that encapsulates the numeric fields behavior.
TIntegerField	TNumericField	A class for implementing the behavior of the integer fields. Integer fields can hold values from –2,147,483,648 to 2,147,483,647.
TSmallIntField	TIntegerField	A class for implementing the behavior of small-integer fields. Small-integer fields can hold values from –32768 to 32767 (i.e., signed 16-bit whole numbers).
TWordField	TIntegerField	A class for implementing the behavior of integer fields. Word fields can hold values from 0 to 65535 (unsigned 16-bit whole numbers).
TAutoIncField	TIntegerField	A class for implementing the behavior of autoincrement fields. Autoincrement fields can hold values from –2,147,483,648 to 2,147,483,647, and are used as a counter for the records in the dataset. Each record is given a unique value in an autoincrement field. Such fields are commonly used to provide a unique primary key value for a record.
TFloatField	TNumericField	A class for implementing the behavior of float fields. Floating-point fields can hold values from $\pm5.0 * 10^{-324}$ to $1.7 * 10308$ with an accuracy of 15 digits.
TCurrencyField	TFloatField	A class for implementing the behavior of currency fields. Currency fields use the Double (not Currency!) data type to store and manipulate their values. Currency fields can hold values from $\pm5.0 * 10^{-324}$ to $1.7 * 10308$ with an accuracy of 15 digits.
TBCDField	TNumericField	A class for implementing the behavior of binary-coded decimal (BCD) fields. BCD values provide greater precision and accuracy than floating-point numbers. TBCDField uses the Currency type to work with data from BCD fields because Delphi does not have a native type for BCD. Therefore, TBCDField limits the precision of the BCD values it can support to four decimal places and 20 significant digits. The underlying database table may include values that require greater precision.
TLargeIntField	TNumericField	A class for implementing of behavior of fields containing 64-bit integer values.
TDateTimeField	TField	A class for implementing the behavior of date-time fields. Date-time fields contain combined date and time information (timestamps).
TDateField	TDateTimeField	A class for implementing the behavior of date fields. Date fields contain date values (without any time value).
TTimeField	TDateTimeField	A class for implementing the behavior of time fields. Time fields contain time values without date.
TStringField	TField	A class for implementing the behavior of string fields. The maximum possible length of this field is 8192 characters, but some databases may only support smaller string fields.
TWideStringField	TStringField	A class for implementing the behavior of wide string fields. Wide string fields are similar to simple string fields except that their length is virtually unlimited and the server returns the field as a wide string. An example of a wide string field is the Unicode field in Microsoft SQL Server.
TGuidField	TStringField	A class for implementing the behavior of fields storing Globally Unique Identifiers (GUIDs).

TField descendant	Direct ancestor	Description
TBooleanField	TField	A class for implementing the behavior of Boolean fields. Boolean fields can hold values of True or False.
TBlobField	TField	A class for implementing the behavior of BLOB fields. BLOB (binary large object) fields are database fields that contain raw binary data of arbitrary length. The data types stored in this field are described in the header of the binary data.
TMemoField	TBlobField	A class for implementing the behavior of memo fields. Memo fields are a form of binary large object (BLOB) fields for storing multi-line text.
TGraphicField	TBlobField	A class for implementing the behavior of graphic fields. Graphics fields are a form of binary large object (BLOB) field for storing graphic data. This data includes a BLOB header describing the encoding of the graphical value.
TBinaryField	TField	An abstract class for encapsulating the behavior of untyped binary fields.
TBytesField	TBinaryField	A class for implementing the behavior of bytes fields. A bytes field value is a set of unformatted bytes of fixed size.
TVarBytesField	TBytesField	A class for implementing the behavior of variable bytes fields. A variable bytes field value is a set of bytes of variable size. The actual length of the value is stored in the first two bytes.
TVariantField	TField	A class for implementing the behavior of Variant fields.
TAggregateField	TField	A class for implementing the behavior of aggregate fields, which represent an aggregate value from a client dataset (e.g., a calculation that summarizes the data in a set of records).
TInterfaceField	TField	An abstract class for encapsulating the behavior of fields that contain pointers to interfaces (IUnknown) as data.
TIDispatchField	TInterfaceField	A class for implementing the behavior of fields that contain pointers to IDispatch interfaces as data.
TObjectField	TField	An abstract class for encapsulating the behavior common to the TADTField, TArrayField, TDataSetField, and TReferenceField classes.
TADTField	TObjectField	A class for implementing the behavior of fields that contain Abstract Data Type (ADT) values, which are user-defined types, similar to structures and created on the server.
TReferenceField	TObjectField	A class for implementing the behavior of reference fields, which store a pointer or reference to another persistent object.
TArrayField	TObjectField	A class for implementing the behavior of array fields, which consist of a set of fields of the same type.
TDataSetField	TObjectField	A class for implementing the behavior of dataset fields, which contain a reference to nested datasets that exist in some object-oriented databases (e.g., Oracle 8) and client datasets.

All TField components are nonvisual and are not visible even at design time. They are associated with a dataset component and used to provide data to data-aware components connected to this dataset.

These components have many common properties, such as the Alignment property to specify how data is displayed and DisplayWidth to specify the number of digits to display. The TField class also defines several AsXXX properties that are used to represent the field's value as Boolean (AsBoolean), Currency (AsCurrency), String

(AsString), Variant (AsVariant), and so on. The latter two are frequently used in Delphi ADO applications to perform conversions from "native" data types to other data types, e.g., MyString := TIntegerField.AsString.

The TFieldList Class

The TFieldList class is used by a dataset to obtain a list of field names in the database table. The field names in the list are listed sequentially, and child fields of an object field type appear after the "parent" object field in the list. This class really just provides a way to get all of the TFields associated with a TDataset.

The TFieldDefs and TFieldDef Classes

The TFieldDefs class is a collection used by a dataset to manage the field definitions (TFieldDef class for each field) that must be used to create field objects, which correspond to fields in the database table. These definitions are used when creating a new database table. The properties and methods of the TFieldDefs class are used to access a specific field definition, add or delete field definitions, calculate the number of fields, and copy a set of field definitions to another table.

The TFieldDefList Collection

The TFieldDefList collection is used by a dataset to create a complete list of field names that correspond to the objects in the FieldDefs property. TFieldDefs with object field types such as TADTField and TArrayField have TFieldDef objects for these object types that contain FieldDefs to hold the TFieldDef objects of their child fields.

A TFieldDefList with object field types lists child TFieldDef objects of object fields sequentially after the parent TFieldDef in order to represent the metadata linearly, as opposite to the TFieldDefs collection that represents the metadata hierarchically.

The TIndexDefs Collection and TIndexDef Class

The TIndexDefs collection stores the list of available index definitions (TIndexDef objects) for a dataset. It can be used to add or delete index definitions for the table you are creating or the client dataset, or to create the indexes of the database table.

The TIndexDef class represents a particular index definition in the TIndexDefs collection. The index definition can be used for determining the index name and other characteristics (e.g., ascending or descending, case-sensitive, etc.) or identifying the underlying fields or expression. If a dataset represents a physical database table or client dataset, the TIndexDef objects are used for creating indexes or to obtain information about them.

The TIndexOptions Set and TIndexOption Type

TIndexOptions is a set of attributes (TIndexOption type) that applies to a specific index. A TIndexOptions value can include zero or more of the following TIndexOption values:

Value	Meaning
ixPrimary	This index is the primary key index of the table.
ixUnique	Each value in the index is unique.
ixDescending	The index imposes a descending sort order.
ixExpression	The index is based on an expression (this is applicable only for BDE access to dBase tables; see Chapter 1 for details).
ixCaseInsensitive	The index sorts records without regard to case.
ixNonMaintained	The index is not automatically updated when the data is edited (see Chapter 1 for details).

It should be mentioned that not all databases support using all possible index options. To find out what kinds of indexes are supported by a particular database, refer to the vendor-supplied documentation.

Components and Events

One of the advantages of components is the ability to receive events and create appropriate event handlers within the development environments. The Delphi ADO Components supports three kinds of events—*Delphi notification events*, *Delphi database events*, and *ADO kernel events*.

Delphi Notification Events

Delphi notification events are of the TNotifyEvent type and do not have event-specific parameters. Such events are simply used to notify the component and the application code inside the event handler that a specific event occurred. The notification events have only one parameter—Sender of the TObject type that can be used to find the object that caused the event. Some of these events come in pairs—the BeforeXXX event is fired <u>before</u> the action occurs and the AfterXXX event is fired <u>after</u> the action is completed.

For example, most of the events inherited by the TADOConnection component from the TCustomConnection class are notification events. They are shown below.

```
AfterConnect     AfterDisconnect     BeforeConnect     BeforeDisconnect
```

Moreover, as you can guess, its Sender parameter gives us access to the instance of the TADOConnection component that causes this event. We will talk about these and other events in the following chapters where we will look at the ADO components in more details.

In some cases, we can receive the notification events of the TDataSetNotifyEvent type. The only difference between the ordinary notification event and the dataset notification event is that the latter contains the DataSet parameter, which points to the TDataSet object instead of TObject, as in the case of ordinary notification events.

When to Implement Event Handlers

You need to implement event handlers for notification events when you want to keep track of what is going in your code. On some rare occasions, you can access the Sender or DataSet parameter to modify some of the properties before the action takes place or find the result after the action was completed. In most cases, there are other events—Delphi database events and ADO kernel events—that can be used to check or modify the parameters.

Delphi Database Events

Another type of event we may encounter when using ADO components are Delphi database events, i.e., events that come from the Delphi data access components and contain parameters that provides more information about the event.

Several DataSetNotifyEvent events in the form of Before/After event pairs are shown in the following table.

BeforeXXX Event	AfterXXX Event	Description
BeforeCancel	AfterCancel	Occurs before and after an application cancels changes
BeforeClose	AfterClose	Occurs before and after an application closes a dataset
BeforeDelete	AfterDelete	Occurs before and after an application deletes the active record in a dataset
BeforeEdit	AfterEdit	Occurs before and after dataset enters edit mode
BeforeInsert	AfterInsert	Occurs before and after an application inserts a record
BeforeOpen	AfterOpen	Occurs before and after an application opens the dataset
BeforePost	AfterPost	Occurs before and after an application posts a change to the active record
BeforeScroll	AfterScroll	Occurs before and after an application scrolls to another record
AfterRefresh	BeforeRefresh	Occurs before and after an application has updated the records in the dataset

Two more notification events should be mentioned here. OnCalcFields is fired when an application recalculates calculated fields, and OnNewRecord occurs when a new record is inserted or appended by an application.

There also can be events of the TDataSetErrorEvent type, which come from the TDataSet class and are available for its descendants—the ADODataSet, ADOQuery, ADOStoredProc, and ADOTable components. This event has three parameters:

■ DataSet parameter of the TDataSet type, which indicates the dataset that causes an error.

■ E parameter of the EDatabaseError type, which points to the exception error message. To access the error message, use the E.Message syntax, as with all other standard Delphi exceptions.

■ Action parameter of the TDataAction type, which indicates the possible response to the error. There can be three types of responses—daFail to abort the erroneous operation and show an error message, daAbort to silently abort the operation, and daRetry to retry the operation.

The following table shows TDataSet events of the `TDataSetErrorEvent` type.

Event	Cause
OnDeleteError	An attempt to delete a record fails
OnEditError	An attempt to edit a record fails
OnPostError	An attempt to post a record fails

The TDataSet class also has the OnFilterRecord event of the TFilterRecordEvent type that occurs for each active record when the filtering is enabled. This event has two parameters. The `DataSet` parameter of the TDataSet type indicates the dataset where the event occurs, and the Boolean `Accept` parameter allows us to accept or deny the record to be filtered according to some conditions. Later in this book we will see how to use the Filter and Filtered properties of the TCustomADODataSet class and its descendants to perform the same tasks.

As with other Delphi database events we may encounter, it should be mentioned that the LoginEvent, available in the TCustomConnection object, is fired when logging to the database occurs.

When to Implement Event Handlers

In most cases, we need to implement the Delphi database event handlers to take care of some error conditions that may occur during the course of our application. We can check the error status of the operation with the DataSetErrorEvent on the dataset level, or find the cause of the error on the ADO object level with the help of the ADO kernel events discussed below.

ADO Kernel Events

These events are shown in the Miscellaneous group (if we arrange properties and events in the Object Inspector by category). As the name implies they come directly from the ActiveX Data Objects kernel—the library, where all ADO objects are implemented. Actually, only two objects of the ADO objects set support event—the Connection object and the Recordset object. There are two kinds of such events—ones that are fired before some operation and ones that are fired after the operation is completed. Such ADO events usually come in pairs of the WillXXX event and the XXXComplete event.

Note: As we have seen above, some Delphi notification events also comes in pairs—in this case the syntax is BeforeXXX and AfterXXX.

The following table shows some of the Will/Complete event pairs available for ADO objects.

WillXXX Event	XXXComplete Event	Class
OnWillConnect	OnConnectComplete	TADOConnection
OnWillExecute	OnExecuteComplete	TADOConnection
OnWillChangeField	OnFieldChangeComplete	TCustomADODataSet
OnWillChangeRecord	OnRecordChangeComplete	TCustomADODataSet
OnWillChangeRecordset	OnRecordsetChangeComplete	TCustomADODataSet
OnWillMove	OnMoveComplete	TCustomADODataSet

Each such event contains a set of parameters that allows us to examine the details of the action—in the case of the WillXXX event—or check the status of the operation or cancel it—in the case of the XXXComplete event—through the EventStatus code or Errors collection.

There are several other ADO events, which are called after some action is completed. For example, the InfoMessage event of the TADOConnection component is fired when some additional information is available from the data provider. The table below shows events available for the TADOConnection and TCustomADODataSet classes.

Event	Class
BeginTransComplete	TADOConnection
CommitTransComplete	TADOConnection
RollbackTransComplete	TADOConnection
Disconnect	TADOConnection
FetchProgress	TCustomADODataSet
FetchComplete	TCustomADODataSet
EndOfRecordset	TCustomADODataSet

When to Implement Event Handlers

You need to implement the ADO kernel event handlers when you want to keep track of what is going on in your application in order to be able to fine tune or check parameters before the action takes place or to find the status of the operation just completed and evaluate the possible error conditions and take appropriate actions. Later in this book, we will give you more detailed examples of event handlers for ADO components and will show you how to use them in your code.

Components and Data-Aware Controls

One of the powerful features of Delphi is a set of data-aware components that can be used to show and edit data from nearly any data source to which the Delphi application is able to connect. These components are available on the Data Controls page of the Component Palette and can be used in Delphi ADO applications. The components available in Delphi 5 are shown on the following page.

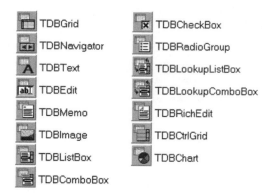

The following table briefly describes the purpose of the data-aware components available in Delphi.

Component	Purpose
TDBChart	Used to represent data graphically
TDBCheckBox	Use to represent values that can be selected or deselected
TDBComboBox	Used to represent values in the combo box
TDBCtrlGrid	Used as a placeholder for other data-aware components
TDBEdit	Used to represent text values with read/write permissions
TDBGrid	Used to show the contents of the database in the grid format
TDBListBox	Used to represent values in the list box
TDBLookupComboBox	Used to select values from another dataset
TDBLookupListBox	Used to select values from another dataset
TDBMemo	Used to represent multiline text fields
TDBNavigator	Used to navigate through the dataset
TDBRadioGroup	Used to represent a group of values
TDBRichEdit	Used to represent multiline text fields with text formatting commands
TDBText	Used to represent text values with read-only permissions

See Chapter 11 for detailed information on using these components.

To use the Delphi data-aware components with ADO components, we use the universal "glue"—the DataSource component, which serves as an interface between the TDataSet-based component and the data-aware component. Although it is part of the BDE components page, this component must be used to send data from all datasets, including ADO, InterBase, and custom ones. Data source components also link datasets in master-detail relationships.

All DataControls components have a DataSource property. This property points to the TDataSource component from the DataAccess page of the Component Palette. This is shown in the following figure.

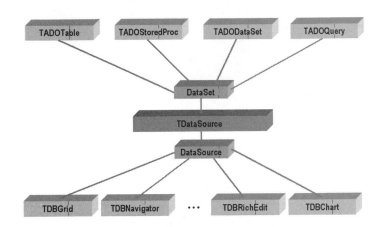

Therefore, you just need to put one of the ADO components on your form—TADODataSet, TADOTable, TADOQuery, or TADOStoredProc—and then you connect it with the data-aware control through two properties. First, you set the DataSet property of the DataSource component to one of the ADO components available and then you set the DataSource property of one of the data-aware controls to match the DataSource component name. If you connect to the database, you can browse your data even in design time.

Access to Underlying ADO Objects

All ADO components are implemented with extensibility in mind. Suppose Microsoft issues a new version of Data Access Components, for example, the new version of ADO, ADO 2.5, in Microsoft Windows 2000. In this case, you will not be able to use the new functionality of ADO objects and will be tied to the current version. The only way to get the new set of components is to wait for Inprise to issue an update or, even worse, a new version of Delphi.

To avoid this, the ADOExpress developers allow us to use the current functionality of ADO objects installed on the computer. This is done through special properties of TCustomADODataSet class and TADOCommand and TADOConnection components, which gives us access to the underlying ADO Objects. These properties are listed in the following table.

Component	Property	ADO Object
TADOCommand	CommandObject	_Command
TADOConnection	ConnectionObject	_Connection
TRDSConnection	DataSpaceObject	DataSpace
TADODataSet	RecordSet	_RecordSet
TADOQuery	RecordSet	_RecordSet
TADOTable	RecordSet	_RecordSet
TADOStoredProc	RecordSet	_RecordSet

Note the underscore (_) in the names of the ADO objects. This is done to distinguish them from Delphi objects and to avoid possible conflicts with some Delphi VCL definitions.

We will see examples of how to use these properties in separate chapters dedicated to these components.

Conclusion

In this chapter, we provided you with an introduction to the Delphi database architecture. We have discussed:

- The data access mechanisms used in Delphi
- The main parts of the Delphi database application
- The components that implement data access
- The components that are responsible for showing and editing data and how they receive data

We have also learned about three types of Delphi database-related events and now we understand how data-aware controls are used in Delphi ADO applications.

Starting with the next chapter, we will take a deeper look at each component in ADOExpress. We will start with the TADOConnection component, which gives us the ability to connect to various data sources.

THE TADOCONNECTION COMPONENT

In this chapter, we begin to look at the Delphi ADO components. As we have already learned from the previous chapter, this set of Delphi components implements the functionality of Microsoft ActiveX Data Objects. In this set, there are two components that provide the direct implementation of the ADO objects—the TADOConnection component and the TADOCommand component. The other Delphi components—TADODataSet, TADOTable, TADOQuery, and TADOStoredProc—do not have the ADO counterparts. They can be treated as Delphi data access components with ADO-specific functionality borrowed from the RecordSet object and other ADO objects.

In this chapter, we will explore the TADOConnection component, which is the Delphi version of the ADO Connection object. This component is used to connect to various ADO data sources. First, we will discuss the properties, methods, and events of the TADOConnection component, and then we will give several examples of how to use it.

Properties

The TADOConnection component contains several properties that, along with the ConnectionString property, can be used to set the options of the connection before opening it.

Attributes Property

The Attributes property, defined in the ADO Connection object, is used to set transactional facilities of an ADOConnection component, to control retaining commits and aborts. Its value can be one or more of the following constants:

- xaCommitRetaining—indicates that a new transaction automatically starts after a call to the CommitTrans method. The ADO equivalent for this constant is adXactCommitRetaining.

- xaAbortRetaining—indicates that a new transaction automatically starts after a call to the RollbackTrans method call. The ADO equivalent for this constant is adXactAbortRetaining.

- The combination of xaCommitRetaining and xaAbortRetaining indicates that a new transaction automatically starts after an existing transaction finishes.

The Attributes property is implemented as a set. The default value of this property is an empty set. To include one or both constants, use the following code:

```
//Set the xaCommitRetaining attribute

ADOConnection1.Attributes := [xaCommitRetaining];

// Set both attributes

ADOConnection1.Attributes := [xaCommitRetaining,
  xaAbortRetaining];

// Clear attributes

ADOConnection1.Attributes := []; // Empty set
```

Note that not all providers support transactions. To check whether a particular provider supports transactions, check the value of the Transaction DDL property after opening the connection. For example:

```
If ADOConnection1.Properties['Transaction DDL'] <> Nil Then
begin
  S := 'Transactions are supported.';
  S := S + ' Level = ' +
  IntToStr(
    ADOConnection1.Properties['Transaction DDL'].Value
  );
  ShowMessage(S);
end;
```

If the value of the Transaction DDL property is equal to 8, then DDL (data definition language) and DML (data manipulation language) transactions are supported. Smaller values of this property indicate that DDL statements are not supported, and a 0 value indicates that transactions are not supported at all.

Note: In ADO 2.1, only OLE DB Provider for ODBC Drivers, OLE DB Provider for Jet, OLE DB Provider for SQL Server, OLE DB Provider for Oracle, and OLE DB Provider for Index Server support transactions.

The CommandCount Property

This property, defined in the ADO Connection object, indicates the number of TADOCommand components that are associated with this TADOConnection component. This property is significant only if one or more TADOCommand components use this TADOConnection component through its Connection property.

The following example shows how to obtain the CommandText properties of all TADOCommand components associated with the TADOConnection component.

```
procedure TForm1.Button1Click(Sender: TObject);
var
 I : Integer;
begin
 with ADOConnection1 do
 begin
For I := 0 to CommandCount-1 do
  begin
{Get its Name and Text (SQL Statements)}
   Memo1.Lines.Add(
    Commands[I].Name + '—>'+ #9 +
    Commands[I].CommandText
   );
  end;
end;
end;
```

```
ADOConnection Demo                      _ □ ×

  [  Run  ]

 ADOCommand1—>   select Author from Authors
 ADOCommand2—>   select * from Publishers
 ADOCommand3—>   select ISBN, Notes, PubID from Titles
```

The CommandTimeout Property

This property, defined in the ADO Connection object, specifies in seconds how long to wait before the command will be considered unsuccessful. The default value for the CommandTimeout property is 30 seconds. If the value of this property is equal to 0, the provider will wait until the command is executed or canceled.

The Commands Property

This property can be used to access one of the TADOCommand components that is associated with this TADOConnection component. The Commands property provides an indexed array of commands where indexes range from 0 to CommandCount–1. See the CommandCount property above.

The Connected Property

Using this property, we can find out if our connection is active or not and change its state. The default value for the Connected property is `False`, meaning that the connection is closed. Setting this property to `True` opens the connection.

The ConnectOptions Property

Using this property, we can specify whether the connection is synchronous or asynchronous. The default value for the ConnectOptions property is `coConnectUnspecified`, meaning that this is a synchronous connection. This type of connection can be used in most scenarios. Use the asynchronous connections only when you are trying to connect to a server with a long response time.

Value	Meaning	ADO Constant
coConnectUnspecified	This is a synchronous connection	adConnectUnspecified
coAsyncConnect	This is an asynchronous connection	adAsyncConnect

Note: There is no direct equivalent for this property in the ADO Connection object. For this object, the connection options in the form of the ConnectOptionEnum constants are used as an `Options` parameter of the Open method. For example:

```
procedure TForm1.Button1Click(Sender: TObject);
begin
  With ADOConnection1 do
  begin
   ConnectionObject.Open(
     'Provider=Microsoft.Jet.OLEDB.4.0;'
    +' Data Source=c:\data\northwind.mdb;',
     '', '', adConnectUnspecified
   );
   ADODataSet1.Active := True;
  end;
end;
```

The ConnectionObject Property

This property gives us direct access to the underlying ADO Connection object. Use this object in cases when you need to get or set properties not implemented by the

TADOConnection component, or to call additional methods of the ADO Connection object.

The ConnectionString Property

This property, defined in the ADO Connection object, is used to specify detailed information for connections to the data source. At design time, we use the ConnectionString Editor to build the ConnectionString property from a set of dialog boxes, while at run time we should specify the proper string that consists of the following four arguments.

Argument	Meaning
Provider	Specifies the name of the provider. Cannot be used with the FileName argument.
FileName	Specifies the name of the file with the provider-specific connection information. Cannot be used with the Provider argument.
RemoteProvider	Specifies the provider name for the RDS connection
RemoteServer	Specifies the server name for the RDS connection

All other arguments specified in the ConnectionString property are passed directly to the provider. For example, below is the typical ConnectionString for ODBC provider to connect to Microsoft Access database:

```
'Provider=MSDASQL;Driver={Microsoft Access Driver (*.mdb)};
DBQ=c:\data\northwind.mdb'
```

Note that besides the `Provider` argument in this example, there are two extra arguments—Driver and DBQ. These go directly to the provider.

The ConnectionTimeout Property

This property, defined in the ADO Connection object, specifies in seconds how long to wait before the connection will be considered unsuccessful. The default value for the ConnectionTimeout property is 15 seconds. If the value of this property is equal to 0, the provider will wait until the connection is established or canceled.

The CursorLocation Property

This property, defined in the ADO Connection object, specifies the location of the cursor engine. CursorLocation can have two values indicating whether this is the default client-side cursor (`clUseClient`) or a server-side cursor (`clUseServer`).

Using the client-side cursor gives us the ability to retrieve all data to the local machine and perform such operations as sorting and filtering on it.

Note that when we use SQL statements with a WHERE clause, only the reduced dataset is returned to the local machine. The client-side cursor can also be used to create disconnected recordsets.

A server-side cursor is less flexible, but it can be used to operate on large datasets that may not fit the local disk space. Note that many servers only support forward-only datasets, which allow you to iterate the resulting dataset only in the forward direction.

 Note: Changing this property affects only those connections established after this property is changed; the existing connections are not affected.

The DataSetCount Property

Use this property to find how many open TCustomADODataSet components are associated with this TADOConnection component. Using the DataSetCount property with the DataSets property described below allows us to iterate through the array of TCustomADODataSet components. This is a Delphi-specific property.

The DataSets Property

This property can be used to access one of the TCustomADODataSet components that is associated with this TADOConnection component. The DataSets property provides an indexed array of datasets, where indexes range from 0 to DataSetCount–1. See the DataSetCount property above. This is a Delphi-specific property.

The following example shows how to iterate the DataSets array to activate the datasets associated with the TADOConnection component and to extract the name of any TCustomADODataSet component and its CommandText property.

```
procedure TForm1.Button1Click(Sender: TObject);
var
 I : Integer;
begin
 With ADOConnection1 do
  begin
   Open;
{If at least one DataSet is associated}
    For I := 0 to DataSetCount-1 do
     begin
{Activate DataSet}
       DataSets[I].Active := True;
{Get its name}
       Memo1.Lines.Add(DataSets[I].Name +
         '-->' + #9 +
{and CommandText}
         (DataSets[I] as TADODataSet).CommandText);
     end;
  end;
end;
```

```
ADOConnection Demo                _ □ ×
┌─────────┐
│  Run    │
└─────────┘
ADODataSet1-->   Categories
ADODataSet2-->   Customers
ADODataSet3-->   Suppliers
```

 Note: In this example all three TADODataSet components use the CommandType property set to cmdTable with different table names in its CommandText property.

The DefaultDatabase Property

This property, defined in the ADO Connection object, is used to specify the default database used by the TADOConnection component and its underlying ADO Connection object. The DefaultDatabase property will be overwritten if the database to use is specified in the ConnectionString property. The following example shows how to use this property.

```
procedure TForm1.Button1Click(Sender: TObject);
begin
 With ADOConnection1 do
  begin
   ConnectionString := 'Provider=SQLOLEDB.1;' +
     'Persist Security Info=False;User ID=sa;' +
     'Data Source=maindesk';
{Set the default database}
   DefaultDatabase  := 'pubs';
   Open;
   ADODataSet1.CommandType := cmdTable;
   ADODataSet1.CommandText := 'authors';
   ADODataSet1.Active := True;
  end;
end;
```

The Errors Property

This property gives us access to the Errors collection of the underlying ADO Connection object. This collection contains errors that occur at the OLE DB provider level. By using the properties of the Errors collection, we can get its description and other information that can help us find the cause of the error that occurred. We will cover the Errors collection later in this chapter.

The InTransaction Property

This property can be used to find out if the transaction is currently active. If the TADOConnection component is in the transaction state, the InTransaction property will contain a True value; otherwise it will contain False. This is a Delphi-specific property.

The transaction is activated by calling the BeginTrans method. You can check the value of the InTransaction property before calling this method to avoid nested transactions. Once the transaction is committed by the CommitTrans method or canceled by the RollbackTrans method, the value of the InTransaction property becomes False.

The IsolationLevel Property

This property is used to specify the level of the transaction isolation. The transaction isolation level determines how other transactions interact with yours, and whether they can see your changes when they work on the same database objects. The value specified by this property comes into effect when you initiate the transaction by calling the BeginTrans method. In some cases the provider may change the level of transaction isolation if the one that was specified with the IsolationLevel property is not available.

The IsolationLevel property can have one of the following values:

Value	Meaning	ADO Constant
ilBrowse	Allows you to view uncommitted changes in other transactions	adXactBrowse
ilChaos	You cannot overwrite any pending changes from another user (more highly isolated transactions)	adXactChaos
ilCursorStability	You can view changes in other transactions only after they have been committed	adXactCursorStability
ilIsolated	The transactions are completely isolated from other transactions	adXactIsolated
ilReadCommitted	The same as ilCursorStability	adXactReadCommitted
ilReadUncommitted	The same as ilBrowse	adXactReadUncommitted
ilRepeatableRead	You cannot see changes made in other transactions unless you requery the recordset	adXactRepeatableRead
ilSerializable	The same as ilIsolated	adXactSerializable
ilUnspecified	The provider is using a different isolation level than you specified but the level cannot be determined by the provider	adXactUnspecified

Note: This property is the Delphi equivalent of the IsolationLevel property of the ADO Connection object. Its possible values are the equivalents of the ADO IsolationLevelEnum constants.

The KeepConnection Property

Use this property to keep the application connected to a datasource even if there are no active TADODataSet components associated with this connection. The default value for this property is True, which means that the connection will be kept for applications that use the remote database servers or frequently open and close datasets. This reduces traffic across the network and makes applications work faster since there is no need to initialize and reestablish the connection each time the dataset is accessed. This is a Delphi-specific property.

The LoginPrompt Property

Use this property to show the login dialog box for entering the user ID and password to connect to a database. This property should be used only in situations where the ConnectionString property does not contain security information. This is a Delphi-specific property.

The Mode Property

This property, defined in the ADO Connection object, indicates the permissions available to the connection for modifying data. The Mode property can have one of the following values:

Value	Meaning	ADO Constant
cmRead	Read-only permissions	adModeRead
cmReadWrite	Read/write permissions	adModeReadWrite
cmShareDenyNone	Other users cannot open connection with any permissions	adModeShareDenyNone
cmShareDenyRead	Other users cannot open connection with read permissions	adModeShareDenyRead
cmShareDenyWrite	Other users cannot open connection with write permissions	adModeShareDenyWrite
cmShareExclusive	Other users cannot open connection	adModeShareExclusive
cmUnknown	Permissions cannot be determined or have not yet been set; this is the default value	adModeUnknown
cmWrite	Write-only permissions	adModeWrite

Note: The value you can set on the Advanced tab of the Data Link Properties dialog box does not affect the value of the Mode property.

The Properties Property

This property gives us access to the Properties collection of the underlying ADO Connection object. The Properties collection contains one or more Property objects that specify details for the current connection. Most of the properties that can be found in the Properties collection are dynamic properties, i.e., you should access them by name rather than by index within the collection. You can use the Properties collection to fine-tune the connection properties before opening the connection, and check them after the connection is established; in this case, the properties become read-only.

The Provider Property

This property, defined in the ADO Connection object, indicates the name of the provider used by the TADOConnection component. The default value for this property is MSDASQL.

Note that this property is set automatically after the connection is opened if the provider is specified through the ConnectionString property.

Let's create the following example where we specify the value for the ConnectionString property manually, at run time. Before the connection is opened, the default provider is used. After the ConnectionString property is set, the provider specified in it is used:

```
procedure TForm1.FormCreate(Sender: TObject);
begin
 With Memo1.Lines, ADOConnection1 do
  begin
   Add('--- Connection is closed ---');
{Check the provider}
   Add('Provider = ' + Provider);
  end;
end;

procedure TForm1.Button1Click(Sender: TObject);
begin
 With Memo1.Lines, ADOConnection1 do
  begin
{Specify the connection string at run time}
   ConnectionString := 'Provider=Microsoft.Jet.OLEDB.4.0;' +
    'Password=""; User ID=Admin;' +
    'Data Source=C:\DATA\NORTHWIND.MDB;Mode=Share Deny None';
{Open the connection}
   Open;
   Add('--- Connection is opened ---');
{Check the provider}
   Add('Provider = ' + Provider);
  end;
end;
```

The State Property

This property allows us to find out what the component does. By checking the value of the State property, we can determine if the ADOConnection component is connecting to the datasource, executing the connection, fetching rows to the resulting recordset, open but idle, or closed and idle.

The State property can have one of the following values depending on the state the ADOConnection component is in:

Value	Meaning	ADO Constant
stClosed	The Connection object is closed	adStateClosed
stConnecting	The Connection object is connecting to the datasource	adStateConnecting
stExecuting	The Connection object executes the command	adStateExecuting
stFetching	The Connection object is fetching records	adStateFetching
stOpen	The Connection object is open	adStateOpen

Note: This property is the Delphi equivalent of the State property of the ADO Connection object, and its values are the values of the ADO ObjectStateEnum constants.

The Version Property

This property, defined in the ADO Connection object, contains the ADO version number. To check the version number of the currently installed ADO library, you don't need to specify any values for the ADOConnection component properties; simply place the component into your form and use its Version property. For example:

```
procedure TForm1.FormCreate(Sender: TObject);
begin
 Edit1.Text := ADOConnection1.Version;
end;
```

Note that this property allows us to find only the number of the major revision of the ADO library. To find more detailed information, check the file version number of the ADO library file. There is an example later in this chapter on how to do so.

Methods

The TADOConnection component exposes eleven methods. Some of these methods are direct implementations of the ADO Connection object methods, while others were added at the component level to extend its functionality.

The BeginTrans Method

This method, defined in the ADO Connection object, is used to begin a new transaction and return the level of nested transactions. The result returned by this method is 1 for the top-level transaction, 2 for the first nested transaction, and so on. This value should be considered only in cases where you need to keep track of nested transactions.

The BeginTrans method triggers an OnBeginTransComplete event, and changes the value of the InTransaction property to True.

The BeginTrans method should be used only with open connections, i.e., before calling this method you need to perform the following check:

```
procedure TForm1.Button1Click(Sender: TObject);
var
 NLevel : Integer;
begin
 With ADOConnection1 do
  begin
{Check if we already connected}
   If Not Connected then
{If not — open connection}
    Open;
{Begin transaction}
   NLevel := BeginTrans;
  end;
end;
```

Note: The Attributes property is used to set transactional facilities of a TADOConnection component to control retaining commits and aborts. See the Attributes property.

The Cancel Method

This method aborts any pending attempt to connect asynchronously (`ConnectOptions := coAsyncConnect`) to a datasource through the Open or Execute methods.

This method directly calls the Cancel method of the underlying ADO Connection object.

The Close Method

This method, defined in the ADO Connection object, closes the currently opened connection. Calling the Close method triggers the OnDisconnect event.

The CommitTrans Method

This method, defined in the ADO Connection object, writes all changes made by the current transaction (after the call to the BeginTrans method) to the datasource and ends it. If you have nested transactions, the CommitTrans method commits the inner-most one. The following code shows the logic flow:

```
BeginTrans  { High-level transaction }
  { Changes goes here }
BeginTrans  { Nested transaction }
  { Changes goes here }
CommitTrans  { Save changes made by nested transaction }
CommitTrans  { Save changes made by high-level transaction }
```

CommitTrans triggers an OnCommitTransComplete event, and changes the value of the InTransaction property to `False`.

The Execute Method

Use this method to execute queries, SQL statements, or stored procedures. There are two overloaded versions of this method:

```
procedure Execute(const CommandText: WideString;
  var RecordsAffected: Integer; const ExecuteOptions:
TExecuteOptions = [eoExecuteNoRecords]);

function Execute(const CommandText: WideString;
  const CommandType: TCommandType = cmdText;
  const ExecuteOptions: TExecuteOptions = []): _Recordset;
```

The `CommandText` argument specifies the text of the command to execute. This can be the SQL statement, table name, stored procedure name, and so on, including some provider-specific text.

The first version of the Execute method is used for commands that do not return recordsets. By default, its `ExecuteOptions` argument is set to `eoExecuteNoRecords`, meaning that the provider should not return the resulting recordset if any exists. The `RecordsAffected` argument specifies a variable that will contain the number of records affected by the command executed with this method.

The second version of the Execute method is used to execute commands that return the resulting recordsets. By default, its CommandType property is set to `cmdText`, meaning that we will execute a SQL statement. The resulting recordset is available as the result of this function's return value and is of the ADO Recordset object (`_Recordset`) type.

We can use the resulting recordset as is, i.e., iterate through it at the Fields level, or assign it to the RecordSet property of the TADODataSet component. Consider the following example:

```
procedure TForm1.Button1Click(Sender: TObject);
var
 RS : _RecordSet;
begin
 With ADOConnection1 do
```

```
  begin
{Execute Command and obtain resulting recordset}
   RS := Execute('SELECT * FROM CUSTOMERS');
{Assign it to the ADODataSet.RecordSet property}
   ADODataSet1.RecordSet := RS;
{Open ADODataSet}
   ADODataSet1.Active := True;
  end;
end;
```

The following example shows how to iterate through the resulting recordset at the low level:

```
procedure TForm1.Button2Click(Sender: TObject);
var
 RS : _RecordSet;
 I  : Integer;
begin
 With ADOConnection1 do
  begin
{Execute Command and obtain resulting recordset}
   RS := Execute('SELECT * FROM CUSTOMERS');
   With RS do
    begin
{Move to the first record}
      MoveFirst;
{Shows fileds names}
      For I := 0 to Fields.Count-1 do
       Memo1.Lines.Add(Fields[I].Name);
{
 More records manipulations here ...
}
    end;
  end;
end;
```

Note: For more information on CommandType and ExecuteOptions, look in the next chapter, where we discuss the TADOCommand component.

The GetFieldNames Method

This method returns the names of the fields in a table. The connection should be opened before calling this method. The GetFieldNames method expects two parameters—the name of the table to inspect and a string list to fill with the names of the fields. A string list must exist before calling this method. An example of this method usage is shown below. This is a Delphi-specific method.

The GetProcedureNames Method

This method returns the names of the stored procedures found in the database. The connection should be opened before calling this method. GetProcedureNames expects one parameter—a string list to fill with the names of the fields. A string list must exist before calling this method. An example of this method usage is shown below. This is a Delphi-specific method.

The GetTableNames Method

This method returns the names of the tables found in the database. The connection should be opened before calling this method. The GetTableNames method expects two parameters. The first is a string list to fill with the names of the fields. A string list must exist before calling this method. The second parameter indicates whether the names of the system tables should be included in the list. Consider the following example.

```
procedure TForm1.Button1Click(Sender: TObject);
begin
 With ADOConnection1 do
   begin
{Open Connection}
    Open;
{Get the list of the available tables}
    GetTableNames(ListBox1.Items, CheckBox1.Checked);
{Get the list of the available stored procedures}
    GetProcedureNames(ListBox3.Items);
   end;
end;

procedure TForm1.CheckBox1Click(Sender: TObject);
begin
 With ADOConnection1 do
   begin
    If Connected then
     begin
{
 Refresh the tables list box according to the current
 state of the SysTables checkbox
}
     GetTableNames(ListBox1.Items, CheckBox1.Checked);
{Clear the fields list}
     ListBox2.Items.Clear;
    end;
   end;
end;

procedure TForm1.ListBox1Click(Sender: TObject);
```

```
begin
 With ListBox1 do
  begin
{Show the name of the selected table}
   Edit1.Text := 'Table : ' + Items[ItemIndex];
{and get the list of fields within it}
   ADOConnection1.GetFieldNames(Items[ItemIndex], ListBox2.Items);
  end;
end;
```

In this example, we have three list boxes—the first to show the names of tables available in the database, the second to show the fields in the selected table, and the third to show the list of stored procedures. The SysTables checkbox is used to toggle the list of the system tables. GetTableNames is a Delphi-specific method.

The Open Method

This method, defined in the ADO Connection object, opens a connection to a datasource specified in the ConnectionString property. There are two overloaded Open methods available. The first one takes no parameters and simply opens a connection.

The second one takes two parameters—UserID and Password, which are used to connect to a secured database. This version of the Open method can be used if we did not supply the login information through the ConnectionString property. In this case the LoginPrompt property should be set to False so a login dialog does not appear.

The OpenSchema Method

This method, defined in the ADO Connection object, can be used to obtain the database schema information from the provider specified in the ConnectionString property. The OpenSchema method takes four parameters shown in the following table.

Parameter	Description
Schema	One of the siXXX constants indicating the type of schema to retrieve
Restrictions	An array of column names to filter the results. This depends on the schema selected for querying
SchemaID	GUID for a provider-specific schema
DataSet	TADODataSet-type component or its descendant to receive the results

As we have already seen, the Delphi TADOConnection component implements three methods to obtain various information from the database—GetFieldNames, GetProcedureNames, and GetTableNames. All of these methods use the OpenSchema method to retrieve information from the database. Using this method, we can create various procedures of our own, such as one that returns the names of the tables along with their types:

```
procedure TForm1.GetTableNamesTypes;
var
 Tables : TADODataSet;
begin
 try
  Tables := TADODataSet.Create(nil);
  ADOConnection1.OpenSchema(siTables, EmptyParam,
   EmptyParam, Tables);
  While Not Tables.EOF do
   begin
    Memo1.Lines.Add(Tables.Fields.FieldByName('TABLE_NAME').Value
     + #9 + Tables.Fields.FieldByName('TABLE_TYPE').Value);
    Tables.Next;
   end;
 finally
  Tables.Free;
 end;
end;
```

ADOConnection Demo window showing:

```
Alphabetical List of Products    VIEW
Categories                       TABLE
Category Sales for 1997          VIEW
Current Product List             VIEW
Customers                        TABLE
Employees                        TABLE
Invoices                         VIEW
MSysAccessObjects                ACCESS TABLE
MSysACEs                         SYSTEM TABLE
MSysCmdbars                      ACCESS TABLE
MSysIMEXColumns                  ACCESS TABLE
MSysIMEXSpecs                    ACCESS TABLE
MSysObjects                      SYSTEM TABLE
MSysQueries                      SYSTEM TABLE
MSysRelationships                SYSTEM TABLE
Order Details                    TABLE
Order Details Extended           VIEW
Order Subtotals                  VIEW
Orders                           TABLE
Orders Qry                       VIEW
```

Or, if we are looking for information on one particular table, we can call the OpenSchema method with the following arguments:

```
Table:='Customers';
ADOConnection1.OpenSchema(siTables,
  VarArrayOf([Null, Null, Table]), EmptyParam, Tables);
```

The parameter of the VarArrayOf function is an array that contains the possible values in resulting dataset columns and plays the role of *filters*. If some of the values in this array are not null, the resulting dataset will contain only rows, where an appropriate column value is equal to the specified array member.

In the example above, the 'Customers' string is in the third position of this array for the selected siTables schema, because the name of the tables in the resulting dataset are in the third column, with other column values being insignificant.

For more information on possible column names used in different schemas, refer to the Microsoft Platform SDK.

Tip: To quickly find the meaning of columns for particular schema, use DBGrid to show the results of executing the OpenSchema method with the Schema parameter of interest, and theEmptyParam values of the Restrictions and SchemaID parameters.

Here we specify the restrictions, as we are interested in only one particular table. Take a look at the example below:

```
procedure TForm1.Button1Click(Sender: TObject);
begin
 with ADOConnection1 do
 begin
  Open;
{Get list of tables available}
  GetTableNames(ListBox1.Items);
 end;
end;

procedure TForm1.ListBox1Click(Sender: TObject);
begin
{When user selects table from a list box}
 With ListBox1 do
{Show its information}
  GetTableInfo(Items[ItemIndex]);
end;

procedure TForm1.GetTableInfo(Table: WideString);
var
 Tables : TADODataSet;
begin
```

```
Memo1.Lines.Clear;
try
  Tables := TADODataSet.Create(nil);
{Obtain the information for the particular table}
  ADOConnection1.OpenSchema(siTables,
    VarArrayOf([Null, Null, Table]), EmptyParam, Tables);
{Show it}
    Memo1.Lines.Add('TableName  = ' + #9 +
      Tables.Fields.FieldByName('TABLE_NAME').Value);
    Memo1.Lines.Add('TableType  = ' + #9 +
      Tables.Fields.FieldByName('TABLE_TYPE').Value);
    Memo1.Lines.Add('Created    = ' + #9 +
      Tables.Fields.FieldByName('DATE_CREATED').AsString);
    Memo1.Lines.Add('Modified   = ' + #9 +
      Tables.Fields.FieldByName('DATE_MODIFIED').AsString);
finally
  Tables.Free;
end;
end;
```

Let's take a look at two more examples. The first one will show data types supported by the provider. Here is the source code:

```
procedure TForm1.Button2Click(Sender: TObject);
var
  RS: TADODataset;
begin
  Memo1.Lines.Clear;
  With ADOConnection1 do
```

```
begin
 Open;
 try
  RS := TADODataSet.Create(Nil);
  OpenSchema(siProviderTypes, EmptyParam, EmptyParam, RS);
  While Not RS.EOF do
  begin
   Memo1.Lines.Add('Data Type : ' +
    RS.Fields.FieldByName('TYPE_NAME').Value +
    #9 + 'Column Size : ' +
    RS.Fields.FieldByName('COLUMN_SIZE').AsString);
   RS.Next;
  end;
 finally
  RS.Free;
 end;
 Close;
 end;
end;
```

Knowing the data types supported by the provider will allow us to avoid some incompatibility errors and make our code more robust.

The GetTableNames method described above supports only tables. But what should we do if, for example, we need to get a list of views? Borland Knowledge Base suggests using the OpenSchema method. But how? Here is the code that does the job:

```
procedure TForm1.Button3Click(Sender: TObject);
var
 RS: TADODataset;
begin
 Memo1.Lines.Clear;
 With ADOConnection1 do
  begin
```

```
  Open;
  try
   RS := TADODataSet.Create(Nil);
   OpenSchema(siViews, EmptyParam, EmptyParam, RS);
   While Not RS.EOF do
   begin
    Memo1.Lines.Add(
      RS.Fields.FieldByName('TABLE_NAME').Value);
     RS.Next;
   end;
  finally
   RS.Free;
  end;
  Close;
 end;
end;
```

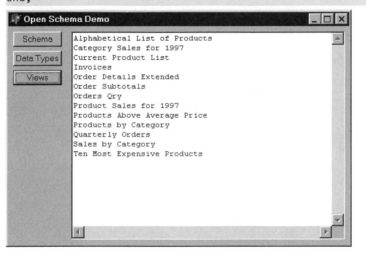

The list of schemas available through the OpenSchema method can also contain catalogs, collations, columns, indexes, primary keys, procedures, and views, to name a few. In addition, we can specify provider-specific schemas. For example, if we use the Microsoft Jet 4.0 OLE DB Provider, we can query for user information (called *user roster*) as well as such objects like forms, reports, and macros. Check the documentation that comes with your OLE DB provider for more information.

Note: As an alternative to the OpenSchema method, we can use properties and methods of the ADOX objects. For more information refer to Chapter 16.

Variants

A Variant is a data type implemented in Delphi to support Automation, which is part of the COM technology underlying the ADO that allows us to use services of ADO and OLE DB libraries. Starting with Delphi 3.0, there is an OleVariant data type that can hold Automation-compatible data types.

We can say that one of the main purposes of the Variant data type is to be able to use a variable whose data type is not specified at compile time. The type of the variant can be changed at run time and can be one of the types in the TVarData structure, defined in the System unit. This structure is shown below.

```
TVarData = packed record
  VType: Word;
  Reserved1, Reserved2, Reserved3: Word;
  case Integer of
    varSmallint: (VSmallint: Smallint);
    varInteger:  (VInteger: Integer);
    varSingle:   (VSingle: Single);
    varDouble:   (VDouble: Double);
    varCurrency: (VCurrency: Currency);
    varDate:     (VDate: Double);
    varOleStr:   (VOleStr: PWideChar);
    varDispatch: (VDispatch: Pointer);
    varError:    (VError: LongWord);
    varBoolean:  (VBoolean: WordBool);
    varUnknown:  (VUnknown: Pointer);
    varByte:     (VByte: Byte);
    varString:   (VString: Pointer);
    varAny:      (VAny: Pointer);
    varArray:    (VArray: PVarArray);
    varByRef:    (VPointer: Pointer);
end;
```

As we can see, variants can be simple data types like integers, floating-point values, strings, Booleans, currency, date, and time, but also can contain Automation objects.

Delphi supports a set of procedures and functions that can be used with variants. They are shown in the table below.

Procedure/Function	Description
VarAsType	This function converts a variant to a specified type.
VarCast	This procedure converts a variant to a specified type. This is the same as the VarAsType function.
VarClear	This procedure clears a variant, making it unassigned.
VarCopy	This procedure copies one variant into another.
VarFromDateTime	This function returns a variant for the specified date and time.
VarIsArray	Returns True if variant is an array.
VarIsEmpy	Returns True if variant is unassigned.
VarIsNull	Returns True if variant is Null.

Procedure/Function	Description
VarToDateTime	Returns the TDateTime value contained in a variant.
VarToStr	Converts a variant to a string.
VarType	Returns the type of the variant.

We can use the functions listed above in our Delphi ADO applications to perform conversions to and from various data types suitable for the particular piece of code.

The OleVariant data type is similar to the Variant data type with the only difference being that the OleVariant data type only supports Automation-compatible data types.

In some cases, we deal with *variant arrays*, which are arrays of variants that can be of different sizes and can contain various types allowed in variants, except ShortString and AnsiString. Using variant arrays is the only way to pass binary data to Automation servers since there are no pointers in the land of COM.

To create a variant array, use the VarArrayCreate or VarArrayOf functions defined in the System unit. To change the size of the variant array, use the VarArrayRedim function. To find the number of dimensions in a variant array, there is a VarArrayDimCount function. The VarArrayLowBound and VarArrayHighBound functions return the lower and upper bounds of an array, and the VarArrayRef returns a reference to the specified variant array. VarArrayLock and VarArrayUnlock are used to lock the array in memory and to unlock it.

The RollbackTrans Method

This method, defined in the ADO Connection object, cancels all changes made since the last call of the BeginTrans method and ends the transaction. The Rollback method triggers an OnRollbackTransComplete event, and changes the value of the InTransaction property to False.

See also the BeginTrans method, which initiates a transaction, and CommitTrans method, which saves changes.

Events

The TADOConnection component supports fourteen events, which we will cover in this section. Instead of listing them alphabetically, we'll examine these events in the order in which they occur in standard situations and what we can do in the event handler for each event. Note that all events with the source specified as Delphi in the following tables are defined in the TCustomConnection class.

Connection Events

As we have learned, there are several ways to open a connection. Regardless of the way we choose to open it, we will get the following sequence of events:

Event	Type	Source
BeforeConnect	TNotifyEvent	Delphi
OnWillConnect	TWillConnectEvent	ADO Kernel
OnLogin	TLoginEvent	Delphi
OnConnectComplete	TConnectErrorEvent	ADO Kernel
AfterConnect	TNotifyEvent	Delphi

As we can see from the above table, there are two notification events—BeforeConnect and AfterConnect—that simply notify us that some events occurred, and three more specific events—OnWillConnect, OnLogin, and OnConnectComplete—that contain more information that is available to the event handler to explore and manipulate. Let's look at each event in more detail.

The BeforeConnect Event

This event occurs immediately before establishing a connection and simply notifies us about that fact. The BeforeConnect event is a Delphi-specific event and occurs <u>before</u> the code really calls the ADO kernel. The Sender parameter of this event indicates the ADOConnection component, so you can access it by a simple typecast:

```
procedure TForm1.ADOConnection1BeforeConnect(Sender: TObject);
var
 Conn : TADOConnection;
begin
 Conn := Sender as TADOConnection;
 Memo1.Lines.Add(#9+'Connecting using '+ Conn.Provider);
end;
```

The OnWillConnect Event

This is the wrapper around the standard ADO event. This event occurs after a request to start a connection but <u>before</u> a connection starts. The event handler receives the following parameters:

Parameter	Type	Description
Connection	TADOConnection	Indicates the TADOConnection component that initiated the connection. This is the same as the Sender parameter in the BeforeConnect event.
ConnectionString	WideString	Contains the connection string—provider name, data source name, and security information for the connection. This is the same as the contents of the ConnectionString property.
UserID	WideString	Contains the user name to use in the connection.
Password	WideString	Contains the password to use in the connection.
ConnectOptions	TConnectOption	Indicates the connection options. See the ConnectOptions property.
EventStatus	TEventStatus	Indicates the status of the event—success or failure.

All parameters except the `Connection` parameter can be changed in the event handler. The `EventStatus` parameter can have one of the following values.

Value	Meaning
esCancel	This operation can be canceled.
esCantDeny	This operation cannot be canceled and requests for cancellation will be ignored.
esErrorsOccured	There were errors during execution.
esOK	There were no problems with this command execution.
esUnwantedEvent	Indicates that events for this operation are no longer required.

The OnLogin Event

This event occurs when we set the LoginPrompt property to True and there is no security information specified in the ConnectionString property. This event can be used in situations where we allow users to enter the user name and password to connect to a database. In the event handler for this event we can check, for example, that no one is trying to log on as a system administrator.

The OnConnectComplete Event

This is the wrapper around the standard ADO event. This event occurs <u>after</u> starting a connection either by calling the Open method or Execute method or setting the Connected property to True. The event handler receives the following parameters:

Parameter	Type	Description
Connection	TADOConnection	Indicates the TADOConnection component that initiated the connection. This is the same as the Sender parameter in the BeforeConnect event.
Error	Error	Provides access to the ADO Error object that can be used to obtain more detailed information about the error.
EventStatus	TEventStatus	Indicates the status of the event—success or failure

In the event handler for the OnConnectComplete event, we can examine the details of the connection just established and check if there are any errors.

The AfterConnect Event

This notification event occurs <u>after</u> a connection is established. This Delphi-specific event simply informs us that the connection is established. Use the OnConnectComplete event to get more information about the connection.

Disconnection Events

When we close the currently open connection through the Close method or by setting the Connected property to False, the following sequence of events occurs:

Event	Type	Source
BeforeDisconnect	TNotifyEvent	Delphi
OnDisconnect	TDisconnectEvent	ADO Kernel
AfterDisconnect	TNotifyEvent	Delphi

As we can see, there are two Delphi notification events and one ADO kernel event. This event contains additional information on the connection.

The BeforeDisconnect Event

This notification event occurs immediately <u>before</u> the connection has been closed. This Delphi-specific event simply informs us that the connection is being closed. Use the OnDisconnect event to get more information about the connection.

The OnDisconnect Event

This ADO event occurs <u>after</u> a connection ends. The event handler receives the following parameters:

Parameter	Type	Description
Connection	TADOConnection	Indicates the TADOConnection component that initiated the connection. This is the same as the Sender parameter in the BeforeConnect event.
EventStatus	TEventStatus	Indicates the status of the event—success or failure

In the event handler for the OnDisconnect event, we can check whether the disconnection was successful or not and inform users that the connection was dropped.

The AfterDisconnect Event

This notification event occurs immediately <u>after</u> the connection has been closed. This Delphi-specific event simply informs us that the connection is being closed. Use the OnDisconnect event to get more information about the connection.

Commands and Events

When we use the Execute method of the ADOConnection component, for example, with the following simple code:

```
procedure TForm1.Button1Click(Sender: TObject);
begin
 with ADOConnection1 do
  begin
   Execute('SELECT * FROM CUSTOMERS');

  end;
end;
```

these two events occur in the following order:

Event	Type	Source
OnWillExecute	TWillExecuteEvent	ADO Kernel
OnExecuteComplete	TExecuteCompleteEvent	ADO Kernel

The OnWillExecute event occurs <u>before</u> the command starts to execute, and the OnExecuteComplete event occurs just <u>after</u> a command finishes executing. Let's look at these events in more detail.

The OnWillExecute Event

The OnWillExecute event occurs <u>before</u> the command starts to execute. Its event handler receives a set of arguments describing the execution properties. It is possible to check or modify them before a command is executed.

Parameter	Type	Description
Connection	TADOConnection	Indicates the TADOConnection executing the command.
CommandText	WideString	Contains the SQL command or name of the stored procedure to be executed.
CursorType	TCursorType	Indicates the type of cursor for the recordset that will be created upon the execution.
LockType	TADOLockType	Indicates the lock type for the recordset that will be created upon the execution.
ExecuteOptions	TExecuteOptions	Execution options that were set with the Options argument of the Execute method.
EventStatus	TEventStatus	Indicates the status of this event. Setting this argument to esCancel will cancel the command execution.
Command	_Command	Indicates the Command object executing the command. If the Command object was not used, this argument contains the nil value.
Recordset	_Recordset	Indicates the Recordset object that will contain the results of the command execution. Recordsets are only used with SQL SELECT statements. In other cases, this argument will contain the nil value.

The following example of an event handler for the OnWillExecute event shows the values of several arguments passed to the handler:

```
procedure TForm1.ADOConnection1WillExecute(
  Connection: TADOConnection;
  var CommandText: WideString; var CursorType: TCursorType;
  var LockType: TADOLockType; var CommandType: TCommandType;
  var ExecuteOptions: TExecuteOptions;
  var EventStatus: TEventStatus;
  const Command: _Command; const Recordset: _Recordset
);
var
  S : String;
begin
  Memo1.Lines.Add('OnWillExecute Event');
  Memo1.Lines.Add(#9'Command = ' + CommandText);
  S := #9'CursorType = ';
  case CursorType of
```

```
   ctUnspecified      : S := S + 'Unspecified';
   ctOpenForwardOnly : S := S + 'OpenForwardOnly';
   ctKeyset           : S := S + 'Keyset';
   ctDynamic          : S := S + 'Dynamic';
   ctStatic           : S := S + 'Static';
 end;
Memo1.Lines.Add(S);
S := #9'LockType = ';
case LockType of
  ltUnspecified     : S := S + 'Unspecified';
  ltReadOnly        : S := S + 'ReadOnly';
  ltPessimistic     : S := S + 'Pessimistic';
  ltOptimistic      : S := S + 'Optimistic';
  ltBatchOptimistic : S := S + 'BatchOptimistic';
end;
Memo1.Lines.Add(S);
S := #9'CommandType = ';
case CommandType of
  cmdUnknown        : S := S + 'Unknown';
  cmdText           : S := S + 'Text';
  cmdTable          : S := S + 'Table';
  cmdStoredProc     : S := S + 'StoredProc';
  cmdFile           : S := S + 'File';
  cmdTableDirect    : S := S + 'TableDirect';
end;
Memo1.Lines.Add(S);
S := #9'ExecuteOptions = [';
If eoAsyncExecute            in ExecuteOptions
  then S := S + ' AsyncExecute';
If eoAsyncFetch              in ExecuteOptions
  then S := S + ' AsyncFetch';
If eoAsyncFetchNonBlocking  in ExecuteOptions
  then S := S + ' AsyncFetchNonBlocking';
If eoExecuteNoRecords        in ExecuteOptions
  then S := S + ' ExecuteNoRecords';
Memo1.Lines.Add(S+']');
end;
```

Here is the output for the simple command shown at the beginning of this section:

```
OnWillExecute Event
 Command = SELECT * FROM CUSTOMERS
 CursorType = Unspecified
 LockType = Unspecified
 CommandType = Text
 ExecuteOptions = []
```

The OnExecuteComplete Event

The OnExecuteComplete event occurs just <u>after</u> a command finishes executing. Its event handler receives a set of arguments describing the status of the execution. We can examine them to find out, for example, if the command completed successfully and how many records it affected.

Parameter	Type	Description
Connection	TADOConnection	Indicates the TADOConnection that executed the command.
RecordsAffected	Integer	Contains the number of records that were affected by the command.
Error	Error	Contains an Error object describing the error that occurred during execution. This argument is set only if EventStatus is equal to esErrorsOccured.
EventStatus	TEventStatus	Indicates the status of this event. If it is equal to esErrorsOccured, then the Error object contains additional information.
Command	_Command	Indicates the Command object executing the command. If Command object was not used, contains the nil value.
Recordset	_Recordset	Indicates the Recordset object that contains the results of the command execution. Recordsets are only used with SQL SELECT statements. In other cases, this argument will contain the nil value.

Here is an example of the event handler that shows how many records were affected by the command, and provides information on errors if any take place.

```
procedure TForm1.ADOConnection1ExecuteComplete(
  Connection: TADOConnection;
  RecordsAffected: Integer; const Error: Error;
  var EventStatus: TEventStatus; const Command: _Command;
  const Recordset: _Recordset
);
begin
 Memo1.Lines.Add(^M^J'OnExecuteComplete Event');
 Memo1.Lines.Add(#9'Records Affected = ' +
  IntToStr(RecordsAffected));
 If EventStatus = esErrorsOccured then
  Memo1.Lines.Add(Error.Description);
end;
```

For example, if we misspell the name of the table in the query:

```
Execute('SELECT * FROM CUSTOMERZ'); // Note Z instead of S !!!
```

we will get the following error message (from the Error.Description property):

```
The Microsoft Jet database engine cannot find the input table or query
'CUSTOMERZ'.  Make sure it exists and that its name is spelled correctly.
```

We will talk about the Error object in more detail later in this chapter.

Transaction Events

As we have learned in this chapter, the TADOConnection component supports transactions through three methods—BeginTrans, CommitTrans, and RollbackTrans. Each of these methods fires an appropriate event upon completion—OnBeginTransComplete, OnCommitTransComplete, and OnRollbackTransComplete. These events, their types, and source are shown in the following table:

Event	Type	Source
OnBeginTransComplete	TBeginTransCompleteEvent	ADO Kernel
OnCommitTransComplete	TConnectErrorEvent	ADO Kernel
OnRollbackTransComplete	TConnectErrorEvent	ADO Kernel

The OnBeginTransComplete Event

This event is fired <u>after</u> the BeginTrans method has been completed. The event handler receives the following parameters:

Parameter	Type	Description
Connection	TADOConnection	Indicates the TADOConnection component that initiated the connection.
TransactionLevel	Integer	Indicates the new transaction level for the transaction.
Error	Error	Contains an Error object describing the error that occurred during execution. This argument is set only if EventStatus is equal to esErrorsOccured.
EventStatus	TEventStatus	Indicates the status of this event. If it is equal to esErrorsOccured, then the Error object contains additional information.

We can use this event to start some actions that should be performed after the transaction has successfully started.

The OnCommitTransComplete Event

This event is fired <u>after</u> the CommitTrans method has been completed. The event handler receives the following parameters:

Parameter	Type	Description
Connection	TADOConnection	Indicates the TADOConnection component that initiated the connection.
Error	Error	Contains an Error object describing the error that occurred during execution. This argument is set only if EventStatus is equal to esErrorsOccured.
EventStatus	TEventStatus	Indicates the status of this event. If it is equal to esErrorsOccured, the Error object contains additional information.

We can use this event, for example, to end some actions that were started in the OnBeginTrans event handler or perform other actions that should be initiated when the transaction has been completed successfully.

The OnRollbackTransComplete Event

This event is fired <u>after</u> the RollbackTrans method has completed. The event handler receives the same parameters as the OnCommitTransComplete event.

Parameter	Type	Description
Connection	TADOConnection	Indicates the TADOConnection component that initiated the connection.
Error	Error	Contains an Error object describing the error that occurred during execution. This argument is set only if EventStatus is equal to esErrorsOccured.
EventStatus	TEventStatus	Indicates the status of this event. If it is equal to esErrorsOccured, the Error object contains additional information.

We can use this event to initiate some actions after the transaction has rolled back, i.e., failed.

Miscellaneous Events

The last event that may occur while using the TADOConnection component is the OnInfoMessage event.

The OnInfoMessage Event

The event handler of the OnInfoMessage event receives the following parameters:

Parameter	Type	Description
Connection	TADOConnection	Indicates the TADOConnection component that initiated the connection.
Error	Error	Contains an Error object describing the error that occurred during execution. This argument is set only if EventStatus is equal to esErrorsOccured
EventStatus	TEventStatus	Indicates the status of this event. If it is equal to esErrorsOccured, then the Error object contains additional information

Unlike other events we have discussed, it is hard to indicate when this event occurs. In most cases, it happens when a provider returns some additional information. In this situation, we can examine the Error object to retrieve this information. For example:

```
procedure TForm1.ADOConnection1InfoMessage(Connection:
 TADOConnection; const Error: Error; var EventStatus:
 TEventStatus);
var
 I : Integer;
```

```
E : ADODB.Error;
begin
Memo1.Lines.Add(#9+Error.Description);
For I := 0 to Connection.ConnectionObject.Errors.Count-1 do
  begin
  E := Connection.ConnectionObject.Errors[I];
  Memo1.Lines.Add(E.Description);
  end;

end;
```

In most cases, this event occurs when we try to connect to the ODBC data sources.
Here are some examples of the information you can receive:

```
// Connecting to the Access Database through ODBC:

[Microsoft][ODBC Driver Manager] Driver's SQLSetConnectAttr failed

// Connecting to the SQL Server Database through ODBC:

[Microsoft][ODBC SQL Server Driver][SQL Server]Changed database context to
'pubs'.
[Microsoft][ODBC SQL Server Driver][SQL Server]Changed language setting to
us_english.
```

In the example above, we see how to retrieve error (or warning) information from the
Error object. Now it is time to take a deeper look at the Error object and Errors collection. These are discussed in the next section.

The Errors Collection and the Error Object

We have encountered the Error object several times in this chapter. Now is a good time
to look at this object in more detail. The Errors collection available through reference
to the underlying ADO Connection object contains one or more Error objects that store
information for a single provider error or warning. As we have seen, this collection can
also be used to extract additional information with, for example, the help of the
OnInfoMessage event.

The Errors Collection

The Errors collection exposes two methods—the Clear method used to remove all
objects from it and the Refresh method that updates the information stored in this collection. The Count property indicates the number of Error objects currently stored in
the collection.

The Error Object

The Error object does not have any methods. It exposes the seven properties described below:

Property	Meaning
Description	Contains the string with the short error description.
HelpContext	Indicates the context ID for the topic in the help file specified in the HelpFile property. If there is no help for this error, this property will contain 0.
HelpFile	Contains the fully qualified path to the help file. If there is no such a file, this property will contain an empty string.
NativeError	Indicates the provider-specific error code for the error.
Number	Indicates the unique number that corresponds to this error.
Source	Contains the source of the error, that is, the name of the object or application that generated it.
SQLState	Indicates the error code (five-character string that follows the ANSI SQL standard) for the error that occurred while processing the SQL statement.

Note that the Error object represents provider-specific errors, not ADO errors. ADO errors are exposed through OLE exceptions, and should be caught through the standard try..except or try..finally blocks.

Also keep in mind that there can be more that one Error object associated with the current operation. Check the Count property of the Errors collection and use this property as the counter to iterate through it.

To be sure that you will receive only the errors associated with the operation just performed, always call the Clear method of the Errors collection before initiating the operation.

Using the TADOConnection Component

In this section, we will give you several examples of how to use the TADOConnection component in Delphi ADO applications. We will start with a more detailed discussion of how to connect to ADO datasources.

Several Ways to Connect

The TADOConnection object provides several ways to connect to a datasource, depending on your need. The simplest way is to set the ConnectionString property value at design time. To do this, click on the ellipsis button at the ConnectionString property in the Object Inspector. This will open the ConnectionString dialog box, which is divided into two parts.

The upper edit box allows us to supply the name of a data link file, while the lower one is used to create a connection string. Let's look at the connection string part first.

Using Connection Strings

Pressing the Build key opens the standard OLE DB Data Link Properties dialog box, which has four tabs. The Provider tab is used to select one of the OLE DB providers available on the computer. The default value is OLE DB Provider for ODBC Drivers.

You may choose any particular provider depending on your needs. For this example, let's use Microsoft Jet 4.0 OLE DB Provider.

Press the Next button to move to the Connection tab; this tab is different for each OLE DB provider. The figure below shows the edit boxes available for the Jet Provider to work with Access databases and other datasources supported by Jet 4.0.

Here we can supply the name of the database we are planning to use and the user name and password for the password-protected databases. In addition, we can test the connection to be sure that everything works fine (at least at the connection side). At this step, we have supplied the minimum information for the ADOConnection object to be able to open a database. Now we can either press the OK button to set the connection string, or move to the other two tabs.

The Advanced tab allows us to set the access permissions for the database. The default value is Share Deny None.

We can change the access rights here. For example, to open a database exclusively, we should set the Share Exclusive option.

The All tab shows all the properties supported by the provider. Once again, this list depends on the type of provider selected. At this step, we can manually set the properties required for our connection, or just use the default values. To modify a property, select it and click on the Edit Value button.

After we have set all the information required for our connection, we can press the OK button. This will return us to the ConnectionString dialog box with the Use Connection String edit box filled with the connection string we have build. Once again, pressing the OK button sets the ConnectionString property value.

The resulting string for our example may look like this:

```
Provider=Microsoft.Jet.OLEDB.4.0;Data Source=C:\DATA\Northwind.mdb;Persist
Security Info=False
```

Note that the ConnectionString contains the name of the provider, the name of the datasource, and security information. Delphi also automatically fills the value of the Provider property, which in our example is:

```
Microsoft.Jet.OLEDB.4.0
```

Using Data Link Files

As we have mentioned, instead of the connection string, we can use the data link file. To do so, we need to select the Use Data Link File edit box and click on the Browse button. This will give us a list of data link files available at the default folder, which is usually located at the Program Files\Common Files\SYSTEM\ole db\Data Links folder. This folder is opened when we press the Browse button in the ConnectionString dialog box. If our data link files are stored in another folder, we can select it using the Select Data Link File dialog box.

After we have selected a data link file and pressed the OK button, the ConnectionString property is set to the following value:

```
FILE NAME=D:\Program Files\Common Files\SYSTEM\ole db\Data Links\DBDEMOS.udl
```

The Provider property in this case will have the following value:

```
D:\Program Files\Common Files\SYSTEM\ole db\Data Links\DBDEMOS.udl
```

The data link file allows us to separate the compiled application from the exact location of the data source (for those who have worked with BDE, the concept of data link files may sound familiar; they play the same role as BDE aliases). In case we move the database to another location, all we need to do is to change the contents of the data link file.

Creating Data Link Files

If we need to create a data link file, we can do this either manually or programmatically. To create a data link file manually, perform the following steps:

1. Right-click on your desktop and choose **New | Microsoft Data Link** from the pop-up menu.
2. Specify the name of the file.
3. Right-click on the file and select the Properties command.
4. In the Properties dialog box, specify the information required—the type of provider, name of the database, and extra parameters if needed.

 Tip: To create a data link file in Windows 2000, create a new text file, and save it with a .udl extension. Double-click this file to open the Data Link Properties dialog box.

To create a data link file programmatically, use the CreateUDLFile procedure that is implemented in the ADODB unit. We should supply three parameters to it: the filename of the newly created data link file, the name of the provider, and the name of the data source. After we are set, we call this procedure and the new .udl file will be created in the current directory.

Here is an example of how we can use this procedure:

```
CreateUDLFile('adodemo.udl','MSDASQL.1', 'GALLERY');
```

Note: You should supply the .udl extension in the filename.

Microsoft Windows stores all data link files in the Program Files\Common Files\System\OLE DB\Data Links folder. To add your newly created file to this folder, you should first obtain its name. The DataLinkDir function, also implemented in the ADODB unit, returns the path to the above-mentioned folder by looking up the location in the registry. So, to store our own data link file in this folder, we should call the CreateUDLFile procedure in this way:

```
CreateUDLFile(DataLinkDir+'\adodemo.udl',
 'MSDASQL.1', 'NORTHWIND');
```

Note: The slash (\) symbol precedes the name of the data link file.

Converting the UDL File to a Readable String

We have talked about the data link files that can be created and selected with the help of some ADODB unit's functions. If we look at the UDL file, we will find that this is a binary file, i.e., its contents can't be manipulated as a string like a connection string. But with the help of an OLE DB interface we can convert the contents of the data link file back into a string.

To do so we need to use the LoadStringFromStorage method of the IDataInitialize interface (discussion of this interface is beyond the scope of this book). Here is the source of the UDL2Str function that accepts the filename of the .udl file and returns its contents as a string:

```
function UDL2Str(FileName: WideString) : WideString;
var
 DI : IDataInitialize;
 CS : PWideChar;
begin
// Get access to the IDataInitialize interface
 DI := CreateComObject(CLSID_DataLinks) as IDataInitialize;
// and call its LoadStringFromStorage method
 OleCheck(DI.LoadStringFromStorage(PWideChar(FileName),
```

```
  CS));
 Result := CS;
end;
```

Note: You should put the OLE DB and ComObj units into the Uses clause.

The resulting string can look like one shown below:

```
Provider=Microsoft.Jet.OLEDB.4.0;Data Source=D:\Program Files\Common
Files\Borland Shared\Data\DBDEMOS.mdb
```

Setting the Connection String Programmatically

In the section above, we have seen two ways to set the values of the ConnectionString property through the ConnectionString dialog box at design time. While this can be useful in most cases, there can be situations where we need to set its value in our application.

```
with ADOConnection1 do
 begin
  Provider := 'Microsoft.Jet.OLEDB.4.0';
  Properties['Data Source'].Value := 'c:\data\NorthWind.mdb';
  Open;
 end;
```

This method can be used to allow users to choose from several databases. Just add the OpenDialog component and assign its FileName property to the 'Data Source' property value as shown below:

```
with ADOConnection1 do
 begin
  Provider := 'Microsoft.Jet.OLEDB.4.0';
  If OpenDialog1.Execute then
   begin
    Properties['Data Source'].Value := OpenDialog1.FileName;
    Open;
   end;
 end;
```

Accessing Provider Properties

As we have already mentioned, the Properties property of the TADOConnection component give us access to the Properties collection of the underlying ADO Connection object. This collection contains various provider-specific properties that can be accessed either by name or by index. Each provider has its own set of properties. Some of them are available before we establish the connection and in most cases are read/write. After the connection is established, the properties become read-only.

Specifying only the provider name, either through the ConnectionString properties or through the Provider property without opening the database, will give us a list of the provider-specific properties. For more information, see Chapter 3 or refer to the documentation that comes with the specific OLE DB provider.

The Attributes property of the Properties property allows us to check whether a property is read-only or read/write. For example:

```
with ADOConnection1 do
  For I := 0 to Properties.Count-1 do
  begin
    S := VarToStr(Properties[I].Name) + '=' +
      VarToStr(Properties[I].Value);
    if Properties[I].Attributes AND adPropRead = adPropRead
    Then S := S + ' [Read]';
    if Properties[I].Attributes AND adPropWrite = adPropWrite
    Then S := S + ' [Write]';
    Memo1.Lines.Add(S);
  end;
```

Finding the Version of ADO Library

We already know how to find the version number by using the Version property of the TADOConnection component described earlier in this chapter. In some cases, we need to know more about the version. For example, instead of 2.1 we may need to find the specific build. To do so we need to find the file version of the ADO library itself. In this case, we use the system registry and look for the ADODB.Connection component in the HKEY_CLASSES_ROOT. If we find one, we extract its class ID (CLSID) and use its value to find the inproc server, the COM server that implements the Connection object. This gives us the location of the ADO library. After that, we extract the version resource and get the version information from it. The following code shows how to do this:

```
function GetFileVer(FileName : String) : String;
var
VerSize : DWORD;
Zero    : THandle;
PBlock  : Pointer;
PS      : Pointer;
Size    : UINT;
begin
{** Get size of Version resource **}
VerSize := GetFileVersionInfoSize(PChar(FileName),
  Zero);
If VerSize = 0 Then
  Begin
    GetFileVer := 'Not found';
    Exit;
  End;
{** Allocate memory **}
```

```
GetMem(PBlock, VerSize);
{** Get Version resource **}
GetFileVersionInfo(PChar(FileName), 0, VerSize,
PBlock);
If VerQueryValue(PBlock,
 '\\StringFileInfo\\000004E4\\ProductVersion',PS,Size) Then
 GetFileVer := StrPas(PS)
Else
 If VerQueryValue(PBlock,
 '\\StringFileInfo\\000004B0\\ProductVersion',PS,Size) Then
  GetFileVer := StrPas(PS)
 Else
  GetFileVer := '?.?';
  FreeMem(PBlock, VerSize);
end;
function GetADOVer : String;
var
 Reg   : TRegistry;
 List  : TStringList;
 I     : Integer;
 CLSID : String;
begin
 try
  Reg  := TRegistry.Create;
  List := TStringList.Create;
  With Reg do
   begin
    RootKey := HKEY_CLASSES_ROOT;
    OpenKey('', False);
    GetKeyNames(List);
    for I := 0 To List.Count - 1 do
     if Pos('ADODB.Connection', List[I]) <> 0 Then
     begin
      OpenKey(List[I]+'\CLSID', False);
      CLSID := ReadString('');
     end;
    CloseKey;
    OpenKey('\CLSID\'+CLSID + '\InprocServer32', False);
    GetADOVer := GetFileVer(ReadString(''));
   end;
 finally
  List.Free;
  Reg.Free;
 end;
end;
procedure TForm1.Button1Click(Sender: TObject);
begin
```

```
ShowMessage(GetADOVer);
end;
```

Note: In this example we have used the Registry unit, which must be included in the Uses clause.

One final note: While the TADOConnection.Version property can be used to find the version of ADO, it is assumed that ADO is already installed on the computer. We can use the technique described in this section to find not only the detailed version of ADO but also if it is installed. In this case there is no need to use Delphi ADO components that can fail if there is no ADO kernel available.

Delphi 5 ADO Support Routines

Now we will take a look at two more helper routines that are available in the Delphi 5 ADODB unit and give some examples of its usage.

The GetProviderNames Procedure

This procedure returns a list (TStrings type) of all providers known to your current OLE DB engine. We can use a list box to get a list of providers. This works fine since TListbox.Items property is a collection of strings, defined as a TStrings type.

```
GetProviderNames(ListBox1.Items);
```

The PromptDataXX Functions

The following two functions available in the ADODB unit can be used to ask the user to supply the data source name (PromptDataSource function) and the data link file-name (PromptDataLinkFile function).

The PromptDataSource function expects two parameters—a handle to the window that will host a dialog box and an initial string. This function returns the data source name as a WideString. For example:

```
procedure TForm1.Button1Click(Sender: TObject);
var
 CS : WideString;
begin
 With ADOConnection1 do
  begin
// Show current connection string
   Edit1.Text := ConnectionString;
// If we have not set one
   If ConnectionString = '' Then
// set it right now
```

```
    CS := PromptDataSource(Form1.Handle, '')
  Else
// or allow use to change the current one
  CS := PromptDataSource(Form1.Handle, ConnectionString);
// set the resulting string
  ConnectionString := CS;
 end;
end;
```

The PromptDataLinkFile function allows us to request a data link file (.udl file). It expects two parameters—a handle to the window that will host a dialog box and a name of the initial file. This function returns the data link filename as a WideString. For example:

```
procedure TForm1.Button2Click(Sender: TObject);
var
 CS : WideString;
begin
 With ADOConnection1 do
  begin
// Show current connection string
   Edit1.Text := ConnectionString;
// Propmt user to choose one of the
// data link files available
   CS := PromptDataLinkFile(Form1.Handle, '')
// Form the connection string and set the property
   ConnectionString := 'File Name='+CS;
// Open dataset
   Open;
// and show tables within it
   GetTableNames(Memo1.Lines);
  end;
```

Note: We cannot use the data link filename as is. Instead, we should use the 'File Name=' argument of the connection string to specify to the ADO engine that all connection information is stored within the data link file.

Conclusion

In this chapter, we have learned about the TADOConnection component, its properties, methods, and events, and how to use it to connect our Delphi applications to various data sources.

In the next chapter, we will continue our discussion of Delphi ADO components with the TADOCommand component, which provides us with the ability to execute commands—SQL statements, stored procedures, and so on.

THE TADOCOMMAND COMPONENT

In the previous chapter, we saw how to use the TADOConnection component to connect to various ADO data sources. The topic of this chapter is the TADOCommand component, which is the direct Delphi implementation of the ADO Command object. It is used in Delphi applications to provide the ability to execute commands such as SQL Data Definition Language statements or stored procedures that do not return results. For SQL queries and stored procedures that return results as a recordset, it is better to use one of the other Delphi ADO components—the TADODataSet, described in the next chapter, or TADOQuery and TADOStoredProc, which are discussed in Chapter 8.

Note that it is also possible to use the TADOCommand component to execute such queries and stored procedures, but this requires manipulating the resulting recordset on the ADO RecordSet object level, or using the separate TADODataSet component. Later in this chapter we will see how to access the resulting recordset from our code.

Now let's look at the TADOCommand component's properties and methods, and then see an example of how to use this component.

Properties

The TADOCommand component has several properties, most of which are the Delphi equivalents of the ADO Command object properties, plus several others that are specific for the Delphi implementation of this component.

The CommandObject Property

This property gives us direct access to the underlying ADO Command object. In most cases, there is no real need to directly access this object, since most of its functionality is already implemented on the component level.

The CommandText Property

This property, defined in the ADO Command object, specifies the command to be executed with the Execute method. This can be the string containing the SQL statement, or the name of the table or stored procedure. If the command specified in the CommandText property requires parameters, they can be set through the Parameters property at either design time or run time.

For performance reasons, always specify the type of command in the CommandType property (see below).

The CommandTimeout Property

This property, defined in the ADO Command object, specifies in seconds how long to wait before the command will be considered unsuccessful. The default value for the CommandTimeout property is 30 seconds.

Note: This property is not the same as the TADOConnection component's CommandTimeout property.

The CommandType Property

This property, defined in the ADO Command object, specifies the type of command contained in the CommandText property. The default value for the CommandType property is cmdUnknown, meaning that the underlying ADO Command object should take extra steps to determine the type of command before executing it.

For performance reasons, always indicate the command's type. The possible values of this property are shown in the following table:

Value	Meaning	ADO Constant
cmdStoredProc	The CommandText property contains the name of the stored procedure	adCmdStoredProc
cmdTable	The CommandText property contains the name of the table that sends the following SQL statement to the provider: SELECT * FROM Table_Name	adCmdTable
cmdText	The CommandText property contains the SQL statement. This is the default value.	adCmdText
cmdUnknown	Unknown command type	adCmdUnknown

For more information about the CommandType property, see Chapter 7.

Note: Contrary to what the documentation says, you can use the cmdTable value for the CommandType parameter.

The Connection Property

This property, which is the Delphi equivalent of the ADO Command object's ActiveConnection property, is used to specify the TADOConnection component that is used to connect to the ADO data source. The Connection property can be used to share the connection among several Delphi ADO components. If this is not the case, use the ConnectionString property described below to specify the details of the connection.

Note: ConnectionString and Connection are mutually exclusive properties. You can only set one of them.

The ConnectionString Property

Use this property to specify the information necessary to connect to the ADO data source. At design time you can use the built-in Connection dialog box to supply all the information needed for the selected OLE DB provider. At run time, you should assign an appropriate string to the ConnectionString property. For example:

```
With ADOCommand1 do
 begin
 ConnectionString := 'Provider=SQLOLEDB.1;Persist ' +
   'Security 'Info=False; User ID=sa;' +
   'Initial Catalog=BIBLIO2000;Data Source=maindesk';
 CommandType := cmdTable;
 CommandText := 'Authors';
 Execute;
end;
```

As we have noted above, instead of the ConnectionString property you can use the Connection property to specify the properly initialized ADOConnection object that will be used to connect to the ADO data source.

Note: ConnectionString and Connection are mutually exclusive properties. You can only set one of them.

The ExecuteOptions Property

This property is used to set the options that affect the execution of the command specified in the CommandText property. The possible values of the ExecuteOptions property are shown in the following table.

Value	Meaning	ADO Constant
eoAsyncExecute	The command is executed asynchronously	adAsyncExecute
eoAsyncFetch	The records are fetched asynchronously	adAsyncFetch
eoAsyncFetchNonBlocking	The records are fetched asynchronously and subsequent operations are not blocked	adAsyncFetchNonBlocking

Value	Meaning	ADO Constant
eoExecuteNoRecords	The command does not return a recordset	adExecuteNoRecords

> **Tip:** If you know that the command does not return a recordset, or you are planning to discard the results, set the command to eoExecuteNoRecords to make it run a little bit faster.

Note that there is no direct equivalent of this property in the ADO Command object. For this object, the values of the ExecuteOptionEnum type are added to the cmdType property.

The ParamCheck Property

This property provides a way to switch between two styles of parameter representation within the code of the command—the ":Parameter" style and "?" style. In most cases the default value of the ParamCheck property, which is True, can be used, meaning that a parameter is created for each ":Parameter" style parameter in the code for the SQL statement.

The Parameters Property

Use this property to set the values of the parameters required to successfully execute the SQL query or stored procedure. At design time you can use the built-in Parameters Editor, which shows various attributes of the particular parameter and allows the setting of its values or the changing of some of its attributes.

At run time, you should use the Parameters property to access one or more Parameter objects within it using the CreateParameter method. We will give you examples of how to do this later in this book.

The Prepared Property

This property should be set to True before calling the Execute method to specify that the compiled version of the command should be saved before execution. This needs to be done only for commands that will be executed more than once. In this case the prepared command will be executed faster since its text will be not parsed on subsequent executions.

The Properties Property

This property provides us with direct access to the Properties collection of the underlying ADO Command object. This collection contains one or more Property objects that represent the detailed characteristics of the ADO Command object.

There is no real need to use the Properties property, since the contents of this collection depend on the provider and, in most cases, this collection is empty for the closed Command object and is filled after we run the Execute method. If you really need to explore this collection, first check the number of items in it with the Count property and then iterate it, using the Name, Type, Value, and Attributes properties to get more information about the particular item. For example:

```
procedure TForm1.Button1Click(Sender: TObject);
var
 I : Integer;
begin
 ADOCommand1.Execute;
 For I := 0 to ADOCommand1.Properties.Count-1 do
  begin
   Memo1.Lines.Add
   (
     ADOCommand1.Properties[I].Name + #9 +
     VarToStr(ADOCommand1.Properties[I].Value)
   );
  end;
end;
```

A more detailed discussion of the Properties collection of the ADO Command object is beyond the scope of this book. Refer to the documentation that comes with your particular OLE DB provider to find more information on this topic. For example, a detailed explanation of the properties for the Microsoft Jet provider is available in the "ADO Provider Properties and Settings" article found at MSDN.

The States Property

This property allows us to find out what the component does. By checking the value of the States property, we can determine if the ADOCommand component is connecting to the data source, executing the command, fetching rows to the resulting recordset, is open but idle, or is closed and idle.

The States property can have one of the following values depending on the state of the TADOCommand component:

Value	Meaning	ADO Constant
stClosed	The Command object is closed	adStateClosed
stConnecting	The Command object is connecting to the data source	AdStateConnecting
stExecuting	The Command object is executing the command	AdStateExecuting
stFetching	The Command object is fetching records	AdStateFetching
stOpen	The Command object is open	adStateOpen

 Note: This property is the Delphi equivalent of the State property of the ADO Command object, and its values are the values of the ADO ObjectStateEnum constants.

One final note: There is no direct equivalent for the Name property of the ADO Command object. In the TADOCommand component this property is of the `TComponentName`

type (defined in the TComponent class), and it is used to specify the name of the component, not the name of the command, defined by the TADOCommand component.

Methods

The TADOCommand component defines a set of its own methods as well as implements the methods of the TADOCommand component. Note that there is no Delphi equivalent to the CreateParameter method of the ADO Command object. Instead, you can work directly with the Parameters collection.

The Assign Method

This method is used to create an exact copy of the TADOCommand object. The Assign method copies the following properties to the current TADOCommand object from the one supplied by the argument:

- Connection or ConnectionString (depending on which one is used in the source object)
- CommandTimeout
- CommandType
- CommandText
- Prepared
- Parameters

For example, to copy properties from the ADOCommand1 object to the ADOCommand2 object, we can use the following code:

```
ADOCommand2.Assign(ADOCommand1);
```

The Cancel Method

This method is used to cancel the execution of the currently running command. The Cancel method can be used only with acynchronous commands, i.e., when the ExecuteOptions property is set to eoAsyncExecute or eoAsyncFetch. The Cancel method can be successful only when it is called within the time frame set by the CommandTimeout property.

The Delphi implementation of this method does not add any functionality; it just calls the Cancel method of the underlying ADO Command object.

The Cancel method can be useful for providing a way to abort the execution of queries with a long execution time.

The Execute Method

There are three overloaded versions of this method with different sets of parameters. The simplest one is the Execute method without parameters; it has the following declaration:

```
function TADOCommand.Execute: _Recordset;
```

It executes the command specified in CommandText if the command has no parameters. If the command uses parameters, you can call one of the other two versions of the Execute method with the following declarations:

```
function TADOCommand.Execute(const Parameters: OleVariant): _Recordset;
```

or

```
function TADOCommand.Execute(var RecordsAffected: Integer;
  const Parameters: OleVariant): _Recordset;
```

The first one passes parameters specified in the Parameters argument along with the command, while the second one allows us to find out how many records were affected by the command.

For all three versions, the resulting recordset (if any exists) is returned by this method. This recordset (or the ADO Recordset type) can be used directly or assigned to the RecordSet property of the ADODataSet component:

```
ADODataSet1.RecordSet := ADOCommand1.Execute;
```

to be manipulated on the "higher" Delphi level. For more details, see the "Using the TADOCommand Component" section below.

Note: Contrary to what the documentation says, there is no overloaded Execute function that take the ExecuteOptions option as a parameter.

Events

The TADOCommand component does not have events.

Using the TADOCommand Component

As we mentioned in the introductory part of this chapter, the TADOCommand component can be used to execute commands such as SQL Data Definition Language statements or stored procedures that do not return results. To do so, we need to perform the following steps:

- Set the connection. This can be the ADOConnection object, specified with the Connection or ConnectionString property and built at design time.

- Choose the type of command to be executed and set it in the CommandType property. This can be cmdText for a SQL query, cmdTable to access a single table, or cmdStoredProc to run a stored procedure in the database.

- Depending on the type of command we have chosen, we need to set the value of the CommandText property. This can be the name of the table selected from the combo box (CommandType property := cmdTable), the name of the stored procedure selected from the combo box (CommandType property := cmsStoredProc), or a SQL statement created with the help of the simple query builder.

- We can set the parameters for the SQL statement or the stored procedure if there are any with the Parameters property, and the execution options with the ExecuteOptions property.

- Finally, we use the Execute method to execute the command.

This scenario works fine for both SQL statements or stored procedures that may or may not return the resulting recordset. If we do not care about the results, we simply forget about the recordset returned by the Execute method.

In the case of SQL statements or stored procedures that do return a recordset, there are some limitations. The following simple assignment:

```
ADODataSet1.RecordSet : = ADOCommand1.Execute;
```

brings up a forward-only recordset, which is not suitable to use, for example, with the TDBGrid or TDBNavigator components that work only with the datasets that support bookmarks. Note that the forward-only recordset supports only the Move and MoveNext methods and can be explored only forward; that's why it is called like this.

There are two ways to solve this. First, we can iterate the resulting recordset, obtained like this:

```
var
 RS   : _RecordSet;
...
RS := ADOCommand1.Execute;
```

with our own code. Consider the example below which shows how to fill the StringGrid component with the contents of the recordset:

```
procedure TForm1.Button1Click(Sender: TObject);
var
 RS   : _RecordSet;
 I,J : Integer;
begin
{
 Obtain the resulting recordset, for example with the
 CommandType = cmdText and CommandText set to the name
 of the one of the tables available
}
```

```
  RS := ADOCommand1.Execute;
With RS, StringGrid1 do
  begin
{Move to the first record}
   MoveFirst;
{Set number of cells equal to the number of fields}
   ColCount := Fields.Count;
{Show cell headings = fields names}
   For I := 0 to Fields.Count-1 do
    Cells[I,0] := Fields[I].Name;
{Iterate the recordset}
    I := 1;
   While NOT EOF do
   begin
{Increase StringGrid row count}
     RowCount := RowCount + 1;
     For J :=0 to Fields.Count-1 do
{Fill cells}
     Cells[J,I] := VarToStr(Fields[J].Value);
{Move to the next record}
     MoveNext;
{Increase the counter}
     Inc(I);
    end;
{Set the header}
   FixedRows := 1;
  end;
end;
```

This code does the job, but is limited to showing only fields with character-based contents. To make it "smarter," we need to check the type of the field, and then perform the appropriate conversion before displaying the field contents in the cell. This code works fine in many cases, and can replace the DBGrid component as shown below.

As you can see, this example nearly mimics the look and feel of the DBGrid component and works well with character-based fields.

In cases where we need a more sophisticated way to output the values of the recordset, we can use the standard interface components. This will give us the ability to show the contents of one record at a time. Let's look at the example below.

```
var
 RS    : _Recordset;
...
procedure TForm1.Button1Click(Sender: TObject);
begin
 RS := ADOCommand1.Execute;
 RS.MoveFirst;
 Edit1.Text := VarToStr(RS.Fields[2].Value);
 Edit2.Text := VarToStr(RS.Fields[3].Value);
 Edit3.Text := VarToStr(RS.Fields[4].Value);
end;
procedure TForm1.SpeedButton1Click(Sender: TObject);
begin
 If Not RS.EOF Then
  begin
   RS.MoveNext;
   Edit1.Text := VarToStr(RS.Fields[2].Value);
   Edit2.Text := VarToStr(RS.Fields[3].Value);
   Edit3.Text := VarToStr(RS.Fields[4].Value);
  end;
end;
```

This may not be the best way to use Delphi ADO components, but it gives us an idea of how to solve situations in which straightforward methods do not work.

Another way is to fill the ClientDataset component with recordset data. In this case, we can use standard data-aware Delphi components such as DBGrid and DBNavigator.

And one final note before we end this chapter. We can use the Filter property to specify records that should meet some criteria. To do so, we need to set the Filter property. For example:

```
RS.Filter := 'Name Like ''W%''';
```

will return only companies with names starting with the letter "W." The filter is applied on the recordset already received by the client application, so we need to place the Filter property after we have called the Execute method:

```
procedure TForm1.Button1Click(Sender: TObject);
begin
 RS := ADOCommand1.Execute;
```

```
RS.Filter := 'Name Like ''w%''';
RS.MoveFirst;
...
end;
```

We will see more examples of using the Filter property later in this book.

Conclusion

In this chapter, we have looked at the TADOCommand component, which, in most cases, can be used to provide the ability to execute SQL statements or stored procedures that do not return results. As we have seen, this component has limited functionality and should be used when you try to port the existing Visual Basic or Active Server Pages code into your Delphi applications. As we will see in the following chapters, there are more powerful Delphi ADO components available that are more suited for command execution. One such component is the TADODataSet component, which is built on top of the ADO Command and ADO Recordset objects. We will look at this component in the next chapter.

THE TADODATASET COMPONENT

In this chapter, we will introduce the TADODataSet component—a direct descendant of the TCustomADODataSet class that can be used to retrieve data from one or more tables in a data source and accessible through ADO. Using this component, we can get all data from the table, set filters to retrieve only the data that meets some criteria, perform SQL queries, run user-defined and system stored procedures, and save recordsets into a file and load them.

Note that the TADODataSet component cannot be used with several types of SQL statements, such as DELETE, INSERT, or UPDATE, since these statements do not return results in a recordset. If you need to run these SQL statements, you should use the TADOCommand component, discussed in Chapter 6, or the TADOQuery component, described in Chapter 8.

The TADODataSet component, with the help of the TCustomADODataSet class, brings together two data access technologies. The first one is implemented in ADO (through the RecordSet and Command objects), and the second one is implemented in the Delphi data access architecture. As a result, we have a component that, on one hand, can be used to access ADO data sources and, on the other hand, is "compatible" with the Delphi database architecture, including usage of data-aware controls.

First, we will look at the properties, methods, and events of the TADODataSet component, and then we will present several examples of how to use this component in Delphi applications.

Properties

The TADODataSet component inherits all properties from its direct ancestor—the TCustomADODataSet class—and adds only one new property of its own—the RDSConnection property. First, let's look at the properties defined in the

TCustomADODataSet class. These properties can be organized in several functional groups as shown in the following table.

Group	Properties
Connection Properties	Connection, ConnectionString
Commands Properties	CommandText, CommandTimeout, CommandType, ExecuteOptions
Cursor Properties	CursorLocation, CursorType, LockType
Field Properties	EnableBCD
Index Properties	IndexField, IndexFieldCount
Parameters Properties	ParamCheck, ParametersPrepared
Records Properties	CanModify, MaxRecords, RecNo, RecordCount, RecordSet, RecordSetState, RecordSize, RecordStatus
Sorting and Filtering Properties	Filter, Filtered, FilterGroup, Sort
Miscellaneous Properties	BlockReadSize, CacheSize, MarshalOptions, Properties

Let's look at these property groups in more detail. Note that some of these properties were covered in previous chapters. For example, the connection properties were described in Chapter 5, and command and parameters properties were introduced in Chapter 6. Here we will discuss the properties that are new for us.

Cursor Properties

We already covered the CursorLocation property when we described the TADOConnection component. As we know, there can be two cursor locations—the client-side cursor and the server-side cursor. The CursorType property specifies the type of cursor used in the ADO dataset before it is opened. This property determines how we can navigate through the recordset and the types of locks we can set. The five types of cursors, defined by the TCursorType type (which is equivalent to the ADO CursorTypeEnum values), are described in the following table:

Value	Meaning	ADO Constant
ctDynamic	Allows viewing of data source changes made by other users; supports adding, changing, and deleting records and bidirectional navigation.	adOpenDynamic
ctKeyset	Has most of the properties of the dynamic cursor, but does not show the changes made by other users.	adOpenKeyset
ctOpenForwardOnly	Forward-only cursor that allows navigating the recordset only in the forward direction. Offers the fastest performance but lacks flexibility.	adOpenForwardOnly
ctStatic	This is like a shapshot of a recordset at a point of time. Supports bidirectional navigation and does not show the changes made by other users.	adOpenStatic
ctUnspecified	The type of cursor was not specified.	-

To specify the record-locking behavior for editing operations, we can use the LockType property. It has the TADOLockType type and can have one of the following values (which is equivalent to the ADO LockTypeEnum values):

Value	Meaning	ADO Constant
ltBatchOptimistic	Used with the UpdateBatch method to update multiple records in a single operation.	adLockBatchOptimistic
ltOptimistic	Optimistic locking; records are locked only when data is updated.	adLockOptimistic
ltPessimistic	Pessimistic locking; the recordset remains locked during all editing operations.	adLockPessimistic
ltReadOnly	Used for recordsets that cannot be edited.	adLockReadOnly
ltUnspecified	The type of lock was not specified.	-

Field Properties

The EnableBCD property is used to specify how to map fields to field classes. There can be floating-point and binary coded decimal (BCD) types of the field. The following table shows how to use this property:

EnableBCD	Field Mapping	Comments
True	adDecimal -> TBCDField adNumeric -> TBCDField	Uses Currency type, supports four decimal places and 20 significant digits
False	adDecimal -> TfloatField adNumeric -> TFloatField	Can hold values in the range from 5.0 * 10-324 to 1.7 * 10308 with an accuracy of 15 digits

Index Properties

This group of properties gives us access to indexes. The IndexFields property of the TField type contains the definitions of the indexes in the table. This is the array of the TField objects that describe an individual index in the table.

The IndexFieldCount property returns the number of fields that comprise the current key. Its value is 1 for single-column indexes or the number of fields for multicolumn indexes.

Records Properties

The CanModify property allows us to find out if we can update the recordset or not. The MaxRecords property specifies how many records to return as the result of a query. The default value for this property is 0, meaning that all records must be returned. There are several things to note:

■ This property can be changed only for the closed recordset.

■ Not all providers support this property. For example, it is not supported by the Jet 4.0 OLE DB Provider. In this case, we must use the TOP n predicate in a Jet SQL statement. For example:

```
SELECT TOP 10 * FROM Orders
```

The RecNo property indicates the ordinal position of the active record in the recordset, and the RecordCount property gives us the total number of records in the recordset. We can use these properties to show the current position in the recordset. For example:

```
procedure TForm1.DBNavigator1Click(Sender: TObject;
 Button: TNavigateBtn);
const
 Rec : String = 'Record %d of %d records';
begin
 With ADODataSet1 do
  Edit1.Text := Format(Rec, [RecNo, RecordCount]);
end;
```

OrderID	CustomerID	EmployeeID	OrderDate	RequiredDate	ShippedDate	ShipVia	Freight
10954	LINOD	5	17.03.98	28.04.98	20.03.98	1	
10955	FOLKO	8	17.03.98	14.04.98	20.03.98	2	
10956	BLAUS	6	17.03.98	28.04.98	20.03.98	2	
10957	HILAA	8	18.03.98	15.04.98	27.03.98	3	
10958	OCEAN	7	18.03.98	15.04.98	27.03.98	2	
10959	GOURL	6	18.03.98	29.04.98	23.03.98	2	
10960	HILAA	3	19.03.98	02.04.98	08.04.98	1	
10961	QUEEN	8	19.03.98	16.04.98	30.03.98	1	
10962	QUICK	8	19.03.98	16.04.98	23.03.98	2	
10963	FURIB	9	19.03.98	16.04.98	26.03.98	3	
10964	SPECD	3	20.03.98	17.04.98	24.03.98	2	
10965	OLDWO	6	20.03.98	17.04.98	30.03.98	3	
10966	CHOPS	4	20.03.98	17.04.98	08.04.98	1	
10967	TOMSP	2	23.03.98	20.04.98	02.04.98	2	
10968	ERNSH	1	23.03.98	20.04.98	01.04.98	3	

Note: The same code can be placed in the TDataSource OnDataChange event handler to get the same results.

The RecordSet property gives us direct access to the underlying ADO Recordset object. We can use this to use properties and methods of this object that are not implemented at the component level.

The RecordSetState property indicates the current state of the ADO Recordset object, i.e., what it is doing now. The object can have the following states:

Value	Meaning	ADO Constant
stClosed	The recordset is closed	adStateClosed
stConnecting	The recordset is currently connecting to the data source	adStateConnecting
stExecuting	The recordset is currently executing a command	adStateExecuting
stFetching	The recordset is currently fetching records	adStateFetching
stOpen	The recordset is open	adStateOpen

The RecordSize property indicates the size of the record in the recordset and the RecordStatus property indicates the status of the current record relative to batch updates or other bulk operations.

Sorting and Filtering Properties

We can use the Sort property to specify the sorting order for the recordset. This property can contain the name of a single field or a comma-separated list of fields.

Let's look at the following example. Suppose we have a recordset that is displayed in the string grid. We can use three buttons to sort the grid by one of the columns (associated with the field) in ascending or descending order, or reset the initial order of records:

```
{Sort in ascending order}
procedure TForm1.Button1Click(Sender: TObject);
begin
 ADODataSet1.Sort := 'CustomerID ASC';
end;

{Sort in descending order}
procedure TForm1.Button2Click(Sender: TObject);
begin
 ADODataSet1.Sort := 'CustomerID DESC';
end;

{Reset intial order}
procedure TForm1.Button3Click(Sender: TObject);
begin
 ADODataSet1.Sort := '';
end;
```

We can also add two radio buttons to specify the sorting order and attach the event handler to the OnTitleClick event of the DBGrid component with the following code:

```
procedure TForm1.DBGrid1TitleClick(Column: TColumn);
begin
 If RadioButton1.Checked then
  ADODataSet1.Sort := Column.FieldName + ' ASC'
 Else
  ADODataSet1.Sort := Column.FieldName + ' DESC'
end;
```

This will allow us not only to set the sorting order—ascending or descending—but to sort on any field by clicking on its name in the DBGrid component.

Using the Filter and Filtered properties, we can extract information that meets some criteria. To do so, we first specify the criteria in the Filter property, and then change the value of the Filtered property to True. We will see an example of using these properties later in this chapter.

The FilterGroup property is used to specify the filter based on the update status of individual rows. This property is used with the Filtered property set to True and the LockType property set to ltBatchOptimistic. The FilterGroup property can have one of the following values:

Value	Meaning	ADO Constant
fgAffectedRecords	Only records affected by the last Delete, Resync, UpdateBatch, or CancelBatch method will be seen	adFilterAffectedRecords
fgConflictingRecords	Records that failed the last update will be seen	adFilterConflictingRecords
fgFetchedRecords	Records in the current cache will be seen	adFilterFetchedRecords
fgNone	The current filter will be removed	adFilterNone
fgPendingRecords	Only records that were changed but have not been updated will be seen	adFilterPendingRecords
fgPredicate	Records that have just been deleted will be seen	adFilterPredicate

Miscellaneous Properties

There are four properties that fall into the miscellaneous category—BlockReadSize, CacheSize, MarshalOptions, and Properties property.

The BlockReadSize property is used to enable or disable the block read mode. If the value of this property is greater than zero (this indicates the number of buffers in each block) and you call the Next method, data-aware controls are not updated and data events are not fired. Setting this property to a value greater than zero also changes the value of the State property—it becomes equal to dsBlockRead. The block read mode is disabled if the value of the BlockReadSize property is zero.

The CacheSize property indicates how many records will be fetched from the recordset at one time and stored in the local cache. The default value is one record; this is also the minimum allowed value.

The MarshalOptions property specifies how records are marshaled back to the server. There are two options—either all records are sent back (MarshalOptions := moMarshalAll)or only the records that were modified in the local recordset are sent back (MarshalOptions := moMarshalModifiedOnly). The last option greatly improves performance since less data is sent back to the server. This property can be used only with client-side, disconnected recordsets.

The Properties property gives us an access to the Properties collection of the underlying ADO Recordset object.

The last property of the TADODataSet component that we will cover here is the RDSConnection property.

The RDSConnection Property

This property indicates the remote dataset component used by the TADODataSet component. If we use the RDSConnection component to get the recordset, then we don't need to use the Connection property. Instead, we should fill the ConnectionString property with the appropriate information of the DataFactory for the RDSConnection component and use the CommandText property to either link to some of the business objects or set the SQL statements of the query.

At design time, we simply choose one of the RDSConnection components available in the application, while at run time we should assign the value of the TRDSConnection type to this property.

For more information on RDS, see Chapter 20.

Methods

There are two additional methods defined by the TADODataSet component—the CreateDataSet method and the GetIndexNames method. All other methods are inherited from the TCustomADODataSet object and its ancestors. Let's look at them first and then discuss the methods added by the TADODataSet component itself.

The BookmarkValid Method

This method is used to test if the specified bookmark is valid, i.e., if it has a value assigned to it. If the bookmark is valid, the BookmarkValid method returns True; otherwise it returns False.

Bookmarks are used to mark records in a dataset and to quickly return to those records when needed. The following bookmark-related methods of the TADODataSet component are available:

- GetBookmark to create a bookmark
- BookmarkValid to check a bookmark
- GotoBookmark to move to a bookmarked record
- FreeBookmark to free memory allocated for a bookmark

The CancelBatch Method

If the recordset was opened in batch update mode, this method cancels a pending batch update. The AffectRecords parameter specifies which records will be affected by the CancelBatch method, and can have one of the following values:

Value	Meaning	ADO Constant
arAll	The default value; all pending updates will be canceled	adAffectAll
arCurrent	Only updates for the current records will be canceled	adAffectCurrent
arFiltered	Only updates for the records that match the current filter will be canceled	adAffectGroup

Note that after the CancelBatch method completes, we may check the Errors collection to see if there were any problems. Also, it may make sense to set the current record position to the first record, because the current record may be unknown after the CancelBatch method completes.

The CancelUpdates Method

This method cancels any changes made to the current record or to a new record prior to calling the Update method. The newly added record will be discarded.

If the addition of a new record was canceled, the record that was current before adding the new one will once again be your current record.

The Clone Method

The Clone method creates an exact copy of the ADODataSet. Calling this method replaces the current recordset with the one available at the ADODataSet specified as the argument. The LockType argument with the default value of ltUnspecified specifies the lock type for the new recordset. The other value for the LockType argument is ltReadOnly, meaning that the recordset cannot be edited. Cloning recordsets is a more efficient way to create a copy of one since all operations will be performed on the client side.

Note that the Clone method can be used only for recordsets that support bookmarks. Also note that changes in one recordset will be visible in all its clones until you call the Requery method for the original recordset.

The Close Method

This method closes the data set and causes all unposted changes to be lost. Calling this method sets the Active property to False.

The CompareBookmarks Method

This method can be used to compare one bookmark to another. Given the two bookmarks (of TBookmark type) passed as arguments, this method returns 0 if bookmarks are the same, −1 if the first one is less than the second one and 1 if the first bookmark is greater than the second one.

The CreateBlobStream Method

This method is used with a BLOB (Binary Large OBject) field or compatible type in the dataset to create a stream for reading and writing from it. When calling this method, you need to specify the field as the value of TField type (not the string with its name, as the documentation suggests!), and the type of the stream to be created. The Mode argument can have one of the following values:

Value	Meaning
bmRead	The stream is for reading
bmWrite	The stream is for writing
bwReadWrite	The stream is for both reading and writing

This method creates a TStream-compatible stream that can be used to manipulate the contents of a BLOB field.

There is a TADOBlobStream class, implemented in ADODB unit, that should be used with Delphi ADO components when we need to read or write BLOB field data.

The DeleteRecords Method

Use this method to delete the current record or group of records. The DeleteRecords method takes one argument that specifies how many records are to be deleted and can have one of the following values.

Value	Meaning	ADO Constant
arAll	All records will be deleted	adAffectAll
arAllChapters	All child records (chapters) will be deleted. For more information on child records, see Chapter 11.	adAffectAllChapters
arCurrent	Only the current record will be deleted	adAffectCurrent
arFiltered	Only records that match the current filter will be deleted	adAffectGroup

Before deleting records, use the Supports method to check if the deletion is supported. This method is covered later in this chapter.

FilterOnBookmarks Method

This method allows us to set a filter based on the array of bookmarks passed as an argument. After assigning the value of the Filter property of the underlying ADO RecordSet object the FilterOnBookmarks method sets the Filtered property to True.

The GetBlobFieldData Method

Use the GetBlobFieldData method to retrieve the value of the BLOB field into a dynamic array of bytes and returns the size of the buffer.

You rarely need to use this method. Rather, use the SaveToStream method to save the contents of the BLOB field into a stream. This gives you more flexibility since the stream can be created either in memory or on a disk.

The GetFieldData Method

This method can be used to fill the buffer with the value of the current field. This method has three prototypes shown below.

- `function TCustomADODataSet.GetFieldData(Field: TField; Buffer: Pointer): Boolean;`
- `function TCustomADODataSet.GetFieldData(Field: TField; Buffer: Pointer; NativeFormat: Boolean): Boolean;`
- `function TCustomADODataSet.GetFieldData(FieldNo: Integer; Buffer: Pointer): Boolean;`

You can either indicate the Field in question by specifying the `TField`-compatible value or its number and supplying a pointer to a buffer that will hold the value of the field. The `NativeFormat` argument indicates whether we need to obtain the value as is (`NativeFormat` equals `True`) or convert it before storing in the buffer.

The IsSequenced Method

Use this method to check if you can navigate through the records using RecNo property or not.

The LoadFromFile Method

This method allows us to load a previously save recordset from a file. Use the SaveToFile method to save a recordset to a file. If a recordset was successfully loaded, it will be automatically opened.

This method works both with the ADTG (Advanced Data Tablegram) files and XML files. For more information look at the SaveToFile method later in this chapter:

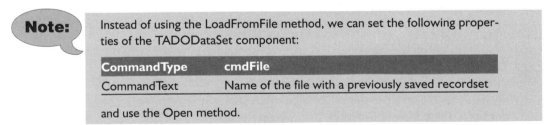 Instead of using the LoadFromFile method, we can set the following properties of the TADODataSet component:

CommandType	cmdFile
CommandText	Name of the file with a previously saved recordset

and use the Open method.

The Locate Method

Use this method to locate a specified record and make that record to be current. The Locate method takes three arguments:

- KeyFields—a list of field names, separated by semicolons, on which a search will be performed.
- KeyValues—a list of values that should match the fields. If multiple fields are specified for KeyFields, this will be a variant array.
- Options—search options. This can be loCaseInsensitive to specify that key fields and key values are matched without regard to case or loPartialKey to specify that that key values can include partial data.

If a match is found, the Locate method returns True and makes that record current; otherwise it returns False.

The following example shows how to locate a record that contains Queso in the ProductName column:

```
Locate('ProductName', 'Queso', [loPartialKey]);
```

Note that we have specified only the partial string that the contents of the ProductName column should match.

If we are looking for more than one column, we should use the array of variants to specify the values we are looking for. This can be done either through the static variant array or through dynamic variant array, created with the VarArrayOf function. For example:

```
Locate('ProductName; CategoryID',
 VarArrayOf(['Ikura', 8]),[loPartialKey]);
```

The Lookup Method

We can use the Lookup method to search for the first row that matches specified search criteria and retrieve field values from it. This method expects three arguments

- KeyFields—a list of field names on which to search, with names being separated with semicolons.
- KeyValues—a variant array of values to match the key fields.
- ResultFields—a string containing a list of field names, separated by semicolons, whose values must be returned for the row found.

The Lookup method returns a variant array with the values from the fields specified in the ResultFields argument. Here is a simple example of how to use the Lookup method:

```
procedure TForm1.Button2Click(Sender: TObject);
var
 S   : String;
 Res : Variant;
begin
 With ADODataSet2 do
 begin
  Open;
  S := 'ProductName;UnitsInStock';
  Res := Lookup('ProductName', 'Ikura', S);
  Edit1.Text := Res[0];   // Shows ProductName
  Edit2.Text := Res[1];   // Shows UnitsInStock
 end;
end;
```

The NextRecordset Method

This method can be used to access a secondary and subsequent recordsets if any. The NextRecordset method is useful when we execute a set of SQL statements, some of which return a recordset. In this case, we receive the first recordset, manipulate it, and then call the NextRecordset method to obtain the next recordset.

This method fills the RecordsAffected property with the number of records in the returned recordset and returns the ADO Recordset-compatible recordset that must be assigned to the Recordset property of ADODataSet component to be accessible.

Note: This method is not supported by the Jet engine, i.e., you cannot use it against Microsoft Access databases.

The Open Method

Use this method to open a recordset. Contrary to the Open method of the underlying ADO Recordset object, this method does not have arguments and simply sets the Active property to True. This method triggers the BeforeOpen and AfterOpen notification events.

The Requery Method

Use this method to refresh the recordset. The Requery method re-executes the command or SQL statement on which the recordset is based. It takes one argument—Options in the form of TExecuteOptions that can be used to specify the characteristics of the execution operation. We have discussed `TExecuteOptions` in the previous chapter.

Running this method is equivalent of using the Close and Open methods. The difference is that we cannot change the values of the CursorLocation, CursorType, and LockType properties while the recordset is open, so the Requery method refreshes the recordset using the values of these properties that are already set.

To change the values of these properties, first close the recordset with the Close method and then reopen it with the Open method.

The SaveToFile Method

This method can be used to save a recordset to a file. It takes two arguments—the full path to the file to save a recordset in and the format in which the recordset will be saved. The second parameter can have one of the following values:

Value	Meaning	ADO Constant
pfADTG	The recordset is saved in the "native: Microsoft binary format."	adPersistADTG
pfXML	The recordset is saved as an XML file	adPersistXML

The SaveToFile method allows us to have disconnected datasets that can be used by mobile users. We will have the complete example of this later in this chapter.

The ADTG (Advanced Data Tablegram) file has the layout described in the table below.

Section	Size (Bytes)	Contents
Header	9	ADTG stream signature and various global information
HandlerOptions	27	Options for the stream reader
ResultDescriptor	33	Information about the recordset, column count and base table count
ResultContext	Variable	Property settings for the rowset
TableDescriptor	13 + Len(TableName) + 2 * KeyColumns	Information about each base table used by the recordset. This is required for updating the recordset
ColumnDescriptor	Variable	Information about each column in the recordset
RowData	Variable	Actual data for the recordset

Note: The filename remains open from the first call to the SaveToFile method until the Close method is called. Any subsequent calls to the SaveToFile method overwrite its contents. Other applications can only read from this file while it is open.

The Seek Method

This method uses the current index to locate specified records. The `KeyValues` argument specifies the column values to search for and the `SeekOption` (default value is `soFirstEQ`)—the type of comparison to be made. The following values can be specified for the `SeekOption` argument:

Value	Meaning	ADO Constant
soAfter	Record pointer is positioned just after a matching record	adSeekAfter
soAfterEQ	Record pointer is positioned at the matching record or just after it	adSeekAfterEQ
soBefore	Record pointer is positioned just before a matching record	adSeekBefore
soBeforeEQ	Record pointer is positioned at the matching record or just before it	adSeekBeforeEQ
soFirstEQ	Record pointer is positioned at the first matching record in any or at the end of the dataset	adSeekFirstEQ
soLastEQ	Record pointer is positioned at the last matching record if any or at the end of the dataset	adSeekLastEQ

Here is an example of how to use this method.

```
procedure TForm1.Button1Click(Sender: TObject);
begin
 With ADODataSet1 do
  begin
   If Seek('London', soFirstEQ) Then
   begin
   // Matching record found...
   end;
  end;
end;
```

If there are more than one column value in the KeyValues argument, use the variant arrays to specify it.

To successfully use this method the following properties should be set:

Property	Value
IndexName	Name of the index to use
CommandType	cmdTableDirect
CursorLocation	clUseServer
CursorType	ctKeySet

 Note: To see if the currently selected provider supports the Seek method, use the Supports method described below.

The Supports Method

Use this method to find if recordset supports certain types of cursor operations specified with the CursorOptions argument. The CursorOptions argument can have one or more of the following values:

Value	Meaning	ADO Constant
coAddNew	Recordset supports addition of new records	adAddNew
coApproxPosition	Recordset supports absolute position—the RecNo property	adApproxPosition
coBookmark	Recordset supports bookmarks	adBookmark
coDelete	Recordset support record deletion	adDelete

Value	Meaning	ADO Constant
coFind	Recordset supports the finding of records through the Locate method	adFind
coHoldRecords	Recordset will keep changes without committing if we will retrieve more data	adHoldRecords
coIndex	The IndexName property can be used to specify the index	adIndex ✗
coMovePrevious	Recordset supports backward movement	adMovePrevious
coNotify	Recordset supports notifications and will return events	adNotify
coResync	Recordset supports data updates with the Resync method	adResync
coSeek	Recordset supports finding records with the Seek method	adSeek ✗
coUpdate	Recordset supports records updates	adUpdate
coUpdateBatch	Recordset supports records updates with the UpdateBatch method	adUpdateBatch

The Supports method can be used to query one or more cursor operations in question. For example, to find if there is support for the Seek method, we call the Supports method the following way:

```
With ADODataSet1 do
  If Supports([coSeek]) then
{Seek method is supported}
...
  Else
{Seek method is not supported}
else
```

To query for more that one value, use the following call:

```
With ADODataSet1 do
  If Supports([coAddNew, coDelete, coUpdate]) then
{All of the operations are supported}
...
Else
  {One of more operations is not supported}
else
```

With the help of Delphi RTTI (Run-Time Type Information) functions, we can check if all of the types of cursor operations are supported in the following loop:

```
uses
 TYPINFO;

...

procedure TForm1.Button1Click(Sender: TObject);
var
TI  : PTypeInfo;
 I  : Integer;
 S  : String;
begin
```

```
// Open dataset
ADODataSet1.Open;
// Get type info for the TCursorOptions
TI := PTypeInfo(TypeInfo(TCursorOptions));
// and iterate through it
For I := Integer(Low(TCursorOption)) to
  Integer(High(TCursorOption)) do
  begin
// get one TCursorOptions option's name
    S := GetEnumName(TypeInfo(TCursorOption), I);
// and value
    S := S + #9 + IntToStr(I);
// And chack if it is supported
    If ADODataSet1.Supports([TCursorOption(I)]) Then
      Memo1.Lines.Add(S + #9 + 'True')
    Else
      Memo1.Lines.Add(S + #9 + 'False')
  end;
end;
```

The UpdateBatch Method

This method writes all pending batch updates to the disk. The AffectRecords argument (default value is arAll) determines how many records will be affected. The following table shows possible values for this argument.

Value	Meaning	ADO Constant
arAll	All records in the recordset will be updated	adAffectAll
arCurrent	Just the current record will be updated	adAffectCurrent
arFiltered	All records matching the current Filter will be updated	adAffectGroup

Note: The CursorType property must be set to ctKeySet or ctStatic and the LockType property must be set to ltBatchOptimistic.

The UpdateStatus Method

This method indicates the cached update status of the current record. The UpdateStatus method can return one of the following values:

Value	Meaning
usDeleted	The current record was deleted, but the deletion has not yet been applied
usInserted	The current record was inserted, but the insertion has not yet been applied
usModified	There are unapplied modifications for the current record
usUnmodified	There is no unapplied cached updates for the current record

Besides the methods described above, the TADODataSet component introduces two new methods that will be discussed in the following sections.

The CreateDataSet Method

This method creates the recordset for an ADO dataset. The CreateDataSet method is called automatically by an ADO dataset, and in most cases there should be no reason for applications to use this method directly. One of the reasons why we need to use this method is the situation when we need to create a recordset on the fly.

The GetIndexNames Method

This method fills the list of strings (of the TStrings type) with the names of the all indexes available in a table. You can use either the standard visual components to store the list of index names, such as Memo, ListBox or ComboBox or some instance of the TStringList object. For example:

```
procedure TForm1.Button1Click(Sender: TObject);
begin
 ADODataSet1.Active := True;
{Get list of indexes into the Memo component}
 ADODataSet1.GetIndexNames(Memo1.Lines);
end;
```

or

```
{Global Variables}
var
 List  : TStringList;

procedure TForm1.FormCreate(Sender: TObject);
begin
{Create the string list}
 List := TStringList.Create;
end;

procedure TForm1.FormDestroy(Sender: TObject);
begin
{Destroy the string list}
 List.Free;
end;

procedure TForm1.Button1Click(Sender: TObject);
begin
 ADODataSet1.Active := True;
{Save the list of Indexes available}
 ADODataSet1.GetIndexNames(List);
end;
end.
```

Events

All of the events available for the TADODataSet component are inherited from the TCustomADODataSet object and TDataSet object.

All of the events declared in the TCustomADODataSet class are ADO Recordset object events. These 12 events can be organized into the groups with Will/Complete pairs (with some exceptions) as shown in the table below:

Group	Events
Data retrieval events	OnFetchProgress and OnFetchComplete
Field change events	OnWillChangeField and OnFieldChangeComplete
Record change events	OnWillChangeRecord and OnRecordChangeComplete
Recordset change events	OnWillChangeRecordset and OnRecordsetChangeComplete
Navigation events	OnWillMove, OnMoveComplete and OnEndOfRecordset

Let's look at these event groups in more detail. We will start with the data retrieval events.

Data Retrieval Events

The data retrieval events can be used to notify the progress of the operation (OnFetchProgress event) and its completeness (OnFetchComplete event).

The OnFetchProgress event is fired during the asynchronous data retrieval operation, and its event handler receives the following parameters:

Parameter	Type	Description
DataSet	TCustomADODataSet	Indicates the TADODataSet component that fired this event.
Progress	Integer	Indicates the number of records already received since the start of the retrieval operation.
MaxProgress	Integer	Indicated the total number of records to be retrieved.
EventStatus	TEventStatus	Indicates the status of the event—its success or failure. See the description of TEventStatus type in Chapter 5.

For example:

```
procedure TForm1.ADODataSet1FetchProgress(
 DataSet: TCustomADODataSet;
 Progress, MaxProgress: Integer; var EventStatus: TEventStatus);
const
 Info : String = '%d of %d records retrieved';
begin
 Memo1.Lines.Add(Format(Info,  [Progress, MaxProgress]));
end;
```

The OnFetchComplete event indicates that the fetching operation completed, and all records were retrieved to the resulting recordset. The event handler receives the following parameters:

Parameter	Type	Description
DataSet	TCustomADODataSet	Indicates the TADODataSet component that fired this event.
Error	Error	Contains the Error object that describes the error occurred during the execution. This argument is set only if the EventStatus is equal to esErrorsOccured.
EventStatus	TEventStatus	Indicates the status of the event—its success or failure.

Field Change Events

There are two field change events that are fired when the contents of the current field will change (OnWillChangeField event) and after a field has changed (OnFieldChangeComplete event).

The OnWillChangeField event handler receives the following parameters:

Parameter	Type	Description
DataSet	TCustomADODataSet	Indicates the TADODataSet component that fired this event.
FieldCount	Integer	Number of Field objects within the Fields array.
Fields	OleVariant	Array of Field objects with pending changes.
EventStatus	TEventStatus	Indicates the status of the event—its success or failure.

We can use this event to check use input before posting changes to the datatset.

The OnFieldChangeComplete event handler receives the following parameters:

Parameter	Type	Description
DataSet	TCustomADODataSet	Indicates the TADODataSet component that fired this event.
FieldCount	Integer	Number of Field objects within the Fields array.
Fields	OleVariant	Array of Field objects with completed changes.
Error	Error	Contains Error object that describes the error occurred during the execution. This argument is set only if the EventStatus is equal to esErrorsOccured.
EventStatus	TEventStatus	Indicates the status of the event—its success or failure.

Record Change Events

There are two events that are fired when the contents of the one or more records will change (OnWillChangeRecord event) and after the changes are completed (OnRecordChangeComplete event).

The OnWillChangeRecord event handler receives the following parameters:

Parameter	Type	Description
DataSet	TCustomADODataSet	Indicates the TADODataSet component that fired this event.
Reason	TEventReason	Indicates the reason an event has occurred.
RecordCount	Integer	The number of records changing.

Parameter	Type	Description
EventStatus	TEventStatus	Indicates the status of the event—its success or failure.

The Reason parameter describes the reason an event has occurred and can have one of the following values:

Value	Meaning
erAddNew	A new row was added.
erClose	The recordset was closed.
erDelete	An existing row was deleted.
erFirstChange	A record is changed for the first time.
erMove	The recordset's row pointer moved.
erMoveFirst	The recordset's row pointer moved to the first row.
erMoveLast	The recordset's row pointer moved to the last row.
erMoveNext	The recordset's row pointer moved to the next row.
erMovePrevious	The recordset's row pointer moved to the previous row.
erRequery	The recordset was refreshed with the Requery method.
erResynch	The recordset was resynchronized with the Resynch method.
erUndoAddNew	A row insert operation was canceled.
erUndoDelete	A row delete operation was canceled.
erUndoUpdate	An update operation was canceled.
erUpdate	An existing row was modified with new values.

The event handler for the OnRecordChangeComplete event receives the following parameters:

Parameter	Type	Description
DataSet	TCustomADODataSet	Indicates the TADODataSet component that fired this event.
Reason	TEventReason	Indicates the reason an event has occurred.
RecordCount	Integer	The number of records changing.
Error	Error	Contains an Error object that describes the error occurred during the execution. This argument is set only if the EventStatus is equal to esErrorsOccured.
EventStatus	TEventStatus	Indicates the status of the event—its success or failure.

Recordset Change Events

The two recordset change events are fired when the recordset will change (OnWillChangeRecordset event) and after it has been changed (OnRecordsetChangeComplete event).

The event handler for the OnWillChangeRecordset event receives the following parameters:

Parameter	Type	Description
DataSet	TCustomADODataSet	Indicates the TADODataSet component that fired this event.
Reason	TEventReason	Indicates the reason an event has occurred.
EventStatus	TEventStatus	Indicates the status of the event—its success or failure.

The event handler for the OnRecordsetChangeComplete event receives the following parameters:

Parameter	Type	Description
DataSet	TCustomADODataSet	Indicates the TADODataSet component that fired this event.
Reason	TEventReason	Indicates the reason an event has occurred.
Error	Error	Contains Error object that describes the error occurred during the execution. This argument is set only if the EventStatus is equal to esErrorsOccured.
EventStatus	TEventStatus	Indicates the status of the event—its success or failure.

Let's look at the order the three prior pairs of events will fire during the course of an update. Suppose we have our data shown in the DBGrid component and we have changed the content of one of the cells and then moved to another row. This will produce the following events:

```
OnWillChangeRecord
 OnWillChangeField
 OnFieldChangeComplete
OnRecordChangeComplete
OnWillChangeRecord
OnRecordChangeComplete
```

When we delete a record, the following events will be fired:

```
OnWillChangeRecord
OnRecordChangeComplete
OnWillChangeRecord
OnRecordChangeComplete
```

Adding a new record will cause a lot of events—the pair of OnWillChangeRecord and OnRecordChangeComplete events plus the OnWillChangeField and OnFieldChangeComplete events for each field in a record.

```
OnWillChangeRecord
OnRecordChangeComplete
```

This pair will be fired for each field in a record.

```
OnWillChangeField
OnFieldChangeComplete
```

```
...
```

```
OnWillChangeRecord
OnRecordChangeComplete
```

The last type of events we will discuss here is navigational events that may occur during the navigation through the records.

Navigation Events

When we navigate through the records, there are three events that may occur. The OnWillMove event is fired before the current position in the recordset is changed. The OnMoveComplete event is fired after the current position in the recordset changes and the OnEndOfRecordset event indicates that we have tried to move to a row past the end of the recordset. Let's look at the order of navigation events from the DBNavigator component's point of view.

When we press the Next Record or Prior Record buttons (or call the Next or Prior methods of the TADODataSet component), we will receive the following pair of events:

```
OnWillMove
OnMoveComplete
```

Pressing the First Record or Last Record buttons (or calling the First or Last methods of the TADODataSet component) will cause the following events:

```
OnWillMove
OnMoveComplete
OnWillMove
OnEndOfRecordset
OnMoveComplete
OnWillMove
OnMoveComplete
```

 Note: If you are using Delphi data-aware controls, you may receive different sets of navigation events than shown here. This depends on the way the particular data-aware control fetches data from the data source.

Now let's look at each of the navigation events in more detail.

The event handler for OnWillMove event receives the following parameters:

Parameter	Type	Description
DataSet	TCustomADODataSet	Indicates the TADODataSet component that fired this event.
Reason	TEventReason	Indicates the reason an event has occurred.
EventStatus	TEventStatus	Indicates the status of the event—its success or failure.

The event handler for the OnMoveComplete event receives the following parameters:

Parameter	Type	Description
DataSet	TCustomADODataSet	Indicates the TADODataSet component that fired this event.
Reason	TEventReason	Indicates the reason an event has occurred.
Error	Error	Contains Error object that describes the error occurred during the execution. This argument is set only if the EventStatus is equal to esErrorsOccured.
EventStatus	TEventStatus	Indicates the status of the event—its success or failure.

The event handler for the OnEndOfRecordset event receives the following parameters:

Parameter	Type	Description
DataSet	TCustomADODataSet	Indicates the TADODataSet component that fired this event.
MoreData	WordBool	True if it is possible to append more data to the recordset while processing this event, False otherwise.
EventStatus	TEventStatus	Indicates the status of the event—its success or failure.

After we have learned about the properties, methods and events of the TADODataSet component, let's look at how we can use it in our Delphi programs.

Using the TADODataSet Component

We can use the TADODataSet component to perform various tasks depending on the value of the CommandType property. Generally speaking, we can use this component for:

- Getting all of the fields from a table
- Getting all of the fields that meet the specified criteria
- Running a stored procedure
- Running a system stored procedure
- Loading a saved recordset file

Let's look at the examples for each action we can perform with the TADODataSet component. For all of the examples below, we will use the Northwind database on the Microsoft SQL Server 7.0. First, we need to set the connection. This can be done in one of two ways for all TCustomADODataSet descendants—either through the separate TADOConnection component, or through the ConnectionString property. For simplicity we will use the latter way and set the following value for the ConnectionString property:

```
Provider=SQLOLEDB.1; Persist Security Info=False; User ID=sa; Initial Catalog=
Northwind; Data Source=maindesk
```

Note that the name of the server (the Data Source parameter) may be different for different computers. After that, we can either set all other properties at design time, and immediately view the results in some data-aware controls, or set them at run time. We will give you examples of how to do that both ways.

Let's place the TButton, the TDataSource, and the TDBGrid component into our form. Next, we need to connect the TDBGrid with the TDataSource component (through the DBGrid.DataSource property), and connect the TDataSource component to the TADODataSet component through the DataSet property.

Now we are ready to see some examples of how to use the TADODataSet component in Delphi ADO applications.

Getting All of the Fields From a Table

To get all of the fields from a table, we should set the CommandType property to either cmdTable or to cmdTableDirect value. When we use the cmdTable value, we actually send the SELECT * FROM table_name SQL statement to the provider, whereas when the cmdTableDirect value is used, the name of the table itself is send to the provider. Note that not all providers support direct table names, so use the cmdTable value to avoid errors.

After we have set the value of the CommandType property to either the cmdTable or cmdTableDirect, we can choose the name of the table from the CommandText property at design time. Now, if we will change the value of the Active property from False to True, we will get a list of all of the fields from the selected table in the DBGrid component.

At run time, we can either hard-code the name of the table or use the GetTableNames method of the TADOConnection component to get a list of the tables available.

In the example below, the first method is shown.

```
procedure TForm1.Button1Click(Sender: TObject);
begin
{We need to get all of the fields from a table}
 ADODataSet1.CommandType := cmdTable;
{The table will be 'CUSTOMERS'}
 ADODataSet1.CommandText := 'CUSTOMERS';
{Open the connection}
 ADODataSet1.Active := True;
end;
```

To use a list of available tables, we need to modify our example a little bit. First, we need to add two more components—the ComboBox component and TADOConnection component. After that, in the OnClick event handler for the Button, we will write the following code:

```
procedure TForm1.Button1Click(Sender: TObject);
begin
 With ADODataSet1 do
  begin
{Associate the ConnectionString with the ADOConnection}
   ADOConnection1.ConnectionString := ConnectionString;
{We need to get all of the fields from a table}
   CommandType := cmdTable;
{Retrieve a list of tables availabe}
   ADOConnection1.GetTableNames(ComboBox1.Items, False);
{Reset the combobox}
   ComboBox1.ItemIndex := 0;
  end;
end;
```

and in the OnClick event handler for the ComboBox we write the following lines:

```
procedure TForm1.ComboBox1Click(Sender: TObject);
begin
 With ComboBox1, ADODataSet1 do
  begin
{Close the connection if it is active}
   Close;
{Set the value of the CommandText property to the name
of the table selected in the combobox}
   CommandText := Items[ItemIndex];
{Open the connection}
   Active := True;
  end;
end;
```

What we have created here is a little browser that allows us to browse through the tables available in the ADO data source.

It would be great if we could set some criteria to analyze the information stored in a table we have selected. We will look at how to do this in the next section.

Setting the Criteria

Getting all values from all of the fields may be great help on some occasions, but in most cases we need to extract only the information that meets some criteria. This can be done either through the Filter property, or with the SQL statement when the CommandType property is equal to the cmdText value.

First, let's look at the example of the Filter property usage. This string property allows us to perform some analysis on the data. For example, we can find all customers from the United Kingdom listed in the CUSTOMERS table by setting the following value of the Filter property:

```
Country = 'UK'
```

To see the result at design time, we need to set the value of the Filter property to an appropriate criteria, and the toggle the value of the Filtered property to switch between the whole list of records (the value is False) and the Filtered one (the value is True).

To be able to set the filter at run time, we will add two more components to our application—the Edit component and the CheckBox component. In the OnClick event handler for the CheckBox component, we will write the following code:

```
procedure TForm1.CheckBox1Click(Sender: TObject);
begin
 If Edit1.Text <> '' Then
  begin
{Set the filter text}
   ADODataSet1.Filter := Edit1.Text;
{Toggle the Filtered value}
   ADODataSet1.Filtered := CheckBox1.Checked;
  end;
end;
```

All other source remains intact from the previous example except the two extra lines in the OnClick event handler of the ComboBox component that now looks like this (the new lines are shown in bold).

```
procedure TForm1.ComboBox1Click(Sender: TObject);
begin
 With ComboBox1, ADODataSet1 do
  begin
{Remove the Filter}
   Filtered := False;
   Edit1.Text := '';
{Close the connection if it is active}
   Close;
{Set the value of the CommandText property to the name
```

```
of the table selected in the combobox}
   CommandText := Items[ItemIndex];
{Open the connection}
   Active := True;
  end;
end;
```

Now we are able to set the criteria to filter our records. For example, we can find what suppliers are available in Germany by setting the following filter:

```
Country = 'Germany'
```

If we are looking for suppliers in Germany that are located in the city of Berlin, we need to set the following filter:

```
Country = 'Germany' AND
City = 'Berlin'
```

Using this filter we can select the orders that were shipped after January 15, 1998:

```
ShippedDate > 15.01.98
```

or query for any other information, for example, orders shipped to the United States:

```
ShippedDate > 15.01.98 AND ShipCountry = 'USA'
```

In other words, you can use the Filter property to run any reasonable query on the fields values of the single table in the database. This can be used as an alternative to the SQL statements.

You should pay attention to the order of comparison statements. For example, using OR and AND together does not work because you need to expand the Filter out. In other words, (A=1 OR A=2) AND (B=1) will not work; it must be expanded to (A=1 AND B=1) OR (A=2 AND B=1).

It should be mentioned, however, that using the Filter property means, that all records of the table are sent from the database server to the client application, and just this application carries out a job of separating the necessary rows. In the case of using SQL statement with an equivalent WHERE clause, records separation is provided by a database server, and the client application receives data that is already filtered. So, using the Filter property makes sense only when the size of the recordset is not big.

Now, let's change the CommandType property to cmdText. This will allow us to use the SQL statements against one or more tables in the database. At design time we can invoke the simple built-in SQL editor by pressing the ellipsis button in the Object Inspector near the CommandText property. This SQL editor lists tables and fields available in the data source in the left pane and allows us to build SQL statements either automatically or manually in the right pane.

When we use this SQL editor to build SQL statements automatically, we are limited with only simple SELECT statement that allows us to choose a table and one or more

fields from it. To enter more complex statements we can extend the one that was built automatically, for example, by adding the WHERE clause or any other keywords, or just enter the entire SQL statement from scratch.

Pressing the OK button sets the value of the CommandText property that is sent to the database engine for processing.

At run time we can either use the previously created SQL statement that is hard-coded as the value of the CommandText property or build our own.

> **Note:** Sometimes it may be wise to store queries in the resources. This way, if something changes in the underlying database, we don't need to change the source code of the application.

There can be two options to do so. We can use, for example, a list of pre-build statements iterating through it and assigning appropriate values to the CommandText property, or we can invoke the SQL editor. To do so, we need to add the SQLEDIT unit into the Uses clause of our application and call the EditSQL function as shown on the example below:

```
procedure TForm1.Button2Click(Sender: TObject);
var
 SQL : String;
begin
{If Ok button was pressed}
 If EditSQL(SQL,
  ADOConnection1.GetTableNames,
  ADOConnection1.GetFieldNames)
{Assign the SQL query text to the CommandText property}
then ADODataSet1.CommandText := SQL;
end;
```

The EditSQL function is implemented in the SQLEDIT unit and has the following declarations:

```
Function EditSQL(var SQL : String; AGetTableNames :
TGetTableNamesProc; AGetFieldNames : TGetFieldNamesProc) :
Boolean;
Function EditSQL(var SQL : TStrings; AGetTableNames :
TGetTableNamesProc; AGetFieldNames : TGetFieldNamesProc) :
Boolean;
```

The first parameter is a String or TStrings type value that will be used to store the resulting SQL statement. The two other parameters are pointers to functions that return a list of tables and fields in a database. For obtaining these pointers, we can use the methods of the TADOConnection component—the GetTableNames and GetFieldNames respectively. The EditSQL function returns True if the OK button was pressed, and False otherwise (the Cancel button was pressed).

In Chapter 9, we will discuss the SQL language statements in more detail.

Running a Stored Procedure

Using the TADODataSet component, we can run user-defined stored procedures that are available in the database. To do so at design time, we need to set the CommandType property to the cmdStoredProc value, and to select one of the available stored procedures from the list at the CommandText property in the Object Inspector.

After that we should check to see if there are any parameters required for the stored procedure we have just selected. To do so, we need to press the ellipsis button near the Parameters property in the Object Inspector. This will bring the Parameters Editor dialog box. For example, the CustOrderHist stored procedure in the Northwind database requires one parameter—the CustomerID.

Clicking on the line with the name of the parameter will bring the Object Inspector where we can check its type, other properties, and set its value. For our example, we will set the value of the CustomerID parameter to BOLID. After closing the Parameters Editor dialog box, we can set the Active property to True, and look at the results returned by this stored procedure.

Name	Value
RETURN_VALUE	0
@CustomerID	BOLID

If we need to run the stored procedure at run time, we need to perform the following steps.

1. Set the CommandType property to the cmdStoredProc value
2. Set the CommandText property to the name of the stored procedure
3. Set the values for parameters by accessing the Parameters collection
4. Activate the connection to retrieve the results

The example below shows how to set a parameter value for the CustOrderHist stored procedure.

```
procedure TForm1.Button1Click(Sender: TObject);
begin
 With ADODataSet1 do
  begin
{Disconnect if we are connected}
   Close;
   ADOConnection1.ConnectionString := ConnectionString;
{We will run a stored procedure}
   CommandType := cmdStoredProc;
{Set its name ...}
   CommandText := 'CustOrderHist;1';
{... and parameter}
   Parameters.ParamByName('CustomerID').Value := 'BOLID';
{Open the connection}
   Active := True;
  end;
end;
```

We will discuss stored procedures in more detail in Chapter 10.

Note: In the example below, we have used the CustOrderHist;1 stored procedure name instead of the CustOrderHist you can find in the Microsoft SQL Server Enterprise Manager. This name is returned by the OpenSchema method indicating the version number of the stored procedure.

Running a System Stored Procedure

Some database servers comes with a wide range of system stored procedures, that can be used to perform various system tasks. For example, the Microsoft SQL Server 7.0 supports a huge list of system stored procedures that has the SP_XXX and XP_XXX names. While we do not intend to discuss the system stored procedures in detail here, we will show you how to use the TADODataSet component to call the SP_HELPFILE system stored procedure that returns the location of the current database.

To run a system stored procedure, set the CommandType property to the cmdText value, and enter the name of the system stored procedure in the CommandText property. Consider the example below:

```
procedure TForm1.Button1Click(Sender: TObject);
begin
 With ADODataSet1 do
  begin
{Disconnect if we are connected}
   Close;
   ADOConnection1.ConnectionString := ConnectionString;
{We will run a system stored procedure}
   CommandType := cmdText;
{Set its name}
   CommandText := 'SP_HELPFILE';
{Open the connection}
   Active := True;
  end;
end;
```

![TADODataSet Demo window showing a Run button and a grid with columns fileid and filename. Row 1: D:\MSSQL7\DATA\northwnd.mdf, Row 2: D:\MSSQL7\DATA\northwnd.ldf]

If the system stored procedure requires parameters, you can set it the same way as the user-defined stored procedure—through the Parameters collection.

Note: For more information on the Microsoft SQL Server system stored procedures, consult the *SQL Server Books Online* that comes with the product.

Loading a Saved Recordset File

If we set the value of the CommandType property to the cmdFile value, we will be able to work with the recordsets stored in the files. As we already know, such recordsets can be created with the SaveToFile method that is available in the TCustomADODataSet class and its descendants.

At design time, as well as at run time, we need to set the following properties to be able to open the recordset in file:

Property	Value
CommandType	cmdFile
CommandText	File name where the recordset is stored
ConnectionString	Provider name and security information if needed

Consider the following example:

```
procedure TForm1.Button1Click(Sender: TObject);
begin
 With ADODataSet1 do
  begin
{Disconnect if we are connected}
   Close;
{Specify the Provider}
   ConnectionString := 'Provider=SQLOLEDB.1;' +
    'Persist Security Info=False;User ID=sa';
{We will use the recordset in file}
   CommandType := cmdFile;
{Specify the file name}
   CommandText := 'c:\cust.dat';
{Open the connection}
   Active := True;
  end;
end;
```

This gives us an ability to work with disconnected recordsets previously saved to a file. In fact, by using this possibility, we can implement the *briefcase model* of data processing. This model can be described in the following example.

Imagine a user that must travel with a computer. He can connect to the database server at his office, retrieve some data by using a query, save it to a file on a hard drive of his computer, take this computer home (or to a business trip), and begin to edit this data. He can periodically save edited data to a file, and retrieve it to continue editing. He can also return to his office, connect to the database server and try to upload his version of the data from a file. This model of processing data is called the *briefcase model*.

Another way of using this model is to save the query result to a file, and then forget about the database server at all. We can, for example, create any reference book by placing such files on a CD, along with MDAC and executable file to retrieve the data. This executable file can contain code similar to shown in the example above.

Of course, we need to know how to create such "briefcase" files. For doing this, we need to use the SaveToFile and LoadFromFile methods of the TADODataSet component.

Let's create an example of implementing the briefcase model. For doing this, we need to create a new project, place the TADOConnection, the TADODataSet, the TDataSource and the TDBGrid components into our form. Next, we need to connect the TDBGrid with the TDataSource component (through the DataSource property of the former one), the TDataSource component to the ADODataSet component through the DataSet property, and the TADODataSet component to the TADOConnection component through the Connection property. Let's also place four TButton components into our form and set their caption properties to Connect, Save, Load, and Update.

Now we need to connect our TADOConnection component to the Northwind database on the MS SQL Server 7.0, and set the CommandType property of the TADOConnection component to cmdText, and the CommandText property to 'SELECT * FROM customers'.

Then, we will create OnClick event handlers for these buttons:

```
const
 FileName = 'c:\cust.dat';
procedure TForm1.SaveButtonClick(Sender: TObject);
begin
 ADODataSet1.SaveToFile(FileName);
end;

procedure TForm1.LoadButtonClick(Sender: TObject);
begin
 ADODataSet1.LoadFromFile(FileName);
 ADODataSet1.Open;
end;

procedure TForm1.ConnectButtonClick(Sender: TObject);
begin
 ADOConnection1.Connected := NOT ADOConnection1.Connected;
 ADoDataSet1.Active := ADOConnection1.Connected;
end;

procedure TForm1.UpdateButtonClick(Sender: TObject);
begin
 ADOConnection1.Connected := True;
 ADODataSet1.UpdateBatch;
end;
```

The first and the second event handlers save the recordset from TADOConnection component to a file and retrieve it correspondingly. The third event handler connects our application to and disconnects it from the database server. The fourth event handler saves the edited recordset to a database server by calling the UpdateBatch method.

Conclusion

In this chapter, we have seen how to use the TADODataSet component to perform various tasks. Let us outline what we have just learned. The following table shows the minimal requirements for each task.

Task	Steps Required
Get all of the fields from a table	■ Set the CommandType property to cmdTable or cmTableDirect; ■ Set the name of the table in the CommandText property
Get all of the fields that meet the specified criteria	■ Set the CommandType property to cmdTable or cmTableDirect; ■ Set the name of the table in the CommandText property; ■ Specify the value for the Filter property; or ■ Set the CommandType property to cmdText; ■ Specify the SQL statement in the CommandText property;
Run a stored procedure	■ Set the CommandType property to the cmdStoredProc value, ■ Set the name of the stored procedure in the CommandText property; ■ Specify parameters in the Parameters collection
Run a system stored procedure	■ Set the CommandType property to the cmdText; ■ Specify the name of the system stored procedure in the CommandText property; ■ Specify parameters in the Parameters collection;
Load a saved recordset file	■ Set the CommandType property to cmdFile; ■ Specify the name of the file in the CommandText property; ■ Specify the provider name and security information in the ConnectionString property;

In the next chapter we will discuss three more Delphi ADO components—TADOTable, TADOQuery, and TADOStoredProc.

MORE DELPHI ADO COMPONENTS

In the previous chapter, we saw how to use the TADODataSet component to retrieve data from one or more tables in a data source. Here we will take a look at three more TCustomADODataSet component descendants that, unlike the TADODataSet component, are used for more specific tasks.

For example, the TADOTable component can be used to extract data from a single table, the TADOQuery component is used to execute various SQL queries, and the TADOStoredProc component is best suited to run user-defined and system stored procedures.

The structure of this chapter will be the same as the previous ones. First, the description of the component and its properties, methods, and events are provided, and then there are several examples that illustrate its usage.

We will start with the TADOTable component, which can be used to extract data from a single table.

The TADOTable Component

The TADOTable component is used when we need to work with a single table in a data source. We can extract all data available in a table, or set some criteria (or filter, in terms of this component) to get only certain data. This ability gives us a way to analyze data, but the filter's functionality is limited. To perform more sophisticated analysis, we should use the SQL queries. This is a task for the TADOQuery component, discussed later in this chapter.

You may ask what the difference is between the TADOTable component and the TADODataSet component with the CommandType property set to cmdTable. Don't they behave the same way? The answer to this question is yes and no. Yes, as we saw in the previous chapter, we can use the TADODataSet component to extract data from a single table, and set the filters to get exactly the data we need.

However, the TADOTable component, as well as the TADOQuery and TADOStoredProc components, allow us to simply migrate from BDE applications; they mimic the basic functions of the corresponding BDE data-access components: TTable, TQuery, and TStoredProc.

Properties

Besides the properties inherited from the TCustomADODataSet class, the TADOTable component introduces five new properties that are described below.

The MasterFields Property

This property is used along with the MasterSource property to specify one or more fields in a master table used in a master-detail relationship. Before setting the value of this property, specify the name of the TDataSource component that provides data from the master table using the MasterSource property.

The MasterSource Property

This property of the TDataSource type specifies the TDataSource component that provides data from the master table in a master-detail relationship. The MasterSource property is used in conjunction with the MasterFields property, which specifies a list of fields used from a master table.

Note that you cannot link the MasterSource property to a data source that points to itself. If you have a self-referencing table like the Employees table in the Northwind database, you need to create two components to capture the relationship in the master-detail form. Also note that the MasterSource property really ends up pointing to the DataSource property of the TCustomADODataset. Since its declaration specifies the GetDataSource function as the reader, this resolves to the TCustomADODatasete.GetDataSource function, which in turn returns the DataSource property.

The ReadOnly Property

If this Boolean property is set to True, the retrieved data cannot be altered by the user. The default value for the ReadOnly property is False, meaning that users can delete, insert, and update data. The ReadOnly property manipulates the LockType property of the underlying ADO Recordset object—if the ReadOnly property is True, then the ltReadOnly value is used; otherwise the ltOptimistic value of this property is used.

The TableDirect Property

This Boolean property specifies the CommandType property of the underlying ADO Command object used to retrieve data from a table. If the value of this property is True, then the CommandType property is set to cmdTableDirect; otherwise it is set to cmdTable.

As we have said in the previous chapter, not all providers support queries with direct table names, so use the TableDirect property set to `False` to avoid errors.

The TableName Property

This property specifies the name of the database table we will use to extract data. At design time, you can choose one of the tables available in a combo box in the Object Inspector. To change the value of this property at run time, disconnect the TADOTable component from a database.

Methods

Besides the standard constructor and destructor, the TADOTable component reimplements the GetIndexNames method, which can be used to get a list of indexes available for a table. You can use either the standard visual components to store the list of index names, such as Memo, ListBox, or ComboBox, or some instance of the TStringList object.

Events

The TADOTable component does not introduce its own events; all of the events available for this component are inherited from the TCustomADODataSet object and TDataSet object.

Using the TADOTable Component

As we have already said, we can use the TADOTable component to retrieve data from a single table. We saw an example of this in the previous chapter when we used the `cmdTable` value of the TADODataSet component's CommandType property.

A more interesting possibility is using the MasterSource and MasterFields properties to create master-detail relationships that are also called *one-to-many relationships* (these were discussed in Chapter 1). To better understand what can be done using such relationships, we will create an example in which, without writing any code, we will connect two tables from the Northwind database stored on the Microsoft SQL Server. To do this, we need the following components:

■ TADOConnection component to connect to the database

■ Two TADOTable components, each for its own table in the database

■ Two TDataSource components to link tables with data-aware controls and each other

■ TDBNavigator, TDBEdit, and TDBGrid components to navigate the dataset and display the data

First, we need to specify the data source. This is done through the ConnectionString property of the TADOConnection component. In our example, it has the following value:

```
'Provider=SQLOLEDB.1; Persist Security Info=False; User ID=sa;' + 'Initial Cat-
alog=Northwind; Data Source=MAINDESK;' +
'Locale Identifier=1049; Connect Timeout=15;' +
'Use Procedure for Prepare=1; Auto Translate=True;' +
'Packet Size=4096; Workstation ID=MAINDESK'
```

After specifying the connection string, we can set the Connection property of both TADOTable components to ADOConnection1, since both of them will use the same database.

Next, we need to set the DataSet property of the DataSource1 component to ADOTable1, and the DataSet property of the DataSource2 component to ADOTable2.

Then, we should connect the data-aware controls to appropriate data sources, and, in particular, set the DataSource property of the DBNavigator1 and DBEdit1 components to DataSource1, and the DataSource property of the DBGrid1 component to DataSource2.

Now comes the tricky part—specifying the relationship between two tables. First, let's select tables. The ADOTable1 component will be attached to the Customers table, and the ADOTable2 component to the ORDERS table. After that, we can set the DataField property of the DBEdit1 component to CompanyName by selecting it from the drop-down list in the Object Inspector.

All we need to do now is set two properties of the ADOTable2—MasterSource and MasterFields. First, we should set the MasterSource property. Since we are linking two tables, the value of this property will be DataSource1—the data source that points to our first table. Now, we should specify the list of fields. This is done by pressing the ellipses button near the MasterFields property in the Object Inspector. Doing this will display the Field Link Designer, which can be used to visually specify links between tables.

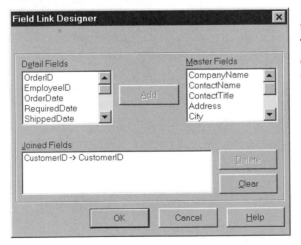

For our example, we will select the CustomerID fields in both tables. That's it. Now we set the Active property for both TADOTable components to True, and run our application.

As you can see from the above figure, the result of linking two tables in the master-detail form gives us the ability to retrieve only data that belongs to the currently selected customer.

One flaw we have found in this approach is that the detail table cannot be filtered, i.e., you cannot set the Filter property for the ADOTable2 used in our example. That means that you will receive all data associated with the customer, not just the rows you need.

Another flaw is that inserting detail records will not automatically fill in the master field with the master value as it does for other datasets.

Some of the filtering problems can be solved using SQL statements. To do so, we need another component—the TADOQuery component, which is a part of the Delphi ADO components set. We will look at this component in the next section.

The TADOQuery Component

The TADOQuery component can be used to specify SQL statements that access one or more tables in a data source. This means that we can extract data with the SELECT statement, create and modify tables and other database objects with ALTER TABLE, CREATE TABLE, DROP TABLE, INSERT, DELETE, and UPDATE statements, and execute stored procedures defined in a data source.

Similar to the TADOTable component, described in the section above, the TADOQuery component does not differ very much from the TADODataSet component we discussed in the previous chapter. In other words, the TADOQuery component provides the same functionality as the TADODataSet with the CommandType property set to the cmdText value. As we will see later, the TADOQuery component adds several new properties and methods, but this is the only difference between these two components. It seems that the TADOQuery component, as well as the TADOTable and TADOStoredProc components, were implemented in Delphi to make the transition from BDE-based applications to ADO-based applications a little bit smoother.

Properties

The TADOQuery component inherits all its properties from the TCustomADODataSet and TDataSet classes and adds the following properties of its own.

The DataSource Property

This property can be used to link two tables using SQL statements. The DataSource property should specify the data source that will be used to supply the values for the parameters in the SQL query. Later in this chapter, we will give you an example of how to use this property.

The RowsAffected Property

This property can be used to find the number of the rows that were affected by the SQL query. This property will have a zero value if no rows were updated or deleted during query processing. Note that this property indicates the rows in the dataset, and not the rows returned to the client application. That is why we cannot use the RowsAffected property when we select data from a data source using the SELECT statement. To do so, we need to inspect the resulting recordset, and find the value of its RecordCount property:

```
NumRows := ADOQuery1.Recordset.RecordCount;
```

The SQL Property

This property of the TStrings type is used to specify one or more SQL statements to be executed. The execution begins when we call the ExecSQL or Open method of the TADOQuery component or set its Active property to True.

Unlike the TADODataSet component, there is no special built-in property editor for the SQL query. Instead, you have to press the ellipsis button at the SQL property in the Object Inspector to display the standard Strings List Editor, and there is nothing left to do but enter the SQL code manually. Hopefully, this will change in a future version of Delphi.

At run time we use the SQL property just like any other TStringList type variable. For example:

```
procedure TForm1.Button1Click(Sender: TObject);
begin
 with ADOQuery1.SQL do
  begin
   Clear;
   Add ('SELECT * ');
   Add ('FROM ORDERS');
  end;
end;
```

It needs to be made clear that Delphi does not perform any checking of the SQL statements entered in the Strings List Editor for the SQL property. It is up to you (or the database server) to evaluate the SQL query and to correct any errors or reject the entire statement. We suggest using the TADODataSet CommandText property editor to visually build simple SELECT queries and then copy and paste them into the SQL property of the TADOQuery component. For more complex queries, use the tools that come with the database products, i.e., QueryDesigner in Microsoft Access, SQL Server Query Analyzer in Microsoft SQL Server, or other appropriate tools. We hope that in future versions of Delphi this situation will change, and Inprise will come up with more sophisticated query building tools of its own.

Methods

Besides the standard constructor and destructor, the TADOQuery component introduces only one new method—ExecSQL.

The ExecSQL Method

This method is used to execute the SQL query that is stored in the SQL property. As we already know, the TADOQuery component provides several ways to execute the SQL query. The following rules apply:

■ Use the ExecSQL method to execute the INSERT, UPDATE, DELETE, CREATE TABLE, ALTER TABLE, and DROP TABLE SQL statements.

■ Use the Open method or set the Active property to True to execute the SELECT statements.

Note: Note that you can improve the performance of your application if you set the Prepared property to True before executing your SQL query for the first time using the ExecSQL method. This should be done only for queries intended to be executed more than once. Setting this property to True forces the database server to compile and optimize the query and place it on the database server cache. In this case, calling the ExecSQL method results in executing a query from this cache that has already been compiled and optimized.

Otherwise, calling the ExecSQL method of the TADOQuery component with the Prepared property set to False results in recompiling and reoptimizing this query, which decreases the performance if this query is executed several times.

Events

The TADOQuery component does not introduce its own events; all of the events available for this component are inherited from the TCustomADODataSet object and the TDataSet object.

Using the TADOQuery Component

In the section about the TADOTable component we created an example of a master-detail relationship between two tables in the Northwind database on the Microsoft SQL Server. We noted that there is no way to set the criteria to filter the resulting records since the detail table does not support the Filter and Filtered properties. Let's see whether this problem can be solved with the help of TADOQuery component.

First, we will reimplement the functionality of our previous example. To do so, we will need the same set of components, but we will change one of the TADOTable components to TADOQuery component. The components we will use are:

- TADOConnection component to connect to the database
- One TADOQuery component to specify the SQL query
- One TADOTable component to connect to the Customers table in the database
- Two TDataSource components to link the table and the query with data-aware controls
- TDBNavigator, TDBEdit, and TDBGrid components to navigate the dataset and show the data

As in the previous example, we assign the ConnectionString property of the ADOConnection1 component to the Northwind database and specify this connection as the Connection property of the ADOQuery1 and ADOTable1 components.

Next, we associate the TDataSource components with ADOQuery1 and ADOTable1 components. In particular, we need to set the DataSet property of the TDataSource1 component to ADOTable1, and the DataSet property of the TDataSource2 component to ADOQuery1.

Now, the most significant part follows. As you recall, we connected two tables—ORDERS and Customers—by the CUSTOMERID field. In this example, we will set the Customers table as the TableName property of the ADOTable1 component. The DBEdit1 component will show the contents of the COMPANYNAME field from the Customers table, so we need to set its DataSource property to DataSource1, and its DataField property to CompanyName.

Now we need to specify the relationship between these two tables, which are the Orders table and the Customers table.

Let's think about what we need to query for. We need to find all customers in the ORDERS table whose CUSTOMERID is equal to CUSTOMERID in the Customers table. In other words, we need to execute the following query:

```
/*** Select all fields from CUSTOMERS and ORDERS tables ***/
SELECT * FROM Customers, Orders
/*** where both CUSTOMERID fields are equal ***/
WHERE Orders.CustomerID = Customers.CustomerID
/*** and order the result by CUSTOMERID ***/
ORDER BY Customers.CustomerID
```

If it is not clear to you what this SQL statement does, keep reading, as we will explain these statements in the next chapter. For now, just try to understand the comments for each statement.

This SQL statement does the job, but we want to implement the exact functionality of the previous example. To do so, we need to specify the DataSource property of the ADOQuery1 component. Set its value to DataSource1 to connect with the Customers table, and then enter the following two lines in the String List Editor for the SQL property:

```
SELECT * FROM ORDERS
 WHERE ORDERS.CUSTOMERID = :CUSTOMERID
```

This looks nearly the same as the previous query, except that instead of CUSTOMERS. CUSTOMERID, we have used the parameter. This means that instead of hard-coding something, we will supply the value at run time.

Our parameter has the CUSTOMERID name, which is the name of the field in the Customers database! And the value for this parameter comes from the appropriate field. All we need to do is to add the BeforeScroll event handler of the TADOTable component. Here is its code:

```
procedure TForm1.ADOTable1BeforeScroll(DataSet: TDataSet);
begin
{Close Connection}
 With ADOQuery1 do
  begin
   Close;
   Active := True;
  end;
end;
```

This event is fired when the current record position in the dataset is changed. Now we can run our example application. It looks like the one we created for the TADOTable component earlier in this chapter.

OrderID	CustomerID	EmployeeID	OrderDate	RequiredDate	ShippedDate
10323	KOENE	4	07.10.96	04.11.96	14.10.96
10325	KOENE	1	09.10.96	23.10.96	14.10.96
10456	KOENE	8	25.02.97	08.04.97	28.02.97
10457	KOENE	2	25.02.97	25.03.97	03.03.97
10468	KOENE	3	07.03.97	04.04.97	12.03.97
10506	KOENE	9	15.04.97	13.05.97	02.05.97
10542	KOENE	1	20.05.97	17.06.97	26.05.97
10630	KOENE	1	13.08.97	10.09.97	19.08.97
10718	KOENE	1	27.10.97	24.11.97	29.10.97
10799	KOENE	9	26.12.97	06.02.98	05.01.98
10817	KOENE	3	06.01.98	20.01.98	13.01.98
10849	KOENE	9	23.01.98	20.02.98	30.01.98

Now we can solve the problem with data filtering. It is easy since we now have the SQL query that drives the data extraction. For example, if we need to filter orders that were received in 1998 and later, we simply add the following line to our SQL property:

```
AND ORDERDATE > '12/31/97'
```

Now our SQL query should look like this:

```
SELECT * FROM ORDERS
WHERE ORDERS.CUSTOMERID = :CUSTOMERID
AND ORDERDATE > '12/31/97'
```

Take a look at the result in the following figure:

Now we can slightly improve this example and add the browsing facilities. We will do this by adding the second TDBGrid component that will show the list of all Customer IDs in our database. When we click on a particular ID, the details will be shown in the first TDBGrid component. This will allow us to get rid of TDBNavigator and be able to jump to any record within a recordset in no particular order.

We need to add the second TDBGrid component, set its DataSource property to DataSource1 (linked with the ADOTable1 component with the Customers table in our example), and specify the columns we would like to see in it. Since we are interested only in the CUSTOMERID field, we can delete all other fields. To do so, we call the

Columns Editor for the DBGrid1 component, use the Add all fields command, then delete the fields we don't need, and close the editor. The following figure shows the modified version of our example application.

In this section, we have seen how to use the TADOQuery component to specify the SQL queries, how to create queries with parameters, and how to implement the master-detail relationship. We also mentioned that this component can be used to execute stored queries. You can use it to perform such tasks, but from our point of view, it is better to use the TADOStoredProc component, which is specially designed for this. We will discuss this component in the following section.

The TADOStoredProc Component

The TADOStoredProc component is the last component in the Delphi ADO components set that we will discuss here. Like the two components described earlier in this chapter, the TADOStoredProc component can also be treated as a specific version of the more general TADODataSet component that was introduced in the previous chapter. The only difference between the TADODataSet component with the CommandType property set to the cmdStoredProc value, and the TADOStoredProc component is that the latter has an extra property—ProcedureName, which is used to specify the stored procedure we want to run. In the TADODataSet component, the CommandText property was used for this purpose.

Properties

The TADOStoredProc component inherits all its properties from the TCustomADODataSet class and adds only one new property of its own—ProcedureName.

This property is used to specify the name of the stored procedure we want to run. At design time, all stored procedure names are available from the combo box in the Object Inspector. At run time, we should assign one of the valid stored procedure names to the ProcedureName property.

Methods

The TADOStoredProc component does not introduce its own methods besides the standard constructor and the ExecProc procedure that executes the stored procedure specified with the ProcedureName property. All of its methods are inherited from the TCustomADODataSet and TDataSet classes.

Events

The TADOStoredProc component does not introduce its own events. All of the events available for this component are inherited from the TCustomADODataSet object and the TDataSet object.

Stored Procedures and Parameters

In the previous chapter, as well as in the section dedicated to the TADOQuery component, we have mentioned parameters that can be supplied to the SQL query and stored procedure. Here we will discuss parameters in more detail.

Parameters allow us to use the same set of SQL statements several times; we simply change the value of one or more variables in it and run the query again and again. The same is true for stored procedures, which are sets of SQL statements stored on the database. Stored procedures are used to perform various tasks, and in many cases they return result to the client. For more information about stored procedures, and how they are created and implemented in databases, see Chapter 10.

If the SQL query or stored procedure requires parameters, they should be supplied in the Parameters collection, which is exposed as a property with the same name. This property is implemented in the TCustomADODataSet class, and inherited by both the TADODataSet and TADOStoredProc components. The Parameters collection is the direct implementation of the same collection of the ADO Command object. It consists of zero or more Parameter objects that also come directly from ADO.

Parameters Collection

This collection contains parameters for a stored procedure or SQL query, defined with the ProcedureName property of the TADOStoredProc component, the SQL property of the TADOQuery component, or the CommandText property of the TADODataSet component. To find the number of parameters, check the Count property.

Properties

This section describes the properties available in the Parameters collection.

The Command Property

This property provides us with direct access to the underlying ADO Command object. There is no need to use the Command property in most cases; we will only see this if in future versions of ADO there are some extensions of the ADO Command object that will not be implemented directly at the component level. In this situation you will need to access the ADO Command object directly to get the extra functionality.

The Items Property

This property represents a collection of individual parameters in the form of zero or more TParameter object. Each item in the Items collection contains a detailed description of the parameter attributes. For more information, see the description of the Parameter object later in this chapter.

The ParameterCollection Property

This property gives us access to the Parameters collection of the underlying ADO Command object. You rarely need to access this collection directly. Almost all its functionality is already implemented on the Delphi ADO components level.

The ParamValues Property

This property is used to get or set values of parameters when we access them by name instead of indexes in the Items collection.

Methods

Beside the methods inherited from the standard TCollection object, such as Add, Clear, Delete, and Insert, the Parameters collection contains several specific methods, which are listed below:

Method	Description
AddParameter	This method adds a new parameter (of the TParameter type) to the collection. The AddParameter method only creates an empty parameter with default attributes that should be initialized later through the properties of the TParameter object.
AppendParameters	Used by the TParameters class to add a ADO Parameter object into an ADO Parameters collection for the underlying Command object
AssignValues	This method can be used to copy parameter values from one TParameters collection to another. For example, you can use this method to copy parameters from one TADOStoredProc component into another.
CreateParameter	Use this method to create a new parameter (of the TParameter type) and add it to the Parameters collection. The difference between AddParameter and CreateParameter is that the first one adds the new parameters with default or empty attributes, while the last one allows us to specify all required attributes instantly.
FindParam	This method returns the specified parameter. If one is found, this method returns the TParameter object; otherwise it returns nil.
GetParamList	Use this method to get a list of parameters available for the query or stored procedure.
IsEqual	This method allows us to compare two TParameter objects to check if they are equal or not.
ParamByName	Use this method to find the parameter specified by name. If one is found, this method returns the TParameter object; otherwise it returns nil.
ParseSQL	This method parses a SQL statement for parameters and adds a new TParameter object for each parameter found within it.
Refresh	Use this method to refresh the Parameters collection.

The following example shows how to use the ParseSQL method and iterate through the Parameters collection.

```
procedure TForm1.Button1Click(Sender: TObject);
const
 ParaCount = 'Total %d parameter(s) found';
 ParaData  = 'Parameter %d' + #9 + 'Name = %s';
var
 SQL : String;
```

```
 I   : Integer;
begin
{Specify the SQL statement}
 SQL := 'SELECT * FROM ORDERS ' +
  'WHERE ORDERS.CUSTOMERID = :CUSTOMERID ';
 With ADOStoredProc1.Parameters do
  begin
{Extract parameters}
   Memo1.Lines.Add(ParseSQL(SQL, True));
{Refresh the Parameters collection}
   Refresh;
{Show how many parameters we have}
   Memo1.Lines.Add(Format(ParaCount, [Count]));
   Memo1.Lines.Add(^M^J);
{If we have parameters, show their names}
     For I := 0 to Count - 1 do
      Memo1.Lines.Add(
       Format(ParaData, [I, Items[I].Name])
       );
  end;
end;
```

Now that we are familiar with the Parameters collection, let's look at the Parameter object, which represents an individual parameter within this collection.

Parameter Object

The Parameter object represents an individual parameter within the Parameters collection. We can access it by iterating the Items collection of the Parameters collection, or access the individual parameters by using one of its methods, such as ParamByName or FindParam.

Properties

The Parameter object has several properties that describe the attributes of the parameter.

The Attributes Property

This property contains the attributes of the individual parameter. The Attributes property is of the TParameterAttributes type and can have one or more of the following values:

Value	Meaning	ADO Constant
psLong	This value indicates that the parameter accepts long data	adParamLong
psNullable	This value indicates that the parameter accepts null values	adParamNullable
psSigned	This is the default value that indicates the parameter accepts signed values	adParamSigned

Note: The ADO equivalents of these constants are the `ParameterAttributesEnum` values.

The DataType Property

This property contains the data type of the individual parameter. The DataType property can have one of the TDataType values that correspond to the `TFieldType` type that is defined in the DB unit. The following table shows how Delphi data types map to ADO data types (the `DataTypeEnum` values):

ADO	Delphi
adEmpty	ftUnknown
adTinyInt	ftSmallInt
adSmallInt	ftSmallInt
adError	ftSmallInt
adInteger	ftSmallInt
adUnsignedInt	ftSmallInt
adBigInt	ftLargeInt
adUnsignedBigInt	ftLargeInt
adUnsignedTinyInt	ftWord
adUnsignedSmallInt	ftWord
adSingle	ftFloat
adDouble	ftFloat
adCurrency	ftBCD
adBoolean	ftBoolean
adDate	ftDate
adDBDate	ftDate
adDBTime	ftTime
adDBTimeStamp	ftDateTime
adFileTime	ftDateTime
adDBFileTime	ftDateTime
adChar	ftWideString
adVarChar	ftWideString
adVarWChar	ftWideString
adLongVarChar	ftMemo
adLongVarWChar	ftMemo
adLongVarBinary	ftBlob
adBinary	ftBytes
adVarBinary	ftVarBytes
adChapter	ftDataSet
adPropVariant	ftVariant
adVariant	ftVariant
adIUnknown	ftInterface
adIDispatch	ftIDispatch
adGUID	ftGUID

ADO	Delphi	
	EnableBCD := True	**EnableBCD := False**
adDecimal	ftBCD	ftFloat
adNumeric	ftBCD	ftFloat
adVarNumeric	ftBCD	ftFloat

The conversion between the two types is implemented in the ADODB unit.

The Direction Property

This property specifies the direction of the parameter, that is, whether it is an input parameter, output parameter, or input/output parameter, or if the parameter is a return value from a stored procedure. The Direction property can have one of the following values of the TParameterDirection type:

Value	Meaning	ADO Constant
pdInput	The parameter is used to pass information to a stored procedure or SQL statement.	adParamInput
pdInputOutput	The parameter is used to pass information to and return information from a stored procedure or SQL statement.	adParamInputOutput
pdOutput	The parameter is used to return information from a stored procedure or SQL statement.	adParamOutput
pdReturnValue	The parameter is used to receive the return values from a stored procedure or SQL statement.	adParamReturnValue
pdUnknown	The direction of the parameter is not known	adParamUnknown

Note: The ADO equivalents of these constants are the ParameterDirectionEnum values.

The Name Property

This property contains the name of the parameter. The name of the parameter identifies it within the Parameters collection and may not be the same as the name of the parameter defined in the stored procedure or SQL statement.

The NumericScale Property

This property is used to specify the scale of numeric values of the parameter, i.e., the number of decimal places or digits to the right of the decimal point is in it. This property, as well as the Precision property described later, is required only for the Numeric data types.

The ParameterObject Property

This property gives us direct access to the underlying ADO Parameter object. In most cases there is no need to use this property.

The Parameters Property

This property indicates the Parameters collection to which this parameter belongs.

The Precision Property

This property is used to specify the degree of precision, i.e., the maximum number of digits allowed for Numeric data types. This property, as well as the NumericScale property described above, is required only for the Numeric data types.

The Properties Property

This property gives us direct access to the Properties collection of the underlying ADO Parameter object. This property is read-only.

The Size Property

Use this property to specify the maximum size (in bytes or characters) of the parameter. This property is only meaningful for the String data types like CHAR and VARCHAR.

The Value Property

This property contains the value assigned to the parameter. There are two ways to assign the above-mentioned property values for the parameter. We can either use the AddParameter method to create a new parameter and then directly access its properties to set its values, or use the CreateParameter method to specify all of the values in one call. In the latter case, the names of the parameters of this method, such as Name, DataType, Direction, Size, and Value, correspond to the same properties of the Parameter object.

Methods

There are several methods of the Parameter object that can be used to manipulate it. We will discuss these below.

The AppendChunk Method

We can use this method to append large text or binary data to a parameter that has the psLong attribute. The data can be supplied as a single piece or in several pieces. The first call to this method (after the parameter attributes are set) overwrites all existing data, while subsequent calls add data to an existing one.

The Assign Method

This method can be used to create a Parameter object that is an exact copy of another existing parameter.

The LoadFromFile Method

Use this method to load the contents of a file into a parameter. When calling the LoadFromFile method, you specify the name of the file and the type of the data to be loaded from it.

The LoadFromStream Method

This method allows us to load the contents of a memory stream into a parameter.

Using the *TADOStoredProc Component*

Now that we have described various properties and methods of the Parameters collection and its Parameter objects, let's take a look at an example using the TADOStoredProc component. Here we will implement the StoredProcDump utility, which will allow us to study stored procedures that are available for the database on the selected data source. This utility should be able to list stored procedures, show their parameters with various attributes, and show the source code for the selected stored procedure.

Overview of the StoredProcDump Utility and its Implementation

First, let's make an assumption. For simplicity, we will work with Microsoft SQL Server 7.0. You can extend the functionality of this utility yourself by adding extra code and data source support if needed.

The steps that the StoredProcDump utility should perform are:

1. Connect to the data source specified in ConnectionString.
2. Obtain a list of stored procedures available for the database.
3. Allow user to select one of the stored procedures available to examination.
4. Show selected stored procedure's parameters and attributes.
5. Show source code for the selected stored procedure.

It should be clear from this outline what functionality we need to implement. Let's do it, step by step.

To implement this utility, we will use the following components:

- TADOConnection component to connect to the database
- TADOStoredProc component to give us access to the parameters of the stored procedure
- TADODataSet component to extract the source code of the stored procedure
- TButton to initiate our application, TComboBox to provide a list of available stored procedures, TListView component to show attributes of parameters, and the Memo component to output the source code

The first thing we need to do is to connect to the data source. We will do this by adding the following line to the OnClick event handler for the Button1 component:

```
{Connect to the data source}
 ADOConnection1.Connected := True;
```

Next, we need to obtain a list of stored procedures available for the database. This can be done with the help of the GetProcedureNames method of the TADOConnection component:

```
var
 SL: TStringList;
…
{Get list of stored procedures}
 ADOConnection1.GetProcedureNames(SL);
```

For reasons that will become clear a little bit later, we need to remove the version information from the stored procedure name. The following code does this:

```
{Strip version info}
 For I := 0 to SL.Count-1 do
  begin
   P := Pos(';1', SL.Strings[I]);
   Item := SL.Strings[I];
   If P > 0 Then
    begin
     Delete(Item, P, 2);
     SL.Delete(I);
     SL.Insert(I, Item);
    end;
  end;
```

Now we are ready to load the list of available stored procedures to the ComboBox:

```
{Add stored procedures names into the ComboBox}
 ComboBox1.Items := SL;
{Reset ComboBox}
 ComboBox1.ItemIndex := 0;
```

Now we need to create an OnClick event handler for the ComboBox1 component. Here is the code:

```
{If one procedure selected, show its parameters and source}
procedure TForm1.ComboBox1Click(Sender: TObject);
begin
 with ComboBox1 do
  begin
   ADOStoredProc1.ProcedureName := Items[ItemIndex];
   ShowParams;
  end;
end;
```

What we are doing here is assigning the name of the stored procedure we have selected from the ComboBox to the ProcedureName property of our ADOStoredProc component. Next, we call the ShowParams procedure. Here is the code with comments where some user interface parts are involved:

```delphi
procedure TForm1.ShowParams;
var
  I        : Integer;
  P        : TParameter;
  S        : String;
  ListItem : TListItem;
begin
{Clear ListView}
{**
The Refresh method should be called before we
can access parameters properties
**}
ADOStoredProc1.Parameters.Refresh;

with ADOStoredProc1 do
  begin
    for I := 0 to Parameters.Count-1 do
      begin
      P := Parameters.Items[I];
      With ListView1 do
      begin
       S := '';
       ListItem := Items.Add;
       ListItem.Caption := P.Name;
       If paSigned   in P.Attributes then S := 'paSigned';
       If paNullable in P.Attributes then S := 'paNullable';
       If paLong     in P.Attributes then S := 'paLong';
       ListItem.SubItems.Add(S);

       ListItem.SubItems.Add(StrDataType[Integer(P.DataType)]);
       case P.Direction of
        pdUnknown      : ListItem.SubItems.Add('pdUnknown');
        pdInput        : ListItem.SubItems.Add('pdInput');
        pdOutput       : ListItem.SubItems.Add('pdOutput');
        pdInputOutput  : ListItem.SubItems.Add('pdInputOutput');
        pdReturnValue  : ListItem.SubItems.Add('pdReturnValue');
       end;
       ListItem.SubItems.Add(IntToStr(P.NumericScale));
       ListItem.SubItems.Add(IntToStr(P.Precision));
       ListItem.SubItems.Add(IntToStr(P.Size));
       ListItem.SubItems.Add(IntToStr(P.Value));
      end;
     end;
   end;
 ProcSource(Memo1.Lines);
```

end;

Note: The StrDataType function is used to convert the integer value of the data type into an appropriate string. Its source code is available on the companion CD-ROM.

As you can see from the source code above, here we iterate through the Parameters collection, extract available parameters, and show its attributes in the ListView1 component. At the end of this procedure, we call the ProcSource procedure that should show the source of the currently selected stored procedure. Here is the code:

```
procedure TForm1.ProcSource(SL: TStrings);
var
 I : Integer;
begin
{Retrieve the Source}
 With ADODataSet1 do
  begin
{Connect to the data source}
   Connection := ADOStoredProc1.Connection;
{
 Call the Systetem Stored Procedure SP_HELPTEXT with
 the name of our stored procedure
}
   CommandText := 'exec sp_helptext ''' +
    ADOStoredProc1.ProcedureName + '''';
{Active the connection}
   Active := True;
{Move to the first record}
   First;
   SL.Clear;
{Iterate through the records}
   For I := 0 to RecordCount-1 do
    begin
{To collect source code strings}
     SL.Add(Fields[0].Value);
    Next;
    end;
{Disconnect...}
   Active := False;
  end;
end;
```

To obtain the source of the stored procedure we are using the system stored procedure SP_HELPTEXT, implemented in Microsoft SQL Server 7.0. This solution ties us to the specific DBMS tool, but later, in Chapter 16, we will learn how to use the features of this ADO extension to obtain the same source code.

The complete source code for the StoredProcDump utility is available on the companion CD-ROM. You are free to modify and extend it for your needs.

One final note. We think that this utility can be of a great help when you are learning about stored procedures and trying to figure out what is at your disposal. As you can see, it works perfectly well with both system stored procedures and user-defined stored procedures. Chapter 10 contains more information about user-defined stored procedures.

Conclusion

In this chapter we learned about three Delphi ADO components—TADOTable, which can be used to extract data from a single table, TADOQuery, used to execute SQL queries, and TADOStoredProc, which is best suited for running stored procedures. As we have seen here, all these components behave nearly the same as the TADODataSet component that was described in the previous chapter.

This chapter ends our tour of the Delphi ADO components. In the next chapter, we discuss the basics of the structured query language (SQL), which is used to extract data from various data sources and to update, create, or delete database objects.

INTRODUCTION TO STRUCTURED QUERY LANGUAGE

In the previous chapter, we saw several examples of structured query language statements that were used to retrieve data from a dataset with the help of some Delphi ADO components and underlying ADO objects. Now is a good time to take a look at the SQL language and learn its major features. In this chapter, you will learn the role of SQL, its purpose, and major statements, and will receive several examples of the following data operations:

- Retrieving data
- Summarizing data
- Adding data
- Deleting data
- Updating the database
- Protecting data
- Creating a database

To learn SQL in more detail, refer to *Learn SQL* by José A. Ramalho, Wordware Publishing, 1999.

Introduction

Structured query language (SQL, pronounced "S-Q-L" or "sequel") is a nonprocedural language that is used to handle data in relational database systems. It is a set of commands used to access data stored in virtually any database. Currently SQL is the language of choice to access and manipulate data stored in relational databases.

SQL started as an IBM research project in the early 1970s and was created to implement E.F. Codd's relational model. It was born under the name of SEQUEL (for Structured English Query Language), then become SEQUEL/2, and then simply SQL. The official standard for SQL was initially published by ANSI in 1986 (this is the version most commonly implemented today) and since then has been expanded twice—in 1989 (a minor revision) and 1992 (so the current implementation of SQL is called SQL92). ANSI is working on the SQL3 standard that will have several new object-oriented extensions.

There are three levels of compliance to the ANSI standard: Entry, Intermediate, and Full. Many major companies such as IBM, Informix, Microsoft, Oracle, and Sybase have their own implementations of SQL based on the ANSI standard with some vendor-specific extensions.

For further details, refer to the vendor documentation. You may find the following references useful:

- Microsoft Jet Engine: *Microsoft Jet Database Engine Programmer's Guide*, Microsoft Press, 1997

- Microsoft SQL Server: *Transact-SQL Reference*, part of the SQL Server Books Online; available on the product's CD-ROM

- Oracle: *Oracle8 SQL Reference*, part of the Oracle 8 HTML documents; available on the product's CD-ROM

How SQL Works

Let's look at how SQL works. Suppose the computer system has a database with important information, such as production, sales, inventory, or payroll data. The database is controlled by a database management system (DBMS). When we need to retrieve data from a database, we use the SQL language to make a request. The DBMS processes the SQL request, retrieves the requested data, and returns it to us. The process of requesting data from a database and receiving back the results is called a *database query*. This is illustrated in the figure below:

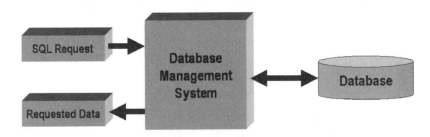

As we will see later, SQL is more than a query language. It has expanded beyond its initial purpose and also can be used to define the structure and organization of data; to manipulate data by adding new data, removing it, and modifying it; to restrict the access to databases; to share data; and to maintain data integrity.

Note: Note that SQL is not a database management system, nor is it a stand-alone product. It is an integrated part of a DBMS, and it serves as a language and a tool to communicate with the DBMS.

SQL Statements

SQL provides statements for different types of functions within a database. The SQL language consists of about 40 statements, each requesting a specific action from the DBMS. Following is a brief description of each of the categories of SQL statements and a list of statements by category.

Data Definition Language (DDL)

Data definition language statements allow us to create, alter, and drop databases and objects within it, such as tables and views. These statements provide access to database objects through granting and revoking roles, allow us to analyze the information on a table or index, and control auditing options. The DDL statements are shown below:

Statement	Description
CREATE TABLE	Used to add a new table to the database
DROP TABLE	Used to remove a table from the database
ALTER TABLE	Used to change the structure of an existing table
CREATE VIEW	Used to create a new view in the database
DROP VIEW	Used to remove a view from the database
CREATE INDEX	Used to build an index for a column
DROP INDEX	Used to remove the index for a column
CREATE SCHEMA	Used to add a new schema to the database
DROP SCHEMA	Used to remove a schema from the database
CREATE DOMAIN	Used to add a new data value domain
ALTER DOMAIN	Used to change a domain definition
DROP DOMAIN	Used to remove a domain from the database

Data Manipulation Language (DML)

Data manipulation language statements allow us to query and manipulate data in the existing database objects. Note that these statements do not implicitly commit the transaction on which they are invoked. The DML statements are shown in the following table:

Statement	Description
SELECT	Used to retrieve data from the database
INSERT	Used to add new rows of data to the database
DELETE	Used to remove rows of data from the database

Statement	Description
UPDATE	Used to modify existing database data

Note that sometimes the SELECT statement has its own category called data query language (DQL).

Transaction Control Language (TCL)

Transaction control language statements are used to manage changes made by the data manipulation language statements. The TCL statements are shown in the following table:

Statement	Description
COMMIT	Used to end the current transaction and commit the changes
ROLLBACK	Used to abort the current transaction and ignore the changes
SET TRANSACTION	Used to set the data access characteristics of the current transaction

Data Control Language (DCL)

Data control language statements, sometimes called access control statements, are used to perform administrative functions that grant and revoke privileges for using the database, a set of tables within the database, or specific SQL commands. The DCL statements are shown in the following table:

Statement	Description
GRANT	Used to grant user access privileges
REVOKE	Used to remove user access privileges

Cursor Control Language (CCL)

Cursor control language statements are used to define a cursor and to prepare SQL statements for execution and other operations. The cursor control language statements are shown in the following table.

Statement	Description
DECLARE CURSOR	Used to define a cursor for a query
EXPLAIN	Used to describe the data access plan for a query. Note: This statement is an SQL extension used in Microsoft SQL Server 7.0. It may not work in other DBMSs. For example, in Oracle you should use the EXPLAIN PLAN statement
OPEN CURSOR	Used to open a cursor to retrieve query results
FETCH	Used to retrieve a row of query results
CLOSE CURSOR	Used to close a cursor
PREPARE	Used to prepare a SQL statement for dynamic execution
EXECUTE	Used to dynamically execute a SQL statement
DESCRIBE	Used to describe a prepared query

All SQL statements have the same basic form shown below.

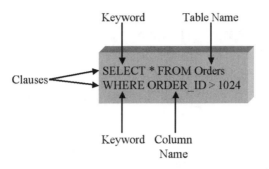

Every SQL statement begins with a verb, a keyword that defines what the statement does; this can be SELECT, INSERT, DELETE, or any other allowed SQL command. Part of the statement is one or more clauses that specify the data to be acted upon. Every clause begins with a keyword such as FROM or WHERE. The specific structure varies from statement to statement; many clauses contain table or column names while other clauses may contain additional keywords, constants, or expressions.

ANSI/ISO SQL92 Keywords

Some of the keywords defined in the ANSI SQL standard cannot be used to name database objects (tables, columns, or users) and are reserved. These keywords are shown below:

ABSOLUTE	CROSS	GET	NEXT	SPACE
ACTION	CURRENT	GLOBAL	NO	SQL
ADD	CURRENT_DATE	GO	NOT	SQLCODE
ALL	CURRENT_TIME	GOTO	NULL	SQLERROR
ALLOCATE	CURRENT_TIMESTAMP	GRANT	OCTET_LENGTH	SQLSTATE
ALTER	CURRENT_USER	GROUP	OF	SUBSTRING
AND	CURSOR	HAVING	ON	SUM
ANY	DATE	HOUR	ONLY	SYSTEM_USER
ARE	DAY	IDENTITY	OPEN	TABLE
AS	DEALLOCATE	IMMEDIATE	OPTION	TEMPORARY
ASC	DEC	IN	OR	THEN
ASSERTION	DECIMAL	INDICATOR	ORDER	TIME
AT	DECLARE	INITIALLY	OUTER	TIMESTAMP
AUTHORIZATION	DEFAULT	INNER	OUTPUT	TIMEZONE_HOUR
AVG	DEFERRABLE	INPUT	OVERLAPS	TIMEZONE_MINUTE
BEGIN	DEFERRED	INSENSITIVE	PAD	TO
BETWEEN	DELETE	INSERT	PARTIAL	TRAILING

BIT	DESC	INT	POSITION	TRANSACTION
BIT_LENGTH	DESCRIBE	INTEGER	PRECISION	TRANSLATE
BOTH	DESCRIPTOR	INTERSECT	PREPARE	TRANSLATION
BY	DIAGNOSTICS	INTERVAL	PRESERVE	TRIM
CASCADE	DISCONNECT	INTO	PRIMARY	TRUE
CASCADED	DISTINCT	IS	PRIOR	UNION
CASE	DOMAIN	ISOLATION	PRIVILEGES	UNIQUE
CAST	DOUBLE	JOIN	PROCEDURE	UNKNOWN
CATALOG	DROP	KEY	PUBLIC	UPDATE
CHAR	ELSE	LANGUAGE	READ	UPPER
CHARACTER	END	LAST	REAL	USAGE
CHAR_LENGTH	END-EXEC	LEADING	REFERENCES	USER
CHARACTER_ LENGTH	ESCAPE	LEFT	RELATIVE	USING
CHECK	EXCEPT	LEVEL	RESTRICT	VALUE
CLOSE	EXCEPTION	LIKE	REVOKE	VALUES
COALESCE	EXEC	LOCAL	RIGHT	VARCHAR
COLLATE	EXECUTE	LOWER	ROLLBACK	VARYING
COLLATION	EXISTS	MATCH	ROWS	VIEW
COLUMN	EXTERNAL	MAX	SCHEMA	WHEN
COMMIT	EXTRACT	MIN	SCROLL	WHENEVER
CONNECT	FALSE	MINUTE	SECOND	WHERE
CONNECTION	FETCH	MODULE	SECTION	WITH
CONSTRAINT	FIRST	MONTH	SELECT	WORK
CONSTRAINTS	FLOAT	NAMES	SESSION	WRITE
CONTINUE	FOR	NATIONAL	SESSION_USER	YEAR
CONVERT	FOREIGN	NATURAL	SET	ZONE
CORRESPONDING	FOUND	NCHAR	SIZE	
COUNT	FROM	NULLIF	SMALLINT	
CREATE	FULL	NUMERIC	SOME	

The SQL standard also includes a list of potential keywords that will become keywords in future versions of the standard. These are shown in the following table:

AFTER	EQUALS	OLD	RETURN	TEST
ALIAS	GENERAL	OPERATION	RETURNS	THERE
ASYNC	IF	OPERATORS	ROLE	TRIGGER
BEFORE	IGNORE	OTHERS	ROUTINE	TYPE
BOOLEAN	LEAVE	PARAMETERS	ROW	UNDER
BREADTH	LESS	PENDANT	SAVEPOINT	VARIABLE
COMPLETION	LIMIT	PREORDER	SEARCH	VIRTUAL
CALL	LOOP	PRIVATE	SENSITIVE	VISIBLE
CYCLE	MODIFY	PROTECTED	SEQUENCE	WAIT
DATA	NEW	RECURSIVE	SIGNAL	WHILE
DEPTH	NONE	REF	SIMILAR	WITHOUT
DICTIONARY	OBJECT	REFERENCING	SQLEXCEPTION	

EACH	OFF	REPLACE	SQLWARNING
ELSEIF	OID	RESIGNAL	STRUCTURE

The SQLTest Application

Before diving into the details of SQL, we need a test bed, that is, a Delphi application that will allow us to enter various SQL statements and immediately see the results of their execution. We will use the TADOQuery component as an execution "engine" for the SQL statements we will create during the course of this chapter. The SQLTest application is very simple.

Begin by putting the following components into the main form of the new project: TADOConnection, TADOQuery, TButton, TMemo, TDataSource, and TDBGrid. Connect the TADOQuery component with the TADOConnection component through the Connection property, specify the Northwind.mdb database (which was described in Chapter 1) in the ConnectionString property of the TADOConnection component, then use the TDataSource component to associate the TDBGrid with the TADOQuery component. Enter the following code in the OnClick event handler for the TButton component:

```
procedure TForm1.Button1Click(Sender: TObject);
begin
 If Memo1.Lines.Count > 0 Then
  With ADOQuery1 do
  begin
   Close;
   ADOQuery1.SQL := Memo1.Lines;
   ADOQuery1.ExecSQL;
  end;
end;
```

Save your application and run it. We are ready to start our journey in the land of structured query language.

Note: Instead of the Northwind database, you can use any other database you have. Just make sure that you have created a backup copy of it before experimenting with various SQL statements.

Working with SQL Operators

Throughout the remainder of this chapter, we will use the application created above to study different SQL operators used for retrieving, adding, deleting, and updating data, changing metadata, and other operations.

Retrieving Data

Data retrieval is the most common operation performed with the SQL language. The SELECT statement is one of the most important statements in the language. It is used to retrieve data into a dataset. The basic syntax for the SELECT statement is:

```
SELECT column-list
FROM table-list
[WHERE where-clause]
[ORDER BY order-by-clause]
```

SELECT statements must include SELECT and FROM clauses; other clauses, such as the WHERE and ORDER BY, are optional.

The SELECT statement is used to specify which columns to include in the resulting dataset. The asterisk (*) indicates all fields from a table. For example:

```
SELECT *
```

To indicate a single column, use the following syntax:

```
SELECT CompanyName
```

To choose multiple columns, use the syntax below:

```
SELECT CompanyName, ContactName, ContactTitle
```

To include multiple tables in the SELECT statement, where the column name is the same in one or more tables, we need to refer to the fully qualified version of the column name. For example:

```
SELECT Customers.CompanyName, Shippers.CompanyName
```

The FROM Clause

To specify the names of the tables from which to select records, we use the FROM clause. For example:

```
SELECT * FROM Customers
```

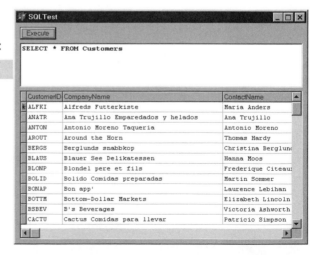

This will return all fields from the Customers table.

If we wish to return only the CompanyName and ContactName columns, we could enter the following SELECT statement:

```
SELECT CompanyName, ContactName FROM Customers
```

To query more than one table at a time, we can use the following SELECT statement:

```
SELECT Customers.CompanyName, Shippers.CompanyName
FROM Customers, Shippers
```

The WHERE Clause

To restrict or filter the results returned by the SELECT statement, we can use the optional WHERE clause. The syntax for the WHERE clause is:

```
WHERE expression1 [{AND | OR} expression2 [...]]
```

For example, instead of receiving the full list of products, we can restrict the rows to only those products in which `CategoryID = 4`:

```
SELECT * FROM Products
WHERE CategoryID = 4
```

We can use various expressions with the WHERE clause. For example:

```
SELECT * FROM Products
WHERE CategoryID = 2 AND SupplierID > 10
```

or

```
SELECT ProductName, UnitPrice FROM Products
WHERE CategoryID = 3 OR UnitPrice < 50
```

or

```
SELECT ProductName, UnitPrice FROM Products
WHERE Discontinued IS NOT NULL
```

The IS NOT NULL statement means that a particular column of the resulting dataset may not have empty values.

We can use one of the six relational operators defined in SQL to specify the criteria for the WHERE clause. These operators are shown below:

Operator	Meaning
<	Is less than
<=	Is less than or equal to
<>	Is not equal to

Operator	Meaning
=	Is equal to
>	Is greater than
>=	Is greater than or equal to

Besides the simple comparison operators, we can use a number of special comparison operators listed in the following table:

Operator	Meaning
ALL	Used in conjunction with comparison operators to test against values in a list
ANY	Used in conjunction with comparison operators to test against values in a list
BETWEEN	Compares a range of values including bounds of the range specified
IN	Tests against values in a list
LIKE	Compares a character pattern

Let's look at some examples of these operators. To use wild cards to find the data that matches a particular pattern, we can use the keyword LIKE:

```
SELECT CompanyName, ContactName
FROM Customers
WHERE CompanyName LIKE "M%"
```

In this pattern, the "%" symbol (percent) replaces any substring, and the "_" symbol (underscore) replaces any symbol. The same result can be achieved with the following query:

```
SELECT CompanyName, ContactName
FROM Customers
WHERE CompanyName BETWEEN 'M' AND 'N'
```

In the last case, we can "extend" the search range. For example, to find companies with names starting with letters A to C, so BETWEEN does not include the endpoints.

```
SELECT CompanyName, ContactName
FROM Customers
WHERE CompanyName BETWEEN 'A' AND 'D'
```

Using the LIKE keyword, we can narrow our search by supplying more complex patterns for comparison. For example, to find all companies that include "bl" in their name, we use the following query:

```
SELECT CompanyName, ContactName
FROM Customers
WHERE CompanyName LIKE '%bl%'
```

The pattern "%bl%" indicates that we are looking for any number of symbols before and after the letters "bl" in the company name.

Using the IN operator, we can give a list of values that the field value should match. For example:

```
SELECT CompanyName, ContactName
FROM Customers
WHERE  CustomerID IN ('ALFKI', 'BERGS', 'VINET')
```

The AND, OR, and NOT Operators

We have already seen how we can use the AND operator for logical operation when we need to combine the two values. For example, the following query returns a list of customers that are located in the United States and have names that start with "S":

```
SELECT CompanyName, ContactName
FROM Customers
WHERE CompanyName LIKE 'S%' AND Country = 'USA'
```

The OR operator allows us to choose only one of the conditions listed, while the NOT operator is used to exclude an option from the resulting set. We can use the OR operator to find, for example, all customers that are located in California or whose names start with the "S" letter (but located anywhere in the world):

```
SELECT CompanyName, ContactName
FROM Customers
WHERE CompanyName LIKE 'S%' OR Region='CA'
```

In this case, we will receive all records where the CompanyName field meets the first condition, plus all records where the Region field meets the second one.

Now let's see an example for the NOT operator. To exclude customers from the resulting recordset, we can use the following query:

```
SELECT CompanyName, ContactName
FROM Customers
WHERE Country NOT IN ('USA', 'UK')
```

This gives us a list of customers located in all countries except the United States and United Kingdom.

The ORDER BY Clause

The optional ORDER BY clause can be used to sort the resulting data by one or more columns. To specify the sorting order—either ascending or descending—use the ASC or DESC keywords. The ascending order is the default. The syntax for the ORDER BY clause is:

```
ORDER BY column1 [{ASC | DESC}] [, column2 [{ASC | DESC}] [,…]
```

To order employees alphabetically by last and then by first name, we can use the following SQL statement:

```
SELECT LastName, FirstName, Title
FROM Employees
ORDER BY LastName, FirstName
```

If we need to specify the descending sort order, for example, to list products from the most expensive to the least expensive, we use the DESC keyword:

```
SELECT ProductName, UnitPrice
FROM Products
ORDER BY UnitPrice DESC
```

```
SELECT ProductName, UnitPrice
FROM Products
ORDER BY UnitPrice DESC
```

ProductName	UnitPrice
Cote de Blaye	263.5
Thuringer Rostbratwurst	123.79
Mishi Kobe Niku	97
Sir Rodney's Marmalade	81
Carnarvon Tigers	62.5
Raclette Courdavault	55
Manjimup Dried Apples	53
Tarte au sucre	49.3
Ipoh Coffee	46
Rossle Sauerkraut	45.6
Schoggi Schokolade	43.9
Vegie-spread	43.9
Northwoods Cranberry Sauce	40

Joining Tables

As we have already seen, we can create queries that extract data from multiple tables. One of the ways to do this is to join tables on one or more columns. Note that without joining the following query will produce the arithmetic product of two or more input tables (known as a Cartesian product):

```
SELECT ProductName, CategoryName
FROM Products, Categories
```

while the one shown below will give us the right result:

```
SELECT ProductName, CategoryName
FROM Products, Categories
WHERE Products.CategoryID = Categories.CategoryID
```

Compare the results of these two queries shown in the figures below.

The syntax for joining tables is:

```
SELECT column-list
FROM table1, table2
WHERE table1.column1=table2.column2
```

The following examples are specific for Microsoft Access and Microsoft SQL Server, and may not work in other database management systems. However, we think this functionality is essential.

There can be several types of joins. For example, the following SQL statement performs an inner join, which shows only the matching rows in both tables:

```
SELECT ProductName, CategoryName
FROM Products INNER JOIN Categories
ON Products.CategoryID = Categories.CategoryID
```

An outer join allows us to include all rows from one table while choosing only matching rows from the other table. For example:

```
SELECT ProductName, CategoryName
FROM Products LEFT OUTER JOIN Categories
ON Products.CategoryID = Categories.CategoryID
```

The above example is a left outer join. There can also be a right outer join, which returns all rows from the table on the right side of the join and matching rows from the other table:

```
SELECT ProductName, CategoryName
FROM Products RIGHT OUTER JOIN Categories
ON Products.CategoryID = Categories.CategoryID
```

When we combine the two outer joins, we create a full outer join that returns all data from both tables:

```
SELECT ProductName, CategoryName
FROM Products FULL OUTER JOIN Categories
ON Products.CategoryID = Categories.CategoryID
```

To get all combinations of rows from two tables (the Cartesian product) we can use the CROSS JOIN keyword without specifying the joining condition:

```
SELECT ProductName, CategoryName
FROM Products CROSS JOIN Categories
```

If there are more than two tables in the query, we can use nested joins.

The GROUP BY Clause

To create a resulting dataset that summarizes data in a table or set of tables, we use the GROUP BY clause. Here is the syntax for this clause:

```
GROUP BY {column1} [, …]
```

The following query joins two tables and then sorts them by CustomerID. For each CustomerID, it then creates a single row in the resulting dataset. Then it counts the number of OrderIDs for each CustomerID and shows this number:

```
SELECT Customers.CustomerID, COUNT (Orders.OrderID)
FROM Customers INNER JOIN Orders
ON Customers.CustomerID = Orders.CustomerID
GROUP BY Customers.CustomerID
```

In the previous query we used the aggregate function COUNT in the SELECT clause to number the values. Here is a list of common aggregate functions.

Function	Purpose
AVG	Returns a mean or average
COUNT	Counts the number of non-null values for a column
MAX	Returns the largest value in the column
MIN	Returns the smallest value in the column
SUM	Returns the sum of the values for a column
STDEV	Returns the sample standard deviation for the column. This function is specific to Microsoft Access and Microsoft SQL Server. In Oracle it is called STD.
STDEVP	Returns the population standard deviation for the column. This function is specific to Microsoft Access and Microsoft SQL Server.
VAR	Returns the sample variance for the column. This function is specific to Microsoft Access and Microsoft SQL Server. In Oracle it is called VARIANCE.
VARP	Returns the population variance for the column. This function is specific to Microsoft Access and Microsoft SQL Server.

In addition to the above listed aggregate functions we can use mathematical and character functions that are shown in the following tables.

Function	Purpose
ABS	Returns an absolute value; negative numbers are converted to positive and positive numbers are not changed
CEIL	Rounds up a decimal value
FLOOR	Rounds down a decimal value
GREATEST	Returns the largest of the two values. This function is specific to Microsoft Access and Microsoft SQL Server.
LEAST	Returns the smallest of the two values. This function is specific for Microsoft Access and Microsoft SQL Server.
MOD	Returns the remainder of value1 divided by value2
POWER	Returns value1 to the power of value2
ROUND	Rounds value1 to value2 decimal places
SIGN	Returns a minus if the value is less than zero; returns a plus otherwise
SQRT	Returns the square root of value

Function	Purpose
LEFT	Returns the specified number of the leftmost characters from the string. This function is specific to Microsoft Access and Microsoft SQL Server.
RIGHT	Returns the specified number of the rightmost characters from the string. This function is specific to Microsoft Access and Microsoft SQL Server.
UPPER	Converts the string to all uppercase letters
LOWER	Converts the string to all lowercase letters
INITCAP	Converts the string to initial caps
LENGTH	Returns the length of the string, that is, the number of characters in it
LPAD	Pads the string on the left with the specified character to make it specified characters long
RPAD	Pads the string on the right with the specified character to make it specified characters long
SUBSTR	Extracts letters from the string beginning at the specified position

The HAVING Clause

The HAVING clause has the same purpose as the WHERE clause, but it is used with aggregated data. For example:

```
SELECT Customers.CustomerID, COUNT (Orders.OrderID)
FROM Customers INNER JOIN Orders
ON Customers.CustomerID = Orders.CustomerID
GROUP BY Customers.CustomerID
HAVING COUNT(Orders.OrderID) >= 10
```

This query works like the previous one, but the resulting set includes only customers that have made ten or more orders.

The ALL and DISTINCT Keywords

So far we have seen how to extract all or specified columns from one or more tables. To control the duplicate records we can use the ALL or DISTINCT keywords with the

SELECT clause. The DISTINCT keyword specifies that we need only the unique names, while the ALL keyword returns all rows. For example, to extract the names of the countries we are dealing with, we can use the following query:

```
SELECT DISTINCT Country FROM Customers
```

Note that the ALL keyword is used by default. If we specify more than one column name along with the DISTINCT keyword, we will receive different rows in the resulting dataset, but some values in the same field of different rows could be identical.

```
SELECT DISTINCT Country, City FROM Customers
```

Note the following:

```
USA     Chicago
USA     Miami
USA     New York
...
UK      London
UK      Manchester
...
France    Paris
France    Lyon
...
```

The TOP Keyword

We can use the TOP keyword to return the top *n* rows or top *n* percent of rows from a table. For example, the following query returns the first 10 products in the table:

```
SELECT TOP 10 * FROM PRODUCTS
ORDER BY ProductName
```

This query returns the first quarter of the records in the table:

```
SELECT TOP 25 PERCENT * FROM PRODUCTS
ORDER BY ProductName
```

Data Modification Statements

So far we have learned the basic SQL statements used to query data. In addition, SQL can be used to update and delete records, copy records to other tables, and perform many other operations. Here we will take a look at the following statements: UPDATE, DELETE, and INSERT.

The UPDATE Statement

To change values in one or more columns in a table we use the UPDATE statement. The syntax for this statement is:

```
UPDATE table
SET column1 = expression1 [, column2 = expression2] [,…]
[WHERE criteria]
```

The expression in the SET clause can be a constant or the result of a calculation. For example, to increase the price of all products that cost less than $10, we can use the following query:

```
UPDATE Products
SET UnitPrice = UnitPrice * 1.1
WHERE UnitPrice < 10
```

The DELETE Statement

To delete rows from tables we use the DELETE statement. It has the following syntax:

```
DELETE
FROM table
[WHERE criteria]
```

Caution: The WHERE clause is optional, but if you don't include it, you will delete all of the records from the table.

To delete all discontinued items from the Products table, we can use the following query:

```
DELETE
FROM Products
WHERE Discontinued IS NULL
```

Note that it is a good idea to use the SELECT statement with the same syntax as the DELETE statement so you can look at the records you want to delete before actually deleting them. Here is the SELECT statement for the previous deletion query:

```
SELECT ProductName
FROM Products
WHERE Discontinued IS NULL
```

We can use more complex criteria in the WHERE clause to specify exactly which rows we intend to delete. For example, we can delete customers who have not placed orders since a specified date. First, we execute the following SELECT statement to find what we will delete:

```
SELECT CompanyName
FROM Customers
WHERE Customers.CustomerID NOT IN
  (SELECT CustomerID FROM Orders WHERE OrderDate > #01/01/96#)
```

Then we change the SELECT statement to the DELETE statement:

```
DELETE FROM Customers
WHERE Customers.CustomerID NOT IN
  (SELECT CustomerID FROM Orders WHERE OrderDate > #01/01/96#)
```

 Note: When using Date, Time, and DateTime fields in SQL statements, refer to your database server documentation for the correct syntax to specify the date and time values.

The INSERT Statement

To add new rows to a table, we use the INSERT statement. The syntax is:

```
INSERT [INTO] table
( [column_list]
  { VALUES ( { DEFAULT | NULL | expression }
} [, …]
)
```

To add new a customer to the Customers table, we can use the following statement:

```
INSERT INTO Customers
(CustomerID, CompanyName)
VALUES
('XYZFO', 'XYZ Deli')
```

Data Definition Statements

There are several SQL data definition statements that can be used to create, alter, and drop databases and objects within them. Here we will look at the following statements: CREATE TABLE, ALTER TABLE, and DROP.

The CREATE TABLE Statement

To create a new table we use the CREATE TABLE statement. It has the following syntax:

```
CREATE TABLE table
(  column1 type1 [(size1)][CONSTRAINT column-constraint1]
[, column2 type2 [(size2)][CONSTRAINT column-constraint2]
[, ...]]
[CONSTRAINT table-constraint1 [,table-constraint2 [, ...]]]);
```

You specify the name of the column, its data type (supported by the DBMS in use), an optional size parameter, and one of the two types of constraints (using a CONSTRAINT clause), either single-column index or table index. The following query creates a table named Simple with four columns—LastName, FirstName, Email, and HomePage:

```
CREATE TABLE Simple
(FirstName varchar(50) NOT NULL,
  LastName varchar(50) NOT NULL,
  EMail    varchar(50),
  HomePage varchar(255)
)
```

We can extend this table by adding the PersonID field, which will be used as the primary key:

```
CREATE TABLE Simple
( PersonID Integer NOT NULL PRIMARY KEY,
  FirstName varchar(50) NOT NULL,
  LastName  varchar(50) NOT NULL,
  EMail     varchar(50),
  HomePage  varchar(255)
)
```

Now we specify that the combination of the LastName and FirstName must be unique:

```
CREATE TABLE Simple
( PersonID Integer NOT NULL PRIMARY KEY,
  FirstName varchar(50) NOT NULL,
  LastName  varchar(50) NOT NULL,
  EMail     varchar(50),
  HomePage  varchar(255),
 CONSTRAINT SimpleConstraint UNIQUE
 (FirstName, LastName)
)
```

Using the SELECT statement and the keyword INTO we can create new tables based on criteria specified in the WHERE statement. For example:

```
SELECT *
INTO NewOrders
FROM Orders
WHERE OrderDate > #1/1/97#
```

This SQL query will create a table called NewOrders, which will contain order details for orders issued since January 1, 1997.

The ALTER TABLE Statement

To change the schema of an existing table, we can use the ALTER TABLE statement. By using this statement we can add a new column or delete a constraint. There are four forms of the ALTER TABLE statement.

The first form is used to add a column to a table:

```
ALTER TABLE table ADD [COLUMN] column datatype [(size)]
[CONSTRAINT single-column-constraint]
```

We specify the name of the table, the name of the new column, its data type, and its size, which can be omitted for some data types but is required for others. Additionally, we can specify an optional index for the column. For example, to add the column Phone to the Simple table created above, we can use the following statement:

```
ALTER TABLE Simple ADD Phone varchar(30)
```

The second form of the ALTER TABLE statement is used to add constraints to a table:

```
ALTER TABLE table ADD CONSTRAINT constraint
```

This allows us to create only indexes that are unique or serve as primary or foreign keys.

The third form of the ALTER TABLE statement is for removing a column from a table:

```
ALTER TABLE table DROP [COLUMN] column
```

The COLUMN keyword is optional. For example:

```
ALTER TABLE Simple DROP Phone
```

Note that to remove the indexed columns you must first remove its index. This can be done with the fourth form of the ALTER TABLE statement:

```
ALTER TABLE table DROP CONSTRAINT index
```

Here is an example for this statement:

```
ALTER TABLE Simple DROP CONSTRAINT PrimaryKey
```

The DROP Statement

To remove tables or indexes, we can use the DROP statement, which has two forms. The first form is used to remove a table from a database:

```
DROP TABLE table
```

The second form is used to remove an index:

```
DROP INDEX index ON table
```

Other SQL Statements

As we mentioned in the beginning of this chapter, there are approximately 40 SQL statements. We have covered a lot of them to help you become familiar with the language. Some of the statements that were not covered in this chapter are:

- CREATE statements such as CREATE DATABASE, CREATE VIEW, and CREATE TRIGGER. We will see the latter two in the next chapter.
- ALTER statements such as ALTER DATABASE, ALTER VIEW, and ALTER TRIGGER
- DROP statements such as DROP DATABASE, DROP VIEW, and DROP TRIGGER
- BEGIN TRANSACTION, COMMIT TRANSACTION, and ROLLBACK TRANSACTION, used to execute a group of multiple statements as a single logical entity
- DECLARE CURSOR, OPEN, and FETCH to work with cursors

- GRANT and REVOKE statements to add or remove permissions for database objects and CREATE USER, ALTER USER, DROP USER, CREATE GROUP, ALTER GROUP, and DROP GROUP to manage users and groups

Conclusion

In this chapter, we have covered the basic components of SQL. In particular, we have learned that:

- SQL is a nonprocedural language used to handle data in relational database systems. The most recent official standard for SQL was published by ANSI in 1992 and the current implementation of SQL is called SQL92. SQL is supported by many DBMS vendors.
- We can use the SELECT statement to query for information stored in tables. The WHERE clause can be used to restrict queries to specific records.
- The GROUP BY clause can be used to create a resulting dataset that summarizes data in a table or set of tables.
- To combine information that was extracted from multiple tables we can join them.
- To perform database modifications we use the INSERT, UPDATE, and DELETE statements.
- The CREATE, ALTER, and DROP statements can be used to create, modify, and delete databases and objects within them.

In the next chapter, we will discuss several other database objects, such as stored procedures, views, and triggers. We will see how to create and use them and how to manipulate them from our Delphi ADO programs.

WORKING WITH DATABASE OBJECTS

In the previous chapter, we saw how to use the structured query language to extract information from database tables, perform database modifications, and create, alter, and drop databases and objects within them. Here we will provide more details on several database objects that may be found in databases. The objects covered in this chapter are stored procedures, views, and triggers.

We mentioned in Chapter 1 that most server DBMSs support views, triggers, and stored procedures. Views are also supported in many desktop DBMSs, such as Access, dBase, and Clipper.

It should be mentioned that triggers and stored procedures must be created with procedural SQL extensions. These extensions must contain operators for describing algorithms, such as do...while, if...then...else, etc., that are nonexistent in SQL itself. Unlike SQL, these extensions are not standardized, and different DBMSs use different syntax for them. However, discussing differences in SQL extensions for different DBMSs are out of the scope of this book. To illustrate how we can use views, triggers, and stored procedures, we have chosen Microsoft SQL Server 7.0, as it is one of the more popular SQL servers accessible through OLE DB and ADO.

Please note that implementing these objects in your DBMS and storing them may differ from the examples shown in this chapter. Also, before trying to create these objects, ask your database administrator for appropriate permissions.

It should also be mentioned that some ODBC drivers do not support using stored procedures in client applications. In this case, you cannot use them through OLE DB providers for ODBC drivers, even if your DBMS itself supports them. However, they still can be called from triggers.

For the examples in this chapter, we will use the Northwind database located on the Microsoft SQL Server 7.0.

We will start with views, then discuss stored procedures, which we have already encountered in Chapters 5, 6, and 7, and will end this chapter with a general overview of triggers.

Views

Recall from Chapter 1 that a *view* is a virtual table, usually created as a subset of columns from one ore more tables. A view is only a description of the specific SELECT statement stored in the database; it does not contain any records itself. In most cases, views can be used as a security mechanism by granting permissions on a view but not on the tables that supply its data. Using this method, users will never have access to the individual tables.

Listed below are some characteristics of a view:

■ A view behaves like a table

■ A view does not store any data

■ A view may include more than one table

To create a view, we use the CREATE VIEW statement. The ALTER VIEW statement is used to modify a view, and the DROP VIEW statement is used to remove a view.

The CREATE VIEW Statement

The CREATE VIEW statement allows us to create a view for the current database. The syntax for the view resembles the SQL SELECT statement with some extra statements around it. Here is the simplified syntax:

```
CREATE VIEW view_name
[WITH ENCRYPTION]
AS
 select_statement
```

The view_name argument specifies the name of the view. The [WITH ENCRYPTION] keyword used in Microsoft SQL Server can help hide the source code of the CREATE VIEW statement in the syscomments table.

The AS keyword specifies the actions the view is to take. This SELECT statement defines the view. In it, we can use more than one table and other views. Note that the SELECT statement cannot include the ORDER BY, COMPUTE, or COMPUTE BY clauses or the INTO keyword, and cannot reference a temporary table.

The ALTER VIEW Statement

To change a previously created view, we can use the ALTER VIEW statement, which has the same syntax as the CREATE VIEW statement. Its main purpose is to make some modifications in an existing view. One situation in which we would need to change the view is when the permissions for the table are changed or need to be changed. In this case, we use the GRANT statement on the SELECT statement in the view.

The DROP VIEW Statement

We use the DROP VIEW statement to remove one or more views from the current database when we no longer need the view. Note that if we have dropped a table, we must explicitly drop all views on that table. When using this statement, we specify the name of the view (or views) to remove. After the view is removed, all information about it is deleted from system tables.

Another case in which we need to drop a view is when the structure of the underlying table (or tables) has been changed since the view was originally created. In this case, we drop the view and then re-create it with the CREATE VIEW statement.

Creating and Using Views

We use the CREATE VIEW statement to create a view that allows us to extract data that meets some criteria. A view is created in the current database and stored as a separate object in this database.

The best way to create a view is to create a SELECT statement first and then add the appropriate statements to it. Let's look at the view called Products by Category that is included in the Northwind database. Here is its source code:

```
CREATE VIEW "Products by Category" AS
 SELECT Categories.CategoryName, Products.ProductName,
  Products.QuantityPerUnit, Products.UnitsInStock,
  Products.Discontinued
FROM Categories INNER JOIN Products ON Categories.CategoryID =
  Products.CategoryID
WHERE Products.Discontinued <> 1
```

The first string is marked with the bold font; this shows the only difference between a view and an ordinal SELECT statement that does the real job. The SELECT statement specified in this view selects fields from two tables. From the Categories table CategoryName is selected, while the ProductName, QuantityPerUnit, UnitsInStock, and

Discontinued fields are selected from the Products table. Then the data in the two tables is joined by the CategoryID field and the only products that are still produced (see the criteria in the WHERE keyword) are included in the resulting recordset. Here is the result of executing this view:

Let's create a view that shows all territories in the eastern region. This view will be based on the following SQL query:

```
SELECT Territories.TerritoryDescription,
   Region.RegionDescription
 FROM Territories INNER JOIN
   Region ON Territories.RegionID = Region.RegionID
 WHERE Territories.RegionID = 1
```

After we have tested that this SELECT statement returns the results we are looking for, we add the CREATE VIEW statement to transform it into a view:

```
CREATE VIEW EastTerr AS
SELECT Territories.TerritoryDescription,
   Region.RegionDescription
FROM Territories INNER JOIN
   Region ON Territories.RegionID = Region.RegionID
WHERE Territories.RegionID = 1
```

Since this view returns a list of territories in the eastern region, we have given it the name EastTerr.

Instead of creating a view manually, we can use the tools that come with the database management systems. The figure below shows how the same view can be built visually with the help of tools that are part of the Microsoft SQL Server.

The upper part of the view designer allows us to specify the fields and joins between tables. The next part is used to set aliases, criteria, and output characteristics of the fields. Then comes the source code for the SELECT statement and the results of its execution.

To use views in Delphi we can use either the TADODataSet component or the TADOTable component. These were described earlier in the book, but here we will briefly refresh your memory.

To use a view with the TADODataSet component, we either set the CommandType property equal to cmdTable (as we recall, the view behaves like a table) and manually enter its name for the CommandText property, or use the CommandType property equal to cmdText and enter the following SQL statement for the CommandText property:

```
SELECT * FROM view_name
```

> **Note:** At the time of this writing, the TADODataSet component did not show the list of views for the CommandType property equal to cmdTable. This was fixed in the unofficial patch for the ADODB unit and hopefully will be included in the Delphi 5update.

Using the TADOTable component, we specify the name of the view in the TableName property. This can be done only manually; the TADOTable component does not show views in the drop-down list box for the TableName property. Nevertheless, this approach works fine. The following figure shows the "code-less" Delphi application that uses the EastTerr view.

Before we end our brief look at views, let's see how we can get more information about them. In Microsoft SQL Server 7.0, we can use the following system stored procedures:

- To get information on a view, use the sp_help system stored procedure. For example, sp_help EastTerr will return information about the view created earlier in this section.

- To retrieve source code of the view, use the system stored procedure called sp_helptext.

- To find the list of tables the view depends on, use the sp_depends system stored procedure.

- To rename a view, use the sp_rename system stored procedure.

In this section, we have seen how to use views to get information that satisfies some criteria. In the Northwind database, more than one region exists. To get a list of all of them we need to implement four different views—one for each region. This task can be simplified if we can pass RegionID as a parameter. This can be done with the help of stored procedure—the topic of the next section.

Stored Procedures

A *stored procedure* is a precompiled collection of SQL statements that are stored as a named unit in the database and executed as one piece of code. Stored procedures can take and return user-supplied parameters. When we define a stored procedure, SQL Server compiles it and stores it in a shared procedure cache. After that, multiple users can make use of the same precompiled code. When an application uses a procedure, it passes parameters, if there are any. SQL Server then executes the stored procedure without recompiling.

There are several performance gains when we use stored procedures. First, in comparison with ordinary SQL queries sent from a client application, they take less time to prepare for execution, since they are already precompiled and stored. Second, the network traffic is reduced because a smaller amount of data is transmitted and there is no extra disk activity with running the stored procedure; it is already in cache. The following diagram shows the client application invoking a stored procedure:

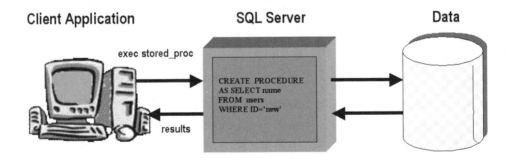

Stored procedures are automatically recompiled whenever changes are made to objects they affect; this ensures that they are always up to date. As we have already mentioned, stored procedures can accept parameters. This allows a single procedure to be used by multiple applications using different sets of input data.

Stored procedures are typically used to enforce data integrity and business rules. In the latter case, we gain additional flexibility since if the business rule changes, we only need to alter the code of the stored procedure without touching the client application itself.

There are data definition SQL statements to create, modify, and delete stored procedures—CREATE PROCEDURE, ALTER PROCEDURE and DROP PROCEDURE. We will look at them in the following next sections.

The CREATE PROCEDURE Statement

The CREATE PROCEDURE statement is used to create a stored procedure. This statement has the following simplified syntax:

```
CREATE PROC proc_name
[
  {@parameter data_type} [= default] [OUTPUT]
]
[...]
AS
  sql_statements
```

The proc_name argument sets the name of the new stored procedure. This name must be unique within the database. The @parameter argument specifies a parameter in the procedure. We can declare one or more parameters in the CREATE PROCEDURE statement. If there is no default value for the parameter, it must be supplied by the user when the procedure is called. There is a maximum of 1,024 parameters available for a stored procedure. By default, parameters are nullable.

The data_type argument specifies the data type of the parameter. All data types are supported. The default keyword can be used to set the default value for the parameter; it can be either a constant or NULL. If a default value is specified, the procedure can be called without specifying a value for that parameter. If the procedure uses this parameter with the LIKE keyword, its default value can contain wildcard characters (%, _, [], and [^]).

The OUTPUT keyword indicates that the parameter is a return parameter, which returns information to the caller.

The AS keyword specifies the actions the procedure is to take in the form of any number of SQL statements.

A stored procedure created with the CREATE PROCEDURE statement will be stored in the current database. In the Microsoft SQL server, its name is stored in the sysobjects system table, and the source code for it is stored in the syscomments table.

The ALTER PROCEDURE Statement

T he ALTER PROCEDURE statement is used to change an already existing stored procedure. This statement has the same syntax as the CREATE PROCEDURE statement. An example of when we need to change the stored procedure is to encrypt it after it was fine-tuned in order to hide its source code.

The DROP PROCEDURE Statement

This statement is used to remove one or more stored procedures from the current database when it is no longer needed. The DROP PROCEDURE statement takes one argument—the name of the stored procedure or stored procedures to be removed.

When a stored procedure is dropped, information about this procedure is removed from the sysobjects and syscomments system tables.

Creating and Using Stored Procedures

In the section about views, we mentioned that it would be nice to supply our view with a parameter that contains the RegionID to select one of the four regions available in the Northwind database. Let's look once again at the SELECT query that returns territories for some region. Here is the code for it:

```
SELECT Territories.TerritoryDescription,
   Region.RegionDescription
FROM Territories INNER JOIN
   Region ON Territories.RegionID = Region.RegionID
WHERE Territories.RegionID = 1
```

To be able to choose a different region, we need to change the criteria in the WHERE statement in the last line of the query. Thus, by using the variable (let's call it RegID) we can easily select one of the four regions available without affecting the other statements in this query.

There are four regions in the Northwind database numbered from 1 to 4. That means that the RegID variable should have an integer type. The code for the stored procedure is shown below:

```
CREATE PROCEDURE ShowRegion
 @RegID int
AS
SELECT Territories.TerritoryDescription,
   Region.RegionDescription
FROM Territories INNER JOIN
   Region ON Territories.RegionID = Region.RegionID
WHERE Territories.RegionID = @RegID
```

Note how we have left almost all the code of the SELECT query intact (it is shown in italics) and only attached the CREATE PROCEDURE statement with the name of our newly created stored procedure (the first line), the declaration of the parameter (the second line), and the AS keyword, which marks the start of the statements that perform this operation.

The figure below shows the result of executing this stored procedure in the SQL Server Query Analyzer for RegID equal to 2.

It should be clear that we can use stored procedures for more than implementing extended versions of views or "smart" SELECT statements. Stored procedures also provide very powerful mechanisms that allow us to automate many routine tasks.

In Delphi we can use the TADODataSet component or TADOStoredProc component to execute stored procedures. In the case of the TADODataSet component, we specify the value of the CommandType property as cmdStoredProc and select the name of the procedure in the CommandText list box. When we use the TADOStoredProc component, we set the name of the stored procedure to the value of the ProcedureName property.

In both cases, we supply parameters as the value of the Parameters property. This can be done either at design time or at run time. In the chapter about the TADOCommand component, we mentioned the CreateParameter method that can be used to create parameters at run time. Let's see an example of how to use it. Suppose we have a form that allows us to get a list of territories for each region. The code is based on our ShowRegion stored procedure created earlier in this section.

The first thing we need to do is create a parameter. This can be done in the OnCreate event handler for our form.

```
procedure TForm1.FormCreate(Sender: TObject);
begin
 With ADODataSet1 do
 begin
  Parameters.CreateParameter(
   'RegID', ftInteger, pdInput, 1, 0);
 end;
end;
```

Here we supply the following arguments to the CreateParameter method:

- The name of the parameter—RegID in our example
- Its data type—integer (ftInteger)
- Its type—input parameter here (pdInput)
- The size of the parameter (1)
- Its default value (0)

The specified parameter will be created and stored in the Parameters collection of the TADODataSet component.

Next, we need some way to set the value of the parameter of our stored procedure. This is done in the SetVal procedure, which takes one argument—the new value for the parameter:

```
procedure TForm1.SetVal(Value: Integer);
begin
 With ADODataSet1 do
 begin
  Close;
  Parameters[1].Value := Value;
  Active := True;
 end;
end;
```

Here we check if our TADODataSet component is active and make it inactive before changing the value of the parameter. Then we access the Parameters collection and set the new value of its second element (the first element of the Parameters collection always is the output value of the stored procedure).

Now we need some interface element in order to select one of the four regions of interest. Since regions must be exclusive, we use a group of four radio buttons. Each radio button has its Tag property equal to the number of the region it represents. This allows us to create a common OnClick event handler for all four radio buttons:

```
procedure TForm1.RadioClick(Sender: TObject);
begin
 SetVal((Sender as TRadioButton).Tag);
end;
```

The figure below shows our application in action:

In Microsoft SQL Server 7.0, we can also use the following system stored procedures to work with our stored procedures:

- sp_stored_procedures— shows a list of stored procedures

- sp_helptext—shows the source code for the stored procedure

- sp_depends—displays information about stored procedure dependencies

- sp_procoption—sets or shows procedure options
- sp_recompile—recompiles the stored procedure the next time it runs

■ sp_rename—changes the name of the stored procedure

System Stored Procedures

Since we are talking here about Microsoft SQL Server, it is worth mentioning the huge set of system stored procedures implemented within it. The names of system stored procedures are prefixed with SP_ and XP_ and they are stored in the master database. We have already described some of the commonly used system stored procedures earlier in this chapter.

To give you a taste of the available system stored procedures, here is a short list:

System Stored Procedure	Description
sp_configure	Used to display or change global configuration settings for the server
sp_databases	Used to obtain a list of databases that reside on the server or are accessible through it
sp_datatype_info	Used to get information about the supported data types
sp_help	Used to get general information about a database object
sp_helpdb	Used to get information about a specified database or all databases
sp_helpfile	Used to find the physical names and attributes of files associated with the current database.
sp_monitor	Outputs statistics about Microsoft SQL Server
xp_msver	Used to obtain server version information and related values

As we have already seen in Chapter 7, we can use system stored procedures in our Delphi ADO applications. We can either select a master database and then choose the name of the system stored procedure from the CommandText or ProcedureName list box, or enter its name manually.

The last topic we will cover in this chapter is a brief introduction to another commonly used database object called a trigger.

Triggers

In the first chapter, we briefly described triggers and how they are used in databases. Now here is a definition. A *trigger* is a special kind of stored procedure that automatically executes when data in a specified table is inserted, deleted, or updated through the INSERT, DELETE, or UPDATE SQL statements. Depending on which data modification statement invoked the trigger, it is called an *insert trigger*, *delete trigger*, or *update trigger*.

Note: Some databases support different triggers to be executed before and after inserting, deleting, and updating records. Also note that most DBMSs support creating several triggers for the same event. In this case, you may need to define an order in which they will be executed.

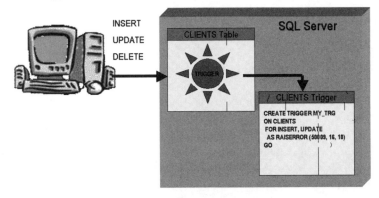

Triggers are often used to enforce referential integrity, perform cascading deletes (*cascading* is the process whereby changes to a parent are propagated to the child), archive deleted or changed data, keep track of table modifications, or call other user-defined and system stored procedures.

Since the trigger is invoked automatically by the DBMS itself (Microsoft SQL Server in our example), there is no way to call it from the client application.

Triggers can indirectly activate other triggers. If the currently invoked trigger contains the code to modify another table with its own trigger, the other trigger will be invoked. This trigger can invoke another trigger and so on. These are called nested triggers. Microsoft SQL Server supports up to 32 levels of nested triggers.

Like many other database objects, triggers are created with the CREATE statement. To change the trigger, we use the ALTER statement ,and to erase it, we use the DROP statement. In the following sections, we will briefly look at the basic syntax of these statements and then we will create a trigger that can be indirectly invoked from our Delphi ADO application and used to show some results.

The CREATE TRIGGER Statement

This statement creates a new trigger for a specified table for any INSERT, DELETE, or UPDATE statement. Here is the simplified syntax for this statement:

```
CREATE TRIGGER trigger_name
ON table_name
FOR {INSERT, UPDATE, DELETE}
    [WITH ENCRYPTION]
AS
    sql_statements
```

The `trigger_name` argument specifies the name of the trigger. This name must be unique within the database. The `table_name` argument is the table on which the trigger is executed. Only "real" tables should be used, i.e., you cannot specify the name of the view here.

The {INSERT, UPDATE, DELETE} keywords specify which data modification statements activate the trigger. At least one of the keywords must be specified.

The optional [WITH ENCRYPTION] keyword can be used to hide the source code for the CREATE TRIGGER statement; it will not be visible in the syscomments table.

The AS keyword specifies a list of SQL statements that define the actions the trigger is to take. Here we can use any SQL statements except these listed below:

ALTER DATABASE	ALTER PROCEDURE	ALTER TABLE
ALTER TRIGGER	ALTER VIEW	CREATE DATABASE
CREATE DEFAULT	CREATE INDEX	CREATE PROCEDURE
CREATE RULE	CREATE SCHEMA	CREATE TABLE
CREATE TRIGGER	CREATE VIEW	DENY
DISK INIT	DISK RESIZE	DROP DATABASE
DROP DEFAULT	DROP INDEX	DROP PROCEDURE
DROP RULE	DROP TABLE	DROP TRIGGER
DROP VIEW	GRANT	LOAD DATABASE
LOAD LOG	RESTORE DATABASE	RESTORE LOG
REVOKE	RECONFIGURE	
TRUNCATE TABLE	UPDATE STATISTICS	

Note that triggers should not return data to the user. There must be only one trigger for each INSERT, DELETE, or UPDATE event, but one trigger can handle one or more of these events.

In CREATE TRIGGER statements, it is possible to use two special tables. The deleted and inserted tables have the same structure as the table on which the trigger is defined and contain the old and new values of the rows changed by the user action. For example, we can use the following SQL statement to find out which records have been deleted:

```
SELECT * FROM deleted
```

The following table shows the contents of the deleted and inserted tables for each possible modification action.

Action	Contents of the Inserted Table	Contents of the Deleted Table
INSERT	Inserted rows	-
DELETE	-	Deleted rows
UPDATE	New valued for modified rows	Old values for modified rows

The ALTER TRIGGER Statement

This statement has the same syntax as the CREATE TRIGGER statement discussed above. It is used to change the contents of the existing trigger. For example, if we have decided that some trigger, defined for all three actions, should not be invoked when the rows are deleted, we should use the same statement as we have used to create this trigger but remove the UPDATE keyword from the FOR keyword.

The DROP TRIGGER Statement

This statement deletes one or more triggers from the database. When using this statement, we specify the name of the trigger (or triggers) to remove. Note that the trigger will be removed when the table it was created for is dropped.

Creating and Using Triggers

There are many examples of various triggers that enforce referential integrity, perform cascading deletes, and accomplish other tasks. For purposes of this chapter, we will create a trigger that will be used to keep track of table modifications. Let's say we have a group of managers in which every manager can insert, delete, and alter data about the customers. To be able to keep track of these changes, the senior manager need some mechanism to do so. One of the ways to implement such a mechanism is to create a trigger.

First, we need to add two new fields that will store the information. We will call them UpdatedBy (here we will store the name of the manager who updated the record) and UpdatedWhen (to store the date when the record was updated). Then we will create the trigger that will be called KeepTrack. Here is the SQL code for this trigger:

```
CREATE TRIGGER KeepTrack ON Customers
FOR INSERT, UPDATE
AS
UPDATE Customers
SET Customers.UpdatedBy   = USER_NAME(),
    Customers.UpdatedWhen = GETDATE()
FROM inserted, Customers
WHERE inserted.CustomerID = Customers.CustomerID
```

As we can see from the source code, this trigger will be fired on every INSERT and UPDATE operation performed on the Customers table. This trigger will save the name of the manager (user) in the Customers.UpdatedBy field and the current date and time in the Customers.UpdatedWhen. The information will be extracted from the temporary table called Inserted.

Now we can create a Delphi application that will show us who made modifications to the records of the Customers table and when they were made. Here is an illustration of this demo application:

As we can see from the figure above, the trigger created earlier in this chapter allows us to keep track of modifications and insertions in the table.

Using triggers, we can create powerful applications in which the trigger code is implemented on the server and the Delphi ADO application provides the mechanisms of firing it.

Information about triggers can be found in the system tables. The **sysobjects** table stores information about the trigger itself and its type, while the **syscomments** table contains the trigger's source code.

Conclusion

In this chapter, we have looked at several database objects—stored procedures, views, and triggers. We have learned that:

- A view is a virtual table, usually created as a subset of columns from one or more tables. We use the CREATE VIEW statement to create a view, the ALTER VIEW statement to modify it, and the DROP VIEW statement to remove it. To use views in Delphi, we can use either the TADODataSet component or the TADOTable component.

- A stored procedure is a precompiled collection of SQL statements that are stored as a named unit in the database and executed as one piece of code. There are data definition SQL statements to work with stored procedures—CREATE PROCEDURE to create a procedure, ALTER PROCEDURE to modify it, and DROP PROCEDURE to remove it. In Delphi, we can use the TADODataSet component or the TADOStoredProc component to execute stored procedures. We can also use the system stored procedures in Delphi ADO applications.

- A trigger is a special kind of stored procedure that automatically executes when data in a specified table is inserted, deleted, or updated through the INSERT, DELETE, or UPDATE SQL statements. Triggers are created with the CREATE

TRIGGER statement, modified with the ALTER TRIGGER statement, and deleted with the DROP TRIGGER statement.

Now we have enough information to be able to create a complex Delphi ADO application. We will start to do this in the next chapter, and will continue to extend its features in Chapters 12 and 13.

BUILDING DATABASE
APPLICATIONS

In this chapter, we will discuss several topics related to the creation of Delphi database applications using ADO data sources. We will start with the TDataSource component and Delphi data-aware controls, which can be used to show, edit, and navigate data, and we will show how to use and customize grids, how to use components for editing a single field, and how to select which component is better to use to represent a particular field.

Then we will discuss how the descendants of the TField object are used in applications, and show how to create calculated and lookup fields using these objects. After that we will show how to create and use nested datasets using Microsoft Data Shaping and the TDataSetField object.

Then we will spend some time discussing data validation techniques and database error trapping in Delphi applications. And at the end of this chapter we will discuss how to edit and use data modules.

Using Data-Aware Controls

Back in Chapter 4, we briefly mentioned a set of Delphi data-aware components that can be used to show, edit, and navigate data. These components are available on the Data Controls page of the Component Palette and can be used in Delphi ADO applications. Here we will look at these components in more detail. The list of components we will discuss here is shown in the following table.

Component	Purpose
TDBCheckBox	Used to represent values that can be selected or deselected
TDBComboBox	Used to represent values in the combo box
TDBCtrlGrid	Used as a placeholder for other data-aware components
TDBEdit	Used to represent text values with read/write permissions
TDBGrid	Used to show the contents of the database in the grid format
TDBListBox	Used to represent values in the list box
TDBLookupComboBox	Used to select values from another dataset
TDBLookupListBox	Used to select values from another dataset
TDBMemo	Used to represent multiline text fields
TDBNavigator	Used to navigate through the dataset
TDBRadioGroup	Used to represent a group of values
TDBRichEdit	Used to represent multiline text fields with text formatting commands
TDBText	Used to represent text values with read-only permissions

Note: The TDBChart component will be described in the next chapter.

Delphi data-aware components can be divided into two groups. The first one, called "multi-field" components, consists of the TDBGrid component and the TDBCtrlGrid component. These components can show data from several database fields and records at a time.

Other Delphi data-aware components are "single-field" components. That means that these components, such as the TDBEdit or TDBMemo component, can show data from only one database field at a time.

Among Delphi data-aware components, there is also a component that does not belong to either of these two groups because it does not show any data. It is called TDBNavigator, and is used to navigate through the dataset.

We will start with the multi-field components—TDBGrid and TDBCtrlGrid—then describe the TDBNavigator component, and provide you with the details of how to use the single-field components. Before we jump into the discussion of data-aware components, we need to understand the role of the TDataSource component.

The Role of the TDataSource Component

As we already mentioned in Chapter 4, the TDataSource component serves as a "universal glue" used to create a "bridge" between the data-aware components and the TDataSet-based components, which, in the case of ADO, are the TADODataSet, TADOQuery, TADOStoredProc, and TADOTable components.

In most database applications, the TDataSource component usually is connected to one of the TDataSet-based components, like TADOTable or TADOQuery, and with one or more data-aware controls—TDBGrid, TDBEdit, and so on. The link between the

TDataSet-based components and data-aware controls is done using the following properties and events:

- The DataSet property of the TDataSource component identifies the name of the TDataSet-based component. This can be done either at design time (using the Object Inspector to select one of the available datasets) or at run time.

- The Enabled property of the TDataSource component activates or deactivates the link between the TDataSet-based components and data-aware controls. If the value of this property is `True`, which is the default value, then the data-aware controls display the data. Using this property with the `False` value allows us to temporarily disconnect data-aware controls from the dataset. This can be useful, for example, to prevent the blinking of controls during search operations on a huge set of data.

- The AutoEdit property of the TDataSource component sets the editing functions of the data-aware control. When the value of this property is `True` (the default value), the Edit method of the TDataSet-based component is called automatically when the user tries to modify the contents of a data-aware control. When the value of this property is `False`, we should explicitly call the Edit method to perform the data modifications. This can be done by pressing the Edit button of the TDBNavigator component.

- The OnDataChange event (of the `TDataChangeEvent` type) occurs when a field in the current record has been changed and the application moves to another field or record, using, for example, the Next or Prior method of the TDataSet-based component. The event handler for this event receives two arguments. The first one (of the `TObject` type) indicates the source of the event, while the second argument specifies the field (of the `TField` type) that has been changed. The value of the Field argument may be `nil` when more than one of the fields has been changed at once. This may occur when we move from one record to another.

- The OnUpdateData event occurs when the user attempts to change the data in the current record. In the handler of this event (which is of the `TNotifyEvent` type), we can perform some data validation before its real posting.

- The OnStateChange event occurs when the value of the State property of the TDataSet-based component, which is connected to the TDataSource component, changes.

To find the current state of the associated TDataSet-based component, we can use the State property. The TDataSet-based component can be in one or more of the states, described by the `TDataSetState` type, which consist of the following values:

Value	Meaning
dsInactive	The dataset is inactive, i.e., closed. Its data is not available.
dsBrowse	The data can be browsed, but not edited. This state is the default state for the open dataset.
dsEdit	The data in the current record is being edited.

Value	Meaning
dsInsert	The current record is being inserted. The data can be edited, and then the record can be posted or discarded.
dsSetKey	Only TTable, TADOTable, and the TClientDataSet components can be in this state. It means that a search operation is currently in progress, and data cannot be inserted or modified.
dsCalcFields	Indicates the OnCalcFields event is in progress.
dsFilter	Indicates the OnFilterRecord event is in progress.
dsNewValue	The NewValue property of a field is being accessed. This is an internal state.
dsOldValue	The OldValue property of a field is being accessed. This is an internal state.
dsCurValue	The CurValue property of a field is being accessed. This is an internal state.
dsBlockRead	Calls to the Next method will not update the data-aware controls.
dsOpening	The dataset in now in the process of opening.

When the state of the associated TDataSet-based component changes, the OnStateChange notification event occurs. In the handler for this event, we can perform various actions depending on the current state of the component. For example, at some stages of the TDataSet-based component's lifetime some user functions associated with menu items or buttons can be disabled or enabled.

The following example shows how to create an event handler for the OnStateChange notification event, in which we show the current state in the Edit component:

```
procedure TForm1.DataSource1StateChange(Sender: TObject);
var
 S : String;
begin
 With Sender as TDataSource do
  begin
// Clear the edit box
   Edit1.Text := '';
// Determine the current state
   Case State of
     dsInactive    : S := 'Inactive';
     dsBrowse      : S := 'Browse';
     dsEdit        : S := 'Edit';
     dsInsert      : S := 'Insert';
     dsSetKey      : S := 'SetKey';
     dsCalcFields  : S := 'CalcFields';
     dsFilter      : S := 'Filter';
     dsNewValue    : S := 'NewValue';
     dsOldValue    : S := 'OldValue';
     dsCurValue    : S := 'CurValue';
     dsBlockRead   : S := 'BlockRead';
     dsInternalCalc : S := 'InternalCalc';
     dsOpening     : S := 'Opening';
   end;
```

```
// and show it
   Edit1.Text := S;
  end;
end;
```

Now that we understand the role the TDataSource component plays in Delphi ADO applications, let's outline the main properties of all data-aware controls available in Delphi's Visual Component Library.

Main Properties of Data-Aware Controls

There are three main properties that are essential for using data-aware controls in Delphi applications. The DataSource property is used to specify the source of data for the control. It is of the `TDataSource` type, and we must use the TDataSource-based component as its possible value. At design time, we simply choose an appropriate data source from a list box, while at run time, we assign the value of the DataSource property to one of the data sources currently available.

While the DataSource property specifies the source of data, the DataField property (which exists only for single-field components) is used to specify the field whose value will be displayed in the control. Once again, at design time, we choose one of the fields from the list box, while at run time, we supply a string with the name of the field.

The last property we will discuss here is the Field property. This property, as well as the previous one, exists only in single-field components since the multi-field components use more than one field. The Field property is of the `TField` type, and it provides access to the database field whose contents are shown in the control.

The Field property allows us to set some properties that are not available in the data-aware component itself. For example, we can specify the alignment of the field's data within the data-aware control, the input mask, and several other characteristics. To do this programmatically, we simply refer to the Field property and use its properties. TField objects will be discussed later in this chapter.

Now we can start a detailed discussion of the data-aware controls available in Delphi. The first one we will look at is the TDBGrid component.

Using the TDBGrid Component

We can use the TDBGrid component to represent data in a tabular grid that looks like a spreadsheet. This component allows us to browse and edit data, as well as customize its output. Each cell in the TDBGrid component is tied to the appropriate TField object, and by using this object, we can specify the columns' visibility, display format, ordering, and other properties.

In its simplest form, the TDBGrid component outputs as much data as fits in it, allowing us to scroll both horizontally and vertically to view more data. Note that this component is the best way to get a quick overview of the contents of the dataset attached to it at design time.

Let's look at how we can use its properties, methods, and events to perform some actions. The main property of the TDBGrid component is the Options property, which allows us to fine-tune it. This property is a set of the TDBGrid options that represents the following features of the TDBGrid component:

Option	Description
dgEditing	Indicates whether the editing functions are supported. This is ignored if the dgRowSelect option is set.
dgAlwaysShowEditor	Indicates whether the editing functions are always enabled. Used with the dgEditing option.
dgTitles	Indicates whether the column titles are shown.
dgIndicator	Indicates whether the indicator is shown near the first column. The indicator is used to mark the current row.
dgColumnResize	Specifies whether columns can be resized and moved.
dgColLines	If set, the lines between columns will be shown.
dgRowLines	If set, the lines between rows will be shown.
dgTabs	Indicates whether the Tab and Shift+Tab keys can be used to navigate through the grid.
dgRowSelect	Specifies whether the user can select an entire row.
dgAlwaysShowSelection	If set, the focus rectangle will be shown for the selected cell.
dgConfirmDelete	If set, the confirmation dialog box appears before the row is deleted.
dgCancelOnExit	Indicates whether the newly inserted but not modified record will be ignored upon exiting.
dgMultiSelect	Allows the selecting of more than one row at a time.

The TDBGrid component has a lot of methods that are primarily used to perform some custom functions, depending on the user functions. Discussion of these methods can take an entire chapter itself and is left for our readers to investigate.

Now we will show you two examples of TDBGrid manipulation. The first one will allow us to dynamically set the new alignment for all cells. To do so, we will place a group of radio buttons—one for left-justified text, one for centered text, and one for right-justified text. The Tag property of each radio button corresponds to an appropriate value of the TAlignment type. To change the alignment of all the columns, we need to set the Alignment property of the underlying TField object. The following code shows how to do this:

```
procedure TForm1.RadioButton1Click(Sender: TObject);
var
 I : Integer;
begin
 With DBGrid1 do
  begin
// Set the alignment of all cells
```

```
    For I := 0 to FieldCount-1 do
      Fields[I].Alignment :=
// according to one of the selected radio-buttons
        TAlignment((Sender as TRadioButton).Tag);
    end;
end;
```

In the following example, we will implement data sorting in the grid by clicking the column name. When we click the title of the column, the OnTitleClick event occurs, and we can use its event handler to perform the sorting. This is done by specifying the new value of the Sort property in the underlying dataset component. In the following example, we use the TADOTable component attached to the TDBGrid component:

```
procedure TForm1.DBGrid1TitleClick(Column: TColumn);
begin
 ADOTable1.Sort := Column.FieldName;
end;
```

Grids and Columns

Each column in the TDBGrid component is represented by the TColumn object, which is stored in the TDBGridColumns collection and is accessible through the Columns property. There are several methods of this collection that are of particular interest:

- The SaveToFile and LoadFromFile methods can be used to save the column headings, properties, and the names of the associated fields (not the data as the documentation suggests!) into a file and retrieve it from the file later.

- The SaveToStream and LoadFromStream methods work the same way with streams.

- The RestoreDefaults method removes custom changes made to the columns of the grid and sets its properties to default values

- The RebuildColumns method deletes all existing columns and creates a new set of columns from the underlying dataset.

As we have said earlier, the TColumn object represents one column in a TDBGrid and is accessible through the TDBGridColumns collection. We can use this object to check and change the visual characteristics and data binding for a particular column. Beside the visual characteristics of the column, we can specify the alignment of the text in the column (the Alignment property), the style of the button available in the column (the ButtonStyle property), and the column's background color, font, title, and width. Through the Title property, we can set the alignment, caption, color, and font for the column's title.

The major data binding properties are the Field and FieldName properties that tie this column to the field in the record. To find the grid where the column resides, we can use the Grid property, and if this column has a parent column (in the case of nested datasets, which will be discussed later in this chapter), it will be available through the ParentColumn property. If there is a drop-down list or lookup field associated with the column, its number of rows can be specified in the DropDownRows property. The pick list associated with the column is specified through the PickList property.

We create a pick list simply by supplying the strings for the PickList property of the column in the Object Inspector. At run time, we may load this list from a file and assign it to the same property of the particular column. For example:

```
DBGrid1.Columns[1].PickList.LoadFromFile(
  'c:\data\prodlist.txt'
);
```

In both cases, after we have defined the contents of the list, it is available for our users to select values from.

To create a lookup list (a list of possible values for this field to select from), we simply associate a lookup field with the column. Later in this chapter, we will see how to create lookup fields; see the "Using the TField Objects" section below.

As we have said above, there can be a button associated with the column. To do so, we need to specify its type, which must be auto (the ButtonStyle property set to cbsAuto) for pick lists and lookup fields. There also can be an ellipsis button (the ButtonStyle property set to cbsEllipsis) or no button at all (ButtonStyle property set to cbsNone).

When the user presses the ellipsis button, our application receives the OnEditButtonClick notification event. In the handler for this event, we can perform any imaginable task. For example, we can provide the user with a custom list of data for the selected field. After a selection is made, we can set the field data to the selected value. This can be done by accessing the appropriate TField object through the SelectedField property of the TDBGrid component.

Custom Drawing in the TDBGrid Component

In some cases, we may need some attention from the users of our application. This can be attained in different ways. For example, we can create some visual effects on rows or cells in the grid. To do so, we need to create an event handler for the OnDrawColumnCell event that occurs when the grid's cell needs to be painted. As we will see later in this section, by accessing the underlying canvas, we can draw nearly anything either in one of the cells or in the whole row.

The event handler for the OnDrawColumnCell event receives a set of arguments shown in the following table:

Argument	Type	Meaning
Sender	TObject	Indicates the object that fired this event. In our case, this is the instance of the TDBGrid component.
Rect	TRect	Indicates the location of the cell in canvas.
DataCol	Integer	Contains the index of the column in the Columns array.
Column	TColumn	The column to be painted.
State	TGridDrawState	Indicates the state of the column. Can be gdSelected (the cell is currently selected), gdFocused (the cell has input focus), or gdFixed (the cell is the non-data cell like column header).

Since one of the ancestors of the TDBGrid component is the TCustomControl class (which is the base class for all windowed controls that support custom drawing), we can access its Canvas property to draw anything we want on its surface. To do so, we will use the Delphi methods that are equivalent to the standard Windows API functions. For more information, we suggest reading *The Tomes of Delphi 3: Win32 Graphical API* (Wordware Publishing). It contains in-depth coverage of the Windows API with many examples in Object Pascal.

Now we will create several examples of custom drawing in rows and cells of the TDBGrid component. We will start with a situation in which we need to change the foreground and background colors of some rows in the TDBGrid component, for example, to highlight it. We can use the following code to do this:

```
procedure TForm1.DBGrid1DrawColumnCell(Sender: TObject; const Rect: TRect;
  DataCol: Integer; Column: TColumn; State: TGridDrawState);
begin
// If Country = USA
 If ADOTable1.FieldByName('Country').Value = 'USA' then
 begin
// Set the gray background
  DBGrid1.Canvas.Brush.Color := clGray;
// and white letters
```

```
  DBGrid1.Canvas.Font.Color  := clWhite;
// draw background
  DBGrid1.Canvas.FillRect(Rect);
// and text
  DBGrid1.Canvas.TextOut(
    Rect.Left+2, Rect.Top+2, Column.Field.Text);
  end;
end;
```

Note that this code works fine only for cells with the default text alignment. If we change the alignment from left-justified to centered or right-justified, our highlighted rows will be shown left-justified because we start to output the contents of the cell two pixels above and to the left of it; see the arguments for the TextOut method in the code. This is shown on the figure below.

To solve this problem, we need to create extra code to find the current alignment and to draw the contents of the cell according to it. Here is the improved code that works with the three possible types of text alignment (the new lines are shown in **bold**):

```
procedure TForm1.DBGrid1DrawColumnCell(Sender: TObject; const Rect: TRect;
  DataCol: Integer; Column: TColumn; State: TGridDrawState);
var
 TextWidth : Integer;
 Middle    : Integer;
 Text      : String;
begin
// If Country = USA
 If ADOTable1.FieldByName('Country').Value = 'USA' then
 begin
  Text := Column.Field.Text;
```

```
  TextWidth := DBGrid1.Canvas.TextWidth(Text);
// Set the gray background
  DBGrid1.Canvas.Brush.Color := clGray;
// and white letters
  DBGrid1.Canvas.Font.Color  := clWhite;
// draw background
  DBGrid1.Canvas.FillRect(Rect);
// and text accoringly to the current justification
  case Column.Alignment of
// Text is left-justified
  taLeftJustify  : DBGrid1.Canvas.TextOut(
    Rect.Left+2, Rect.Top+2, Text);
// Text is right-justified
  taRightJustify : DBGrid1.Canvas.TextOut(
    Rect.Right-2-TextWidth, Rect.Top+2, Text);
// Text is centered
  taCenter       : begin
                     Middle := (Rect.Right-Rect.Left) DIV 2;
                     Middle := Middle + Rect.Left;
                     DBGrid1.Canvas.TextOut(
                       Middle-(TextWidth DIV 2)-2, Rect.Top+2,
                       Text);
                   end;
  end;
 end;
end;
```

SupplierID	CompanyName	ContactName	ContactTitle
1	Exotic Liquids	Charlotte Cooper	Purchasin
2	New Orleans Cajun Delights	Shelley Burke	Order Adr
3	Grandma Kelly's Homestead	Regina Murphy	Sales Rep
4	Tokyo Traders	Yoshi Nagase	Marketing
5	Cooperativa de Quesos 'Las Cabras'	Antonio del Valle Saavedra	Export Adr
6	Mayumi's	Mayumi Ohno	Marketing
7	Pavlova, Ltd.	Ian Devling	Marketing
8	Specialty Biscuits, Ltd.	Peter Wilson	Sales Rep
9	PB Knackebrod AB	Lars Peterson	Sales Age
10	Refrescos Americanas LTDA	Carlos Diaz	Marketing
11	Heli Su?waren GmbH & Co. KG	Petra Winkler	Sales Mar
12	Plutzer Lebensmittelgro?markte AG	Martin Bein	Internation
13	Nord-Ost-Fisch Handelsgesellschaft mbH	Sven Petersen	Coordinat
14	Formaggi Fortini s.r.l.	Elio Rossi	Sales Rep
15	Norske Meierier	Beate Vileid	Marketing
16	Bigfoot Breweries	Cheryl Saylor	Regional
17	Svensk Sjofoda AB	Michael Bjorn	Sales Rep
18	Aux joyeux ecclesiastiques	Guylene Nodier	Sales Mar

Custom Grid Demo

Note: In the examples above, we have not considered the size and name of the font. In real applications, you must consider extending the code for various possible font/size combinations to be sure it will work fine on all computers.

If we need to change the appearance of a particular cell in the grid, we can use the same event handler with slightly modified criteria in the If statement (shown in **bold** in the example below):

```
procedure TForm1.DBGrid1DrawColumnCell(Sender: TObject; const Rect: TRect;
  DataCol: Integer; Column: TColumn; State: TGridDrawState);
var
 Text : String;
begin
 If ((ADOTable1.FieldByName('Country').Value = 'USA')
 AND (Column.FieldName = 'SupplierID')) Then
 begin
  Text := Column.Field.Text;
  DBGrid1.Canvas.Brush.Color := clGray;
  DBGrid1.Canvas.Font.Color  := clWhite;
  DBGrid1.Canvas.FillRect(Rect);
  DBGrid1.Canvas.TextOut(
   Rect.Left+2, Rect.Top+2, Text);
 end;
end;
```

Custom Grid Demo

SupplierID	CompanyName	ContactName	ContactTi
1	Exotic Liquids	Charlotte Cooper	Purchasin
2	New Orleans Cajun Delights	Shelley Burke	Order Adn
3	Grandma Kelly's Homestead	Regina Murphy	Sales Rep
4	Tokyo Traders	Yoshi Nagase	Marketing
5	Cooperativa de Quesos 'Las Cabras'	Antonio del Valle Saavedra	Export Adi
6	Mayumi's	Mayumi Ohno	Marketing
7	Pavlova, Ltd.	Ian Devling	Marketing
8	Specialty Biscuits, Ltd.	Peter Wilson	Sales Rep
9	PB Knackebrod AB	Lars Peterson	Sales Age
10	Refrescos Americanas LTDA	Carlos Diaz	Marketing
11	Heli Su?waren GmbH & Co. KG	Petra Winkler	Sales Mar
12	Plutzer Lebensmittelgro?markte AG	Martin Bein	Internation
13	Nord-Ost-Fisch Handelsgesellschaft mbH	Sven Petersen	Coordinat
14	Formaggi Fortini s.r.l.	Elio Rossi	Sales Rep
15	Norske Meierier	Beate Vileid	Marketing
16	Bigfoot Breweries	Cheryl Saylor	Regional
17	Svensk Sjofoda AB	Michael Bjorn	Sales Rep
18	Aux joyeux ecclesiastiques	Guylene Nodier	Sales Mar

Sometimes we may need to alter the value of the field to be shown in the column. This can be done by using the TextOut method of the TDBGrid component's Canvas property. In the previous examples, we extracted the text of the cell into the Text variable. We can use this variable to change the current text of the cell without changing the real value of the underlying field. The following example shows how to do this:

```
procedure TForm1.DBGrid1DrawColumnCell(Sender: TObject; const
  Rect: TRect; DataCol: Integer; Column: TColumn; State:
  TGridDrawState);
var
 Text : String;
begin
// For only one column
 If Column.FieldName = 'SupplierID' Then
 begin
```

```
// Is States
 If ADOTable1.FieldByName('Country').Value = 'USA'
  Then Text := 'In the USA'
// If somewhere else
 Else
  Text := 'Anywhere';

// Show the text we have selected

  DBGrid1.Canvas.Brush.Color := clGray;
  DBGrid1.Canvas.Font.Color  := clWhite;
  DBGrid1.Canvas.FillRect(Rect);
  DBGrid1.Canvas.TextOut(
   Rect.Left+2, Rect.Top+2, Text);
  end;
end;
```

Instead of the text in the above example, we can use some special symbols such as the symbols from the Webdings font to mark the cells. The following example shows how to do this:

```
procedure TForm1.DBGrid1DrawColumnCell(Sender: TObject; const Rect: TRect;
  DataCol: Integer; Column: TColumn; State: TGridDrawState);
var
 Text : String;
begin
 If Column.FieldName = 'SupplierID' Then
 begin
 If ADOTable1.FieldByName('Country').Value = 'USA'
// Select the character to represent the States
  Then Text := Chr(254)
 Else
```

```
// Select the character to represent the rest of the world
  Text := Chr(251);

// Choose font, size and draw the character
  DBGrid1.Canvas.Font.Name  := 'Webdings';
  DBGrid1.Canvas.Font.Size  := -12;
  DBGrid1.Canvas.FillRect(Rect);
  DBGrid1.Canvas.TextOut(
    Rect.Left+2, Rect.Top, Text);
  end;
end;
```

In the example above, we use the 🌐 symbol to indicate the supplier in the United States and the 🗺 symbol to indicate the customer anywhere in the world.

Now we will show a final example of how we can use the custom draw features in the TDBGrid component. This time we will use small icons in one of the cells. To do so, we need to add the TImageList component into our project, and add at least two images to it. The image with index 0 will indicate the supplier is in the United States, while the image with index 1 will indicate the supplier is located anywhere else in the world. Here is the code that demonstrates this technique:

```
procedure TForm1.DBGrid1DrawColumnCell(Sender: TObject; const Rect: TRect;
  DataCol: Integer; Column: TColumn; State: TGridDrawState);
var
 Image  : TBitmap;
 Middle : Integer;
begin
// Create new empty bitmap
```

```
try
  Image := TBitmap.Create;
  If Column.FieldName = 'SupplierID' Then
  begin
  If ADOTable1.FieldByName('Country').Value = 'USA'
// Get image for US
    Then ImageList1.GetBitmap(1, Image)
  Else
// Or the image for the rest of the world
    ImageList1.GetBitmap(0, Image);

// And draw it in the cell
    DBGrid1.Canvas.Brush.Color := clWhite;
    DBGrid1.Canvas.FillRect(Rect);
    Middle := (Rect.Bottom-Rect.Top) DIV 2;
    Middle := Middle + Rect.Top;
    DBGrid1.Canvas.Draw((Rect.Left+Rect.Right-Image.Width) DIV 2,
      Middle-(Image.Height DIV 2)+2, Image);
    end;
// Destroy image
  finally
    Image.Free;
  end;
end;
```

	SupplierID	CompanyName	ContactName	ContactTit
	♀	Exotic Liquids	Charlotte Cooper	Purchasin
	⚙	New Orleans Cajun Delights	Shelley Burke	Order Adm
	⚙	Grandma Kelly's Homestead	Regina Murphy	Sales Rep
▶	♀	Tokyo Traders	Yoshi Nagase	Marketing
	♀	Cooperativa de Quesos 'Las Cabras'	Antonio del Valle Saavedra	Export Adi
	♀	Mayumi's	Mayumi Ohno	Marketing
	♀	Pavlova, Ltd.	Ian Devling	Marketing
	♀	Specialty Biscuits, Ltd.	Peter Wilson	Sales Rep
	♀	PB Knackebrod AB	Lars Peterson	Sales Age
	♀	Refrescos Americanas LTDA	Carlos Diaz	Marketing
	♀	Heli Su?waren GmbH & Co. KG	Petra Winkler	Sales Man
	♀	Plutzer Lebensmittelgro?markte AG	Martin Bein	Internation
	♀	Nord-Ost-Fisch Handelsgesellschaft mbH	Sven Petersen	Coordinat
	♀	Formaggi Fortini s.r.l.	Elio Rossi	Sales Rep
	♀	Norske Meierier	Beate Vileid	Marketing
	⚙	Bigfoot Breweries	Cheryl Saylor	Regional
	♀	Svensk Sjofoda AB	Michael Bjorn	Sales Rep
	♀	Aux joyeux ecclesiastiques	Guylene Nodier	Sales Man

In this section, we have seen how we can use the custom draw techniques to implement various highlights for the rows and cells in the TDBGrid component.

This ends our tour of the TDBGrid component. Now we move to another multifield component called the TDBCtrlGrid component.

Using the TDBCtrlGrid Component

The TDBCtrlGrid component is used to create a grid in which each cell can contain one or more data-aware controls. Such grids are used to display fields of records without any additional navigation controls, like in the TDBGrid component discussed above. There may be one or more rows visible at a time, as well as one or more columns in such a grid. To set the number of rows, we use the RowCount property; the number of columns is set through the ColCount property.

The number of rows and columns depends on how many data-aware controls we are planning to insert into the cell of the grid, its size, location, and so on. So, there are no general rules for these two properties; they depend on the particular application. The following two screen shots show how to use the same data in one- and two-column grids.

Two other properties of the TDBCtrlGrid component—AllowDelete and AllowInsert—determine whether the user can delete the current record (using the Ctrl+Del key combination) and insert a new record (using the Ctrl+Ins key combination). The way we scroll the contents of the grid, either vertically or horizontally, can be changed with the Orientation property.

Using the OnPaintPanel event handler, we can perform some custom drawing of the grid's cell. In our example, we can mark all records with discontinued products with a dark background. The following example shows how to do this:

```
procedure TForm1.DBCtrlGrid1PaintPanel(DBCtrlGrid: TDBCtrlGrid;
  Index: Integer);
var
 R : TRect;
begin
 With DBCtrlGrid1 do
  begin
// Create a rectangle from the panel (cell)
  With R do
   begin
    R.Top    := 0;
    R.Left   := 0;
    R.Bottom := PanelHeight;
    R.Right  := PanelWidth;
   end;
// Check is the current product is discontinued
   If DataSource1.DataSet.FieldByName('Discontinued').Value =
   True
   then
    begin
// If yes, change the panel's background
     Canvas.Brush.Color := clGray;
     Canvas.FillRect(R);
    end;
  end;
end;
```

Please note that not all of the data-aware controls can be placed into the TDBControlGrid.

So far, we have seen two data-aware multirecord components that can be used to show and edit data without additional navigation tools. In both components discussed above—TDBGrid and TDBCtrlGrid—we used the scroll bars to move from one record to another. Delphi VCL provides a handy component called TDBNavigator that can be used for more precise navigation. We will discuss this component in the next section.

Navigating the Records: The TDBNavigator Component

The TDBNavigator component can be used to navigate the records with a set of buttons. By using the buttons of the TDBNavigator component we can move not only to the next and previous records of the dataset, but also jump to the first and last records, as well as initiate editing; insert, delete, and update records; and refresh the data in the dataset. This set consists of ten buttons, listed in the following table:

Button	Value	Actions	Method
First	nbFirst	Goes to the first record	First()
Previous	nbPrior	Goes to the previous record	Prior()
Next	nbNext	Goes to the next record	Next()
Last	nbLast	Goes to the last record	Last()
Insert	nbInsert	Inserts a blank record	Insert()
Delete	nbDelete	Deletes the current record	Delete()
Edit	nbEdit	Initiates editing of the current record	Edit()
Post	nbPost	Posts the current record	Post()
Cancel	nbCancel	Cancels the changes	Cancel()
Refresh	nbRefresh	Refreshes the data	Refresh()

Using the VisibleButtons property, we can select which buttons appear in the component. This can be useful, for example, when we need to disable the editing functions. In this case, we make visible only the First, Next, Previous, and Last buttons. To illustrate this feature, let's create a short example. Here we have two options—navigate through the database in read-only mode or in read/edit/write mode. Both options are available as a radio button. When our form is created, we save the current set of buttons in the FullSet variable (of the TNavigateBtn type), assuming that by default we have a full-featured TDBNavigator component. When the Read-Only radio button is pressed, we remove some buttons from the component, and when the Read/Edit radio button is pressed, we restore them. Here is the code that implements this:

```
var
 FullSet : Set of TNavigateBtn;

// On form creation : Save the full set of buttons
procedure TForm1.FormCreate(Sender: TObject);
begin
 FullSet := DBNavigator1.VisibleButtons;
```

```
end;

// "Read-Only" clicked—reduce the set of buttons
procedure TForm1.Button1Click(Sender:
TObject);
begin
  DBNavigator1.VisibleButtons := [nbFirst,
nbPrior,
    nbNext,nbLast];
end;

// "Read/Edit" clicked—restore the full set
procedure TForm1.Button2Click(Sender:
TObject);
begin
  DBNavigator1.VisibleButtons := FullSet;
end;
```

To find out which navigator button was pressed, we use the event handler for the OnClick method. It receives two arguments—the Sender argument (of the TObject type) and the Button argument (of the TNavigateBtn type). The Button argument indicates the button that was pressed, and can have one of the values shown in the Value column in the above table.

The TDBNavigator component contains a method to simulate the button click—the BtnClick method—that can be used to control the navigation from the code. Note that this is like calling the appropriate method of the datasource's dataset object associated with the TDBNavigator component.

Setting the ShowHint property to True will show the default hints associated with each button of the TDBNavigator component. To change the text of the hints, you need to access the Hints array. Set the new text for the button you need, or set the empty string (' ') to leave the default text.

On some rare occasions, we may implement the navigation functions in our application with buttons of our own using the TButton component, the TBitBtn component, or the TSpeedButton component. Note that the last one does not receive the focus, so its usage is limited only by mouse operations. With any of these button types, we use the appropriate method shown in the Method column in the table above. Just keep in mind that some operations, like posting or deleting records, may require confirmation from the user.

Earlier in this chapter, we saw two components—the TDBGrid component and the TDBCtrlGrid component—that are used to represent data from several fields of the record or several records at once. We have also discussed how we can use the TDBNavigator component to navigate the data. Now it's time to talk about the single-field data-aware controls available in Delphi.

Using Single-Field Data-Aware Controls

In this section, we will discuss a set of Delphi data-aware controls used to represent the values of a single field of the record. We have divided these controls into the following groups:

- Text boxes and memos—the TDBText, TDBEdit, TDBMemo, and TDBRichEdit components
- List boxes and combo boxes—the TDBListBox, TDBComboBox, TDBLookupListBox, and TDBLookupComboBox components
- Graphics—the TDBImage component
- Check boxes and radio buttons—the TDBCheckBox component and TDBRadioGroup component

We will start with the components that are used to show single-line and multi-line text information.

Text Boxes and Memos

Delphi VCL contains four data-aware controls to represent the contents of the various table fields in a text form. The simplest one is the TDBText component, which is a data-aware label used to display the value of the field. This is a read-only control. Since the data for this control comes from the database, there is no way to determine its minimum and maximum size. Always set the Autosize property to True to avoid possible truncation of long text.

To be able to edit the text in the field, we use the TDBEdit component, which is the data-aware version of the standard edit box. Using the properties of the TFied object, which represents the underlying field attached to the TDBEdit component, we can specify the mask (TField.EditMask) and display format (TField.DisplayFormat) for date-time and numeric fields.

If we have BLOB text fields in a database, we can show its contents either in the TDBMemo component or in the TDBRichEdit component. Both of them support multiline text and various editing functions. The TDBRichEdit component is used when we have RTF-formatted text. If this is not the case, we use the TDBMemo component. The following screen shot shows what happens when we use the TDBEdit component and TDBRichEdit component to show the RTF-formatted text from one of the fields of the Employees table in the Northwind database.

List Boxes and Combo Boxes

The set of Delphi data-aware controls contains two pairs of list boxes and combo boxes. They are TDBListBox, TDBComboBox, TDBLookupListBox, and TDBLookupComboBox. The first two components are used to present a fixed list of values that can be inserted into a particular field. They are data-aware because they are connected to one of the fields in a table, and one of the values chosen in such a component becomes the new value for this field. As you may guess, the only difference between the TDBListBox and TDBComboBox component is that the latter one takes up less space on the form.

The last two components—TDBLookupListBox and TDBLookupComboBox—are used to display a list of possible values from a lookup field. This gives us more flexibility since the list can be stored in the table in a database and when its contents are updated, the contents of the component are automatically updated too.

Graphics

The TDBImage data-aware component is used to display graphical data stored in BLOB fields. This component works with the clipboard, allowing us to copy images from the database and save them into it. There are not many properties and methods in this component, and most of them are the same as in the TImage component.

If you have tried to use the TDBImage component with graphical data stored in Microsoft Access, Microsoft Visual FoxPro, or Microsoft SQL Server databases, you are probably familiar with the "Bitmap Image is not valid" message. The problem here is that in BLOB fields of the above-mentioned databases, the graphical image is stored not as the "raw" data, but as an OLE object with the OLE storage header attached at the beginning of the real graphical data. This header contains information about the type of object, the application that created it, and other information for the OLE kernel to be able to operate with it. The TDBImage component, implemented in Delphi VCL, is based on the TPicture class, which supports only "pure" graphical data.

To access the data itself, we must ignore this header. The exact size of the header is 78 bytes according to Earl F. Glynn (EarlGlynn@att.net), who wrote the Delphi code to avoid this problem. Here is a modified version of Earl's code that solves the "Bitmap Image is not valid" problem. We have tested this code with both Microsoft Access and Microsoft SQL Server. It should work with Microsoft Visual FoxPro as well.

```
procedure TForm1.ADOTable1AfterScroll(DataSet: TDataSet);
var
 Bitmap  : TBitmap;
 BS      : TADOBlobStream;
begin
// Create ADO BLOB Stream
 try
  BS := TADOBlobStream.Create(ADOTable1Photo, bmRead);
// Skip OLE Storage header
  BS.Seek(78, soFromBeginning);
```

```
// Create bitmap
 Bitmap := TBitmap.Create;
// Load graphics from a stream
 Bitmap.LoadFromStream(BS);
// Show it
 DBImage1.Picture.Graphic := Bitmap;
// Clear memory
finally
 Bitmap.Free;
 BS.Free;
end;
end;
```

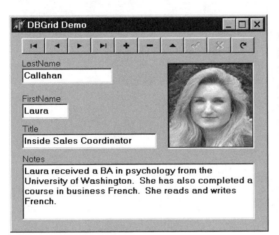

Place this code in the AfterScroll event handler of any of the ADO components you use to access the table with the graphical data. The TADOBlobStream object (defined in the ADODB unit) used here is the stream object used to read and write BLOB fields (TBlobField and its descendants) in ADO datasets.

For those readers who are looking for more general solutions, we suggest creating a descendant of the TADOBlobStream class to make the things more automated, as well as allow saving pictures back to the database, or wait until Borland provides better support for graphical BLOBs in Microsoft databases.

Check Boxes and Radio Buttons

The last two data-aware controls we will cover here are the TDBCheckBox component and the TDBRadioGroup component.

The TDBCheckBox component is a data-aware check box used to display or set a Boolean or Boolean-like data field, i.e., the field can have only two values, represented visually by a checked and an unchecked box. This component has two string properties that allow assigning the values of the underlying field. In the checked state, the ValueChecked property contains a set of the possible values for the field. If any of the values specified in this property (a semicolon-delimited list) matches the value of the field, the check box will be checked. The ValueUnchecked property is used in unchecked states.

Let's look at the following example. The Products table in the Northwind database has a Discontinued field that can have either a False value for a product that is available to order or True for a discontinued product. Since we have only two possible values for this field (and its type is `TBooleanField`), we can use the TDBCheckBox component to represent its contents.

The TDBRadioGroup component is used to create a data-aware group of radio buttons. The best way to explain how to use this component is to create an example. Let's look at the Orders table in the Northwind database. Here we have a ShipVia field that contains a ShipperID for one of the three companies that does the actual shipping of the ordered products. Since each order can be shipped by only one of the shipping companies, we can represent them with a set of mutually exclusive buttons, placed within the TDBRadioGroup component. This is shown on the screen shot below.

This example was created using the following steps.
1. Place the TADOConnection component into a form and connect it to the Northwind database.
2. Place the TDataSource component, attach it to the TADOTable component, and select the Orders table.
3. Place the set of TDBEdit fields to show the OrderID, OrderDate, ShippedDate, and ShipName fields.
4. Add another TADOTable component. This time select the Shippers table.
5. Next, place the TDBRadioGroup component, and set its DataSource property to DataSource1 and its DataField property to ShipVia.
6. Then, write the following OnCreate event handler for Form1:

```
procedure TForm1.FormCreate(Sender: TObject);
begin
 with ADOTable2, DBRadioGroup1 do
 begin
  Open;
  First;
  while NOT EOF do
   begin
    Items.Add(FieldByName('CompanyName').Value);
```

```
     Values.Add(FieldByName('ShipperId').Value);
     Next;
   end;
  Close;
 end;
end;
```

Here we have filled the Items and Values properties of the TDBRadioGroup component. The first of them contains strings that are shown in the application near the radio buttons, while the second one contains values that must be stored in the appropriate fields. The ADOTable2 component is used only to supply the DBRadioGroup1 component with these two sets of strings.

7.   Finally, place the TDBNavigator component to be able to navigate through the Orders table.

This ends our discussion of the Delphi data-aware controls. In the next section, we will see how to use the TField objects that lay behind all data-aware controls we have described in this chapter.

Using the TField Objects

In this section, we will discuss how to use the TField objects. We briefly reviewed the TField class and its descendants in Chapter 4. Now we will show you how to use them in Delphi ADO applications.

Creating TField Objects

Any descendant of an abstract TField class represents a particular field in a dataset (either retrieved from a database or obtained by another way, e.g., by performing calculations). It contains information about the name and data type of this field (from the client application's point of view), and some extended attributes of the field that are not stored in a database but are often used in client applications. Such attributes can include visibility, display label, alignment, edit mask, and constraints.

By default, TField objects are created dynamically at run time when the dataset is being opened. In this case, these extended attributes are based on the metadata retrieved from a database (e.g., display labels of fields are the same as real field names in a table or in a query result).

We can also create such TField objects at design time. This gives us the ability to manually define all extended attributes we may need. In addition, using these objects may prevent additional calls to a database server for retrieving metadata; instead, the data stored in TFields objects will be used.

To illustrate how to create TFields objects at design time, let's create a new project and place the TADOConnection and TADOTable components on a form. Then we will connect the ADOConnection1 component with the Northwind database, set the

Connection property of the ADOTable1 component to ADOConnection1, and set its TableName property to OrderDetails.

If we right-click the ADOTable1 component and select the Fields Editor item from the pop-up menu, we will receive an empty window with four navigating buttons at the top. Now we need to fill this empty window with the list of TField objects. To do this, we right-click on the window and select the Add Fields item from the pop-up menu. The Add Fields dialog with the list of available fields will appear. In this dialog, we select the necessary fields, and press the OK button to add them. The selected fields are now available in the Fields Editor, as shown below. These fields are also known as *persistent fields* because we defined them at design time and they are stored in the DFM file.

Any item shown in the Fields Editor corresponds to a newly generated TField descendant that represents a particular field of the dataset. The particular class of this object depends on the data type of the field in a dataset.

If we select some fields in the Fields Editor, we can drag them to the form. This displays the TDataSource component and some data-aware controls for editing these fields, as shown in the figure at right.

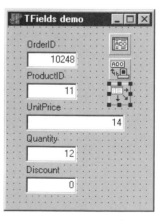

Properties of the TField Objects

The TField class and its descendants have many properties that describe extended attributes of the dataset fields.

These properties can be organized into several functional groups as shown in the following table:

Group	Properties
Appearance Properties	Alignment
	DisplayLabel
	DisplayText
	DisplayName
	DisplayWidth
	EditMask
	Visible
Read/Assign Properties	AsBoolean
	AsCurrency
	AsDateTime
	AsFloat
	AsInteger
	AsString
	AsVariant
	ReadOnly
	Required
	Size
	Text
	ValidChars
Lookup Properties	Lookup
	LookupList
	LookupField
	LookupDataSet
	LookupCache
	LookupResultField
	KeyFields
Field Properties	FieldKind
	FieldNo
	FieldName
	FullName
	Dataset
	DataSize
	DataType
	Origin
	ParentField
Index Properties	Index
	IsIndexField

Group	Properties
Value Properties	Value
	IsNull
	NewValue
	OldValue
	CurValue
	AutoGenerateValue
	Calculated
	DefaultExpression
Constraint Properties	HasConstraint
	CustomConstraint
	ImportedConstraint
	ConstraintErrorMessage
Records Properties	CanModify
	MaxRecords
	RecNo
	RecordCount
	RecordSet
	RecordSetState
	RecordSize
	RecordStatus

The most used properties are the lookup properties, the constraint properties, and those responsible for the appearance of the field, and for reading and assigning the field value.

The properties responsible for the appearance change the way the field's data is shown in a client application, such as its alignment and automatic formatting of the field data. For example, if we set the DisplayFormat property of the ADOTable1Discount component that represents the Discount field in the previous example to '0.00', we will get the value of this field with two decimal digits. The '0' character in this format is a digit placeholder. It should be mentioned that we can set different formats for positive, negative, and zero values. In this case, we must separate different format strings by semicolons.

Among the properties responsible for reading and assigning the field value are the AsXXX properties (AsBoolean, AsString, AsCurrency, AsDateTime, AsFloat, AsInteger, AsVariant) that allow us to assign the field value to a variable of the appropriate type, which may not be the same as the data type of the field itself. Otherwise, the Value property returns the field value in the variable of the same or similar data type as the field type itself.

The FieldKind property is used to determine whether a particular field is a data field, a *calculated field* (which will be discussed in the next section), or a *lookup field*. In practice, this value is usually set at design time.

Lookup properties are used when we need to use *reference tables* in Delphi ADO applications. We will discuss them in the "Creating Lookup Fields" section later in this chapter. Finally, we need to briefly mention the properties responsible for data validation in a client application.

In Chapter 1, we discussed constraints, database objects responsible for restrictions on the database data. If a user tries to insert data that does not satisfy the restrictions defined in a constraint, the database server generates an exception or sends an error message to the client application. This mechanism of data validation does not depend on a client application because all data validity examination is provided by and performed on a database server.

However, in some cases, this is not convenient because it requires a call to a database server. To check the value entered into the field before the entire record has been edited, we can save the intermediate results and check if there is a database constraint error fired by a server. Otherwise, the user must wait until the entire record is posted to receive all constraint error messages.

In the case of BDE data sources, this problem can be solved by using custom constraints in a client application. These constraints are SQL statements in the CustomConstraint property values of an appropriate TField object. The ConstraintErrorMessage property of the same component contains a string to be shown to the user when there is a constraint violation in a field he has finished editing. Unfortunately, we could not find a way to force these properties to work with ADO data sources. Instead, we recommend using the OnExit event of the appropriate data-aware control to perform data validation. This can be done as shown in the example below:

```
procedure TForm1.DBEdit1Exit(Sender: TObject);
begin
 if ADOTable1UnitPrice.Value < 5 then
 begin
  ShowMessage ('The UnitPrice must be greater than 5');
  DBEdit1.SetFocus; //continue editing the invalid data
 end;
end;
```

Another way to set data restrictions is to use the OnValidate event (it will be fired when the user finishes editing data before writing to the dataset):

```
procedure TForm1.ADOTable1UnitPriceValidate(Sender: TField);
begin
 if ADOTable1UnitPrice.Value < 5 then
 begin
  ShowMessage ('The UnitPrice must be greater than 5');
  DBEdit1.SetFocus; //continue editing the invalid data
 end;
end;
```

Now we know enough to create some custom TField objects used in client applications. These are calculated fields, lookup fields, and fields containing nested datasets.

Creating Calculated Fields

Sometimes users need additional information that is available directly from a dataset. For example, if an OrderDetails table contains the UnitPrice field, the Quantity field, and the Discount field, it does not make sense to store the resulting payment in the same table, because it could be calculated using these fields. However, users may want to see this value.

There are two ways to provide them with such information. One way that has already been discussed in the previous chapter is to create a view containing these fields and the result of the calculations. This is effective only if we need to show data without editing it, because in this case all calculations are provided by a database server. However, as we already know, views do not contain any data—they are only stored queries. Therefore, if we want to edit data and receive the result of such calculation simultaneously, we need to refresh a view while editing/saving data to force these calculations. This results in additional calls to the database server, and decreases the performance of our application.

Another way to show the results of calculations is to use calculated fields. This is based on performing calculations directly in a client application without calling a database server (and without creating any additional objects in a database). We will see how to do this below.

Let's reopen the previous project in which we created several TField descendants for the OrderDetails table, which is accessible through the TADOTable component. We may need to show the value of the resulting payment for the particular ordered product. To do so, open the Fields Editor, right-click on it, and select the New field... item from the pop-up menu. The New Field dialog appears.

Set the Name property of the new field to PaymentDue. The Name property of the TField component we are creating will be filled automatically, but if we do not like this name, we can rename it. Then it is necessary to set the field type in the Type combo box (this means that we select the name of the TField descendant). In our example it will be the BCD type that corresponds to the TBCDField class, because the TADOTable1UnitPrice object that represents the UnitPrice field belongs to this class.

Finally, we need to select the Calculated item in the Field type radio group.

After pressing the OK button, we see that there is a new PaymentDue item in the Field Editor. Let's drag it and drop it on our form.

Now we need to write the code to perform the calculation itself. To do this, we handle the OnCalcFields event of the ADOTable1 component. This event occurs when a client application tries to obtain values from calculated fields in a dataset. Here is the code:

```
procedure TForm1.ADOTable1CalcFields(DataSet: TDataSet);
begin
 //Calculate the payment due
 ADOTable1PaymentDue.Value:=
 //Payment due is equal to UnitPrice*Quantity
 ADOTable1UnitPrice.Value*ADOTable1Quantity.Value*
 // and we need to take discount into account
 (1-ADOTable1Discount.Value);
end;
```

After compiling and running this application, we can obtain the results of the calculations as shown in the figure below:

It should be mentioned that the AutoCalcField property of the dataset component can be used to control the way the OnCalcFields events are fired.

Setting this property to False reduces the number of calculations; for example, in this case OnCalcFields will not be called when changes are made to individual fields within a record.

Note: Remember that such calculated fields are available only in the client application where they are defined. No new database fields will be created in this case, and no calculated values will be stored in a database.

If the FieldKind property is set to fkCalculated, the results of the calculations are not stored in a dataset.

Creating Lookup Fields

Many databases contain tables called *reference tables*. In most cases, such tables contain a numeric (or short string) primary key field, and one or more fields (sometimes called *descriptive fields*) that could be long strings or belong to other data types.

Imagine that a user inputs data to the table that contains a digital or short string foreign key (in the case of the OrderDetails table, it is a ProductID value). It is obvious that selecting a product name (e.g., Ravioli Angelo) from a product list is preferable for the user than typing the corresponding ProductID value found in the product list. Using the product name also reduces errors.

To provide users with a string list to select from rather than having them enter values, we can use *lookup fields*. These usually contain easily understandable string data from a reference table corresponding to the foreign key values. The string data replaces these foreign key values in a client application. Similar to the previous case, these fields are available only inside a client application and do not exist as database fields. Now we will look how to create and use the lookup fields.

Let's return to our previous example. To create a lookup field for the dataset in use, we will place another TADOTable component for creating a reference dataset in which our application will find strings corresponding to numeric values of the ProductID field. In order to have a reference dataset, we will set the Connection property of the ADOTable2 component to `ADOConnection1`, and the TableName property to the Product table.

The next step is to open the Fields Editor for the OrderDetails dataset, and create a new field in it. In the New Field dialog, set the Name property of the new field to `ProductName`, select the string type, which corresponds to the TStringField class, from the Type combo box, and set its length to 50 characters. (Be sure to take into account the length of the appropriate database field in the reference table when deciding what this value will be.)

When we select the Calculated item in the `Field` type radio group, the Lookup definition group of controls becomes available to be edited. In this group:

The Dataset value is the name of the reference dataset (in this case it is the ADOTable2 component).

Key Fields is the foreign key field (or a set of fields separated by a semicolon) that are to be replaced.

Lookup Keys is the field (or a set of fields) that is a primary key of the reference dataset.

The Result Field is a string field in the reference dataset to be shown instead of the replaced foreign key field of the original dataset.

For our example, the values of these properties are shown in the figure below:

The next step is to replace the TDBEdit component for editing the ProductID field with the TDBLookupComboBox component, and set its DataSource and DataField properties to the same values as the corresponding properties of the deleted TDBEdit component. It should be mentioned that we can drag the lookup field from the Fields Editor to the form to receive the TDBLookupComboBox component with all necessary properties already defined.

Now the user of this application can select the product name from the combo box instead of typing numbers, as shown in the figure below:

When the user selects an item from the combo box, an appropriate value of the replaced foreign key field (in this case it is the ProductID field of the TADOTable1 dataset) changes to the value of the corresponding primary key of the reference table.

We can also obtain the same results without using calculated fields. In this case, we need to use the second TDataSource component connected to the TADOTable2 component. We also need to set the following properties of the TDBComboBox component:

- ListSource—the TDataSource component that connected with the lookup dataset (in our example, it is equal to DataSource2)

- KeyField—the field of the lookup dataset that has the same values as the values in the original field (in our example, it is equal to ProductID)

- ListField—the field of the lookup dataset in which data is shown instead of the actual field (in our example, it is equal to ProductName)

 Note: The TDBGrid component also could display the list of lookup values instead of the actual ID.

Using Data Shaping for Creating Nested Datasets

In all previous examples, we have used datasets that contained only *atomic* values, such as strings, numbers, images, memos, etc. In some cases, the data in a dataset field may be more complex. For example, it may be convenient to have dataset fields that contain special data types, such as tables or arrays. To implement these fields in Delphi, we can use several descendants of the TField class (for example, TArrayField, TDataSetField, TADTField, etc.).

In Chapter 1, we mentioned that some object-oriented databases (e.g., Oracle 8) can have tables with such complex field types. If such a field contains a table, this table is called *nested*. It is obvious that tables with such fields (or queries to these tables) can be represented in datasets with appropriate complex data. However, at the time of this writing, OLE DB providers supporting such features of object-oriented databases were still not available.

Nevertheless, it does not mean that using datasets with nested tables cannot be done from Delphi ADO applications. Starting in version 2.0, ADO provides the Hierarchical Cursor feature, which enables us to define a child Recordset object as the value of a field in a parent recordset. Hierarchical recordset objects can be nested to any depth required (that is, it is possible to create children recordset objects of children recordset objects, and so on).

Setting the Connection String for Data Shaping

Hierarchical recordsets can be created in Delphi through the Data Shaping Service for OLE DB. The OLE DB provider for this service was described in Chapter 3.

When we use the MSDataShape OLE DB provider with the Microsoft Access version of the Northwind database, the connection string could look like this:

```
Provider=MSDataShape.1;
Persist Security Info=False;
Data Source=c:\data\NorthWind.mdb;
Data Provider=Microsoft.Jet.OLEDB.4.0
```

If we are using the MSDataShape OLE DB provider with the Microsoft SQL Server version of the Northwind database, the connection string may look like this:

```
Provider=MSDataShape.1;
Persist Security Info=False;
Connect Timeout=15;
Data Source=MAINDESK;
User ID=sa;
Initial Catalog=Northwind;
Data Provider=SQLOLEDB.1
```

Please note that your versions of these connection strings may differ from the ones shown above.

The next step in creating an application with nested datasets is to create a database query that returns the underlying recordset. This can be done with the Shape command, which is described below.

The Shape Command

The Shape command defines the structure of a hierarchical recordset, and the commands necessary to populate it with data. This command contains one or more queries, which return a recordset. These queries are usually created in SQL.

The Shape Append command adds to the parent recordset a complex field that contains a child recordset. Its syntax is shown below:

```
SHAPE  {parent_query} [[AS] alias]
APPEND {child_query}
RELATE (parent_field TO child_field)
```

The parent_query and child_query arguments are simple SQL queries that must return recordsets. The parent_field is the field in the parent_recordset returned by the parent_query, and the child_field is the field in the child_recordset returned by the `child_query`. These fields are used to create a relation between recordsets. For example, we can use the following Shape command:

```
SHAPE  {SELECT * FROM Customers}
APPEND ({SELECT * FROM Orders}
RELATE CustomerID TO CustomerID)
```

Shape commands can be nested. This means that the `parent_query` or `child_query` can be another Shape command.

Another Shape command is the Compute command, which executes an aggregate function on the rows of the `child_recordset` to generate a `parent_recordset` and then places the `child_recordset` to the field in the newly generated `parent_recordset`. The syntax of this command is shown below:

```
SHAPE { child_query } [[AS] alias]
COMPUTE aggregate_expression
[BY group_field_list]
```

Here, `aggregate_expression` is a list of fields operated on by an aggregate function. The recordset is referred to by its alias in the aggregate function.

The aggregate functions could be SUM, AVG, MIN, MAX, COUNT, STDEV, or ANY, and their argument must be the field of the child recordset.

Creating Applications with Nested DataSets

Now we know enough to start creating applications with a nested dataset based on a recordset retrieved with the Shape command.

Let's create a new project, place the TADOConnection component on its form, and set its ConnectionString property similar to one of the two connection strings shown earlier. If we use the standard property editor for the ConnectionString property, we need to select the MSDataShape provider, and set the Data Provider value, the Initial Catalog value, and the DataSource value manually.

The next step is to place the TADODataSet component to the form, and set its Connection property to the ADOConnection1 component. Now we can set its CommandText property as shown below:

```
SHAPE  {SELECT * FROM Customers}
APPEND ({SELECT * FROM Orders}
RELATE CustomerID TO CustomerID)
```

Then we add the TDataSource and TDBGrid components and set the Active property of the ADODataSet1 component to `True` to see the resulting dataset. We will see that the resulting dataset, along with the fields corresponding to the database fields, has an additional Products field that is of the `TDataSetField` type. If we compile and run this application, and then click on the cell in the Products column of the DBGrid1 component, we obtain a new pop-up window with the detail records from a Products table with the same CategoryID value that is in the current record of the parent dataset.

It should be mentioned that the pop-up window could also be shown programmatically with the following OnClick event handler for the TButton component:

```
procedure TForm1.Button1Click(Sender: TObject);
begin
  DBGrid1.ShowPopupEditor(DBGrid1.Columns[4]);
end;
```

The ShowPopupEditor method of the TDBGrid component is used to show a window that represents a nested dataset in a column where the TDataSet field is shown.

Clicking the Show details button displays the pop-up window with the detail records, as shown in the figure below:

What we have done here is created a special kind of master/detail relationship provided in a single dataset.

If we need to create an application where the nested dataset is shown in a separate grid, we can use the DataSetField property of the TADODataSet component. To illustrate this, we will extend our example. First, we will create the TFields objects for the TADODataSet1 component, then add a second TADODataSet component, a second TDataSource component, and a second TDBGrid component to show the nested dataset content. Now we will set the DataSetField property of the TADODataSet2 component to ADODataSet1Products. This gives us an application similar to the master/detail application, but both master and detail records are stored inside the same dataset.

Using the Shape command is not the only way to create nested datasets. Another way of creating them is to use the TClientDataSet component. This will be discussed in Chapter 21.

Error Trapping

Any robust application—whether a database application or any other program—must contain an error trapping mechanism to prevent message boxes from appearing and to provide ways to save data.

In Delphi ADO applications, we can use the standard Delphi exception handling mechanisms to handle possible errors and close applications without loss of data. The general rule is to protect the code blocks that may cause an error to occur with a special set of Delphi commands. For example, we can use the try-except-end block to protect the block of code as shown in the syntax below:

```
// Begin protected block
try
// Do some operations here
// If exception occurs
except    // the execution will jumps here
  on Exception do
// handle the exception
end;
// Execution continues here. End of protected block
```

Another block that can be used in Delphi is the try-finally-end block, which is used to protect the resources; its syntax is shown below:

```
// Allocate the resource
try
// Use the resource
finally
// Free the resource
end;
```

The first type of exception handling code contains the on Exception do statement that is used to perform some actions. This can be a custom error message, code that is more sophisticated, or actions performed by default (at the Delphi or the operating system level). The last case has some severe limitations, especially since we cannot control the default actions.

In Delphi ADO applications, we should be aware of two types of exceptions—ones that are generated by the Delphi database engine and are in the form of EDatabaseError and EADOError, and OLE exceptions (EOLEError, EOLEException, and EOLESysError) that comes from the OLE kernel inside the Microsoft Windows operating system. This does not mean that we should ignore other types of exceptions that may occur in our application.

Database Exceptions

The main database exception we may encounter is in the form of the EDatabaseError type. This exception indicates a database error. A more specific form for ADO is the EADOError type, which is raised with some ADO errors that may occur in applications.

OLE Exceptions

Since the ADO Express components that implement ADO support in Delphi are built as wrappers around the ADO objects and we may use some other ADO extensions, we should pay attention to the OLE errors that may occur in our applications. In most cases, such errors can be avoided with properly installed support libraries required by the Delphi ADO applications. But sometimes we need to perform extra checking, especially when we create objects from the ADOX, ADO MD, or JRO libraries and use their properties and methods. Note that it is a good practice to use the Assigned function to check a newly created object before using it.

Information on Exceptions

All of the types of exceptions mentioned above are derived from the Exception class, which has a set of properties and methods that can be used to provide more information about the exception.

The Message property indicates the text of the error message to be displayed, while the HelpContext property may contain the help context identifier that provides extra information about the error. Note that the HelpContext property is rarely used. We can use the Message property in our exception handling code to show a message on the screen, save the message and some extra information in the log file, or extract some information from it to combine with our own error message.

Using Data Modules

Sometimes it may be convenient to store all non-visual components for data access together in a dedicated location. Delphi provides a container object called the TDataModule object that can be used for this. Using it is optional, but it is convenient, especially if the application contains several forms to edit or show the same database tables or queries.

At design time, the TDataModule object provides a visual container into which we can place non-visual components. To create this object at design time, we need to select the Data Module item from the New page of the Object Repository. Delphi 5 comes with a visual tool called Data Module Designer that can be used to visually set some properties of the data access components. The right pane of its window is a container where we place non-visual components. Using the tree view control in the left pane, we can easily navigate all data access components and objects available in this data module, including TField descendants.

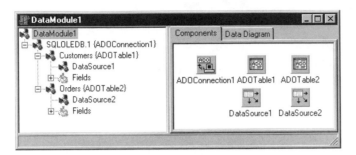

Note: It is also possible to place any non-visual component on the data module, for example, TTimer, TImageList, etc.

If you use several forms that refer to the same data module, check that the data module is created before it is released from your forms.

If we select the Data Diagram page of the Data Module Designer, we will receive an empty container, in which we can drag any object from the tree view control with the list of data access objects, as shown in the following figure:

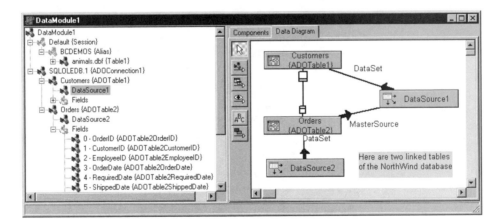

We can see that all links between objects are shown at this diagram.

Unfortunately, the Data Module Designer is substantially a BDE-oriented tool. For BDE data access components, it provides some additional services, such as setting the master/detail relationships with the TDataSource component appearing automatically, selecting the lookup table, setting properties of data access objects using drag-and-drop, and retrieving field lists in the TTable and graphical representations of TQuery. Unfortunately, these features are not available for the ADO data sources. Moreover, attempts to set master/detail relationships or to select the lookup table by drag-and-drop operations results in an error message despite the fact that these tables can be linked in such relationship by placing a TDataSet component and setting its properties.

Note: Some of these bugs were fixed in the Delphi Update Pack 1. For example, now you can build master/detail relationships visually. We suggest installing the Delphi Update Pack 1 as soon as possible to make your work with data modules more comfortable.

Conclusion

In this chapter, we discussed how to create Delphi database applications using ADO data sources. We have learned that:

- Delphi data-aware components can be divided into two groups—"multi-field" components, which can show data from several database fields and records at a time, and "single-field" components, which can show data from only one database field at a time.

- If we want to represent data in a tabular grid, we need to use the TDBGrid component. This component allows us to browse and edit data, and can be customized to show pick lists, nested datasets, and custom images.

- If it is necessary to create a grid in which each cell can contain one or more data-aware controls, use the TDBCtrlGrid component.

- To navigate records in datasets, use the TDBNavigator component.

- The TDBText and TDBEdit components can be used to show fields that could be represented as a string. TDBText is preferable when the field shown should not be edited by the user; otherwise, it is better to use the TDBEdit component.

- To show BLOB text field, use the TDBMemo component when the text is not formatted, and the TDBRichEdit component otherwise.

- The TDBListBox and TDBComboBox components are used to present a fixed list of values that can be inserted into a particular field. The TDBLookupListBox and TDBLookupComboBox components are used to display a list of possible values from a lookup field.

- The TDBImage data-aware component is used to display graphical data stored in the BLOB fields.

- The TDBCheckBox component is a data-aware check box that is used to display or edit a Boolean or similar to Boolean data field.

- The TDBRadioGroup component is used to create a data-aware group of radio buttons.

In addition, we have shown how to display images from Microsoft SQL Server and Microsoft Access.

In this chapter, we have also discussed how to use the TField class descendants. Now we know how to create the TFields objects at design time, how to create calculated and lookup fields, and nested datasets using these objects. We have learned that:

■ To use `reference tables` in applications, we need to use lookup fields.

■ To perform calculations that are not stored in a database, we can create calculated fields.

■ To create nested datasets, we can use the Microsoft Data Shaping to obtain nested recordsets, and TDataSet field object to use such recordsets in Delphi.

Then, we have talked about error trapping and in particular we have discussed that:

■ In Delphi ADO applications, we should be aware of the two types of exceptions—the ones that are generated by Delphi database engine and are in the form of `EDatabaseError` and `EADOError`, and OLE exceptions (`EOLEError`, `EOLEException` and `EOLESysError`) that comes from the OLE kernel inside Microsoft Windows operating system.

At last, we have discussed how we can create and use data modules in Delphi applications. Now we know that using data modules is convenient when we need to place data access objects together to provide centralized handling, especially if we create an application with several forms serving the same database tables or queries.

One Delphi data-aware component—the TDBChart component—still has not been discussed. In the next chapter we will see how to use it as well as how to create different types of charts based on a database data.

BUSINESS GRAPHICS WITH ADO

We have spent the previous chapter discussing various Delphi data-aware controls, the TField object, and data-validation and error-trapping techniques. There we saw how to use multi-field and single-field components to represent and edit data from the fields of the database.

Here we will discuss the last data-aware component available in the Delphi VCL. This component—TDBChart—is used to add various charting capabilities and business graphics to our Delphi ADO applications. Note that the TDBChart component is part of the TeeChart library that contains two more charting components. This library was created by the Spanish company teeMach, SL. Its Standard version has been licensed by Borland to be included in the Professional and Enterprise versions of Delphi and Borland C++Builder products.

We will start with a brief description of the TeeChart library itself, then move to more detailed explanations of the TDBChart component and the objects it uses. Then we will discuss creating Delphi ADO applications that use charts and provide you with examples of creating a simple pie chart, using several series, using the Gantt series, and using standard functions.

All the examples in this chapter use data from the Northwind database located either on the Microsoft SQL Server 7.0 or in Microsoft Access 2000.

Introduction to the TeeChart Library

Here we will briefly discuss the general organization of the TeeChart library and the components that are included in it. Let's start with some definitions:

- A *chart* is a graphical representation of data.
- A group of related data points that are plotted in a chart is called a *data series*. Usually, each data series in a chart has a unique appearance, e.g., unique color, pattern, or bar form. If the chart legend is used, each series can be represented in it. We can plot one or more data series in a chart, except for pie charts, which have only one data series.

- A *legend* is a part of a chart that identifies the colors (or patterns, etc.) assigned to the data series or categories in a chart.

- An *axis* is a line that borders one side of the plot area, providing a reference for measurement or comparisons in a chart. For most charts, data values are plotted along the value axis, which is usually vertical (the y-axis), and categories are plotted along the category axis, which is usually horizontal (the x-axis).

- A *data label* provides additional information about a single data point or an entire series. It can show values, series names, categories, percentages, or combinations of them.

- *Walls* are plain surfaces that are used to set the three-dimensional border of the chart.

The major components of the chart are shown below:

The main component of the TeeChart library is the TChart component, which defines a set of properties, methods, and events used by itself and its descendants—the TDBChart and TQRChart components.

The Charting Components

The TChart component, which resides on the Additional page of the Delphi Component Palette, is the Delphi TPanel-based component that can be used to provide the "non-database-aware" charting capabilities for Delphi applications. We will see an example of using this component in Chapter 15.

The TDBChart component is built on the base of the TChart component (through the TCustomChart class) and extends the set of properties, methods, and events of the

TChart component with the abilities to extract data from data sources. In this chapter, we will see how to use ADO data sources to provide the data for the TDBChart component.

One more component—the TQRChart component—needs to be mentioned here. It allows us to embed TChart or TDBChart components into reports created with QuickReports bands. See Chapter 13 for details.

Since we are talking here about business graphics with ADO, our focus will be on the TDBChart component. The list of properties and methods of the TDBChart component is very huge and it does not make sense to discuss all of them here. Note that some properties of this component are available only at run time.

Series

The TDBChart component serves as a container for TChartSeries objects. These objects hide all the charting logic from the programmer; all we need to do is to supply the right source of the data and set several properties that determine the visual characteristics of the chart.

In TeeChart library, all series are derived from the TChartSeries class. This class defines a set of properties, methods, and events for all types of series implemented in this library. The list of properties and methods of the TChartSeries class is too huge to be discussed here, so we will look only at the most essential part of it.

The DataSource property is used to specify the source of data for the series. When we use the TChart component, its series can contain a set of random values, a function, or no data at all. In the latter case, we supply the data at run time. When we use the TDBChart component, its series can also refer to any TDataSet-based component (for example, to the TADODataSet component) or to a single record. To assign this property to a particular series, we need to use the TDBChart property editor, in which we can select a particular series and set its DataSource property (and all necessary subproperties specific for the particular type of the series) at the DataSource tab.

The XValues and YValues properties (of the TChartValueList type) are used to specify the values of the x- and y-axes. The XLabel property contains the horizontal series labels. To specify the function used on the series, we set the FunctionType property to one of the TTeeFunctionTypes defined in the library. There are several functions in the TeeChart library—TAddTeeFunction, TSubstractTeeFunction, TMultiplyTeeFunction, TDivideTeeFunction, TAverageTeeFunction, THighTeeFunction, and TLowTeeFunction. These functions are used to perform some statistical calculations on the series data. Examples of its usage are provided in the "Using Standard Functions" section of this chapter. The Title property is used by the TChartLegend to draw the series descriptions. Series must be "attached" to the TDBChart component through the ParentChart property.

There are 11 standard series types in the Standard version of the TeeChart library included in Delphi. Each type has its own specific properties and events that can be used to customize the chart.

Marks

Each series has a Marks property (TSeriesMarks component) that serves as a "hint" for each series point. Marks can be visible or invisible and attached to the series through the ParentSeries property. We can control the type of pen used to draw the mark (Arrow property), its length (ArrowLength property), background color, style, font, and position characteristics (Positions property). To find the Marks index of the clicked mark, we use the Clicked method; this allows us to make our charts interactive.

To assign the Marks property for the particular series we need to use the TDBChart property editor where we can select a particular series and then select the necessary characteristics of the marks, such as background color, font, style, and so on.

Axis

The TChartAxis component is used to draw the axis of a chart. There are five properties of this type—LeftAxis, RightAxis, TopAxis, BottomAxis, and DepthAxis. Axis is connected to the chart through the ParentChart property. The TChartAxis component has a lot of properties and methods that allows us to fine-tune it according to our needs. It is possible, for example, to perform a custom drawing on the axis through the CustomDraw method, and respond to user clicks through the Clicked method, which returns the coordinates of the point that was clicked on the axis.

Legend

Another component used while displaying charts is the TChartLegend component. This component draws a rectangle that is filled with the chart series titles or series values. The contents of the legend can be switched through the Legend property. The legend can be placed at the top, left, right, or bottom side of the chart.

Walls

To control the drawing of the chart's left and bottom walls, the TChartWall component is used. The walls are specified through the LeftWall and BottomWall properties of the TDBChart component, while the ParentChart property ties the wall to its "owning" component. The size of the walls can be set through the Size property, and the Color and Brush properties are used to fill the walls.

The components that form the parts of the chart are shown in the following figure:

TChart Component

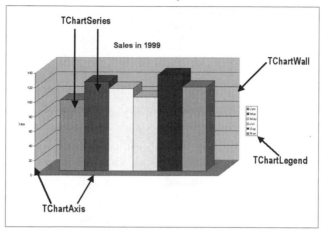

> **Note:** The help file for the TeeChart library that comes with Delphi contains many errors, is incomplete, and does not even support navigation with the standard Windows Help buttons. A slightly improved version (in which you can at least use the Back key and access the Contents, Index, and Search panes) can be found at the teeMach, SL Web site (http://www.teechart.com).

The Chart Property Editor

To set the properties of the TDBChart component at design time, we can use the built-in Chart Property Editor. This property editor can be called by clicking the right mouse button on the TDBChart component and selecting the Edit Chart command from the pop-up menu.

The Chart Property Editor consists of two main panes— the Chart tab and the Series tab.

The first step is to add the type of series used in the chart by pressing the Add button. The TeeChart Gallery appears in which we can select standard series, functions, extended series, and sample series.

After that, we can jump to the Series tab, select the DataSource page, and specify the source of the data. In Delphi

ADO applications, we use the Dataset type. The rest of the work with the Chart Property Editor consists of setting additional parameters for the chart. This can be done on the Axis, Titles, Legend, Panel, Paging, Walls, or 3D pages for the Chart itself, or on Format, General, and Marks pages for the Series.

By switching to the form and back to the Chart Property Editor, we can see the immediate results, as well as use the Print Preview function to find how our chart will look.

When the chart is complete, i.e., all the colors, labels, and titles are set, we can copy it into the clipboard or save it into a file as a bitmap, Windows metafile, enhanced metafile, or TEE-file. All this can be done without compiling our application!

As we already know, all of the properties that are set through the Chart Property Editor can be changed at run time through the appropriate properties of the components that comprise the chart.

Now that we have discussed the main features of the TeeChart library, let's look in more detail at the types of series that can be used in charts created with the TDBChart component. The following section is devoted to series types, the classes that implement them, and their DataSource properties, and describes the possible usage for each type of series.

Types of Series Used in Charts

In this section, we will describe the different types of series that can be used in Delphi applications with the TeeChart library that comes with Delphi. The types of series that are available are shown in the table below.

Series Type and Class	DataSource Properties	Description
Line—TLineSeries	XValues, YValues, XLabel	We use the line series when we have a set of points that need to be connected to each other. The Line series outputs points by drawing a line between them.
Fast Line—TFastLineSeries	XValues, YValues, XLabel	The fast line series is similar to the line series. It is used when we need to draw charts and to add new points to it with high performance. It can present high volumes of data restricted only by available memory. This series has no clicking support and no marks .

Series Type and Class	DataSource Properties	Description
Bar—TBarSeries 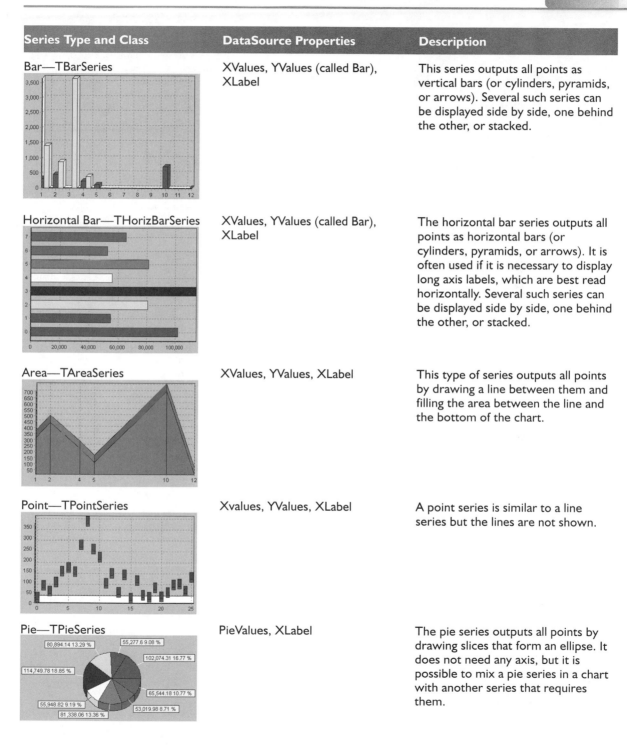	XValues, YValues (called Bar), XLabel	This series outputs all points as vertical bars (or cylinders, pyramids, or arrows). Several such series can be displayed side by side, one behind the other, or stacked.
Horizontal Bar—THorizBarSeries	XValues, YValues (called Bar), XLabel	The horizontal bar series outputs all points as horizontal bars (or cylinders, pyramids, or arrows). It is often used if it is necessary to display long axis labels, which are best read horizontally. Several such series can be displayed side by side, one behind the other, or stacked.
Area—TAreaSeries	XValues, YValues, XLabel	This type of series outputs all points by drawing a line between them and filling the area between the line and the bottom of the chart.
Point—TPointSeries	Xvalues, YValues, XLabel	A point series is similar to a line series but the lines are not shown.
Pie—TPieSeries	PieValues, XLabel	The pie series outputs all points by drawing slices that form an ellipse. It does not need any axis, but it is possible to mix a pie series in a chart with another series that requires them.

Series Type and Class	DataSource Properties	Description
Arrow—TArrowSeries 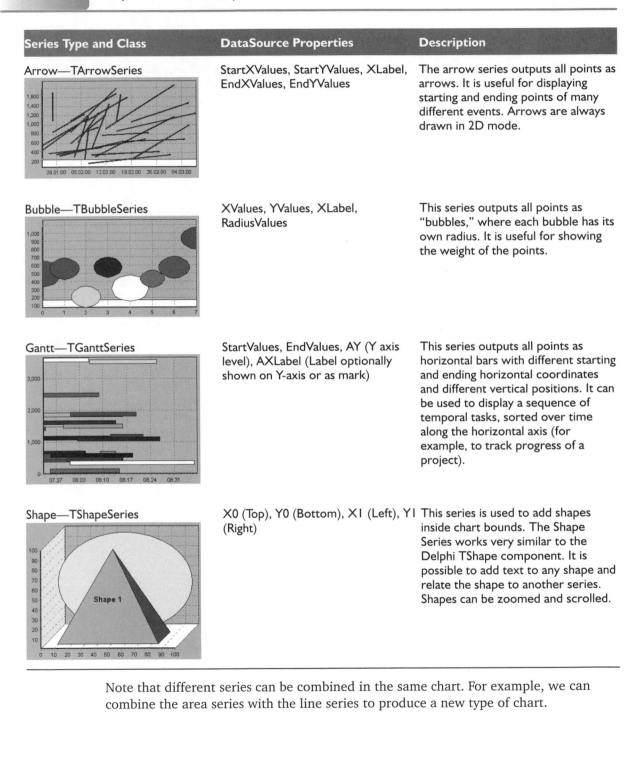	StartXValues, StartYValues, XLabel, EndXValues, EndYValues	The arrow series outputs all points as arrows. It is useful for displaying starting and ending points of many different events. Arrows are always drawn in 2D mode.
Bubble—TBubbleSeries	XValues, YValues, XLabel, RadiusValues	This series outputs all points as "bubbles," where each bubble has its own radius. It is useful for showing the weight of the points.
Gantt—TGanttSeries	StartValues, EndValues, AY (Y axis level), AXLabel (Label optionally shown on Y-axis or as mark)	This series outputs all points as horizontal bars with different starting and ending horizontal coordinates and different vertical positions. It can be used to display a sequence of temporal tasks, sorted over time along the horizontal axis (for example, to track progress of a project).
Shape—TShapeSeries	X0 (Top), Y0 (Bottom), X1 (Left), Y1 (Right)	This series is used to add shapes inside chart bounds. The Shape Series works very similar to the Delphi TShape component. It is possible to add text to any shape and relate the shape to another series. Shapes can be zoomed and scrolled.

Note that different series can be combined in the same chart. For example, we can combine the area series with the line series to produce a new type of chart.

The TeeChart Pro Library

As we have already mentioned, the version of the TeeChart library that comes with Delphi and C++Builder is only a subset of the TeeChart library that is available as a separate product. Below we will briefly outline the main features of the Professional version of this library.

The TeeChart Pro library provides 11 standard series types, nine extended series types, six custom sample series types (TRadarSeries, TContourSeries, TPoint3DSeries, TBezierSeries) and 16 statistical functions including Moving Averages, Curve Fitting, and Trends. It supports 2D, 3D, and OpenGL 3D rendering with the support of your own 3D rendering mechanism, such as VRML rendering or DXF exporting. There is a new visual component—TDraw3D—for 3D generic drawing (non-chart related).

To work inside the Internet applications, there is an ability to retrieve chart binary files from Internet URL addresses through the LoadChartFromURL procedure.

Besides the basic charting components we have described earlier in this chapter, there is a set of additional components that resides on the TeeChart tab on the Component Palette:

- The TSeriesDataSet component enables the connection of a TDBGrid to data in a TChart or TDBChart.

- The TChartScrollBar component is used to add scroll bars to a chart.

- The TDraw3D component represents a panel with 3D canvas drawing capabilities.

- The TTeeCommander component associates the navigation bar with a TChart or TDraw3D component. This navigation bar can be used to rotate the chart, displace it, zoom it, and change its 3D depth

- The TChartEditor component allows us to include the customized version of the Chart Editor that can be used at run time.

- The TChartPreviewer component is used to preview charts at run time.

- The TTccOpenGL component changes the Canvas mode of the TChart or TDraw3D to OpenGL.

The TeeChart Pro library also supports a run-time Chart Editor.

Note: You can download the evaluation version of the TeeChart Pro library for Delphi 5 from the teeMach, SL Web site at http://www.teechart.com.

Now we have enough information about the TeeChart library to start to use it in our Delphi ADO applications. The rest of this chapter will provide you with examples of how to add charts into applications using ADO data sources.

Creating Applications with Charts

In this section, we will create several examples containing different charts based on data from the Northwind database. The first of them will contain a simple pie chart, and the second one will show how to use multiple bar series and change the chart data dynamically. The third example will contain a Gantt chart, and the fourth example will show how to use standard functions.

Creating a Simple Pie Chart

Our first chart will be a simple pie chart. We will use the Category Sales for 1997 view that can be found in the Views list of the Northwind database.

Let's create a new application and place the TADOConnection component on its form, set its LoginPrompt property to `False`, and set its ConnectionString property to the `Northwind` database.

The next step is to place the TADODataSet component on the form, and set its Connection property to `ADOConnection1`, its CommandType property to `cmdText`, and its CommandText property to the following:

```
SELECT * FROM [Category sales for 1997]
```

The resulting dataset for this query contains two fields—CategorySales (TBCDField) and CategoryNames (TWideStringField).

Then we need to set the Active property of the TADODataSet component to `True`.

Now let's place the TDBChart component on the form, right-click on it, and select the Edit Chart item from its pop-up menu. The property editor of the TDBChart component will appear.

In order to select the chart type, click the Chart tab in this editor, press the Add button, and select the Pie item from the TeeChart gallery.

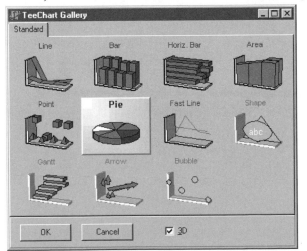

Now we can set the common properties for this chart, e.g., the chart title and its font, the legend display, the vertical and horizontal offset, the content of labels (and whether they are shown at all), the angle of the chart rotation if it is shown as a three-dimensional cylinder, and so on.

After setting the common chart properties, we will set some properties of the chart series. To do this, we need to click the Series tab of the TDBChart property editor, and select the necessary series from the combo box at the top of the selected the tab sheet.

The main property of this series is the DataSource property. To set it, we must click the Data Source tab of the page control on the current Series page. When we select the DataSet item from the combo box at the top of the Data Source tab sheet, an additional panel with some controls for setting the DataSource sub-properties appears. For this example, we will set the Pie property; it must contain numeric values (the CategorySales column values in this case).

The next step is to set the field that must supply data for labels. It would be nice to use the CategoryName field, but unfortunately, this component does not support WideString fields, and they are just ignored by the TDBChart component. We will solve this problem using several other components later in this book. Nevertheless, do not worry about this; most of these problems can be solved and we will show you how.

The simplest way to be able to use data from the WideString fields is to create a calculated field for the ADODataSet1 component that is of TStringField type (see the previous chapter to find out how to create calculated fields), and use it for creating labels. Let's leave the TDBChart property editor, create TField objects for TADODataSet1, then create a new calculated field and name it CategoryName_1. Finally, it is necessary to create the OnCalcField event handler of the ADODataSet1 component:

```
procedure TForm1.ADODataSet1CalcFields(DataSet: TDataSet);
begin
   ADODataSet1CategoryName_1.Value :=
   String(ADODataSet1CategoryName.Value);
end;
```

Now we can return to the TDBChart property editor, and select this field name as the supplier for label text.

Then, we can set some visible properties for this series, such as how to show marks, format data, and draw borders. To do this, we can select other tabs of the page control shown above.

As we use calculated fields to show labels, we can see them properly only at run time. So, let's compile and run the application:

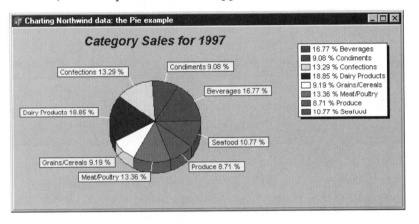

In this example, we have seen how to create a simple pie chart. This type of chart can only contain a single series. In the next example, we will see how to create multiple-series charts.

Using Several Series

This example is a little bit more complicated. It will contain several series, and its data will change dynamically at run time. Let's, for example, output average sales by month for the particular country selected by the user for different years in different series.

First, let's create a new view on the database server that will supply data for this chart. It must provide us with the sum of payments for orders in particular months and in particular countries, so we need to use the GROUP BY clause. In addition, the resulting dataset must contain a number representing the month and a number representing the year, so we need to use the Month and Year functions available in Microsoft SQL Server queries and views. Also, we need to pay discounts into account. The SQL source code for our view is shown below:

```
CREATE VIEW dbo.[Order subtotal by country]
AS
SELECT
    [Order Details].OrderID, SUM(CONVERT(money,
    [Order Details].UnitPrice * [Order Details].Quantity *
    (1-[Order Details].Discount)
    / 100) * 100) AS Subtotal, Customers.Country,
    Customers.CustomerID, Orders.OrderDate,
    Orders.ShippedDate, Orders.RequiredDate,
    { fn MONTH(OrderDate) } AS Ord_Month,
```

```
       { fn YEAR(OrderDate) } AS Ord_Year
FROM [Order Details] INNER JOIN
    Orders ON
    [Order Details].OrderID = Orders.OrderID INNER JOIN
    Customers ON
    Orders.CustomerID = Customers.CustomerID
GROUP BY [Order Details].OrderID, Customers.Country,
    Customers.CustomerID, Orders.OrderDate,
    Orders.ShippedDate, Orders.RequiredDate
```

Next, we will create a new application and, similar to the previous example, place the TADOConnection component on its form, set its LoginPrompt property to False, and set its ConnectionString property to the Northwind database.

The next step is to add the TADODataSet component that will contain the list of countries to select from. It must have the Connection property set to ADOConnection1, and its CommandText property must be the following:

```
SELECT DISTINCT Country FROM Customers
```

Let's set its Active property to True. Then we need to add the TDataSource component and the TDBGrid component connected with it to the form in order to show the list of countries. Later, we will create several detail datasets for it.

We create detail datasets by placing three TADODataSet components (one for each year) on the form. They have the same Connection property as the previous one. Their CommandText properties must be the following:

```
SELECT SUM(Subtotal) AS sum_in_month, Country, Ord_Month,
    Ord_Year
FROM [Order subtotal by country]
WHERE [Order subtotal by country].Ord_Year = 1996
GROUP BY Ord_Month, Country, Ord_Year
SELECT SUM(Subtotal) AS sum_in_month, Country, Ord_Month,
    Ord_Year
FROM [Order subtotal by country]
WHERE [Order subtotal by country].Ord_Year = 1997
GROUP BY Ord_Month, Country, Ord_Year
SELECT SUM(Subtotal) AS sum_in_month, Country, Ord_Month,
    Ord_Year
FROM [Order subtotal by country]
WHERE [Order subtotal by country].Ord_Year = 1998
GROUP BY Ord_Month, Country, Ord_Year
```

These datasets must be detail datasets in three master-detail relationships. Therefore, we will set their DataSource property to DataSource1, and their MasterFields property to Country. Then, we can set their Active properties to True.

Now we can place the TDBChart component to the form, open its property editor, and create three bar series in it with names like "1996," "1997," and "1998." For each of them, we need to select an appropriate TADODataSet component as the data source, and set the Bar value as Sum_in_month and the X value and Labels value as Ord_Month. The following figure shows the setup for the first bar series:

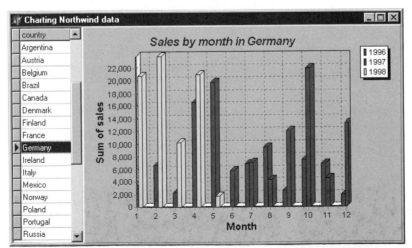

When the user navigates the country list, the chart must change its data. In order to make the chart refresh its series and show the current country name in the chart title, we will create the AfterScroll event handler of ADODataSet1 component:

```
procedure TForm1.ADODataSet1AfterScroll(DataSet: TDataSet);
begin
 //Refresh all series in the chart
 DBChart1.RefreshData;
 //Change its title
 DBChart1.Title.Text[0]:=
 'Sales by month in '+ADODataSet1.Fields[0].AsString;
end;
```

Now we can compile, run, and test our application. Notice that navigating the DBGrid1 component results in changes to the chart data and title.

Note: The RefreshData method forces TDBChart to retrieve all series points from all datasets that supply them with data. This method is not available for the TChart component.

Using Gantt Series

The next example will show how to use "unusual" series, such as Gantt series. This type of series is used when we need to control time periods for different processes, such as the time between shipment dates and required dates of orders. This value can be either positive, if the order is "well-timed", or negative, if the order is overdue. Therefore, we will use the TRadioGroup component to select what types of orders we will present—well-timed or overdue.

The Orders table contains several hundred records. In order to make the chart understandable, we must provide options for selecting the year and month when the orders were made. So, we need to create a master-detail relationship similar to the one in the previous example.

First, let's create a new application and, similar to the two previous examples, place the TADOConnection component on its form, set its LoginPrompt property to `False`, and set its ConnectionString property to be connected to the Northwind database. Then, we need to place the TADODataSet component with the Connection property equal to `ADOConnection1`, and the CommandText property containing the following string:

```
SELECT DISTINCT Year(ShippedDate) AS Ship_year,
Month(ShippedDate) AS Ship_month FROM Orders WHERE
ShippedDate IS NOT NULL
```

This query will contain a list of "year-and-month" pairs available in the Orders table.

Let's set the Active property of the ADODataSet1 component to `True`, and add the TDataSource and TDBGrid components connected with it to the form, in order to show the list of years and months.

Then let's place another TADODataSet component on the form, set its Connection property to `TADOConnection1`, and set its CommandText property to the following query:

```
SELECT * FROM [Order subtotal by country] WHERE
ShippedDate<RequiredDate AND ShippedDate IS NOT NULL
```

This query returns the order subtotals for the well-timed orders.

Now we need to set the master-detail relationship. To do so, we need to set the DataSource property of the TADODataSet2 component to `DataSource1`, and the MasterFields property to the `Ship_month;Ship_year` pair of values. To do this, we need to link the Ord_month field of the ADODataSet2 with the Ship_month field of the ADODataSet1, and the Ord_year field of the ADODataSet2 with the Ship_year field of the ADODataSet1.

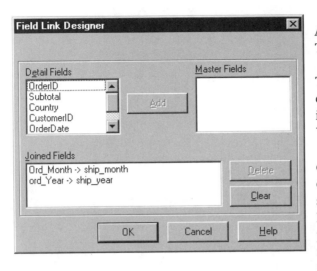

The next step is to set the Active property of the last placed TADODataSet component to True.

To create a chart, let's place the TDBChart component on the form, create a Gantt series in it, and set its DataSet property to the TADODataSet2 component.

This series requires start and end times for each "point" in the chart. To define them, we need to set the Start property to the RequiredDate field name, the End property to the ShippedDate field name, and the Y property to the Subtotal field name.

Note: Generally, we can also select a field that points to another record in the same dataset to show the next process or task (if any), with the end of the "point" being connected by a line with the start of the "point" selected as the next task.

Then, we place the TRadioGroup component on the form and add two strings ("Well-timed orders" and "Overdue orders") to its Items property. It is also necessary to create the OnClick event handler for the RadioGroup1 component in order to change the text of the query in the TADODataSet2 component at run time. The source code for this event handler is shown below.

```
procedure TForm1.RadioGroup1Click(Sender: TObject);
begin
 //Close the detail dataset
 ADODataSet2.Close;
 if RadioGroup1.ItemIndex = 1 then
 //Overdue orders selected, so ShippedDate>RequiredDate
  ADODataSet2.CommandText :=
   StringReplace(ADODataSet2.CommandText,'<','>',[rfReplaceAll])
 else
 //Well-timed orders selected, so ShippedDate<RequiredDate
  ADODataSet2.CommandText :=
 StringReplace(ADODataSet2.commandtext,'>','<',[rfReplaceAll]);
 //Open the detail dataset
 ADODataSet2.Open;
 //Change the chart title
 DBChart1.Title.Text[0] :=
  RadioGroup1.Items[RadioGroup1.ItemIndex];
```

```
//Refresh series in the chart
DBChart1.RefreshData;
end;
```

This event handler changes the CommandText property of the ADODataSet2 component, depending on what type of order is selected in the RadioGroup1 component, and refreshes the chart data and title.

Finally, similar to the previous example, we need to refresh data in the chart when the master dataset is being navigated. Here is the code for this:

```
procedure TForm1.ADODataSet1AfterScroll(DataSet: TDataSet);
begin
  DBChart1.RefreshData;
end;
```

If we run our application, we will see that both navigating the DBGrid1 component and clicking the radio buttons results in changes to the chart data.

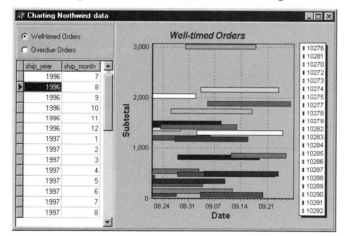

Using Standard Functions

With TeeChart chart components, we can create series that represent calculated functions. A function may act upon two series to create its source data. All functions can accept two arguments that are series of the chart. Here is the list of standard functions available in the TeeChart library:

Function Name	Meaning
Add	Calculates a sum of values for corresponding points in two series
Subtract	Subtracts values of the second series from appropriate values of the first series
Multiply	Multiplies values for corresponding points in two series
Divide	Divides values of the first series to appropriate values of the second series
High	Calculates the highest value for corresponding points in two series

Function Name	Meaning
Low	Calculates the lowest value for corresponding points in two series
Average	Calculates the average value for corresponding points in two series

To show how to use functions, let's edit the chart created previously in this chapter. Let's open its property editor, add the next series, and set its DataSource property to Function. Then we will select the Subtract function, and the 1998 and 1997 series for its arguments.

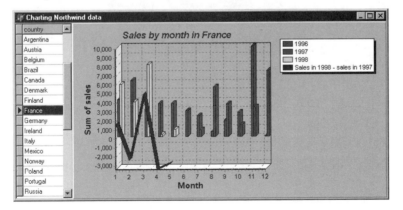

If we run this application, we will see that a new series appears, containing values that are equal to the difference between values of the 1998 and 1997 series.

Conclusion

In this chapter, we saw how to use charting in Delphi ADO applications. We have learned that:

- The TeeChart library consists of the TChart, TDBChart, and TQRChart components and a set of classes to provide Delphi applications with charting capabilities.

- The key property of the TDBChart component is the SeriesList property, which contains a collection of TChartSeries objects.

- The TChartSeries object is used to represent a set of points describing a function. Any chart contains one or more series. There are several descendants of the TChartSeries class used for presenting different types of series.

- The key property of the TChartSeries object is the DataSource property. This property can refer to any TDataSet descendant, and can also refer to one of the standard functions that act upon other series.

In this chapter, we created several charts, including charts with multiple series and with data that is changed at run time.

As we have seen, charting is a good way to present data for business analysis. However, there may be a need for some additional representation of the data besides charting, such as a special kind of document called database reports. We will show how to create such documents in the next chapter.

CREATING REPORTS WITH ADO COMPONENTS

In the previous chapter, we saw how to use business graphics in Delphi ADO applications. We learned how to create different types of charts and several series, use functions in charts, and use the ADO data sources to supply data for them. Now we are ready to learn how to create database reports. In this chapter, we will discuss how to create and use database reports with ADO components.

Reports are printed documents containing, as a rule, some data from databases. To generate reports, we usually use some special reporting tools. One example of such a tool is Crystal Reports from Seagate Software. To create reports in Delphi applications we can use either the run-time versions of such reporting tools or a set of VCL components. One set of components, QuickReport from QuSoft (http://www.qusoft.com), comes with Delphi.

The QuickReport components can be found in the QReport page of the Component Palette. These components allow us to create reports based on data from database tables and queries, string lists, and text files. The principle of designing reports with QuickReport components is very simple and based on Delphi Form Designer.

Types of Reports

There are different types of database reports. The most common are:

- *List (or tabular) reports* that look like a table, with rows containing data of a single dataset record. These reports can contain one or more similar columns of the same structure.

- *Label reports* that contain rectangular areas of the same width and height for each dataset record.

- *Master-detail* reports that contain data from more than one linked dataset, with detail records following the appropriate master record.

There are also other kinds of reports, which can be combinations of the ones listed above.

The Main Parts of a Report

Generally, a database report consists of several parts shown in the figure below (in terms of QuickReport, they are called *bands*). Note that any of them can be optional.

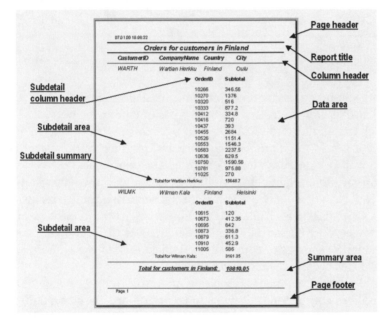

The first part of the report is the *report title*, which, as a rule, contains the name of the report, and, sometimes, the date and time of report generation or data selection criteria. This part is printed only on the first page of the report.

The *page header* and *page footer* are printed at the top and bottom of each page (although sometimes the page header can be absent on the first page of the report). One of them usually contains the page number, and sometimes the page header also contains the name of the report. The date and time may also be placed in the page header or footer. In the case of a very large report, they can be slightly different from the beginning to the end of the same report, since it may take some time to produce it.

The *column header* is often used in list reports. It is printed on the top of each column. Usually the column header is printed once per page, following the page header or the report title. If the report contains more than one column (multi-column report), the column header is printed once per column. In many cases, it is used to print field names (or their replacements) in list reports.

The most important part of the database report is the *data area*, which must contain database records. As previously mentioned, in list reports one record usually occupies one line, and in label reports (which are often used to generate address labels), one record usually occupies a rectangle of predefined width and height.

The *summary area* can contain totals of numeric fields or other summary information. This area usually follows the data area.

If we use datasets linked by a master-detail relationship, we need to use subdetail areas to print detail records linked to a particular master record. Very often, such detail records are printed after the appropriate master record. Moreover, subdetail areas can have summaries, headers, and footers of their own.

Introduction to QuickReports Components

Here we will briefly overview the QuickReports components. They can be divided into three distinct groups—layout components, data printing components, and data exporting components. We will start with the layout components.

Layout Components

Layout components are responsible for providing different report areas such as headers, footers, data areas, etc. They are containers for components responsible for printing data. Among them are the TQuickRep, TQRBand, TQRSubDetail, TQRStringsBand, TQRGroup, and TQRChildBand components.

The TQuickRep Component

TQuickRep is the main reporting component. This component is a descendant of an abstract TCustomQuickRep class. It serves as a container for all other layout components and can be placed on a form. Since this form does not contain any meaningful information for the application user, it does not make sense to show it.

The main property of this component is the DataSet property that specifies the TDataSet descendant, which supplies data for the report. Another useful property is the Bands property, which indicates the bands that should appear on the report.

In addition, we can use the Options property to define whether the first page header and last page footer are printed and whether this report is being compressed in memory before printing. The ReportTitle property is used to set the report title.

The most commonly used methods of this component are Preview and Print. The Preview method is used to generate the report and create a screen preview of it. From the preview window, we can choose whether or not to print the report. The Print method is used to send the report to a printer. To export the report to a format different from its native QRP format, we can use the ExportToFilter method.

For more information about the TQuickRep component, refer to the documentation that comes with your copy of Delphi.

Next we will discuss components that represent report bands. All of them are descendants of the TQRCustomBand class (TQRBand, TQRChildBand, TQRSubDetail, etc.).

The TQRBand Component

The TQRBand component is used to create different bands for the report. Its main property is the BandType property that indicates which role this band will play in the report. The possible values for this property are shown in the table below:

Value	Meaning
rbTitle	This band represents the report title that must be printed on the first page of the report.
rbPageHeader	This band represents the page header that is printed at the top of each page. You can prevent it from appearing on the first page by using the Options property of the TQuickRep component.
rbPageFooter	This band represents the page footer that is printed at the bottom of each page. You can prevent it from appearing on the last page by using the Options property of the TQuickRep component.
rbDetail	This band represents one record of the dataset specified with the DataSet property in the data area. It is printed once for every record.
rbSummary	This band controls a summary area.
rbSubDetail	This band represents a data area for detail datasets in master-detail relationships. It is used by the TQRSubDetail component.
rbColumnHeader	This band controls a column header that is printed at the top of each column on all pages of a report.
rbGroupHeader	This band represents a header band for groups and subdetail bands. It is printed at the beginning of a group or before a set of subdetail bands.
rbGroupFooter	This band represents a footer band for groups and subdetail records. It is printed at the end of a group or after a set of subdetail bands.
rbChild	This band is a continuation of another band.

The TQRBand component can be placed on a TQuickRep component. At design time, we can use a TQuickRep property editor to set which bands this report consists of:

Other useful properties of the TQRBand component are the HasChild and ChildBand properties. The first one defines whether this band has a child band, i.e., the band that must be printed after it. The second property defines the name of the child band.

The LinkBand property is used to force printing of two different bands on the same page.

The ForceNewPage and ForceNewColumn properties are used to print this band always on the top of the page or on the top of the column, respectively.

We can operate the printed data programmatically by using the event handlers for the AfterPrint and BeforePrint events that are fired by this component.

The TQRSubDetail Component

This component can be used to create a master-detail report. It is responsible for printing detail records for any master record. Its main property is the Dataset property, which must contain the name of the detail dataset. The Master property must be set to the name of the TQuickRep component. The Bands property of the TQRSubDetail component defines whether this subdetail band has header and footer bands, and the HeaderBand and FooterBand properties define their names.

Note that the master-detail relationship between the datasets themselves must also be set up properly. For more details, see Chapter 8.

Also note that this component allows us to create multi-level master-detail relationships. In this case, the Master property can be set to the other TQRSubDetail component.

To change the data or its appearance before it is sent to printer, we can create the handler for the OnNeedData event that is fired by this component.

The TQRStringsBand Component

The TQRStringsBand component is a report band that makes it possible to create reports without connection to any dataset. It is responsible for printing a list of strings that are contained in its Items property (of the TStrings type). One instance of the band is printed for each entry in the string list.

The TQRGroup Component

This component is used when it is necessary to divide a report into logical groups. The TQRGroup component plays a role as a group header band and can have an optional group footer band.

The TQRGroup component finishes printing the current group and begins printing a new one when the result of its Expression property changes.

The FooterBand property indicates the name of the footer band for a group. The Master property is used to select what part of the report the grouping should apply to. The ReprintOnNewPage property indicates whether the group header is reprinted at the top of every page if a group occupies more than one page.

The TQRChildBand Component

This component is used to create a *child band*—a band that is a continuation of another ("parent") band. This can be necessary if the "parent" band contains elements that are not constant (for example, memos with variable size). In this case, all controls that follow such a control can be placed on the TQRChildBand component. The properties of this component are similar to the properties of the TQRBand component.

TheParentBand property indicates its parent band. The LinkBand property of the TQRChildBand component can be set to the "parent" band when it is necessary to print these bands on the same page.

Data Printing Components

Data printing components are an essential part of the QuickReport component. They must be placed on different report bands. Their appearance and behavior depend on which band contains this particular component. There are data-aware and non-data-aware data printing components. For example, the TQRDBText, TQRDBRichText, and TQRDBImage components are data aware, while the TQRLabel, TQRSysData, TQRMemo, TQRRichText, TQRShape, and TQRImage components are not. The TQRExpr and TQRExprMemo components can contain expressions based on data from database fields, and the TQRChart component can include a chart based on a data from a dataset. Let's briefly look at the data printing components that are part of QuickReport.

The TQRLabel and TQRDBText Components

The TQRLabel component is not data aware. It is a descendant of the TQRCustomLabel class, and is used for printing static text contained in its Caption property. This component has the usual Alignment, AutoSize, AutoStretch, Lines, WordWrap, Caption, Color, and Font properties that specify its appearance on a report. To manipulate the properties of the TQRLabel component at run time, we can use the event handler for its OnPrint event.

The TQRDBText component, unlike the previous one, is a data-aware descendant of the TQRCustomLabel class. It is used to print number, date/time, text, and memo fields (except formatted memo fields) from a dataset. The TQRDBText component can have a variable height to fit to the text length of the particular record. To do so, set its AutoStretch property to True.

The main properties of the TQRDBText component are DataSet, which points to a TDataSet descendant (not to a TDataSource component!), DataField, which indicates the field of the dataset that must be printed, and Mask, which defines an output format of the printed data.

Both of these components also have the usual Alignment, AutoSize, AutoStretch, Lines, WordWrap, Caption, Color, and Font properties that specify their appearance on a report.

The TQRExpr Component

This component is also a descendant of the TQRCustomLabel class and can be used to calculate an expression, defined in its Expression property, during report generation. Expressions can be based on dataset fields, but this is not required.

The TQRExpr component has its own property editor, and we will discuss how to use it later in this chapter.

The ResetAfterPrint property is used if we want to reset the expression result to 0 after the contents of this component are printed. This is usually used for printing totals in group footers. The Master property is used to recalculate the expression during dataset navigation. This allows us to calculate sums and counts for sets of records. The Mask property is used for formatting the expression in a report.

TQRExpr also has the usual Alignment, AutoSize, AutoStretch, Lines, WordWrap, Caption, Color, and Font properties that specify its appearance on a report.

The TQRSysData Component

This component is used for printing system information, such as report title, date, time, and current page number. Its Data property defines the type of system information to be printed, and its Text property contains text that could be printed near the system data value.

This component also has the usual Alignment, AutoSize, and Font properties that specify its appearance on a report.

The TQRMemo and TQRExprMemo Components

The TQRMemo component is used to print large multiline texts. It is also a descendant of the TQRCustomLabel class and is not data aware.

The TQRExprMemo component, which is also a descendant of the TQRCustomLabel class, is used for printing memo text with embedded expressions. These expressions are substituted with their values during report generation. Expressions can be based on dataset fields, but this is not required.

An example of an expression memo text is shown below:

```
Dear {Name},
Your order # {OrderID} is processed.
All ordered items will be delivered at {OrderDate}.

Regards,
Jack Green,
Sales manager.
```

Both of these components have the usual Alignment, AutoSize, AutoStretch, Lines, WordWrap, Caption, Color, and Font properties that specify their appearance on a report.

The TQRRichText and TQRDBRichText Components

The TQRRichText is a non-data-aware component used to print formatted memo text. This text can be contained in its Lines property, or in a TRichEdit component that is associated through the ParentRichEdit property of the component.

The TQRDBRichText component is data aware, and is used to print formatted memo fields stored in BLOB fields. To make the height of this control accommodate the length of the text, we can set its AutoStretch property to True.

The TQRImage and TQRDBImage Components

The TQRImage component is not data aware. It is used to print images in the report in any graphics formats supported by the VCL. The AutoSize, Center, and Stretch properties are responsible for fitting the picture to the control, centering it, and resizing the TQRImage to fit the image inside it. The Picture property contains a reference to the image to be printed.

The TQRDBImage component is data aware. It can be used to print images stored in BLOB fields in tables in graphics formats supported by the VCL.

The AutoSize, Center, and Stretch properties are responsible for fitting the picture to the control, centering it, and resizing the TQRDBImage to fit the image inside it.

The DataSet property points to a TDataSet descendant, and the DataField property indicates the field of this dataset that must be printed.

The TQRChart Component

This component can be used to print business charts based on data from datasets. The TQRChart component links TChart or TDBChart components with QuickReports, allowing them to be embedded to report bands.

The TQRShape Component

This non-data-aware component is used to draw rectangles, circles, and lines on a report's surface. To specify the shape to draw and how to draw it, we can use the Shape, Pen, and Brush properties of this component.

Data Exporting Components

Components for exporting data allow us to save the report as an ASCII text file (TQRTextFilter component), HTML page (TQRHTMLFilter component), or comma-separated value (TQRCSVFilter component) file that can be opened in most spreadsheet packages like Microsoft Excel or Lotus 1-2-3. To allow the user to export all reports in his application to one of these formats, we need to place an appropriate component on one of the TQuickRep components in the application.

The TQRTextFilter Component

This component allows us to export the report to a text file. If the TQRTextFilter component is placed on any TQuickRep component in the application, the Text file option will appear in the Save to file dialog in the report preview form. Note that all reports can also be saved as ASCII files with the ExportToFilter method of the TQuickReport component.

The TQRCSVFilter Component

This component allows us to export the report to a CSV file. If the TQRCSVFilter component is placed on any TQuickRep component in the application, the CSV file option will appear in the Save to file dialog in the report preview form. Note that all reports can also be saved as CSV files with the ExportToFilter method of the TQuickReport component.

The TQRHTMLFilter Component

This component allows us to export the report to an HTML file. If the TQRHTMLFilter component is placed on any TQuickRep component in the application, the HTML file option will appear in the Save to file dialog in the report preview form. Note that all reports can also be saved as HTML files with the ExportToFilter method of the TQuickReport component.

We have covered a lot of components, and now it's time to see most of them in action. The rest of this chapter will show you how to use the QuickReport components in Delphi ADO applications.

Using QuickReport Components with ADO

In this section, we will learn how to use the QuickReport components in our Delphi ADO applications. We will cover the following topics:

- Using templates
- Creating custom reports
- Creating master-detail reports
- Using expressions
- Using business graphics
- Using memo fields and images in reports
- Creating reports using ADO recordsets
- Creating custom preview forms
- Saving reports in different formats

We will start with a discussion of how to use Delphi Object Repository templates to create reports.

Using Templates

The simplest way to create a list report is to use the QuickReport Wizard, which can be launched by clicking the icon on the Business page of the Delphi Object Repository. Unfortunately for us, this wizard can be used only with BDE data sources, and does not support ADO data sources.

Besides the QuickReport Wizard, there are three report templates on the Forms page of the Object Repository. The QuickReport List template is used to create list reports, the QuickReport Labels template can help us create label reports, while the QuickReport Master/Detail template allows us to create master-detail reports.

Click on the QuickReport Labels icon. This will give us a new form with the report template. This form contains a TQuickRep component, which contains a TQRBand component, a TQRLabel component with some comments, and a TTable component.

Now we need to delete the TQRLabel, which contains a comment and is not necessary here, and the TTable component, along with the DB and DBTables units from the Uses clause. The TTable component is used to access data through BDE, and in our ADO applications we simply do not need it. Instead, we will use the TADOConnection and the TADODataSet components in our report. Unfortunately, the Object Repository does not contain any ADO-enabled report templates, but you can create and add them if you need to.

Now we can set the ConnectionString property of the ADOConnection1 component to the Northwind database on the Microsoft SQL Server 7 or Access 2000. Then we connect the ADODataSet1 component to the ADOConnection1 component through its Connection property, specify the ADODataSet1.CommandType property as cmdTable, and select the Customers table from the list of available tables. After that, we set the Active property of the ADODataSet1 to True and connect QuickRep1 component to ADODataSet1 through the DataSet property. If you forget to set the DataSet property of the TQuickRep component, your report will consist of only one record from this dataset.

The next step is to place some TQRDBText components on DetailBand1 (in this case it is the only band of the report), and set their DataSet property to ADODataSet1. Then, let's set their DataField property to CompanyName, Address, City, and Country. We can also change the Font property of these components, if necessary, and set the Frame property of the DetailBand1 component to allow frames to be drawn around it.

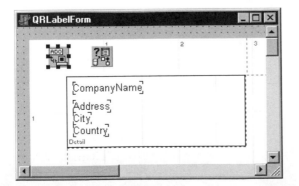

If we want to know what the printed report will look like, we can select the Preview option from the pop-up menu of the TQuickRep component. The following screen shot shows the Print Preview page for our report.

If we don't like the results of the preview, we can continue editing the report in the Form Designer by changing properties of existing components or adding other components until the results satisfy us.

To show and print this report at run time, we simply place the TButton component on the main form of the application, refer to the report form in the main form in the Uses clause, and create the following OnClick event handler for the Button1 component:

```
procedure TForm1.Button1Click(Sender: TObject);
begin
   QRLabelForm.QuickRep1.Preview;
end;
```

Here we use the Preview method of the TQuickRep component to show the report in a standard preview window.

Creating Custom Reports

In addition to using templates, we can manually create reports. The simplest way to do this is to select the Report icon from the New page of the Object Repository.

This brings up an empty report form. We can right-click on it, and select the Report Settings command from the pop-up menu. Then, we need to select the kinds of band this report will contain. For example, let's select the Page Header, Page Footer, Detail

Band, and Column Header check boxes (or set the corresponding properties in the QuickReport.Bands property). In addition, let's enable the printing of the first page header and the last page footer and set the ReportTitle property of the TQuickRep to Customers of Northwind Traders.

Leaving the current number of columns equal to one, we obtain an empty list report, which is the most common type of report. Note that our report contains several different TQRBand components. We will use the TADOConnection and TADODataSet components that are the same as in the previous example (you can just copy and paste them), and we will set the DataSet property of the QuickRep1 component to ADODataSet1.

Now we can place some TQRDBText components on the DetailBand1, and set their DataSet property to ADODataSet1. Then, we set their DataField property to the following values (by selecting them from the pop-up list): CustomerID, CompanyName, Country, City, and Address. Then, we place four TQRLabel components (one for each field selected earlier) on ColumnHeaderBand1, arrange them, and set their Caption property to appropriate field names or any other meaningful text.

After that, we can use some TQRSysData components. For purposes of this example, we will place two of them on the page footer and set their Data property to qrsDateTime and qrsPageNumber, respectively. We can also add some additional text to these components, for example, "Page #". The third TQRSysData component placed on PageHeaderBand1 will have its Data property equal to qrsReportTitle. The results of our manipulations are shown on the screen shot below.

Using the Print Preview command, we can preview this report to find how it will look on paper.

In this example, we have created a list database report using the data from only one dataset. However, very often we need to create more complicated reports based, for example, on two or more linked datasets. This is covered below.

Creating Master-Detail Reports

To create a *master-detail report*—a report based on two or more linked datasets—we can either use the QuickReport Master/Detail template from the Forms page of the Object Repository or create all necessary bands manually.

First we create a new report and place all possible bands on it. In addition, let's add the TQRSubDetail component to a report and set its Master property to the TQuickRep component. Then, we need to set the Bands.HasHeader and Bands.HasFooter properties to True. This adds two additional bands that are the header and footer bands for subdetail records.

The next step is to place the TADOConnection component on the report. It can have the same ConnectionString property as in the previous example.

Now we can place two TADODataSet components on the report and set their Connection property to the ADOConnection1 component and their CommandType property to cmdText. Now we need to insert the following query into the CommandText property of the ADODataSet1 component:

```
SELECT CustomerID, CompanyName, City, Country
FROM Customers
WHERE Country='Finland'
```

In addition, let's insert the following query into the CommandText property of the ADODataSet2 component:

```
SELECT CustomerID, Orders.OrderID, Subtotal
FROM Orders, [Order Subtotals]
WHERE Orders.OrderID=[Order Subtotals].OrderID
```

Then, we need to set the master-detail relationship between these datasets. To do this, we need to place the TDataSource component on the report, set its DataSet property to ADODataSet1, set the DataSource property of the ADODataSet2 component to DataSource1, and then set its DataField property to CustomerID (we can use the property editor to do so). This links our datasets in the master-detail relationship.

The next step is to set the DataSet property of the QRSubDetail1 component to ADODataSet2.

Now, we can place some TQRDBText components on the QRSubDetail component and the DetailBand1 component. It is also necessary to bind them with the appropriate datasets (by selecting the DataSet property) and appropriate fields (by selecting the DataField property). The results of our manipulations are shown on the screen shot below.

In this example, we have created a master-detail report. However, the summary areas for master and detail datasets in this report are still empty. To calculate summaries, we need to use expressions. This is covered below.

Using Expressions

Most reporting tools allow using expressions in reports. QuickReport also provides this feature. To calculate an expression we can use the TQRExpr component. It should be placed on an appropriate band, and its Expression property must be set through an appropriate property editor. This property editor allows us to use expressions, database fields, variables, and functions (including aggregate functions such as sums and averages).

Let's extend our previous example with expressions. To do this, we need to place two TQRExpr components on the SummaryBand1 and set the Expression property of the first of them to simple text string:

```
'Total for customers in Finland: '.
```

The Expression property of the second TQRExpr component must be set to

```
SUM(ADODataSet2.Subtotal)
```

by selecting the function name, the dataset name, and the field name in the Expression Wizard as shown below.

We also need to set the Master property of the TQRExpr component to QRSubDetail1 and the ResetAfterPrint property to True.

The next step is to place two TQRExpr components on the group footer of the subdetail band. The Expression property of the first of them must be set to:

```
'Total for '+ADODataSet1.CompanyName+': '
```

This expression contains one of the fields of the master record that is not represented in this subdetail band, but is present in the nearest detail band connected with the master dataset in the master-detail relationship. The Expression property of the second TQRExpr component will be set to:

```
SUM(ADODataSet2.Subtotal)
```

and the Master property of this component needs to be also set to QRSubDetail1. We also need to set the ResetAfterPrint property of this component to True. In this case, it is essential, because this band will be printed several times. This property defines what data is really summarized—the fields of all previously printed detail records, or just of the subset of detail records following the master one. This results in calculating sums only for a subset of detail records following the particular master record. The resulting report is shown on the screen shot below.

To find how the report will look, we can use the Print Preview command. From the screen shot below, you can see that all summaries are calculated correctly both for the master data set and the detail set.

Note that all calculations defined in such expressions are provided by a client application. If we need to provide calculations that involve a large amount of data or several linked datasets, and this data must not be printed, we can create and use, for example, stored procedures (these were discussed in Chapter 10). This allows us to make the database server perform all calculations without sending unneeded data to the client application.

Using Business Graphics in Database Reports

There are many custom report types that cannot be created by using templates, for example, reports that contain business graphics. To create such a report, we can add the TQRChart component to the list or master-detail report.

Creating a chart report is similar to creating the master-detail report shown above. The datasets used for this report are the Customers and Orders tables of the Northwind database. You can copy and paste the TADOConnection component from the previous example (or use it directly by referring to the previous report form), and then add two TADODataSet components to the report, set their CommandType properties to cmdTable. Set the cmdText property of the ADODataSet1 component to Customers, and the cmdText property of the ADODataSet2 component to Orders. Then we need to link the tables with a master-detail relationship. To do this, it is necessary to place the TDataSource component on the report, set its DataSet property to the ADODataSet1, set the DataSource of the ADODataSet2 component to DataSource1, and then set its DataField property to CustomerID.

The next step is to set the DataSet property of the QRSubDetail1 component to ADODataSet2, and the DataSet property of the TQuickRep component to the ADODataSet1. If necessary, we can place some TQRDBText components on the QRSubDetail component and the DetailBand1 component, and link them with the appropriate dataset fields. We can also create some summaries in this report.

After these preparations, we can expand the vertical size of the DetailBand1 component. Then, let's place the TQRChart on to the DetailBand1 and double-click on it to open its property editor.

Now we need to edit this chart. Let's add one series to the chart (let it be a Horizontal Bar series). In the Chart page, we need to click the Add button and select a linear graph from the TeeChart Gallery.

The next step is to click the Series tab of the TQRChart property editor, select the created series, and click the DataSource tab. After selecting the DataSet option from

the combo box control, additional interface elements will appear in this page. Then we need to select the ADODataSet2 from the DataSet combo box control. It is also necessary to select the fields of this dataset that become X values (bars in the case of horizontal bars), Y values, and point labels. Name these OrderDate, Freight, and OrderDate respectively.

Now click the Close button. Our report contains a horizontal bar chart.

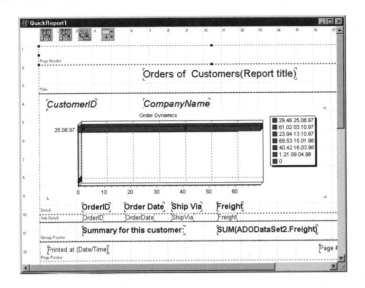

We can also edit other chart appearance parameters like titles, angles, and the colors of walls and axes. You can refer to the previous chapter for details on how to do this.

To see how the report will look, use the Print Preview command.

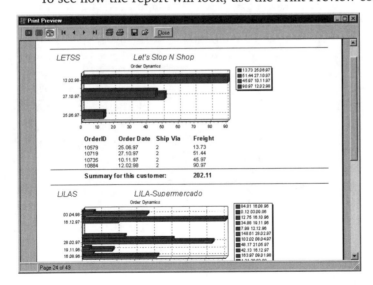

Using Memo Fields and Images in Reports

To print images, we may use either the TQRImage component, which is suitable for printing non-data-aware images (e.g., company logo, etc.), or the TQRDBImage component, which allows us to print graphical images from the fields of database tables. Note that printing graphical images from the fields of tables is still not supported in most professional report generators.

To illustrate how to create a report with images and memos, let's use the Employees table of the Northwind database. We need to create a new list report, put the TADOConnection and TADODataSet components into it, and connect them with the Northwind database and Employee table.

The next step is to connect the TADODataSet component to the TADOConnection component and set its CommandType property to cmdText. Then select the Employees table name from the list of available tables and set its Active property to True. It is necessary to set the DataSet property of the QuickRep1 component to ADODataSet1.

Now let's increase the height of the DetailBand1 and place the TQRImage and TQRDBText components on it. Then, we need to set the DataSet property of the TQRDBText component to ADODataSet1 and the DataField property to Notes. Set the AutoStretch property of the QRDBText1 component to True in order to fit its size to the text length. Also, we need to set the AutoSize property of the QRImage1 component to True in order to fit its size to the image size. Finally, set the WordWrap property of the QRDBText1 to True (in order to allow this field to be shown as a multi-line text). Thus, we have created the report shown at the figure below.

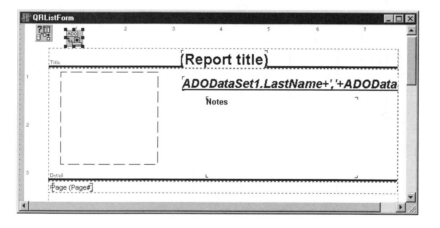

Why do we use the TQRImage component instead of the TQRDBImage component? The reason is the "Bitmap Image is not valid" problem that was discussed in Chapter 11. This problem arises because Microsoft Access and Microsoft SQL Server store images with the OLE Storage header, while Delphi image components including TQRImage and TQRDBImage can display only "pure" graphical data. So, we need to handle the BeforePrint event of an appropriate TQRBand component that occurs before a band is about to be printed (or shown in a preview window). In this event handler, we will extract an image from the database, remove the OLE Storage header, and put the image itself in the band:

```
procedure TQRListForm.DetailBand1BeforePrint(Sender: TQRCustomBand; var
PrintBand: Boolean);
var
  Bitmap  : TBitmap;
  BS      : TADOBlobStream;
```

```
begin
 // Create ADO BLOB Stream
 try
  BS := TADOBlobStream.Create(ADODataSet1Photo, bmRead);
  // Skip OLE Storage header
  BS.Seek(78, soFromBeginning);
  // Create bitmap
  Bitmap := TBitmap.Create;
  // Load graphics from a stream
  Bitmap.LoadFromStream(BS);
  // Show it
  QRImage1.Picture.Graphic := Bitmap;
  // Clear memory
 finally
  Bitmap.Free;
  BS.Free;
 end;
end;
```

Note: The approach shown above requires persistent fields that can be created using the Fields Editor of the appropriate data set.

We can also handle the AfterScroll event of the TADODataSet component instead of the BeforePrint event of the appropriate report band to get the same results.

Of course, you can see images only during run time. So, we need to refer to this report from the main form and initiate a preview of this report from it (for example, by placing a button on the main form and handling its OnClick event).

Note: We need to place the reference to the report form into the Auto-create forms list in the Project Options dialog box. This will guarantee that the report form will be created before we will try to access it.

Let's look at the preview of this report. We can see that the height of the text itself and the height of the appropriate band changes according to the length of the text in the current record.

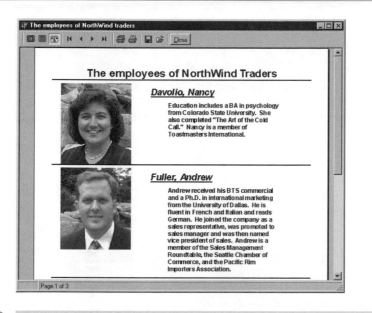

Note: If you need to place some report elements below such auto-stretched components, set the HasChild property of the appropriate band to True and place all these components on the new TQRChildBand component.

Creating Reports Using ADO Recordsets

In the previous examples, we have created all reports using ADOExpress components. It is convenient but not necessary. Here we will show how to create a very simple report using the ADO Recordset object directly.

Let's create a new empty list report, delete all TDataSet descendants from it, place the TQRMemo component on it, and set this component's font to Courier. Then, like in the previous example, we will set the AutoStretch property to True, the AutoSize property to False, and the WordWrap property to True (to allow this field to be shown as multiline text).

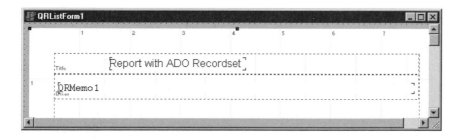

This report must not be connected to any dataset because it manipulates the ADO recordset directly. That means that we must generate all text to be printed programmatically, and cannot use the Print Preview feature at design time.

To generate the text to be printed, we will handle the BeforePrint event of the TQuickRep component:

```
procedure TQRListForm1.QuickRep1BeforePrint(Sender:
 TCustomQuickRep; var PrintReport: Boolean);
var  DSN: String;
     RST: _Recordset;
begin
 //Delete the previous output
 QRMemo1.Lines.Clear;
 //Create the Recordset object
 OleCheck(CoCreateInstance(CLASS_Recordset, nil, clsctx_all,
 IID__Recordset, RST));
 //Set the Data Source
 DSN := 'Provider=SQLOLEDB.1;Integrated Security=SSPI;'
 + 'Persist Security Info=False;Initial Catalog=Northwind;'
 +  'Data Source=MAINDESK;Locale Identifier=1049; '
 +  'Connect Timeout=15; Use Procedure for Prepare=1;'
 +  'Auto Translate=True;Packet Size=4096; '
 +  'Workstation ID=MAINDESK';
 //Open the Recordset
 RST.Open('SELECT * FROM Customers',DSN,adOpenForwardOnly,
 adLockReadOnly, adCmdUnspecified);
 //Fill the QRMemo with the printer text
 Repeat
  QRMemo1.Lines.Add(RST.Fields[0].value+ '  '
  + RST.Fields[1].value + ' (' + RST.Fields[8].value + ')');
  RST.move(1, EmptyParam);
 Until RST.Eof;
end;
```

We can still use the TADODataSet component (RST := ADODataset1.Recordset) but in the example above we have shown you another method of using ADO objects.

Note: Please note that your version of the string in the DSN variable may differ from the one shown in the code above.

In this example, we just added strings to the Lines property of the TQRMemo component—one for each record in the recordset. As we have already mentioned, we can see this report only at run time. Here is how it may look:

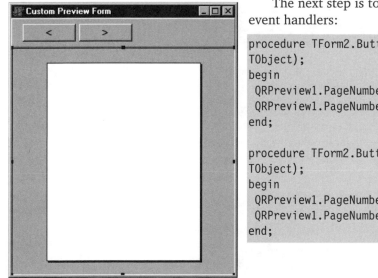

Creating Custom Preview Forms

In all the previous examples in this chapter, we used the standard QuickReport preview form. However, if we want to change the appearance or behavior of this form, we can create our own preview forms. To do this, we must use the TQRPreview component.

Let's create a form, place the TQRPreview component on it, and place two buttons to navigate the multi000000000page report.

The next step is to create appropriate event handlers:

```
procedure TForm2.Button1Click(Sender:
TObject);
begin
 QRPreview1.PageNumber :=
 QRPreview1.PageNumber-1;
end;

procedure TForm2.Button2Click(Sender:
TObject);
begin
 QRPreview1.PageNumber :=
 QRPreview1.PageNumber+1;
end;
```

Now we need to refer to this custom preview form from all report forms and from the form which calls this custom preview (in our example, it is the main form of the application).

We can place a check box on the main form and the necessary set of buttons (one for each report to show/print it). Let's also set the Tag properties of the buttons to values from 1 to 6. It is also necessary to refer to all report forms in the unit of the main form of our application.

The next step is to create a procedure that can be used as an OnPreview event handler for each report in the application:

```
procedure TForm1.CustomPreview(Sender: TObject);
begin
 Form2.QRPreview1.QRPrinter := TQRPrinter(Sender);
end;
```

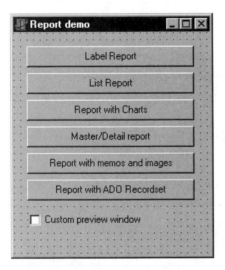

Now we need to create a common OnClick event handler for all six buttons to allow the user to select the kind of preview form to use—standard or custom.

```
procedure TForm1.Button1Click(Sender: TObject);
var CurrRpt: TQuickRep;
begin
with Sender as TButton do begin
 //select what of six reports is to preview
 case Tag of
  1:   CurrRpt:=QRLabelForm.QuickRep1;
  2:   CurrRpt:=QuickReport3;
  3:   CurrRpt:=QuickReport1;
  4:   CurrRpt:=QRMDForm.QuickRep1;
  5:   CurrRpt:=QRListForm.QuickRep1;
  6:   CurrRpt:=QRListForm1.QuickRep1;
 end;
 if Form1.CheckBox1.Checked then
  //the custom preview form is used
  begin
   //show the custom preview form
   Form2.Show;
```

```
    //and set the OnPreview event handler for the selected report
    CurrRpt.OnPreview:=CustomPreview;
  end else begin
    //the standard preview form is used
    //hide the custom preview form
    Form2.Hide;
    //and reset the OnPreview event handler
    CurrRpt.OnPreview:=nil;
  end;
  //preview the report
  CurrRpt.Preview;
  end;
end;
```

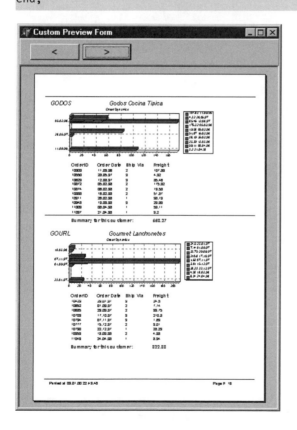

In this code, we change the name of the TQuickRep component to preview. The visibility of the custom preview form depends on the Checked property of the CheckBox1 component on the main form.

Now all six of our reports must be previewed in our custom window. You can also switch between the standard and custom preview forms using the check box in the main form.

Saving Reports in Different Formats

Generally, the QuickReport reports can be saved in the proprietary format QRP. However, it is also possible to save reports as ASCII, HTML, or CSV files (we already mentioned this possibility early in the chapter). To do this, we need to place the TQRTextFilter, TQRHTMLFilter, or TQRCSVFilter components on any report form of the application.

After that, all reports of application can be saved in the format supported by the chosen TQRxxxFilter components. A report saved in the HTML format and then opened in a Web browser is shown below:

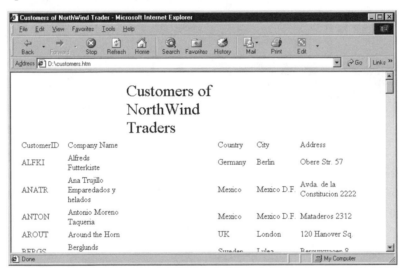

Other Ways of Creating Reports

We have spent this chapter looking at the QuickReport components that come as part of your Delphi package. Note that using these components is not the only way to create and print reports. For example, we can use other reporting tools, such as Crystal Reports from Seagate Software. In this case, it is possible to include such reports in applications by using the reporting engine API functions from our own code. Often, such reporting tools may also contain ActiveX controls, which encapsulate this API. They can be embedded in the Component Palette for use in Delphi applications. Sometimes VCL components for Delphi are included in professional versions of some reporting tools.

And, finally, some reporting tools can be Automation servers. In these cases, it is possible to manipulate them from Delphi applications by creating Automation Controllers. One of the best examples of such Automation servers is Microsoft Office. Using the Automation controller we can perform almost all of the operations of Word, Excel, or PowerPoint. This gives us an opportunity to use these tools to create reports.

Conclusion

In this chapter, we saw how to use the QuickReport components to create database reports for Delphi ADO applications. We discussed the main parts of reports, reviewed the QuickReport components that are included in Delphi, and showed how to create different kinds of reports with them, including master-detail reports, and reports with charts, images, and memos. We also learned how to create QuickReport reports based on recordsets.

We also discussed how to calculate summaries and use business graphics in reports. Presenting data in the form of charts and obtaining summaries are facilities necessary for data analysis and decision support. But in many cases, creating simple charts or calculating summary values is not enough to make an important decision, and more complicated data analysis is required. The next two chapters will show you how to provide such analysis using OLAP—online analytical processing.

14

OLAP BASICS

In this chapter, we will discuss using ADO for online analytical processing (OLAP)—the data management techniques that are widely used in decision support systems and data warehousing. We will also discuss the two ways of implementing OLAP with ADO and Delphi: using client-side OLAP with the help of the Decision Cube components in Delphi VCL, and using server-side OLAP, based on the MS SQL Server 7.0 OLAP services.

First, we will present an overview of the basic terms used in OLAP, then we will discuss the Decision Cubes.

OLAP Basics

As a rule, enterprise information systems consist of different user applications. These include applications for data analysis and decision support, obtaining trends, receiving statistics, and other tasks. They usually have an advanced user interface that includes business graphics and provides functionality for obtaining various aggregate data—sums, counts, averages, maximum and minimum values, and so on.

Behind the user interface of such decision support applications is an implementation of such analysis that is based on OLAP.

What are OLAP and Data Warehousing?

OLAP—*online analytical processing*—is a popular technology for multidimensional business analysis. It is based on the multidimensional data model that will be discussed later in this chapter. The concept of OLAP was described in 1993 by Dr. E.F. Codd, a well-known database researcher and developer of the relational database model. Currently, OLAP support is implemented in different databases and tools. For example, most database servers provide OLAP facilities, sometimes as separate specialized data storages and tools for operating them (e.g., ORACLE Express OLAP, Microsoft SQL Server 7.0 OLAP Services, and so on).

OLAP is a key component in data warehousing. *Data warehousing* is the process of collecting and sifting data from different information systems and making the resulting information available to end users for analysis and reporting. Data warehouses can be used to describe these stores of collected and summarized information that is available for users to browse.

In most cases, there is no easy way to find the information in relational databases that is necessary for making a decision. For example, the data structures can be difficult for the end user to understand, or the user's questions are too complex when expressed in SQL.

Take the following example. To get an answer to the question "Who are the top customers in each region for the year 1998 arranged by quarter?" we must execute many queries to obtain a two-dimensional subset of aggregate values and then show this subset to the user. That is why any OLAP implementation contains advanced query tools which hide the database complexity from the end user.

In discussing OLAP tools, we should say that OLAP facilities also can be found in development tools and office applications. Unlike server-side OLAP, such as Oracle Express OLAP or Microsoft SQL Server 7.0 OLAP Services, these facilities usually implement client-side OLAP. For example, within Microsoft Excel 2000, a new PivotTable dynamic view function provides connectivity between Excel spreadsheets and OLE DB Provider for SQL Server OLAP Services. This gives us the ability to create a local subset from a larger set of aggregate data from the database server.

As for Delphi, its Enterprise version comes with a set of client-side OLAP components, which can be found in the Decision Cube page of the Component Palette. Later in this chapter, we will look at them in more detail.

Using OLE DB Provider for SQL Server OLAP Services, Delphi applications can also connect to server-side OLAP storages to retrieve aggregate data for end users. In this chapter and the next we will see how to create such applications.

Before we start to create decision support applications, let's spend some time discussing multidimensional cubes, and what data they contain.

What are Decision Cubes?

In this section, we will discuss the Decision Cube and OLAP concepts in details. To provide a simple example of what multidimensional analysis is, we will use the Northwind database on Microsoft SQL Server, and will create a view based on several tables from it. Here is the SQL source code for this view:

```
CREATE VIEW Ord_pmt AS
SELECT [Order Details].OrderID, Orders.OrderDate,
    CONVERT(varchar, Orders.CustomerID) AS CustomerID,
    CONVERT(varchar, Customers.Country) AS Country,
    CONVERT(varchar, Customers.City) AS City,
    SUM(CONVERT(money, [Order Details].UnitPrice *
    [Order Details].Quantity *
    (1 - [Order Details].Discount) / 100) * 100) AS Payment,
```

```
    CONVERT(varchar,Shippers.CompanyName) AS CompanyName,
    Orders.Freight,
    CONVERT(varchar, Employees.LastName)
    AS EmployeeName
FROM [Order Details] INNER JOIN
    Orders ON
    [Order Details].OrderID = Orders.OrderID INNER JOIN
    Customers ON
    Orders.CustomerID = Customers.CustomerID INNER JOIN
    Shippers ON
    Orders.ShipVia = Shippers.ShipperID INNER JOIN
    Employees ON
    Orders.EmployeeID = Employees.EmployeeID
GROUP BY [Order Details].OrderID, Orders.OrderDate,
    Orders.Freight, Customers.Country, Customers.City,
    Orders.CustomerID, Employees.LastName,
    Shippers.CompanyName
```

Once called, this view will return a dataset with nearly complete information on all the orders that will be used in the examples in this chapter.

Before we continue with the Decision Cube, we need to make the following comments.

■ Delphi Decision Cube components do not support Wide String data. That is why we retrieve all string data as *non-Unicode* strings using the SQL Server built-in CONVERT function.

■ Dividing by 100 and then multiplying by the same value for the Payment field is the procedure for rounding this value.

If we use Microsoft Access, the above view may look like the one shown below:

```
SELECT [Order Details].[OrderID], [Orders].[OrderDate],
       [Orders].[CustomerID],
       [Customers].[Country], [Customers].[City],
       SUM(([Order Details].[UnitPrice]*
       [Order Details].[Quantity]*
       (1-[Order Details].[Discount])/100)*100) AS Payment,
       [Shippers].[CompanyName], [Orders].[Freight],
       [Employees].[LastName] AS EmployeeName
FROM Shippers INNER JOIN
((Employees INNER JOIN
(Customers INNER JOIN Orders ON [Customers].[CustomerID]=[Orders].[CustomerID])
ON [Employees].[EmployeeID]=[Orders].[EmployeeID]) INNER JOIN [Order Details] ON
[Orders].[OrderID]=[Order Details].[OrderID]) ON
[Shippers].[ShipperID]=[Orders].[ShipVia]
GROUP BY [Order Details].[OrderID], [Orders].[OrderDate],
         [Orders].[Freight], [Customers].[Country],
         [Customers].[City], [Orders].[CustomerID],
         [Employees].[LastName], [Shippers].[CompanyName];
```

The resulting recordset, obtained by using the view created above, for CustomerID, OrderDate, CompanyName, Freight, Country, and Payment fields may look like the one in the table below.

CustomerId	OrderDate	CompanyName	Freight	Country	Payment
VINET	07.04.96	Federal Shipping	32.38	France	440
TOMSP	07.05.96	Speedy Express	11.61	Germany	1863.4
HANAR	07.08.96	United Package	65.83	Brazil	1552.6
VICTE	07.08.96	Speedy Express	41.34	France	654.06
VINET	09.02.96	United Package	1.15	France	121.6
HANAR	07.10.96	United Package	58.17	Brazil	1444.8
VINET	08.06.96	Speedy Express	6.01	France	538.6
BERGS	08.12.96	United Package	92.69	Sweden	1488.8
TOMSP	02.14.97	Speedy Express	14.68	Germany	246.24
BERGS	08.14.96	Speedy Express	8.98	Sweden	613.2
TOMSP	05.26.97	United Package	1.43	Germany	240.1
BERGS	02.12.97	Federal Shipping	3.5	Sweden	1031.7
BERGS	02.13.97	Speedy Express	9.3	Sweden	174.9
...	...	...	...	...	...

What is the aggregate data that can be obtained from such a table or view? Usually they can answer the following typical questions:

■ What is the sum of payments for French customers' orders?

■ What is the sum of payments for orders shipped by Speedy Express in the first quarter of 1996?

■ How many orders from French customers were shipped by Speedy Express?

■ How many orders from French customers were processed in the first quarter of 1997 and shipped by Speedy Express?

These questions will, of course, differ, depending on the type of business.

Since we are working with the data that resides in a database, we need to translate these human-readable questions into SQL queries. For example:

```
--
-- What is the sum of payments for French customers'
  orders? --
--
SELECT SUM (Payment) FROM Ord_pmt
 WHERE Country='France'

--
-- What is the sum of payments for orders shipped by Speedy --
-- Express in the first quarter of 1996?                    --
--
SELECT SUM (Payment) FROM Ord_pmt
 WHERE CompanyName='Speedy Express'
 AND OrderDate BETWEEN 'December 31, 1995' AND 'April 1, 1996'
```

```
--
-- How many orders from French customers were shipped --
-- by Speedy Express?                               --
--
SELECT count(*) FROM Ord_pmt
 WHERE Country='France'
 AND CompanyName='Speedy Express'


--
-- How many orders from French customers were processed in --
-- the first quarter of 1997 and shipped by Speedy Express? --
--
SELECT COUNT(*) from Ord_pmt
 WHERE Country='France'
 AND OrderDate BETWEEN 'December 31, 1996' AND 'January 1, 1998'
 AND CompanyName='Speedy Express'
```

Note: In some cases, such text queries can be translated to SQL equivalents with the help of Microsoft English Query. This topic, however, is beyond the scope of this book.

As we might expect, the result returned by executing any of the queries shown above will return some number. As you can see from the SQL query source code, we can replace "France" with "Austria" or any other country name, execute this query again, and obtain another value. By doing this with all customer names, we can obtain a set of values similar to those shown below:

Country	Sum (Payment)
Argentina	8119.10
Austria	128003.84
Belgium	33824.85
Brazil	106925.77
Canada	50196.30
Denmark	32661.02
Finland	18810.05
France	81358.31
Germany	230284.62
Ireland	49979.90
…	…

This table contains aggregate data and can be considered as a one-dimensional set of values. Now let's look at the second and the third queries, which contain two conditions in the WHERE clause. Note that using GROUP BY, we can achieve similar results.

```
--
-- What is the sum of payments for orders shipped by Speedy --
-- Express in the first quarter of 1996?                    --
--
SELECT SUM (Payment) FROM Ord_pmt
 WHERE CompanyName='Speedy Express'
 AND OrderDate BETWEEN 'December 31, 1995' AND 'April 1, 1996'


--
-- How many orders from French customers were shipped --
-- by Speedy Express?                                 --
--
SELECT count(*) FROM Ord_pmt
 WHERE Country='France'
 AND CompanyName='Speedy Express'
```

If we run these queries and change the Country value or the CompanyName value for every country or company name we have in the database, we will get a two-dimensional set of values shown in the following table:

Country	Federal Shipping	CompanyName Speedy Express	United Package
Argentina	4	5	7
Austria	13	12	15
Belgium	8	3	8
Brazil	17	31	35
Canada	16	4	10
Denmark	7	6	5
Finland	9	8	5
France	21	27	29
Germany	28	41	53
Ireland	6	4	9
...	...	...	...

This set of values is called a *cross table* or *pivot table*. Creating such tables from the original data is a simple data processing function found in many spreadsheet packages, such as Microsoft Excel. Note that by using CROSS JOINs or subqueries, we can achieve similar results.

Now let's look at the fourth query:

```
--
-- How many orders from French customers were processed in --
-- the first quarter of 1997 and shipped by Speedy Express? --
--
SELECT COUNT(*) from Ord_pmt
 WHERE Country='France'
 AND OrderDate BETWEEN 'December 31, 1996' AND 'January 1, 1998'
```

```
AND CompanyName='Speedy Express'
```

This query contains three conditions in the WHERE clause. Therefore, if we want to get all possible results for this query, we must supply different data for all three parameters. As the result, we will get a three-dimensional set of values that can be presented as a cube shown below:

Country	Federal Shipping	Speedy Express	United Package
Argentina	0	0	0
Austria	3	4	1
Belgium	0	0	2
Brazil	3	2	8
Canada	0	0	4
Denmark	3	0	0
Finland	3	1	0
France	4	7	4
Germany	8	6	10
Ireland	2	1	2
Italy	0	2	1
Mexico	7	0	2
Norway	0	0	1
Poland	1	0	0
Portugal	2	1	1
Spain	1	2	3
Sweden	3	2	1
Switzerland	1	0	2
UK	4	3	3
USA	8	4	11
Venezuela	5	3	0

(1998, 1997, 1996 along the depth axis)

Every cell of this cube contains a numeric value that results from a query similar to the query shown above, but with different parameter values in the WHERE clause.

If we slice the cube by a plane parallel to one of the cube edges, we get different types of two-dimensional tables. Such tables are called *cross-sections* (or slices) of such cube. Examples of such slices are shown below:

Orders in the USA

CompanyName	Year		
	1996	1997	1998
Federal Shipping	8	15	17
Speedy Express	4	19	8
United Package	11	26	14

Orders delivered by Federal Shipping

Country	Year 1996	1997	1998
Argentina	0	1	3
Austria	3	7	3
Belgium	0	4	4
Brazil	3	9	5
Canada	0	10	6
Denmark	3	3	1
Finland	3	3	3
stright France	4	10	7
Germany	8	15	5
Ireland	2	4	0
...	...	...	...

If we create a sample query with four or more conditions in the WHERE clause, we will get a four-dimensional (or five-dimensional, six-dimensional, etc.) set of values.

It should be clear that along with sums and counts, we can also put into the cube cells maximum, minimum, and average values, i.e., aggregate SQL functions, such as MIN, MAX, AVG, COUNT, and so on, described in Chapter 9. These aggregate values are called *summaries*, and variables used in queries are called *dimensions*. The original source data that is summarized (e.g., payments) is called *measures*.

Within each dimension of the cube, data can be organized into a hierarchy that represents detail levels of the data. For instance, within the OrderDate dimension, there can be the following levels: years, quarters, months, and days.

This multidimensional data model makes it simple for users to formulate complex queries, arrange data in a report, switch from summary to detailed data, and filter or slice data to create different subsets.

As we have mentioned earlier in this chapter, such multidimensional analysis can be provided both on a database server and inside a client application. We will begin with a short discussion of the possible ways of implementing client-side OLAP.

Client-Side OLAP Applications in Brief

In this section, we will briefly discuss creating Delphi client-side OLAP applications with Decision Cube components. Then we will explain the advantages and disadvantages of this method.

Implementing Client-Side OLAP

As we have said before, Delphi Enterprise includes a set of Decision Cube components for implementing client-side OLAP. These components provide a convenient user interface for creating analytical applications. However, there are several difficulties when using them with ADO data sources.

First, the Decision Cube components do not support TWideStringField fields. That means that we need to obtain the resulting dataset without such fields (such as we have done in the view created earlier in this chapter). However, this way of solving the problem of unsupported WideString data in Decision Cube components is not universal. For example, we may have insufficient privileges to create database views. In this case, we need to create calculated fields that contain non-Unicode versions of the WideString fields and use them to create cube dimensions, or redefine all WideString fields as TString fields by replacing all *"WideString"* substrings to *"String"* substrings in the appropriate *.pas and *.dfm files.

Second, the TDecisionQuery component that contains a specialized form of TQuery and is used to define the data in a Decision Cube is a fully BDE-oriented component. In Delphi 5, it does not work with ADO data sources at all.

We can, of course, replace the TDecisionQuery component with any ADO dataset component (e.g., TADOQuery), and enter the query for calculating the summaries manually. The following is an example of such a query:

```
SELECT CustomerID, OrderDate, CompanyName, Country,
SUM(Payment) as SUM_Pmt, COUNT(Payment) as CNT_Pmt
FROM Ord_pmt
GROUP BY OrderDate, Country, CustomerID, CompanyName
```

In this case, we can create an application with a convenient user interface containing grids, charts, and controls to hide, show, expand, and collapse dimensions, and, at design time, it will look attractive. However, and this is the third problem, the run-time behavior for such an application is strange: Not all of the data is presented correctly (for example, some data may be lost), indexes for cubes are calculated significantly more slowly than at design time, the Decision Cube capacity appears to be low even if a dataset is small, and so on.

Transferring data to the client dataset does not improve the situation. In fact, this is the most serious reason not to use these components with ADO data sources. However, we expect that these problems may be solved in the next version of Delphi.

A radical way to solve the problems described above is to edit the source code of the Decision Cube components. However, if you do this, you should not expect any support from Borland if you have any problems with such components.

How should you implement client-side OLAP for ADO data sources rather than use the Decision Cube? First, you can create an application (called an *Automation controller*) that will drive Microsoft Excel through its Automation objects; in this case, your applications could provide all Excel PivotTable services for your users. However, your users must have Microsoft Excel installed on their computers.

Second, you can calculate summaries in your code and use non-data-aware grids and charts, as was shown in Chapters 11 and 12.

Pros and Cons of Client-Side OLAP Applications

In this section, we will show the advantages and disadvantages of using client-side OLAP.

The advantage of client-side OLAP applications is that we can provide online analytical processing possibilities for any data source, since we are using the Universal Data Access mechanisms. It does not matter whether this data source provides OLAP services itself. In fact, client-side OLAP is the most common way to analyze data on desktop databases, SQL servers that do not have their own OLAP implementations (such as InterBase), data that comes from various ODBC and OLE DB data sources, and so on. Unfortunately, that is all that can be said about the advantages of this approach.

The disadvantages of client-side OLAP are very serious, and you must keep them in mind when creating such applications.

First, client-side OLAP applications can consume a lot of memory and produce heavy traffic, as they bring a lot of data from the database server to the client application. Therefore, the amount of such data should be estimated correctly, and these estimations must include the possible growth of database in the future. In addition, this restricts the number of dimensions. Generally, for any client-side OLAP tool, using more than six is not recommended.

Second, at the time of this writing, the particular Delphi implementation of client-side OLAP components is not applicable for using with ADO data sources. We hope this is changed in the next version of Delphi.

As we mentioned in the introduction to this chapter, another way to create OLAP applications is to use server-side OLAP. As we will see in the next part of this chapter, server-side OLAP is free from such problems as bringing all summaries back to the client application. It can also be used with large data sources.

Below we will see how to use server-side OLAP extensions implemented in Microsoft SQL Server 7.0 along with Delphi ADO components or ADO MD extensions.

We will begin by creating OLAP cubes with the Microsoft SQL Server OLAP Manager. Then we will create several applications for querying such cubes using the OpenSchema method and Multidimensional Expressions (MDX)—extensions of the SQL language for querying OLAP cubes. Moreover, in the next chapter, we will show you how to use ADO MD extensions in Delphi server-side OLAP applications.

Microsoft SQL Server 7.0 OLAP Services

In this section, we will discuss the architecture of Microsoft SQL Server OLAP Services and will show you how to use ADO MD extensions and create applications that use these services.

OLAP Services Architecture

Microsoft SQL Server 7.0 OLAP Services consist of server and client components. The client components can also be used as middle-tier software in multitier systems. These client and server components are shown in the diagram below:

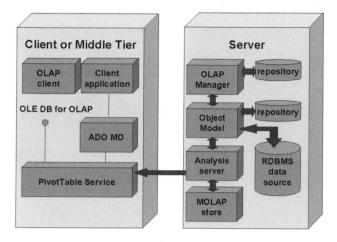

On the server side, the OLAP server operates as a Microsoft Windows NT service and provides the core computational functionality. OLAP Manager is the built-in administrative user interface for OLAP Services. It can be executed, for example, on a client or middle-tier computer. OLAP Manager allows the database administrator to design OLAP data models, access information in RDBMS stores, design aggregations, and populate OLAP data stores. The OLAP metadata definitions are stored in a special repository.

It is essential that OLAP Services can access source data not only in SQL Server, but in any data source which is be available through OLE DB data providers.

On the client side, OLAP Services includes a component called PivotTable Service. This service is designed to connect OLAP client applications to the OLAP Services server. All access to data managed by OLAP Services is provided by this service through the OLE DB for OLAP interface.

Creating OLAP Cubes

Before creating any Delphi application, we need to create an essential part of a whole server-side OLAP system. This part is a multidimensional OLAP cube, which is stored and maintained by a database server.

We assume that you have already installed Microsoft SQL Server 7.0. Now, we need to add the SQL Server 7.0 OLAP Services that comes as part of the Microsoft SQL Server 7.0 and can be found in the SQL Server 7.0 Components list in the second installation screen.

After Microsoft SQL Server 7.0 OLAP Services are installed, it is necessary to start the OLAP Manager. This will allow us to connect to Microsoft SQL Server and look at the list of repositories containing cube definitions.

The first step is to create a new OLAP database (let's name it NorthWindOLAP). This can be done by right-clicking on a Server node in the tree view in the left part of the OLAP Manager, and selecting the New Database option. The next step is to create a new cube by right-clicking on a Cube node of a newly created database, and selecting the New Cube option. Then we can use either the Cube Editor or the Cube Wizard. For our example, we will select the Cube Wizard and follow the dialog boxes that will appear.

In the first dialog box, we need to select the data source for our cube. To do this, click the New Data Source button, select OLE DB Provider for MS SQL Server, and fill in the properties to connect to the Northwind database. Next, choose a fact table containing data for summaries. Let it be our Ord_pmt view, created earlier in this chapter.

The next page of the wizard asks which numeric values should be used as cube measures (as we already know, measures are the source data for creating summaries). In the Ord_pmt view, there are three numeric fields—OrderID, Freight, and Payment. Let's select both the Freight and Payment fields as cube measures.

In the next dialog, we need to define dimensions of the cube. Press the New Dimension button to open the Dimension Wizard. To create all necessary dimensions, we need to run the Dimension Wizard four times—once for each dimension.

The first dimension is OrderDate. In the first dialog box of the Dimension Wizard, we will select the same Ord_pmt view as a dimension source. Generally, the source of the dimension can be any other table or view that is in the lookup relationship with the fact table or view.

In the second dialog, we need to select the type of dimension. Choose a time dimension. In the third dialog, choose the date/time hierarchy type. Since our data contains no time, we will select the "Year, Quarter, Month, Day" type of hierarchy. We also can point to where a year starts. This is very useful when, for example, the fiscal year is different from the calendar year.

Finally, we name the created dimension Date, and browse all hierarchy levels of this dimension:

The next step is to create another dimension. Let's choose the Country/City/ CustomerId dimension. In fact, it contains three levels of "geographical" hierarchy, because in this example a customer resides in a particular city and country. Therefore, we should select the Country, City, and CustomerId fields as the levels of the hierarchy of this dimension, which will be called Cust as shown on the screen shot below:

The third dimension is very simple. It contains only the CompanyName field (we will call this dimension Shipment). Finally, the fourth dimension also contains only one field—EmployeeName (we will call this dimension Employee).

After creating all four dimensions, we need to save the cube. Let's name it Payment_Cube. After this step, the Cube Editor window will appear.

Now we have a cube definition stored in a database. However, it is also essential to calculate and store its data. So, we need to design a data storage with the Storage Design Wizard. This can be done by selecting Tools | Design Storage from the Cube Editor menu bar.

When we start the Storage Design Wizard, it will ask what type of data storage to create. We have the following options:

- MOLAP (Multidimensional OLAP)—All data, both source and aggregates, is stored in a multidimensional database. This is recommended for use with analytical applications.

- ROLAP (Relational OLAP)—All data is stored in a relational database. This is recommended for applications that are responsible for both data modification and analysis.

- HOLAP (Hybrid OLAP—Aggregate data is stored in a multidimensional database, and source data is stored in a relational database.

For our example, we will select the MOLAP data storage. Then we can set some storage options to specify a necessary balance of the storage size and the performance of user query execution.

To process the cube, i.e., to calculate aggregate data, we select the Tools | Process Cube menu item.

After processing the cube, we can view its data by selecting the View | Data option from the Cube Editor menu. In the Cube Editor, we can drag and drop dimensions, show and hide dimensions, expand and collapse hierarchy levels, move dimensions from columns to rows, and filter cube data by selecting possible values.

Thus, we have prepared all necessary server data. We have created an OLAP cube based on a previously created view. This cube has the four dimensions shown in the following table:

Dimension name	Level(s)	Description
Cust	Country, City, CustomerId	Geographical hierarchy for registered customers
Date	Year, Quarter, Month, Day	Date hierarchy for processed orders
Shipment	CompanyName	List of shipping companies
Employee	EmployeeName	List of employees

In addition, this newly created cube has two measures:

Measure Name	Description
Payment	Payment for a particular order
Freight	Freight expenses for a particular order

This means we have created the cube with aggregate data. This data can be accessed from client applications by querying it. However, before querying cubes, our users may need to know what cubes are contained in multidimensional databases, and their dimensions, hierarchies, levels, and members. In other words, a user needs to know what query parameters could be used. In the next section, we will show you how to do this using the OpenSchema method of the TADOConnection component.

Retrieving Cube Metadata in Delphi Applications

How do we obtain information about cubes, and their dimensions, hierarchies, levels, and members in Delphi applications? Let's recall that we have already learned how to do this with "ordinal" relational databases. In the chapter about the TADOConnection component, we discussed the OpenSchema method that is used for retrieving metadata from databases accessible through OLE DB providers.

The OLAP cube created with Microsoft SQL Server 7.0 OLAP Services can belong to a multidimensional database that cannot be relational. But, in spite of this, they are accessible via Microsoft OLE DB Provider for OLAP Services. So, to retrieve the cube metadata, we can use the OpenSchema method of the ADO Connection object that is accessible through the Delphi TADOConnection component.

Looking carefully at the list of possible values of the TSchemaInfo parameter, we can find some of them concerning cubes. They are siCubes, siDimensions, siHierarchies, siLevels, siMeasures, siProperties and siMembers. By using them as the first parameter in the OpenSchema method, we can retrieve information on cubes, dimensions, hierarchies, levels, measures, and members in a particular multidimensional database.

Let's create an example showing how to use this method to retrieve cube metadata. To do this, we need to create a new Delphi project, and place the TComboBox, TButton, TDBGrid, TDBNavigator, TADOConnection, TADODataSet, and TDataSource components on a form. Then, let's set the DataSource value of the

DBNavigator1 and DBGrid1 components to DataSource1, and the DataSet property of the DataSource1 component to ADODataSet1. Fill the Items value of the TComboBox component with the following strings:

- siCubes
- siDimensions
- siHierarchies
- siLevels
- siMeasures
- siProperties
- siMembers

Then let's set up the Connection property of the ADOConnection1 component. We need to select Microsoft OLE DB Provider for OLAP Services as a provider name, input or select the computer name with the multidimensional database as the data source name, insert the user name and password, and then select the name of the multidimensional database from which we want to retrieve the metadata.

The next step is to create the OnClick event handler for the Button1 component:

```
procedure TForm1.Button1Click(Sender: TObject);
var
 SI : TSchemaInfo;
 I  : Integer;
begin
//Select a type of metadata query
 case ComboBox1.ItemIndex of
  0: SI := siCubes;
  1: SI := siDimensions;
  2: SI := siHierarchies;
  3: SI := siLevels;
  4: SI := siMeasures;
  5: SI := siProperties;
  6: SI := siMembers;
 end;
 //Retrieve results of the metadata query to ADODataSet1
 ADOConnection1.OpenSchema(SI,EmptyParam,
  EmptyParam,ADODataSet1);
 //Open a query result
 ADODataSet1.Open;
 //Change appearance of the DBGrid
 for I:=0 to DBGrid1.Columns.Count-1  do
  DBGrid1.Columns[I].Width:=80;
end;
```

Finally, let's initialize the ItemIndex property of the ComboBox1 component:

```
procedure TForm1.FormCreate(Sender: TObject);
begin
 ComboBox1.ItemIndex := 0;
end;
```

Now we can compile and run this application. An example of its output is shown below:

To filter the retrieved metadata, we specify the criteria that the metadata must meet. These criteria must be the second parameter of the OpenSchema method and may contain an array of values for filtered columns of the resulting dataset. For example, if we want to show only the members of the Employee dimension of the Payment_Cube cube of the NorthWindOLAP multidimensional database, we may write the following code:

```
Cr1 := WideString('NorthWindOLAP');
Cr2 := WideString('Payment_Cube');
Cr3 := WideString('Employee');
Criteria := VarArrayOf([Cr1,Null,Ccr2,Cr3]);
ADOConnection1.OpenSchema(siMembers,Criteria,
 EmptyParam,ADODataSet1);
```

Thus, we have learned how to retrieve the cube metadata into the client Delphi application. This will help us find which cubes are available, and their dimensions, hierarchies, levels, and members. That means that we have enough information to query the cube.

However, in most cases, we are interested in both cube metadata and cube data. Generally, it is necessary to query the cube to obtain its slices, and then show them in a client application. These queries are based on the knowledge about the cube metadata.

Now it is time to create queries that can be used in client Delphi applications. The multidimensional expressions (MDX) are used for this task. Multidimensional expressions are SQL extensions used for querying cubes accessible through OLE DB Provider for OLAP Services. We will give you a brief description of these SQL language extensions in the next section.

Using Multidimensional Expressions (MDX)

OLE DB for OLAP is a set of COM interfaces designed to extend OLE DB for efficient access to multidimensional data. To specify queries to multidimensional data stored in SQL Server OLAP cubes, OLE DB for OLAP employs multidimensional expressions (MDX), which are extensions of SQL.

Before we look at multidimensional expressions, we need to create a test application to execute MDX queries.

The MDX Test Application

This application will allow us to enter various MDX statements and immediately see the results of their execution. To do this, we will slightly modify a test application used in Chapter 9.

Here is the list of modifications that should be done for the SQL Test application:

- Change the ConnectionString property of the TADOConnection component. In this case, we need to select Microsoft OLE DB Provider for OLAP Services, and then select the server name and database name as usual. In our example, we will specify the initial catalog as NorthWindOLAP (e.g., the name of our database, which contains the previously created cube).

- Slightly change the OnClick event handler for the Button1 component:

```
procedure TForm1.Button1Click(Sender: TObject);
var i:integer;
begin
 If Memo1.Lines.Count > 0 Then
 try
  With ADOQuery1 do
  begin
   Close;
 SQL := Memo1.Lines;
 Open;
  end;
   //Change appearance of the DBGrid
   for I :=0 to DBGrid1.Columns.Count-1  do
   DBGrid1.Columns[i].Width:=100;
 except
  ShowMessage('Invalid MDX query');
 end;
end;
```

After that, our test application is ready for use.

Note: Sometimes, after the value of the SQL property is changed, this application generates the EAccessViolation exception but continues its execution. The try..except block in the code above is used to prevent the error message from appearing.

Overview of Multidimensional Expressions (MDX)

Now we can begin our tour of MDX queries. To create such queries, we need to use the cube metadata returned by the OpenSchema method of the ADO Connection object, and to test them, we can run a test application created earlier in this chapter.

The MDX Syntax

The simplest form of an MDX query is:

```
SELECT axis_specification ON COLUMNS,
axis_specification ON ROWS
FROM cube_name
WHERE slicer_specification
```

The axis_specification can be thought of as the member selection for the axis, where a member is an item in a dimension or measure. An axis_specification value includes an optional dim_props value, which enables querying of dimension, level, and member properties.

The dim_props value has the following syntax:

```
[DIMENSION] PROPERTIES property [, property...]
```

The syntax of the property value depends on the property queried.

Property	Syntax	Notes
Dimension ID	dimension_name.ID	
Dimension name	dimension_name. NAME	
Level ID	[dimension_name].level_name.ID	The dimension name is optional if it is not required for level qualification
Level name	[dimension_name].level_name.NAME	
Member property	level_name.member_property_name	

We can use the [] braces to describe dimension names, levels of a hierarchy, and members. If an axis specification consist of several definitions, they can be separated with commas and included together in the {} braces. The examples in the following sections illustrate how to define axis specifications.

The slice specification for the WHERE clause is optional. If it is not used, the returned measure will be the default for this cube. Unless you actually query the measures dimension, you should always use a slice specification.

The MEMBERS Function

The simplest form of an axis specification or member selection involves taking the MEMBERS of the required dimension, including those of the special measures dimension:

```
SELECT Measures.MEMBERS ON COLUMNS,
[cust].MEMBERS ON ROWS
FROM [Payment_Cube]
```

This expression satisfies the requirement to query the recorded measures for each customer along with a summary at every defined summary level. Alternatively, it displays the measures for the Cust hierarchy. When running this expression, we find that the first row is unnamed; it is generated by default and is called "All." This row contains summaries for measures for all customers.

The result of this query is shown in the figure below:

In addition to taking the MEMBERS of a dimension, a single member of a dimension can be selected. For example:

```
SELECT Measures.MEMBERS ON COLUMNS,
{[cust].[Country].[France],
[cust].[Country].[Germany]} ON ROWS
FROM [Payment_Cube]
```

This expression queries the measures summarized for the orders in France and Germany:

The CHILDREN Function

To actually query the measures for the members making up both these countries (France and Germany in our example), it is necessary to query the CHILDREN of the required members:

```
SELECT Measures.MEMBERS ON COLUMNS,
{[cust].[Country].[France].CHILDREN,
[cust].[Country].[Germany].CHILDREN}  ON ROWS
FROM [Payment_Cube]
```

What is the difference between CHILDREN and MEMBERS? The MEMBERS function returns the members for the specified dimension or dimension level, while the CHILDREN function returns the child members for a particular member within the dimension. For example, in the query above, [cust].[Country].[France].CHILDREN are cities in France, but [cust].[City].MEMBERS are all cities where customers reside.

The DESCENDANTS Function

Both CHILDREN and MEMBERS functions can be used in formulating expressions, but they do not allow drilling down to a lower level within the hierarchy. This can be done with the DESCENDANTS function. This function allows us to go to the next level in depth. It has the following syntax:

```
DESCENDANTS(member, level [, flags])
```

If the flags parameter is omitted, the members at the specified level will be included. For example:

```
SELECT {[Measures].[Payment]} ON COLUMNS,
(DESCENDANTS([cust].UK, [City])) ON ROWS
FROM [Payment_Cube]
```

In our example in the rows axis, we will receive the members of the City level of the Cust hierarchy for the UK member of the Country level, as shown in the figure below:

The same result can be obtained if we use the SELF flag value.

If we use the AFTER flag, we will drill down to the depth in the next level of the hierarchy in the rows axis. For example:

```
SELECT {[Measures].[Payment]} ON COLUMNS,
(DESCENDANTS([cust].UK, [City], AFTER) ) ON ROWS
FROM [Payment_Cube]
```

In our example, we will receive several rows for all customers in the United Kingdom.

If we use the BEFORE flag, we will receive the higher level of a hierarchy on the axis. In our example, we will receive only one row for the UK member.

Finally, if we use the BEFORE_AND_AFTER flag value, we will receive several rows for the next level of a hierarchy, and the row for the highest level. For example:

```
SELECT {[Measures].[Payment]} ON COLUMNS,
(DESCENDANTS([cust].UK, [City], BEFORE_AND_AFTER) ) ON ROWS
FROM [Payment_Cube]
```

The Slicer Specifications

To define what data must be output, we need to define a slicer specification. Let's look at the following example:

```
SELECT {[Date].CHILDREN} ON COLUMNS,
([cust].MEMBERS)ON ROWS
FROM [Payment_Cube]
WHERE Payment
```

Here we will obtain a two-dimensional set of summaries of payments for any customer and any year.

The next example shows shipment expenses for the second quarter of 1998:

```
SELECT {[Shipment].children} ON COLUMNS,
([cust].members)ON ROWS
FROM Payment_Cube
WHERE ([Date].[Year].[1998].[Quarter 2])
```

In this example, we have defined how to select a specific data range in the slicer specification.

Note: Slicing does not affect selection of the axis members. It affects only the values that go into them. This is not the same as filtering, because filtering reduces the number of axis members.

This was a brief introduction to MDX queries. In fact, we can also use calculated expressions (including conditional expressions), create slices for comparing parallel periods (e.g., January 1997 and January 1998), provide for filtering and sorting data, use calculated members (dimension members, whose value is calculated at run time), and provide many other useful facilities.

Now we can modify our test application by adding predefined queries. To do this, let's add the TComboBox component and fill it with the following strings:

- Freight by Year for all customers
- Payment by Year for all customers
- Payment and Freight for all customers

Then let's create an OnChange event handler for the ComboBox1 component as shown below:

```
procedure TForm1.ComboBox1Change(Sender: TObject);
var
 I : Integer;
begin
 I := ComboBox1.ItemIndex;
 Memo1.Lines.Clear;
 case I of
 0: Memo1.Lines.Add(
     'SELECT {[Date].children} ON COLUMNS,' +
     chr(13)+chr(10) +
     '([cust].members) ON ROWS FROM Payment_Cube WHERE Freight'
     );
 1: Memo1.Lines.Add(
     'SELECT {[Date].children} ON COLUMNS,' +
     chr(13)+chr(10)+ ([cust].members) ON ROWS ' +
     'FROM Payment_Cube WHERE Payment'
     );
 2: Memo1.Lines.Add(
     'SELECT  {[Measures].Freight, ' +
     '[Measures].Payment}' + chr(13)+chr(10)
     +'ON COLUMNS,([cust].members) ON ROWS FROM Payment_Cube '
     );
 end;
end;
```

Now we can compile and run our application. After selecting the type of query from the combo box and pressing the button, the appropriate result set is shown in a grid:

In this section, we have learned how to create a simple Delphi client for SQL Server OLAP Cube using an appropriate OLE DB Provider and ADO components.

Conclusion

In this chapter, we introduced online analytical processing (OLAP). We have learned that:

- OLAP is a popular technology for multidimensional business analysis and a key component in data warehousing based on the multidimensional data model.

- The basic idea of OLAP is creating multidimensional cubes that contain calculated summaries based on aggregate SQL functions.

- Within each dimension of the cube, data can be organized into a hierarchy that represents detail levels of the data.

We have also discussed two ways of implementing OLAP in Delphi application—client-side and server-side. Now we know that:

- Client-side OLAP can be applicable only if the number of dimensions is not very high, and the predictable amount of summarized data is not large, as such applications bring all summaries from the database server to the client application.

- Server-side OLAP is applicable to large amounts of data, because such applications bring only required summaries to the client application.

We have also discussed one of the possible implementations of the Delphi server-side OLAP—using the OLAP extensions implemented in Microsoft SQL Server 7.0 along with Delphi ADO components.

We have described how to create a multidimensional cube, how to process it, and how to access the cube metadata and data from Delphi. Now we know that:

- To access the OLAP cubes stored in Microsoft SQL Server multidimensional databases, we need to use the OLE DB Provider for OLAP Services.

- To retrieve information about cubes, and their dimensions, hierarchies, levels, and members, we can use the OpenSchema method of the ADO Connection object.

- To query cubes and retrieve their data to Delphi applications, we can use the multidimensional expressions, which are SQL language extensions to query multidimensional databases.

Using Delphi ADO components is not the only way to retrieve cube metadata and data. In the case of using OLE DB provider for OLAP Services, ADO object hierarchy is extended with additional objects, collections, and methods that are specially designed to use OLAP cube data. These extensions are known as ADO MD (ADO multidimensional). In the next chapter, we will see how to use these objects in Delphi applications.

OLAP AND ADO MULTIDIMENSIONAL

In the previous chapter, we talked about online analytical processing (OLAP) and discussed two ways of implementing OLAP with ADO and Delphi—client-side and server-side. We also discussed a server-side OLAP implementation based on using the OLAP extensions implemented in Microsoft SQL Server 7.0 along with Delphi ADO components. However, there is another way to create server-side OLAP applications. This is based on using ADO Multidimensional Extensions (ADO MD), which are Automation objects designed to retrieve OLAP cube metadata and related data. In this chapter, we will discuss these objects and will show you how to use them in Delphi ADO applications.

Using ADO MD Extensions

As we have already learned from the previous chapters, the Microsoft Data Access Components (MDAC) contain more than core ADO objects. Version 2.1 comes with some extensions, including ADO extensions to work with multidimensional data. These extensions, called ADO MD Extensions, first appeared in ADO 2.0 and have since been widely used in various database solutions.

In this section, we will take a look at ADO MD Extensions, and their object model and features, and will give you some examples of how to use them in Delphi applications. Note that all this functionality comes with a single installation file—MDAC_TYP.EXE. It, along with ADO Extensions for DDL and Security (ADOX) and Jet and Replication Objects (JRO), is available on any computer that has the core MDAC files installed. The ADO Extensions for DDL and Security (ADOX) and Jet and Replication Objects (JRO) are covered later.

ADO Multidimensional

Like all other interfaces in Microsoft Data Access Components, ADO MD consists of a set of objects. The following diagram shows the objects that come with ADO MD, and how they are related to each other.

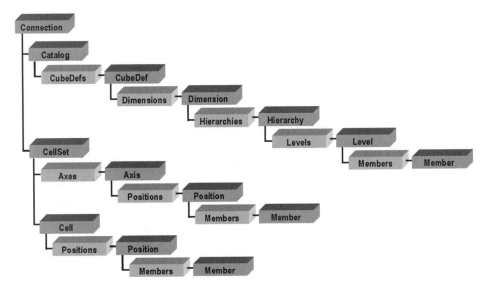

As we can see from the above diagram, the main objects of ADO MD are Catalog and CellSet. The Catalog object contains all information that describes the OLAP storage properties. It has some properties and methods, as well as several collections that contain information on cubes, dimensions, hierarchies, levels, and members.

The CellSet object contains all information that describes the result of a multidimensional query. It has some properties, methods, and collections that contain information about axes and cells of the MDX query result.

Type Libraries

To be able to view the contents of the ActiveX objects and Automation servers, we need access to some kind of description. This description can be found in a *type library*, which stores the type information about the objects implemented within ActiveX objects and Automation servers. Through the type library, we can find the characteristics of an object—the number and type of the interfaces it supports, the names and addresses of the members of each interface, and so on. Using the type library, we can even invoke a member of a particular interface.

Type libraries are binary files either with the .TLB extension or part of the EXE or DLL file with the ActiveX object or Automation server, and contain the following information:

- Descriptions of one or more objects implemented in the ActiveX object or Automation server. This includes interfaces, IDispatch interface, CoClass, and so on, as well as their methods.

- Information about data types—enumerations, structures, unions, and aliases.

- References to other type libraries.

To create a type library, we use the Delphi Type Library editor or any other appropriate tool, such as Microsoft IDL compiler. Using the ICreateTypeLib, ICreateTypeLib2, IcreateTypeInfo, and ICreateTypeInfo2 interfaces, we can create type libraries programmatically.

In Delphi, we need to create type libraries only when we create COM objects, ActiveX controls, Automation objects, and ASP components. These topics are not discussed in this book.

In the following section, we will examine how to browse the contents of the type libraries and how to use the type libraries in Delphi applications.

Browsing Type Libraries

We can use Delphi's built-in Type Library editor to browse the contents of the type library. To do so, we use the File | Open command and select Type Library in the Files of type combo box in the Open dialog. This will give us the ability to open files with .TLB, .DLL, .OCX, .EXE, and .OLB extensions. Next, we specify the type library we are interested in. To do so, we need to know its exact location. The best way to do this is to use the System Registry to find where the type library is stored. But this is time-consuming work since you first need to find an appropriate Class ID, then look under the other key for the type library path. To simplify this operation, we have created a Type Library List utility that does the job—it shows the exact locations of all type libraries registered in the system. Here is the Delphi code for its main procedure:

```
const
 TLB   = '\TypeLib\';   {Path to the Type Library information}
 WIN32 = '\0\win32\';   {Path to the Type Library File}


procedure TForm1.Button1Click(Sender: TObject);
var
 Reg        : TRegistry;
 KeyList    : TStringList;
 SubKeyList : TStringList;
 Name       : String;
 Path       : String;
 I,J        : Integer;
 ViewItem   : TListItem;
begin
{Create an instance of the TRegistry Class}
 Reg        := TRegistry.Create;
{and two StringLists}
```

```pascal
  KeyList    := TStringList.Create;
  SubKeyList := TStringList.Create;
  With Reg do
   begin
     RootKey := HKEY_CLASSES_ROOT;
{Open the HKCR\TypeLib\ branch}
     OpenKey(TLB, False);
{And get the names of all keys within it}
     GetKeyNames(KeyList);
{If everything is Ok}
     If KeyList.Count > 0 Then
{Iterate through the keys and get the subkeys names within each}
     For I := 0 to KeyList.Count-1 do
      begin
{Open one key}
       OpenKey(TLB+KeyList[I], False);
{Get Subkeys}
       GetKeyNames(SubKeyList);
       CloseKey;
{For each subkey within a key}
       For J := 0 to SubKeyList.Count-1 do
        begin
{Get the name of the type library}
         OpenKey(TLB+KeyList[I]+'\'+SubKeyList[J], False);
         Name := ReadString('');
         If Name <> '' Then
          begin
           CloseKey;
{ and its path}
         OpenKey(TLB+KeyList[I]+'\'+SubKeyList[J]+WIN32, False);
           Path := ReadString('');
           If Path <> '' Then
           begin
{Show it}
            ViewItem := ListView1.Items.Add;
            ViewItem.Caption := Name;
            ViewItem.SubItems.Add(Path);
           end;
           CloseKey;
          end;
        end;
      end;
   end;
{Clear memory}
  SubKeyList.Free;
  KeyList.Free;
  Reg.Free;
end;
```

The following output will appear when you run this utility:

Now we can find where a type library is stored in the file system, and easily open it with the Delphi Type Library editor. Select the Microsoft ActiveX Data Objects 2.1 Library, which is located in the PROGRAM FILES\COMMON FILES\SYSTEM\ADO\ MSADO15.DLL folder. The figure below shows how it looks within the Delphi Type Library editor:

You can browse the type library opened in the editor and look at the objects, methods, events, and constants implemented within the library, and even save it to the IDL or MIDL file that will be opened in the Delphi code editor. This will make the type library more readable, but it will be a C-like file. To create a Delphi interface unit that can be used to work with the type library, we need to import it into our project. This can be done with the Project | Import Type Library command. Later in this chapter and the next two chapters, we will use this command to work with the ADO extensions—ADO MD, ADOX, and JRO—from our Delphi programs.

When we run this command, we will be presented with the list of type libraries registered in the system. This list is similar to the output from the Type Library List utility created earlier:

As you can see from the adjacent figure, choosing one of the available type libraries gives us a list of classes implemented within it, and the ability to specify the Component Palette page for the component wrapper that will be generated by Delphi and the name of the unit to store the resulting Delphi code. Note that creating the component wrappers for ADO type libraries as well as for several other type libraries does not makes sense; it will just waste space on the Component Palette. So, uncheck the Generate Component Wrapper check box.

After you are done, either press the Install button to create a new file and add it to a new or existing package, or press the Create Unit button to create a new file and add it to your project. In both cases, you will get the XXX_TLB.PAS file, where the XXX will be replaced with the name of the type library. For example, the Microsoft ActiveX Data Objects 2.1 Library has the ADODB name, so the resulting Delphi interface unit will have the ADODB_TLB.PAS name.

Now that you have the type library interface file in hand, you can include its name in the USES clause of your unit and enjoy the objects, methods, and constants implemented in the library.

Note that there is no easy way to use the events of the COM and Automation objects. To be able to do so, we need to implement event sinking, which is beyond the scope of this introduction.

The other utility that may be handy for looking into type libraries is the Microsoft OLEVIEW utility that comes with the Platform SDK. It allows us to view the Registry entries for the type library, as well as its contents. The ITypeLib Viewer provides a way to browse through the IDL source code looking for enums, interfaces, CoClasses, TypeDefs, and so on.

As the Delphi Type Library editor, this utility can be used only for browsing through the type library; it generates only an IDL file that is not usable in Delphi.

A final note before we move to the next topic: If you want to jump into the dark waters of COM interfaces and create your own type library browser, you can consider the ITypeLib, ITypeLib2, ITypeInfo, ITypeInfo2, and ITypeComp interfaces and their methods.

Now we have a Delphi unit for the type library, and are ready to use it in our applications. Let's look at how to do this.

Using Type Libraries

In order to use the object and its properties and methods from the type library, we need to include the Delphi unit in the USES clause of our unit. Then we should create instances of the objects we are planning to use. This can be done in several ways.

The first way is to declare the variable of the appropriate type and either call the CoXXX.Create method to create an instance of the object (where XXX is the name of the object to be created), or use the standard Delphi CreateCOMObject procedure to do so.

The other way is to create a Variant-type variable and use one of the methods listed above.

Let's take a look at an example. Suppose we have created a Delphi unit for the type library that describes the object in the ADOX library (MSADOX.DLL). This library (discussed in more detail in the next chapter) contains several objects for data definition and security.

The first object we need to create in order to successfully use other ADOX objects is the Catalog object that represents the whole database. To do so, we create a variable of the _Catalog type and call the CoCatalog.Create method:

```
procedure TForm1.OpenCatalog;
var
 Catalog      : _Catalog;
begin
 Catalog := CoCatalog.Create;
{
 other catalog manipulation code goes here
}
end;
```

We can also use the CreateCOMObject function with the same result. Here is the code:

```
procedure TForm1.OpenCatalog;
var
 Catalog      : _Catalog;
begin
 Catalog      := CreateCOMObject(StringToGUID('ADOX.Catalog')) as
 _Catalog;
{
 other catalog manipulation code goes here
}
end;
```

Note that while calling the CreateCOMObject function, we specify the globally unique identifier (GUID) parameter in the form of StringToGUID('ADOX.Catalog').

What are the advantages of using a variable of the specified type? One of the main advantages here is that we can use the Code Insight features of the code editor in the Delphi IDE.

```
procedure TForm1.OpenCatalog;
var
  Catalog      : _Catalog;
begin
  Catalog := CoCatalog.Create;
  Catalog.|
         ┌────────────────────────────────────────┐
         │ function    Get_Tables : function: Tables       ▲ │
         │ function    Get_ActiveConnection : function      │
         │ procedure   _Set_ActiveConnection : proce        │
end;     │ procedure   Set_ActiveConnection : proced        │
         │ function    Get_Procedures : function: Proc      │
end.     │ function    Get_Views : function: Views         ▼ │
         └────────────────────────────────────────┘
```

This is very handy if we quickly need to locate a property or method, especially in cases where Delphi implements its own methods to get and set the values of the properties instead of the ones defined in the type library.

```
procedure TForm1.OpenCatalog;
var
  Catalog      : _Catalog;
begin
  Catalog := CoCatalog.Create;
  Catalog.Set_ActiveConnection(
                        const pVal: IDispatch

end;
```

The same functionality of the code editor works for argument names and types for the methods of the object. But we pay a high price since we need to supply all the arguments of the method, even those that have default values and are not significant for the particular call. This may make our code more complicated and even slow the development process.

This problem can be solved if we use Variants (discussed in the chapter about the TADOConnection component) instead of particular object types. Here is an example of how we can do this:

```
procedure TForm1.OpenCatalog;
var
  Catalog      : Variant;
begin
  Catalog := CoCatalog.Create;
  {
  other catalog manipulation code goes here
  }
end;
```

In this case, we lose the luxury of using the Code Insight features of the code editor, but we will end up with more readable code.

Note that the created objects are freed when the variable goes out of scope. Also, we can free the previously created object by using its Free method (if any), or assign the object variable to the UnAssigned value.

Accessing ADO MD from Delphi

Since ADO MD is not supported in Delphi 5 on the components level, we need to use the type library to access ADO MD objects. This type library is contained in the msadomd.dll file. To use this type library, choose the Project | Import Type Library command from the main menu, and in the list of available type libraries, select the Microsoft ActiveX Data Objects (Multidimensional) 1.0 Library.

If you have already imported the ADOX type library (ADOX is discussed in the next chapter), rename TCatalog to TADOMDCatalog to avoid conflicts with the already declared Delphi TCatalog class. It is also best to uncheck the Generate Component

Wrapper check box because we only need to create a Pascal (*.pas) file to access ADO MD objects.

Pressing the Create Unit button results in generating the ADO MD_TLB.PAS file, which is the interface unit to the ADO MD type library. In most of the examples in this chapter, we assume the ADOMD_TLB.PAS file is included in the Uses clause.

Note: We will use some COM and ADO functions, so we need to include the COMOBJ and ADODB units to the Uses clause.

Now we are ready to discuss each object in the ADO MD object model in details. We will start with the Catalog object, then discuss the objects that represent the cube's metadata. After that, we will look at the CellSet object and the other objects that represent the MDX query results.

The Catalog Object

The Catalog object contains all information that describes cubes in an OLAP storage. This object has several collections that allow us to manipulate cubes and their dimensions, hierarchies, levels, and members. All this functionality is available through appropriate collections containing objects of the particular type.

Now we will look at the methods, properties, and collections exposed by the Catalog object.

Properties of the Catalog Object

The Catalog object exposes two properties: ActiveConnection and Name.

The ActiveConnection property can be used to get or set information on the connection to the data source. In Delphi, this property is not available directly. Instead, there are three methods for providing access to it:

- To get ActiveConnection, use the Get_ActiveConnection method with no parameters; this method returns the IDispatch interface.

- To set ActiveConnection, use the _Set_ActiveConnection method that takes one parameter—a WideString.

- You can also use the Set_ActiveConnection method that expects a parameter in the form of IDispatch. In this case, we need to supply the valid instance of the ADO Connection object that can be obtained, for example, from the ConnectionObject property of the TADOConnection component.

The Name property indicates the name of the catalog. It returns a WideString value and is read-only. This property is available both directly and by using the Get_Name method.

Note: The Get_XXX methods are available only when we use Automation with co-classes and interfaces.

Collections of the Catalog Object

The Catalog object exposes only one collection—the CubeDefs collection that allows us to retrieve names of available cubes belonging to the specific catalog.

This collection contains a set of CubeDef objects that represent a multidimensional catalog or schema of the specific OLAP storage. The CubeDefs collection is available both directly and by using the Get_CubeDefs method.

Now we need to look at objects available through the CubeDefs collection—the CubeDef objects that, in the ADO MD object model, are situated one level below the Catalog object.

The CubeDef Object

The CubeDef object that is available through the CubeDefs collection of the Catalog object contains detailed information for a single cube and represents a specific OLAP cube.

Properties of the CubeDef Object

The CubeDef object exposes two properties: Name and Description.

The Name property indicates the name of the cube. It returns a WideString value and is read-only. This property is available both directly and by using the Get_Name method.

The Description property indicates the optional description of the cube. It returns a WideString value and is read-only. This property is available both directly and by using the Get_Description method.

Collections of the CubeDef Object

The CubeDef object exposes two collections: Properties and Dimensions.

The Properties collection contains provider-supplied properties of the OLAP cube. For Microsoft OLE DB Provider for OLAP Services, the following properties are available:

Property	Meaning
CatalogName	This property specifies the name of the catalog (storage) to which this cube belongs.
SchemaName	This property specifies the name of the schema to which this cube belongs.
CubeName	This property specifies the name of the cube.
CubeType	This property specifies the type of the cube.
CubeGUID	This property specifies the cube GUID.
CreatedOn	This property specifies the date and time when the cube was created.
LastSchemaUpdate	This property specifies the date and time when the schema was updated.
SchemaUpdatedBy	This property specifies the user ID of the person who did the last schema update.
DataUpdatedBy	This property specifies the user ID of the person who did the last data update.
Description	This property contains a description of the cube.

Note: The property list for other OLE DB providers for OLAP Services (if any) may differ from the one above. It depends on the particular implementation of the provider.

Later in this chapter, we give you an example of how to use the Properties collection.

This collection contains a set of Dimension objects that represent dimensions of the OLAP cube. This collection is available both directly and by using the Get_Dimensions method of the CubeDef object.

The Dimension Object

The Dimension object, which is available through the Dimensions collection of the CubeDef object, contains detailed information for a single cube and represents a specific dimension used in the OLAP cube.

Properties of the Dimension Object

The Dimension object exposes three properties: Name, UniqueName, and Description.

The Name property indicates the name of the dimension. It returns a WideString value and is read-only. This property is available both directly and by using the Get_Name method of the Dimension object.

The UniqueName property indicates the unique name of the dimension. It returns a WideString value and is read-only. This property is available both directly and by using the Get_UniqueName method of the Dimension object.

The Description property contains an optional description of the dimension. It returns a WideString value and is read-only. This property is available both directly and by using the Get_Description method of the Dimension object.

Collections of the Dimension Object

The Dimension object exposes two collections: Properties and Hierarchies.

The Properties collection contains provider-supplied properties of the dimension. For Microsoft OLE DB Provider for OLAP Services, the following properties are available:

Property	Meaning
CatalogName	This property specifies the name of the catalog (storage) which contains the cube that uses this dimension.
SchemaName	This property specifies the name of the schema to which this cube belongs.
CubeName	This property specifies the name of the cube that uses this dimension.
DimensionName	This property specifies the name of the dimension.
DimensionUniqueName	This property specifies the unique name of the dimension.
DimensionGUID	This property specifies the dimension GUID.
DimensionCaption	This property specifies the label or caption associated with the dimension.
DimensionOrdinal	This property specifies the ordinal number of the dimension among the group of dimensions of the cube.
DimensionType	This property specifies the dimension type.
DimensionCardinality	This property is equal to the number of members in the dimension.
DefaultHierarchy	This property specifies the unique name of the default hierarchy for this dimension.
Description	This property specifies a description of the dimension.

Note: The property list for other OLE DB providers for OLAP Services may differ from those shown above. The content of the property list depends on the implementation of the OLE DB provider.

The Hierarchies collection contains a set of Hierarchy objects, which represent a specific hierarchy of the dimension. This collection is available both directly and by using the Get_Hierarchies method of the Dimension object.

The Hierarchy Object

The Hierarchy object, which is available through the Hierarchies collection of the Dimension object, represents a specific hierarchy of the OLAP cube dimension.

Properties of the Hierarchy Object

The Hierarchy object exposes three properties: Name, UniqueName, and Description.

The Name property indicates the name of the hierarchy. It returns a `WideString` value and is read-only. This property is available both directly and by using the Get_Name method.

The UniqueName property indicates the unique name of the hierarchy. It returns a WideString value and is read-only. This property is available both directly and by using the Get_UniqueName method of the Hierarchy object.

The Description property indicates the optional description of the hierarchy. It returns a WideString value and is read-only. This property is available both directly and by using the Get_Description method of the Hierarchy object.

Collections of the Hierarchy Object

The Dimension object exposes two collections: Properties and Levels.

The Properties collection contains provider-supplied properties of the hierarchy. For Microsoft OLE DB Provider for OLAP Services, the following properties are available:

Property	Meaning
CatalogName	This property specifies the name of the catalog (storage) which contains the cube that uses the dimension with this hierarchy.
SchemaName	This property specifies the name of the schema to which this cube belongs.
CubeName	This property specifies the name of the cube that uses the dimension with this hierarchy.
DimensionUniqueName	This property specifies the unique name of the dimension.
HierarchyName	This property specifies the name of the hierarchy.
HierarchyUniqueName	This property specifies the unique name of the hierarchy.
HierarchyGUID	This property specifies the hierarchy GUID.
HierarchyCaption	This property specifies the label or caption associated with the hierarchy.
DimensionType	This property specifies the type of dimension to which this hierarchy belongs.
HierarchyCardinality	This property is equal to the number of members in the hierarchy.
DefaultMember	This property specifies the unique name of the default member for this hierarchy.
AllMember	This property specifies the unique name of the member at the highest level of rollup in the hierarchy.
Description	This property specifies a description of the hierarchy.

Note: The property list for other OLE DB providers for OLAP Services may differ from the one shown above. It depends on the implementation of the OLE DB provider.

The Levels collection contains a set of Level objects that represent a specific level of the hierarchy. This collection is available both directly and by using the Get_Levels method of the Hierarchy object.

The Level Object

The Level object, which is available through the Levels collection of the Dimension object, represents a specific level of a hierarchy of the OLAP cube dimension.

Properties of the Level Object

The Level object exposes five properties: Caption, Depth, Name, UniqueName, and Description.

The Caption property indicates the text caption used when displaying the level. It returns a `WideString` value and is read-only. This property is available both directly and by using the Get_Caption method of the Level object.

The Depth property indicates the number of levels this specific level is from the root of the hierarchy. It returns a SmallInt value and is read-only. This property is available both directly and by using the Get_Depth method of the Level object.

The Name property indicates the name of the level. It returns a `WideString` value and is read-only. This property is available both directly and by using the Get_Name method of the Level object.

The UniqueName property indicates the unique name of the level of a hierarchy. It returns a `WideString` value and is read-only. This property is available both directly and by using the Get_UniqueName method of the Level object.

The Description property indicates an optional description of the level. It returns a `WideString` value and is read-only. This property is available both directly and by using the Get_Description method of the Level object.

Collections of the Level Object

The Level object exposes two collections: Properties and Members.

The Properties collection contains provider-supplied properties of the level. For Microsoft OLE DB Provider for OLAP Services, the following properties are available:

Property	Meaning
CatalogName	This property specifies the name of the catalog (storage) that contains the cube.
SchemaName	This property specifies the name of the schema to which this cube belongs.
CubeName	This property specifies the name of the cube.
DimensionUniqueName	This property specifies the unique name of the dimension.
HierarchyUniqueName	This property specifies the unique name of the hierarchy to which this level belongs.
LevelName	This property specifies the name of the level.
LevelUniqueName	This property specifies the unique name of the level.
LevelGUID	This property specifies the level GUID.
LevelCaption	This property specifies the label or caption associated with the level.
LevelNumber	This property specifies the distance of the level from the root of the hierarchy

Property	Meaning
LevelCardinality	This property is equal to the number of members in the level.
LevelType	This property specifies the type of the level.
Description	This property specifies a description of the level.

Note: The property list for other OLE DB providers for OLAP Services may differ from the one shown above. It depends on the implementation of the OLE DB provider.

The Members collection contains a set of the Member objects that represent a specific member of the level of a hierarchy. This collection is available both directly and by using the Get_Members method of the Level object.

The Member Object (of a Level in a CubeDef)

The Member object, which is available through the Members collection of the Level object, represents a specific member of the level of a hierarchy.

In ADO MD, there are two types of Member objects. The first one is for members of levels in CubeDef objects, and the second one is for members of positions along axes in CellSet objects. The CellSet objects type is discussed later.

Properties of the Member Object

The Member object (of a level in a CubeDef) exposes nine properties: Caption, Name, UniqueName, LevelDepth, LevelName, ChildCount, Parent, Type, and Description.

The Caption property indicates the text caption used when the member is shown. It returns a `WideString` value and is read-only. This property is available both directly and by using the Get_Caption method of the Member object.

The Name property indicates the name of the member. It returns a `WideString` value and is read-only. This property is available both directly and by using the Get_Name method of the Member object.

The UniqueName property indicates the unique name of the member. It returns a `WideString` value and is read-only. This property is available both directly and by using the Get_UniqueName method of the Member object.

The LevelDepth property indicates the number of levels from the root of the hierarchy to the member. It returns an `Integer` value and is read-only. This property is available both directly and by using the Get_LevelDepth method of the Member object.

The LevelName property indicates the name of the level of a member. It returns a `WideString` value and is read-only. This property is available both directly and by using the Get_LevelName method of the Member object.

The ChildCount property is approximately equal to the number of members for which the current member is the parent. It returns an `Integer` value and is read-only. This property is available both directly and by using the Get_ChildCount method of the Member object.

Note: This property contains an estimation of the number of children, and not the exact value. To obtain the exact number of children, use the Count property of the Children collection. However, if the number of children in the collection is large, calculating this value can be a time-consuming process.

The Parent property returns the Member object that is the parent for the current member in the hierarchy. A member at the top level of a hierarchy has no parent. This property is only supported on Member objects belonging to a Level object.

Note: Referencing this property when using the Member object representing a member of a position along an axis in the CellSet object results in an error.

The Type_ property indicates the type of the current Member object (it was renamed after generation of ADO MD_TLB.PAS from the original Type name to avoid conflicts with a Delphi reserved word). It returns an Enumeration type (named as MemberTypeEnum) value and is read-only.

This property can have one of the following values:

Name	Value	Meaning
adMemberRegular	1	The member represents an instance of a business entity (it is the default value).
adMemberMeasure	2	The member belongs to the Measures dimension. It represents a quantitative attribute.
adMemberFormula	4	The member is calculated using a formula expression.
adMemberAll	8	The member represents all members of the level.
adMemberUnknown	16	The type of member cannot be determined.

The Description property indicates the description of the member (optional). It returns a WideString value and is read-only. This property is available both directly and by using the Get_Description method of the Member object.

Collections of the Member Object

The Member object exposes two collections: Children and Properties.

The Children collection contains members for which this member is the hierarchical parent. Members of the last level will have zero members in this collection. Thus, such collections implement a hierarchical structure of members in levels of dimensions.

This collection is only supported on Member objects belonging to a Level object.

Note: Referencing this collection when using the Member object representing a member of a position along an axis in the CellSet object results in an error.

The Properties collection contains provider-supplied properties of the member. For Microsoft OLE DB Provider for OLAP Services, the following properties are available:

Property	Meaning
CatalogName	This property specifies the name of the catalog (storage) that contains the cube.
SchemaName	This property specifies the name of the schema to which this cube belongs.
CubeName	This property specifies the name of the cube.
DimensionUniqueName	This property specifies the unique name of the dimension.
HierarchyUniqueName	This property specifies the unique name of the hierarchy to which this level belongs.
LevelUniqueName	This property specifies the unique name of the level.
LevelNumber	This property specifies the distance of the level from the root of the hierarchy.
MemberOrdinal	This property specifies the ordinal number of the member.
MemberName	This property specifies the name of the member.
MemberUniqueName	This property specifies the unique name of the member.
MemberType	This property specifies the type of the member.
MemberGUID	This property specifies the member GUID.
MemberCaption	This property specifies the label or caption associated with the member.
ChildrenCardinality	This property is equal to the number of children of the member.
ParentLevel	This property specifies the level number of the member's parent
ParentUniqueName	This property specifies the unique name of the member's parent.
ParentCount	This property is equal to the number of parents of this member.
Description	This property specifies a description of the member.

Note: The property list for other OLE DB providers for OLAP Services may differ from the one shown above. It depends on the implementation of the OLE DB provider.

We have just discussed all ADO MD objects that are responsible for representing the cube metadata. Now it is time to look at the objects responsible for representing the cube data. We will begin with the CellSet object, and then will discuss other objects that represent the MDX query results.

The CellSet Object

The CellSet object contains the result of a multidimensional query and provides an array-like access to it. This object contains collections that allow us to retrieve information about axes and cells, and also about their positions and members.

Let's look at the methods, properties, and collections exposed by the CellSet object.

Properties of the CellSet Object

The CellSet object exposes four properties: ActiveConnection, Source, State, and FilterAxis.

The ActiveConnection property can be used to get or set information on the connection to the data source. In Delphi, this property is not available directly. Instead, we can use the following methods:

- To get ActiveConnection, we can use the Get_ActiveConnection method with no parameters. This method returns the IDispatch interface.

- To set ActiveConnection, we can use the _Set_ActiveConnection method that takes one parameter—a WideString.

- We can also use the Set_ActiveConnection method, which expects a parameter in the form of IDispatch. In this case, we need to supply a valid instance of the ADO Connection object. It can be obtained, for example, from the ConnectionObject property of the TADOConnection component.

The Source property indicates the source of an MDX query. It returns an IDispatch value. This property can be read both directly and by using the Get_Source method of the CellSet object. To set this property, we need to use the Set_Source method with the OleVariant parameter, or the _Set_Source method, which has a WideString parameter that contains a valid MDX query.

The State property indicates whether this CellSet is open or closed. It is an integer property, which can be one of the following values:

Name	Value	Meaning
adStateClosed	0	The CellSet is closed.
adStateOpen	I	The CellSet is open.

Note: We can set this property by using the Open or Close methods of the CellSet object.

The FilterAxis property specifies an Axis object containing filter information for the current Cellset. This property is used to obtain information on the dimensions that were used to slice the data. This axis usually has one row.

Note: The Axis returned by the FilterAxis property is not contained in the Axes collection of a Cellset object.

Collections of the CellSet Object

The CellSet object exposes three collections: Properties, Axes, and Items.

The Properties collection contains dynamic properties defined by the OLE DB provider. All of them can be referenced only through this collection. For a detailed description of this collection, see the "ADO MD Collections" section later in this chapter.

Note: The list of Cellset properties depends on the implementation of the OLE DB provider.

The Axes collection contains a set of the Axis objects that represent an axis of the specific cellset. We will discuss Axis objects later. Usually, there are two axes in this collection—one for columns and one for rows. This collection is available both directly and by using the Get_Axes method of the CellSet object.

The Item collection is a two-dimensional collection of Cell objects. Any of them can be retrieved using its coordinates. An example of using this collection is provided later in the chapter.

Methods of the CellSet Object

The Cellset object exposes two methods: Open and Close.

The Open method changes the State property of the CellSet object. It accepts two OleVariant parameters. They are DataSource and ActiveConnection. The first specifies the text of a valid MDX query, and the second is the connection string. An example of using this method is provided later in this chapter.

The Close method sets the State property of the CellSet object to 0.

Now that we have discussed methods, properties, and collections of the CellSet object, let's look at the Axis object, which is one level below the CellSet object.

The Axis Object

The Axis object, which is available through the Axes collection or through the FilterAxis property of the CellSet object, represents a specific axis of the cellset. It contains collections to access selected members of one or more dimensions.

Properties of the Axis Object

The Axis object exposes two properties: Name and DimensionCount.

The Name property indicates the name of the axis. It returns a WideString value and is read-only. This property is available both directly and by using the Get_Name method of the Axis object.

The DimensionCount property indicates the number of dimensions of an axis. It returns an Integer value and is read-only. This property is available both directly and by using the Get_DimensionCount method of the Axis object.

Collections of the Axis Object

The Axis object exposes two collections: Positions and Properties.

The Positions collection contains the Position objects that make up an axis. The Position object available through this collection will be discussed later.

The Properties collection contains dynamic properties defined by the OLE DB provider. All of them can be referenced only through this collection. For a detailed description of this collection, see the "ADO MD Collections" section later in this chapter.

 Note: The list of Axis object properties depends on the implementation of the OLE DB provider.

The Cell Object

The Cell object, which is available by using the Item method of the CellSet object, represents the data in a cell at the intersection of the cellset axes.

Properties of the Cell Object

The Cell object exposes three properties: Value, FormattedValue, and Ordinal.

The Value property specifies the value of the current cell. It returns a `Variant` value. This property is available both directly and by using the Get_Value method of the Cell object.

The FormattedValue property returns a `WideString` value representing the Value property formatted for display. This property is available both directly and by using the Get_FormattedValue method of the Cell object.

The Ordinal property specifies the ordinal value of the current Cell within the cellset. It returns an `Integer` value. This property is available both directly and by using the Get_Ordinal method.

Collections of the Cell Object

The Cell object exposes two collections: Properties and Positions.

The Properties collection contains provider-supplied properties of the cell. The following properties are available for Microsoft OLE DB Provider for OLAP Services:

Property	Meaning
BackColor	This property specifies the background color to use when displaying the cell.
ForeColor	This property specifies the foreground color to use when displaying the cell.
FormatString	This property specifies the value in a formatted string.
FontName	This property specifies the font used to display the cell value.
FontSize	This property specifies the font size used to display the cell value.
FontFlags	This property specifies the bit mask detailing effects on the font.

Note: The property list for other OLE DB providers for OLAP Services may differ from these. It depends on the implementation of the OLE DB provider.

The Positions collection contains the Position objects that make up an axis. See the Position object for details.

The Position Object

The Position object, which is available through the Positions collection of the Cell object, represents a set of one or more members of different dimensions that defines a point along an axis. This object is also available through the Positions collection of the Axis object.

Collections of the Position Object

The Position object exposes only one collection: Members.

The Members collection contains one or more related Member objects that make up an axis. See the Member object (of a position along an axis in a cellset) for details.

The Member Object (of a Position Along an Axis in a Cellset)

The Member object that is available through the Members collection of the Position object represents a specific member of the position along an axis. As we already know, in ADO MD there are two types of Member objects, for members of levels in CubeDef objects and for members of positions along axes in CellSet objects. Now we will discuss the Member object for members of positions along axes in CellSet objects.

Properties of the Member Object

The Member object of a Position along an Axis exposes ten properties. They are described below.

The Caption property indicates the text caption used when displaying the member. It returns a `WideString` value and is read-only. This property is available both directly and by using the Get_Caption method.

The Name property indicates the name of the member. It returns a `WideString` value and is read-only. This property is available both directly and by using the Get_Name method.

The UniqueName property indicates the unique name of the member. It returns a `WideString` value and is read-only. This property is available both directly and by using the Get_UniqueName method.

The LevelDepth property indicates the number of levels from the root of the hierarchy to a member. It returns an `Integer` value and is read-only. This property is available both directly and by using the Get_LevelDepth method.

The LevelName property indicates the name of the level of a member. It returns a `WideString` value and is read-only. This property is available both directly and by using the Get_LevelName method.

The ChildCount property is approximately equal to the number of members for which the current member is the parent. It returns an `Integer` value and is read-only. This property is available both directly and by using the Get_ChildCount method.

Note: For Member objects in a cellset, the maximum possible value of the ChildCount property is 65536. If the actual number of children exceeds 65536, the value returned will also be 65536.

The Type_ property indicates the type of the current Member object (it was renamed after generation of ADOMD_TLB.PAS from the original Type name to avoid conflicts with a Delphi reserved word). It returns an `Enumeration` type (named as MemberTypeEnum) value and is read-only.

This property can have the same values as the Type_ property of the Member object of a level in a CubeDef. See the appropriate section earlier in this chapter for details.

The Description property contains the description of the member (optional). It returns a `WideString` value and is read-only. This property is available both directly and by using the Get_Description method of the Member object.

The DrilledDown property indicates whether the member is drilled down. It returns a `WordBool` value and is read-only. You can also use the Get_DrilledDown method to access this property or read it directly.

Note: Referencing this property when using the Member object representing a member of a hierarchy level of the dimension in a CubeDef object results in an error.

The ParentSameAsPrev property indicates whether the parent of this member is the same as the parent of the immediately preceding member. It returns a `WordBool` value and is read-only. We can also use the Get_ParentSameAsPrev method to access this property or read it directly.

Note: Referencing this property when using the Member object representing a member of a hierarchy level of the dimension in a CubeDef object results in an error.

Collections of the Member Object

The Member object exposes two collections: Children and Properties.

The Properties collection contains provider-supplied properties of the member. The list of available properties for Microsoft OLE DB Provider for OLAP Services is the same as the list of available properties for the Member object of a level in a CubeDef. See the appropriate section earlier in this chapter for details.

The Children collection contains child members of the current member on the next lower level in the hierarchy.

Note: The Children collection is always empty for a member of a cellset.

The ADO MD Collections

Several objects in the ADO MD collections expose collections that contain objects discussed above. This is shown in the following table:

Object	Exposes Collections
Catalog	CubeDefs
CubeDef	Dimensions, Properties
Dimension	Hierarchies, Properties
Hierarchy	Levels, Properties
Level	Members, Properties

Object	Exposes Collections
CellSet	Axes, Properties, Item
Axis	Positions, Properties
Cell	Positions, Properties
Position	Members, Properties
Member	Properties, Children (for Members of the Position of the Axis)

The Properties Collection

This collection contains dynamic properties defined by the OLE DB provider. These properties can only be referenced through this collection.

The Property Object

Any dynamic Property object that is available through the Properties collection has four built-in subproperties of its own:

Name	Type	Meaning
Name	WideString	Specifies the name of the property
Type	SmallInt	Specifies the data type of the property
Value	Variant	Contains the property setting
Attributes	Integer	Contains provider-specific characteristics of the property

Note: The properties list of the ADO MD objects depends on the implementation of the OLE DB provider.

Other Collections

All ADO MD collections, except the Properties collection, expose two properties and one method to access their content.

Properties of a Collection

All ADO MD collections, except the Properties and Items collections, expose two properties: Count and Item.

The Count property returns the number of objects in the current collection. It returns an Integer value and is read-only.

The Item property (which in the case of using interfaces is accessible through the Get_Item method) returns a specific member of a collection by its name or ordinal number.

Note: If an object corresponding to the ordinal number cannot be found in the collection, an error occurs. It should also be mentioned that some collections do not support names of objects. For these collections, it is necessary to use ordinal number references.

Methods of a Collection

All ADO MD collections, except the Properties collection, expose one method: Refresh.

The Refresh method updates the objects in the collection to correspond to the current catalog's schema.

Now that we have learned about the objects in the ADO MD object model, we are ready to create some examples that will show how to use these objects, and their collections, properties, and methods in our Delphi applications.

ADO MD Usage Examples

Now we will create several examples to illustrate how to use the ADO MD objects discussed above. We will show how to use the Catalog object to retrieve cube metadata, and how to use the CellSet object and its collections to retrieve cube data.

Using the Catalog Object and its Collections

To show how to use the Catalog object and its collections, we will create three examples. The first one will show how to get cube names and properties. The second will illustrate how to obtain dimension properties. And, finally, the third will demonstrate how to obtain the names of levels and members.

Getting Cube Names and Properties

In our first example, we will get a list of cubes within a selected catalog. To do this, we need to iterate the CubeDefs collection of the Catalog object, extract the CubeDef object, and get its properties. We will show cubes available in a tree structure, so we need to use a TTreeView component from the Win32 page of the Component Palette that will be placed on a form along with a TButton component.

First, we need to create an instance of a Catalog object. Here is the code to do this:

```
Catalog1 := CoCatalog.Create;
```

This line of code creates a COM object based on the object name.

We store the Catalog1 variable and the CubeDef1 variable in the global declaration section. Later, we will add some more variables there.

Please note that we need to add the reference to the ADOMD_TLB unit to the Uses clause.

```
var
  Form1      : TForm1;
  DS         : WideString;
  Catalog1   : ICatalog;
  CubeDef1   : CubeDef;
  CubeNode   : TTreeNode; //Nodes for the TTreeview component
```

```
CubeDefNode : TTreeNode;
RootNode    : TTreeNode;
```

Next, we need the name of the data source where the tables are stored:

```
procedure TForm1.Button1Click(Sender: TObject);
begin
 DS := 'Provider=MSOLAP.1;Persist Security Info=False;'+
       'User ID=sa;Data Source=MAINDESK;'+
       'Connect Timeout=60;Initial Catalog=NorthWindOLAP;'+
       'Client Cache Size=25;Auto Synch Period=10000';
 CubeList(DS);
end;
```

All functionality of this example is implemented inside the CubeList procedure, which can be split into two parts: the TreeView1 initialization part and the cubes iteration part. In the first part, we create a root node and a child node for cubes. Next, we connect our selected data source to the Catalog object:

```
Catalog1._Set_ActiveConnection(OleVariant(DataSource));
```

Then the data source will be opened, and we can iterate through the cubes within it. First, we check that we have cubes. This is not necessary, since any actual storage should have at least one cube. We do this just to show you how to use the Count property of the CubeDefs collection:

```
If Catalog1.CubeDefs.Count > 0 then
 begin
  //do something with the Catalog object ...
 end;
```

Now we enter the loop, where at each step we extract one CubeDef object at a time and show it in the TreeView1 component. Here is the code we use for this:

```
    For I := 0 to Catalog1.CubeDefs.Count-1 do
     begin
      CubeDef1    := Catalog1.CubeDefs[I] as CubeDef;
      CubeDefNode :=
      TreeView1.Items.AddChild(CubeNode, CubeDef1.Name);
      //do something else with a CubeDef1 object ...
     end;
```

Now we need to get the CubeDef object properties by iterating its Properties collection and showing them in the TreeView1 component.

Then we enter the loop, where at each step we extract one Property object at a time and show its name and value in the TreeView1 component. To do this, we use the Name and the Value properties of the Property object. Here is the code:

```
    For J :=0 to CubeDef1.Properties.Count - 1 do
     begin
      TreeView1.Items.AddChild(CubeDefNode,
      CubeDef1.Properties[J].Name + '=' +
        VarToStr(CubeDef1.Properties[J].Value));
     end;
```

Thus, the full source code of the CubeList procedure will look like this:

```
procedure TForm1.CubeList(DataSource: WideString);
var
 I,J  : Integer;
begin
 Catalog1 := CoCatalog.Create;
 TreeView1.Items.Clear;
 RootNode := TreeView1.Items.Add(nil, 'Catalog');
 CubeNode := TreeView1.Items.AddChild(RootNode, 'Cubes');
 Catalog1._Set_ActiveConnection(OleVariant(DataSource));
  for I := 0 to Catalog1.CubeDefs.Count-1 do
   begin
    CubeDef1     := Catalog1.CubeDefs[I] as CubeDef;
    CubeDefNode :=
     TreeView1.Items.AddChild(CubeNode, CubeDef1.Name);
    for J := 0 to CubeDef1.Properties.Count - 1 do
     begin
      TreeView1.Items.AddChild(CubeDefNode,
      CubeDef1.Properties[J].Name+'='+
      VarToStr(CubeDef1.Properties[J].Value));
     end;
   end;
end;
```

After saving and compiling this project, we can obtain the following output in the TreeView1 component:

Getting Dimension Properties

In our second example, we will get a list of dimensions and their properties within a selected catalog. To do this, we will iterate the Dimensions collection of the CubeDef object, extract the Dimension object, and get its properties. It is a modified version of the previous example, so it also uses a TTreeView component.

As in the previous case, we also need to create an instance of the Catalog object. In addition, we need to create the Dimension object. So, we will add the following lines to the global declaration section:

```
var
 Form1        : TForm1;
 DS           : WideString;
 Catalog1     : ICatalog;
 CubeDef1     : CubeDef;
 Dimension1   : Dimension;
 CubeNode     : TTreeNode; //Nodes for the TTreeview component
 RootNode     : TTreeNode;
 CubeDefNode  : TTreeNode;
 DimNode      : TTreeNode;
```

As all functionality is implemented inside the CubeList procedure, we need to modify it as shown below:

```
procedure TForm1.CubeList(DataSource: WideString);
var
 I : Integer;
begin
 Catalog1 := CoCatalog.Create;
 TreeView1.Items.Clear;
 RootNode := TreeView1.Items.Add(nil, 'Catalog');
 CubeNode := TreeView1.Items.AddChild(RootNode, 'Cubes');
 Catalog1._Set_ActiveConnection(OleVariant(DataSource));
  for I := 0 to Catalog1.CubeDefs.Count-1 do
  begin
   CubeDef1     := Catalog1.CubeDefs[I] as CubeDef;
   CubeDefNode :=
     TreeView1.Items.AddChild(CubeNode, CubeDef1.Name);
   if CubeDef1.Dimensions.Count > 0 then
    ShowDimProp;
  end;
end;
```

This procedure looks like the one from the previous example. But there are some differences. As in the previous case, we need to connect the Catalog object to our selected data source, and then iterate through the cubes within it. Also, as in the previous case, we enter the loop, where at each step we extract one CubeDef object at a time and show it in the TreeView1 component.

But we also need to obtain dimensions and their properties for each cube. To do this, we call the ShowDimProp procedure. Its code looks like this:

```
procedure TForm1.ShowDimProp;
var
 I,J : Integer;
begin
 for J := 0 to CubeDef1.Dimensions.Count-1 do
 begin
  Dimension1 := CubeDef1.Dimensions[J] as Dimension;
  DimNode    :=
   TreeView1.Items.AddChild(CubeDefNode,Dimension1.Name);
   for I := 0 to Dimension1.Properties.Count - 1 do begin
   TreeView1.Items.AddChild(DimNode,
     Dimension1.Properties[I].Name + '=' +
     VarToStr(Dimension1.Properties[I].Value));
    end;
 end;
end;
```

Let's look at this procedure in more detail. First, we need to get the Dimension collection of the CubeDef1 object, check whether it contains at least one dimension, iterate it, obtain the Dimension object from it, and add its name to the TreeView1 component:

```
procedure TForm1.ShowDimProp;
var
 I,J : Integer;
begin
 for J := 0 to CubeDef1.Dimensions.Count-1 do
  begin
   Dimension1 := CubeDef1.Dimensions[J] as Dimension;
  //add a node for this dimension and output its properties
 end;
end;
```

Finally, we need to get the Dimension1 object properties by iterating its Properties collection and show them in the TreeView1 component. To do this, we enter the loop, where at each step we extract one Property object at a time and show its name and value in the TreeView1 component. Here is the code we use for this:

```
 for I := 0 to Dimension1.Properties.Count - 1 do
  begin
   TreeView1.Items.AddChild(DimNode,
    Dimension1.Properties[I].Name + '=' +
    VarToStr(Dimension1.Properties[I].Value));
  end;
```

After saving and compiling this project, we can obtain a list of the Dimension properties in the TreeView1 component, as shown in the figure below:

Getting Names of Hierarchies, Levels, and Members

In our third example, we will get a list of all objects inside the selected catalog, i.e., cubes, dimensions, and their hierarchies, levels, and members. To do this, we will iterate all collections of all objects within the hierarchy of the Catalog collections. It is also a modified version of the previous example, so it also uses a TTreeView component.

As in the previous example, we also need to create an instance of the Catalog and Dimension objects, and, in addition, instances of the Hierarchy, Level, and Member objects. So, we need to change the global declaration section:

```
var
  Form1             : TForm1;
  DS                : WideString;
  Catalog1          : ICatalog;
  CubeDef1          : CubeDef;
  Dimension1        : Dimension;
  Hierarchy1        : Hierarchy;
  Level1            : Level;
  Member1           : Member;
  CubeNode          : TTreeNode;
  RootNode          : TTreeNode;
  CubeDefNode       : TTreeNode;
  HierNode          : TTreeNode;
```

```
LevelNode              : TTreeNode;
NodeName               : String;
```

As the functionality is implemented inside the CubeList procedure, we need to modify it once again, as shown below:

```
procedure TForm1.CubeList(DataSource: WideString);
var
 I : Integer;
begin
 Catalog1 :=  CoCatalog.Create;
 TreeView1.Items.Clear;
 RootNode := TreeView1.Items.Add(nil, 'Catalog');
 CubeNode := TreeView1.Items.AddChild(RootNode, 'Cubes');
 Catalog1._Set_ActiveConnection(OleVariant(DataSource));
  for I := 0 to Catalog1.CubeDefs.Count-1 do
  begin
   CubeDef1 := Catalog1.CubeDefs[I] as CubeDef;
   CubeDefNode :=
    TreeView1.Items.AddChild(CubeNode, CubeDef1.Name);
   if  CubeDef1.Dimensions.Count > 0 then
    DimList;
  end;
end;
```

This procedure is almost the same as in the previous example, although there are some differences. As in the previous case, we need to connect the Catalog object to our selected data source, and then iterate through the cubes within it. Also, as in the previous case, we enter the loop, where at each step we extract one CubeDef object at a time and show it in the TreeView1 component.

Then we need to obtain dimensions for each cube. To do this, we call the DimList procedure. Its code looks like this:

```
procedure TForm1.DimList;
var
 I : Integer;
begin
 for I := 0 to CubeDef1.Dimensons.Count-1 do
 begin
  Dimension1 := CubeDef1.Dimensions[I] as Dimension;
  DimNode :=
   TreeView1.Items.AddChild(CubeDefNode, Dimension1.Name);
  HierarchyList;
 end;
end;
```

Instead of iterating the Property collection of the Dimension1 object, we need to iterate its Hierarchies collection.

To obtain a list of hierarchies of the dimension, we call the HierarchyList procedure. It looks like this:

```
procedure TForm1.HierarchyList;
var
 I : Integer;
begin
 For I := 0 to Dimension1.Hierarchies.Count-1 do
 begin
  Hierarchy1 := Dimension1.Hierarchies[I] as Hierarchy;
  NodeName := Hierarchy1.Name;
  If Hierarchy1.Name = ''
   Then NodeName := 'Hierarchy';
  HierNode := TreeView1.Items.AddChild(DimNode, NodeName);
   LevelList;
 end;
end;
```

Here we enter the loop, where at each step we extract one Hierarchy object at a time and show it in the TreeView1 component. Be sure to comment the following line:

```
if Hierarchy1.Name = '' then NodeName := 'Hierarchy';
```

This is used for a case in which the Name property of the Hierarchy object returns an empty string. Our cube just contains unnamed Hierarchy objects, one for each dimension.

At the next step, if there are levels in this collection, we need to iterate the Levels collection of the Hierarchy object. The LevelList procedure is designed for this:

```
procedure TForm1.LevelList;
var
 I : Integer;
begin
 for I := 0 to Hierarchy1.Levels.Count-1 do begin
  Level1 := Hierarchy1.Levels[I] as Level;
  LevelNode :=
   TreeView1.Items.AddChild(HierNode, Level1.Name);
   MemberList;
 end;
end;
```

Here we enter the loop, where at each step we extract one Level object at a time and show it in the TreeView1 component.

Finally, we need to iterate the Members collection of the Level object with the MemberList procedure:

```
procedure TForm1.MemberList;
var
 I : Integer;
begin
 for I := 0 to  Level1.Members.Count - 1 do begin
  Member1 := Level1.Members[I] as Member;
  TreeView1.Items.AddChild(LevelNode, Member1.Name);
 end;
end;
```

Here, we enter the loop, where at each step we extract one Member object at a time and show it in the TreeView1 component.

After saving and compiling this project, we can obtain the output shown at right in the TreeView1 component.

We have just created an example that shows cube metadata in a treeview. This information is necessary for creating MDX queries, which results in retrieving cube data to the CellSet object. The next two examples will illustrate how to do this.

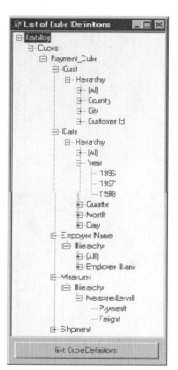

Using CellSet Objects

To show how to use the CellSet object and its collections, we will create two examples. The first one will show how to retrieve the members of positions along Axis objects of the Axes collection of the CellSet object, how to retrieve the Cells values using the Item method, and how to place all obtained values into a grid. The second one will illustrate how to retrieve the same data to the client dataset.

Retrieving Cells to a Grid

In this example, we will create a CellSet object and put the values of its cells into a grid. Also, we will draw a chart with the CellSet content. To do this, we need to iterate through all Cell values available by using the Item method of the CellSet object.

Let's start a new project and place the TStringGrid, TButton, and TChart components on a form. Also, we will place on the form the TComboBox component (we will fill it with names of some predefined MDX queries) and the TMemo component (it will contain the text of an MDX query, which can be edited by the user).

First, let's prepare a set of predefined MDX queries, and place their names in the ComboBox1.Items property, for example:

ComboBox1.Items	MDX Query
Payments by year for all countries	SELECT {[Date].children} ON COLUMNS, ([cust].children) ON ROWS FROM Payment_Cube WHERE Payment
Payments by quarter for 1997 for all countries	SELECT {[Date].[Year].[1997].children} ON COLUMNS, ([cust].children) ON ROWS FROM Payment_Cube WHERE Payment
Payments by year for all customers	SELECT {[Date].[Year].members} ON COLUMNS, ([cust].[Customer ID].members) ON ROWS FROM Payment_Cube WHERE Payment
Payments by year for customers in Germany	SELECT {[Date].[Year].members} ON COLUMNS, ([cust].[Country].[Germany].children) ON ROWS FROM Payment_Cube WHERE Payment

The MDX query text itself will be placed in the Lines property of the Memo1 component. To do this, we need to create the OnChange event handler for the ComboBox1 component:

```
procedure TForm1.ComboBox1Change(Sender: TObject);
var
 I : Integer;
begin
 I:=Combobox1.ItemIndex;
 Memo1.Lines.Clear;
 case I of
  0: Memo1.Lines.Add('SELECT {[Date].CHILDREN} ON COLUMNS,'+
     ' ([Cust].CHILDREN)ON ROWS from Payment_Cube'+
     ' WHERE Payment');
  1: Memo1.Lines.Add('SELECT {[Date].[Year].[1997].CHILDREN}'+
     ' ON COLUMNS, ([Cust].CHILDREN)ON ROWS ' +
     ' FROM Payment_Cube WHERE Payment');
  2: Memo1.Lines.Add('SELECT {[Date].[Year].MEMBERS} '+
     ' ON COLUMNS, ([Cust].[Customer ID].MEMBERS)ON ROWS'+
     ' FROM Payment_Cube WHERE Payment');
  3: Memo1.Lines.Add('SELECT {[Date].[Year].MEMBERS}'+
     ' ON COLUMNS,([Cust].[Country].[Germany].CHILDREN) '+
     ' ON ROWS FROM PaymentCube WHERE Payment');
 end;
end;
```

This event handler places the appropriate text of an MDX query when the user selects an item from the ComboBox1. In addition, the user can just edit the Memo1 content at run time to retrieve CellSets that result from the custom MDX queries.

Second, we need to provide a variable to work with when creating an instance of the CellSet object. We store this variable in the global declaration section:

```
var
  Form1   : TForm1;
  DS      : WideString;
  Cellset1 : ICellSet;
```

Next, we need the name of the data source where the cubes are stored:

```
procedure TForm1.Button1Click(Sender: TObject);
begin
 DS := 'Provider=MSOLAP.1;Persist Security Info=False;'+
       'User ID=sa;Data Source=MAINDESK;'+
       'Connect Timeout=60;Initial Catalog=NorthWindOLAP;'+
       'Client Cache Size=25;Auto Synch Period=10000';
 CellGrid(DS);
 CellChart;
end;
```

The functionality of this example is implemented inside the CellGrid procedure, the source code of which looks like this:

```
procedure TForm1.CellGrid(DataSource: WideString);
var
 I, J : Integer;
 V    : OleVariant;
begin
 CellSet1:=CreateOleObject('ADOMD.Cellset');
 CellSet1.Open(Memo1.Text,DataSource);
 StringGrid1.ColCount:=CellSet1.Axes[0].Positions.Count+1;
 StringGrid1.RowCount:= CellSet1.Axes[1].Positions.Count+1;
 for J:=1 to CellSet1.Axes[1].Positions.Count do
  StringGrid1.Cells[0,J]:=
   CellSet1.Axes[1].Positions[J-1].Members[0].Caption;
 for I:=1 to CellSet1.Axes[0].Positions.Count do
 begin
  StringGrid1.Cells[I,0]:=
   CellSet1.Axes[0].Positions[I-1].Members[0].Caption;
  for J:=1 to CellSet1.Axes[1].Positions.Count do
  begin
  V:=VarArrayCreate([0,1], varVariant);
  V[0] := I-1;
  V[1] := J-1;
   if Cellset1.Item[PSafeArray(TVarData(V).VArray)].
     FormattedValue <> ''
   then
     StringGrid1.Cells[I,J] :=
     Cellset1.Item[PSafeArray(TVarData(V).VArray)].Value
   else
     StringGrid1.Cells[I,J]:='0';
```

```
  end;
 end;
CellSet1.Close;
CellSet1 := nil;
end;
```

First, in this procedure we must create an instance of the CellSet object:

```
CellSet1:=CoCellSet.Create;
```

Second, we need to open this CellSet using the text of an MDX query taken from the Memo1 component:

```
CellSet1.Open(Memo1.Text,DataSource);
```

Third, we need to find out how many columns and rows the StringGrid1 component must contain. To do this, we use the Count properties of the Positions collections of the Axis objects, which belong to the Axes collection of the CellSet object:

```
StringGrid1.ColCount := CellSet1.Axes[0].Positions.Count + 1;
StringGrid1.RowCount := CellSet1.Axes[1].Positions.Count + 1;
```

As we have discussed earlier in this chapter, usually there are two Axis objects in the Axes collection—one for columns (Axes[0]) and the other for rows (Axes[1]). As we need to have an additional row for column names and an additional column for row names, we add one to the value of the Count properties for both axes.

Fourth, we need to fill the first column of the StringGrid1 component with the row names. To do this, we will iterate all Position objects of the Positions collection of the appropriate Axis object (in this case, it is the CellSet1.Axes[0] object). We can get the row name from the Caption property of the primary item of the Members collection of such Position objects:

```
for J := 1 to CellSet1.Axes[1].Positions.Count do
StringGrid1.Cells[0,J] :=
 CellSet1.Axes[1].Positions[J-1].Members[0].Caption;
```

Next, let's fill the first row of the StringGrid1 with the column names by iterating all Position objects of the Positions collection of the appropriate Axis object (now it is the CellSet1.Axes[0] object):

```
for J := 1 to CellSet1.Axes[0].Positions.Count do
begin
 StringGrid1.Cells[J,0] :=
  CellSet1.Axes[0].Positions[J-1].Members[0].Caption;
 //fill this column by values
end;
```

Then let's fill the rest of the StringGrid1 components with the CellSet content. To do this, we need to obtain the necessary values by using the Value property of Cell objects that are returned by the Item method of the CellSet object:

```
V := VarArrayCreate([0,1], varVariant);
V[0] := I-1;
V[1] := J-1;
 if CellSet1.Item[PSafeArray(TVarData(V).VArray)].
   FormattedValue <> ''
 then
   StringGrid1.Cells[I,J] :=
     CellSet1.Item[PSafeArray(TVarData(V).VArray)].Value
 else
   StringGrid1.Cells[I,J]:='0';
end;
```

Note that here we use the argument of the PSafeArray type, as it is defined in the ADOMD_TLB.PAS file (this also requires referring to the ActiveX unit in the Uses clause). When using Automation with Variants (also called late binding), we need to use the CellSet.Item[I,J] syntax.

We put zero value in all empty cells of StringGrid1. This component does not require that empty cells be filled, but because we will be creating a chart with this data, it is necessary to have valid numbers in these cells.

Finally, we need to close the CellSet object and empty the Variant variable:

```
CellSet1.Close;
CellSet1 := nil;
```

To make our application more attractive to users of our application, we will create a chart with the StringGrid1 data. The CellChart procedure is designed to do this:

```
procedure TForm1.CellChart;
var
 I,J     : Integer;
 ASeries : THorizBarSeries;
 y       : Real;
 X       : String;
begin
 Chart1.SeriesList.Clear;
 for I := 1 to StringGrid1.ColCount-1 do
 begin
  ASeries := THorizBarSeries.Create(Chart1);
  Chart1.AddSeries(ASeries);
  ASeries.Marks.Visible := False;
  ASeries.Title := StringGrid1.Cells[i,0];
  for J := 1 to StringGrid1.RowCount-1 do
  begin
   X:=StringGrid1.Cells[0,J];
```

```
   Y:=StrToFloat(StringGrid1.Cells[I,J]);
   Chart1.Series[I-1].AddX(Y,X);
  end;
 end;
end;
```

Note that we need to refer to the Series unit in the Uses clause. First, we need to clear the series list of the Chart1 component:

```
Chart1.SeriesList.Clear;
```

Then we need to iterate all columns to create appropriate series in the chart:

```
for I := 1 to StringGrid1.ColCount-1 do
begin
 ASeries := THorizBarSeries.Create(Chart1);
 Chart1.AddSeries(ASeries);
 ASeries.Marks.Visible := False;
 ASeries.Title := StringGrid1.Cells[I,0];
 //add points to this series
end;
```

Finally, we need to add points to all specific series:

```
for J := 1 to StringGrid1.RowCount-1 do
begin
 X := StringGrid1.Cells[0,J];
 Y := StrToFloat(StringGrid1.Cells[I,J]);
 Chart1.Series[I-1].AddX(Y,X);
end;
```

The result of retrieving cells to a string grid and a chart is shown in the following illustration:

Retrieving Cells to a Client Dataset

The next example will show you how to retrieve the Cell object values to the client dataset. This is useful if we need to perform some data manipulation in a client application, e.g., sorting, filtering, or generating reports or HTML contents.

In this example, we will create a CellSet object and put the values from its cells into the TClientDataSet component. As in the previous example, we will draw a chart based on the data from the CellSet object. To do this, we will also iterate through all Cell values available using the Item method of the CellSet object.

Let's create a new Delphi project and place the TClientDataSet, TDBGrid, TDBNavigator, TButton, and TChart components on a form. Also, we will place on the form the TComboBox component (as in the previous example, we will fill it with the names of predefined MDX queries) and the TMemo component (it will contain the text of MDX query, which can be edited by the user).

As in the previous example, for the reasons explained above, we will use Automation with Variants instead of using co-classes, and will create a set of predefined MDX queries. When the data source is selected, we call the CDSFill procedures, passing the data source name as an argument, and then call the CDSChart procedure to draw a chart using the CellSet data.

The functionality of this application is implemented inside the CDSFill procedure, the source code of which looks like this:

```
procedure TForm1.CDSFill(DataSource: WideString);
var
 I,J : Integer;
 V   : OleVariant;
begin
 CellSet1 := CoCellSet.Create;
 CellSet1.Open(Memo1.Text,DataSource);
 with ClientDataSet1 do
 begin
  Close;
  DisableControls;
  with FieldDefs do
  begin
   Clear;
   with AddFieldDef do
   begin
    Name := 'rows';
    DataType := ftString;
   end;
   for I := 1 to CellSet1.Axes[0].Positions.Count do
   begin
    with AddFieldDef do
    begin
     Name :=
     CellSet1.Axes[0].Positions[I-1].Members[0].Caption+
     ' ('+IntToStr(CellSet1.Axes[0].Positions[I-1].Ordinal)
     +')';
     DataType := ftFloat;
    end;
   end;
  end;
  CreateDataSet;
  Open;
  for J:=1 to CellSet1.Axes[1].Positions.Count  do
  begin
   Append;
   Fields[0].Value :=
    CellSet1.Axes[1].Positions[J-1].Members[0].Caption;
   for I := 1 to CellSet1.Axes[0].Positions.Count do
   begin
    V :=VarArrayCreate([0,1], varVariant);
    V[0] := I-1;
    V[1] := J-1;
    if Cellset1.Item[PSafeArray(TVarData(V).VArray)].
      FormattedValue <> ''
    then
     Fields[I].Value :=
     Cellset1.Item[PSafeArray(TVarData(V).VArray)].Value
```

```
    else
      ClientDataSet1.Fields[I].Value:=0;
    end;
    EnableControls;
  end;
  CellSet1.Close;
  CellSet1 := nil;
 end;
end;
```

First, in this procedure we must create an instance of the CellSet object and open it:

```
CellSet1 := CoCellSet.Create;
 CellSet1.Open(Memo1.Text,DataSource);
```

Second, we need to create the first field of the client dataset. It will contain the row names, so it will be a string type:

```
with ClientDataSet1 do
begin
 Close;
 DisableControls;
 with FieldDefs do
 begin
  Clear;
  with AddFieldDef do
  begin
   Name := 'rows';
   DataType := ftString;
  end;
  //create fields and define their name and type
 end;
 //fill the ClientDataSet1.with data
end;
```

Third, we need to create fields to store the CellSet data. The names can be the same as the names of the appropriate Member objects on the positions along the horizontal axis of the cellset.

These fields must be of a Float type since they contain financial values.

```
with AddFieldDef do
begin
 Name :=
  CellSet1.Axes[0].Positions[i-1].Members[0].Caption + ' ('+
  IntToStr(CellSet1.Axes[0].Positions[i-1].Ordinal) + ')';
 DataType := ftFloat;
end;
```

We need to comment this code. The reason for using the Ordinal property in the field name is that field names must be unique in the dataset. However, we can have the same Caption properties for different positions. For example, look at the following MDX query:

```
SELECT {[Date].[1997].[Quarter 1], [Date].[1998].[Quarter 1]} ON COLUMNS,
([cust].CHILDREN) ON ROWS FROM PaymentCube
WHERE Payment
```

The result of this query will contain two columns with the same name—Quarter 1. But, in this case, we cannot use these names as field names. As for the Ordinal value, it is unique, so we can add this value to the field name.

We can, of course, provide another way to obtain unique names of your fields. For example, it is possible to use the UniqueName property of the appropriate member instead of using the Caption property:

```
with AddFieldDef do
begin
  Name :=
    CellSet1.Axes[0].Positions[I-1].Members[0].UniqueName;
  DataType := ftFloat;
end;
```

Next, we need to create the client dataset and open it:

```
CreateDataSet;
Open;
```

Now we need to iterate the CellSet rows and add each of them to the client dataset. First, we need to append a record to the client dataset:

```
for J := 1 to CellSet1.Axes[1].Positions.Count  do
begin
  Append;
  //fill this record with data
end;
```

Second, we need to insert data into the first field of the created record. It will be the name of the Cellset row. So, we need to use the Caption property of the primary member of the current Position object that is an item of the Positions collection of the appropriate axis. In this case, it is the CellSet1.Axes[1] object:

```
Fields[0].Value :=
CellSet1.Axes[1].Positions[J-1].Members[0].Caption;
```

Third, we need to fill the remaining fields of the record. The values to be inserted are the Value properties of the Cell objects that are the results of retrieving the Item collection members of the CellSet object:

```
for I := 1 to CellSet1.Axes[0].Positions.Count do
begin
 V:=VarArrayCreate([0,1], varVariant);
 V[0] := I-1;
 V[1] := J-1;
 if Cellset1.Item[PSafeArray(TVarData(V).VArray)].
   FormattedValue <> ''
  then
   Fields[I].Value :=
   Cellset1.Item[PSafeArray(TVarData(V).VArray)].Value
  else
   ClientDataSet1.Fields[I].Value:=0;
end;
```

Note that here we use the argument of the PSafeArray type, as it is defined in the ADOMD_TLB.PAS file (this also requires referring to the ActiveX unit in the Uses clause). When using Automation with Variants (also called late binding), we need to use the CellSet.Item[I,J] syntax.

And finally, we need to close the CellSet object and empty the appropriate variable:

```
CellSet1.Close;
CellSet1 := nil;
```

Now we will create a chart with the ClientDataSet1 data. The CDSChart procedure is designed to do this:

```
procedure TForm1.CDSChart;
var
 I       : Integer;
 ASeries : THorizBarSeries;
 Y       : Real;
 X       : String;
begin
 Chart1.SeriesList.Clear;
 for I :=1 to ClientDataSet1.Fields.Count-1 do
 begin
  ASeries := THorizBarSeries.Create(Chart1);
  Chart1.AddSeries(ASeries);
  ASeries.Marks.Visible := False;
  ASeries.Title := ClientDataSet1.Fields[I].FieldName;
  ClientDataSet1.First;
  while not ClientDataSet1.EOF do
  begin
   X := ClientDataSet1.Fields[0].Value;
   Y := ClientDataSet1.Fields[I].Value;
   Chart1.Series[I-1].AddX(Y,X);
   ClientDataSet1.Next;
```

```
  end;
 end;
end;
```

Note that we need to refer to the Series unit in the Uses clause. First, we need to clear the series list of the Chart1 component:

```
Chart1.SeriesList.Clear;
```

Second, we need to iterate all columns to create appropriate series of the chart:

```
for i:=1 to ClientDataSet1.Fields.Count-1 do
begin
 ASeries := THorizBarSeries.Create(Chart1);
 Chart1.AddSeries(ASeries);
 ASeries.Marks.Visible:=False;
 ASeries.Title := ClientDataSet1.Fields[i].FieldName;
 //add points to this series...
end;
```

Then we need to add points to all specific series:

```
ClientDataSet1.First;
while not ClientDataSet1.eof do
begin
 X := ClientDataSet1.Fields[0].Value;
 Y := ClientDataSet1.Fields[I].Value;
 Chart1.Series[I-1].AddX(Y,X);
 ClientDataSet1.Next;
end;
```

The result of retrieving cells to the client dataset and an applicable chart is shown on the following page:

In these two examples, we have shown how to retrieve cube data using MDX queries to a client application. Now you can see that by using ADO MD extensions, you can create applications with charting possibilities similar to those with Decision Cube client-side OLAP components. However, unlike the Decision Cube applications, using ADO MD has a great advantage: Such applications do not require bringing a lot of data to the client application. In this case, all necessary calculations are done by the database server, and the end user obtains only the required data.

Conclusion

In this chapter, we have discussed creation of server-side OLAP Delphi applications using ADO MD objects. Now we know that:

- The main objects of ADO MD are Catalog and CellSet.
- The Catalog object contains all information that describes the OLAP storage properties. It has some properties and methods, as well as several collections that contain information on cubes, dimensions, and their hierarchies, levels, and members.
- The CellSet object contains all information that describes a result of a multidimensional query. It has some properties, methods, and collections that contain information on axes and cells of the MDX query result.
- To retrieve the cube metadata, such as cube name, names of dimensions, hierarchies, levels, and members, we can use the ADO MD Catalog object.

- To access the cube data, we need to use the ADO MD CellSet object, which opens an MDX query.

We have also created several examples of creating server-side OLAP applications, illustrating how to retrieve cube metadata and cube slices based on MDX queries. We have seen that this way of creating analytical applications can be used with large data sources because such applications bring only the data required in the MDX query.

ADO MD, which was discussed in this chapter, is just one of the ADO extensions available in MDAC 2.1. There are two other extensions in this version of MDAC: ADO Extensions for DDL and Security (ADOX), which allows using Automation to manipulate metadata in databases, e.g., to create tables, views, and procedures, set the field properties, and so on, and Jet and Replication Objects (JRO), which provides some replication features specific to the Microsoft Jet Database Engine. We will discuss these extensions in the following two chapters.

USING ADOX IN DELPHI APPLICATIONS

In the previous chapter, we started to discuss the additional components of the Microsoft Data Access Components (MDAC) library and learned how we can use ADO Multidimensional—an ADO extension for working with multidimensional data that first appeared in ADO 2.0. ADO Version 2.1 comes with two more extensions that can be used in Delphi projects: ADO Extensions for DDL and Security (ADOX) and Jet Replication Objects (JRO).

In this chapter, we will look at the ADO Extensions for DDL and Security (ADOX) library, its object model, and features, and give you some examples of how to use them. Note that all this functionality comes with a single installation file—MDAC_TYP.EXE.

The ADOX Library

We already know that ADOX stands for *ADO Extensions for DDL and Security*, and that's why its set of objects can be discussed from two points of view—the objects to access the data definition, and security extensions.

The data definition part of the ADOX library gives us access to the underlying structure of the database. It allows us to get a list of tables, columns, and properties, as well as to obtain a list of views and stored procedures. In many cases, ADOX can be considered as the object-oriented version of the OpenSchema method of the Connection object that we discussed back in Chapter 5. To obtain such information (called *metadata*), we can use both approaches, but from our point of view, the objects and methods of the ADOX library are easier to use.

The security extensions part of the ADOX library allows us to manipulate users and groups, get and set owners of database objects, and perform other related tasks. Once again, all of this can be achieved through the appropriate set of SQL statements, but the object-oriented approach implemented in the ADOX library is easier to use and is often more intuitive.

Like all other interfaces in Microsoft Data Access Components, ADOX consists of a set of objects. The following diagrams show the objects that come with ADOX and their relationships:

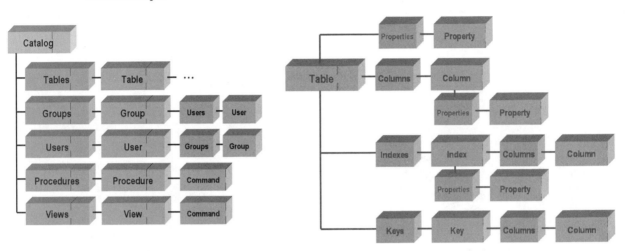

As we can see from the diagrams above, the main object of ADOX is Catalog. It contains all information that describes the schema information of a data source. It has some properties and methods, as well as several collections that contain information on tables, columns, indexes, keys, procedures, and views, as well as groups and users.

We will start our overview of the ADOX library with the Catalog object, but before we do this, we must be able to access this library from our Delphi code. This is described in the next section.

Accessing ADOX from Delphi

Since ADOX support in Delphi 5 was not implemented at the components level, we need to use the type library to access ADOX objects. To do so, choose **Project | Import Type Library** command from the main menu and in the Import Type Library dialog box select **Microsoft ADO Ext. 2.1 for DDL and Security (Version 2.1)**.

To avoid conflicts with already declared Delphi classes, rename TTable to TADOXTable, TColumn to TADOXColumn, and TIndex to TADOXIndex. For consistency and easy identification, we can also rename the TGroup and TUser classes to TADOXGroup and TADOXUser. Note that this only applies if the Generate Component Wrappers check box is checked.

Then press the Install button and choose either the default package (dcluser50.dpk) or the new one (i.e., adox.dpk). If you're not going to use the component, don't install a package; just press the Create Unit button. If you are going to use the component, then you need to compile the package to install the component to the palette.

In both cases, we will end up with the ADOX_TLB.PAS file, which is the Pascal language conversion of the contents of the ADOX type library. In the examples throughout this chapter, we will assume that the ADOX_TLB.PAS file is included in the Uses clause.

Note: Since we will use some COM functions as well as several routines implemented in ADO Express, we will need to include the COMOBJ and ADODB units in the Uses clause.

Now we are set and ready to look at each object in the ADOX object model in detail. For obvious reasons we will start with the Catalog object.

The Catalog Object

The Catalog object contains all information that describes the schema information of a data source. This object contains collections that allow us to manipulate tables, procedures, and views within the data, and obtain or provide security information on the groups and users level. All this functionality is available for us through the appropriate collections; each collection contains zero or more objects of the particular type.

Besides providing the schema information, the Catalog object can be used to create new catalogs and, with the help of other ADOX objects, tables and columns within them. This object-based approach is easier and clearer than the SQL data definition statements we saw in Chapter 9. Depending on the provider, we can get access to the whole set of features implemented in the Catalog object, or just a subset of them.

Note: The current version of ADOX, ADOX 2.1, is fully implemented only for the Microsoft OLE DB Provider for the Microsoft Jet Database Engine, i.e., all functionality is available for the Access databases. See notes for each particular object for more details.

Let's look at the methods, properties, and collections exposed by the Catalog object.

Methods of the Catalog Object

The Catalog object exposes three methods, which are used to create a new Catalog (Create method), and to get and set the owner of an object (GetObjectOwner and SetObjectOwner, respectively).

The Create Method

This method can be used to create a new catalog. In the current implementation (ADOX version 2.1) you can only create a new Access database (.mdb file). This method is called with an appropriate connection string and can return a connection string that was used to create a data source. Below is an example of what you can get with the following connection:

```
Provider=Microsoft.Jet.OLEDB.4.0;
Data Source= c:\data\demo.mdb

Provider=Microsoft.Jet.OLEDB.4.0;
Password="";
User ID=Admin;
Data Source=c:\data\demo.mdb;
Mode=Share Deny None;
Extended Properties="";
Locale Identifier=1033;
Jet OLEDB:System database="";
Jet OLEDB:Registry Path="";
Jet OLEDB:Database Password="";
Jet OLEDB:Engine Type=5;
Jet OLEDB:Database Locking Mode=1;
Jet OLEDB:Global Partial Bulk Ops=2;
Jet OLEDB:Global Bulk Transactions=1;
Jet OLEDB:New Database Password="";
Jet OLEDB:Create System Database=False;
Jet OLEDB:Encrypt Database=False;
Jet OLEDB:Don't Copy Locale on Compact=False;
Jet OLEDB:Compact Without Replica Repair=False;
Jet OLEDB:SFP=False
```

Later in this chapter, we will see how to check some of the properties of the connection.

This method is not supported for the following providers:

- Microsoft SQL Server OLE DB Provider
- Microsoft OLE DB Provider for ODBC
- Microsoft OLE DB Provider for Oracle

The GetObjectOwner Method

Use this method to get the user or group name of an object's owner. It takes two parameters—the name of the object we are looking for and its type. The type of the object can be one of the following constants:

Constant	Value	Meaning
adPermObjProviderSpecific	-1	The object is of a provider-specific type.
adPermObjTable	1	The object is a table.
adPermObjColumn	2	The object is a column.
adPermObjDataBase	3	The object is a database.
adPermObjProcedure	4	The object is a procedure.
adPermObjView	5	The object is a view.

A third, optional parameter should be used only when the type of the object is adPermObjProviderSpecific. In that case, it is of `Variant` type, and it should contain the valid GUID of an object. Here is the prototype for the GetObjectOwner method:

```
function GetObjectOwner(const ObjectName: WideString;
 ObjectType: ObjectTypeEnum;
 ObjectTypeId: OleVariant): WideString;
```

The following example shows how to get the owners of all tables inside the Catalog object:

```
// Global Declaration
 Catalog : TADOXCatalog;

procedure TForm1.ListOwners;
var
 Table    : TADOXTable;
 I        : Integer;
 S        : String;
begin
 Memo1.Lines.Clear;
 S := 'Name = %s; Owner= %s';
 Table := CoTable.Create;
 For I := 0 to Catalog.Tables.Count-1 do
  begin
   Table := Catalog.Tables[I];
   Memo1.Lines.Add(Format(S, [Table.Name,
     Catalog.GetObjectOwner(
       Table.Name,
```

```
        adPermObjTable,
        EmptyParam
      )])));
  end;
  Table._Release;
end;

procedure TForm1.Button1Click(Sender: TObject);
var
 DS  : WideString;
begin
 Catalog := CoCatalog.Create;
 DS := 'Provider=Microsoft.Jet.OLEDB.4.0;';
 DS := DS + 'Data Source=c:\data\northwind.mdb;';
 DS := DS + 'Jet OLEDB:System Database=';
 Ds := DS +
  GetSysDBPath;
 Catalog._Set_ActiveConnection(OleVariant(DS));
 ListOwners;
end;
```

Note: If you are using the Jet Provider, you should set a security database before you can access the GetObjectOwner method. Thus, the connection string should contain a reference like the one shown below:

```
Jet OLEDB:System Database=d:\Program Files\Microsoft
Office\Office\System.mdw
```

To programmatically find the path to the security database, we can use the following function:

```
function GetSysDBPath : String;
const
 SoftPath   = 'Software\Microsoft\';
 JetPath    = 'Jet\4.0\Engines';
 AccessPath = 'Office\9.0\Access\InstallRoot\';
var
 R     : TRegistry;
 SysDB : String;
begin
 try
  R := TRegistry.Create;
  R.RootKey := HKEY_LOCAL_MACHINE;
  R.OpenKey(SoftPath+JetPath, False);
// Read the name of the security database
  SysDB := R.ReadString('SystemDB');
  R.CloseKey;
  R.OpenKey(SoftPath+AccessPath, False);
```

```
// and determine the full path to it
   Result := R.ReadString('Path')+ SysDB;
  finally
    R.Free;
  end;
end;
```

The SetObjectOwner Method

Use this method to set the user or group name of an object's owner. It takes the same parameters as the GetObjectOwner method. If you are using the Jet Provider, you should set a security database as described above. The following example shows how to set the new owner of the first table in the Catalog object:

```
Catalog.SetObjectOwner(Catalog.Tables[0].Name, adPermObjTable, 'Alex',
EmptyParam);
```

Properties of the Catalog Object

The Catalog object exposes only one property: ActiveConnection, which can be used to get or set the information on the connection to the data source. In can be of two types: an ADO Connection object or a valid ADO connection string.

In Delphi, this property is not available directly. Instead, there are three methods as shown below.

To get ActiveConnection, use the Get_ActiveConnection method with no parameters. This method returns an OleVariant (String).

To set ActiveConnection, use the _Set_ActiveConnection method, which takes one parameter—an OleVariant (String). For example:

```
//
// Obtain the Data Source from the standard dialog box
//
DataSource := PromptDataSource(Application.Handle, '');
//
// if we have one
//
 If DataSource <> '' Then
  begin
//
// assign it to the Catalog.ActiveConnection property
//
   Catalog._Set_ActiveConnection(DataSource);
  end;
```

You can also use the Set_ActiveConnection method, which expects a parameter in the form of IDispatch. In this case, you should supply the valid instance of the ADO

Connection object. It can be obtained, for example, from the ConnectionObject of the TADOConnection component.

Note:

The value returned by the Get_ActiveConnection method is the same as the result of the Create method described above.

To set the ActiveConnection property for an ADO Connection object, use the ConnectionObject property of the ADOConnection class.

Collections of the Catalog Object

The Catalog object exposes five collections that allow us to go deeper inside the schema information of a data source. These collections are shown in the table below:

Collection	Meaning	Object
Tables	Collection of the tables within this catalog	Table
Procedures	Collection of the stored procedures within this catalog	Procedure
Views	Collection of the views within this catalog	View
Groups	Collection of the user group accounts within this catalog	Group
Users	Collection of the user accounts within this catalog	User

Now that we have discussed methods, properties, and collections of the Catalog object, let's look at what every object available through its collections can provide for us. One level below the Catalog object is the Table object.

The Table Object

The Table object, which is available through the Tables collection of the Catalog object, contains detailed information for a single table. As with the Catalog object, not all of the features of the Table object are implemented in the current release of ADOX library:

- For the Microsoft SQL Server OLE DB Provider, properties for the existing tables are read-only and properties for new tables are read/write.

- For the Microsoft OLE DB Provider for ODBC, properties for the existing tables are read-only and properties for new tables are read/write. The Append and Delete methods of the Tables collection are not implemented.

- For the Microsoft OLE DB Provider for Oracle, properties for the existing tables are read-only and properties for new tables are read/write. The Append and Delete methods of the Tables collection are not implemented.

Properties of the Table Object

The Table object exposes five properties that contain detailed information for a single table: its creation and modification dates, name, type, and parent catalog.

The DateCreated Property

This property allows us to find the date the table was created. As Microsoft documentation indicates, if this value is Null, the property is not supported by the provider. That does not mean that we can compare the DateCreated property to zero; because this property is of the Variant type, we should perform the following comparison:

```
If Not VarIsNull (Table.DateCreated) Then
  Created := ' [Created at: ' + VarToStr(Table.DateCreated) +']';
```

Note: To get the value of this property for a newly created table, you should first call the Refresh method of the Tables collection.

The DateModified Property

This property allows us to find the date the table was last modified. The same comparison as with the DateCreated property should be used:

```
If Not VarIsNull (Table.DateModified) Then
  Modified := '; Modified at: ' + VarToStr(Table.DateModified) +
']';
```

Note: To get the value of this property for a newly created table, you should first call the Refresh method of the Tables collection.

The Name Property

This property contains the name of the table. It is read-only for tables already in the collection, and is read/write for the newly created table.

The ParentCatalog Property

This property is used to access the Catalog object that owns this table. If you set this property to an open Catalog, you will get access to provider-specific properties. Then you can set these properties before appending a table to a Catalog object.

Later in this chapter, we will give you an example of how to use this property.

The Type Property

This read-only property allows us to find the type of the table. It can be SYSTEM TABLE, TABLE, or GLOBAL TEMPORARY.

The following example shows how to find the type of the table by comparing the first letter of the Type property against S (for SYSTEM TABLE), T (for TABLE), or G (for GLOBAL TEMPORARY).

```
Case Table.Type_[1] of
// SYSTEM TABLE
     'S' : TreeView1.Items.AddChild(SysTblNode, Name);
// TABLE
     'T' : begin
             TblNode :=
               TreeView1.Items.AddChild(OrdTblNode, Name);
             BrowseColumns(Table, TblNode);
           end;
// GLOBAL TEMPORARY
     'G' : TreeView1.Items.AddChild(TmpTblNode, Name);
   End;
```

For Access tables (accessible through the Jet OLE DB Provider), there also can be the following values of the Type property: ACCESS TABLE, LINK, PASS-THROUGH, and VIEW. These are shown in the following table:

Table Type	Meaning
ACCESS TABLE	This is an Access system table.
LINK	This is a linked table from a non-ODBC data source.
PASS-THROUGH	This is a linked table from an ODBC data source.
VIEW	This is a view.

Collections of the Table Object

The Table object exposes four collections that can be used to access columns, indexes, keys within a table, and the properties of a table. These collections are shown in the following table:

Collection	Meaning	Object
Columns	Collection of columns within a table	Column
Indexes	Collection of indexes associated with the table	Index
Keys	Collection of keys associated with the table	Key
Properties	Provider-specific properties of the table	Property

The Properties Collection

This collection contains properties of the Table object. In ADOX 2.1, the Table object can have the following properties:

Property	Meaning
Jet OLEDB:Cache Link Name/Password	This Boolean property specifies whether authentication information for the link to a remote ODBC data source should be cached in the Microsoft Jet database. This property should be used only in conjunction with the Jet OLEDB: Create Link property when it is set to True.

Property	Meaning
Jet OLEDB:Create Link	This Boolean property indicates whether the Append method of the Tables collection is used to create a link to a remote data source or to create a table in the native store.
Jet OLEDB:Exclusive Link	This Boolean property indicates whether a link should be created so that the remote source is opened exclusively. This property should be used only in conjunction with the Jet OLEDB: Create Link property when it is set to `True`.
Jet OLEDB:Link Datasource	This string property sets or returns the database used to create a linked table. This property should be used only in conjunction with the Jet OLEDB: Create Link property when it is set to `True`.
Jet OLEDB:Link Provider String	This string property sets or returns the connection string used to connect to a remote ODBC data source to create a linked table. This property should be used only in conjunction with the Jet OLEDB: Create Link property when it is set to `True`.
Jet OLEDB:Remote Table Name	This string property sets the name of the remote table used to create a linked table. This property should be used only in conjunction with the Jet OLEDB: Create Link property when it is set to `True`
Jet OLEDB:Table Hidden In Access	This Boolean property indicates whether this table is shown in Microsoft Access.
Jet OLEDB:Table Validation `Rule`	This string property specifies the expression that will be evaluated before the record will be saved in the table.
Jet OLEDB:Table Validation Text	This string property specifies the string that will be displayed when the validation rule is broken.
Temporary Table	This Boolean property indicates whether the table is temporary. Its value is always `False` for the Microsoft Jet OLE DB provider.

To get and set values of the Table object properties, we should use the "named properties" syntax. For example:

```
{
 Get the Jet OLEDB:Table Validation Text property value
}
VText :=
 Table.Properties['Jet OLEDB:Table Validation Text'].Value;
```

Note: The properties described above are not available through the Properties collection through indexes. In most cases, you will get the value of the Properties.Count property equal to 0. That does not mean that there are no properties for this table; use the "named properties" syntax shown above.

The Column Object

This object and its properties represent one column (i.e., field) in a table, index, or key. It does not have methods, just a set of properties to get detailed information for a single column.

Properties of the Column Object

The properties of the Column object give us detailed information for a single table. Using them, we can collect some valuable information about the column, including its type, defined size, attributes, numeric scale, and so on.

The Attributes Property

This property allows us to get or set the following attributes of the table—whether a particular column has a fixed length, can contain Null values, or both. The default value for this property is 0, meaning that the column is neither fixed nor nullable. The Attributes property can contain one or both of the following constants:

Constant	Value	Meaning
adColFixed	1	The Column has a fixed length.
adColNullable	2	The Column can contain Null values.

To get or set the value of this property we should use the OR or AND operations. For example:

```
If (Column.Attributes AND adColNullable) = adColNullable Then
 ShowMessage('This Column can contain Null values');
else
 ShowMessage('This Column cannot contain Null values');
```

The DefinedSize Property

This property sets or returns the maximum size of the column. The default value is 0. To get the actual size of the column value, you can use the ActualSize property of the Field object, which is available through the ADO Recordset object. See Chapter 7 for more details.

The Name Property

This property contains the name of the column. Its string value is read-only for existing columns and read/write for columns intended to be appended into the Columns collection.

The NumericScale Property

This property contains the scale if the column values are of adNumeric or adDecimal type and is ignored for all other data types. The default value is zero. The value of this property is read-only for existing columns and read/write for columns intended to be appended into the Columns collection.

The ParentCatalog Property

This property is used to access the Catalog object that owns this column. If you set this property to an open Catalog, you will get access to provider-specific properties, which you can set properties before appending a column to a Columns collection of a table.

Later in this chapter, we will provide an example of how to use this property.

The Precision Property

This property contains the maximum precision of data values in the column if the column values are of adNumeric or adDecimal type; it is ignored for all other data types. The default value is zero. The value of this property is read-only for existing columns and read/write for columns intended to be appended into the Columns collection.

The RelatedColumn Property

For key columns, this property contains the name of the related column in the related table. The default value is an empty string. The value of this property is read-only for existing columns and read/write for columns intended to be appended into the Columns collection.

The SortOrder Property

For the columns in the Indexes collection, this property indicates the sorting order of the column. It can be one of the following values:

Constant	Value	Meaning
adSortAscending	1	The column is sorted in ascending order.
adSortDescending	2	The column is sorted in descending order.

The Type Property

This property indicates the data type for the values stored in this column. The default value is adVarChar. Some of the data types and their equivalents for Microsoft Access are shown in the table below:

ADOX Data Type	Microsoft Access Data Type
adBoolean	Yes/No
adUnsignedTinyInt	Number/Byte
adCurrency	Currency
adDate	Date/Time
adDecimal	Number/Decimal
adDouble	Number/Double
adSmallInt	Number/Integer
adInteger	Number/LongInteger
adLongVarBinary	OLE Object
adLongVarWChar	Memo
adSingle	Number/Single
adVarWChar	Text

The value of this property is read-only for existing columns and read/write for columns intended to be appended into the Columns collection.

Collections of the Column Object

The Column object exposes only one collection: Properties.

The Properties Collection

This collection contains properties of the Column object. In ADOX 2.1, the Table object can have the following properties:

Property	Meaning
Autoincrement	This Boolean property specifies whether the values of the column are auto-incremented for the new record.
Default	This Boolean property specifies the default value for a column.
Description	This string value indicates the description given for the column.
Fixed Length	This Boolean value indicates whether a column is of fixed or variable length.
Increment	This long property sets the value for auto-incremented columns.
Jet OLEDB:Allow Zero Length	This Boolean property specifies whether this column can contain zero-length strings.
Jet OLEDB:Autogenerate	This Boolean property indicates whether or not the GUID should be automatically generated for the `adGUID` data type.
Jet OLEDB:Column Validation Rule	This string property specifies the expression that will be evaluated before the column is inserted in the set.
Jet OLEDB:Column Validation Text	This string property specifies the string that will be displayed when the validation rule is broken
Jet OLEDB:Compressed UNICODE Strings	This Boolean property indicates the need for compression of Unicode strings. Used only with Jet 4.0.
Jet OLEDB:Hyperlink	This Boolean property specifies whether this column is a hyperlink.
Jet OLEDB:One BLOB Per Page	This Boolean property specifies the way BLOBs are stored in the databases.
Nullable	This Boolean property indicates whether this column can have Null values.
Primary Key	This Boolean property specifies whether the column is part of the primary key.
Seed	This long property sets the seed value for the auto-incremented columns.
Unique	This Boolean property specifies whether the column allows unique values.

Note: Before accessing properties of the Column object, the ParentCatalog property must be set to the Catalog object that owns the table where this column resides.

The Index Object

The Index object can be used to access properties of a single index in a table. This object does not have methods.

Properties of the Index Object

The Index object has five properties: Clustered, IndexNulls, Name, PrimaryKey, and Unique.

The Clustered Property

This property allows us to check whether the index is clustered or not. The default value is False, meaning that it is not clustered. For existing indexes this property is read-only; you can change its value only for indexes intended to be appended into the Indexes collection.

The IndexNulls Property

This property specifies the actions taken for an index that contains Null value. The IndexNulls property can have the following values:

Constant	Value	Meaning
adIndexNullsAllow	0	Null values are allowed.
adIndexNullsDisallow	1	Null values are not allowed. This is the default value for the IndexNulls property.
adIndexNullsIgnore	2	Null values are ignored.
adIndexNullsIgnoreAny	4	Null values are ignored for multicolumn keys.

For existing indexes this property is read-only; you can change its value only for indexes intended to be appended into the Indexes collection.

The Name Property

This property holds the name of the index. Its string value is read-only for existing indexes and read/write for indexes intended to be appended into the Indexes collection.

The PrimaryKey Property

This property allows us to check whether the index is the primary key of the table. The default value is False, meaning that the index is not the primary key. For existing indexes this property is read-only; you can change its value only for indexes intended to be appended into the Indexes collection.

The Unique Property

This property indicates whether the keys in the index must be unique. The default value is False, meaning that the keys must not be unique. For existing indexes this property is read-only; you can change its value only for indexes intended to be appended into the Indexes collection.

Collections of the Index Object

The Index object exposes two collections: Columns and Properties.

The Columns Collection

This collection contains the Column object for each column in the index. See the Column object for more details.

The Properties Collection

This collection contains provider-specific properties for the Index if any. The following table shows standard and Jet OLE DB Provider specific properties:

Property	Meaning
Auto Update	This Boolean value specifies whether the index is automatically maintained or not. For the Jet Provider its value is always True.
Clustered	This Boolean value indicates whether the index is clustered.
Fill Factor	This long property specifies the fill factor of the index. For the Jet OLE Provider its value is always 100.
Initial Size	This long property specifies the initial size of the index. For the Jet Provider its value is always 4096 for one page.
NULL Collation	This long property indicates how Null values are sorted in the index. For the Jet Provider its value is always 4; the Null values are collated at the low end of the list.
NULL Keys	This long property indicates whether Null keys are allowed. For the Jet Provider its value is always 1.
Primary Key	This Boolean property indicates whether the index is the primary key.
Sort Bookmarks	This Boolean property indicates whether the index must sort repeated keys by bookmark. For the Jet Provider its value is always False.
Temporary Index	This Boolean property indicates whether the index is temporary. For the Jet Provider its value is always False.
Index Type	This long property specifies the type of the index. For the Jet Provider its value is always 1.
Unique	This Boolean property indicates whether index keys must be unique.

The Key Object

This object gives us access to a table key that can be primary, foreign, or unique. The Key object does not have any methods.

Properties of the Key Object

The Key object's five properties allow us to get or set some of its attributes.

The DeleteRule Property

For the primary key this property contains rules to apply when it is deleted. It can be one of the following values:

Constant	Value	Meaning
adRINone	0	Indicates that deletes are not cascaded. This is the default value.
adRICascade	I	Indicates that deletes are cascaded.
adRISetNull	2	Indicates that for deletes the foreign key should have Null value.
adRISetDefault	3	Indicates that for deletes the foreign key should have its default value.

The Name Property

This property holds the name of the key. Its string value is read-only for existing keys and read/write for keys intended to be appended into the Keys collection.

The RelatedTable Property

For the foreign key, this property contains the name of the foreign table. You can use the RelatedColumn property of the Column object to find the column in the related table.

The Type Property

This property specifies the type of the key. It can be one of the following values:

Constant	Value	Meaning
adKeyPrimary	I	Indicates that the key is a primary key
adKeyForeign	2	Indicates that the key is a foreign key
adKeyUnique	3	Indicates that the key is a unique key

The UpdateRule Property

For the primary key, this property contains rules to apply when it is updated. It can be one of the following values:

Constant	Value	Meaning
adRINone	0	Indicates that updates are not cascaded. This is the default value
adRICascade	I	Indicates that updates are cascaded
adRISetNull	2	Indicates that for updates the foreign key should have Null value
adRISetDefault	3	Indicates that for updates the foreign key should have its default value

Collections of the Key Object

The Key object exposes one collection: Columns.

The Columns Collection

This collection contains the Column object for each column in the key. See the Column object for more details.

The Procedure Object

The Procedure object can be used to get access to a stored procedure, which is the set of SQL statements that can be executed on the server. The way this object is implemented, it does not contains the SQL statements for the stored procedure itself, but rather points to an ADO Catalog object that implements this stored procedure. The Procedure object does not contain methods and collections. Only four properties are available to manipulate its contents.

Properties of the Procedure Object

The Procedure object exposes four properties that can be used to get and set its associated SQL statements, creation and modification dates, and name.

The Command Property

This property sets or returns an ADO Catalog object that implements this stored procedure. In Delphi, the Command property is available through the Get_Command method that returns an OleVariant variable of VarDispatch type. This gives us a reference to an IDispatch interface of the Command object. This object itself has the Get_CommandText method or CommandText property that contains the source of the stored procedure.

The following example shows how to get the source code for the stored procedure:

```
procedure TForm1.ShowProcProperties(Proc: Procedure_);
var
 Disp : IDispatch;
 Cmd   : TADOXCommand;
begin
 Disp := Proc.Get_Command;
 Cmd   := Disp as TADOXCommand;
 Memo1.Lines.Clear;
 Memo1.Lines.Add(Cmd.Get_CommandText);
end;
```

The typical output for this code, taken for the Sales by Year stored procedure in the Northwind.mdb database, is shown below:

```
SELECT DISTINCTROW Orders.ShippedDate, Orders.OrderID, [Order
Subtotals].Subtotal
FROM Orders INNER JOIN [Order Subtotals] ON Orders.OrderID=[Order
Subtotals].OrderID
WHERE (((Orders.ShippedDate) Is Not Null))
ORDER BY Orders.ShippedDate;
```

The DumpProc example on the CD-ROM will help you to browse through the stored procedure inside the databases and to study its sources.

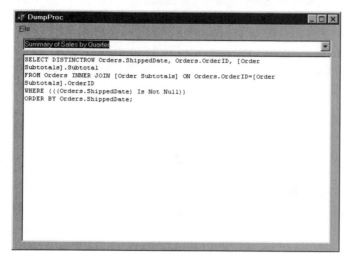

To create a new procedure, you do the reverse operation. First, you create a new Command object, assign the source for the stored procedure to its CommandText property, and then store the reference to it in the Command property of the Procedure object.

In the current version of ADOX (ADOX 2.1) this property is not supported for the following providers:

- Microsoft SQL Server OLE DB Provider
- Microsoft OLE DB Provider for ODBC
- Microsoft OLE DB Provider for Oracle

The DateCreated Property

This property specifies the date the stored procedure was created. Its value is read-only for the procedures already in the collection and read/write for newly created procedures. To see the value of this property for newly appended procedures, you need to call the Refresh method of the Procedures collection.

The DateModified Property

This property specifies the date the stored procedure was last modified. Its value is read-only for the procedures already in the collection and read/write for newly created procedures. To see the value of this property for newly appended procedures, you need to call the Refresh method of the Procedures collection.

The Name Property

This property specifies the name of the procedure. Its value is read-only for the procedures already in the collection and read/write for newly created procedures. To see the value of this property for newly appended procedures, you need to call the Refresh method of the Procedures collection.

The View Object

The View object is used to access views in the catalog. Views are special kinds of SQL queries stored in the database and used to create virtual tables from other tables in the database. These queries have no parameters and return a set of records.

This object is implemented the same way as the Procedure object discussed above: It does not contain the SQL statements itself, but rather provides a reference to an ADO Catalog object that implements this view. The View object does not contain methods or collections.

Note: For Microsoft Access databases, the View object also represents standard select queries.

Properties of the View Object

The View object has four properties to manipulate its contents.

The Command Property

This property sets or returns an ADO Catalog object that implements this view. In Delphi, the Command property is available through the Get_Command method that returns an OleVariant variable of VarDispatch type. This gives us a reference to an IDispatch interface of the Command object. This object itself has the Get_CommandText method or CommandText property that contains the source of the view.

The following example shows how to get the source code for the stored procedure:

```
procedure TForm1.ShowViewsProperties(OneView: View);
var
 Disp : IDispatch;
 Cmd  : TADOXCommand;
begin
 Disp := OneView.Get_Command;
 Cmd  := Disp as TADOXCommand;
 Memo1.Lines.Clear;
 Memo1.Lines.Add(Cmd.Get_CommandText);
end;
```

The typical output for this code, taken from the Current Product List View in the Northwind.mdb database, is shown below:

```
SELECT [Product List].ProductID, [Product List].ProductName
FROM Products AS [Product List]
WHERE ((([Product List].Discontinued)=No))
ORDER BY [Product List].ProductName;
```

The DumpView example on the CD-ROM will help you to browse through the views inside the databases and to study its sources.

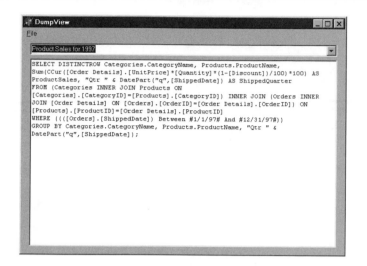

To create a new view, you do the reverse operation. First, you create a new Command object, assign the source for the view to its CommandText property, and then store the reference to it in the Command property of the View object.

In the current version of ADOX (ADOX 2.1), this property is not supported for the following providers:

- Microsoft SQL Server OLE DB Provider
- Microsoft OLE DB Provider for ODBC
- Microsoft OLE DB Provider for Oracle

The DateCreated Property

This property specifies the date the view was created. Its value is read-only for views already in the collection and read/write for newly created views. To see the value of this property for newly appended views, you need to call the Refresh method of the Views collection.

The DateModified Property

This property specifies the date the view was last modified. Its value is read-only for views already in the collection and read/write for newly created views. To see the value of this property for newly appended views, you need to call the Refresh method of the Views collection.

The Name Property

This property specifies the name of the view. Its value is read-only for views already in the collection and read/write for newly created views. To see the value of this property for newly appended views, you need to call the Refresh method of the Views collection. The following example shows how to access this property to build a list of all views within a database:

```
procedure TForm1.BuildList(VList: Views);
var
 I  : Integer;
begin
 ComboBox1.Items.Clear;
 For I := 0 to VList.Count-1 do
  begin
   ComboBox1.Items.Add(VList[I].Name);
  end;
  ComboBox1.ItemIndex := 0;

end;
```

We have finished looking at the objects that form the first part of ADOX—the ADO Extensions for Data Definition Language. As we have seen, these objects allow us to get detailed schema information for the data source and to create new databases and tables with records and indexes from scratch. Later in this chapter, we will see some examples of how to use these objects.

The last two objects of the ADOX object model—the Group object and the User object—are security extensions for ADO, implemented within the ADOX library.

Security Extensions for ADO

The current version of ADOX supports only security objects for the Microsoft Jet OLE DB Provider. In future versions, namely ADO 2.5, there will be support for other providers.

Microsoft Jet database engine employs a user level security system. That means that objects themselves do not have passwords as is, rather they have permissions granted to user and group accounts. This is similar to the network security implemented in such operating systems as Microsoft Windows NT and NetWare. After a user is authenticated by logging on with a password, he receives permissions to some objects within a database. These can be, for example, update permissions or read-only permissions.

Permissions are assigned to users and groups on objects. When a user tries to perform certain actions, Microsoft Jet database engine checks to see if the user or any of the groups to which that user belongs have the necessary permission.

All security information is stored in the System Database called the Access Workgroup Information File. By default, it is called SYSTEM.MDW, and its path is:

```
HKEY_LOCAL_MACHINE\SOFTWARE\Microsoft\Office\9.0\Access\Jet\4.0\Engines
```

under subkey SystemDB.

This system database stores users, groups, logon passwords, and the internal Security Identifier (SID) for each user and group.

To use the security features of Microsoft Jet database engine, we need to supply the name of the appropriate workgroup information file in the connection string. For example:

```
Provider=Microsoft.Jet.OLEDB.4.0;
Data Source=C:\DATA\Northwind.mdb;
Jet OLEDB:System database=d:\Program Files\Microsoft Office\Office\System.mdw
```

This information is available through the Jet OLEDB:System Database property of the Connection object. For example:

```
Edit1.Text := VarToStr(
  ADOConnection1.Properties['Jet OLEDB:System Database']);
```

So, before accessing the security features from the code, we should check if the system database was used to initiate a connection. This can be done by comparing the value of this property against an empty string.

The ADOX object model exposes two objects—Group and User—as well as Groups and Users collections that can be used to create and manage security user accounts. The two main methods, GetPermissions and SetPermissions, are used to set permissions on database objects.

The Group Object

For the secured database this object represents a group account that has access permissions to the data. This object can be used to set or get permissions on database objects. The Group object exposes two methods, one property, and one collection.

This object is not supported for the following providers:

- Microsoft SQL Server OLE DB Provider
- Microsoft OLE DB Provider for ODBC
- Microsoft OLE DB Provider for Oracle

Methods of the Group Object

The Group object has two methods: GetPermissions and SetPermissions.

The GetPermissions Method

This method returns the permissions for a group on a specified object. The result of the GetPermissons method execution is a combination of one or more adRightXXX constants. The following table shows possible values for these constants:

Constant	Value	Meaning
adRightRead	-2147483648	The user or group has permission to read the object.
adRightNone	0	The user or group has no permissions for the object.
adRightDrop	256	The user or group has permission to remove objects from the catalog.
adRightExclusive	512	The user or group has permission to access the object exclusively.
adRightReadDesign	1024	The user or group has permission to read the design for the object.
adRightWriteDesign	2048	The user or group has permission to modify the design for the object.
adRightWithGrant	4096	The user or group has permission to grant permissions on the object.
adRightReference	8192	The user or group has permission to reference the object.
adRightCreate	16384	The user or group has permission to create new objects of this type.
adRightInsert	32768	The user or group has permission to insert the object. For objects such as Tables, the user has permission to insert data into the table.
adRightDelete	65536	The user or group has permission to delete data from an object. For objects such as tables, the user has permission to delete data values from records.
adRightReadPermissions	131072	The user or group can view but not change the specific permissions for an object in the catalog.
adRightWritePermissions	262144	The user or group can modify the specific permissions for an object in the catalog.
adRightWriteOwner	524288	The user or group has permission to modify the owner of the object.
adRightMaximumAllowed	33554432	The user or group has the maximum number of permissions allowed by the provider. Specific permissions are provider-dependent.
adRightFull	268435456	The user or group has all permissions on the object.
adRightExecute	536870912	The user or group has permission to execute the object.
adRightUpdate	1073741824	The user or group has permission to update the object. For objects such as tables, the user has permission to update the data in the table.

The object type is one of the adPermObjXXX constants listed above in the section on the GetObjectOwner method of the Catalog object. Here is the prototype for this method:

```
function  GetPermissions(Name: OleVariant;
 ObjectType: ObjectTypeEnum;
 ObjectTypeId: OleVariant): RightsEnum;
```

The SetPermissions Method

This method is the counterpart to the GetPermissions method and is used to set the group permissions for an object. Here is the prototype for the SetPermissions method:

```
SetPermissions(Name: OleVariant;
    ObjectType: ObjectTypeEnum;
    Action: ActionEnum;
    Rights: RightsEnum;
    Inherit: InheritTypeEnum;
    ObjectTypeId: OleVariant
);
```

In addition to the name of the object and its type, the SetPermissions method takes three more parameters that indicate the type of the permission action to set (adAccessXXX constants), individual permissions (adRightXXX constants), and the type of permissions inheritance (adInheritXXX constants).

The following table shows the possible values for the permission inheritance constants:

Constant	Value	Meaning
adInheritNone	0	Default. No inheritance occurs.
adInheritObjects	1	Non-container objects in the container inherit the permissions.
adInheritContainers	2	Other containers that are contained by the primary object inherit the entry.
adInheritBoth	3	Both objects and other containers contained by the primary object inherit the entry.
adInheritNoPropogate	4	The adInheritObjects and adInheritContainers flags are not propagated to an inherited entry.

Properties of the Group Object

The Group object has one property: Name.

The Name Property

This property specifies the name of the Group account.

Collections of the Group Object

The Group object exposes one collection: Users.

The Users Collection

This collection of User objects contains all users that belong to this group.

The User Object

For the secured database this object represents a single user account that has access permissions to the data.

This object is not supported for the following providers:

- Microsoft SQL Server OLE DB Provider
- Microsoft OLE DB Provider for ODBC
- Microsoft OLE DB Provider for Oracle

Methods of the User Object

The User Object has three methods: ChangePassword, GetPermissions, and SetPermissions.

The ChangePassword Method

This method is used to change the user password. It takes two string parameters—one for the current password and one for the new one. Blank password is indicated by an empty string.

The GetPermissions Method

This method returns the permissions for a user on a specified object. The result of the GetPermissons method execution is a combination of one or more adRightXXX constants.

The object type is one of the adPermObjXXX constants listed in the section about the Catalog object's GetObjectOwner method.

The SetPermissions Method

This method is the counterpart to the GetPermissions method and is used to set the user permissions for an object. Beside the name of the object and its type, the SetPermissions method takes three additional parameters that indicate the type of the permission action to set (adAccessXXX constants), individual permissions (adRightXXX constants), and type of permissions inheritance (adInheritXXX constants).

Properties of the User Object

The User object has one property: Name.

The Name Property

This property specifies the name of the user.

Collections of the User Object

The User object exposes one collection: Groups.

The Groups Collection

This collection of Group objects contains all groups to which the user belongs.

ADOX Collections

Several objects in the ADOX object model expose collections that contain objects, as discussed above. These are shown in the following table:

Object	Exposes Collections
Catalog	Tables
	Procedures
	Views
	Groups
	Users
Table	Columns
	Indexes
	Keys
Index	Columns
Key	Columns
Group	Users
User	Groups

All ADOX collections have three methods and two properties, discussed below.

Methods of a Collection

There are three methods of a collection that can be used to manipulate its contents. The Add method is used to add an item to the collection, the Delete method removes an item from the collection, and the Refresh method refreshes the contents of the collection.

The Delete and Refresh methods have the same syntax for all collections shown in the table above. For each type of collection, use the appropriate syntax of the Append method.

The Tables.Append Method

This method adds a new Table object to the Tables collection. The Tables.Append method expects one parameter of the `OleVariant` type; this should be a variable of the `Table` type. For example:

```
Table := CoTable.Create;
Table.Name := 'Customers';
{
  Add Table to the Tables Collection
}
Catalog.Tables.Append(Table);
```

Before appending a new Table object to the Tables collection, you should set at least its Name property and the appropriate parameters if needed. The parameters of the Table object are available through the ParentCatalog property. Later in this chapter, we will discuss in more detail how to create a new Table object and how to set its parameters. See the "Creating a Database from Scratch" section later in this chapter.

The Tables.Append method is not supported for the following providers:

- Microsoft OLE DB Provider for ODBC
- Microsoft OLE DB Provider for Oracle

The Columns.Append Method

This method adds a new Column object to the Columns collection of the table. See the Indexes.Append and Keys.Append methods below for a discussion of appending columns to the Indexes and Keys collections.

The Columns.Append method expects three parameters: the name of the column, its data type, and its maximum size. The example below shows how to use this Append method:

```
Table.Columns.Append('FIRSTNAME', adVarWChar, 128);
Table.Columns.Append('LASTNAME',  adVarWChar, 128);
```

The Indexes.Append Method

This method adds a new Index object to the Indexes collection of the table. The Indexes.Append method expects two parameters: the new Index object (or its name) that will be added into the collection, and a list of column names contained in the Index in the form of a variant array.

The Indexes.Append method is not supported for the following providers:

- Microsoft OLE DB Provider for ODBC
- Microsoft OLE DB Provider for Oracle

The Keys.Append Method

This method appends a new Key object to the Keys collection of the table. The Keys.Append method expects five parameters, shown in the following table:

Parameter	Description
Key	Indicates the Key object to append or its name.
KeyType	Specifies the type of the key. See the Type property of the Key object for more information.
Column	Indicates the name of the column that the key applies to.
RelatedTable	Specifies the name of the related table. Used only for foreign keys.
RelatedColumn	Specifies the name of the related column. Used only for foreign keys.

The Keys.Append method is not supported for the following providers:

- Microsoft SQL Server OLE DB Provider
- Microsoft OLE DB Provider for ODBC

■ Microsoft OLE DB Provider for Oracle

The Procedures.Append Method

This method adds a new procedure to the Procedures collection of the Catalog object. The Procedures.Append method expects two parameters: the name of the new procedure and the Command object that contains the text of this procedure.

The Procedures.Append method is not supported for the following providers:

■ Microsoft SQL Server OLE DB Provider

■ Microsoft OLE DB Provider for ODBC

■ Microsoft OLE DB Provider for Oracle

The Views.Append Method

This method adds a new view to the Views collection of the Catalog object. The Views.Append method expects two parameters: the name of the new view and the Command object that contains the text of this view.

The Views.Append method is not supported for the following providers:

■ Microsoft SQL Server OLE DB Provider

■ Microsoft OLE DB Provider for ODBC

■ Microsoft OLE DB Provider for Oracle

The Groups.Append Method

This method adds a new group to the Groups collection of the Catalog object. It expects one parameter: the Group object to be appended or the name of the group.

The Groups.Append method is not supported for the following providers:

■ Microsoft SQL Server OLE DB Provider

■ Microsoft OLE DB Provider for ODBC

■ Microsoft OLE DB Provider for Oracle

The Users.Append Method

This method is used to add a new user to the Users collection of the Catalog object. It expects two parameters: the User object to be added or its name and an optional password for the new user.

The Users.Append method is not supported for the following providers:

■ Microsoft SQL Server OLE DB Provider

■ Microsoft OLE DB Provider for ODBC

■ Microsoft OLE DB Provider for Oracle

The Delete Method

This method removes an item from the collection. You can call this method either with the index number of the item within the collection or with the name of the item. For example:

```
Catalog.Tables.Delete(10);
```

or by using the name of the item:

```
Catalog.Tables.Delete('Customers');
```

The Keys.Delete, Procedures.Delete, and Views.Delete methods are not supported for the following providers:

- Microsoft SQL Server OLE DB Provider
- Microsoft OLE DB Provider for ODBC
- Microsoft OLE DB Provider for Oracle

The Indexes.Delete method is not supported for the following providers:

- Microsoft OLE DB Provider for ODBC
- Microsoft OLE DB Provider for Oracle

The Refresh Method

The Refresh method refreshes the contents of the collection. After calling this method the changes in the collection becomes visible; that is, the newly appended items will be available and the deleted items will be no longer available.

Properties of a Collection

There are two properties exposed by the Collection object: Count and Item.

The Count Property

The Count property gives us the number of objects within the collection. For example:

```
For I:= 0 to Catalog.Tables.Count-1 do
  begin
  // Do something with tables here...
  end;
```

The Item Property

The other property is the Item property. It can be omitted. To access an item within a collection, you can use the following syntax:

```
ShowMessage(
 VarToStr(Catalog.Tables['Customers'].DateCreated)
 );
```

Or you can use the Item property as shown below:

```
ShowMessage(
  VarToStr(Catalog.Tables.Item['Customers'].DateCreated)
);
```

Now that we have looked at the ADOX object model and learned what objects are in it and their methods, properties, and collections, we are ready to write some ADOX code.

ADOX Usage Examples

We will create two examples. The first one will show you how to get schema data of a particular database, while the other will demonstrate creating a new database from scratch. Note that we must include the ADOX_TLB unit in the Uses clause to make the following examples work correctly.

Getting a List of Tables

In our first example, we will get a list of all tables within a selected database. To do this, we will iterate the Tables collection of the Catalog object, extract the Table object, and get its properties. We will show tables available in a tree structure, so we will use a TTreeView component from the Win32 page of the Component Palette. Place it into a form along with a TButton component.

First, we need to create an instance of a Catalog object. Here is the code to do so:

```
Catalog := CoCatalog.Create;
```

Next, we need the name of the data source where the tables are stored. We use the standard Delphi function PromptDataSource (discussed in Chapter 4) to get one and save the value it returns in the global variable DS:

```
procedure TForm1.Button1Click(Sender: TObject);
begin
  DS := PromptDataSource(Application.Handle, '');
  If DS <> '' Then
    begin
      BrowseData(DS);
    end;
end;
```

As you can see, we put this code in the Button1.OnClick event handler; when the user presses the button he sees the data source selection dialog. When one is selected, i.e., DS variable is not an empty string, we call the BrowseData procedure, passing the data source name as an argument.

The real stuff is implemented inside the BrowseData procedure, the source code of which looks like this:

```
procedure TForm1.BrowseData(DataSource: WideString);
var
 OrdTblNode   : TTreeNode;
 SysTblNode   : TTreeNode;
 TmpTblNode   : TTreeNode;
 RootNode     : TTreeNode;
 Table        : TADOXTable;
 I            : Word;
begin
 TreeView1.Items.Clear;
 RootNode    := TreeView1.Items.Add(nil, 'Database');
 SysTblNode := TreeView1.Items.AddChild(RootNode, 'SysTables');
 OrdTblNode := TreeView1.Items.AddChild(RootNode, 'Tables');
 TmpTblNode := TreeView1.Items.AddChild(RootNode, 'Global
Temporary');

// Connect Data Source to Catalog
 Catalog._Set_ActiveConnection(DataSource);
// Iterate through tables
   For I := 0 to Catalog.Tables.Count-1 do
    begin
     Table := Catalog.Tables[I] as TADOXTable;
     Case Table.Type_[1] of
// SYSTEM TABLE
      'S' : TreeView1.Items.AddChild(SysTblNode, Table.Name);
// TABLE
      'T' : TreeView1.Items.AddChild(OrdTblNode, Table.Name);
// GLOBAL TEMPORARY
      'G' : TreeView1.Items.AddChild(TmpTblNode, Table.Name);
    End;
    end;
 end;
```

This procedure can be separated into two parts: the TreeView initialization part and the table iteration. In the first part we create the root node and three child nodes—one for each table type we may encounter—system table, table, and global temporary table. Next, we connect our selected data source to the Catalog object:

```
Catalog._Set_ActiveConnection(DataSource);
```

The data source will be opened and we can traverse through the tables within it through a loop, where at each step we extract one Table object at a time. Here is the code we use for this:

```
For I := 0 to Catalog.Tables.Count-1 do
  begin
    Table := Catalog.Tables[I] as TADOXTable;
  end;
```

As we already know, there can be three types of tables within a database. To distinguish between them we check the Type_ property of the Table object (note the underscore!), which is of WideString type. So, we can check the first letter and decide where this particular table belongs—the System Tables branch, the Tables branch, or the Global Temporary branch.

Working with Columns

Now that we have learned how to create a list of tables available in the selected database, we can go deeper and obtain information about the columns within the table. The following example shows how to do this for a particular table:

```
procedure TForm1.ListBox1Click(Sender: TObject);
var
 Table    : TADOXTable;
 ViewCol  : TListColumn;
 ViewItem : TListItem;
 I        : Integer;
begin
 ListView1.Columns.Clear;
 ListView1.Items.Clear;
 ViewCol := ListView1.Columns.Add;
 ViewCol.Caption := 'Column Name';
 ViewCol.Width := (ListView1.Width DIV 4)-1;
 ViewCol := ListView1.Columns.Add;
 ViewCol.Caption := 'Data Type';
 ViewCol.Width := (ListView1.Width DIV 4)-1;
 ViewCol := ListView1.Columns.Add;
 ViewCol.Caption := 'Max Length';
 ViewCol.Width := (ListView1.Width DIV 4)-1;
 ViewCol.Alignment := taCenter;
 ViewCol := ListView1.Columns.Add;
 ViewCol.Caption := 'Nullable';
 ViewCol.Width := (ListView1.Width DIV 4)-1;
 ViewCol.Alignment := taCenter;

 Table := CoTable.Create;
 Table := Catalog.Tables[ListBox1.ItemIndex];
```

```
With Panel1 do
begin
 Caption := Table.Name;
 If Not VarIsNull (Table.DateCreated) Then
  Caption := Caption + ' [Created at: ' +
   VarToStr(Table.DateCreated);
 If Not VarIsNull (Table.DateModified) Then
  Caption := Caption + '; Modified at: ' +
   VarToStr(Table.DateModified) + ']';
end;
For I := 0 to Table.Columns.Count-1 do
 begin
  ViewItem := ListView1.Items.Add;
  ViewItem.Caption := Table.Columns[I].Name;
  ViewItem.SubItems.Add(GetDataType(Table.Columns[I].Type_));
  ViewItem.SubItems.Add(
   IntToStr(Table.Columns[I].DefinedSize));
   If (Table.Columns[I].Attributes AND adColNullable) =
    adColNullable Then
    ViewItem.SubItems.Add('Yes')
   Else
    ViewItem.SubItems.Add('No')
 end;
 Table := Nil;
end;
```

ADOX Columns

File

Invoices [Created at: 13.09.95 10:51:44; Modified at: 19.11.99 20:51:11]

	Column Name	Data Type	Max Length	Nullable
AllCust	Address	adVarWChar	60	Yes
Alphabetical Lis	City	adVarWChar	15	Yes
Categories	Country	adVarWChar	15	Yes
Category Sales f	CustomerID	adVarWChar	5	Yes
Current Product	Customers.Com...	adVarWChar	40	Yes
Customers	Discount	adSingle	0	Yes
Employees	ExtendedPrice	adCurrency	0	Yes
Invoices	Freight	adCurrency	0	Yes
MSysAccessObject	OrderDate	adDate	0	Yes
MSysACEs	OrderID	adInteger	0	No
MSysCmdbars	PostalCode	adVarWChar	10	Yes
MSysIMEXColumns	ProductID	adInteger	0	Yes
	ProductName	adVarWChar	40	Yes
	Quantity	adSmallInt	0	Yes
	Region	adVarWChar	15	Yes
	RequiredDate	adDate	0	Yes
	Salesperson	adVarWChar	255	Yes
	ShipAddress	adVarWChar	60	Yes
	ShipCity	adVarWChar	15	Yes
	ShipCountry	adVarWChar	15	Yes

The source code for the GetDataType functions, which return the data type for a particular column, is shown below:

```
function TForm1.GetDataType(DT: Integer): String;
begin
 Case DT of
    0 : GetDataType := 'adEmpty';
    2 : GetDataType := 'adSmallInt';
    3 : GetDataType := 'adInteger';
    4 : GetDataType := 'adSingle';
    5 : GetDataType := 'adDouble';
    6 : GetDataType := 'adCurrency';
    7 : GetDataType := 'adDate';
    8 : GetDataType := 'adBSTR';
    9 : GetDataType := 'adIDispatch';
   10 : GetDataType := 'adError';
   11 : GetDataType := 'adBoolean';
   12 : GetDataType := 'adVariant';
   13 : GetDataType := 'adIUnknown';
   14 : GetDataType := 'adDecimal';
   16 : GetDataType := 'adTinyInt';
   17 : GetDataType := 'adUnsignedTinyInt';
   18 : GetDataType := 'adUnsignedSmallInt';
   19 : GetDataType := 'adUnsignedInt';
   20 : GetDataType := 'adBigInt';
   21 : GetDataType := 'asUnsignedBigInt';
   64 : GetDataType := 'adFileTime';
   72 : GetDataType := 'adGUID';
  128 : GetDataType := 'adBinary';
  129 : GetDataType := 'adChar';
  130 : GetDataType := 'adWChar';
  131 : GetDataType := 'adNumeric';
  132 : GetDataType := 'adUserDefined';
  133 : GetDataType := 'adDBDate';
  134 : GetDataType := 'adDBTime';
  135 : GetDataType := 'adDBTimeStamp';
  136 : GetDataType := 'adChapter';
  137 : GetDataType := 'adDBFileTime';
  138 : GetDataType := 'adPropVariant';
  139 : GetDataType := 'adVarNumeric';
  200 : GetDataType := 'adVarChar';
  201 : GetDataType := 'adLongVarChar';
  202 : GetDataType := 'adVarWChar';
  203 : GetDataType := 'adLongVarWChar';
  204 : GetDataType := 'adVarBinary';
  205 : GetDataType := 'adLongVarBinary';
 end;
end;
```

Now we are able to list tables and columns within it. The final thing we need to know about the database is what kind of indexes and keys it contains. We will see how to obtain such information next.

Getting a List of Indexes and Keys

As we already know from earlier in this chapter, each Table object contains two collections—Indexes and Keys—which allow us to find the indexes and keys for this table. Let's extend our example and add two TMemo components to show a list of indexes and keys available for each selected table. Here is the code for this:

```
{Indexes and Keys}
Memo1.Lines.Clear;
Memo2.Lines.Clear;
For I := 0 to Table.Indexes.Count-1 do
  Memo1.Lines.Add(Table.Indexes[I].Name);
For I := 0 to Table.Keys.Count-1 do
  Memo2.Lines.Add(Table.Keys[I].Name);
```

This code just outputs a list of indexes and keys and does not show any extra information, but it can be easily extended to show additional properties of the Index and Key objects. We will leave this as an exercise for our readers.

Working with Groups and Users

Using the Groups and Users collections of the Catalog object we can obtain a list of users and groups for the database in question. The following example shows how to iterate through the Users collection and obtain all users available for the table along with the names of the groups to which they belong:

```
procedure TForm1.Button1Click(Sender: TObject);
var
 I,J  : Integer;
 User : TADOXUser;
 S    : String;
begin
 DS := 'Provider=Microsoft.Jet.OLEDB.4.0;';
 DS := DS + 'Data Source=c:\data\northwind.mdb;';
 DS := DS + 'Jet OLEDB:System Database=';
 DS := DS + GetSysDBPath;

 Catalog._Set_ActiveConnection(DS);
 For I := 0 to Catalog.Users.Count-1 do
  begin
   S := Catalog.Users[I].Name;
   For J := 0 to Catalog.Users[I].Groups.Count-1 do
    S := S + ' [' + Catalog.Users[I].Groups[J].Name + ']';
   Memo1.Lines.Add(S);
  end;
end;
```

Through the examples provided above, we have seen how to use the ADOX library to extract various information about the database. In the next section, we will see how to use this library to create a new database and its objects.

Creating a Database from Scratch

Earlier we mentioned that one of the advantages of using ADOX is that we can create new databases without using SQL Data Definition Language. The following example shows how to do this:

```
procedure TForm1.Button1Click(Sender: TObject);
const
 BaseName =  'c:\data\demo.mdb';
 DS       =  'Provider=Microsoft.Jet.OLEDB.4.0;Data Source='+BaseName;
var
 Catalog  : TADOXCatalog;
 Table    : TADOXTable;
 Column   : TADOXColumn;
 Index    : TADOXIndex;

begin
{Create an instance of ADOX Catalog}
 Catalog  := CoCatalog.Create;
{If database exists, delete it}
 If FileExists(BaseName) Then DeleteFile(BaseName);
{Create new MDB file}
 Catalog.Create(DS);
{Specify the active connection}
 Catalog._Set_ActiveConnection(DS);

 Table          := CoTable.Create;
 Table.Name     := 'Customers';
 Table.ParentCatalog := Catalog;
{Start to add columns}

 Column := CoColumn.Create;
 With Column do
  begin
   ParentCatalog := Catalog;
   Name    := 'CustID';
   Type_   := adInteger;
   Properties['Autoincrement'].Value := True;
   Properties['Description'].Value   := 'Customer ID';
  end;
 Table.Columns.Append(Column, 0, 0);
 Column := Nil;

 Column := CoColumn.Create;
 With Column do
  begin
   ParentCatalog := Catalog;
   Name          := 'FirstName';
```

```
   Type_       := adVarWChar;
   DefinedSize := 64;
   Properties['Description'].Value    := 'Customer First Name';
  end;
 Table.Columns.Append(Column, 0, 0);
 Column := Nil;

 With Table.Columns do
  begin
   Append('LastName',  adVarWChar, 64);
   Append('Phone',     adVarWChar, 64);
   Append('Notes',     adLongVarWChar, 128);
  end;

 Table.Columns[4].Attributes := adColNullable;

{To catch an error}
 try
  Catalog.Tables.Append(Table);
 finally
Catalog := Nil;
end;
end;
```

Let's look at the code line by line. First, we create a new instance of the Catalog object that gives us access to the already existing database or allows us to create a new one:

```
Catalog := CoCatalog.Create;
```

Then we delete the database if it already exists. This step is needed to be able to create a new database only; if you are planning to modify the existed one, you must use the _Set_ActiveConnection method instead of the Create method used here.

```
{If database exists, delete it}
 If FileExists(BaseName) Then DeleteFile(BaseName);
{Create new MDB file}
 Catalog.Create(DS);
```

After our new database is created, we can add tables and columns to it. This is explained in the next section.

Adding Tables and Columns

The first thing we need to do is to create a new instance of the Table object, assign its name, and specify the ParentCatalog property, which will give us access to the provider-specific properties:

```
Table        := CoTable.Create;
Table.Name   := 'Customers';
Table.ParentCatalog := Catalog;
```

Next, we can start adding columns. As we already know, there are two ways to do this. The first way is to create an instance of the Column object, set its properties, and use the Append method of the Columns collection to add this new column to the table. This is shown in the example below:

```
Column := CoColumn.Create;
With Column do
 begin
  ParentCatalog := Catalog;
  Name    := 'CustID';
  Type_   := adInteger;
  Properties['Autoincrement'].Value := True;
  Properties['Description'].Value   := 'Customer ID';
 end;
Table.Columns.Append(Column, 0, 0);
Column := Nil;
```

Note that by using this method we can access the Properties collection of the Column object.

If we just want to add columns and specify its names, types, and size, we can use the Append method without creating a Column object. This is shown in the example below:

```
With Table.Columns do
 begin
  Append('LastName',  adVarWChar, 64);
  Append('Phone',     adVarWChar, 64);
  Append('Notes',     adLongVarWChar, 128);
 end;
```

To set the attributes of a particular column, we can access its Attributes property through the Columns collection, as shown below:

```
Table.Columns[4].Attributes := adColNullable;
```

After the columns are defined, we can add the Table object to the Catalog object. In the example below, we use the try-finally-end block to skip the error that may occur. Our experience shows that this OLE error occurs randomly without any reason and does not prevent the creation of the database itself and objects within it.

```
{To catch an error}
 try
  Catalog.Tables.Append(Table);
 finally
```

```
Catalog := Nil;
end;
```

In this section, we have seen how to create a new database and add tables and columns to it. Using the objects from the ADOX library, we can also create indexes and keys. This is shown in the next section.

Adding Indexes and Keys

Let's add the index to the LastName column in the table created above. To do this we first need to create an instance of the Index object. Then we can specify its properties and add this newly created index to the Indexes collection of the table. The following example shows how to do this:

```
Index := CoIndex.Create;
With Index do
 begin
  Name := 'LastNameIndex';
  IndexNulls := adIndexNullsDisallow;
  Columns.Append('LastName', adVarWChar, 64);
  Columns['LastName'].SortOrder := adSortAscending;
 end;
Table.Indexes.Append(Index, EmptyParam);
```

Using the Keys collection of the Table object, we can add primary, foreign, or unique keys. The code below shows how to add a primary key:

```
Table.Keys.Append('LastNameKey', adKeyPrimary,
  Table.Columns[2], '', '');
```

When we are using a foreign key, we also need to specify the RelatedTable and RelatedColumn parameters that are now used for primary keys and are left blank in the example above. Since the foreign key is mostly used in one-to-many relationships between two tables, both tables must exist before we can add a foreign key. Like many other database objects, keys can be added to existing tables to create new relationships, as well as to newly created tables.

Adding Views and Procedures

Using the ADOX library we can create views and stored procedures, and add them to the database. Let's start with views, which as we already know are only a description for a specific SELECT statement stored in the database. For purposes of our example we will use the Northwind database and a simple view called AllCust. This view will simply return all records from the Customers table. Here is the source code to create this view:

```
procedure TForm1.Button1Click(Sender: TObject);
const
 BaseName =  'c:\data\northwind.mdb';
 DS       =  'Provider=Microsoft.Jet.OLEDB.4.0;Data Source='
  + BaseName;
var
 Catalog  : TADOXCatalog;
 Command  : TADOCommand;
begin
 Catalog  := CoCatalog.Create;
 Catalog._Set_ActiveConnection(DS);
 Command := TADOCommand.Create(Self);
 With Command do
  CommandText := 'SELECT * FROM CUSTOMERS';
 Catalog.Views.Append('AllCust', Command.CommandObject);
 Catalog := Nil;
 Command.Free;

// Execute view and output the results
ADODataSet1.CommandType := cmdText;
ADODataSet1.CommandText := 'SELECT * FROM ALLCUST';
ADODataSet1.Active := True;
end;
```

First, we created instances of the Catalog object and Command component. Then, we specified the CommandText property of the Command component and simply added it to the Views collection of the Catalog object. After that, we used the TADODataSet component to output the results returned by the newly created view in the TDBGrid.

Now we will create a new procedure, called the parameterized command (query) in Microsoft Jet. Here is the source code that shows how to do this:

```
procedure TForm1.Button1Click(Sender: TObject);
const
 BaseName =  'c:\data\northwind.mdb';
 DS       =  'Provider=Microsoft.Jet.OLEDB.4.0;Data Source='
  + BaseName;
var
 Catalog   : TADOXCatalog;
 Command   : TADOXCommand;
 Parameter : TParameter;
begin
 Catalog  := CoCatalog.Create;
 Catalog._Set_ActiveConnection(DS);
 Command := CoCommand.Create;

{Microsoft Jet Specific Syntax}

 Command.CommandText := 'PARAMETERS [CustID] Text;'
  + 'SELECT * FROM Customers WHERE CustomerId = [CustId]';

 Catalog.Procedures.Append('CustomerById', Command);

 With ADODataSet1 do
  begin
   CommandType := cmdStoredProc;
   CommandText := 'CustomerById';
   Parameter := Parameters.AddParameter;
   Parameter.Name  := 'CustomerId';
   Parameter.Value := 'BOLID';
   Active := True;
  end;
end;
```

To create a procedure, we use the same set of steps as with the view, but specify different text for the CommandText property of the Command object and append the resulting command to the Procedures collection. After our procedure is stored in the database, we can use it. To do this, we set the appropriate properties of the TADODataSet component, create a new Parameter object (for some unknown reasons the parameter in our procedure cannot be seen by the TADODataSet component, and check the results.

Conclusion

In this chapter, we have learned a lot about ADOX—ADO Extensions for DDL and Security. We have talked about the purpose of this additional library that comes as part of the Microsoft Data Access Components and discussed its object model and the objects it exposes. We have seen how to use this library from the Delphi applications and provided several examples of schema manipulation techniques.

In particular, we considered:

- The ADOX object model
- Accessing ADOX from Delphi
- Objects that are exposed by the ADOX and their methods, properties, and collections
- Security issues for working in multi user environments
- Examples of getting the schema information for a sample database
- Examples of creating a database from scratch, adding tables, columns, indexes, keys, procedures, and views into it

In the next chapter, we will learn how to use the Jet and Replication Objects (JRO) library that provides some features specific to the Microsoft Jet Database Engine.

WORKING WITH JRO OBJECTS

In this chapter, we will look at the last extension library available for ActiveX Data Objects—the Microsoft Jet and Replication Objects (JRO) library. Unlike the ADO library itself and its ADOX and ADO MD extensions, the JRO library provides some features that are specific to the Microsoft Jet Database Engine. Its functionality is mostly applicable to Microsoft Access databases.

Using the Microsoft Jet and Replication Objects library, you can add the following functionality to your applications:

- Create database replicas and synchronize them
- Compact databases
- Set password on databases
- Set encryption on databases
- Write pending data changes to the database and retrieve the most recent data from the database

The JRO library exposes two objects—the JetEngine object and the Replica object—and one collection—the Filters collections. The object model for the JRO library is shown below:

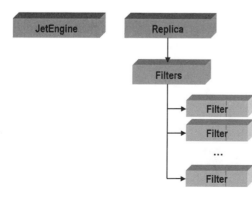

The JetEngine object represents the Jet Database Engine and gives you control of it. Using its methods, you can compact a database, set its password and encrypt it, as well as specify the system database, Registry information, and other options.

The Replica object is used to manipulate replicated databases. Using this object, you can create new replicas, set their options, synchronize the changes between two replicated databases, and check if any conflicts occur during synchronization.

The Filters collection consists of zero or more Filter objects. Each Filter object is used to create a partial replica and sets criteria that limits the records that become replicated.

Database Replication: A Brief Introduction

Before we discuss the features provided with the JRO library we should understand what database replication is and how it is supported in Microsoft Access through the Microsoft Jet Engine.

This brief introduction is not intended to cover all the specifics of replication. For more information, see *Microsoft Jet Database Engine Programmer's Guide*, available from Microsoft Press.

Database replication is a way to create copies of databases in which data or database design changes are shared between copies. Database replication provides us with a mechanism for sharing changes without having to copy the entire database over and over again. The original database is called the *design master* and copies of the database are called *replicas*. A set of copies, including the design master, is called the *replica set,* and replication can be done between any members of a set.

In each replica set, there can be only one design master. This is where you make design changes to tables, queries, and other objects. Each member of the set can also contain local objects—those objects that will not be replicated in future replications. By default, when you create a design master from a database to be replicated, all objects in this database are replicable. Using some methods of the JRO library, you can make some of the objects in the design master local. All new tables and queries created in a design master are considered local and should be first marked as replicable to be distributed to other members of the replica set.

Using the JRO library, you can create full or partial replicas. In the case of a *full* (or *complete*) *replica*, all the data and objects marked as replicable are copied to the replica. In contrast, with a *partial replica* only a subset of the data from the design master is copied to the replica. The partial replica is based on criteria, similar to the SQL WHERE clause. This is called a *filter.* Such a filter defines the rules that limit the records transferred during replication.

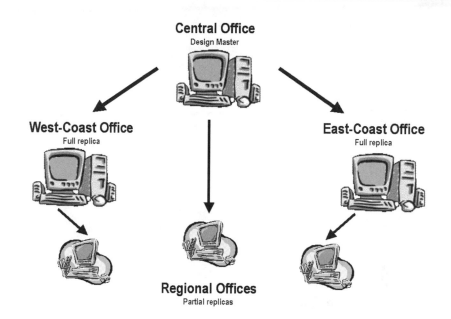

In talking about replications, we should mention *synchronization*, which is the process that ensures that every copy of the database contains the same set of objects and data. During synchronization only the data and design of the objects that have changed is updated. Synchronization can be *bi-directional* and *single-directional*. In bi-directional synchronization, changes are propagated both ways, while in single directional synchronization, changes always occur from the design master to replicas.

Microsoft Jet supports *direct* and *indirect* synchronization. Direct synchronization is when the synchronization process has a direct connection to both replicas. This gives us the ability to immediately read and write updates. Indirect synchronization is used in cases where there is no direct connection to the remote replica. All updates are collected locally and applied when the connection is available.

Now that we are familiar with the basic terms of replication, let's take a look at the JRO library and its objects, properties, and methods.

Accessing the JRO Library from Delphi

Like the other ADO extensions covered in this book, the JRO library is not represented in the current version of Delphi as a set of components. Thus, before using the objects, you must include the type library in your Delphi project. To do so, you need to open a new project and run the **Project | Import Type Library** command from the main menu. In the Import Type Library dialog box select **Microsoft Jet and Replication Objects 2.1 Library (Version 2.1)** and press the **Install** button to create the package, or the **Create Unit** button to create just a single interface unit.

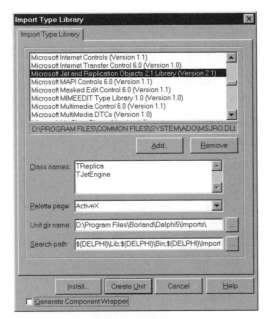

This will give you the JRO_TLB unit that must be included in your code to access the objects exposed by the JRO library.

 Note: The Microsoft Jet and Replication Objects library is implemented in the MSJRO.DLL file in the Program Files\Common Files\System\ADO\ folder.

After the JRO_TLB unit is included in your USES clause, you can create objects through their appropriate coclasses—CoJetEngine and CoReplica, respectively, or use the CreateCOMObject function to do so. For more information, see the examples provided later in this chapter. Please refer to the general discussion of using type libraries in Chapter 15.

Now that we have learned what replication is for, and how to access the Jet and Replication Objects library from your Delphi code, let's look at the features provided with the JRO library and how to use them to create replicas and perform other database manipulations.

The JetEngine Object

The JetEngine object represents the Jet Database Engine and gives you control of it. Using its methods you can compact a database, set its password, and encrypt it, as well as specify the system database, Registry information, and other options.

The CompactDatabase Method

This method creates a new, compacted version of the database and allows you to specify if the copy should be password protected and encrypted. The CompactDatabase method takes two parameters: the ADO connection string for the source database and the destination database. The ADO connection string for the destination database should describe the new database that will be created as a result of compaction of the source database. Note that the CompactDatabase method <u>requires</u> that the source and destination databases be different, at least by name or location, and the destination file should not exist before calling the CompactDatabase method.

The following example shows how to compact the Northwind.mdb database stored in the C:\Data\ folder and create a new compacted copy named Newnorth.mdb in the D:\Data\ folder.

```
const
 Provider = 'Provider=Microsoft.Jet.OLEDB.4.0;';
 SrcMDB   = 'c:\data\northwind.mdb';
 DstMDB   = 'd:\data\newnorth.mdb';

procedure TForm1.Button1Click(Sender: TObject);
var
 JetEng    : JetEngine;
 Src       : WideString;
 Dest      : WideString;
begin
 JetEng := CoJetEngine.Create;

 Src  := Provider + 'Data Source=' + SrcMDB;
 Dest := Provider + 'Data Source=' + DstMDB;

 If FileExists(DstMDB) Then DeleteFile(DstMDB);

 JetEng.CompactDatabase(Src, Dest);

 JetEng := Nil;
end;
```

To see the results of compaction, we can add two edit boxes to our form and show the initial size of the database and the size of its compacted version. For example:

The code for this example is given below:

```
const
 Provider = 'Provider=Microsoft.Jet.OLEDB.4.0;';
 SrcMDB   = 'c:\data\northwind.mdb';
 DstMDB   = 'd:\data\newnorth.mdb';

procedure TForm1.Button1Click(Sender: TObject);
var
 JetEng    : JetEngine;
 Src       : WideString;
 Dest      : WideString;
 SearchRec : TSearchRec;
begin
 JetEng := CoJetEngine.Create;

 if FindFirst(SrcMDB, faAnyFile, SearchRec) = 0 then
   Edit1.Text := IntToStr(SearchRec.Size div 1024) + ' K';
 FindClose(SearchRec);

 Src  := Provider + 'Data Source=' + SrcMDB;
 Dest := Provider + 'Data Source=' + DstMDB;

 If FileExists(DstMDB) Then DeleteFile(DstMDB);
 JetEng.CompactDatabase(Src, Dest);

 if FindFirst(DstMDB, faAnyFile, SearchRec) = 0 then
   Edit2.Text := IntToStr(SearchRec.Size div 1024) + ' K';
 FindClose(SearchRec);

 JetEng := Nil;
end;
```

This allows us to find how much we gain by compacting a database or performing other calculations.

Without going into the inner depths of the Microsoft Jet Engine, let's outline what really happens when we compact a database:

- Tables pages are reorganized and reside in adjacent database pages after compaction. This gives us greater performance since the table is no longer fragmented.

- Unused space is reclaimed by deleting objects and records that are marked as deleted.

- AutoNumber fields are reset so the next allocated value will be in the continuous sequence from the highest value currently set.

- The table statistics used in the query optimizations are updated.

■ Since the database statistics changed, all queries are flagged so they will be recompiled the next time the query is executed.

Besides the simple compaction of a database, we can use the CompactDatabase method to modify other database properties. The table below lists the possible values that can be used in the connection string for the destination database:

Property	Meaning
Locale Identifier	Allows changing the collation order for string comparisons in the database. If omitted, the same locale identifier as in the source database will be used.
Jet OLEDB:Engine Type	Allows changing the database version for the destination database. This gives us a way to "upgrade" databases. You can use the following values: ■ 1 for Jet 1.0 ■ 2 for Jet 1.1 ■ 3 for Jet 2.x ■ 4 for Jet 3.x ■ 5 for Jet 4.x
Jet OLEDB:Encrypt Database	Allows us to indicate whether the database should be encrypted
Jet OLEDB:Don't Copy Locale on Compact	Allows us to specify whether to use the database sort order or per-column locale settings
Jet OLEDB:Compact Without Relationships	Allows us to indicate whether relationships are copied into the compacted version of the database
Jet OLEDB:Compact Without Replica Repair	Allows us to indicate whether to repair damaged replicated databases

The following example shows how to encrypt the destination database:

```
const
 Provider = 'Provider=Microsoft.Jet.OLEDB.4.0;';
 SrcMDB   = 'c:\data\northwind.mdb';
 DstMDB   = 'd:\data\newnorth.mdb';

procedure TForm1.Button1Click(Sender: TObject);
var
 JetEng    : JetEngine;
 Src       : WideString;
 Dest      : WideString;
begin
 JetEng := CoJetEngine.Create;

 Src  := Provider + 'Data Source=' + SrcMDB;
 Dest := Provider + 'Data Source=' + DstMDB;

{Encrypt Database}
 Dest := Dest + ';Jet OLEDB:Encrypt Database=true';
```

```
If FileExists(DstMDB) Then DeleteFile(DstMDB);
JetEng.CompactDatabase(Src, Dest);

JetEng := Nil;
end;
```

Note that the encryption only hides data from the low-level tools like hex-dumping utilities. Consider the figure to the right. The left column shows the "normal" contents of the database, while the right column shows the same data after the encryption.

Encrypted databases can still be opened with Microsoft Access or with the ADO/ADOX code. To make your data secure, consider using passwords. In most cases, data encryption is necessary before sending data across networks or storing it on media.

The RefreshCache Method

This method is used to force any pending writes to the database and refresh memory with the most current data from the database. The RefreshCache method expects one parameter of the _Connection type: an open ADO Connection object for which the cache is to be refreshed.

The RefreshCache method needs to be used only in multi user applications, where its forced writes to disk can release locks in memory, thus increasing performance of the application.

The example below shows how to use this method:

```
procedure TForm1.Button1Click(Sender: TObject);
var
 JetEng    : JetEngine;
begin
 JetEng := CoJetEngine.Create;
 ADOConnection1.Open;

 JetEng.RefreshCache(ADOConnection1.ConnectionObject
   as ADODB_TLB._Connection);

 ADOConnection1.Close;
 JetEng := Nil;
end;
```

Note that we need to explicitly set the type of the ConnectionObject parameter since the Delphi type library parser creates a JRO_TLB unit, which refers to the ADODB_TLB unit, while the ADOConnection1.ConnectionObject object type is defined in the `ADOINT` unit. Since both definitions of the ConnectionObject point to the same data type, this activates the incompatibility error message:

```
Incompatible types: 'ADOInt._Connection' and 'ADODB_TLB._Connection'
```

This error can be avoided with the technique shown above.

The Replica Object

As we will see below, the real power of the Microsoft Jet and Replication Objects library is hidden behind the Replica object, which gives us various properties and methods to create replicas of the database.

Properties of the Replica Object

The Replica object exposes several properties, which are discussed below.

The ActiveConnection Property

The ActiveConnection property indicates the ADO Connection object for the Replica object. In Delphi, this property has the `IDispatch` type so we can only supply the ConnectionObject value of the ADOConnection component to it. For example:

```
procedure TForm1.Button1Click(Sender: TObject);
var
 JetRep : Replica;
begin
 JetRep := CoReplica.Create;
 ADOConnection1.Open;
 JetRep.ActiveConnection := ADOConnection1.ConnectionObject;
{
   ...
   Replication goes here
   ...
}
 ADOConnection1.Close;
 JetRep := Nil
end;
```

To use the ADO connection string to specify the ActiveConnection property value, we should consider the _Set_ActiveConnection method shown below:

```
const
 Provider = 'Provider=Microsoft.Jet.OLEDB.4.0;';
 SrcMDB   = 'd:\data\demo.mdb';

procedure TForm1.Button1Click(Sender: TObject);
var
 JetRep : Replica;
```

```
 Src    : WideString;
begin
 JetRep := CoReplica.Create;

 Src  := Provider + 'Data Source=' + SrcMDB;
 JetRep._Set_ActiveConnection(Src);
{
   ...
   Replication goes here
   ...
}
 JetRep := Nil
end;
```

The ConflictFunction Property

This property points to the name of a function that will be used to resolve conflicts during synchronization. The ConflictFunction property is usable only from the Visual Basic for Applications (VBA) code within Microsoft Access.

The ConflictTables Property

This property indicates the list of tables and associated conflict tables. The ConflictTables property is read-only and its value is set by the Microsoft Jet Engine in the case of conflicts during the synchronization of two replicas. The resulting recordset (of the _Recordset type) contains two columns: TableName, which indicates the first table, and ConflictTableName, which indicates the conflicting table.

The DesignMasterId Property

This read-only property uniquely identifies the design master in a replica set and is in the form of a GUID. In very rare situations, you can use DesignMasterId to check if the design master in use is the real design master for the current replica set by comparing the values of this property.

The Priority Property

This property sets the relative priority of the replica during conflict resolution. Priorities range from 0 to 100, and the replica with the highest priority value wins. If the priority values of replicas are equal, the replica with the lowest ReplicaId wins. For global replicas, the value of the Priority property is 90 percent of the parent replica's priority. Local and anonymous replicas have this value set to 0; this value can't be changed.

The ReplicaId Property

This property indicates a unique identifier for a database replica in the form of a GUID. The ReplicaId is read-only and its value is automatically generated when the replica is created.

The ReplicaType Property

The ReplicaType property indicates the type of replica. It can have one of the following values:

Constant	Value	Meaning
jrRepTypeNotReplicable	0	Indicates that the database is not replicable
jrRepTypeDesignMaster	1	Indicates that the database is the design master
jrRepTypeFull	2	Indicates that the database is a full replica
jrRepTypePartial	3	Indicates that the database is a partial replica

This property can be used to check if the database is replicable before calling the CreateReplica method. For example:

```
If JetRep.ReplicaType = jrRepTypeNotReplicable then
  {
  Database is not replicable. We can make it replicable
  or simply eject user at this stage
  }
Else
  {
  Database is replicable. We can create replica
  }
```

The jrRepTypeFull and jrRepTypePartial values are used with the CreateReplica method to set the type of the new replica.

The RetentionPeriod Property

This property indicates how many days replica histories should be kept. The RetentionPeriod property can have values from 5 to 32,000 days. The default value is 60 for databases that were made replicable through ADO code or Replication Manager and 1000 for databases that were made replicable with Microsoft Access.

 Note: This property can be set only on a design master database.

The Visibility Property

This property indicates the visibility of the replica to other replicas. Replica visibility can be global, local, or anonymous, and is set when the replica is first created. The Visibility property can take the following values:

Constant	Value	Meaning
jrRepVisibilityGlobal	1	Global replica. Can synchronize with any other global replica in the set. A global replica is typically the design master.
jrRepVisibilityLocal	2	Local replica. Can synchronize only with its parent, which is the global replica it was created from.

Constant	Value	Meaning
jrRepVisibilityAnon	4	Anonymous replica. Can synchronize only with its parent. No replica is aware of an anonymous replica, which has a priority of 0.

The following example shows how to create an anonymous replica:

```
const
 Provider = 'Provider=Microsoft.Jet.OLEDB.4.0;';
 SrcMDB   = 'd:\data\demo.mdb';

procedure TForm1.Button1Click(Sender: TObject);
var
 JetRep : Replica;
 Src    : WideString;
begin
 JetRep := CoReplica.Create;

 Src  := Provider + 'Data Source=' + SrcMDB;
 JetRep._Set_ActiveConnection(Src);

 JetRep.CreateReplica('d:\data\democopy.mdb', 'AnonReplica',
  jrRepTypeFull, jrRepVisibilityAnon, -1, jrRepUpdFull);

 JetRep := Nil
end;
```

Methods of the Replica Object

The methods of the Replica object can be used to create replicas, check the replicability of objects (tables, queries, forms, reports, and macros) in the database, make the database replicable, populate a partial replica, and perform synchronization between two replicas.

The CreateReplica Method

This method creates a new replica of the current replicable database. It takes the following parameters:

Parameter	Type	Description
ReplicaName	String	Specifies the name and path of the replica to be created.
Description	String	Specifies the description of the replica to be created.
ReplicaType	Integer	Sets the type of the replica. Can be jrRepTypeFull (the default value) or jrRepTypePartial.
Visibility	Integer	Sets the visibility of the replica. Can be jrRepVisibilityGlobal, jrRepVisibilityLocal, or jrRepVisibilityAnon. The default value is jrRepVisibilityGlobal.
Priority	Integer	Sets the priority of the replica for use during conflict resolution. See the Priority property above.

Parameter	Type	Description
Updatability	Integer	Sets the type of updates allowed. Can be jrRepUpdFull (the replica can be updated) or jrRepUpdReadOnly (the replica is read-only).

 Note: The ActiveConnection property should be set before calling this method and the source database should be replicable.

The GetObjectReplicability Method

This method is used to find whether the object is replicated or will be replicated. For databases that are not replicable (ReplicaType = jrRepTypeNotReplicable) this method returns True for all objects. This indicates that the object will be replicated if the database is replicable. For replicable databases, this method returns False for all new objects. To set object replicability we should use the SetObjectReplicability described below.

The GetObjectReplicability method takes two parameters. The first one specifies the name of the object, and the second one specifies its type.

The following example shows how to use this method:

```
If JetRep.GetObjectReplicability('Customers','Tables')
  then
    ShowMessage('[Customers] table can be replicated later')
```

The MakeReplicable Method

This method makes the database replicable. The first parameter indicates the connection string to the database that is to be made replicable. The second parameter indicates whether changes are tracked by row (False) or column (True). The following example shows how to make the database replicable:

```
const
 Provider = 'Provider=Microsoft.Jet.OLEDB.4.0;';
 SrcMDB   = 'd:\data\north.mdb';

procedure TForm1.Button1Click(Sender: TObject);
var
 JetRep : Replica;
 Src    : WideString;
begin
 JetRep := CoReplica.Create;

 Src  := Provider + 'Data Source=' + SrcMDB;
 JetRep._Set_ActiveConnection(Src);

 If JetRep.ReplicaType = jrRepTypeNotReplicable Then
   {
```

```
  Database is not replicable. We can make it replicable
  }
 begin
  ShowMessage('Not Replicable');
  JetRep.ActiveConnection := Nil;
  JetRep.MakeReplicable(Src, True)
  if JetRep.Get_ActiveConnection <> Nil Then
   ShowMessage('Operation Succeed')
 end
Else
 {
  Database is replicable. We can create replica
 }
 ShowMessage('Already Replicable');
 JetRep := Nil;
end;
```

> **Note:** If the database is already replicable, an error occurs. In addition, if the operation is successful, the value of the ActiveConnection property will change.

The PopulatePartial Method

This method is used to populate a partial replica. The PopulatePartial method is similar to the Synchronize method, but it synchronizes any changes in the partial replica with the full replica, removes all records in the partial replica, and then repopulates the partial replica based on the current replica filters. Here is an example of how to use this method:

```
const
 Provider = 'Provider=Microsoft.Jet.OLEDB.4.0;';
 SrcMDB   = 'd:\jet\north.mdb';
 DstMDB   = 'd:\jet\cust.mdb';
 Table    : WideString = 'Customers';
 Criteria : WideString = 'Country=''USA''';

procedure TForm1.Button1Click(Sender: TObject);
var
 JetRep : Replica;
 Src    : WideString;
begin
 JetRep := CoReplica.Create;

 Src  := Provider + 'Data Source=' + SrcMDB;
 JetRep._Set_ActiveConnection(Src);
{Create Partial Replica}
 JetRep.CreateReplica('d:\jet\cust.mdb', 'Partial Replica',
  jrRepTypePartial, jrRepVisibilityGlobal, 0, jrRepUpdFull);
```

```
JetRep.ActiveConnection := nil;
JetRep := nil;

JetRep := CoReplica.Create;

{Open Partial Replica}
Src := Provider + 'Data Source=' + 'd:\jet\cust.mdb';
Src := Src + ';Mode=Share Exclusive';
JetRep._Set_ActiveConnection(Src);

{Add Filter}
JetRep.Filters.Append(Table, jrFilterTypeTable, Criteria);

{Populate}
JetRep.PopulatePartial('d:\jet\north.mdb');

JetRep := Nil
end;
```

The SetObjectReplicability Method

This method is used to set whether or not an object will be replicated with the next call to the CreateReplica method. SetObjectReplicability takes three parameters: the name of the object, its type (Table or Query) and the Boolean value that makes the object replicable (True) or not.

The Synchronize Method

This method is used to synchronize two replicas. There are three parameters for this method:

Parameter	Type	Description
Target	String	The path and file name of the replica with which to synchronize. This can also be the name of a synchronizer that manages the target replica or the Internet server where the target replica is contained.
SyncType	Integer	Sets the type of synchronization. Can have one of the following values: ■ jrSyncTypeExport—to export changes from the current database to the target database ■ jrSyncTypeImport—to import changes from the target database to the current database ■ jrSyncTypeImpExp—to exchange changes between the current and target databases

Parameter	Type	Description
SyncMode	Integer	Sets the method of synchronization. Can have one of the following values: ■ jrSyncModeIndirect—indicates indirect synchronization ■ jrSyncModeDirect—indicates direct synchronization ■ jrSyncModeInternet—indicates indirect synchronization over the Internet

 Note: To use indirect synchronization over the Internet you should first install the Microsoft Replication Manager. This tool is available in the Microsoft Office 2000 Developer.

Collections of the Replica Object

The Replica object exposes only one collection: the Filters collection that contains one or more Filter objects. Each Filter object specifies replication information.

The Filters Collection

As we mentioned earlier, the Filters collection contains one or more Filter objects. Each Filter object specifies replication information. This collection supports three methods and two properties that are described below.

To append a new Filter object to the Filters collection, we use the Append method that takes three parameters:

Parameter	Type	Description
TableName	String	Specifies the name of the table to which the filter is applied.
FilterType	Integer	Sets the type of the filter. See the FilterType property above.
FilterCriteria	String	Sets the criteria that the record must meet to be included in the replica. See the FilterCriteria property above.

For example, we can set the following filter for the Customers table in the Northwind database:

```
const
 Table    : WideString = 'Customers';
 Criteria : WideString = 'Country=''USA''';

...

JetRep.Filters.Append(Table, jrFilterTypeTable, Criteria);
```

To remove a filter from the Filters collection you must use the Delete method. It takes one parameter: the index of the filter to be removed. After manipulating the Filters collection, such as adding and removing items, you need to call the Refresh method to make all the changes visible.

The Filters collection exposes two properties. The Count property tells us how many items are in the collection, and the Item property allows us to access any particular item. Item is the default property, so you don't have to refer to the Item property to access it. Here is the code that can be used to list all Filter objects in the Filters collection:

```
For I := 0 to JetRep.Filters.Count-1 do
  Memo1.Lines.Add(
    JetRep.Filters[I].TableName + ' ' +
    JetRep.Filters[I].FilterCriteria
  );
```

Note: You should delete only the Filter objects you created. The Filters collection contains several Filter objects that are added by the Jet Engine. These are system tables with names like MSysCmdbars, MSysIMEXColumns, MSysIMEXSpecs, and MSysAccessObjects that are used by the Jet Engine to store system-specific information. You should not delete them.

The Filter Object

The Filter object specifies criteria that limit the recordset of a replicated database. Using filters, you can create partial replicas that contain a subset of the records in a database.

Properties of the Filter Object

The three properties of the Filter object are used to set the criteria, filter type, and name of the table to which it applies.

Note: These properties are available only when you access some objects in the Filters collection. To set these properties you should use the appropriate parameters of the Filters collection's Append method described below.

The FilterCriteria Property

This property sets the criteria that the record must meet to be included in the replica. The string value of the FilterCriteria property is a SQL WHERE clause without the WHERE keyword. The FilterCriteria is set in the Append method of the Filters collection. Once set, the FilterCriteria is read-only.

The FilterType Property

This property indicates the type of the filter. The FilterType can have two values: jrFilterTypeRelationship for filters based on a relationship and jrFilterTypeTable for filters based on a table. The FilterType is set in the Append method of the Filters collection. Once set, the FilterType is read-only.

The TableName Property

This property indicates the name of the table to which the filter applies. The TableName is set in the Append method of the Filters collection. Once set, the TableName is read-only.

Step-by-Step Guide to Replication

We will end this chapter with a short step-by-step guide to replication that will show you how to perform various replication scenarios and what methods and properties of the Replica object are involved in each step.

Creating a Design Master

The first step in every successful replication scenario is to create a design master. To make a database a design master we should make it replicable. To do so we call the MakeReplicable method of the Replica object. Before calling this method, we may check if the database is already replicable by checking whether the ReplicaType property is set to jrRepTypeNotReplicable or jrTypeDesignMaster.

Making Local and Replicable Objects

To find the current replicability status of the object, table, or query in the database, we can use the GetObjectReplicability method of the Replica object. Its status can be either True, meaning that the object is replicable, or False, meaning the object is not replicable, i.e., local.

To change the replicability status of the object, we use the SetObjectReplicability method, using False to make the replicable object local and True otherwise.

Creating a Replica

To create a full replica, we should first open the design master by setting an appropriate value of the ActiveConnection property and then call the CreateReplica method. For the full replica, we should set the ReplicaType parameter to jrRepTypeFull. Using the Updatability parameter we can create replicas that allow changes to the schema and records (jrRepUpdFull) or read-only replicas (jrRepUpdReadOnly). In most cases, we need to create global replicas (the Visibility parameter is set to jrRepVisibilityGlobal), though it is possible to create local replicas (jrRepVisibilityLocal)and anonymous replicas (jrRepVisibilityAnon).

Creating a Partial Replica

To create a partial replica, we call the CreateReplica method and set the ReplicaType parameter to jrRepTypePartial. Then we need to populate the replica with records according to some rules defined with the filter. To do so, we first append the new filter to the Filters collection (using the Append method) and then call the PopulatePartial method of the Replica object.

Data Synchronization

To synchronize two replicas, i.e., to exchange data and design changes, we use the Synchronize method of the Replica object. First, we need to open the source replica (by setting its ActiveConnection property) and then set the type of the synchronization (export, import, or import-export) and the synchronization mode. Remember that direct synchronization (jrSyncModeDirect) is suitable for replicas on local area networks, while indirect synchronization (jrSyncModeInDirect) should be your choice in WAN or dial-up connection environments. Note that there can also be synchronization over Internet (jrSyncModeInternet), but this requires using the Replication Manager that is available as part of the Microsoft Office 2000 Developer.

Conclusion

In this chapter, we have taken a look at the features of the Microsoft Jet and Replication Objects (JRO) library that allows us to perform replication of Microsoft Access databases as well as compact and encrypt them. During the course of this chapter we have seen how to make a database replicable (i.e., how to create a design master), how to create full and partial replicas, and how to synchronize them.

In the next chapter, we will discuss how to deploy our Delphi ADO applications and learn how to find various system information and how to use the InstallShield Express package that comes with Delphi 5.

DEPLOYING DELPHI 5 ADO APPLICATIONS

Creating a Delphi ADO application that uses data from some data source and provides ways to manipulate it is only part of the job. The other part is to be able to successfully deploy this application on the user's computer. In this chapter, we will talk about how we can deploy Delphi ADO applications, what tools to use for this, and issues we should be concerned about.

In this chapter, we will learn when we need to install DCOM and where to get it. We will discuss which MDAC versions are currently available, where to get them, how to install MDAC, and when we do not need to install it.

Also, we will show you how to create an installation using InstallShield Express, a special tool that comes with Delphi 5 Professional and Enterprise editions. We will show you how to include the necessary files into the installation applications, how to specify where they must be placed on the user computer, which System Registry entries are created during installation, and how to force creation of custom Registry entries. We will also provide an example of how to create an installation application that installs both our application and Microsoft Data Access Components.

Before we can start discussing the details, we need to develop a general plan for our product. Let's outline the major part of the product to be deployed and the general steps to be performed in order to successfully install our Delphi ADO application.

What Should Be Installed

Generally, the product ready to be deployed has the following parts:

- One or more executable files. One of them is the main executable of the application, while the others are additional tools, configuration utilities, and so on.

- Other files used by the application. These can be data files, help files, VCL and third-party run-time packages, resource DLLs, and so on.

- Third-party libraries used by the product, including data access libraries. In the case of Delphi ADO applications, these are the MDAC files and, probably, additional ODBC or OLE DB drivers. If our Delphi ADO application uses server DBMS, we need to have the client software of this DBMS installed on the computer.

- Files and software that are not used by the application directly but are necessary for setting up all database environments. An example of this is SQL scripts for creating database objects on the server.

Besides the items shown above, our product may need to use some System Registry entries or some environment variables. Note that the best practice is to use the System Registry to store and extract information and use Windows functions to find the locations of some directories, such as the directory to store temporary files.

After we have found what should be installed, let's define the steps of a successful installation process.

Step-By-Step Installation Plan

From our point of view, the first step of the installation process must be determining the current environment. This includes determining the version of Windows, checking for some core functionality our application relies on, and some additional conditions. We must be sure that our user has all appropriate system files and libraries to be able to use our product. In the case of Delphi ADO applications, we should check the availability and version of Microsoft Data Access Components and, in some cases, the availability and version of Microsoft DCOM. As we will see later in this chapter, there are many different versions of Windows that may not have all of the system components we need. For example, there may be DCOM installed but no MDAC files, no DCOM or MDAC at all, or earlier versions of DCOM and MDAC than we expect to use. We will discuss this in more detail in the next section

After we have found that the current user's environment satisfies our needs, we can install the components of our product; these are one or more executable files and other files used by our application. We must remove any debug information from our executables (refer to your Delphi documentation on how to set an appropriate project options); rebuild the application without packages (if you are not sure which run-time packages are used by it) or create a list of packages used by an application; and specify the icon, help file, and versioning information. Then we must create the final version of our application and other executables that come with the product.

Then all of the files must be collected in one package and an appropriate Setup.exe (or Install.exe) file should be created. This is a job for installation applications. Later in this chapter, in the section called "Creating Installation Applications," we will show you how to use InstallShield Express to create installations.

The third step in our installation is to supply additional files, create data sources, attach necessary databases to the server or create them on the server, and perform other fine-tuning. We will cover this in the section called "Specifying Data Sources and Other Issues" later in this chapter.

In this section, we have created a general step-by-step plan for our installation process. Now it is time to implement these steps. We will start with the user's environment and learn how to find which version and type of Windows operating system is installed, which required components are already available, and how to install the components that are absent in the current configuration.

MDAC and DCOM Installation Issues

In order to run our Delphi ADO application correctly, the target computer must have the recent MDAC files installed on it. The first thing we need to do is to check the version of the operating system installed on the computer. This can be done with the GetVersionEx Windows core API function. This function fills the TOSVersionInfo (TOSVersionInfoEx in Windows 2000) structure with the operating system version information. The following example shows how to use this function to determine the operating system version and perform appropriate tasks:

```
procedure TForm1.Button1Click(Sender: TObject);
const
 WinVer = 'Windows %d.%d';
begin
 OSVerInfo.dwOSVersionInfoSize := SizeOf(OSVerInfo);
 GetVersionEx(OSVerInfo);
 With OSVerInfo do
 begin
  Memo1.Lines.Add(Format(WinVer,
    [dwMajorVersion, dwMinorVersion]
  ));
 Case dwMajorVersion of
  4 :
    Begin
     Case dwPlatformID of
      VER_PLATFORM_WIN32_WINDOWS :        {Windows 9.x}
       Begin
        If dwMinorVersion = 0
         Then // Windows 95
         Else // Windows 98
       End;
      VER_PLATFORM_WIN32_NT      :        {Windows NT}
       Begin
        // Check Service Pack version
       End;
```

```
   End;
   End;
 5 : // We are running Windows 2000
 end;
 end;
end;
```

In the case of Windows NT, we may need the type of NT operating system and the Service Pack version installed on it. The type of Windows NT (either Workstation or Server) can be found by checking the following key in the System Registry:

```
HKEY_LOCAL_MACHINE\SYSTEM\CurrentControlSet\Control\ ProductOptions
```

The value of the ProductType entry gives us the type of the NT. This is shown in the example below:

```
function GetNTType : String;
var
 R: TRegistry;
begin
 R := TRegistry.Create;
 try
 With R do
  begin
    RootKey := HKEY_LOCAL_MACHINE;
    OpenKey('SYSTEM\CurrentControlSet\Control\ProductOptions',
     False);
    Result := ReadString('ProductType');
  end;
 finally
  R.Free;
 end;
end;
```

Note that here we use the Registry unit; it must be specified in the Uses clause of our application.

In our application, we can check the result returned by the GetNTType function. For example:

```
If StrUpcase(GetNTType) = 'WINNT' Then
 ShowMessage('Workstation')
Else
 ShowMessage('Server');
```

To find the Service Pack version installed on the computer running the Windows NT operating system, we must check the following key in the System Registry:

```
HKEY_LOCAL_MACHINE\SYSTEM\CurrentControlSet\Control\Windows\CSDVersion
```

This entry contains the NT Service Pack version installed on the computer. For example, if we have SP4, this entry will be equal to 1024 (4000 hex).

Now we know how to programmatically determine the version of operating system installed on the computer. Depending on the current version, we may need to perform some extra steps.

The simplest case is Windows 2000, which contains MDAC as part of the operating system core files. If our user has this version installed on his computer, we do not need to install MDAC at all.

In the case of Windows NT or Windows 98, we need to check if the MDAC files are already installed; if they are, we need to check the version of these files. If this version is earlier than the one we have tested our application with, we must install MDAC files.

Note: Microsoft has tested MDAC components under Windows NT 4.0 Service Pack 3 and later, so we need to check which NT Service Pack is installed on the user's computer and suggest upgrading to the latest one before installing MDAC components.

If we have found that our user runs Windows 95, we must check if the computer has the DCOM files installed and its version. (DCOM is part of the operating system in Windows NT, Windows 2000, and Windows 98.) If there are no DCOM files found, we must install them first, and then install the current version of MDAC.

Let's start with DCOM. In the next section, we will learn how to find out if it is installed and how to define the currently installed version.

Installing DCOM

As we have mentioned, we need to check the version of DCOM and its availability, primarily under Windows 95; later versions of Windows come with DCOM as part of the operating system. According to Microsoft, in some cases, DCOM may not be installed on a Windows 98 computer. If it has not been installed, we must install DCOM98 before installing MDAC. Note that Microsoft does not allow redistributing DCOM for Windows 98; only DCOM95 can be legally redistributed.

The version of DCOM is stored in the System Registry as a string in the form of "X, XX, X, XXXX". The possible values for the version of DCOM are shown in the following table:

DCOM Version	Comment
4, 71, 0, 3328	DCOM95 and DCOM98 1.3 Release 4.71.0.3328
4, 71, 0, 2618	DCOM95 1.2 Web Release 4.71.0.2618
4, 71, 0, 2612	DCOM 1.2. Release 4.71.0.2612; DCOM98.EXE shipped with Visual Studio 6
4, 71, 0, 1719	DCOM Win98 Gold Release 4.71.0.1719
4, 71, 0, 1718	DCOM95 1.1 Release 4.71.0.1718
4, 71, 0, 1120	DCOM 1.x Release 4.71.0.1120

The following two functions show how to find if DCOM is already installed on the computer and which version it is:

```
{/////////////////////////////////////////////
 CheckForDCOM - returns True or False, indicating
 if DCOM is installed on this computer or not
/////////////////////////////////////////////}
function CheckForDCOM : Boolean;
var
 S : String;
 R : TRegistry;
begin
 Result:= False;
 R := TRegistry.Create;
 try
 With R do
  begin
   RootKey := HKEY_LOCAL_MACHINE;
   OpenKey('SOFTWARE\Microsoft\OLE', False);
   S := StrUpcase(ReadString('EnableDCOM'));
   If S = 'Y' Then
     Result := True;
   CloseKey;
  end;
 finally
  R.Free;
 end;
end;


{//////////////////////////////////////////////////
 GetDCOMVer - returns string with the version of DCOM
//////////////////////////////////////////////////}
function GetDCOMVersion : String;
var
 R : TRegistry;
begin
 Resule := '';
 If CheckForDCOM then
 begin
 R := TRegistry.Create;
 try
 With R do
  begin
   RootKey := HKEY_CLASSES_ROOT;
   OpenKey('CLSID\' +
     '{bdc67890-4fc0-11d0-a805-00aa006d2ea4}' +
     '\InstalledVersion',
     False);
```

```
   Result := ReadString('');
   CloseKey;
  end;
 finally
  R.Free;
 end;
 end;
end;
```

The most current version of DCOM for Windows 95 and Windows 98 can be downloaded from the Microsoft Web site:

http://www.microsoft.com/com/resources/downloads.asp

For Windows 95, we can include the DCOM95.exe executable as part of our installation, copy it to hard disk, and execute it. In order to execute the DCOM95.exe executable, we need to use the ShellExecute function implemented in the Windows kernel and available through the ShellAPI unit that must be included in the Uses clause. Here is an example of how we can run DCOM95.exe using this function:

```
ShellExecute(Handle, 'open', 'c:\mdac\dcom95.exe',
 '', '', SW_SHOWNORMAL);
```

The first argument indicates the handle to the parent window; in our case, this is the Delphi form that we currently using. The second argument specifies the action to be performed, and the third one specifies the file on which to perform the action. The next two arguments are used to specify the parameters to be passed to the executable and the default directory. The last argument specifies how the window should be opened; in our example, we use the default value.

Note that we may want to use the /Q option to invoke the quiet mode of DCOM installation in order to avoid extra message and dialog boxes on the screen. In this case, the call of the ShellExecute function will look like this:

```
ShellExecute(Handle, 'open', 'c:\mdac\dcom95.exe',
 '/Q', '', SW_SHOWNORMAL);
```

If DCOM is not installed under Windows 98, all we can do is to terminate our application with the appropriate message. In this case, users must download DCOM98.exe from the Microsoft site, install it, and then reinstall our application.

After we have checked for the presence of DCOM, and installed it if needed, we must check if the MDAC components are already available on the computer, and if not, install them. We will learn how to do this in the next section.

Installing MDAC

The first step is to find if Microsoft Data Access Components are already installed, and, if so, check the version of ADO. The following example shows how to find out if ADO is installed on the computer:

```
{///////////////////////////////////////////////
 CheckForADO - returns True or False, indicating
 if ADO is installed on this computer or not
 ///////////////////////////////////////////////}
function CheckForADO : Boolean;
var
 R : TRegistry;
begin
 Result := False;
 R := TRegistry.Create;
 try
 With R do
  begin
   RootKey := HKEY_CLASSES_ROOT;
   OpenKey('\ADODB.Connection\CurVer', False);
   If ReadString('') <> '' Then
    Result := True;
   CloseKey;
  end;
 finally
  R.Free;
 end;
end;
```

Note that here we use the Registry unit, so it must be specified in the Uses clause of our application.

If we need to find the version of ADO, we can use the code provided in Chapter 5.

Versions of MDAC 2.1

At the time of this writing, the most recent version of MDAC was version 2.1. It exists in three major releases that are available as part of Microsoft products as well as a Web release.

Version	Comments
2.1.2.4202.3	The most current version of MDAC called MDAC SP2.
2.1.0.4202.1	Web release of MDAC 2.1; also called MDAC 2.1 GA.
2.1.1.3711.11	Installed with Microsoft Office 2000 and Microsoft Internet Explorer 5a. This version contains significant fixes to Microsoft Jet components. This version is also called MDAC 2.1 SP1.

Version	Comments
2.1.1.3711.6	Installed with Microsoft Internet Explorer 5.0. This is a subset of release 2.1.1.3511.11 that contains only core ADO, OLE DB, and ODBC. It does not contain Microsoft Jet or any drivers or providers
2.1.0.3513.2	Original version of MDAC 2.1 shipped with Microsoft SQL Server 7.0. This version was also included in Microsoft SQL Server 6.5 SP5a.

The most current version of MDAC can be downloaded from the Microsoft Web site:

```
http://www.microsoft.com/data/
```

If we have not found MDAC on the computer, we must install it. This can be done by executing the MDAC_TYP.exe with the help of the ShellExecute function, which we have already discussed in this chapter. Here is the code that installs MDAC:

```
ShellExecute(Handle, 'open', 'c:\mdac\mdac_typ.exe',
  '/Q', '', SW_SHOWNORMAL);
```

Here we also use quiet mode to avoid extra dialog boxes on screen.

Now the computer we are running on has all support files to run our application, and we can install its main parts. As we have already indicated, this is a job for installation applications. In the next section, we will see how to create them.

Creating Installation Applications

In this section, we will discuss how to use InstallShield Express for Delphi 5, which comes with Delphi Enterprise and Professional editions. Before we go into the details of how to create an installation application, let's summarize what this application must do. Generally, it must perform the following tasks:

- Copy files (*.exe, *.ocx, *.dll, *.bpl, *.hlp, fonts, data files, etc.) to appropriate directories of the user's hard disk
- Modify the Windows System Registry
- Modify environment variables, if any
- Create program groups and icons, and modify the Windows Start menu
- Restart Windows if necessary

Traditionally, such an installation application must allow the user to specify the destination directory in which to install the application, and to select what parts of an application should be installed; this needs to be done only when we have Typical, Custom, or Compact versions of our product. In most cases, the license agreement and readme file are also presented for the user.

There are several ways to create an installation application. The hardest but most flexible way is to use Windows API and Microsoft Setup and Installation API to create a special Delphi application that will perform all the steps required. This task can be simplified if we use some third-party components. For example, the Mele Systems, LLC (http://www.youseful.com/youseful/default.htm) produces a set of such components, called Youseful Installation Components. This set of 18-plus native VCL components turns an ordinary Delphi/C++ Builder project into an installation program.

The second way is to use some special installation tools. The most popular of these products are listed below:

Product	Vendor	URL
InstallShield Express	InstallShield Software	http://www.installshield.com/
InstallShield Professional	Corporation	
InstallFromTheWeb		
Wise for Windows Installer	Wise Solutions	http://www.wisesolutions.com/
InstallManager		
InstallMaster		
AutoInstall	20/20 Software	http://www.twenty.com
PC-Install		
Microsoft Installer	Microsoft	http://www.microsoft.com

For purposes of our example, we will

- Give our users the ability to select where to install our application
- Let the users select what parts of an application will be installed
- Select which dialog boxes will appear during installation
- Create program groups, application icons, and Start menu items.
- Create distribution media
- Add automatic uninstaller to our product

Unfortunately, this version of InstallShield Express is BDE-oriented and does not support MDAC installation directly from it. Also, we cannot set up ODBC data sources, or create UDL strings with the same convenience as including BDE or creating BDE aliases. Nevertheless, we have already described how to install MDAC and other required files earlier in this chapter.

Creating Installations with InstallShield Express

Imagine that we need to create an installation of a Delphi ADO application. Let's assume that this application is called Sales Data and its main executable is Northwind.exe. This program comes with the Northwind.mdb Access database that must be located in the \DATA subdirectory of the Northwind.exe executable file installation path. The context-sensitive help system is implemented in the Northwind.hlp help file and Northwind.cnt help content files.

If you have not installed InstallShield Express, do this right now by clicking the **InstallShield Express Custom Edition for Delphi** button in the Delphi Setup dialog box.

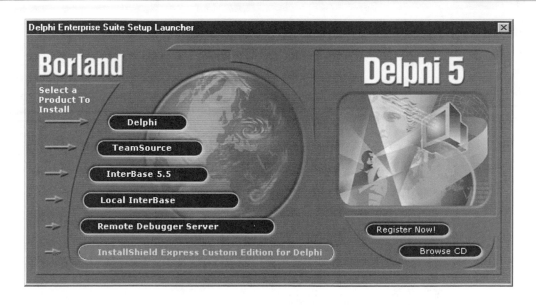

In the following section, we will use the InstallShield Express to create an installation for our application.

Creating the Setup Project

To create an installation application, select the **Express for Delphi 5** item from the Start | Programs | InstallShield Express menu. In the Welcome to the InstallShield Express dialog box, select **Create a New Setup Project**. Then we need to set the project name and select the directory where the InstallShield script will be generated; this script will be used by InstallShield to create the installation program. If we want to provide our users with the ability to select which parts of the application to install, it is necessary to check the Include a custom setup type check box.

After pressing the Create button, we will obtain a setup checklist with a list of steps to be done for creating installation. Each major step has its own dialog box in which we can specify the information for InstallShield to proceed.

Now we need to select the first group of items in this list. In the Set the Visual Design dialog box, select the name of an executable file of the application (in our example it will be Northwind.exe), and set where in the user computer this executable should be installed.

Looking at the Default Destination Directory edit box in the dialog box shown above, we can see that, by default, InstallShield uses the <ProgramFilesDir> variable to identify the location of program files.

The InstallShield Variables

When creating installations, we need to expect that different users can use different paths to install our application, and different target systems have different locations of Windows and Windows System folders, Program Files folders, fonts, common files, etc. To take this into account, InstallShield provides several variables (also called *directory specifiers*) that are replaced with the actual user system data during installation. Commonly used variables are shown in the following table:

Variable Name	Meaning
<INSTALLDIR>	The installation directory selected by the user during the setup process in the Choose Destination Location dialog box (this will be discussed later in this chapter)
<WINDIR>	The main Windows directory on the target system (for example, C:\WINNT)
<WINSYSDIR>	The Windows System directory on the target system (for example, C:\WINNT\System32)
<WINDISK>	The drive letter of the disk containing the Windows directory (for example, C:)

Variable Name	Meaning
<WINSYSDISK>	The drive letter of the disk containing the Windows System directory (for example, C:)
<ProgramFilesDir>	The Program Files directory on the target system (for example, C:\Program Files)
<CommonFilesDir>	The Common Files directory on the target system (for example, C:\Program Files\Common Files)
<SRCDIR>	The source directory from which the application files are copied. For example, if the source files are be installed from a CD-ROM located in the customer's E: drive, the SRCDIR value will be E:
<SUPPORTDIR>	The directory for storing temporary installation files
[group name]	The directory into which that particular group is copied
<WINSYS16DIR>	The 16-bit System directory in Windows NT. In Windows 9.x, this variable is equal to <WINSYSDIR>

In addition, we can define any subdirectory of the directories specified in such a variable. For example, we can define the Data subdirectory of the installation directory as:

```
<INSTALLDIR>\Data
```

The Main Window page of the Set the Visual Design dialog box allows us to select how the main installation screen will look. In particular, we can select the screen color, specify the logo bitmap, if any, and the window title (in our example it will be "NorthWind Traders Sales Data Setup").

The Features page of the Set the Visual Design dialog box contains only one check box—Automatic Uninstaller. It is strongly recommended you leave it checked. In this case, InstallShield will automatically include the uninstallation program and appropriate System Registry entries that will allow the automatic removal of our application files, icons, folders, directories, and Registry entries if the user decides to uninstall it. All installation information, such as the list of created folders and files and Registry entries, will be saved in the *.isu files. Please note that uninstallation capability is one of the Windows 2000 Logo requirements. Note that uninstallation can be performed by using the Add/Remove Components applet from the Control Panel.

The next task in the checklist is the Specify InstallShield Objects for Delphi 5 group. In this dialog box, we can specify run-time packages used by our application, if any, and add them to the set of redistributable files.

The next step in the setup checklist is to specify components and files groups by using the appropriate checklist group and dialog box.

Creating Components, Groups, and Setup Types

The files our application consists of must be organized into groups. These groups will be included in components that can be used to create multiple setup types.

Let's recall that our application consists of the Northwind.exe file, Northwind.hlp and Northwind.cnt help files, and the Northwind.mdb file that should be located in the \DATA subdirectory. For the purposes of our example, we can create three following file groups:

- The Program Files group with the Northwind.exe file
- The Help Files group with the Northwind.hlp and Northwind.cnt files
- The Data Files group with the Northwind.mdb file

These groups are shown in the figure below:

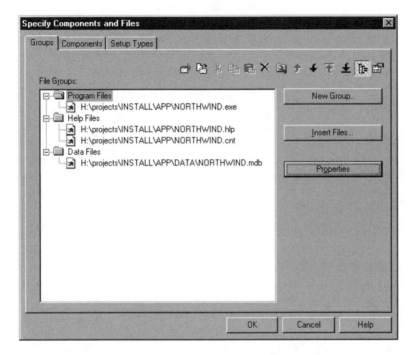

We can either use the Insert Files button to add files to one of the groups or drag files to the group directly from the Windows Explorer.

Having selected any file in a group, we can press the Properties button to study the properties of this file, such as its size, creation date, and version information. This Properties dialog box also contains the Allow Express to Self-register this file check box. If it is checked, the installation application will attempt to register this file on a target computer after copying it. This is useful if we need to deploy ActiveX components or DLLs that must be registered. This feature also works with ordinal executable files; they will be copied in the destination directory and executed.

Pressing the Properties button for the selected file group will bring up a dialog box in which we can set the group properties. For example, we can specify the destination directory for the files in a group, how files will be updated, and the platforms on which this group must be installed. The parameters for the Data Files group for our example are shown in the following figure:

As we have mentioned above, file groups are part of the application components. In our example, we will create two components:

■ Application files that consist of the Program Files group and the Data Files group

■ Help and Tutorial files that consist of the Help Files group

These components are shown in the figure below:

The next step in organizing files in the installation is to create setup types. This version of InstallShield Express provides for either using the default setup type or creating the following three setup types:

■ Typical, which usually includes all components

■ Compact, which usually consists of only those components necessary to run the application

■ Custom, which allows the user to select which components will be installed

In our example, we will include both setup components created above into the Typical and Custom setup types, and the Application Files group into the Compact setup type.

Having organized application files into groups, components, and setup types, we can move to the next step of the creating installation—defining dialog boxes.

Defining Dialog Boxes

In the Dialog Boxes dialog box, we can select the dialog boxes that will appear during the installation process. Using the Settings tab, we can define specific properties (if any) for every dialog box in use. In InstallShield Express, the following dialog boxes are available:

The Dialog Box	Purpose
Welcome Bitmap	This dialog box is used to display a bitmap specified in the Settings page in a child window after the startup message, but before any of the other user dialog boxes.
Welcome Message	This dialog box displays a message welcoming the user to our application's installation. This message could contain, for example, a request to close Windows programs before starting the setup or some copyright information.
Software License Agreement	This dialog box allows us to display a text file with the license agreement, specified in the Settings page.
Readme Information	This dialog box allows you to display a text file with the readme file, specified in the Settings page.
User Information	This dialog box collects the user's name and company to be stored in the Windows Registry.
Choose Destination Location	This dialog box allows the user to select the directory in which to install our application. The directory and path selected by the user will be used to replace the <INSTALLDIR> variable in all installation dialog boxes.
Choose Database Location	This dialog box allows the user to set the directory where data files will be located. If necessary, we can define that this directory will not be deleted if our user uninstalls the application.
Setup Type	This dialog box allows the user to select a Typical, Compact, or Custom installation. If we want to provide these options for our users, this dialog box should be selected.
Custom Setup	This dialog box allows the user to select the components of an application to be installed. It will be displayed only if the user has selected a Custom setup type in the Setup Type user dialog box.
Select Program Folder	This dialog box allows the user to define the program folder in which the application icons will be placed.
Start Copying Files	This dialog box displays the setup type, destination directory, and user information already entered by the user. It allows the user to go back and modify this data.
Progress Indicator	This dialog box shows a graphical representation of the file transfer process.
Billboards	This component allows the display of images during installation (as done during Delphi installation). To show images, we need to create bitmaps or Windows metafiles named Setup1.bmp, Setup2.bmp, etc., or Setup1.wmf, Setup2.wmf, etc., and place them in a directory specified in the Settings page.

The Dialog Box	Purpose
Setup Complete	This user dialog box may consist of two different dialog boxes. The first of them is the Reboot Computer dialog box that informs the user about the end of the installation and asks if he want to reboot. This dialog box will be displayed if the setup encounters any locked or shared files; in this case, they will be replaced after reboot.
	The second dialog box is the launch application dialog box that allows the user to run your application or view the Readme file by selecting a check box and clicking the OK button.

Now that we have defined the dialog boxes that can be used during the installation process and specified their properties, we can move to the next item in the setup checklist.

Creating Registry Entries

The next step in creating an installation program is to define Registry changes necessary for our application. To do this, we need to select the Make Registry Changes group in the checklist, and define necessary subkeys to be created during installation. For example, if we want to create the HKEY_LOCAL_MACHINE\SOFTWARE\NorthWind Traders\Databases System Registry key during setup, we need to press the Add Key button and enter the name of the appropriate key.

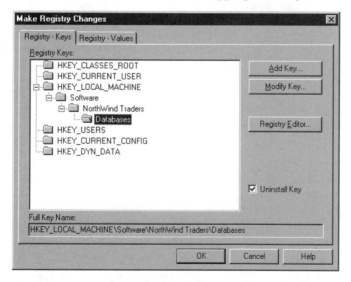

Then we can select the newly created key, click the Registry-Values tab, and press the Add Value button. In the dialog box that appears, we need to define the necessary Registry value name and data, as shown in the figure below:

We have already mentioned that the setup program will automatically create the standard System Registry key with application information that looks like that shown below:

```
HKEY_LOCAL_MACHINE\SOFTWARE\<Company>\<AppName>\<Version>
```

The <Company>, <AppName>, and <Version> key names are the same as the information we already entered in the Application Information dialog box.

For our example, the appropriate Registry entry is the following:

```
HKEY_LOCAL_MACHINE\SOFTWARE\NorthWind Traders\Sales Data\1.0
```

The values of this key are the Company and Name values that will be entered by the user.

Note: This version of InstallShield does not support the serial number input and can't check if it is valid during installation. This functionality is provided by the commercial version of InstallShield.

In addition, if the Automatic Uninstaller feature was selected in the Set the Visual Design dialog box, InstallShield Express will create the Registry keys and values necessary to run InstallShield's uninstallation application on the user's system. These entries are stored under the following key:

```
HKEY_LOCAL_MACHINE\SOFTWARE\Microsoft\Windows\Current Ver-
sion\Uninstall\<AppName>
```

In our example, this key has the following name:

```
HKEY_LOCAL_MACHINE\SOFTWARE\Microsoft\Windows\CurrentVersion\Uninstall\Sales
Data
```

This key contains two values. The first of them is the DisplayName value containing the data from the Application Name field of the Application Information dialog box (this string is used in the Add/Remove Programs applet on the Windows Control Panel). The second is the UninstallString value containing the command to uninstall our application.

The next Registry entry is the App Paths entry stored under the following key:

```
HKEY_LOCAL_MACHINE\SOFTWARE\Microsoft\Windows\CurrentVersion\App
Paths\<AppName.EXE>
```

In our example, this key is the following:

```
HKEY_LOCAL_MACHINE\SOFTWARE\Microsoft\Windows\CurrentVersion\App
Paths\NorthWind.exe
```

The default value of this key will contain the full path of the main executable of the application (NorthWind.exe file in our example).

This information is necessary to allow the user to start our application by selecting the Run item from the Start menu and typing the filename of the main application executable.

Specifying Folders and Icons

The next step in creating installations is to define folders and icons to be created on the target computer. This can be done by selecting the Specify Folders and Icons checklist group.

To specify an icon, we need to select the file for which the icon should be created. Then, we can specify the icon description, Run command parameters, the directory in which this application will be started, where the icon must be placed, and whether we want to create a shortcut key.

Building Disk Images

Having specified folders and icons, we could select the next item from the checklist—Disk Builder. This will bring up the Disk Builder dialog, where we can select the type of distribution media (floppy disks, CD-ROM, etc.). By running Disk Builder, we will create installation application files that should be copied to the distribution media.

It should be mentioned that if we have made mistakes during defining installation parameters (for example, we have created empty file groups, empty application components, or file groups that do not belong to any application component), we will see error messages when creating disk images.

Testing an Installation Application

The Test Run option in the checklist can be used to run the installation application in order to see how it looks, and to browse through the dialog boxes we defined on the early steps. Then we can test the installed application itself to check if we have included all necessary files.

However, running this application on the computer where it was created is not the proper way to test it. For instance, in our example, we have not included MDAC files in the installation. The installed application will run properly on the computer where the installation was created, because we have MDAC installed there. However, it will fail on a computer without MDAC.

To test for missing files or to check the System Registry entries, it is better to test an installation and the installed application on a computer containing only Windows. We need to remember that if we have not written system requirements for our application (for example, "This application requires Windows NT 4.0 Service Pack 5 or later"), a user could try to install this application into Windows 95.

Note: Delphi applications may require some additional files not included in previous 32-bit versions of Windows, for example, the CTL3DV2.dll file. It is essential to test which files are necessary to include in the installation before creating the final set of files.

In the next section of this chapter, we will continue with this example. We have just mentioned that our installation does not contain MDAC files. In the next section, we will show how to create a complex installation of our application using solutions discussed in the previous sections of this chapter.

Completing the Installation

Now we have an installation program called Setup.exe that can be used to install the core files of our product and a set of code that allows us to test the user's environment and to install some system components required for our product—MDAC and DCOM. The last thing we need to do is to combine all this together. Now we will create an Install.exe program that will perform the following tasks:

- Check the user's environment and install the system components if needed
- Run the installation program created with InstallShield
- Create additional files and fine-tune our application

Before we create our Install.exe program, we need to implement a set of short procedures. The source code for this is shown below:

```
{/////////////////////////////////////////////
 Fail if we run Windows 98 and do not have DCOM
/////////////////////////////////////////////}
procedure NoDCOM98;
begin
```

```
  Writeln('Please install DCOM98 before running ' +
    'this application');
  Halt(1);
end;
{/////////////////////////////////////////////////
  Fail if we don't have NT SP4 on the computer
/////////////////////////////////////////////////}
procedure NoSP;
begin
  Writeln('Please install NT Service Pack 4 before ' +
    'running this application');
  Halt(2)
end;
{/////////////////////////////////////////////////
  Install MDAC in quiet mode
/////////////////////////////////////////////////}
procedure InstallMDAC;
begin
  ShellExecute(Null, 'open', 'mdac\mdac_typ.exe',
    '/Q', '', SW_SHOWNORMAL);
end;
{/////////////////////////////////////////////////
  Install DCOM for Windows 95 in quiet mode
/////////////////////////////////////////////////}
procedure InstallDCOM;
begin
  ShellExecute(Null, 'open', 'mdac\dcom95.exe',
    '/Q', '', SW_SHOWNORMAL);
end;
{/////////////////////////////////////////////////
  Install Core files of our application
/////////////////////////////////////////////////}
procedure InstallMain;
begin
  ShellExecute(Null, 'open', 'xxx.exe',
    '', '', SW_SHOWNORMAL);
end;
```

Now we are ready to implement the main procedure of our Install.exe program; it may look like that shown below:

```
begin
  Init; // Create an instance of TRegistry
  {Step 1 - Find version of Windows}
  Case GetWinVer of
    95   : Begin
             {Install DCOM95 if we don't have it}
             If Not CheckForDCOM then InstallDCOM;
```

```
              {Install MDAC if we don't have it}
               If Not CheckForADO then InstallMDAC;
               Install := True;
              End;
   98    : Begin
              {Fail we don't have DCOM under Windows 98}
               If Not CheckForDCOM then NoDCOM98;
              {Install MDAC if we don't have it}
               If Not CheckForADO then InstallMDAC;
               Install := True;
              End;
   1000  : Begin
               If GetNTSPVer < 1024 Then
                 NoSP;
              {Install MDAC if we don't have it}
               If Not CheckForADO then InstallMDAC;
               Install := True;
              End;
   2000  : Begin
                 Install := True;
              End;
 end;
{Step 2 - Install our main application}
 If Install then InstallMain;
{Step 3 - Perform some extra steps}
 DoExtraSteps;
 Done; // Free an instance of TRegistry
end.
```

One piece of code is missing—the DoExtraSteps procedure. In the next section, we will discuss what may be implemented in it.

Specifying Data Sources and Other Issues

It should be obvious that when we create a program that will be executed on another computer, the data source should not be hard-coded into it. Depending on the type of database we are using, there may be different ways to make the data source information "flexible."

If we are using Microsoft Access *.mdb files, we can always open them, for example, from the Data subfolder of the folder where our executable resides. This allows us to build the whole connection string and just append the actual data source into it. For example, we can specify the ConnectionString property of the TADOConnection component (or other Delphi ADO components that have this property) as shown in the following code:

```
With ADOConnection1 do
 begin
 ConnectionString := 'Provider=MSDataShape.1;' +
  'Persist Security Info=False;' +
  'Mode=Share Deny None;' +
  'Data Source= DATA\NORTHWIND.MDB;'
  'Data Provider=Microsoft.Jet.OLEDB.4.0'
  Open;
 end;
```

In the case of data that is accessed through ODBC drivers, we can use the ODBC API, create Registry keys (by saving the appropriate ODBC Registry entries into the *.reg files and importing them using the REGEDIT utility), or use the ODBCCONF utility that comes as part of MDAC to specify ODBC data sources.

The other option is to create and use the Data Link Files that were discussed in Chapter 5. For example, we can provide a connection to the database in our main executable using Data Link File as shown below:

```
procedure TForm1.ConnectButtonClick(Sender: TObject);
begin
 //Set the Connection String using the Data Link File
 ADOConnection1.ConnectionString :=
  'FILE NAME=' + DataLinkDir() + '\NWind.udl';
//Open datasets linked with ADOConnection1
 ADOConnection1.Open;
end;
```

In order to make this code work properly on the user's computer, we need to create a Data Link File during the installation process. In this case, the DoExtraSteps procedure could look like this:

```
procedure DoExtraSteps;
begin
//Create the Data Link File
 CreateUDLFile(DataLinkDir() + '\NWind.udl',
  'Microsoft.Jet.OLEDB.4.0', 'data\northwind.mdb');
end;
```

Note that in the Data Link File we can refer to both absolute and relative paths to point to the database file. It should also be mentioned that creating Data Link Files during installation is preferable to simply copying *.udl files, because the default location for them on the user's computer might differ from the default location on the software developer's computer.

It should be mentioned that if we have created a client/server application, we may need to supply database files that can be deployed on the database server as is or by running a SQL script.

Conclusion

In this chapter, we discussed how we can create installation applications. We have seen how to install MDAC, when and how to install DCOM, and how to create an installation application using InstallShield Express, which comes with Delphi. Now we know that:

- Generally speaking, an application ready for deployment consists of one or more executable files, other files used by the application (for example, data files, help files, VCL packages, resource DLLs, and so on), third-party libraries used by the application, including data access libraries, and files and software that are not used by the application directly but are necessary for setting up the database environment (for example, scripts for creating database objects, etc.).

- To make our Delphi ADO applications work correctly on a user's computer, the Microsoft Data Access Components should be installed. These, in turn, require DCOM to be installed.

- An installation application, as a rule, copies files (*.exe, *.ocx, *.dll, *.hlp, fonts, data files, etc.) to appropriate directories of the user's hard disk; modifies the System Registry, Windows Start menu, and environment variables; creates program groups and icons; and restarts Windows if necessary.

- To create an installation application, we can use InstallShield Express that comes with Delphi. However, it does not provide support for MDAC installation.

- To test the installation application, it is better to run it at a computer containing just Windows.

- In the case of data that is accessed through the ODBC drivers, we can use ODBC API, create appropriate Registry keys, or use the ODBCCONF utility that comes with MDAC.

- For client/server applications, database files or appropriate scripts for creating database objects may be supplied and deployed.

This chapter ends our tour of traditional desktop and client/server database applications.

The following three chapters are devoted to distributed computing. In these chapters, we will discuss when and why we need to use this technology, general concepts, and how it is implemented in Windows DNA-based applications. Then we will discuss applications that use ADO Remote Data Services objects (RDS), and how to create distributed ADO applications using MIDAS—the Borland technology for creating multi-tier applications implemented in Delphi on the VCL level. The remaining chapters discuss ADO applications and Microsoft Transaction Server.

INTRODUCTION TO DISTRIBUTED COMPUTING

In previous chapters, we saw the "traditional" database applications, which are also called *two-tiered* applications. This term means that these applications consist of two distinct parts. One is the database server that provides data services, and the other consists of client applications that provide presentation services, i.e., they present data to the users and interact with them.

Here we will discuss another type of database application—*three-tiered* applications, also called *distributed* applications. In this chapter, we will learn the fundamentals of distributed computing and the general concepts of Windows DNA—Distributed interNet Applications, Microsoft's application development model for the Windows platform. We will also provide a brief description of some particular implementations of the Delphi ADO distributed applications and show how they comply with the Windows DNA concepts.

In the next several chapters, we will see some particular implementations of the Delphi ADO distributed applications, and discuss the implementation details of them.

We will begin with a discussion of distributed computing basics and then move to an introduction of Windows DNA.

Distributed Computing Basics

In this section, we describe when and why multi-tiered applications are preferred over client/server applications, their components, and what the components of such applications are responsible for. Here we do not provide detailed descriptions of the particular three-tier system implementations—these are covered in the next three chapters.

Limitations of Client/Server Applications

Before discussing the general concepts of multi-tier applications in general and Windows DNA architecture, let's look more closely at the "classic" client/server two-tiered database applications.

As we already know from previous chapters (such as Chapter 1), such applications consist of two parts, or tiers—the database server and the client application. We know that the database server is responsible for storing and maintaining data and user-defined business rules that may be implemented in stored procedures, triggers, constraints, and other database objects. In other words, the database server provides both data services and business services. The following diagram shows the two-tiered application architecture:

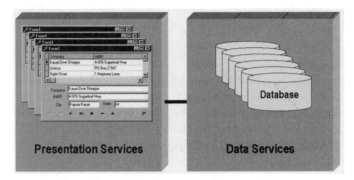

Despite its being widely used for many years, this approach does have limitations, mainly that two-tiered applications could not fully control their critical resources, i.e., resources that are valuable and are required by the application for its reliable functioning. Examples of such resources are database connections and transactions.

In the two-tiered client/server system, the critical application resources can be directly accessed by clients, who can use them any time they wish. That's why it is almost impossible to protect such resources from unexpected client behavior. For example, one of the clients may execute a query that takes up most of the resources of the database server for a long time, making it almost impossible for other clients to work with the data while such a query is executing. This allows any client to put all information systems in an inoperable state, either by accident or on purpose.

Other problems are not so significant, but they also should be taken into account. As we have already mentioned, in a traditional client/server system the business rules can be implemented in database objects, such as triggers, stored procedures, and constraints. In this case, we often cannot debug the server code as easily as the Delphi code. In most cases, writing business rules in this way is similar to coding in old programming languages and legacy operation systems without a development environment. This makes writing and testing such code a time-consuming process.

Additionally, the client application can contain code for data validation and data processing (see Chapter 11 for more details). Here we need to implement data validation and other "client" business rules in all client applications that could be used with this database, and prevent any other way of database access except using these applications. In this case, such applications are called *trusted* applications.

To solve some of the problems discussed above, we can create multi-tier applications. In the next section, we discuss the general concepts of Windows DNA and how we can solve these problems by using this architecture.

Multi-Tier Applications and Windows DNA

Windows DNA is an architecture for creating three-tiered Windows applications. They consist of the following logical parts:

- The presentation services tier (also called *thin clients*)
- The business services tier (also called middle tier)
- The data services tier (typically, the database)

Physically, each part of the Windows DNA applications can be implemented on one or more computers, and vice versa. In some implementations, two or even three logical tiers could be located on the same computer. The following diagram shows the three-tiered Windows DNA applications architecture:

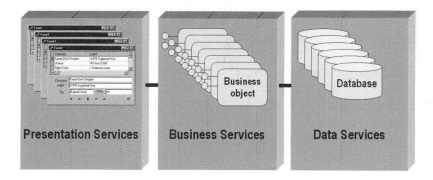

Let's look at each tier in more detail and outline its most significant features.

Presentation Services

The presentation services tier is responsible for interaction with the user, sending the user-supplied data to the middle tier to process, receiving the results of this processing back from the business services, and, presenting them to the user. This tier can be implemented in a Web browser (called an HTML application) or as a standard Windows application.

Core elements of presentation services in Windows DNA are HTML and Dynamic HTML, ActiveX components, and Win32 API functions.

The presentation services can be either interactive or non-interactive.

- The *interactive* presentation services provide feedback to the user immediately after user input. Such services could be implemented, for example, in Delphi applications or as a JavaScript code included into the HTML page and interpreted inside a Web browser.

- The *non-interactive* presentation services provide user feedback only after sending a request to the middle tier and receiving a response from it.

As a rule, if a client is able to download business objects responsible for data validation on a property level and use them, the presentation services implemented in it are interactive. In this case, such a client can check the validity not only of the entire database record but also of a single database field.

Since this book is about Delphi, we will discuss only interactive Windows DNA presentation services.

Business Services

The business services tier is responsible for receiving data from the presentation tier, interacting with the data services to carry out the business operations (for example, processing an order or calculating accounting balance), and providing the results of this business operations to the presentation tier.

This tier could be implemented in the form of business objects that can be created inside applications and libraries. Some business objects can use database access to the data service tier using the Microsoft Universal Data Access (see the introduction to this topic in Chapter 2). This includes the usage of OLE DB and ADO. The core technologies to implement business services are:

- Internet Information Server (IIS), which hosts Web applications and business objects
- Microsoft Message Queue Services (MSMQ), which allows creating applications with asynchronously executing components
- Microsoft Transaction Server (MTS), which allows creating applications with transactions that span components and databases

In Windows 2000, the application services such as MTS and MSMQ are now part of COM+, which is a core element of this platform. The services currently implemented in Internet Information Server are also a core part of the Windows 2000 Server operating system and are called Internet Information Services.

Data Services

The data services tier is responsible for storing and retrieving data, and maintaining data integrity. In other words, data services perform tasks typical for database servers. Core elements of data services in Windows DNA are:

- Microsoft SQL Server for storing relational and non-relational data
- Microsoft Universal Data Access as a mechanism to access this data
- Microsoft Exchange Server for providing document and message workflow through the enterprise

As you can see, the data services could be implemented not only in the form of database servers, but also in the form of file system, e-mail folders, etc. (as with the client/server architecture, this really depends on the OLE DB provider selected).

Business Objects in Brief

In Windows DNA applications, unlike client/server applications, clients cannot directly access critical resources, such as database connections. Instead, clients send requests to special trusted business objects. These objects can perform the business operations according to these requests, and only these objects, not clients, can use critical resources. For example, if such an object is designed for processing orders, it must find the ordered item in a stock database table, mark an appropriate item as unavailable, calculate payments, and add another record to the orders database table.

Business objects use critical resources in a trusted way. Therefore, Windows DNA applications could control those resources all the time they are running, thus making their work stable. It should be noted that before a business object can perform any business operation, it should identify the client that has sent a request, check if the client has the rights to request this business operation, and verify the client's request syntax and data.

To reduce the probability of generating improper requests by clients, Windows DNA applications can use another special type of business objects that help clients to generate proper requests. For example, such objects can contain data that is necessary for the client to create its requests, e.g., results of executing database queries or some validation code. In some cases, such objects can be downloaded from the middle tier and executed on the client.

In the Microsoft article "Designing and Building MS Windows DNA Applications" (Frank E. Redmond III, Microsoft Corporation, June 1999; see Microsoft's MSDN Web site), two terms were introduced—*emissaries* (objects containing data for client needs, perhaps along with some validation rules) and *executants* (objects performing business operations). We think these terms adequately describe different types of business objects, so we will use them through this and following chapters.

Introduction to COM Objects

We have already said that business services are implemented as COM servers in Windows DNA applications. Here we will provide a brief description of what they are.

The *Component Object Model* (COM) is a binary standard that defines how objects are created and destroyed and how they interact with each other. If an application follows the COM standard, it can communicate with other applications executing in different address space and on different computers. To be able to use COM servers on other computers, we rely on *Distributed COM* (DCOM), a COM extension that allows the component technology to work across networks and the Internet.

Because it is a binary standard, COM is language independent, meaning that COM servers can be created with any programming language including Delphi.

The fundamental COM concept is the interface that is a collection of logically related methods. All COM interfaces are descendants of the IUnknown interface. In Delphi, the IUnknown interface is defined the following way:

```
IUnknown = interface
  ['{00000000-0000-0000-C000-000000000046}']
  function QueryInterface(const IID: TGUID; out Obj): HResult; stdcall;
  function _AddRef: Integer; stdcall;
  function _Release: Integer; stdcall;
end;
```

This interface exposes three methods. The first of them is the QueryInterface method that is used to ask the COM object whether it supports a particular interface. The second and third methods of this interface, _AddRef and _Release, are used for incrementing and decrementing a reference counter for an object; when this reference counter become zero, the COM object is destroyed by the operation system.

Any other interfaces that are descendants of the IUnknown interface expose these three methods and some additional specific methods. For example, besides these three methods, the IDispatch interface, which is a direct descendant of the IUnknown interface, exposes four additional methods necessary for the object to be an Automation server:

```
IDispatch = interface(IUnknown)
  ['{00020400-0000-0000-C000-000000000046}']
  function GetTypeInfoCount(out Count: Integer): HResult;
    stdcall;
  function GetTypeInfo(Index, LocaleID: Integer;
    out TypeInfo): HResult; stdcall;
  function GetIDsOfNames(const IID: TGUID; Names: Pointer;
    NameCount, LocaleID: Integer; DispIDs: Pointer): HResult;
    stdcall;
  function Invoke(DispID: Integer; const IID: TGUID;
    LocaleID: Integer;
    Flags: Word; var Params; VarResult, ExcepInfo,
    ArgErr: Pointer): HResult; stdcall;
end;
```

The first of these methods, GetTypeInfoCount, determines whether there is type information available for this interface. The second one, GetTypeInfo, retrieves the type information for this interface if the previous method returns successful. The third method, GetIDsOfNames, converts text names of properties and methods (including arguments) to their identifiers, while the fourth method, Invoke, calls a method or accesses a property in this interface.

Finally, an interface for the custom automation object that is created in this chapter exposes all methods of the IDispatch interface, along with custom methods and properties that we have defined for this custom object:

```
IrdsO = interface(IDispatch)
  ['{D89C2CCD-A738-11D3-B008-0000E8540471}']
  function  Get_Data: _Recordset; safecall;
  property Data: _Recordset read Get_Data;
end;
```

A COM interface defines the parameter types and the syntax for each of its methods, and the COM class provides an implementation for each method of the interface.

COM servers can be executables or dynamic-link libraries that implement one or more COM classes.

All COM servers, classes, and interfaces have a Globally Unique Identifier (GUID). The GUID for an interface is also called an IID—interface identifier (we can see references to IIDs in the definitions of the methods in the code above). A GUID is a 128-bit number that is unique for each COM server, class, or interface. It is the uniqueness of the GUID that is the base of all COM functionality.

Most modern development tools provide wizards for creating COM servers. In Delphi, such a wizard is based on creating a type library that describes COM classes, interfaces, methods, and their parameters, along with a COM class itself (for brief introduction to the concept of type libraries, refer to Chapter 15). Editing the type library results in generating method templates to which we must add the code that implements the real functionality of the method.

Windows DNA Requirements

It is essential to look at reliability issues in Windows DNA applications. We can say that an application is *reliable* if it provides correct results in a multi user environment. Let's consider an example. Imagine two users are trying to order the same unique item from stock. Both clients read the stock database and see that this item is available. They then process the order, providing the necessary financial information, and mark this item as already ordered. Now we have two orders and two payments for a single item from different customers. Obviously such a result is not correct.

To ensure correct results, business objects must perform their operations similar to performing database transactions in server DBMS. In Chapter 1, we discussed database transactions. If we extend a database transaction concept into a non-database world, we could say that a transaction is a set of operations that must be either executed as one unit or not executed at all. Similar to database transaction, the non-database one must also satisfy ACID (atomicity, consistency, isolation, and durability) requirements.

In Windows DNA, transactions are considered critical resources, as they lock records or other resources. This means that clients must not be able to manipulate them directly.

Applications critical for business must be capable of serving client requests any time they need. Such availability depends on both hardware and software availability.

To increase it, we need to create fail-over safe applications, and one of the ways to do this is to use doubling of resources, services, and business objects, and organize this doubling conveniently for the client.

Using Microsoft Message Queue Services, which repeatedly tries to forward each queued message to its destination until either successful delivery or a timeout, we can increase the availability of Windows DNA applications. However, using MSMQ is outside the scope of the book.

The next point we need to mention is that Windows DNA applications should be *scalable*. This means that we need to make them able to serve more and more clients by simply adding resources so the average time of processing a transaction does not grow.

To satisfy the demands of scalability, we need to use resources as little as possible. For example, we need to avoid including any user or network interaction into transactions, hold resources only when they are needed and release them as soon as possible, and make resources available as much as possible (for example, by using resource pooling or sharing). This is possible when we use Microsoft Transaction Server to manage resources and business objects.

Providing load balancing of resources is also desirable for application scalability. This is possible if we use MSMQ for communication between business objects. By using these services, we can simply add servers for processing increasing amount of requests. If several servers process a shared queue of client requests, they are dynamically load-balanced. With MSMQ, each server processes requests from the queue as fast as possible, so it is impossible for one server to be overloaded while another server is waiting for work. However, providing load balancing can be implemented in different ways besides using MSMQ; we will discuss these later in this chapter.

The final Windows DNA applications requirement is to maximize its *interoperability*. That means that this application should be able to use resources and data on other platforms.

Windows DNA 2000

The next step in developing Windows DNA ideas is the concept of Windows DNA 2000, the distributed applications based on the Windows 2000 operating systems family. The core idea of this concept is transforming Web servers from simple HTML page suppliers to Web services that communicate with each other by sending XML messages.

XML is *Extensible Markup Language*, a platform-independent standard for structured data exchange between applications. XML is optimized for delivery over the Web that ensures that structured data will be uniform and independent of applications, vendors, or platforms.

Similar to HTML, an XML source is made up of XML elements, each of which consists of the information between the start and end tags. However, XML allows any set of tags (unlike HTML, which contains a fixed set of tags), and each tag indicates the meaning of the text between tags (in HTML, tags indicate text formatting). The meaning of the tags is defined by the author of the XML document, and is described in the Document Type Definition (DTD) file that should come with the XML data.

A simple example of an XML document is shown below:

```
<?xml version="1.0" ?>
<STAFF xmlns="x-schema:STAFF.DTD">
<employee>
  <name>
    <lastname>Davolio</lastname>
    <firstname>Nancy</firstname>
    <titleof>Ms.</titleof>
  </name>
  <addressinfo>
    <address>507 - 20th Ave. E.</address>
    <city>Seattle</city>
    <region>WA</region>
    <postalcode>98122</postalcode>
    <country>98122</country>
  </addressinfo>
</employee>
```

XML-exchanging services can be accessed through SOAP—*Simple Object Access Protocol*—based on XML/HTTP (HTTP is *HyperText Transfer Protocol* used for sending HTML pages over the Internet), which is independent from platforms, programming languages, and object models. SOAP is a distributed object protocol that, like DCOM, allows clients to call methods on servers. However, it defines standard XML-based conventions for representing requests, responses, and the information contained in them. This allows sending SOAP messages inside standard HTTP requests, which makes it simple to use them over the Internet. The following diagram shows how applications exchange with SOAP messages:

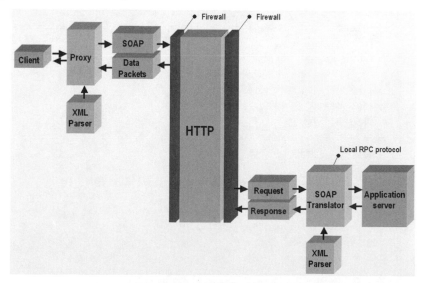

We need to mention that at the time of this writing, SOAP is a protocol that is not yet implemented and still exists only as a specification. You can find details about SOAP at the following sites:

- http://msdn.microsoft.com/xml
- http://www.develop.com/soap

You can find the draft specification of the SOAP protocol at the following sites:

- http://msdn.microsoft.com/xml/general/soaptemplate.asp
- http://www.ietf.org/internet-drafts/draft-box-http-soap-01.txt

Nowadays, XML is an integral part of the Windows DNA. It is used for data delivery and exchange between multiple tiers. Being a platform- and language-independent standard, XML allows us to create unique data formats for specific applications and is an ideal format for server-to-server transfer of structured data. This makes it possible to begin developing the BizTalk Framework, which is a platform-independent e-commerce framework for information exchange between applications and over the Internet. This framework is based on the XML language and includes design tools to implement an XML schema and a set of XML tags used in messages sent between applications over the Internet. Along with providing schemas for documents to exchange, BizTalk also provides a framework for describing data handling rules in order to satisfy industrial standards of processing data.

XML schemas are definitions of common formats for exchanging data among applications. They are also built with XML and contain information about the required tags, structure, and data types of the XML document, as well as relationships between elements in the document.

The XML schema for the XML document shown above may look like the following:

```
<?xml version ="1.0"?>
<Schema name = "STAFF.DTD"
 xmlns = "urn:schemas-microsoft-com:xml-data"
 xmlns:dt = "urn:schemas-microsoft-com:datatypes">
 <ElementType name = "STAFF" content = "eltOnly" order = "seq">
 <element type = "employee" minOccurs = "1" maxOccurs = "*"/>
</ElementType>
 <ElementType name = "employee" content = "eltOnly" order = "seq">
  <element type = "name"/>
  <element type = "addressinfo"/>
 </ElementType>
 <ElementType name = "name" content = "eltOnly"/> order = "seq">
  <element type = "lastname"/>
  <element type = "firstname"/>
  <element type = "titleof"/>
 </ElementType>
 <ElementType name = "addressinfo" content = "eltOnly"/> order = "seq">
  <element type = "address"/>
  <element type = "city"/>
  <element type = "region"/>
```

```
  <element type = "postalcode"/>
  <element type = "country"/>
</ElementType>
<ElementType name = "lastname" content = "textOnly"/>
<ElementType name = "firstname" content = "textOnly"/>
<ElementType name = "titleof" content = "textOnly"/>
<ElementType name = "address" content = "textOnly"/>
<ElementType name = "city" content = "textOnly"/>
<ElementType name = "postalcode" content = "textOnly"/>
<ElementType name = "country" content = "textOnly"/>

</Schema>
```

You can find details on BizTalk and XML schemas at the following Web sites:

- http://msdn.microsoft.com/xml

- http://www.microsoft.com/industry/biztalk/developers/xml/xml.stm

- http://www.xml.com/

- http://www.xmltree.com/

- http://www.marketsite.net/

These schemas are developed and provided by many companies and groups of companies within different industries and are based on the Microsoft BizTalk Framework, which provides a specification for implementing XML schemas. The draft version of this specification can be found at: http://www.biztalk.org.

To programmatically access the structure and data contained in an XML document, we need to use the XML Document Object Model (DOM) that is based on an in-memory tree representation of the XML document and defines the programmatic interface (including the names of the methods and properties).

Another key part of Windows DNA is Collaboration Data Objects (CDO), which allow us to build collaborative Web server applications on Microsoft Exchange Server. These libraries contain COM classes accessible through CDO object model form applications created with scripting languages (e.g., VBScript or JavaScript), and development tools with COM support (e.g., Delphi). However, using CDO is out of the scope of this book.

The next key part of Windows DNA 2000 is the Active Directory services that support a wide range of protocols and data formats. The Active Directory is a service that integrates the Internet concept of a namespace with the operating system's directory services, thus allowing enterprises to unify and manage the multiple namespaces in the heterogeneous software and hardware environments of corporate networks. It uses the Lightweight Directory Access Protocol (LDAP) as its core protocol and can work across operating system boundaries, integrating multiple namespaces. Active Directory can manage application-specific directories. This results in a high level of interoperability required for heterogeneous networks. You can find more details about LDAP at the following sites:

- `http://msdn.microsoft.com/library/backgrnd/html/msdn_windnawp.html`
- `http://msdn.microsoft.com/library/backgrnd/html/dnafaq.htm`

We have discussed the main factors to be taken into account when building Windows DNA applications. Now let's look at how such applications can be implemented with Delphi and ADO.

Delphi Windows DNA Applications

There are many different ways to make a Windows DNA application. In this book, we will discuss the following three major types:

- Applications that use Remote Data Services, which comes with the Microsoft Data Access Components
- Multi-tier applications that use the Borland MIDAS (Multi-tier Distributed Application Services Suite) technology to provide fail-over safe applications
- Transactional applications that use Microsoft Transaction Server to provide reliability of the distributed applications

Each of these three technologies will be described in detail in the following chapters. Here we will only discuss some of their basic concepts.

RDS-Based Applications

Remote Data Service (RDS) is a component that comes as part of Microsoft Data Access Components. RDS enables applications to access OLE DB providers, running either on remote machines or in separate processes on the same machine.

Let's look at how the parts of RDS-based applications map to the different tiers of Windows DNA applications.

The possibility of remote access to OLE DB providers means that by using RDS we can implement business objects that directly access databases by a trusted way (i.e., data access servers that interact with databases directly using OLE DB). These business objects (implemented in COM objects) play the role of emissaries. RDS provides a predefined object—RDS.DataFactory—that is used to perform standard operations of sending and receiving recordsets, but we can also create custom RDS business objects to perform some extra operations.

An RDS client plays the role of presentation tier that could interact with business objects. This presentation tier can be interactive, because RDS clients receive copies of recordsets from business objects for editing and sending them back. These recordsets, also called disconnected recordsets, play the role of emissaries in the distributed application.

The following diagram shows the typical architecture of an RDS-based application:

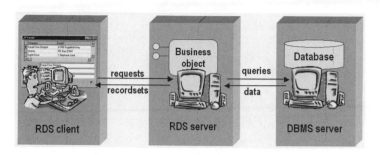

In RDS-based applications, critical resources such as database connections and database transactions are inaccessible from the client directly and satisfy the Windows DNA requirements. In addition, client applications could serve even if the database connection in the data access server is temporary lost. The server also might shut down and restart again on client demand. This increases the availability of the entire application.

We will show in detail how to create RDS clients and custom business objects in the next chapter.

The next technology we will discuss is Borland MIDAS. This technology also allows us to create Windows DNA applications; unlike RDS, however, MIDAS provides some additional functionality to make these applications reliable, scalable, and interoperable.

Borland MIDAS Applications

MIDAS (Multi-tier Distributed Application Services Suite) is a technology for creating data access servers and their clients as Automation servers and Automation controllers, or, in some cases, CORBA (Common Object Request Broker Architecture) servers and clients. MIDAS is implemented in Delphi VCL components and classes, along with some other services. Let's look at how the parts of the MIDAS application map to the Windows DNA tiers.

We have already noted that, in terms of Windows DNA, the data access servers implement the business objects for a business services tier that supplies the clients with data, and their clients play the role of presentation services tier.

These servers and clients send (or *marshal*) datasets between each other back and forth, in order to provide a way to make presentation services interactive.

The MIDAS application architecture is shown in the figure below:

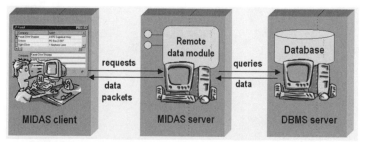

MIDAS servers can play the role of both executant and emissary business objects. They are trusted objects, so they can directly use database connections and database transactions, being real database clients (in this book, we will discuss MIDAS servers that use ADO to access the data services tier).

We definitely could say that the core idea of MIDAS (similar to the idea of ADO and RDS) is using COM and Automation. COM supports a wide list of possible data types. However, if we look through the supported types, we definitely will not find any "dataset" types there. By "dataset type" we mean a non-existent data type which can contain, for example, a result of a database query, i.e., an unpredictable number of rows with an unpredictable number of columns, which have unpredictable data types.

Considering this, we can say that MIDAS is a technology that allows us to convert datasets into COM-compatible data types, use these converted data in the usual way through DCOM, and make a backward conversion. In applications created with Delphi 5, MIDAS data packets can be passed in XML format, which is an industrial standard of data exchange between applications.

Therefore, we can say that we have two types of datasets. There are "real" (or original) datasets that are situated in a data access server process, and client datasets, which are the result of this complex marshalling and are situated in a "thin" client process. Client datasets are local, in-memory copies of the "real" dataset used for user access. We can say that they play the role of emissaries.

Having discussed the basic ideas of MIDAS applications in general, let's note what MIDAS could provide to satisfy the availability demand of Windows DNA.

We have already said in the previous section that availability means that the application (including business objects) must serve client requests any time they need. To make this possible, we need to create fail-over safe applications. In MIDAS, this can be implemented by creating several MIDAS servers with the same functionality that could easily replace each other. To provide fail-over safety, we also need a mechanism to reconnect a client to another server if the current server that attends this client fails. This mechanism can be implemented in special services called directory services, or object brokers (this is not the same core Directory Services implemented in the Windows operating system), separate, or implemented in a client application. Such services accept client requests to seek a server (when the server is required the first time after the client has started, or when a client has "lost" the server it was already connected to) and find an appropriate server for this client. The following diagram shows how the directory service is used in MIDAS applications:

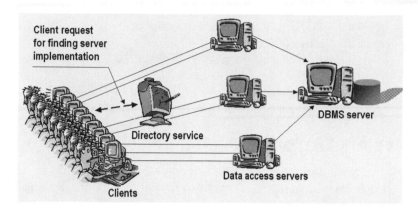

Using the concept of directory services allows MIDAS applications to satisfy the demand of scalability, because directory services can also provide load balancing for such applications. This means that the directory service can split clients almost equally between several servers.

If we need to make MIDAS applications satisfy the interoperability demand of the Windows DNA, we can use a special type of application called a WebMIDAS application. In these applications, the business services tier is complex; it contains the data access servers and their clients that generate XML output interpreted as a JavaScript code by a special parsing service. This JavaScript code, which contains a data snapshot and some data validation rules, is interpreted by JavaScript-enabled Web browsers that take the role of the presentation service tier. The following diagram shows the architecture of a WebMIDAS application:

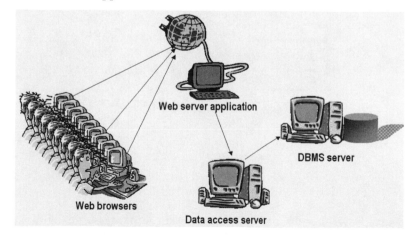

It is essential that the presentation services in WebMIDAS applications are both interoperable (since JavaScript-enabled browsers are available for several platforms, e.g., Windows, Solaris, Digital UNIX, Red Hat Linux, etc.) and interactive (they allow data validation without connecting to the business service tier). It is also essential that generating XML output makes it possible to create applications that are compliant with Windows DNA 2000 concepts.

The details of implementation of the MIDAS applications are discussed in Chapter 21.

The next technology that is widely used in Windows DNA applications is the Microsoft Transaction Server, which is discussed below.

Distributed Applications with MTS Objects

The reliability requirement of Windows DNA applications means that business operations must be performed similar to performing database transactions in server DBMSs. In other words, they must be considered as a transaction in the wider sense (for example, as a transaction including non-database operations). To manage such operations, Microsoft recommends using Microsoft Transaction Server.

MTS objects are in-process Automation servers. They can be executed in a client application address space and, as a rule, play the role of emissaries. However, most of the time, they are executed in an address space of an MTS executable (mtx.exe); in this case, they can play a role of both emissaries and executants. For example, some of them could manage datasets or process database transactions (and could be built the same way as MIDAS data access servers), and some of them could implement a transaction that consists of calling methods of other objects. The following diagram shows how the MTS objects can interact with each other:

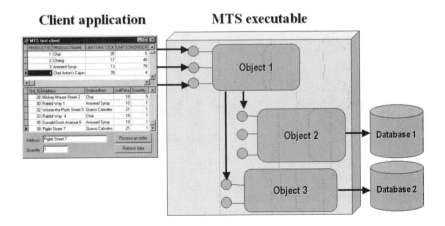

We have already said that to satisfy the demands of scalability, we need to use resources as little as possible. This can be done by using resource pooling or sharing, which is possible with objects operated by Microsoft Transaction Server.

We will show how to create MTS objects using Delphi components and classes in conjunction with ADO in Chapter 22.

Conclusion

In this chapter, we discussed the reasons for using distributed computing in business-critical applications. We have also described the basic concepts of Windows DNA—Distributed interNet Applications. Now we know that:

■ Windows DNA applications consist of three logical tiers: presentation services, business services (called also middle tier), and data services.

■ The presentation services tier is responsible for getting information from the user and sending it to the business services tier to process, receiving the results of this processing from the business services tier, and presenting these results to the user.

■ The business services tier is responsible for receiving user input from the presentation tier, interacting with the data services tier to perform the business operations, and returning their results to the presentation tier.

■ The data services tier is responsible for storing and retrieving data, and maintaining data integrity.

■ In Windows DNA applications, unlike ordinary client/server systems, clients cannot directly access critical resources. Instead, clients send requests to special trusted business objects that are part of the business services tier.

■ To make Windows DNA applications *reliable*, business objects must perform their operations as transactions that are also considered critical resources; this means that client must not be able to manipulate them directly.

■ Windows DNA applications should be *scalable,* meaning that they must be able to serve more and more clients by simply adding resources.

■ The *interoperability* of Windows DNA applications means that this application should be able to use resources and data on other platforms, as well as applications written with different development tools.

We have also reviewed different architectures of distributed systems, and discussed the types of enterprises on which they can be used. Now we know that:

■ Remote Data Services is a component that comes with MDAC and enables applications to access OLE DB providers, running on remote machines. This makes it possible to create trusted business objects serving as data access servers that directly access databases and send recordsets to RDS clients.

■ MIDAS (Multi-tier Distributed Application Services Suite) is a technology of creating data access servers and their clients as Automation servers and Automation controllers implemented in Delphi VCL components and classes.

■ To make MIDAS applications satisfy the availability demand of Windows DNA, we need to create fail-over safe applications that can be implemented by creating several MIDAS servers with the same functionality, and use directory services. Using directory services also allows MIDAS applications to satisfy the demand of scalability, because directory services can also provide load balancing for this application.

- If we need to make MIDAS applications satisfying the interoperability demand of the Windows DNA and compliant with Windows DNA 2000 concepts, we can use WebMIDAS applications.

- To satisfy the demands of reliability and scalability of Windows DNA applications, we can use Microsoft Transaction Server (MTS) to manage distributed and non-database transactions and to provide resource pooling and sharing.

The following three chapters discuss the different ways of creating distributed Delphi applications. The next chapter covers RDS applications that use remote OLE DB data sources.

CREATING RDS-BASED APPLICATIONS

20

In the previous chapter, we discussed the basic concepts of Windows DNA, an architecture describing three-tiered applications implemented on the Windows platform. We also discussed different technologies that could be used to implement Windows DNA applications.

This chapter is devoted to one of these particular technologies—Remote Data Service (RDS)—which is part of Microsoft Data Access Objects, and enables applications to access OLE DB providers that are running on remote machines. With RDS, we can use remote business objects that can access databases available on computers where these objects are instantiated, and supply other applications with the results of querying them. Such business objects are called *data access servers*. These servers can send recordsets obtained from databases that are available for them to the client applications, where they can be manipulated, edited, and sent back.

We will begin with an introduction of RDS concepts in order to provide understanding of this technology.

The RDS Basics

Having already discussed the Windows DNA applications architecture and its features, we know that such applications require keeping most of the application logic at the business service tier, while the client applications, where users manipulate and edit data, provide only the local validation of the data. This means that when creating a Windows DNA application, we need to follow the programming model based on implementing access to the data services in a business object in a middle tier. The RDS provides us with such a programming model, as it implements this concept. RDS allows us to create "thin" clients that use default or custom business objects (or data access servers) implemented in COM servers. These services use the Universal Data Access mechanisms (OLE DB and ADO) to work with data services.

Before discussing the implementation details of RDS-based applications, let's look at how they work in general.

How the RDS Application Works

The typical scenario of using the RDS application may look like this:

- A user runs a client application (implemented as a Windows executable or an HTML application), and creates a request for connection to the business object on the remote computer.

- If the request is correct, an instance of the business object is created on the specified remote computer (it plays the role of *executant*).

- Now the user can send a request containing a query and a connect string to this business object. Note that the connection string will be used by the <u>remote</u> business object, so it must refer to the data sources available on the <u>remote</u> computer. There is no need to make this connection string valid for the computer on which the client application is running, or define appropriate data sources; generally, they are unavailable to the computers on which client applications are running.

- The remote business object connects to a database using the connection string specified in the user request, and, being an *executant*, tries to execute a user query.

- If the query is valid and returns a recordset, the remote business object sends it back to the client application for processing.

- The client application receives the recordset (which plays the role of *emissary* of this business object in a client application) and presents it to the user.

- The user edits the presented data according to his needs.

- Having finished editing the data, the user creates a request to the remote business object to receive the modified records and send them back to the database.

- The business object receives the modified records and tries to upload them to the database server. If the modified records have not been changed by another user since they were downloaded, and satisfy the data integrity rules, all of them will be updated.

- If some records the business object has received from a client application were changed by other users, or do not satisfy the database referential integrity rules, no updates will be made, and an error (in the form of an OLE exception) will occur in the client application. As a rule, in three-tier systems, database locks are not used (otherwise, the user input will be part of a transaction that broke the rules of Windows DNA architecture), so it is quite possible that several users could edit the same records simultaneously. It should be mentioned that starting with MDAC 2.1, the client application theoretically can "know" which particular rows failed to be updated; this information is stored in an array available only through low-level OLE DB interfaces. Analyzing this array requires a lot of OLE DB calls and makes the code more complex than the average ADO application code. Using OLE DB interfaces is out of the scope of this book.

The scenario described above is schematically shown in the diagram below:

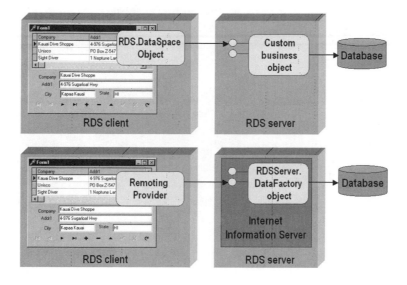

It should be mentioned that both client and server use in-memory data caching, which reduces the number of requests between different tiers of the application.

There can be different variations of this scenario. For example, the client application can save a received recordset to a file and retrieve it later, implementing a briefcase model. Sometimes it is necessary to implement additional methods in a business object. For example, we may need to process collisions that occur when several clients edit the same data in a different way.

It is essential in RDS-based applications that client and server exchange recordsets in three ways. The first way is to use DCOM directly, and the second way is to use the HTTP or HTTPS (secure HTTP) protocol. In the second case, the business object is instantiated inside the Internet Information Server process (and, of course, the RDS-based application requires IIS to be running). The third one is to use both the presentation tier and middle tier on the same computer without any protocols.

Having discussed the basic scenario of processing data in RDS-based applications, we can discuss the objects that are used in such applications.

The RDS Programming Model

The RDS programming model is based on several objects, both in a client application and in a data access server. Here we will discuss them in more detail. We will begin with the client-side objects of RDS-based applications.

The Client-Side Objects

On the client side, RDS uses the following objects:

- The RDS.DataSpace object is used by a client application to communicate with the data access server and to maintain sending recordsets between client and server. This object implements a part of a COM client (called a *proxy*) that is responsible for sending data between client and server (also called *marshaling*). If the HTTP protocol is used for communicating with the server, the server method call in this object is translated into an HTTP Post request with the name (or ProgID) of the COM server to be invoked, the method name, and all input parameters. The output parameters and return values of the called method are transported back as the response to this request. On the client, these parameters and values are unpackaged back into original data types and handled by a client application.

- The client cursor engine provides client-side manipulation of resulting sets; RDS uses it to buffer remote recordsets. In addition, the client cursor engine maintains client updates in its cache. To do this, it contains information about row counts, primary and secondary keys, column names, and timestamps, as well as the actual table data itself. It also provides the mechanism to send updates as a batch to the server with minimum network traffic, by sending only the modified records.

- The OLE DB Persistence provider can save a recordset into a binary stream and create a recordset from such a stream. The cursor engine object uses the OLE DB Persistence provider to send recordsets to the server.

- RDS.DataControl is also a client-side object that is an ActiveX control, which invokes the RDS.DataSpace and RDSServer.DataFactory objects and provides the means for visual controls to access the returned recordset object. This object can be used in Visual Basic and HTML applications (applications running in Microsoft Internet Explorer), so we will not use it in our examples.

The RDS.DataSpace object is the most important one of those listed above because it can be explicitly used in applications. It exposes the InternetTimeout property, which specifies the number of milliseconds to wait before a request times out, and the CreateObject method, which initiates creation of business object on a remote computer.

The CreateObject method of the RDS.DataSpace object accepts two parameters. The first is the ProgID of the business object, and the second is the URL (Uniform Resource Locator) of the computer where the business object will be instantiated (if using HTTP protocol) or the computer name (if using DCOM). If this value is empty, the object will be created locally as an in-process server if it is implemented in a dynamic-link library, or in a separate process if it is implemented as an executable file.

As we can see, the RDS.DataSpace object is used to communicate with the objects on a server side.

The Server-Side Objects

On the server side, RDS uses the following objects:

- The ADISAPI component is the RDS server-side object (also called a *stub*) that receives requests generated by the RDS.DataSpace object when using the HTTP protocol. Inside the address space of the Internet Information Server, it instantiates the business object whose ProgID is specified in the client request and calls the specified method. It implements an HTTP parser, which unpackages the data packets into individual parameters necessary for the method call and also packages the return values and out parameters into data packets. It also initiates converting recordsets to binary streams and back with the help of the OLE DB Persistence provider.

- Business objects are the main components on the server side. They are implemented as COM Automation objects that the client-side components access remotely. These objects typically use ADO to query/update the underlying databases. If such an object is invoked using the HTTP protocol by the RDS.DataSpace object, it exists only when the called method is executed, and is released after the executing method is finished.

- The RDSServer.DataFactory object is a default business object that comes with RDS. It provides read/write access to SQL-based OLE DB data sources but does not contain any logic for data validation or other business rules. We can either use the default RDSServer.DataFactory business object or create a custom one, for example, to perform more complicated data access, validity checks, and so on.

- The Customization Handler component can be used to customize the behavior of the RDSServer.DataFactory object. We can either use the standard MSDFMAP.Handler handler or create our own custom handlers that can intercept calls to RDSServer.DataFactory and execute some custom logic by implementing the IDataFactoryHandler COM interface. However, writing customization handlers is out of the scope of this book.

The RDS business objects are the most important ones in RDS applications, as they implement all business logic and data access in RDS-based applications.

The default business object—RDSServer.DataFactory—exposes the following methods that can be called remotely:

Method	Description
ConvertToString	Converts a recordset to a MIME (Multipurpose Internet Mail Extensions) string that represents the recordset data.
CreateRecordset	Creates an empty disconnected recordset.
Query	Sends an SQL query to the data source to return a recordset. Accepts two parameters—the connection string for database access and an SQL query text.
Refresh	Requeries the OLE DB data source and updates the query results.
SubmitChanges	Submits pending changes of the locally cached updatable recordset to the OLE DB data source.

After reviewing the client-side and server-side RDS objects, we need to discuss how to access remote OLE DB providers.

Remote Connection Issues

There are two ways to establish a remote connection with a business object. The first one is based on using the OLE DB Remoting Provider, and the second one uses the RDS.DataSpace object. Let's look at each method in more detail.

Using the OLE DB Remoting Provider

Using the OLE DB Remoting Provider (MS Remote) is called *implicit remoting*. To implement it in Delphi applications, we need to use the TADOConnection component with a connection string referring to this OLE DB provider. Another possible way of implementing the implicit remoting could be to use the RDS.DataControl object, but this is not a good choice for Delphi applications. This ActiveX control was implemented to be used in HTML applications, and that's why it takes a lot of code to make it work.

In MDAC 2.1, the OLE DB Remoting Provider is an OLE DB service provider that allows client applications to work with recordsets retrieved from a remote server as if they were on the local computer. This provider makes it possible to retrieve and update such recordsets.

Remote data providers are providers running either on another computer, or in a different process on the same computer as the client application. The Remoting Provider, which runs on another computer, communicates over the network using either DCOM or HTTP protocols.

The typical connection string for the OLE DB Remoting Provider looks like the following:

```
const CSTR=
      'Provider=MS Remote; Remote Server=http://MyServer;'    +
      'Remote Provider=SQLOLEDB;DSN=NorthWind;User ID=sa;'
```

In this example, we use the following parameters:

Parameter	Meaning
Remote Server	The name of the computer on which the RDSServer.DataFactory must be instantiated
Remote Provider	The OLE DB provider to access the database from the remote computer
DSN	The Data Source Name necessary to access the database from the remote computer
User ID	The User ID that will be used by the remote business object to login to the database

We will provide an example of how to use this OLE DB provider later in this chapter.

Customizing the RDSServer.DataFactory Behavior

Implicit remoting is based on using the RDSServer.DataFactory object to open and update recordsets. In this case, we may need to provide additional functionality for this object, for example, to add some checks. To do this, we need to use the RDS custom handler that makes it possible to customize RDSServer.DataFactory functionality by intercepting calls made on RDSServer.DataFactory methods for opening and updating recordsets. A custom handler is a COM object that implements the IDataFactoryHandler interface and is installed on the same machine as the RDSServer.DataFactory object. There may be several custom handlers installed on the same machine.

RDS 2.1 comes with a default handler whose behavior can be configured by using an MSDFMAP.INI file installed in the System directory on the server. This handler should be used to control the operations that the RDSServer.DataFactory object can execute on that server.

The typical MSDFMAP.INI file looks like this:

```
[connect default]
Access=ReadWrite

[sql default]
Sql=" "

[sql CustomerById]
Sql="SELECT * FROM Customers WHERE CustomerID = ?"

[connect AuthorDatabase]
Access=ReadOnly
Connect="DSN=MyLibraryInfo;UID=MyUserID;PWD=MyPassword"

[userlist AuthorDatabase]
Administrator=ReadWrite

[sql CustomerByCountry]
Sql="SELECT * FROM Customers WHERE Country = ?"
```

Each section header in the customization file consists of square brackets ([]) containing a type and parameter. The four section types are indicated by the literal strings connect, sql, userlist, or logs. The parameter is the literal string, the default, a user-specified identifier, or nothing.

Part	Description
Connect	This section modifies a connect string.
Sql	This section modifies an SQL query.
Userlist	This section modifies the access rights of a specific user.
Logs	This section specifies a log file that records operational errors.
default	This section is used if no identifier is specified or found.

If the string in a connection string or in an SQL query does not match the identifier in any connect or sql section header, and there is no connect or sql section header with a default parameter, then the client string is used without modification.

The connect section can contain a connect string that replaces the client connection string, or a default access entry that specifies the default read and write operations allowed on this connection.

A replacement connection string entry has the following syntax:

```
Connect=ConnectionString
```

where `ConnectionString` is a replacement for a client connection string.
A default access entry has the following syntax:

```
Access=AccessRights
```

`AccessRights` must have the following values:

- `NoAccess`—User cannot access the data source.
- `ReadOnly`—User can read the data source.
- `ReadWrite`—User can read or write the data source.

The sql section can contain a new SQL string that replaces the client query. The new SQL string may have parameters designated by the "?" character, which can be replaced by corresponding arguments in an identifier in the client query (the appropriate string looks like a function call).

For example, if the client query is

```
"CustomerByCountry('USA')"
```

the SQL section header is

```
[SQL CustomerByCountry]
```

and the new SQL section string is

```
"SELECT * FROM Customers WHERE Country = ?"
```

The MSDFMAP handler will generate the following query

```
"SELECT * FROM Customers WHERE Country = 'USA'"
```

and use this string to query the data source.
A replacement SQL string entry is of the form:

```
SQL=SQLString
```

where `SQLString` is a replacement for the client query.
The userlist section belongs to the connect section with the same section identifier parameter. This section can contain a user access entry, which specifies access rights

for the specified user and overrides the default access entry in the matching connect section. The user access has the following syntax:

```
userName= AccessRights
```

Here, `AccessRights` must have the same possible values as for the default access entry described above.

The logs section contains a log file entry, which specifies the name of a file that records errors during the operation of the RDSServer.DataFactory. The entry in this section must have the following syntax:

```
err= FileName
```

When using customization handlers, the client application must have a reference to it (in the connection string) in the form:

```
Handler=handlernameINIfilename
```

For example, if we use the default MSDFMAP.Handler and the default MSDFMAP.INI file that must be located in the Windows System directory, the following connection string contains the appropriate reference:

```
const CSTR=
    'Provider=MS Remote; Remote Server=http://MyServer;' +
    'Handler=msdfmap.handler,msdfmap.ini '              +
    'Remote Provider=SQLOLEDB; DSN=NorthWind; User ID=sa;'
```

It should be mentioned that we can prevent any connections to the RDSServer.DataFactory business object without using handlers. To do this, we need to set the handlerRequired value to 1 under the following Registry key at the server computer:

```
HKEY_LOCAL_MACHINE\SOFTWARE\Microsoft\DataFactory\HandlerInfo
```

Later in this chapter, we will provide an example of how to use the default customization handler.

Using the RDS.DataSpace Object

The second way to establish a remote connection with a business object is to use the RDS.DataSpace object; this is called *explicit remoting*. In Delphi applications, we need to use the TRDSConnection object that is a VCL wrapper around the RDS.DataSpace object. This component will be discussed later in this chapter.

As we already know, the RDS.DataSpace object can be used to invoke business objects. These objects can be written as COM Automation objects, so they must implement the IDispatch interface. As a rule, such a business object must implement methods that return a recordset to the client application. If the recordset must have read/write access on it, it must be opened with batch-optimistic locking. In addition, if a method of the business object accepts a disconnected recordset in order to apply updates to the database, it is necessary to create a new connection object, set it as the ActiveConnection property of the obtained recordset, and then call the UpdateBatch method.

We will provide examples of how to use the RDS.DataSpace object in Delphi applications and how to create a custom business object later in this chapter.

Having discussed in general what RDS is, what its main objects are, and how it works, we are now ready to look at how the RDS functionality is implemented in the Delphi TRDSConnection component. It is the last ADO Express component that will be discussed in this book.

The TRDSConnection Component

The TRDSConnection component is the VCL wrapper around an RDS.DataSpace object, and it must be used in a client application. In Delphi applications that are "thin" clients, this can be used instead of the TADOConnection component. If a TADODataSet component contains data received from a remote business object, its RDSConnection property could be set to the name of appropriate TRDSConnection component. Note that TRDSConnection can use either the RDS.DataFactory business object or a custom one.

Below we will describe the key properties and methods of this component.

Properties

The TRDSConnection component contains several properties that can be used to set the options of the connection before opening it.

The AppServer Property

This property is used to directly communicate with the business object. It returns an OleVariant.

At run time, this property is used to get direct access to the interface of the business object, for example, for calling its methods. To call the BusinessObjectMethod method with parameter1 and parameter2 arguments, use the following code:

```
RDSConnection1.AppServer.BusinessObjectMethod(
 parameter1, parameter2
);
```

Note that if the ServerName property is not set, the AppServer property refers to the RDS.DataFactory object.

The ComputerName Property

The ComputerName property specifies the name of the computer on which the business object should be instantiated. If this property is empty, the business object is instantiated on the client computer.

If the business object is accessed through the HTTP protocol, ComputerName contains a URL identifying the Web server where an instance of the business object must be created, for example:

```
http://MAINDESK
```

If the business object will be accessed through DCOM, the ComputerName property contains just the name of the computer.

The DataSpaceObject Property

This property gives us direct access to the underlying RDS.DataSpace object. We should use this object when we need to get or set properties not implemented on the TRDSConnection component level, or to call additional methods of the RDS.DataSpace object.

The InternetTimeOut Property

This property specifies the amount of time in milliseconds before a request times out. The InternetTimeOut property is applicable only when we use the HTTP protocol. It is equal to the InternetTimeout property of the underlying RDS.DataSpace object. When the timeout is reached, a client application no longer waits for its result.

The ServerName Property

This property contains the name of the business object in the form of <server_name>.<CoClass_name>; in other words, it specifies the name (ProgID) of the business object.

By default, this value is equal to the RDSServer.DataFactory object. If we want to use the custom business object instead of the default one, we need to specify its name in this property.

When we use the RDSServer.DataFactory object, we can call its Query method, which accepts two parameters—the connection string that will be used by the business object to connect to a database and the SQL query to retrieve data.

Note: It is essential that the connection string is appropriate for the server on which the business object will be instantiated, and not for the client computer.

The Connected Property

This Boolean property specifies whether the TRDSConnection component is connected to the business object. It should be set to True when we need to open the connection, and to False when we need to break it.

The DataSetCount Property

This integer property contains the number of active datasets associated with the TRDSConnection component. This property can be used to determine the number of datasets listed by the DataSets property. This property comes from the TCustomConnection parent.

The DataSets Property

This property returns an array of the TADODataSet objects corresponding to the active datasets associated with the TRDSConnection component. Each object in this array is accessible through the index, from 0 to DataSetCount–1. This property comes from the TCustomConnection parent.

Methods

The TRDSConnection component exposes several methods. The GetRecordset method implements a call to the business object, and the other two methods—Close and Open—were added at the component level to extend its functionality.

The Close Method

This method contains no parameters. It should be called when we need to disconnect from the business object. Before the connection component is deactivated, all associated datasets will be closed. This method comes from the TCustomConnection parent.

 Note: We can also disconnect from the business object by setting the Connected property to False.

It should be mentioned that after closing and reopening the TRDSConnection component, all previously active datasets will not be reopened automatically.

The Open Method

This method also contains no parameters. It is used to establish a connection with the business object on the remote computer. Please note that the Open method will work only when all other properties of the TRDSConnection component are already set correctly. This method comes from the TCustomConnection parent.

 Note: To connect to the business object we can also set the Connected property to True.

The GetRecordSet Method

This method is used to retrieve a recordset from the business object. It accepts two parameters: the SQL query that will be used by the business object to retrieve data from a database and the connection string that should be valid for the computer on which the business object should be instantiated. This function returns the ADO recordset object that could then be assigned to the TADODataSet component.

The GetRecordset method is called automatically by the TADODataSet components associated with the TRDSConnection component.

If we use the default RDSServer.DataFactory business object, we need to supply this method with both parameters. Only in this case, this method calls the Query method of the underlying RDSServer.DataFactory object.

When we use a custom business object, we need to provide the first parameter which, in this case, is equal to the name of this business object. The CommandText and ConnectionString properties of the TADODataSet components associated with the TRDSConnection component will be passed to the business object in order to receive a recordset.

The ConnectionString property of the TADODataSet associated with the TRDSConnection component must be valid for the computer on which the business object should be instantiated, and not for the client computer.

Events

There are four notification events (TNotifyEvent) implemented in TRDSConnection component. They are:

- BeforeConnect event—Occurs immediately before establishing a connection
- AfterConnect event—Occurs after a connection is established
- BeforeDisconnect event—Occurs before dropping a connection
- AfterDisconnect event—Occurs after the connection is closed

Now that we have discussed the properties, methods, and events of the TRDSConnection component, we will provide several examples of how to create RDS-based multi-tier applications with Delphi.

RDS Usage Examples

In this section, we will create three examples. The first one will show how to implement implicit remoting using the OLE DB Remoting Provider. In this example, we will also show how to use the default customization handler.

The second example will show how to use explicit remoting with TRDSConnection the component and the default RDSServer.DataFactory object. In the third example, we will show how to create a custom business object and use it in a client application.

It is best to run all examples provided in this chapter on two computers on the same network; however, it is also possible to use the same computer both for creating and running the RDS client and for instancing server objects.

If you use two different computers, be sure that you have MDAC 2.1 installed on both of them (see Chapter 18 for explanations of how to find if MDAC is installed). We will use "server" for the computer on which the business object will be instantiated, and "client" for the computer on which the client application will be developed and running. If you use the HTTP protocol, be sure the Internet Information Server is running at the server computer, since it hosts business objects.

Using the OLE DB Remoting Provider

Our first example will implement implicit remoting using the OLE DB Remoting Provider. To do this, we need to create a new project on the client computer, and place the TADOConnection on a form and set its ConnectionString property to MS Remote OLE DB Provider.

```
Provider=MS Remote.1;
Connect Timeout=15;
Persist Security Info=False;
User ID=sa;
Initial Catalog=NorthWind;
Remote Server=http://MAINDESK;
Remote Provider=SQLOLEDB;
Internet Timeout=300000;
Transact Updates=True
```

The next step is to place the TADODataSet component, and set its Connection property to the ADOConnection1 component. Then we place the TDataSource component and the TDBGrid component in order to show records retrieved to the ADODataSet1 component from the remote computer.

We also need to set the LockType property of the ADODataSet1 component to ltBatchOptimistic.

Then let's place the TMemo component to enter a query text at run time; this query will be used by the TADODataSet component to retrieve records from the business object at the server computer.

Finally, we will place two buttons on a form. The first button will retrieve records that the business object receives for us from the database. Here is the code for this button's event handler:

```
procedure TForm1.GetButtonClick(Sender: TObject);
begin
//Close the dataset
```

```
ADODataSet1.Close;
//Set the SQL query to be sent to the business object
ADODataSet1.CommandText := Memo1.Text;
//Retrieve the recordset
ADODataSet1.Open;
end;
```

The second button will send all updates made by the user to the business object in order to save them in the database. Here is the code for this button's event handler:

```
procedure TForm1.SendButtonClick (Sender: TObject);
begin
//Send updates to the remote business object
ADODataSet1.UpdateBatch;
//And retrieve the new version of the recordset
GetButtonClick(self);
end;
```

Now let's test this application. Input into the Memo1 component a valid query to the database that is available on the server computer, and press the first button. The DBGrid1 component will receive the result of executing this query by the remote business object, as shown in the figure below:

We can see that this application works correctly when we run one copy of it. However, what happens if several users begin editing the same data with this application simultaneously? To test this, we can run another copy of this application. If we try to change different sets of records in both applications, the first client that updates data will receive back the result of its own update, and the client that updates data later will receive back the results both of its own updates and the other client's updates. However, if the sets of records updated by both clients have at least one common record, only the first update operation will be successful, and the second update operation will fail.

We have already mentioned in this chapter that we can use the low-level OLE DB code to receive an array of values showing which records in the second update operation were already changed by other users. This array can give us some useful information when we try to resolve such conflicts. But it is desirable to have a more convenient way to provide such analysis and to give the user the possibility to make a decision about what to do with any conflicting record included in RDS, along with the possibility to update non-conflicting records in a batch.

We can also try to avoid such conflicts by, for example, retrieving and editing recordsets that are completely different for different users, such as those based on the user name. This can be done by using parameterized queries and stored procedures (for more details, refer to Chapters 9 and 10). Using customization handlers is another way to customize retrieved recordsets.

Using the Default Customization Handler

To see how to use the customization handler, let's slightly modify our example. In the ConnectionString property editor of the TADOConnection component, we will set the Handler property of the MS Remote OLE DB Provider to `MSDFMAPHandler`'s modify the following section in the MSDFMAP.INI file (it is located in the Windows folder of the remote computer):

```
[connect default]
;If we want to disable unknown connect values,
;we set Access to NoAccess
Access=ReadWrite
```

This allows using connections specified in our application if they are not defined in the MSDFMAP.INI file.

In addition, let's add a custom query to this file, for example:

```
[sql CustomerByCountry]
Sql="SELECT * FROM Customers WHERE Country = ?"
```

Now we can run the modified application. Let's input the following text into the Memo1 component:

```
CustomerByCountry('Germany')
```

This results in the list of German customers appearing in the grid.

If we try to create the usual query for the Northwind database, for example:

```
SELECT * FROM Orders
```

this query will fail.

Thus, we have prevented retrieving recordsets of any type other than those defined in the MSDFMAP.INI file on the server computer. Now our application's user can only retrieve partial lists of customers and not any other information from a database.

Using the RDSServer.DataFactory Object

Our second example will show how to use explicit remoting with the TRDSConnection component and the default RDSServer.DataFactory object. It is similar to the previous one, so we can just modify that example.

First, let's delete the TADOConnection component; we do not need it in this example. Instead, let's place the TRDSConnection component on the form and set its ComputerName property to the URL of the server computer. To simplify the code, let's also set its Connected property to True. As for the ServerName property, we will live the default RDSServer.DataFacroty value (as we have already mentioned earlier in this chapter, this means that we will use the default RDS business object, RDSServer.DataFactory).

In this example, we do not need to set any additional properties for the TADODataSet component.

Now let's add some code to the global declaration section:

```
var
Form1 : TForm1;
RS1    : Variant;
QRY    : WideString;

const CS = 'Provider=SQLOLEDB.1;User ID=sa; ' +
           'Initial Catalog=Northwind;'      +
           'Data Source=MAINDESK;'           +
           'Workstation ID=MAINDESK';
```

The OnClick event handlers for buttons should be modified as shown below:

```
procedure TForm1.GetButtonClick(Sender: TObject);
begin
 try
  //create the text of the query to send
  QRY := Memo1.Text;
  //get a recordset fron RDSServer.DataFactory
  //using this query and the connection string
  ADODataSet1.Recordset := RDSConnection1.GetRecordset(QRY,CS);
  //Show the recordset using ADODataSet1
  ADODataSet1.Open;
 except
  ShowMessage('Invalid command');
 end;
end;

procedure TForm1.SendButtonClick(Sender: TObject);
begin
 try
  //commit any current edits
  ADODataset1.Post;
```

```
//create a recordset object
//Fill it with recordset of ADODataSet1
RS1 := ADODataSet1.Recordset;
//send updates to the remote business object
RDSConnection1.AppServer.SubmitChanges(CS,RS1);
except
  ShowMessage('Cannot update data');
end;
RS1 := Unassigned;
//retrieve the updated recordset
GetButtonClick(self);
end;
```

Now we can compile and run this application. Its behavior is not significantly different from the previous example. However, by using the TRDSConnection component, we can instantiate business objects other than the default RDSServer.DataFactory object. We will show how to do this in the following example.

Creating Custom Business Objects

We will begin by creating a new project of an executable file (it will be accessible through DCOM). It is better to reduce the size of the main form of the server application and set its FormStyle property to fsStayOnTop, because its purpose is simply to indicate that the server is running.

The next step is to create a business object; it must be a COM Automation object. To create it, let's open the Delphi Object Repository and select the Automation object item from the ActiveX page. In the Automation Object Wizard dialog box that appears, we need to set the CoClass name of the business object (call it rds0).

The Instancing parameter in this dialog box indicates how the Automation server is launched. The possible values of this parameter are:

Value	Meaning
Internal	The object can only be created internally, and an external application cannot create an instance of the object directly.
Single Instance	Allows only a single copy of the object for each executable (application). In this case, a separate server executable instance will be running for each client.
Multiple Instance	Multiple client applications can connect to the application, and several instances of the business object can be invoked inside the same server executable.

 Note: When a business object is created as in-process server (DLL), the Instancing parameter is ignored.

For our example, we will select the Multiple Instance value of this parameter, which will allow using the same instance of COM Automation server by several client applications.

As for the threading model parameter, let's select the Apartment option. We also will not generate the event support code in this case.

The next step is to create methods of this object that will be accessible for a client application. Generally, there can be methods for obtaining recordsets for the client, for uploading the recordset received from a client to a database, for registering in a database server with a specific user name and password (in this case, they could be input parameters of this method), and so on.

For our example, we will create only one method (let it be called Data) to retrieve a recordset on behalf of the client application. Methods that retrieve recordsets and have no additional parameters can be called by a client application by using the GetRecordset method of the TRDSConnection object.

To create a method, we need to select the View | Type Library item of the main menu to open the Type Library Editor. First, we need to include the ADO 2.1 type library, in order to make it possible to use the recordset data type as the method parameter, as shown in the figure below:

In this editor, it is necessary to select the Irds0 dispatch interface item, press the New Property button on the Type Library Editor toolbar, and select the ReadOnly item from its drop-down menu. Next, we need to set the type of this property to _Recordset*.

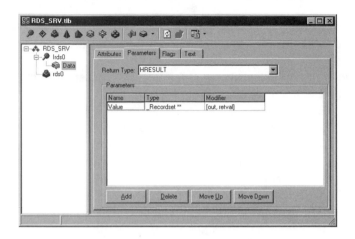

After defining all necessary methods and properties, we need to press the Refresh button on the Type Library Editor toolbar, and then open the module that will contain the implementation code of these methods (it was created automatically by the Automation Object Wizard). Here we will insert the implementation code for this method:

```
function Trds0.Get_Data: _Recordset;
begin
 Result := CoRecordSet.Create;
 Result.CursorLocation := adUseServer;
 Result.Open('SELECT * FROM Customers', CSTR, adOpenStatic,
  adLockBatchOptimistic, adCmdText);
end;
```

We also need to add the following code to the global declaration section:

```
const CSTR=
      'Provider=SQLOLEDB.1;Integrated Security=SSPI;'        +
      'Persist Security Info=False;Initial Catalog=Northwind;'+
      'Data Source=MAINDESK;Locale Identifier=1033;'         +
      'Connect Timeout=15;Use Procedure for Prepare=1;'      +
      'Auto Translate=True;Packet Size=4096;'                +
      'Workstation ID=MAINDESK';
```

The next step is to compile and save the project, then copy the resulting executable file to the server computer, and execute it in order to register its COM server.

Now we can create the client application. It will be similar to the previous example, but now we don't need to have a TMemo component to input queries; in this example, the query text is predefined and is already contained in a business object code.

```
Result.Open('SELECT * FROM Customers', CSTR, adOpenStatic,
  adLockBatchOptimistic, adCmdText);
```

Note that if we need to allow the user to pass in a dynamic query from the client, we need to create a method of the custom business object that accepts a string parameter with a query text and sets it to the CommandText when retrieving a recordset.

Instead, we can place the TEdit component to enter the computer name into it.

First, the global declaration section will be the following:

```
var
  Form2 : TForm2;
  RS    : _Recordset;
```

Second, we need to modify the OnClick event handlers for buttons. Now they are the following:

```
procedure TForm2.GetButtonClick(Sender: TObject);
begin RDSConnection1.ComputerName := Edit1.Text;
 Try
  //connect to the specified computer through DCOM
  //and retrieve a recordset
  RS := RDSConnection1.GetRecordSet('Data','');
  //show it using the ADODataSet1 component
  ADODataSet1.Recordset := RS;
  ADODataSet1.Open;
 except
  ShowMessage('Cannot get data')  ;
 end;
end;

procedure TForm2.SendButtonClick(Sender: TObject);
begin
 try
  //send the recordset back to the business object
  ADODataSet1.UpdateBatch(arAll);
 except
  ShowMessage('Cannot update data');
 end;
 Button1Click(self);
end;
```

It should be mentioned that the RDSConnection1.ServerName property needs to be set to the ProgID of the business object we just created.

Unlike the previous examples, any custom business object serves a single client, so it is "alive" the entire time the client uses it. This improves its response time, as it is not necessary to instantiate it every time a client sends a request to it.

Also note that this is a DCOM executable server that does not require any host application, so we need to enter the computer name, not the URL, in the Edit1 component.

RDS Applications Deployment Issues

Deployment of RDS clients and servers is almost the same as deployment of two-tier database applications discussed in Chapter 18. Both server and client computers must have MDAC installed. The difference is that we do not need to define data sources on a client computer, because they are not used by it. However, they must be defined on the server computer as usual.

If you need to use ODBC data sources in the server computer, they must be defined as system DSNs, both for custom business objects and for RDSServer.DataFactory object. The reason is that when the user logs on to the server using the HTTP protocol anonymously, the user data sources are inaccessible.

Custom business objects that will be invoked using the HTTP protocol must have the ADCLaunch permission. This permission must be set by adding the ProgID of this server to the following Registry key on the server computer:

```
HKEY_LOCAL_MACHINE\SYSTEM\CurrentControlSet\Services\ W3SVC\Parameters\ADCLaunch
```

If a business object is to be invoked using DCOM, the ProgID of this object, along with its ClassID, must be registered on the client. You can use the `regsvr32` utility to do it.

Conclusion

In this chapter, we discussed the basic concepts of Remote Data Services as one of the ways to create Windows DNA applications. We have learned that:

- Remote Data Service is a component that comes with MDAC and enables applications to access OLE DB providers running on remote machines. This makes it possible to create trusted business objects serving as data access servers that directly access databases and send recordsets to "thin" clients.

- The RDS.DataSpace object is a key RDS object used by a client application to communicate with the data access server, and to maintain sending recordsets between client and server.

- The RDSServer.DataFactory object is a default business object that comes with RDS. We can either use the default RDSServer.DataFactory business object or create a custom one to, for example, perform complicated data access, validity checks, and so on.

- The Customization Handler component can be used to customize the behavior of the RDSServer.DataFactory object. We can write a custom handler interface that can intercept calls to RDSServer.DataFactory and execute some custom logic by implementing the IDataFactoryHandler, or use the default MSDFMAP.Handler handler that can be tuned by modifying an appropriate MSDFMAP.INI file.

We have also learned that to establish a remote connection with a business object, we can use two methods:

- The first is to establish a remote connection, also called implicit remoting, based on using the OLE DB Remoting Provider. For Delphi applications, that means we need to use the TADOConnection component with a connection string referring to this OLE DB provider.

- The second way is to establish a remote connection with a business object, also called explicit remoting, using the RDS.DataSpace object. For Delphi applications, this means that we need to use the TRDSConnection object that is a VCL wrapper around the RDS.DataSpace object.

We have also discussed the properties, methods, and events of the TRDSConnection component. To illustrate how to create RDS-based applications with Delphi, we created examples illustrating how to use implicit and explicit remoting, how to use the default customization handler, and how to create a custom business object.

Finally, we also reviewed some specific issues of RDS-based applications deployment.

Having discussed different aspects of using RDS, we can now move to other possible implementations of Windows DNA applications. We will continue our tour of distributed computing with a discussion of Borland MIDAS—the technology for creating data access servers and their clients as Automation servers and Automation controllers that exchange Delphi datasets. This technology is implemented in Delphi VCL components and classes. Compared with RDS, MIDAS provides some additional possibilities to make applications scalable, reliable, and interoperable. We will discuss these in the next chapter.

DISTRIBUTED MIDAS ADO APPLICATIONS

In previous chapters, we discussed the basic concepts of Windows DNA, an architecture describing three-tiered Windows applications, and the RDS technology as one possible implementation of such applications. We have seen that RDS-based applications, in spite of their simplicity, have some disadvantages. For example, at the time of this writing, they do not provide enough services to resolve collisions in multi user environments. That's why RDS is used primarily in applications that present data or create new records but do not require previously created records to be modifiable.

This chapter is devoted to another technology used to create distributed applications—Borland Multi-tier Distributed Application Services Suite (MIDAS)—which is a technology of creating data access servers and "thin" clients as Automation servers and Automation controllers, respectively, that exchange data packets containing dataset data. This technology is implemented in Delphi classes and components and in some separate services.

The MIDAS Basics

In Chapter 19, we discussed that when creating a Windows DNA application, we need to follow the programming model based on implementing access to data services in business objects in a middle tier. Similar to RDS, MIDAS also provides us with such a programming model, allowing us to create "thin" clients that use custom business objects (or data access servers) implemented in COM servers. To work with data services, these servers could use either the Universal Data Access mechanisms (OLE DB and ADO) or BDE.

Let's look at the typical scenario of how a MIDAS application works:

- A user runs a client (implemented as a Windows executable or an ActiveX control) and creates a request for connection to the business object inside a data

543

access server on the remote computer. In MIDAS applications, this business object is called a *remote data module* and is implemented as a COM Automation object.

■ If the request is correct, an instance of the remote data module (which plays the role of *executant*) is created inside a data access server (also called an *application server*) on the specified remote computer.

■ Now the user can send a request containing all necessary data for the remote data module to receive database data into a dataset. As a rule, this request contains a reference to the TDataSetProvider object that gives access to a TDataSet descendant available in the remote data module through its IAppServer interface (in MIDAS applications, this is called an *exported object*). All information necessary for the remote data module to connect to the database (when using ADO, it is the connection string, the SQL query, and other parameters of a dataset) is stored in this exported object. Note that this database connection, as in the case of RDS, will be used by the <u>remote</u> COM Automation object, so it must refer to the data sources available on the <u>remote</u> computer; there is no need to make this database available for the client.

■ The remote data module tries to connect to a database and retrieve the data into the dataset presented by the dataset provider to which the client referred.

■ If the previous operation was successful, and a dataset contains data, the remote data module packs it and sends it back to the client for processing.

■ The client receives the data packets and converts them back to the dataset object. In MIDAS applications, this object is called a *client dataset*. It plays the role of emissary of the "original" dataset stored in the remote data module. Then the client presents the client dataset to the user.

■ The user edits the presented data according to his needs.

■ Having finished editing the data, the user creates a request to the remote data module to receive the modified records and send them back to the database.

■ The remote data module receives the modified records and tries to upload them to the database server. All modified records that satisfy the data integrity rules and were not changed by other users since they were downloaded will be updated.

■ If some records that the remote data module has received from a client were changed by other users or do not satisfy the database referential integrity rules, then only these records will not be updated, and an error (in the form of a client dataset event) will occur in the client. This event can be handled in a client in order to provide a way for the user to make a decision about what to do with a particular conflicting record. We already know from the previous chapter that, as a rule, in three-tier systems database locks are not used in order not to break the rules of Windows DNA architecture, so the simultaneous editing of the same records by several users is quite possible. This means we need to have a convenient mechanism to resolve such collisions.

As with RDS applications, there are different variations of this scenario. For example, the client can save a client dataset to a file and retrieve it later to continue editing data. Sometimes we need to add custom methods to the remote data module (for example, for calculating aggregate values using the database data, or for logging in to the database).

It is essential that in MIDAS applications the client and server can exchange data using DCOM directly, or the TCP/IP or HTTP protocols. With HTTP, the MIDAS application requires Internet Information Server (or Personal Web Server) to be running. We can also use both the presentation tier and middle tier on the same computer (implemented in the same executable or in different executables) with any of these protocols, or just implemented in the same executable.

MIDAS provides some additional features that RDS does not, such as the abilities to send business rules to a client dataset, place data from several linked tables on the same dataset, and increase the availability and scalability of the application by using a set of the same MIDAS servers available on several computers. In this chapter, we will show how to implement such multi-server applications and how to create interoperable InternetExpress applications that allow creating a presentation tier based on JavaScript-enabled browsers.

Having discussed the basic scenario of processing data in MIDAS applications, we now discuss the Delphi components and classes that are used in such applications.

MIDAS Components and Classes

Delphi Enterprise comes with a set of components and classes for creating MIDAS applications. These components are contained in the MIDAS and InternetExpress pages of the Component Palette. Among them is the TDataSetProvider component, which is the only server-side MIDAS component. Other components used in MIDAS clients include several connection components that are descendants of the TCustomConnection class. In addition, there is the TClientDataSet component to cache server data in the client memory (it implements the client dataset) and the TSimpleObjectBroker component to store a collection of computers on which the MIDAS server can be executed.

Let's look at these components and classes in details.

The TRemoteDataModule Class

The TRemoteDataModule objects are used as the storage for data access components (datasets, provider components to provide communications with clients, etc.) and other non-visual components used in data access servers. They are descendants of the TDataModule class and, simultaneously, COM Automation servers that implement the IAppServer interface. All connection components that belong to clients call methods of this interface to access objects that provide data access.

In addition, the unit file for the remote data module can contain a code implementing business rules that must be centralized in the middle tier of a three-tiered application.

The TDataSetProvider Component

The TDataSetProvider component is used in MIDAS servers for two purposes: to provide data from some "real" dataset to a client dataset and to resolve updates from a client dataset back to the original dataset and, possibly, to a database, which this dataset represents. This component is used in data access servers.

The TDataSetProvider component obtains data from a dataset, converts it to data packets, and passes these packets to the client dataset by one of several possible ways (namely, DCOM, TCP/IP, or HTTP protocols). The client dataset receives these data packets, reconstructs the data, and provides them to the user to edit. When the editing is done, and an appropriate method for synchronizing data in a client dataset and a "real" dataset is called, the client dataset places all changed data in a data packet and sends this packet to the provider on the data access server. Upon receiving this packet, the TDataSetProvider component tries to apply the updates back to a database.

This component has a long list of properties and methods. All of its methods are accessible from clients through the IAppServer interface of the remote data module.

The most commonly used properties of the TDataSetProvider component are: Constraints, DataSet, ResolveToDataSet, UpdateMode, Exported, and Options.

The Constraints property defines whether constraints defined for the provider's associated dataset are sent to clients along with the metadata for the dataset in order to allow client datasets to check for constraint violations locally. However, this property is not applicable for ADO data sources, because the data dictionaries containing constraints imported from a database are only supported for BDE data sources.

The DataSet property defines which dataset is represented by the TDataSetProvider component.

The ResolveToDataSet property defines how updates are applied—to the dataset defined in the DataSet property (if this property is equal to True) or directly to the database represented by this dataset (False).

The UpdateMode property specifies how to locate records in the dataset for applying updates (based on all fields, only the key fields, or the key fields and modified fields).

The Exported property indicates whether the TDataSetProvider component is accessible for clients.

The Options property is a set of the following subproperties used to customize how the provider communicates with client datasets:

Option	Meaning
poFetchBlobsOnDemand	BLOB fields are not sent to the clients, and a client must request these values if necessary either using the FetchBlobs method or automatically (if the FetchOnDemand property of the TClientDataSet component is True)
poFetchDetailsOnDemand	When the provider represents the master table in a master-detail relationship, nested detail records are not sent to the client, and a client requests them when necessary, either using the FetchDetails method or automatically (if the FetchOnDemand property of the TClientDataSet component is True)

Option	Meaning
poIncFieldProps	The following field properties are sent along with data to the client: Alignment, DisplayLabel, DisplayWidth, Visible, DisplayFormat, EditFormat, MaxValue, MinValue, Currency, EditMask, DisplayValues
poCascadeDeletes	If the provider represents the master table in a master-detail relationship, and the database supports cascaded deletes as a part of its referential integrity settings, the detail records are deleted automatically when master table records are deleted.
poCascadeUpdates	If the provider represents the master table in a master-detail relationship, and the database supports cascaded updates as a part of its referential integrity settings, the detail records are updated automatically when master table records key values are changed.
poReadOnly	Applying updates to the provider is impossible.
poAllowMultiRecordUpdates	Individual updates that affect multiple records are possible.
poDisableInserts	Inserting new records is impossible (but editing or deleting existing records may be allowed).
poDisableEdits	Modifying existing data values is impossible (but inserting or deleting records may be allowed).
poDisableDeletes	Deleting records is impossible (but editing or inserting records may be allowed)
poNoReset	Ignores the reset flag in calls to the AS_GetRecords method of the IAppServer interface (this flag forces sending records in the data packet starting with the first record independent of the contents of any previously sent data packets).
poAutoRefresh	The client dataset is refreshed when it applies updates. This value is not used in the current version of Delphi.
poPropogateChanges	Changes that are made in the BeforeUpdateRecord and AfterUpdateRecord event handlers are sent back to the client.
poAllowCommandText	The client is allowed to execute a custom SQL query using the GetRecords or Execute method.

The TDataSetProvider is the only MIDAS component used in the data access server. All other components in the MIDAS page of the Component Palette are used to build MIDAS clients. The component that users interact with is the TClientDataSet component.

The TClientDataSet Component

The TClientDataSet component contains a local, in-memory copy of the "real" dataset that is used in "thin" clients. Being the TDataSet class descendant, it has all methods for navigating and editing data. This local copy is independent of databases because it is obtained from a data access server.

The TClientDataSet component can obtain a data packet from the server and store it in the memory cache, which is accessible through its Data property. If a user changes this data packet, the change log is stored separately and is accessible through the read-only Delta property.

The snapshot of data containing this component can be saved to a file and restored from a file using the SaveToFile and LoadFromFile methods. It allows us to implement a briefcase model in multi-tiered applications. This means that the "thin" client can edit data in the off-line mode and occasionally connect to the server to upload the edited data or download the new version of the data. In addition, with this component we are able to create applications with a stand alone, flat-file dataset that does not require using any data access mechanisms. This dataset can be saved to and loaded form a file with such an application.

Along with storing server dataset snapshots, the TClientDataSet component also can send a custom query to the database through the data access server, on the condition that it is allowed by the corresponding TDataSetProvider component on the server.

Sometimes client datasets are used in two-tiered applications. In this case, the TClientDataSet component can call the provider component's methods directly.

In three-tier applications, a "thin" client uses the TClientDataSet component to communicate with the data access server's data provider. The client dataset communicates with a data provider through the remote data module's IAppServer interface, and can receive the list of available providers through the AS_GetProviderNames method of this IAppServer interface. The full list of the IAppServer interface methods that are available for the TClientDataSet component is shown below:

```
IAppServer = interface(IDispatch)
  ['{1AEFCC20-7A24-11D2-98B0-C69BEB4B5B6D}']
  function  AS_ApplyUpdates(const ProviderName: WideString;
  Delta: OleVariant; MaxErrors: Integer;
  out ErrorCount: Integer;
  var OwnerData: OleVariant): OleVariant; safecall;
  function  AS_GetRecords(const ProviderName: WideString;
  Count: Integer; out RecsOut: Integer;
  Options: Integer; const CommandText: WideString;
  var Params: OleVariant;
  var OwnerData: OleVariant): OleVariant; safecall;
  function  AS_DataRequest(const ProviderName: WideString;
  Data: OleVariant): OleVariant; safecall;
  function  AS_GetProviderNames: OleVariant; safecall;
  function  AS_GetParams(const ProviderName: WideString;
  var OwnerData: OleVariant): OleVariant; safecall;
  function  AS_RowRequest(const ProviderName: WideString;
  Row: OleVariant; RequestType: Integer;
  var OwnerData: OleVariant): OleVariant; safecall;
  procedure AS_Execute(const ProviderName: WideString;
  const CommandText: WideString;
  var Params: OleVariant;
  var OwnerData: OleVariant); safecall;
```

In addition, this component must use one of the components responsible for a connection to the server. In the case of using COM, they are the TDCOMConnection, TSocketConnection, and TWebConnection components. These components are discussed in the following sections.

Connection Components

We have already said that a client must use one of the connection components to establish a connection between a client and a remote data access server. When using COM MIDAS servers, they are the TDCOMConnection, TSocketConnection, and TWebConnection components. Any of these components can establish or drop a connection, obtain an IAppServer interface pointer for the data access server, obtain its list of providers, and call its methods. The first of these components allows the client to interact directly with the data access server, and the others require special services to interact with; these services are COM clients of the data access server.

A brief description of these components, how to connect to the server, and what additional services are required are shown in the table below:

Connection Type	Connection Component	Services Required Installed	Running
DCOM	TDCOMConnection	DCOM	None
TCP/IP	TSocketConnection	TCP/IP support	Borland Socket Server ScktSrvr.exe
HTTP	TWebConnection	Internet Information Server or Personal Web Server; HTTPSRVR.DLL must be in the Scripts catalog of the Web server, WININET.DLL in the Windows system directory of a client computer	IIS or PWS

Details of how to use these components and what settings they require to work properly will be discussed in the "MIDAS Connection and Security Issues" section later in this chapter.

The TSimpleObjectBroker Component

The TSimpleObjectBroker component contains a list of servers that can be used to run the data access server. If this component is used, the TSimpleObjectBroker component returns the name of one of the available servers in this list when a connection component requests a server. This component allows clients to find or change one of multiple servers dynamically at run time. In the case of periodical reconnecting clients to servers, clients can continue working even if some servers fail. In other words, this component provides a simple way of implementing the fail-over safety that increases availability of the distributed application.

In addition, the TSimpleObjectBroker component can select servers randomly from its server list, which makes it possible to balance loading of the servers.

Having discussed the components and classes used in MIDAS applications, we will show how to create different types of MIDAS applications. Next we will provide a set of examples that illustrate the main features of this technology.

MIDAS Usage Examples

We will begin our MIDAS tour with a simple MIDAS application using a TCP/IP connection. Then we will show how to implement the briefcase model in MIDAS, how to create a method for user access verification, and how to propagate constraints to a client dataset.

It is best to run all examples provided in this chapter on two computers on the same network; however, it is also possible to use the same computer for creating and running both MIDAS clients and MIDAS servers. As in the previous chapter, we will use "server" for the computer on which the MIDAS server will be executed, and "client" for the computer on which the client application will be executed. The server computer must have access to the database used in the examples.

To test our sample applications, we need to be sure that you have MDAC 2.1 installed on the server computer. If we use the DCOM connection, we need to be sure both computers have DCOM installed (see Chapter 18 for an explanation of how to find if DCOM and MDAC are installed programmatically). If we use the HTTP protocol, we need the Internet Information Server (or Personal Web Server) running on the server computer. If we use the TCP/IP protocol, we need to ensure that TCP/IP support is installed on both computers.

Creating a Simple MIDAS Application

First we will show how to create a simple MIDAS server and then how to develop a simple client for it.

Creating an ADO MIDAS Server

To create a data access server, we will use the Northwind database on MS SQL Server 7.0.

We will begin by creating a new project for the data access server. Its main form will serve as an indicator of a server being running, so it is a good idea to reduce its size and set its FormStyle property to fsStayOnTop. Then we will place a TLabel component on this form and set its Caption property to 0 (zero). This label will be used later as a counter of connected clients. Let's also add the integer variable to store the number of connected clients to the private section of the form, and define the procedure for updating the caption of the label in the public section:

```
type
  TForm1 = class(TForm)
    Label1: TLabel;
```

```
private
  { Private declarations }
  ClientCounter : Integer;
public
  { Public declarations }
  procedure UpdateCounter(Increment: Integer);
end;
```

Also, we will implement the UpdateCounter procedure, as shown below:

```
procedure TForm1.UpdateCounter(Increment: Integer);
begin
  ClientCounter  := ClientCounter+Increment;
  Label1.Caption := IntToStr(ClientCounter);
end;
```

The next step is to open the Object Repository and choose the Remote Data Module icon from its New page. This will bring up the Remote Data Module Wizard dialog box. Here we will enter the remote data module class name (let's call it MyRDM1) and select how many instances of a remote data module our server can create. There are three choices:

■ The Multiple Instance option means that the server can create many instances of a remote data module. This is the default option.

■ The Single Instance option means that the server can create only one instance of a remote data module, so it is necessary to run a separate server process for each client.

■ The Internal option is used if the remote data module is created internally. This means that the client application cannot create it directly, so it is not applicable here.

For our example, we will select the Multiple Instance option. Keep the default value for the Threading Model parameter.

After the remote data module COM class has been created, we need to place the TADOConnection component into it and set its ConnectionString property to connect with the Northwind database. Please note that this connection string will be used by the <u>server</u> computer to connect to the database server, so there is no need to make this database available for the client computer at all, since the client will not use it directly. It is important to input a valid user name and password into the connection string, and then set the Login Prompt property of the TADOConnection component to False. Otherwise, the user access dialog will appear in a data access server that is not accessible for users. This does not mean, of course, that the user access to the database with the user name and password is impossible in a multi-tier system. We will discuss this task later.

Then we place two TADODataSet components on the remote data module and bind them to the ADOConnection1 component, and set their CommandType property to cmdTable and their CommandText properties to Customers (ADODataSet1) and

Orders (ADODataSet2). Then let's bind ADODataSet1 and ADODataSet2 components with a master-detail relationship using the CustomerID field common for these datasets.

The last component to place on the remote data module is the TDataSetProvider component. Let's set its DataSet property to ADODataSet1 and its Exported property to True. The following screen shot shows all the components used in our data access server:

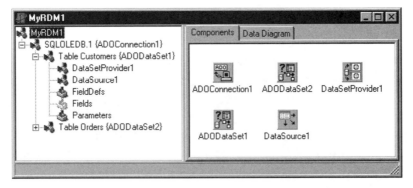

In the remote data module unit, we must refer to the main form.

And finally, let's create two event handlers for the OnCreate and OnDestroy events of the remote data module to update the client counter placed on the main form. The code for these handlers is shown below:

```
procedure TMyRDM1.RemoteDataModuleCreate(Sender: TObject);
begin
  Form1.UpdateCounter(1);
end;

procedure TMyRDM1.RemoteDataModuleDestroy(Sender: TObject);
begin
  Form1.UpdateCounter(-1);
end;
```

Note that generally in apartment-threaded servers, we need to take care of synchronizing access to the main form from different instances of the COM object. However, this is not so critical for this particular example.

The last step in creating a server is to save and compile the server and copy it to the server computer, along with the MIDAS.DLL file that can be found in the Windows System directory of the computer on which Delphi is installed. This library is used by MIDAS components of the created server. As the data access server is a COM server, we need to run it there in order to register it. The MIDAS.DLL library also needs to be registered; you can do this with the Regsvr32.exe utility in the Windows\System directory.

Note that if we plan to use DCOM access to this server, we need to take into consideration the visibility of the server's main form. See the "MIDAS Connection and Security Issues" section for details.

Now that we have a data access server, we are able to create a simple MIDAS client. This is shown in the next section.

Creating a MIDAS Client

In this example, we will use the TCP/IP protocol to reach the server.

Before creating a client, we need to run (or install as a Windows NT service) Borland Socket Server (scktsrvr.exe), which is a dispatch program residing in the Delphi5\Bin directory on the server computer. The client will interact with Socket Server, which receives calls and tries to send them to the data access server using COM. We will discuss in detail the role played by this server and other such services in the "MIDAS Connection and Security Issues" section later in this chapter.

Now let's create a new project, place the TSocketConnection component on the main form, and set its Address property to the IP address of the server computer. You can also use the Host property of this component, and enter the computer name.

Now we need to type the COM object name (ProgID) in the ServerName property in the form of <server_name>.<COM_object_name> (or select it from a pop-up list, if it is available). If we create a client on the server computer, the GUID property will be automatically filled. We can also enter the CoClass GUID of the remote data module manually into the GUID property instead of entering the ServerName property.

The next step is to try to set the Connected property to True. If all other settings are correct, the server starts automatically. The Delphi IDE is now a client of the data access server, and the connection counter on the server main form indicates that one client is connected to the server.

Now let's place the TClientDataSet component on the client main form and set its RemoteServer property to SocketConnection1. The next step is to select the ProviderName property of the TClientDataSet component from the list of available providers (in our case it contains only the DataSetProvider1 value). Then, we can set the Active property of the TClientDataSet component to True.

Now we can place the TDataSource component and the necessary DataControls components on a form (for instance, the TDBGrid component and the TDBNavigator component) in order to present and edit data in the TClientDataSet component.

It should be pointed out that the TClientDataSet component could contain a cached data of two or more tables, which are linked in a master-detail relationship. In this example, the Customers table and the Orders table are linked in a master-detail relationship established in our data access server. This will give us the TClientDataSet component containing all fields corresponding to the real Customers table fields and, in addition, a new TDataSetField corresponding to the related detail records in the Orders table. In other words, TClientDataSet emulates "nested" tables, similar to datasets based on ADO recordsets received using MS DataShape OLE DB provider (this was discussed in the "Using Data Shaping for Creating Nested Datasets" section of Chapter 11).

From the previous section of this chapter, we know that client datasets store both the original uploaded data in their Data property and the change log in their Delta property. To initiate uploading the edited data from the change log, the ApplyUpdates method of the TClientDataSet component must be used. This method takes the changes in the change log and sends them to the data access server. This method has an integer parameter, which indicates how many errors can occur in the server before canceling the update process and rolling back the transaction. If this parameter is equal to −1, it means that there can be any number of server errors. We need to take into account the possibility of errors because, generally, the client will not have complete information about which records were changed by another user since they were downloaded from the server, which of these records were deleted from the database, etc. Therefore, only when an attempt is made to upload edited data are database integrity rule violations or other collisions shown. To provide the ability to upload data, we will place two buttons on a form and then create OnClick event handlers for them. The code for these handlers is shown below:

procedure TForm1.Button1Click(Sender: TObject);

```
begin
  ClientDataSet1.ApplyUpdates(-1);
end;

procedure TForm1.Button2Click(Sender: TObject);
begin
  ClientDataSet1.CancelUpdates;
end;
```

Now we can compile and save our application. Then we can copy it to the client computer (if we developed this application on another one), along with the MIDAS.DLL file; this library is used by MIDAS client components and must be placed in the Windows System directory or the directory where the client executable is located.

Note that MDAC and DBMS client software do not need to be deployed to the client computer at all because the "thin" client does not use them.

Now we can run the client. If we look at the server main form, we can see that the connection counter is equal to 2. The first client is the Delphi IDE; the second client is our running application. By clicking on the ADODataSet2 column in a grid, we can see that the secondary form with the corresponding detail records appears; this is shown in the figure below:

It should be mentioned that both master and detail records can be edited and uploaded with the same ApplyUpdates method of the ClientDataSet1 component. Thus, we have created a simple MIDAS application that satisfies the Windows DNA requirement not to allow "thin" clients to have direct database access and, instead, uses data access servers in a middle tier to get database data.

A final note concerning this example: We have created a "thin" client as a Windows executable. However, we can also implement it as an ActiveX control. This allows us to include it in an HTML page that could be uploaded from a Web server and opened inside Microsoft Internet Explorer 3.0 or higher. Details on creating ActiveX applications are out of the scope of this book.

Having created a simple MIDAS application, we need to take some additional steps to make it reliable. The first step is to provide for its convenient usage in multi user environment. The following example will illustrate how to do this.

multi user Data Processing in MIDAS

One of the important requirements of Windows DNA applications is reliability. This means that such applications must provide correct results in a multi user environment. Here we will show how to provide for multi user data processing in MIDAS applications, and how to use the database security mechanisms in such applications.

Resolving Database Collisions

It is obvious that in a multi-tier system, it is impossible to use locking. This is because the possible time delay between downloading records for editing and uploading the edited record back to the database can be very long to lock database records. Therefore, multi user data processing in multi-tier systems differs from the traditional one. Compared to the current implementation of RDS, MIDAS is superior in this area.

During uploading of the edited data to the database server, the actual version of the uploaded record stored in the database is compared with its previously downloaded version stored in the client dataset cache. If these versions are different, the OnReconcileError event of the TClientDataSet component occurs, and we can handle this event to give our users the ability to decide what should be done. The simplest way to do this is to use the Reconcile Error dialog box from the Dialogs page of the Object Repository.

Let's improve our example by adding this dialog box and referring to it in the Uses clause in the main form unit. This dialog must belong to the Available Forms list in the Project Options dialog (otherwise, it would appear immediately on client startup before any error really occurs).

Then we need to create the OnReconcileError event handler of the ClientDataSet1 component. Its code follows:

```
procedure TForm1.ClientDataSet1ReconcileError(
  DataSet: TClientDataSet; E: EReconcileError;
  UpdateKind: TUpdateKind; var Action: TReconcileAction);
begin
  Action := HandleReconcileError(DataSet, UpdateKind, E);
end;
```

HandleReconcileError is the method of the Reconcile Error dialog that can be found in the Reconcile Error dialog unit.

Now we can compile and save the client, and copy it to the client computer. Then let's execute it twice. In both instances, we will change the same record in different ways and then try to apply updates from both instances of the client. The first attempt will be successful, and the second one will bring up the Reconcile Error dialog as shown in the figure below:

The grid in this dialog contains the field values of the conflicting record that triggered the collision. These are the value to be uploaded (or *modified value*), the value found in a database during the uploading process (or *conflicting value*), and the previously downloaded value (or *original value*). The second user can decide what to do with this record (to edit, to agree with its new version, etc.).

Note that the detail records in "nested" client datasets can also be processed by the same event handler in the case of a collision. Also note that we can modify the Reconcile Error dialog to satisfy our specific requirements (for example, to provide another way of reconciliation).

Having found the solution for resolving possible collisions, we need to pay attention to another problem of multi user data processing in MIDAS applications—providing authorized access to databases from clients through remote data modules. The following example will show how to do it.

User Access Verification

Reliability of Windows DNA applications means that we must prevent unauthorized access to critical resources of the application, such as database connections. This means that in multiuser environments we need to provide a way to use security mechanisms provided by database servers. Let's look at how to do this in MIDAS applications.

To provide authorized access of remote data modules to the database, we will create a method implementing user access verification when connecting to the database server. In addition, we will show on the server main form which users are currently logged on and who else attempted to connect to the database through this data access server.

To do this, let's add the TMemo component to the main form of our server. This component will contain a log where all attempts to connect must be stored.

Now we need to make some changes in our connection string. Here is how it will look now:

```
const
  Cstr = 'Provider=SQLOLEDB.1;Password=%s;'         +
         'Persist Security Info=True;User ID=%s;' +
         'Initial Catalog=Northwind;Data Source=%s';
```

Now we can create the Login method of the remote data module. To do this, we need to open the type library and create a new method of our COM object (using the New | Method option of the pop-up menu of the IMyRDM1 interface).

The parameters of this method are the user name, password, and computer name (DataSource parameter when using Microsoft OLE DB Provider for SQL Server), which are all of the BSTR (or WideString) type. To define them, we need to choose the Parameters tab, press the Add button three times, and rename the default parameters created by the Type Library Editor.

To inform the client whether the Login method is successful, we will add a fourth parameter of VARIANT_BOOL type that must be set to True if this method results in connecting the data access server to the database, and False in other cases. All the defined parameters of the Login method are shown in the following figure:

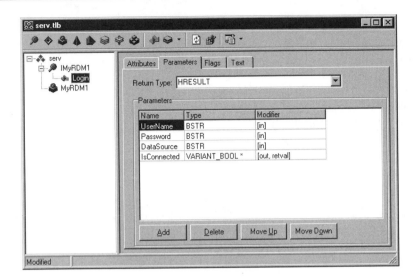

After pressing the Refresh button we can open the remote data module unit and add
the implementation code of the Login method:

```
function TMyRDM1.Login(const UserName, Password,
  DataSource: WideString): WordBool;
const
  cstr = 'Provider=SQLOLEDB.1;Password=%s;'        +
         'Persist Security Info=True;User ID=%s;' +
         'Initial Catalog=Northwind;Data Source=%s';
var
  S : String;
begin
  // Disconnect from the database
  ADOConnection1.Connected := False;
  // Insert real data into the connection string template
  S := Format(cstr, [Password, UserName, DataSource]);
  ADOConnection1.ConnectionString := S;
  try
   //Set the global variable with user name
   Uname := UserName;
   //Try to connect
   ADOConnection1.Connected := True;
   //If successful, the user is now logged on
   Result := True;
  except
   //Inform the system administrator about attempt to connect
   Form1.Memo1.Lines.Add('Somebody attempted to connect+
   'using UserName='+ UserName+' at '+ DateTimeToStr(Now));
   //Reset the global variable with user name
   Uname := '';
   //nobody is now logged on
```

```
    Result:=False;
  end;
end;
```

In this method, we disconnect from the server, insert the user name, password, and data source name in the connection string template, and attempt to reconnect. If this attempt is successful, the method returns True. Otherwise, it returns False, and places a message about the unsuccessful attempt to connect in the log in the Memo1 component on the main form of the server.

We also need to create a remote data module variable that contains the current user name:

```
  private
    Uname : String;
```

In addition, let's create the AfterConnect and AfterDisconnect event handlers for the ADOConnection1 component:

```
procedure TMyRDM1.ADOConnection1AfterDisconnect(Sender: TObject);
begin
  //Inform the system administrator
  //that user has disconnected
  Form1.Memo1.Lines.Add('User '+UName+' has disconnected at '+
    DateTimeToStr(Now));
end;

procedure TMyRDM1.ADOConnection1AfterConnect(Sender: TObject);
begin
  //Inform the system administrator
  //that user has connected
  Form1.Memo1.Lines.Add('User '+UName+' has connected at '+
    DateTimeToStr(Now));
end;
```

These event handlers are necessary to add information about these events to the log shown in the Memo1 component on the main form.

Now we need to save, compile, and copy our server to the server computer.

The next step is to change our Windows multi user client. We will place on the main client form three TEdit components, a TButton component (let's set its Caption property to Login), and a CheckBox1 component (with its Caption property set to Connected). Set he PasswordChar property of the Edit2 component to *.

Let's create the OnClick event handler for the CheckBox1 component:

```
procedure TForm1.CheckBox1Click(Sender: TObject);
begin
  SocketConnection1.Connected := CheckBox1.Checked;
  //Prevent off-line data editing
  if Not CheckBox1.Checked
```

```
then
  ClientDataSet1.Close;
end;
```

This event handler connects the client just to the data access server <u>without</u> connecting the appropriate remote data module to the database.

Now let's create the OnClick event handler for the Login button:

```
procedure TForm1.Button3Click(Sender: TObject);
var
  IsLogged: Boolean;
begin
  if SocketConnection1.Connected then
  Begin
  //Try to connect
   IsLogged := SocketConnection1.AppServer.Login(Edit1.Text,
     Edit2.Text,Edit3.Text);
   //If login fails
   if Not IsLogged then
   begin
     // Inform the user
     ShowMessage('Wrong user name or password');
     //  and make  data unavailable
     ClientDataSet1.Active := False;
   end
   //If login was successful, make data available
   else
     ClientDataSet1.Active := True;
   end ;
end;
```

Here we try to log in to the database. If the login attempt is successful, the client dataset will be opened. Otherwise, we inform the user that his user name and password are wrong.

Now we can save, compile, and test the client. Press the Connect check box, enter the user name, password, and data source name in the appropriate controls, and then press the Login button to connect the remote data module to the database; if successful, the client dataset will open. You can also see all attempts to connect to and disconnect from the database server, as shown in the figure below:

Thus, we have provided user access verification when a client sends a request to the data access server to connect to the database. This allows us to use security mechanisms provided by database servers in clients.

It should be mentioned that we can add to the interface of the remote data module methods implementing any other functionality, for example, calculating aggregate data, running stored procedures, and so on.

As we know from Chapter 19, Windows DNA applications can be interactive and non-interactive. Interactive applications are preferable because they allow users to perform data validation or other manipulation without sending additional requests to the middle tier. The following section will show how to make MIDAS applications more interactive.

Increasing Interactivity of MIDAS Clients

In the following set of examples, we will show how to propagate constraints defined in the data access server to a client dataset, and how to resort and index data in it.

Propagating Business Rules to Clients

To make Windows DNA applications more interactive, we can include some business rules into the middle-tier emissaries that are downloaded to the clients. For MIDAS applications, this means that it is desirable to store business rules in a client dataset. MIDAS provides some possibilities for including business rules into data packets that are downloaded to the client and stored in a client dataset along with data itself. This allows us to provide the data analysis inside the client without connecting to the data access server, thus reducing the network traffic.

To find out if business rules are delivered to a client dataset, we can simply run the client, open the Customers table, and violate the primary key integrity by adding a record with a primary key value that already exists in this table (for our example, it is the CustomerID field). When we try to post this record, we receive an error message: "Key violation." Thus, the client dataset can check some referential integrity violations of data without connecting the server.

Now let's make a little change in our data access server to illustrate propagating database constraints to the client dataset. To do so, we will open the server project, create TField objects for the ADODataSet1 component, and create a constraint and an appropriate error message for one of the fields. See the following example:

```
procedure TMyRDM1.MyRDMCreate(Sender: TObject);
begin
  ADODataSet1Country.CustomConstraint :=
  'Country Name IS NOT NULL';
  ADODataSet1Country.ConstraintErrorMessage :=
      'Please input country name';
      Inc(ClientCount);
      Form1.Label1.Caption:=IntToStr(ClientCount);
end;
```

Now we can compile and save this project, copy the new version of the server to the server computer, and then execute the client application. When we violate the created constraint during editing data in a client dataset and try to post this record locally, we receive the constraint error message defined in the code above.

We can also propagate the extended attributes of fields. To illustrate this, in the server project, we will change some properties of TFields objects (e.g., DisplayLabel and Alignment). Then, let's set the DataSetProvider1 Options property to [poIncFieldProps]—this option makes the TDataSetProvider include extended field attributes to data packets sent to the client. After compiling, saving, and copying the server executable to the server computer, we can run the client and see that these view properties of the table changed.

It should be mentioned, however, that among the custom constraints implemented in the TFields objects, there are also custom database constraints. For example, if we explore the Northwind database and its Customers table with the MS SQL Server Enterprise Manager, we can see that this table contains a server constraint:

```
CompanyName IS NOT NULL
```

It is interesting to check whether this constraint is propagated to the client dataset. To do this, we will run the client that contains the Reconcile Error dialog and add a new record to this table, leaving the CompanyName field empty. If we call the Post method of the client dataset, nothing happens. But when we call the ApplyUpdates method of the client dataset, we will obtain the Reconcile Error dialog with the following error message text:

```
Cannot insert the value NULL into column 'CompanyName', table
'Northwind.dbo.Customers'; column does not allow nulls.
INSERT fails
```

We see that this database constraint is not propagated to the client dataset; we need to try applying updates through the data access server to the database in order to check whether the database constraint is violated.

The TDataSetProvider component has the Constraints property, which controls whether database constraints are passed to the client. This allows client datasets to check for constraint violations locally, without connecting to the data access server. But these constraints must be imported to the data dictionary on the data access server. However, data dictionaries are supported only for BDE data source and are unavailable when we use ADO data sources.

In addition, when using ADO data sources, we cannot create a list of constraints for the entire dataset, as in the case of using BDE. Unfortunately, Delphi ADO data access components do not have the Constraints property, unlike the BDE data access components. Therefore, the possibilities of propagating server constraints provided by MIDAS for ADO data sources are significantly less than the possibilities provided for BDE data sources.

Besides using downloaded constraints, we may also need to provide the ability for our users to manipulate the downloaded data. Resorting data is an often-used manipulation, and it is preferred that a request not be sent to a data access server just to sort the same data in a different order. The example below shows how to solve this task.

Manipulating Data in Client Datasets

Another way to increase interactivity and availability of MIDAS applications is to make the clients able to perform some data manipulations with downloaded data, for example, resorting and indexing, without additional retrieving of data from the data access server.

To sort data in the client dataset, we can use its IndexFieldNames property, or the IndexName property and the AddIndex and DeleteIndex methods.

To illustrate this, let's add the TComboBox component to the client. Later, it will be filled with the names of fields that allow indexing.

Then we need to create two event handlers. The first fills the TComboBox component with the names of fields that allow sorting data by their values (they belong to the TNumericField, TDateTimeField, or TStringField classes or to their descendants, such as TWideStringField, TIntegerField, etc.), and adds appropriate indexes to the client dataset:

```
procedure TForm1.ClientDataSet1AfterOpen(DataSet: TDataSet);
var
  I  : Integer;
  Fn : String;
begin
  //Reset the list of fields
  ComboBox1.Items.Clear;
  for I := 0 to ClientDataSet1.FieldList.Count-1 do
  begin
    //If the field allows indexing
    if (ClientDataSet1.Fields.Fields[I] is  TStringField)
      or (ClientDataSet1.Fields.Fields[I] is  TNumericField)
      or (ClientDataSet1.Fields.Fields[I] is TDateTimeField)
    then
    begin
      Fn := ClientDataSet1.Fields.Fields[i].FieldName;
      //Add the name of field to the field list
      ComboBox1.Items.Add(Fn);
      //Create a new index in a client dataset
      ClientDataSet1.AddIndex(Fn + 'Index', Fn,
        [ixCaseInsensitive],'','',0);
      ClientDataSet1.IndexName := Fn + 'Index';
    end;
  end;
  //Set the initial value in the field list
  ComboBox1.ItemIndex := 0;
```

```
end;
```

The OnChange event handler of the ComboBox1 component is used to select an index on the field selected from the list box, and to resort data in the client dataset:

```
procedure TForm1.ComboBox1Change(Sender: TObject);
var
  Fn : String;
begin
  Fn := ComboBox1.Items.Strings[ComboBox1.ItemIndex];
  //Change the current index
  ClientDataSet1.IndexName := Fn + 'Index';
end;
```

Finally, we need to reset all index definitions before opening the client dataset:

```
procedure TForm1.ClientDataSet1BeforeOpen(DataSet: TDataSet);
begin
  //Reset index definitions in client dataset
  ClientDataSet1.IndexName := 'DEFAULT_ORDER';
end;
```

At run time, all field lists of the TClientDataSet component will be shown in a combo box, and selecting one of them results in resorting records. This is shown in the screen shot below:

Note that there is no need to requery the data access server to show the client dataset data in another sort order.

Having discussed ways to make MIDAS applications more interactive, we need to mention that there is also a way to create interoperable clients for MIDAS applications. This is based on the InternetExpress technology implemented in the InternetExpress components. The InternetExpress application contains the complex business services tier consisting of the MIDAS data access server and its client, which is a Web server application. Users interact with this application through JavaScript-enabled Web browsers, where they can navigate and edit data, and then apply them back. However, they can use the same (or almost the same) data access servers as when using a Windows client, so we will not discuss how to create such clients here. We should note that this technology does not support ADO data access servers with "nested" master-detail datasets but works correctly with similar BDE datasets. This may be fixed in the next version of Delphi.

Having shown what types of Windows DNA applications can be created with MIDAS, we need to spend some time discussing the details of different types of connections with the clients and data access servers used in MIDAS applications. These issues are discussed in the following section.

MIDAS Connection and Security Issues

This section describes the differences between using MS DCOM, sockets, and HTTP connections in MIDAS applications in regard to configuration and the requirements of additional client and server software installation.

Generally, the client must have permission to establish a remote connection with a data access server; it is not advisable that any LAN or Internet user could run any application inside the address space of our computer. Sometimes, the client does not interact directly with the data access server; instead, it interacts with an additional service responsible for security and data exchange (this is true for HTTP and TCP/IP).

We will begin discussing MIDAS connection and security issues from the DCOM connection and some features in DCOM settings necessary for MIDAS applications to work correctly.

Using DCOM

If a client uses the TDCOMConnection component to connect to a data access server, we need to have DCOM installed on both the server and client computer, except when they are running on the same computer. Refer to Chapter 18 for details of how to check if DCOM is installed and where to get it.

To make MIDAS applications work correctly using DCOM, we need to configure DCOM parameters on the server and client computer. Generally, the server computer can be configured with User-Level access or Share-Level access (to check or change this setting, choose the Network applet from the Control Panel and then select the Access Control page in its dialog box).

If we have a primary domain controller in our network, the first step in configuring DCOM at the server computer is to download the Windows NT user list from the primary domain controller to the server computer. Having the Windows NT user list, we can grant or revoke permissions to users or user groups to run our DCOM server; this should be done using the DCOMCNFG utility.

If we do not have a primary domain controller (or have the MIDAS server installed in a computer with the Windows 95 operating system), we need to use Share-Level access. The details of how to configure DCOM in this case are in Dan Miser's "DCOM Configuration" article, which can be found at the DistribuCon company site (http://www.distribucon.com/dcom95.html).

When setting the DCOM connection properties for a server, we need to keep in mind that MIDAS servers may pretend to modify the Windows Registry on startup. Therefore, these servers must be launched remotely on behalf of the user who has permission to edit the Registry of the server computer. This can be done using the Identity tab of the Object Properties dialog of the DCOM configuration utility.

If we want to show the main form of the server using the DCOM type of connection, we need to select the Interactive User option in the Identity tab of your DCOM configuration utility. Otherwise, the main form of the server will be hidden.

Configuring access to the DCOM server on a client computer is not necessary with MIDAS, because the location of the server computer is explicitly pointed to in the ComputerName property of the TDCOMConnection component.

We can summarize the general rule of DCOM access to the MIDAS server as follows: *The access to this specific server is possible for the domain users who have the DCOM client installed on their computers and are granted a permission to access this server.*

Using Sockets

Using sockets allows us to make a non-configurable client, which in most cases does not need any client parts or additional settings of DCOM or any other communication software, except the TCP/IP support.

Note:

When using the TSocketConnection component with the SupportCallback property equal to True, we need to have the Winsock2 library installed on a client computer. For Windows 95, this library can be downloaded from the Microsoft Web site:

http://www.microsoft.com/windows95/downloads/

However, if we do not need to use callback functions of this component, we can set this property to False and not worry whether Winsock2 is installed. Discussing callback functions is out of the scope of the book.

Because using sockets, in most cases, does not require any additional settings and software, it is the best way to provide Internet deployment of clients.

When the client uses the TSocketConnection component to connect to the data access server, the client interacts with the Borland Socket Server that should be running on the server computer. Borland Socket Server accepts client requests and instantiates the remote data module using COM.

In addition, we need to make this particular server available through TCP/IP, or change a mode of running Socket Server to permit using TCP/IP with all COM servers (this can be done by unchecking the Connections/Registered Objects Only menu item of the Borland Socket Server window).

The remote data module wizard automatically adds a call to the EnableSocketTransport procedure to the UpdateRegistry method of the remote data modules; this procedure adds the Registry entries that Scktsrvr.exe uses to check whether clients can access the data access server, and can be removed by calling the DisableSocketTransport procedure. To make a data access server unavailable to connections via sockets, we need to remove these two calls from the UpdateRegistry method in the remote data module unit. After that, the data access server can still be accessible for connections through other protocols.

We can summarize the general rule of access to the server using sockets: *"The access to this specific server is possible for all users who can connect this computer using the TCP/IP protocol, when the Socket Server is running, on condition that either this particular server is registered as available through socket connection, or all COM servers are available through socket connection."*

Using HTTP

Using the HTTP protocol allows us to create clients that can communicate with data access servers protected by a firewall, and use the SSL (Socket Security Layer) provided by WININET.DLL, which is a library of Internet utilities available with Microsoft Internet Explorer 3.0 or higher. Instead of creating the remote data module directly from the client, the TWebConnection component interacts with the special Web server library HTTPSRVR.DLL that comes with Delphi and must be installed in the scripts catalog of the Microsoft Internet Information Server 4.0 or higher, or in Personal Web Server. This library accepts client requests and instantiates the remote data module through COM.

To get access to the data access server through the HTTP protocol, we need to set the ServerName property of the TWebConnection component to the ProgID of the data access server, and the URL property to the URL of the computer on which the data access server will be running, for example:

```
WebConnection1.URL:='http://127.0.0.1/scripts/httpsrvr.dll';
```

As in the case of using sockets, you need to have permission to use the HTTP protocol to connect to the particular server. The remote data module wizard automatically adds a call to EnableWebTransport procedure to the UpdateRegistry method of the remote data modules: This adds the Registry entries that HTTPSRVR.DLL uses to check whether clients can access the data access server, and can be removed by calling the

DisableWebTransport procedure. To make the data access server unavailable to HTTP connections, we need to remove these two calls from the UpdateRegistry method in the remote data module unit. After that, the data access server can still be accessible for connections through other protocols.

The general rule of access to the server using HTTP can be summarized as follows: *"The access to this specific server is possible for all users who can connect this computer using the HTTP protocol, when the Internet Information Server (or Personal Web Server) is running, on condition that either this server is registered as available through HTTP connection, or all COM servers are available through HTTP connection."*

Using Directory Services

According to the requirements of Windows DNA, multi-tier applications should satisfy demands of availability and scalability. Availability means the application must be capable of serving client requests any time they need, and scalability means that an application can serve more and more clients by simply adding resources, with the average processing time of a request not growing.

One of the ways to achieve these purposes is to use several data access servers instead of only one server, and distribute all "thin" clients among these servers to provide their load balancing; this provides scalability of the entire application. In addition, you should provide the ability for any client to be reconnected to another server when the server providing data to it becomes unavailable. This means that the information system is fail-over safe, and such fail-over safety increases availability of the application.

To provide both fail-over safety and load balancing in distributed applications, we can use special services called *directory services*, or *object brokers* (these are not the same as core Directory Services implemented in the Windows operating systems).

The simplest way is to place such a service into a client. To do this, we can use the TSimpleObjectBroker component. It contains a list of servers on which the data access server can run.

When the client requests a server, the TSimpleObjectBroker component randomly passes the name of one of the available servers in its server list. Thus, clients can be distributed between different servers, so it is possible to make the information system load-balanced. If we implement periodical connecting to and disconnecting from the server in the client code, and place this code for connecting the server in a try...except block, the clients could locate servers dynamically at run time and reconnect to another server if necessary.

To show how to use this component, we will modify one of our previous examples. Let's place the TSimpleObjectBroker component on the client form and set the ObjectBroker property of the TSocketConnection component to its name. Then, we need to fill the Servers collection of the SimpleObjectBroker1 component with the list of computer names on which the MIDAS server is installed and registered.

Finally, let's create the OnClick event handler for the Reconnect button as shown below:

```
procedure TForm2.Button1Click(Sender: TObject);
var
  I : Integer;
begin
  try
    // Try to connect to all servers in the
    // TSimpleObjectBroker.Servers collection
    // one by one
    SocketConnection1.Connected := True;
    ClientDataSet1.Active := True;
  except
    ShowMessage('Failed to connect to any of servers');
  end;
end;
```

When using the TSimpleObjectBroker component, the try. . . except block leads to iterating through the Servers collection of this component and attempting to connect to any of them until connecting successfully. The statements between except and end are executed only if all these attempts fail (we can test this, for example, by stopping all Socket Servers on server computers).

The last issue we need to discuss is the deploying and licensing of MIDAS applications.

Deploying and Licensing MIDAS Applications

It was mentioned above that thin client deployment is a very simple process. It demands the MIDAS.DLL library be installed and registered in the Windows\System directory or in the same directory as the client executable. There is no need to include data access libraries, e.g., MDAC and DBMS client software. Otherwise, data access servers need data access libraries to be installed. In addition, they require the MIDAS.DLL library (it must be placed in the Windows System directory and must be registered).

Unlike RDS, which comes with MDAC and therefore does not require licensing, MIDAS, as a rule, requires one. Generally, the MIDAS license is required if the MIDAS data packets are transferred from one computer to another. For example, it is required when using the WebMIDAS application if the data access server and a client are running on different computers, or a Web server and a Web browser are running on different computers. When using several different MIDAS servers on the same computer, only one MIDAS license is required. However, when using directory services and several load-balanced servers, every server computer requires a separate MIDAS license.

Note that the briefcase file that is a result of saving a client dataset to a local file is also a MIDAS data packet. So, any way of transferring it from one computer to another (e.g., by e-mail, FTP, or diskettes) requires a MIDAS license.

A MIDAS license is not required if the data access server and the client are running on the same computer, and it does not matter if they are separate executables or parts of a single compound executable. The stand-alone application that uses a briefcase file also does not require a MIDAS license.

For more details on deployment and licensing issues, refer to John Kaster's article "When Do I Need to Buy a MIDAS License?" (see the Borland Community site `http://community.borland.com`), and to the LICENSE.TXT and DEPLOY.TXT files that come with Delphi.

Conclusion

In this chapter, we discussed creating Windows DNA applications with MIDAS. We have reviewed components and classes used to create MIDAS applications. We have also shown how to create MIDAS data access servers and "thin" clients, and how to make them more interactive, scalable, available, interoperable, and reliable. Now we know that:

- MIDAS is a technology of creating data access servers and thin clients as Automation servers and Automation controllers, respectively, that exchange data packets with Delphi datasets. MIDAS is implemented in Delphi classes and components, and in some separate services.

- Compared with RDS, MIDAS provides some advanced functionality for resolving database collisions in multi user environments by handling the appropriate event.

- MIDAS provides some additional features to propagate business rules from the data access server to the client; however, some of these are still not available for ADO data sources.

- MIDAS allows us to create interoperable JavaScript clients using the InternetExpress technology implemented in the InternetExpress Delphi components.

- MIDAS allows clients to connect data access servers using DCOM, sockets, and HTTP protocols using appropriate TCustomConnection descendants.

- Using socket connections allows us to create non-configurable clients that do not require any additional software installation except MIDAS.DLL and the client itself.

- Using HTTP protocol to connect to the data access server allows for interaction with data access servers that are behind a firewall and use SSL security.

- To increase scalability and availability of MIDAS applications, we can use several data access servers and directory services that could be implemented both separately or in a client using the TSimpleObjectBroker component.

■ A MIDAS license is required if the MIDAS data packets (including briefcase files) are transferred from one computer to another.

Although MIDAS is convenient, it has some disadvantages. In commercial use of multi-tier systems, we need to use server resources effectively, for example, by sharing or pooling them. In addition, according to Windows DNA requirements, business operations must be performed similar to performing database transactions in server DBMS. So, we need to be able to perform transactions that do not belong to the same database or are non-database at all. To solve these two problems, we need to use some special services, such as Microsoft Transaction Server. The next chapter will discuss creating transactional applications with ADO and, in particular, using Microsoft Transaction Server with ADO.

ADO APPLICATIONS AND MICROSOFT TRANSACTION SERVER

In the previous two chapters, we discussed the basic concepts of Windows DNA architecture that describes multi-tier applications on the Windows platform, and two possible ways of implementing such applications with Delphi—RDS technology and Borland MIDAS. Both of these technologies allow us to create business and presentation tiers of Windows DNA applications.

Even though RDS and MIDAS applications are more reliable and scalable than ordinary client/server applications, they still have some disadvantages. Generally speaking, MIDAS servers may require a lot of critical resources (for example, database connections) when they serve a lot of clients. Instantiating a new COM object, especially a data access object, can be a time-consuming process. In this case, it would be better to use *resource pooling* and *object pooling*. This means we have a pool of objects or resources, and if we need one, an object or resource can be taken from this pool without creating or destroying it. However, if we need to use this technique with RDS, we need to implement it manually, as this technology does not provide any implementation of such pooling.

Note: MIDAS servers allow object pooling with the use of the TWebConnection component and HTTPSRVR.DLL. For other types of connections, you can find an example of the manual implementation of object pooling in the Delphi5\Demos\MIDAS\Pooler folder. There is also a sample that shows how to get object pooling to work for other connections.

Another problem is that many real applications require a complex middle tier that consists of several services and business objects, with each of them solving its own task. For example, some of the objects can be responsible for manipulating data in different database servers, so you should have a tool that can integrate them to perform a complicated task, for example, implementing a transaction that affects different database servers.

These problems can be solved by using Microsoft Transaction Server (MTS), which is currently available as a free add-on to Windows NT 4.0 and comes as part of the Windows NT4 Option Pack. MTS is a service that can host in-process COM servers performing different tasks, and provides the ability to pool and share resources (such as database connections) for them.

This chapter covers ADO applications that use distributed transactions, and we will discuss how to create them using MTS. We will show how to create MTS server objects using ADO, how to manage them, and how to implement distributed transactions in them.

The MTS Basics

In this section, we will discuss how MTS works, how it provides database connection pooling, and the requirements of MTS objects.

Before discussing the implementation details of MTS-based applications, we need to know how they work in general.

How an MTS Application Works

Let's look at the typical scenario of how an MTS-based application works:

- A user runs a client application (implemented as a Windows executable or an HTML application) and requests a connection to the business object inside a Microsoft Transaction Server executable process on the remote computer (or, possibly, inside its own address space, but we will not discuss this case here). Generally speaking, an MTS object (implemented as a COM in-process Automation server) can do nearly anything. For example, it can be a data access server.

- If the request is correct, an instance of the context object is created inside an MTS process on the specified remote computer. This context object is personal for a client, unlike the real MTS object, and can interact with a real MTS object that can either be instantiated or reused (it plays the role of *executant*).

- Now the user can send a request to the MTS object to execute one of its methods. Such a method can, for example, retrieve a recordset using the RDS technology, retrieve a MIDAS data packet (they can play a role of *emissary* of the MTS object in a client application), or perform any other job. Moreover, using the method of an MTS object we can instantiate another MTS object. In this case, we will get the "parent" and "child" MTS objects.

- During the execution of the method of any MTS object (both a "child" and a "parent" one), an exception can occur. In this case, the MTS object informs MTS about this exception, MTS informs the caller about it, and performs some other processing of this exception if necessary.

- After the method of the MTS object finishes its job (perhaps using other MTS objects), it informs MTS whether it was successful. In addition, this object informs MTS that it is no longer necessary to this particular client. After that, the object can be destroyed or reused by another client.

As a rule, in database applications, MTS technology is used along with either MIDAS or RDS.

Now let's look at the details of how MTS works, and how we can use it for our purposes.

MTS Features

In this section, we will discuss some MTS features that are necessary for understanding how it works.

Resource and Database Connection Pooling

We have already discussed that *resource pooling* means that we have a pool of resources of a particular type (e.g., database connections), and if we need one, it can be taken from this pool without creating or destroying this resource. To implement such pooling, we can use special objects called *resource dispensers*. These objects cache resources to provide the ability for MTS objects belonging to the same group of MTS objects (called a *package*) to share them. One of the resource dispensers available is the Shared Property Manager; this object makes it possible to use shared properties for several MTS objects.

It should be mentioned that there are other resource dispensers that are widely used. For example, the ODBC resource dispenser enables ODBC connections to be pooled. This pooling is supported by some ODBC 3.0 and ODBC 3.5 database drivers such as the Microsoft ODBC drivers for SQL Server and Oracle. That means that after a connection has been created, used by an application, and then freed when the application has finished with it, the driver holds the connection in a pool in memory. Then, when another application requests a connection, the driver searches the pool for free connections and, if it finds one that matches the requirements, it returns it instead of creating a new one.

You can find out which of the ODBC drivers support database connection pooling in the Connection Pooling page of the ODBC Data Source Administrator.

You can find details of the databases and database drivers that support connection pooling, as well as distributed transactions in the "Microsoft Transaction Server FAQ: Databases and Transactions" article on MSDN. One example of an OLE DB provider that supports connection pooling is the OLE DB Provider for Microsoft SQL Server.

Object pooling is not available in MTS 2.0, but it is implemented in COM+, which combines enhancements to COM and MTS with many new services that are part of the Windows 2000 family of operating systems. To use this feature, MTS provides a persistent context object for each client that can require an object. This context object is not actually a physical object, but only a class factory wrapper. The client interacts directly with this context object instead of the real one. When object pooling will actually be implemented, the object context can take an object from a pool when necessary and return it when it is no longer needed.

Monitoring Database Transactions in MTS

In Chapter 1, we discussed what a transaction is. Generally speaking, the transaction can affect not only tables in the same database, but several different databases (maybe of different types), or include some non-database actions. In this chapter, we will primarily discuss distributed database transactions that can affect tables within different database servers.

To monitor distributed and non-database transactions in MTS objects, the Microsoft Distributed Transaction Coordinator (MS DTC) is used. This service can be activated by Windows Control Panel, or directly from the MTS Explorer. (MS DTC can be also started from MS SQL Server 7.0.)

MS DTC is a system service that coordinates transactions that use multiple resource managers. This means that a task affecting several databases can be committed as a single transaction, even if it uses multiple resource managers, maybe on separate computers. Note that DTC is also a part of Microsoft SQL Server 7.0.

Let's see how a distributed transaction works. When a component requests access to a database, the database driver checks with the appropriate MTS context object whether a transaction is required and, if any, informs the DTC about this. Then the database driver asks the resource manager for the database to start a transaction within it. The component can then manipulate the data in the database using this driver.

If we have two databases that should be modified within the same transaction, the DTC and the first database driver start the database transaction as described above. Then, if the MTS object opens a connection to the second database, the DTC and the second database driver ask this resource manager to start a new internal transaction for the changes that will be made in the second database. Now both databases are holding open transactions.

When the MTS object finishes its job, it calls its own SetComplete method if all was done properly, or the SetAbort method if the transaction should be rolled back. Then, the DTC asks both resource managers to commit or abort their current transaction. So, either all the updates on all the data stores will succeed, or all will be rolled back.

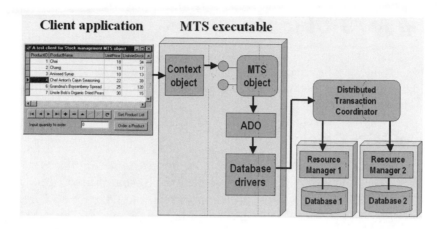

If an object needs to prevent committing or rolling back the distributed transaction, it can call the DisableCommit method. The EnableCommit method allows DTC to commit all open database transactions.

It should be mentioned that parts of the distributed transaction can be implemented in several different objects. We have mentioned earlier in this chapter that some MTS objects ("parent" objects) are able to initiate creation of other MTS objects ("child" objects). If such "child" objects generate an exception during database manipulations, MTS is informed about the need to roll back a transaction. In this case, DTC initiates rolling back the transaction of the "parent" object and notifies a client application about this rollback.

To provide such management, it is necessary to use code that implements different parts of distributed transactions to different MTS objects, and create for them a "parent" object.

Security Features

MTS allows using the Windows NT user list as its own user list. In addition, MTS supports *roles*—sets of users and user groups who are allowed to invoke interfaces of MTS objects included in a specific package. Note that these roles must not be treated as database roles that are sets of grants. Thus, we should not create any additional security mechanisms in the MTS object code.

Having discussed the MTS features, we need to say some words about MTS objects. In particular, we need to discuss the demands they must satisfy, the principles of their development, and how they should be organized in MTS.

Introducing MTS Objects

In this section, we will discuss what MTS objects are, how to create them, how they should be installed to the MTS environment, and what classes in Delphi can be used to create them.

Requirements of MTS Objects

We have already said that MTS objects are in-process Automation servers. This means they are dynamic-link libraries that implement the IDispatch interface.

MTS objects must have a standard class factory and type library (these are automatically created by Delphi MTS Object Wizard and Delphi MTS Data Module Wizard). The type library can be edited to add specific methods (to be used by the MTS executable). In addition, an MTS object must export the DllRegisterServer function; provide for self-registering its CLSID (service identifier), ProgID (server identifier), and implemented interfaces; and contain a type library (the appropriate code is also generated automatically by Delphi wizards for creating MTS objects).

If an MTS object will be used as a shared or pooled object, it must not keep any data from the client application (e.g., the cached data obtained as a result of a client query, the number of the current record in a dataset, etc.). Objects that do not keep data of a particular client are called *stateless objects*, and the appropriate code is called *stateless code*.

Applying this to Delphi applications, we can say that the MTS object must not keep any data of the particular client between calling its methods, such as recordsets obtained by client requests (they should be immediately sent to the caller of the method that retrieved them) or any other client-specific data. Note that MIDAS servers created with Delphi 5 satisfy this demand; all data they retrieve from a database is immediately sent to the client.

When a component has finished executing its method, it calls the SetComplete or SetAbort methods of its context object, which inform MTS that the component has finished the task, and it is no longer necessary to maintain its internal state. If the SetAbort method of a single object is called, the entire transaction in which this object is involved will be rolled back.

In general, in MTS objects it is better to hold database connections as short a time as possible in order to return it to the pool; however, a reference to the object can be stored a long time, because it is a reference to the context object and not the component itself. It is also recommended that the SetComplete method be called as often as possible in order not to hold the component instance in the MTS memory.

How MTS Objects are Organized in MTS

Generally, in-process COM servers are executed in a client application address space. As for MTS objects, they can be executed both in a client application address space and in an address space of an MTS executable (mtx.exe). In other words, MTS hosts these objects.

MTS objects are combined into packages. Each package can contain one or more server objects, of which there are two types. *Library packages* are executed in the client application address space, so it is impossible to implement remote access to them. *Server packages* are executed inside mtx.exe address space that is separate from the client application address space. Therefore, remote access to them is available.

The Registry entries for these COM servers are almost the same as for general in-process servers. The host application for them is, by default, mtxex.dll, which can be found in the WINNT\System32\folder. As for packages, they have separate System Registry entries in the key:

```
HKEY_LOCAL_MACHINE\SOFTWARE\Microsoft\Transaction Server\Packages
```

Any such entry contains information about the package itself and about MTS objects included in it.

Managing MTS objects and packages can be done with the MTS Explorer, which provides a graphical user interface for creating appropriate Registry entries.

Any object installed in MTS has a Transaction Support property that defines how the component will behave within MTS. It has four possible values shown in the table below:

Value	Meaning
Requires a transaction	The component runs within an existing transaction if this transaction already exists. Otherwise, MTS will start a new one.
Requires a new transaction	MTS will start a new transaction each time an instance of the component is activated.
Supports transactions	The component will run within an existing transaction if this transaction already exists. Otherwise, it will run without a transaction.
Does not support transactions	The component will always run outside any existing transactions.

When creating an MTS object using Delphi wizards, we can select the necessary options in the New MTS Object or New MTS Data Module dialog boxes.

Having discussed the MTS objects in general, let's look at Delphi classes that are usually used for creating them.

Delphi Classes for Creating MTS Objects

Delphi Enterprise comes with two classes for creating MTS-based applications. They are the TMtsAutoObject class and the TMtsDataModule class.

We already know that MTS objects are in-process Automation servers with additional features that encapsulate MTS services such as transaction support and security. The TMtsAutoObject class is used to create such objects.

The TMtsDataModule class is provided for the same purposes, but it is also a data module where we can place data access and provider components, as well as other non-visual components. It implements the IAppServer interface that allows us to use the MIDAS connection components and client datasets in client applications.

The methods that are available in both of these classes are shown in the following table:

Method	Description
SetComplete	This method indicates that the MTS object has successfully completed its task and no longer needs to keep its state information. After calling this method, the MTS object is deactivated. If the MTS object is part of a transaction, this method indicates that this part of the transaction can be committed.
SetAbort	This method indicates that any current transaction that includes this MTS object should be aborted. If MTS started a transaction automatically, the transaction will be aborted, and the object will be deactivated. If the MTS object was part of a transaction, the client transaction will fail. Usually, this method is called in the except block of a try...except statement.
EnableCommit	This method indicates that the MTS object can complete its current transaction without releasing state information. It does not allow MTS to deactivate the MTS object. This method permits the current transaction to be completed but does not automatically commit the transaction.
DisableCommit	This method indicates that the MTS object cannot complete its current transaction or release state information until the MTS object calls EnableCommit or SetComplete.
IsInTransaction	This method is called to determine whether the MTS object is currently running in a transaction.
IsCallerInRole	This method accepts the WideString parameter and checks whether the current client is part of the role named by this parameter. It returns True if the client fits the named role.
IsSecurityEnabled	This method checks whether the MTS data module is currently protected by MTS security services.

Debugging Delphi MTS Objects

In discussing MTS objects, we should mention debugging them. First, to debug an MTS object, we need to create a client application that calls methods that must be debugged.

Second, to debug a server object, we need to open its project in the Delphi IDE and set the necessary breakpoints. Then we need to select the Run | Parameters option from the IDE main menu. When using server packages, the host application parameter must be the MTS executable, for example:

```
c:\winnt\system32\mtx.exe
```

When using library packages, this parameter must be the client application executable name.

The Parameters value must contain the appropriate MTS package name:

```
/p:"ADO_MTS_Demo"
```

Note that there are no spaces between the colon and quotes.

Then you can select the Run | Run option from the main menu. After that, you can run the client application outside the IDE, and use it to call the server methods to debug.

It should be mentioned that some problems may arise when we make changes in server object code when testing or debugging it. If the server DLL file is locked when some instances of the server object still exist in the MTS address space, we cannot save the new version of this DLL. To destroy existing instances of the MTS object, we need to find the appropriate package in the MTS Explorer and select the Shutdown option from its pop-up menu. We can also select the My Computer node and select the Shut down server processes option from its pop-up menu to destroy all server objects.

In addition, we can decrease the time of the server object's existence in the inactive state. To do this, we need to select the Properties option from the appropriate package pop-up menu, click the Advanced tab, and set the appropriate value (e.g., zero) of the Shut down after being idle for... parameter. The default value of this parameter is 3 minutes.

Now we are ready to provide several examples of how to create MTS-based multi-tier applications with Delphi.

MTS Usage Examples

We will begin our MTS tour with a simple MTS data access object that manages the Product table in the Northwind database on the Microsoft SQL Server, and a client application to test it. Then, we will create a second MTS object to manage a table in which data about ordered products is stored. The next step will be to create a more complex object to perform a transaction affecting these two tables; this object will instantiate two previous ones inside its own transaction. Finally, we will move the Product table from the Northwind database to the Oracle 8 database, and modify our first MTS object to use this Oracle database instead of the Microsoft SQL Server database, in order to show how distributed transactions are managed using the Distributed Transaction Coordinator.

As in the two previous chapters, the MTS clients and the MTS itself with server objects managed with it can reside either on the same computer, or on different computers in the same domain, because we will use DCOM to connect clients to servers. As in the two previous chapters, we will use "server" for the computer where the MTS server objects will be executed, and "client" for the computer where the client applications will be executed. The server computer must have access to the databases that will be used in the examples.

To transfer the results of queries from servers to clients, we will use the RDS technology, as it does not require MIDAS licenses. So, to test our MTS applications, we need to be sure that MDAC 2.1 is installed on both the client and the server computer. We also must be sure both computers have DCOM installed (see Chapter 18 for explanations of how to find if DCOM and MDAC are installed programmatically).

Before creating MTS objects, we also must be sure that MTS is installed on the server computer. Otherwise, we need to install the Windows NT Option Pack (available on the Microsoft Web site) and select the Transaction Server Components option during installation. Before testing the MTS servers, we also need to start the DTC.

If you are planning to use Oracle to create this example, you must use version 7.3.3 or later, since Oracle 7.3.3. is the first release of Oracle that supports transactions with MTS.

When using the Oracle 8 database, we need to make changes in the following Registry key under which the names of Oracle client libraries are stored:

```
HKEY_LOCAL_MACHINE\SOFTWARE\ Microsoft\Transaction Server\Local Computer\My
Computer
```

By default, the values under this key store the Oracle 7.3 client DLL names in the following string values:

```
OracleXaLib  = "xa73.dll"
OracleSqlLib = "sqllib18.dll"
```

To use the Oracle 8 client software instead of those of Oracle 7.3, we need to change these values to specify the names of the Oracle 8 client libraries:

```
OracleXaLib  = "xa80.dll"
OracleSqlLib = "sqllib80.dll"
```

One last note before creating MTS objects: As we have said before, ODBC 3.0 and 3.5 support distributed transactions. In our examples we will use ODBC and OLE DB Provider for ODBC drivers.

Creating a Simple MTS Application

We will first show how to create a simple MTS server and then show how to develop a simple client for it.

Creating a Server Object

Our first server object will manipulate data in the Products table in the Northwind database on MS SQL Server 7.0. In particular, it will decrement the UnitsInStock and increment the UnitsOnOrder field values (these operations are performed when something is ordered from stock), and send the results of querying this table to the client in order to control the results of these manipulations. Before creating an MTS object itself, we need to create an ODBC data source to access this database from a server computer (call it Northwind_ODBC).

Our first application will consist of the parts shown in the following figure:

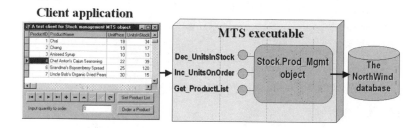

We will begin by creating a new ActiveX library project (call it STOCK.DLL). The next step is to open the Delphi Object Repository, select the MTS Data Module icon from the Multi-tier page, and fill the MTS Data Module Wizard dialog. For an ordinary COM server, we need to input the CoClass Name of the MTS object (let's call it Prod_Mgmt) and select a threading model (for MTS objects, the Apartment model is usually used). Additionally, it is necessary to select a Transaction Support property (in this wizard it is called a *transaction model*) for this object. In this case, we will select the Requires a transaction model; this allows us to use this object as a participant of a transaction initiated by another object. After that, a standard MTS data module and an appropriate type library will be generated.

Now let's place the TADOConnection and TADOCommand components in the MTS data module. The Connection property of the ADOCommand1 component should be set to ADOConnection1, and the ConnectionString property of the ADOConnection1 component should be set to point to the just created ODBC data source for the Northwind database access. See the following example:

```
Provider=MSDASQL.1;
Password="";
Persist Security Info=True;
User ID=sa;
Data Source=NorthWind_ODBC;
Initial Catalog=Northwind
```

We also need to set the LoginPrompt property of the ADOConnection1 component to False to disable the user authentication dialogs at the server computer when the MTS object will be activated.

The next step is to open the type library of the MTS object in order to define its methods. We will create three of them. The first method will decrease the UnitsInStock field value of the selected record (let's call it Dec_UnitsInStock), and the second one will increase the UnitsOnOrder field value of the selected record (let's call it Inc_UnitsOnOrder). Both of them will accept two integer input parameters: the ProductID parameter that identifies the particular record by its primary key field value that is also called ProductID, and the OrdQuantity parameter that is equal to the quantity of ordered products. The third method (let's call it Get_ProductList) will just return a recordset with the results of querying this table to the client application. In order to use the _Recordset** parameter in this method, we need to refer to the

Microsoft ActiveX DataObjects Recordset 2.1 Library in the type library for our STOCK.DLL server. The simplest way to define such a method is to create a read-only property of the _Recordset* type.

The results of editing the type library are shown in the figure below:

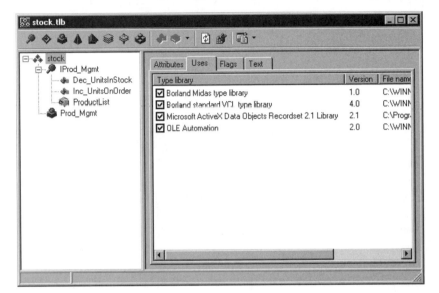

Having defined the MTS object methods, we will press the Refresh button in the Type Library Editor. Now we can implement these methods in the MTS data module unit. As we have said before, the first of them will change the value of the UnitsInStock field. Please note that the possible values in this field are restricted by a database constraint; they cannot be negative. Therefore, this method is a potential source of a database exception. We need to take this into account in its implementation and process such exceptions according to MTS rules, i.e., call the SetAbort method. The following listing shows an implementation of this method:

```
procedure TProd_Mgmt.Dec_UnitsInStock(ProductID,
 OrdQuantity: SYSINT);
begin
 try
  //Connect to the database
  ADOConnection1.Open;
  //Set a command to execute
  ADOCommand1.CommandText := 'UPDATE Products SET '+
  ' UnitsInStock=UnitsInStock-IntToStr(OrdQuantity)+
  ' WHERE ProductID=' +IntToStr(ProductID);
  //Execute a command
  ADOCommand1.Execute;
  //Disconnect from a database
  ADOConnection1.Close;
  //Inform MTS that the object has finished its work
```

```
 //successfully
 SetComplete;
except
 //Disconnect from a database
 ADOConnection1.Close;
 //Inform MTS that the object has finished its work
 //without a success
 SetAbort;
 //Pass an exception to the caller of this object
 raise;
 end;
end;
```

The second method will change the value of the UnitsOnOrder field. Here we will also process a possible exception that can occur not only because of violating a constraint, but for some other reason (for example, a database server becomes unavailable). Here is the code for doing this:

```
procedure TProd_Mgmt.Inc_UnitsOnOrder(ProductID,
 OrdQuantity: SYSINT);
begin
 try
  //Connect to the database
  ADOConnection1.Open;
  //Set a command to execute
  ADOCommand1.CommandText := 'UPDATE  Products SET '+
  ' UnitsOnOrder=UnitsOnOrder+ IntToStr(OrdQuantity)+
  ' WHERE ProductID=' +IntToStr(ProductID);
  //Execute a command
  ADOCommand1.Execute;
  //Disconnect from a database
  ADOConnection1.Close;
  //Inform MTS that the object has finished its work
  //successfully
  SetComplete;
 except
  //Disconnect from a database
  ADOConnection1.Close;
  //Inform MTS that the object has finished its work
  //without a success
  SetAbort;
  //Pass an exception to the caller of this object
  raise;
 end;
end;
```

The third method will query the Product table to receive a list of available products in the form of an ADO recordset. Here is the implementation of this method:

```
function TProd_Mgmt.Get_ProductList: _Recordset;
var
 QRY : string;
begin
   //Set a query text
 QRY := 'SELECT ProductID, ProductName, UnitPrice, ' +
        ' UnitsInStock, UnitsOnOrder from Products ' +
        ' WHERE Discontinued=0';
 try
 //Create a recordset
  Result := CoRecordset.Create;
  Result.CursorLocation := adUseClient;
 //Open the recordset using a query text
  Result.Open(QRY,ADOConnection1.ConnectionString,
  adOpenStatic,adLockBatchOptimistic, adCmdText);
  //Disconnect from a database
  ADOCOnnection1.Close;
  //Inform MTS that the object has finished its work
  // successfully
  SetComplete;
 except
  //Disconnect from a database
  ADOConnection1.Close;
  //Inform MTS that the object has finished its work
  //without a success
  SetAbort;
  //Pass an exception to the caller of this object
  raise;
 end;
end;
```

Note that we also need to refer to the ADODB, ADODB_TLB, and ActiveX units in the Uses clause.

Now we can compile and save this project. The last step is to register it in the MTS environment. If the STOCK.DLL library containing this object is developed on the server computer, this can be done by selecting the Run | Install MTS Objects item from the Delphi IDE menu (in this case, we need to input the name of the new package and where to install this component in the dialog that appears).

If this component is developed in another computer, the just created STOCK.DLL file must be copied to the server computer and registered by using the MTS Explorer. In this case, we can create a new package by right-clicking the My Computer | Packages installed tree node, and selecting the New | Package item from its pop-up menu. Let's call our new package ADO_MTS_Demo. After creating a package, we need to find its name in the tree view, right-click its Components node, and select the New | Component item from its menu. Then we will see a sequence of dialog boxes where we need to answer questions about the DLL name and some other properties, for example, whether this component is already registered in the MTS environment. Also, to register the MTS object, we can drag the DLL from the Windows Explorer to the package in the MTS Explorer.

Now that we have created a simple MTS object and registered it in the MTS environment, we are able to create a client to test its methods. In the next section, we will show how to do this.

Creating an MTS Client

Let's create a new Delphi project and place the TRDSConnection and TADODataSet components on its main form. The ServerName property of the RDSConnection1 component should be set to the ProgID of our MTS object (in our case, it is stock.Prod_Mgmt), and the ComputerName property should be set to the name of the server computer. In this case, we will use the DCOM type of connection, and the MTS object will be executed in the MTS server process, so we need to use the name of the computer, and not its URL (as it was done when we created RDS clients in Chapter 20). We do not need to set any properties of the ADODataSet1 component; it will receive a recordset at run time. However, we need to show this recordset to the users, so we will place the TDataSource, the TDBGrid, and the TDBNavigator components and bind them with the ADODataSet1 component. Then let's place the TEdit component to input the quantity of ordered products, and two buttons to force this application to call methods of the MTS object.

The next step is to create the OnClick event handlers of these buttons. The first of them must retrieve a recordset from an MTS object and show it in a grid. Here is the code for doing this:

```
procedure TForm1.Button1Click(Sender: TObject);
begin
 try
  //Instantiate an MTS object context
  RDSConnection1.Connected := True;
  //Get a recordset from an MTS object
  RS := RDSConnection1.GetRecordset('ProductList','');
  ADODataSet1.Recordset := RS;
  //Show the recordset to the user
  ADODataSet1.Open;
  //Now we can call other methods of the MTS object
  Button2.Enabled := True;
 except
  //Something goes wrong - an MTS object cannot
  //return a recordset
  ShowMessage('Cannot get the product list');
 //Now we cannot call other methods of the MTS object
  Button2.Enabled := False;
 end;
 //Free the MTS object context
```

```
  RDSConnection1.Connected := False;
end;
```

The second one must call two other methods of the MTS object; this emulates processing an order. An implementation of this method is shown in the listing below:

```
procedure TForm1.Button2Click(Sender: TObject);
var
 PID, Quantity : Integer;
begin
 //Identify the product to order by its ProductID
 PID := ADODataSet1.FieldByName('ProductID').AsInteger;
 //Define how many products we need to order
 Quantity := StrToInt(Edit1.Text);
 try
  //Instantiate an MTS object context
  RDSConnection1.Connected := True;
  //Substract the Quantity value from the
  //UnitsOnOrder field value
  RDSConnection1.AppServer.Dec_UnitsInStock(PID, Quantity);
  //Add the Quantity value to the UnitsOnOrder field value
  RDSConnection1.AppServer.Inc_UnitsOnOrder(PID, Quantity);
  Button1Click(self);
 except
  //An exception occurs in MTS
  Showmessage('The order was not processed');
 end;
 //Free the MTS object context
 RDSConnection1.Connected := False;
end;
```

We also need to add the description of the RS variable in the global declaration section:

```
var
  Form1 : TForm1;
  RS    : _Recordset;
```

Now we can save and compile a client application and copy it to the client computer. Let's execute it and press the first button. We will receive a recordset (if we observe the MTS Explorer where this component is shown, we can see that its icon is animated during the process of retrieving a recordset). Then we can select a record in a grid, input an integer value (for example, 1) into the Edit1 component, and press the second button. After that, the data in the grid will be refreshed, and we can see that the UnitsInStock field value was decreased in the selected record, and the UnitsOnOrder value was increased to the value that was entered in the Edit1 component. However, if we try to input a value that exceeds the UnitsInStock value in this record, the database constraint for this field will be violated, an exception will occur in the MTS object, all operations will be cancelled, and we will receive an error message in the client application.

Note that we can find information about committed and aborted transactions by selecting the Transaction Statistics node in the MTS Explorer.

The next step in our MTS examples tour will be the creation of MTS objects that implement a complex transaction consisting of different parts. We will show how to do this in the following section.

Managing Complex Transactions

Now we will create two additional MTS objects. The first one will implement the only method that adds a record to the table where the ordered products are registered (let it be called OrderedProducts, and we will create it before developing this object). It is similar to the previous one. The second object will implement a complex transaction that consists of the following data manipulations:

- Decreasing the UnitsInStock field value of the selected record in the Products table

- Increasing the UnitsOnOrder field value of the same record in the Products table

- Inserting into the OrderedProducts table a new record that contains the name and quantity of the ordered product, along with some additional information obtained from a client application

The parts of this application are schematically shown in the figure below:

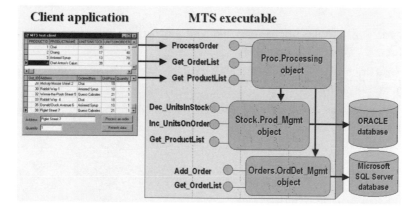

To implement such a transaction, this object will call two "child" objects. The first of them, the Prod_Mgmt object, was created in the previous section; the second one was just described—it will add records to the OrderedProducts table. We will begin by creating it.

Implementing a Complex Transaction

Before creating additional MTS objects, we need to create the OrderedProducts table in the Northwind database. Here is an SQL statement that does the job:

```
CREATE TABLE [dbo].[OrderedProducts] (
  [Ord_ID]      [int] IDENTITY (1, 1) NOT NULL,
  [Address]     [char]        (40)   NULL,
  [OrderedItem] [char]        (50)   NULL,
  [UnitPrice]   [money]              NULL,
  [Quantity]    [int]                NULL
) ON [PRIMARY]
```

Note that we have created the Ord_ID field with an Identity type. We will show later how it behaves when a transaction is rolled back. The Address and Quantity field values will be received from a client application, and the OrderedItem and UnitPrice fields will be obtained from a selected record of the Products table.

Having created a table, we can create a new MTS object. Name the library containing it ORDERS.DLL, and name the object itself OrdDet_Mgmt.

On the MTS data module of this object, we will place the same set of components as in the previous example, with the same property values. Then we need to open the type library of this object and define two methods. The first of them is the Add_Order method, which accepts four arguments:

■ The Addr parameter of BSTR type with the customer address specified by a client application

■ The OrderedItem parameter of BSTR type that will contain the name of the ordered product

■ The UnitPrice parameter of CURRENCY type that will contain the price of a unit of the ordered product

■ The Quantity parameter of Integer type that will contain a quantity of ordered units

The implementation code for this method is shown below:

```
procedure TOrdDet_Mgmt.Add_Order(
 const Addr,
 OrderedItem : WideString;
 UnitPrice   : Currency;
 Quantity    : SYSINT
);
begin
 try
  //Connect to the database
  ADOConnection1.Open;
  //Set the text of a command to execute
  ADOCommand1.CommandText := 'INSERT INTO OrderedProducts '
 + ' VALUES(''' + Addr + ''', ''' + OrderedItem+''', '
```

```
+FloatToStr(UnitPrice) + ', ' + IntToStr(Quantity) + ')';
//Execute a command
ADOCommand1.Execute;
//Disconnect from the database
ADOConnection1.Close;
//Inform MTS that the object has finished its work
// successfully
SetComplete;
except
//Disconnect from the database
ADOCOnnection1.Close;
//Inform MTS that the object has finished its work
//without a success
SetAbort;
//Pass an exception to the caller of this object
raise;
end;
end;
```

The second method will return a recordset with the results of querying the
OrderedProducts table:

```
function TOrdDet_Mgmt.Get_OrderList: _Recordset;
var
 QRY : string;
begin
 //Set a query text
 QRY := 'SELECT * FROM OrderedProducts ORDER BY Ord_ID';
 try
  //Create a recordset
  Result := CoRecordset.Create;
  Result.CursorLocation := adUseClient;
  //Open the recordset
  Result.Open(QRY,ADOConnection1.ConnectionString,
  adOpenStatic,adLockBatchOptimistic, adCmdText);
  //Disconnect from the database
  ADOCOnnection1.Close;
  //Inform MTS that the object has finished its work
  // successfully
  SetComplete;
 except
  ADOConnection1.Close;
  //Inform MTS that the object has finished its work
  //without a success
  SetAbort;
  //Pass an exception to the caller of this object
  raise;
end;
```

```
end;
```

Note that we need to refer to the ADODB, ADODB_TLB, and ActiveX units in the Uses clause.

After compiling and saving this project, we should copy the ORDERS.DLL library to the server computer and install the OrdDet_Mgmt object in the same package where the previous object was installed.

Having created two MTS objects that manipulate two tables, we can design a more complex object that can call them in order to implement its methods. To do this, let's create a new ActiveX library project (let's call this library PROC.DLL) and a new MTS object called Processing. Here we can use the TMtsAutoObject class instead of the TMtsDataModule class (and select the MTS Object icon instead of the MTS Data Module icon in the Object Repository), because this object will not contain any data access components.

Next, we need to select the Requires a new transaction model for it; this means the object requires its own transaction and could not be executed in the transaction of another object. Two previously created objects use the Requires a transaction model, which means they can be executed in a transaction of the object that calls them.

We will define three methods in the type library of this object. Two of them, the Get_OrderList method and the Get_ProductList method, will return recordsets with the results of querying the OrderedProducts table and the Products table, respectively. As in the previous examples, they can be created as methods to get a read-only property, and serve only for presentation purposes. Their implementation is shown in the following listing:

```
function TProcessing.Get_OrderList: _Recordset;
var
 QRY : string;
begin
 try
  //Create an instance of the OrdDet_Mgmt object context
  OleCheck(ObjectContext.CreateInstance(CLASS_OrdDet_Mgmt,
  IOrdDet_Mgmt, FOrdDet));
  //Create a recordset
  Result := CoRecordset.Create;
  Result.CursorLocation := adUseClient;
 //Receive the data from the OrdDet_Mgmt object
   Result := FOrdDet.Get_OrderList;
  //Inform MTS that the object has finished its work
  // successfully
  SetComplete;
 except
  //Inform MTS that the object has failed
  SetAbort;
  //Pass an exception to the caller of this object
  raise;
```

```
 end;
end;

function TProcessing.Get_ProductList: _Recordset;
begin
 try
  //Create an instance of the OrdDet_Mgmt object context
  OleCheck(ObjectContext.CreateInstance(CLASS_Prod_Mgmt,
  IProd_Mgmt, FProd));
  //Create a recordset
  Result := CoRecordset.Create;
  Result.CursorLocation := adUseClient;
  //Receive the data from the Prod_Mgmt object
  Result := FProd.Get_ProductList;
  //Inform MTS that the object has finished its work
  // successfully
  SetComplete;
 except
  //Inform MTS that the object has failed
  SetAbort;
  //Pass an exception to the caller of this object
  raise;
 end;
```

In the implementation of this method, we use the CreateInstance method of the object context, instead of creating an MTS object itself. This allows us to use objects themselves only when they are really necessary, and therefore save server resources. In order to make these methods work properly, we need to add the following definition for variables that will contain references to the two objects to be called from these methods:

```
private
   FProd   : IProd_Mgmt;
   FOrdDet : IOrdDet_Mgmt;
```

We also need to include type libraries of the previous two objects into the current project. The simplest way is to copy the PROC.TLB, PROC_TLB.PAS, STOCK.TLB, and STOCK_TLB.PAS files to the directory of the current project, and include the reference to the PROC_TLB.PAS, and STOCK_TLB.PAS units into the Uses clause, along with the ActiveX, ADODB, and ADOINT units.

The third method, ProcessOrder, will implement a complex transaction that modifies the Product and OrderedProduct tables simultaneously (or does not modify them at all, if a database or other exception occurs during these modifications). This method accepts five parameters:

■ The Prod_Id parameter of Integer type that identifies the record in the Product table that will be modified

- The Prod_Name parameter of BSTR type that will contain the name of the ordered product
- The UnitPrice parameter of CURRENCY type that will contain the price of a unit of the ordered product
- The Quantity parameter of Integer type that will contain the number of ordered units
- The Addr parameter of BSTR type that will contain the customer address supplied by a client application

The implementation of the ProcessOrder method itself can be the following:

```
procedure TProcessing.ProcessOrder(Prod_ID: SYSINT;
  const Prod_Name: WideString; UnitPrice: Currency;
  Quantity: SYSINT;  const Addr: WideString);
begin
 try
  //Create the Prod_Mgmt object context
  OleCheck(ObjectContext.CreateInstance(CLASS_Prod_Mgmt,
  IProd_Mgmt, FProd));
  //Create the OrdDet_Mgmt object context
  OleCheck(ObjectContext.CreateInstance(CLASS_OrdDet_Mgmt,
  IOrdDet_Mgmt, FOrdDet));
  //Add a record to the OrderedProducts table
  FOrdDet.Add_Order(Addr, Prod_Name,UnitPrice,Quantity);
  //Decrease the UnitsInStock field value of the Product table
  FProd.Dec_UnitsInStock(Prod_ID,Quantity);
  //Increase the UnitsOnOrder field value of the Product table
  FProd.Inc_UnitsOnOrder(Prod_ID,Quantity);
  //Inform MTS that the transaction could be committed
  EnableCommit;
 except
  //Inform MTS that the transaction should be rolled back
  DisableCommit;
  //Pass an exception to the client
  raise;
 end;
end;
```

We need to explain some lines of this code. After creating instances of the called objects, we call their methods. In this sequence of called methods, the most "dangerous" method is the second one, as its execution can cause a database exception:

```
FProd.Dec_UnitsInStock(Prod_ID,Quantity);
```

In this case, the results of executing the previous method in this sequence should be rolled back. We will see this later.

After saving and compiling the current project, it should also be copied to the server computer and installed into the same MTS package as the two previous DLLs, as shown in the figure below:

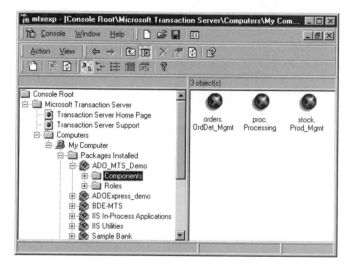

Now we can create a client application to test how these complex transactions work. In the following section, we will show how to do this.

Using Complex Transactions

Let's create a new project, and place the TRDSConnection and two TADODataSet components on its main form. The ServerName property of the RDSConnection1 component should be set to the ProgID of our third MTS object (in our case, it is proc.Processing), and the ComputerName property should be set to the name of the server computer. We do not need to set any properties of the TADODataSet components; they will receive recordsets at run time. To show these recordsets to the users, we will place two TDataSource and two TDBGrid components and bind them with the appropriate TADODataSet component. Then let's place two TEdit components to input the quantity of ordered products and the delivery address, and two buttons to force this application to call methods of the Processing object.

The next step is to set the OnClick event handlers of these buttons. The first of them must retrieve two recordsets from a database using the Processing object and present them in two grids. This is shown in the listing below:

```
procedure TForm1.Button1Click(Sender: TObject);
begin
 try
  //Instantiate the Processing object
  RDSConnection1.Connected := True;
  //Retrieve a Product List
  RS := RDSConnection1.GetRecordset('ProductList','');
```

```
ADODataSet1.Recordset := RS;
ADODataSet1.Open;
//Retrieve an Order List
RS := RDSConnection1.GetRecordset('OrderList','');
ADODataSet2.Recordset := RS;
ADODataSet2.Open;
//Now we can order products
Button2.Enabled := True;
except
 //Some of server objects are unavailable
 ShowMessage('Cannot get data');
 Button2.Enabled := False;
end;
RDSConnection1.Connected:=False;
end;
```

To make this method work properly, we need to refer to the ADODB unit in the Uses clause and add the RS variable description in the global declaration section:

```
var
  Form1 : TForm1;
  RS    : _Recordset;
```

The second event handler initiates a complex transaction, calling the ProcessOrder method:

```
procedure TForm1.Button2Click(Sender: TObject);
begin
 try
  //Instantiate the Processing object
  RDSConnection1.Connected := True;
  //Call its ProcessOrder method
  RDSConnection1.AppServer.ProcessOrder(
  ADODataSet1.FieldByName('ProductID').AsInteger,
  ADODataSet1.FieldByName('ProductName').AsString,
  ADODataSet1.FieldByName('UnitPrice').AsFloat,
  StrToInt(Edit1.Text),Edit2.Text);
  //Refresh data in grids
  Button1Click(self);
 except
  //An exception occurs in one of the server objects
  ShowMessage('Cannot process an order');
  Button2.Enabled := False;
 end;
 RDSConnection1.Connected := False;
end;
```

Now we can compile and save the project, and copy it to the client computer.

Let's run this client application. After pressing the first button, we will receive the data from the Products and OrderedProducts tables to the grids. Then we can select a record in the grid presenting the Product dataset, input an address and the number of ordered units in the appropriate TEdit controls, and press the second button. This results in a complex transaction. If the number of ordered units does not exceed the UnitsInStock field value in the selected record, we will obtain the following results after refreshing data:

- The UnitsInStock field value will be decreased by the Quantity value
- The UnitsOnOrder field value will be increased by the Quantity value
- The new record will appear in the OrderedProducts table

It should be mentioned that if all goes as planned, any newly created record in the OrderedProducts table will have an Ord_Id value equaling the value of this field in the previously created record plus one. But what happens if something goes wrong? Let's input a quantity value that exceeds the UnitsInStock field value in the selected record. In this case, the new record in the OrderedProducts table will be added by the OrdDet_Mgmt object. Then the Prod_Mgmt object will execute its method, which will result in a database exception, the transaction will be rolled back, and the just created record will be deleted from the OrderedProducts table. But the current value of the Identity Ord_Id field will remain unchanged, so if we then try to make a "valid" order, we will see that this Ord_Id field value is skipped; there is no record with this value in the OrderedProducts table. Therefore, the transactions are rolled back when there is an exception in any called method.

You may ask: "Why have you done this the hard way by creating three DLLs, instead of using the obvious transactional mechanisms of the database server?" Yes, this really does not make sense when using the same database. However, the essential feature of MTS and its Distributed Transaction Coordinator is that they allow us to make distributed transactions that affect several different database servers. In our final example, we will illustrate how they work.

Managing Distributed Transactions

To illustrate how to create and use distributed transactions, we will slightly modify our example. Now it will use two tables in two different databases—Microsoft SQL Server 7.0 and Oracle 8.

First, let's copy the Product table from the Northwind database to the Oracle database (in our example, we have used a standard ORCL database that could be created during Oracle installation). We can do it, for example, by using the Microsoft Data Transformation services. Then we should rename the new Oracle Products table PRODUCTS; this means we won't have to modify the texts of queries in our objects.

It is also necessary to create a database constraint for this table by running the following SQL statement in SQL Plus or another SQL tool:

```
ALTER TABLE SCOTT.PRODUCTS
  ADD CONSTRAINT PRODUCTSCHECKCONSTRAINT1
  CHECK (UNITSINSTOCK>-1)
```

The next step is to define the ODBC data source for the Oracle database. Let's call this data source ora_odbc.

Note:

To create MTS objects that connect to Oracle databases, we need to use the Microsoft ODBC Driver for Oracle. The ODBC driver that comes with Oracle 8 itself is appropriate for ordinary ADO client applications, but cannot be used with MTS objects.

Now we need to modify our first Prod_Mgmt object. The only thing that should be done here is to modify the ConnectionString property of the ADOConnection1 component:

```
Provider=MSDASQL.1;
Password=MANAGER;
Persist Security Info=True;
User ID=SYSTEM;
Data Source=ora_odbc
```

Other objects in this example do not use the Products table directly, so we do not need to modify them.

After placing the new version of the STOCK.DLL library on the server computer, we can run the client application again.

Now we can see that distributed transactions are maintained correctly, as in the case of using two tables in the Northwind database. After receiving data from both databases to the grids, selecting a record in the grid showing the Product table, typing an address and the number of ordered units, and pressing the second button, we will receive results similar to those of the previous test. In particular, if the number of ordered units does not exceed the UnitsInStock field value in the selected record, we will see that the UnitsInStock field value will be decreased, the UnitsOnOrder field value will be increased, and the new record will be inserted to the OrderedProducts table. And if a number of ordered units exceeds the UnitsInStock field value, the transaction is rolled back, and the current Ord_Id field value will be skipped in the OrderedProducts table. Therefore, an exception that now occurs in the Oracle database results in a transaction rollback inside an SQL Server database. That is why we use MTS; transaction mechanisms that are used in database servers cannot implement database transactions that span different types of database servers.

Conclusion

In this chapter, we discussed creating transactional ADO applications with MTS. Now we know that:

- Microsoft Transaction Server is a service that can host in-process COM servers performing different tasks, and provides the ability to pool and share resources (such as database connections) for them.

- For monitoring distributed and non-database transactions in MTS objects, the Microsoft Distributed Transaction Coordinator (MS DTC) is used. It is a system service that coordinates transactions that use multiple resource managers.

- MTS objects are in-process Automation servers with additional features that encapsulate MTS services such as transaction support and security.

- If an MTS object will be used as a shared or pooled object, it must be a stateless object.

- MTS objects are combined into packages, of which there are two types. Library packages are executed in the client application address space, and server packages are executed inside the mtx.exe address space.

- Delphi Enterprise comes with two classes for creating MTS-based applications. They are the TMtsAutoObject class and the TMtsDataModule class. The TMtsAutoObject class is used to create MTS objects that do not contain data access components, and the TMtsDataModule class is used to create MTS objects that are also data modules that store data access and provider components, as well as other non-visual components. They implement the IAppServer interface, which allows using the MIDAS connection components and client datasets in client applications.

We also created a set of examples illustrating how to implement different MTS objects. In particular, we have created a simple MTS data access object that manages the Product table in the Northwind database and a client application to test it. Then, we created a second MTS object to manage a table where data about ordered products is stored, and a "parent" object for the previous two ones, which performs a transaction affecting these two tables. Finally, we moved the Product table from the Microsoft SQL Server 7 database to the Oracle 8 database, and modified our first MTS object to use this Oracle database; thus, we have implemented a distributed transaction that spans two different database servers.

Now we can see that using Microsoft Transaction Server is a rather convenient way to create applications that use distributed database transactions.

This discussion of MTS finishes our brief tour of distributed computing with ADO. We have almost finished learning how to create Delphi ADO applications, both ordinary and distributed ones. The last topic that remains to be discussed is the new features of the ADO 2.5 library. This is covered in the next chapter.

USING ADO 2.5

In this chapter, we will look at the future of ADO—version 2.5 of ActiveX Data Objects, which is an integrated part of the Windows 2000 operating system and is available as a separate set of components to be used under the Windows 9x and Windows NT operating systems. We will briefly discuss what is really new in ADO 2.5, and then we will take a more detailed look at the new objects in the ADO object model. We will also create several examples that show how we can use them in Delphi applications.

What is New in ADO 2.5

The new version of Microsoft ActiveX Data Objects contains several new capabilities and bug fixes. In this section, we will briefly outline the new features in ADO 2.5.

The main important feature of ADO 2.5 is that, starting with Windows 2000, it is a standard part of the Windows operating system automatically installed with the other core parts of the system. That means that if you create applications for the Windows 2000 family of operating systems, you don't need to worry about the availability of ADO on the user's computers—it is already installed. The other good news is that being a part of the operating system service, ADO can only be installed or updated by the Microsoft Installer or as a part of the service pack, and the files are now protected by Windows File Protection, which prevents other programs from changing the files needed by the operating system.

ADO 2.5 contains two new objects in the ADO object model—the Record object that represents a row in a Recordset and the Stream object that represents binary data associated with the Record object. Using these objects, we can work with hierarchically organized data found in the file system or in a mail folder. We will discuss the Record and Stream objects in the next section. The following diagram shows the new ADO 2.5 objects in the context of the ADO object model:

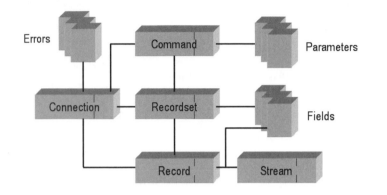

ADO 2.5 allows us to use a Uniform Resource Locator as an alternative to connection strings for accessing the data sources. URL-based connection strings can be used with Connection and Recordset objects, as well as with the new Record and Stream objects introduced in ADO 2.5. One of the OLE DB providers that recognizes the URL-based connection strings is the OLE DB Provider for Internet Publishing that can be used to access the file system over the HTTP protocol.

ADO 2.5 also introduces a special class of providers, called Document Source providers, that are used to manage folders and documents within it. Such providers are used when a Record object represents a document or when a Recordset object points to a folder with documents in it. In this case, the Document Source provider creates a unique set of fields containing the characteristics of the document.

Now that we have outlined the major new features in ADO 2.5, let's discuss them in more detail. We will start by looking at the new objects that are now available in the ADO object model.

The Record Object

This object represents a row in a recordset, a file in a file system, or a message in a mail folder. While rows are supported by the OLE DB providers discussed earlier in this book (see Chapter 3 for more details), the files and messages require a special class of providers, called *Document Source Providers*. These providers supply the characteristics of the file or message as a unique set of fields, accessible through the Fields collection of the Record object.

The Record object's methods, properties, and collections are described below.

Methods

The Record object has seven methods: Cancel, Close, CopyRecord, DeleteRecord, GetChildren, MoveRecord, and Open.

The Cancel Method

This method can be used to terminate the execution of an asynchronous method call. The Cancel method terminates the execution started with the CopyRecord, DeleteRecord, MoveRecord, or Open methods.

An asynchronous method call can be initiated with the adOpenAsync option of the Open method, or by setting the Async argument to True in the CopyRecord, DeleteRecord, and MoveRecord methods.

The Close Method

This method closes the previously opened Record object and frees any associated system resources. Note that this method does not remove the object from memory and it can be reopened later with a call to the Open method.

The CopyRecord Method

This method copies the contents of the Record object to a specified location. The prototype of the CopyRecord method is shown below:

```
function CopyRecord(
 const Source: WideString; const Destination: WideString;
 const UserName: WideString; const Password: WideString;
 Options: CopyRecordOptionsEnum; Async: WordBool): WideString;
safecall;
```

The CopyRecord method has several arguments shown in the table below:

Argument	Type	Meaning
Source	WideString	This optional parameter can be used to specify the URL for the file or directory to be copied. If this parameter is omitted or contains an empty string, the current content of the Record object will be copied.
Destination	WideString	Specifies a string that contains the URL for the location where the Source will be copied.
UserName	WideString	Specifies an optional user ID that may be needed to access the Destination.
Password	WideString	Specifies an optional password that may be needed along with the user ID to access the Destination.
Options	CopyRecordOptionsEnum	Specifies the way the record is copied. See table below for more details.
Async	WordBool	If True, this operation will be performed asynchronously.

Depending on the provider, the CopyRecord method may return the value of the destination.

The Options parameter specifies the way the record is copied. It can have one of the following values:

Constant	Value	Meaning
adCopyUnspecified	-1	This is the default value. It indicates that the default copy will be performed. The copy operation will fail if the Destination already exists.
adCopyOverWrite	1	The copy operation overwrites the Destination if it already exists.
adCopyNonRecursive	2	Only the current directory, but not its subdirectories, will be copied.
adCopyAllowEmulation	4	The copy operation is simulated through download and upload operations.

When using the CopyRecord method, note that the values of the Source and Destination arguments should not point to the same location. In recursive copying (adCopyNonRecursive is not specified in the Options parameter), the Destination argument must not specify a subdirectory of the Source.

The CopyRecord method will fail if the Destination already exists and the adCopyOverWrite option is not used. Also note that when using the adCopyOverWrite option it can be easy to overwrite the entire directory with a single file, so use this option carefully.

The DeleteRecord Method

This method is used to delete a specified location. The DeleteRecord method takes two arguments. The optional Source parameter can be used to specify the URL for the file or directory to be deleted. If this parameter is omitted or contains an empty string, the current location represented by the Record object will be deleted. The second parameter allows us to specify if this operation is synchronous (False) or asynchronous (True).

The prototype of the DeleteRecord method is shown below:

```
procedure DeleteRecord(const Source: WideString;
  Async: WordBool); safecall;
```

After calling this method, the Record object should be closed. If the Record was obtained from the Recordset, the contents of the latter should be updated. This can be done by calling the Requery, Resync, or Update methods, or by closing and reopening the Recordset.

The GetChildren Method

Use this method to retrieve a Recordset that contains the characteristics of the files or directories represented by the Record object.

The prototype for this method is shown below:

```
function  GetChildren: _Recordset; safecall;
```

The following table shows the fields available in the Recordset returned by the GetChildren method for the document source provider:

Field	Type	Description
RESOURCE_NAME	adWChar	Indicates the resource itself in the form of a URL. Read-only.
RESOURCE_PARENTNAME	adWChar	Indicates the parent record in the form of a URL. Read-only.
RESOURCE_ABSOLUTEPARSENAME	adWChar	Concatenation of the previous two values.
RESOURCE_ISHIDDEN	adBoolean	Indicates whether this resource is hidden.
REsOURCE_ISREADONLY	adWChar	Indicates whether this resource is read-only.
RESOURCE_CONTENTTYPE	adWChar	Indicates the MIME content type.
RESOURCE_CONTENTCLASS	adWChar	Indicates the class of the document.
RESOURCE_CONTENTLANGUAGE	adWChar	Indicates the language of the document.
RESOURCE_CREATIONTIME	adDBFileTime	Indicates the time when the resource was created. Read-only.
RESOURCE_LASTACCESSTIME	adDBFileTime	Indicates the time when the resource was last accessed. Read-only.
RESOURCE_LASTWRITETIME	adDBFileTime	Indicates the time when the resource was last written. Read-only.
RESOURCE_STREAMSIZE	adUnsignedBigInt	Indicates the size of the resource. Read-only.
RESOURCE_ISCOLLECTION	adBoolean	If True, the resource is a directory; otherwise it is a simple file.
RESOURCE_ISSTRUCTURED DOCUMENT	adBoolean	If True, the resource is a structured document.
DEFAULT_DOCUMENT	adWChar	If True, the resource represents the default document of a folder or a structured document.
CHAPTERED_CHILDREN	adChapter	Optional. Currently is not used.
RESOURCE_DISPLAYNAME	adWChar	Indicates the name of the resource. Read-only.
RESOURCE_ISROOT	adBoolean	If True, the resource is a root of a collection or structured document. Read-only.

 Note: The set of fields may be different for providers other than document source providers.

The MoveRecord Method

The MoveRecord method can be used to move a file or directory along with its contents to a specified location. The prototype of the MoveRecord method is shown below:

```
function  MoveRecord(
 const Source: WideString;
 const Destination: WideString;
 const UserName: WideString; const Password: WideString;
 Options: MoveRecordOptionsEnum; Async: WordBool): WideString;
safecall;
```

The MoveRecord method has several parameters shown in the table below:

Argument	Type	Meaning
Source	WideString	This optional parameter can be used to specify the URL for the file or directory to be moved. If this parameter is omitted or contains an empty string, the current content of the Record object will be moved.
Destination	WideString	Specifies a string that contains the URL for the location where the Source will be moved.
UserName	WideString	Specifies an optional user ID that may be needed to access the Destination.
Password	WideString	Specifies an optional password that may be needed along with the user ID to access the Destination.
Options	MoveRecordOptionsEnum	Specifies the way the record is copied. See table below for more details.
Async	WordBool	If True, this operation will be performed asynchronously.

Depending on the provider, the MoveRecord method may return the value of the Destination.

The Options parameter specifies the way the record is moved. It can have one of the following values:

Constant	Value	Meaning
adMoveUnspecified	-1	The default move operation will be performed
adMoveOverWrite	1	Overwrites the destination file or directory, even if it already exists
AdMoveDontUpdateLinks	2	The hypertext links of the source Record will not be updated
AdMoveAllowEmulation	4	The move operation is simulated through download, upload, and delete operations

When using the MoveRecord method, note that the values of the Source and Destination arguments should not point to the same location. The MoveRecord method updates all hypertext links in the moved files; this default behavior can be changed if the adMoveDontUpdateLinks option is specified. If the Destination already exists, this method will fail. Use the adMoveOverWrite option to avoid the errors, but remember that in this case one file can overwrite the entire directory.

To get the updated contents of the Record object, reopen it specifying the URL for the new location of the moved files.

The Open Method

This method is used to open an existing Record object or create a new file or directory. The prototype of the Open method is shown below:

```
procedure Open(
  Source: OleVariant; ActiveConnection: OleVariant;
  Mode: ConnectModeEnum;
  CreateOptions: RecordCreateOptionsEnum;
  Options: RecordOpenOptionsEnum;
```

```
const UserName: WideString; const Password: WideString);
safecall;
```

The Open method takes six arguments that are described in the following table:

Argument	Type	Meaning
Source	OleVariant	Indicates the URL for the resource to open, or a row in an open Recordset object.
ActiveConnection	OleVariant	Specifies the connection string or open Connection object.
Mode	ConnectionModeEnum	Indicates the access mode for the resulting opened Record object. See the table below for more details.
CreateOptions	RecordCreateOptionsEnum	Indicates the Record creation options. See the table below for more details.
Options	RecordOpenOptionsEnum	Specifies the options that can be used to open the Record. See the table below for more details.
UserName	WideString	Specifies an optional user ID that may be needed to access the Source.
Password	WideString	Specifies an optional password that may be needed along with the user ID to access the Source.

The Mode parameter can have one of the following values:

Constant	Value	Meaning
adModeUnknown	0	Permissions have not been set or cannot be determined. This is the default value
adModeRead	1	Read-only permissions
adModeWrite	2	Write-only permissions
adModeReadWrite	3	Read/write permissions
AdModeShareDenyRead	4	Other users cannot open this Record with read permissions
AdModeShareDenyWrite	8	Other users cannot open this Record with write permissions
AdModeShareExclusive	12	Other users cannot open this Record with any permissions
AdModeShareDenyNone	16	Other users can open this Record with any permissions
adModeRecursive	4194304	Used with other adModeShareDenyXXX options to specify sharing restrictions for the subrecords of the current Record.

The CreateOptions parameter can have one of the values shown in the following table:

Constant	Value	Meaning
adFailIfNotExists	-1	The Open method will fail if Source does not exist. This is the default value.
AdCreateNonCollection	0	A new Record of the adSimpleRecord will be created.
adCreateCollection	8192	A new collection Record will be created. If the Source is already exists, the Open method will fail.
adOpenIfExists	33554432	An existing Record must be opened.
adCreateOverwrite	67108864	An existing Record will be overwritten and a new one will be created.
adCreateStructDoc	2147483648	A new Record of the adStructDoc will be created.

The Options parameter can have one of the following values:

Constant	Value	Meaning
AdOpenRecordUnspecified	-1	No options are specified. This is the default value.
adOpenAsync	4096	Indicates the asynchronous mode.
adDelayFetchStream	16384	The default Stream associated with the Record will not be fetched.
adDelayFetchFields	32768	The fields associated with the Record will not be fetched.
adOpenSource	8388608	For non-collection records the source for the Record will be opened.

There can be several types of the Source that can be used in the Open method. For example, it can be an absolute URL that points to an existing file or directory, or a relative URL; in this case the ActiveConnection parameter should be used to supply extra information such as a valid Connection object, absolute URL, or a Record object that represents a directory.

The Source can also be an open Recordset object. In this case, the cursor must be positioned to the appropriate record in the Recordset object before calling the Open method.

Properties

The Record object has six properties: ActiveConnection, Mode, ParentURL, RecordType, Source, and State.

The ActiveConnection Property

This property indicates the Connection object that was used to open the current Record object. This property is read-only while the Record object is open, and read/write otherwise.

To get the value of this property in Delphi, we use the Get_ActiveConnection method that returns an OleVariant value. To set the value of this property as a string (like the ConnectionString property of the TADOConnection object), we must use _Set_ActiveConnection, while to indicate the valid ADO Connection object, we must use the Set_ActiveConnection method.

The Mode Property

This property indicates the permissions for modifying data in a Record object. The Mode property is read-only while the Record object is open and read/write when it is closed. By default, the Record object is opened in read-only mode, and the value of the Mode property is adModeRead.

The Mode property has the ConnectModeEnum type. Its possible values are shown in the Open method section above.

The ParentURL Property

This read-only property returns a WideString that contains a fully qualified URL. This URL points to the parent Record of the current Record object. The ParentURL can be an empty string if there is no parent for the current Record object.

The RecordType Property

This read-only property specifies the type of the record represented by the Record object. RecordType has the RecordTypeEnum type and can have one of the following values:

Constant	Value	Meaning
adSimpleRecord	0	The type of the record is simple record. Such records do not contain child records.
adCollectionRecord	I	The type of the record is collection record. Such records contain child records.
adStructDoc	2	The type of the record represents the COM structured storage documents and may contain child records.

The Source Property

This property contains the value of the Source argument passed to the Open method. The Source property can be either an absolute or relative URL, or an IDispatch reference to the opened Recordset object.

To get the value of this property in Delphi, we use the Get_Source method that returns an OleVariant value. To set the value of the Source property as a URL, we must use the _Set_Source method; if we refer to the opened Recordset object, we must use the Set_Source method.

The State Property

This read-only property indicates the state of the Record object. Since this object can execute asynchronous methods, we can use the State property to find whether the object is connecting, executing, or retrieving data.

The State property can have one of the following values:

Constant	Value	Meaning
adStateClosed	0	The Record object is closed.
adStateOpen	I	The Record object is open.
asStateConnecting	2	The Record object is connecting to the data source.
adStateExecuting	4	The Record object executes the command.
adStateFetching	8	The Record object is fetching records.

The default value for this property is adStateClosed.

Collections

The Record object has two collections: the Fields collection, which is described in the section below, and the standard Properties collection.

The Fields Collection

This collection contains one or more Field objects that represent a column in a record. The Count property indicates the number of Field objects in this collection, while the Item property provides access to the particular Field object with which we are already familiar. The methods available for the Fields collection are listed in the following table:

Method	Description
Append	Appends a newly created Field object to the collection
CancelUpdate	Cancels changes in the existing or new Field object after the Update method was called
Delete	Removes the Field object from the collection
Refresh	Updates the collection. To make changes in the Fields collection visible, use the Requery method of the Recordset object
Resync	Resynchronizes the Fields collection
Update	Updates the Fields collection

The Stream Object

The Stream object is used in conjunction with the Record object to access the binary data associated with the record. In addition, the Stream object can be used as is to manipulate binary data without referring to the Record object. This gives us the ability to manipulate binary and text files through the same object model as used for the database manipulation.

In this section, we will look at the methods and properties of the Stream object.

Methods

The Stream object exposes 13 methods, which are described below.

The Cancel Method

This method cancels an asynchronous operation that is initiated with a call to the Open method. In this case the adOpenStreamAsync option is used. See the Open method below.

The Close Method

This method closes the previously opened Stream and frees any associated system resources. Note that this method does not remove the object from memory, and this object can be reopened later by calling the Open method.

The CopyTo Method

Use this method to copy the specified number of bytes (characters) from the current Stream to the one specified with the DestStream argument. The DestStream argument should specify the already opened stream.

The prototype of the CopyTo method is shown below:

```
procedure CopyTo(
 const DestStream: _Stream;
 CharNumber: Integer);
safecall;
```

The CopyTo method copies the specified number of bytes starting from the current Stream position and indicated by the Position property until all of the bytes are copied or the end of the Stream is reached. If the NumChars parameter is equal to –1, all of the bytes from the current position to the end of the Stream will be copied.

Note that the source and destination streams should be of the same type, i.e., both should be adTypeText or adTypeBinary; this can be found by checking the Type_ property of the Stream object.

The Flush Method

Use the Flush method to send the contents of the Stream buffer to the underlying object associated with the Stream. Note that in most of the cases ADO flushed the contents of the Stream buffer itself and there is no need to call this method. Calling the Close method also flushes the Stream buffer.

The LoadFromFile Method

This method is used to load the contents of the file into a Stream object. The file, specified in the FileName argument, must exist.

The prototype of this method is shown below:

```
procedure LoadFromFile(const FileName: WideString); safecall;
```

After calling this method, all of the previous contents of the Stream will be replaced with the contents of the file, and the current positions (the Position property) will be set at the beginning of the Stream.

The Open Method

The Open method is used to open a Stream. The prototype of this method is shown below:

```
procedure Open(
 Source: OleVariant; Mode: ConnectModeEnum;
 Options: StreamOpenOptionsEnum;
 const UserName: WideString; const Password: WideString);
safecall;
```

The Open method takes five parameters that are described in the following table:

Argument	Type	Meaning
Source	OleVariant	Specifies the source of the binary data for the Stream. This can be an absolute URL or a reference to the already opened Record object.

Argument	Type	Meaning
Mode	ConnectModeEnum	Indicates the access mode for the resulting opened Stream object. See the Record.Open method for more details.
Options	StreamOpenOptionsEnum	Specifies the options that can be used to open the Stream. See table below for more details.
UserName	WideString	Specifies an optional user ID that may be needed to access the Source.
Password	WideString	Specifies an optional password that may be needed along with the user ID to access the Source.

The Options argument specifies the options that can be used to open the Stream. It can have one of the following values:

Constant	Value	Meaning
AdOpenStreamUnspecified	-1	The Stream object will be opened with the default options.
adOpenStreamAsync	1	The Stream object will be opened in asynchronous mode.
AdOpenStreamFromRecord	4	The Stream object will be opened and associated with the contents of the Record object.

Note that when we use the Record object as a supplier of the Stream content, we don't need to use the UserName and Password arguments since the Record object is already open. In this case, the access mode of the Record object will be used as the access mode for the Stream object.

When there is no Source argument specified, the Open method will create an empty Stream.

The Read Method

This method is used to read the specified number of bytes (NumBytes argument) from the opened Stream into a variable of the OleVariant type.

The prototype for this method is shown below:

```
function Read(NumBytes: Integer): OleVariant; safecall;
```

If the number of bytes to read is not specified, the whole contents of the Stream will be returned.

The ReadText Method

Use this method instead of the Read method to extract the specified number of characters (NumChars argument) from the text Stream.

The prototype for this method is shown below:

```
function ReadText(NumChars: Integer): WideString; safecall;
```

To read the entire line, we can use the adReadLine constant instead of the number of characters. The adReadAll constant indicates that we need to extract the entire contents of the Stream.

The SaveToFile Method

The SaveToFile method saves the contents of the opened Stream into a file specified by the FileName argument. The second argument, Options, indicates how the file will be created. It can have the following values:

Constant	Value	Meaning
AdSaveCreateNotExist	1	If the specified file does not exist, it will be created.
AdSaveCreateOverWrite	2	If the specified file exists, its contents will be overwritten.

The prototype for this method is shown below:

```
procedure SaveToFile(
 const FileName: WideString; Options: SaveOptionsEnum);
safecall;
```

After the contents of the Stream are saved to a file, the Stream position is set to the beginning of the Stream.

The SetEOS Method

Use the SetEOS method to truncate the open Stream. This method changes the value of the EOS property to the value currently stored in the Position property, making the current position the end of the stream. All data after the end of stream will be lost.

The SkipLine Method

The SkipLine method can be used with the text Stream to skip the entire line while reading from it.

The Write Method

This method writes the contents of the buffer (Buffer argument of the OleVariant type) to the Stream object.

The prototype for this method is shown below:

```
procedure Write(Buffer: OleVariant); safecall;
```

The Write method can be used to replace data in the Stream or to append the data to the end of the Stream; this depends on the current position in the Stream before calling the Write method.

The WriteText Method

Use the WriteText method to write a string to the text Stream. The Options argument specifies whether the line separator will be written to the Stream along with the string. It can have the following values:

Constant	Value	Meaning
adWriteChar	0	Only the specified text string will be written to the Stream.
adWriteLine	1	The text string and the line separator will be written to the Stream.

The prototype for this method is shown below:

```
procedure WriteText(
 const Data: WideString; Options: StreamWriteEnum);
safecall;
```

The WriteText method can be used to replace data in the Stream, or to append the data to the end of the Stream; this depends on the current position in the Stream before calling the WriteText method.

Properties

The Stream object exposes eight properties that are described below.

The Charset Property

This property is used to find the current character set used by the text Stream object or to change it. The data in the text Stream object is stored as Unicode; the Charset property only translates the Unicode data into one of the character sets specified as its value. Before changing the current character set of the Stream, set its Position property to 0 (zero).

The default value for this property is "Unicode," but it can be any of the valid MIME character set strings like "windows-1250," "DOS-862," or "iso-8859-2." To find the MIME character sets supported on your computer, check the following System Registry entry:

```
HKEY_CLASSES_ROOT\MIME\Database\Charset
```

or use the following code to obtain this list programmatically:

```
// Add Registry in the Uses clause

procedure TForm1.Button1Click(Sender: TObject);
const
 MIMECS = 'MIME\Database\Charset';
 Line   = '%25s' + #9 + '%d';
var
 R    : TRegistry;
 L    : TStringList;
 I,CP : Integer;
 S    : String;
begin
 R := nil;
 L := nil;
 try
```

```
  R := TRegistry.Create;
  L := TStringList.Create;
  R.RootKey := HKEY_CLASSES_ROOT;
  R.OpenKey(MIMECS, False);
  R.GetKeyNames(L);
  L.Sort;
  R.CloseKey;
  For I := 0 to L.Count-1 do
   begin
    R.OpenKey(MIMECS + '\' + L[I], False);
// If this is not the charset alias
    If R.ReadString('AliasForCharset') = '' Then
     begin
// find the code page associated with it
      CP := R.ReadInteger('CodePage');
      Memo1.Lines.Add(Format(Line, [L[I], CP]));
     end;
    R.CloseKey;
   end;
 finally
  L.Free;
  R.Free;
 end;
end;
```

The EOS Property

This property indicates whether we are at the end of the Stream. As we already know, we can truncate the Stream by calling the SetEOS method. In this case, the EOS property will be True.

The LineSeparator Property

The LineSeparator property is used to specify the character that will be used as a line separator in the text Stream object. The possible values for this property are shown in the table below:

Constant	Value	Meaning
adCRLF	-1	Carriage return/line feed pair will be used as a line separator. This is the default value.
adLF	10	Line feed symbol will be used as a line separator.
adCR	13	Carriage return symbol will be used as a line separator.

The Mode Property

This property indicates the permissions for the Stream object. If the Stream object is associated with the Record, the default value for this property is adReadOnly; otherwise the default value is adModeUnknown. For the closed Stream object, this property is read/write and it is read-only when the object is open.

The Mode property can be changed with a call to the Open method described above.

The Position Property

The Position property indicates the current position in the opened Stream object. The zero (0) value indicates the beginning of the Stream. A value greater than zero means the number of bytes from the beginning of the Stream.

Note that for both binary and text streams this property is measured in bytes. If you use the text streams with multi-byte characters, you must multiply the Position property by the character size to find the character number in the Stream.

The Size Property

This property indicates the size of the opened Stream, i.e., the number of bytes within it. This property will have the value –1 if the size of Stream is unknown.

The State Property

Use this property to find the current state of the Stream object. Generally, the State property indicates whether the object is opened or closed. If we are using asynchronous operations, we can also determine whether the Stream object is connecting, executing, or fetching. In this case, the State property will be the combination of adStateOpen and a constant that indicates what the object is doing.

The Type_ Property

This property indicates the type of the Stream and the data contained in it. The possible values for this property are shown in the table below:

Constant	Value	Meaning
adTypeBinary	1	This is the binary Stream.
adTypeText	2	This is the text Stream.

Note that the value of this property can be changed only when the current position is at the beginning of the Stream.

Inside the New ADO 2.5 Objects

In Chapter 2, we saw how ADO objects use OLE DB interfaces. To complete this topic, let's briefly look at the inner workings of the new ADO 2.5 objects.

As we already know, ADO is the high-level, object-oriented interface to the OLE DB objects that do the real job of connecting to a data source through the OLE DB provider, extracting data, and performing other data manipulation functions. This means that mostly all of the new features in ADO are implemented on a low level through the appropriate OLE DB interfaces and its methods.

The new ADO objects described above—the Record object and the Stream object—are based on the Record and Stream objects implemented in OLE DB. The OLE DB Row object can be used to create semistructured data stores and includes direct

URL binding support. *Binding* is the process of associating an OLE DB object with a resource named by a URL. OLE DB objects that bind resources named by URL to other OLE DB objects are called *binder objects*. OLE DB 2.5 includes the following binder objects: IBindResource (used to bind to an object named by a URL), ICreateRow (creates and binds to an object named by a URL), and IDBBinderProperties (manipulates binding properties).

The OLE DB Row object contains a set of columns of data and can represent a row in a rowset, the result of a SQL SELECT query, or a node in a tree-structured data-like file within a file system or a message in a mail folder.

The Stream object encapsulates the contents of files, messages, or other streamed objects. This object exposes the IStream interface and can be created from a Row object. All stream objects must expose the ISequentialStream interface that provides forward only reading and writing. The source Row object for a stream can be obtained with a call to the IGetSourceRow.GetSourceRow method. The Row object can then be opened with a call to the IRow.Open method.

To bind to a row, the IBindResource.Bind, ICreateRow.CreateRow, and IScopedOperations.Bind methods are used. For more information on these new OLE DB objects and interfaces, refer to the *OLE DB Programmer's Reference*, which is part of the Microsoft Platform SDK.

To be able to function, ADO 2.5 uses the following OLE DB interfaces: IBindResource, IColumnsInfo, ICreateRow, IDBBinderProperties, and IRow. The new ADO Record object relies on the following methods of OLE DB interfaces:

ADO Record Object	OLE DB Interfaces/Methods
CopyRecord Method	IScopedOperations.Copy
DeleteRecord Method	IScopedOperations.Delete
GetChildren Method	IBindResource.Bind
MoveRecord Method	IScopedOperatons.Move
Open Method	IBindResource.Bind
ParentURL Property	IRow.GetColumns
State Property	IDBAsynchStatus.GetStatus

The other methods, properties, and collections of the Record object are implemented on the ADO level and do not have corresponding OLE DB counterparts.

The ADO Stream object's functionality is based on the IStream OLE DB interface. It uses the following methods of OLE DB interfaces:

ADO Stream Object	OLE DB Interfaces/Methods
CopyTo Method	IStream.CopyTo
Open Method	IBindResource.Bind
Read Method	IStream.StatIStream.Read
SetEOS Method	IStream.SeekIStream.SetSize
SkipLine Method	IStream.SeekIStream.Read
Write Method	IStream.Write
EOS Property	IStream.StatIStream.Seek

ADO Stream Object	OLE DB Interfaces/Methods
Position Property	IStream.Seek
Size Property	IStream.SetSize
State Property	IDBAsynchStatus.GetStatus

The other methods and properties of the Stream object are implemented on the ADO level and do not have corresponding OLE DB counterparts.

OLE DB Provider for Internet Publishing

In Chapter 3, we briefly mentioned the OLE DB Provider for Internet Publishing that can be used to connect to Web servers and access HTML files and folders. Since this provider is widely used by the new ADO 2.5 objects, let's look at it in more detail.

To be able to be "visible" through the OLE DB Provider for Internet Publishing, the Web servers must support either the FrontPage Web Extender Client (WEC) or Web Distributed Authoring and Versioning (WebDAV) protocol extensions.

OLE DB Provider for Internet Publishing requires Microsoft Internet Explorer 5.0 to be installed on the computer. In addition to providing access to folders and files, the provider implements the Windows Explorer Shell Extension called Web Folders.

This provider works on many operating systems and with several Web servers. Here is the list of the platforms supported by the OLE DB Provider for Internet Publishing:

- Microsoft Internet Information Server 4.0 and FrontPage 98
- Microsoft Internet Information Server 4.0 and FrontPage 2000; requires Service Pack 4
- Microsoft Internet Information Server 4.0 and Office 2000 Server Extensions; requires Service Pack 4
- Microsoft Internet Information Server 5.0
- Apache Web Server 1.2 and FrontPage 2000
- Netscape Enterprise Server 3.0 and FrontPage 2000
- Netscape FastTrack Server 2.0 and FrontPage 2000
- O'Reilly WebSite 1.2 and FrontPage 2000
- Stronghold Apache-SSL Web Server 2.0 and FrontPage 2000

The OLE DB Provider for Internet Publishing is shipped as part of the Windows 2000 operating system, Microsoft Internet Explorer 5.0. and Microsoft Office 2000.

- In Windows 2000, the OLE DB Provider for Internet Publishing 1.5 is installed by default.
- The OLE DB Provider for Internet Publishing 1.0 is installed with the typical installation of Microsoft Internet Explorer 5.0.
- The OLE DB Provider for Internet Publishing 1.0 is installed with Microsoft Office 2000 only as part of Microsoft Internet Explorer 5.0 installation.

Supported Methods, Properties, and Collections

Not all of the ADO methods are supported by the OLE DB Provider for Internet Publishing. Here is a list of unsupported or partially supported ADO methods:

ADO Object	Method
Command	CreateParameter
Command	Cancel
Command	Execute; only the adCmdText option is supported
Connection	BeginTrans
Connection	Cancel
Connection	CommitTrans
Connection	Execute; only the adCmdText option is supported
Connection	RollBackTrans
Field	ReadFromFile
Field	WriteToFile
Parameter	AppendChunk
Recordset	Cancel
Recordset	NextRecordset
Recordset	Resync

The list below shows properties currently not supported by the OLE DB Provider for Internet Publishing:

Command.CommandTimeout	Command.State
Connection.CommandTimeout	Connection.DefaultDatabase
Connection.IsolationLevel	Error.HelpContext
Error.HelpFile	Error.SQLState
Field.DataFormat	Parameter.Attributes
Parameter.Direction	Parameter.Name
Parameter.NumericScale	Parameter.Precision
Parameter.Size	Parameter.Type
Parametet.Value	Recordset.AbsolutePage
Recordset.AbsolutePosition	Recrodset.DataMember
Recordset.DataSource	Recordset.MarshalOptions
Recordset.MaxRecords	Recordset.PageCount
Recordset.PageSize	Recordset.StayInSync

Note that since the current version of the OLE DB Provider for Internet Publishing does not support parameters, the following collections are not implemented: Command.Parameters and Parameter.Properties.

Now that we have discussed the new objects in ADO 2.5, and their methods, properties, and collections, we can create several examples that will show these two objects in action. This is the topic for the next part of this chapter.

ADO 2.5 Usage Examples

The first example will show how to use the new Record object to extract folders and file data from the Web server. To give us the luxury of skipping arguments that are not essential for particular method calls, we will use `Variants` instead of real object types. First, we need a set of global variables:

```
var
 Rec  : Variant;  // ADO 2.5 Record Object
 RSet : Variant;  // ADO RecordSet
```

Now, we can write some code that will create a new Record object and fill it with information from the specified URL. To do this, we will create a procedure called OpenRs, that takes three arguments: the URL argument that will specify the URL to open, the Path argument to specify the filename to open, and the List argument that indicates where to store the list of files and subfolders for the current URL.

```
procedure TForm1.OpenRS(URL, Path : Variant;List : TStrings);
begin
 List.Clear;
 List.Add('..');
// Create an instance of the Record object
  Rec  := CoRecord_.Create;
// and an instance of the RecordSet object
  RSet := ADODB_TLB.CoRecordSet.Create;
// Open an URL
  Rec.Open(Path, URL);
 try

  Edit1.Text := URL + Path;
  Case Rec.RecordType of
   adCollectionRecord :
   begin
// Get subfolders and files if any
    RSet := Rec.GetChildren;
    While Not RSet.EOF do
    begin
//  and show them in the list
     List.Add(RSet.Fields[0].Value);    // Add display name
     ParentURL := RSet.Fields[1].Value; // Save ParentURL
     RSet.MoveNext;
    end;
   end;
   adSimpleRecord : ShowContents(Rec);
   adStructDoc    : ShowMessage('StructDoc');
  end;
  finally
```

```
    Rec.Close;
  end;
end;
```

Now we can call this procedure with the following code:

```
OpenRS('URL=http://localhost', '', ListBox1.Items);
```

This will display the list of folders and files in the root directory of the specified Web server, as shown below:

Note that we have added one more item at the top of the list. This item ("..") will allow us to go back to the parent folder. Now we need the code to traverse the directory. We will implement it in the OnClick event handler for the ListBox component. Here is the code for this event:

```
procedure TForm1.ListBox1Click(Sender: TObject);
begin
 With ListBox1 do
 If ItemIndex = 0 Then
  OpenRS('URL='+ParentURL, '', ListBox1.Items)
 Else
  OpenRS('URL='+ParentURL, Items[ItemIndex], ListBox1.Items);
end;
```

Note that for the first item in the list box (its ItemIndex is equal to 0) we call the OpenRs procedure with the empty Path argument, while for the other items we simply supply the name. This allows us to get the list of subfolders and files within the subfolders.

As you can see from the code for the OpenRs procedure, if we have a file (i.e., the Record type is equal to adSimpleRecord), we call the ShowContents procedure that outputs the contents of the file into the Memo component. To be able to do so, we use another new object in ADO 2.5—the Stream object. Here is the code for this procedure:

```
procedure TForm1.ShowContents(R: Variant);
var
 S : Variant;      // ADO 2.5 Stream Object
begin
 Memo1.Clear;
// Create an instance of the Stream object
  S := CoStream.Create;
// Open underlying stream
  S.Open(R, adModeRead, adOpenStreamFromRecord);
 try
// as text file
  S.Type    := adTypeText;
  S.CharSet := 'ascii';
// ... and show its contents
  Memo1.Text := S.ReadText(adReadAll);
 finally
  S.Close;
 end;
end;
```

Note how we open the Stream associated with the Record by supplying it as the first argument of the Open method. In the following section, we will see how to use the Stream object to work with files, rather than the data associated with the particular Record. Also note that in the code above we explicitly set the stream type as text. This allows us to get the contents of any file, not just a text file like HTML file, ASP file, or JavaScript file. To make the code more flexible, we must check the Type property.

Using a Stand-alone Stream

Now let's look at how we can use the Stream object as is, i.e., without associating it with the Record object. The first step is to create a new Stream. The following code shows how to do this:

```
var
 S : Variant;

// Create an instance of the Stream object
 S := CoStream.Create;
// Open it ..
 S.Open;
// .. and specify its character set
 S.Charset := 'Windows-1251';
```

By default, this will be the text Stream, so we can use the WriteText method to add some data into it. The following line of code shows how to use the contents of the Memo component for this purpose:

```
S.WriteText(Memo1.Text);
```

Now we can rewind the current position to the beginning of the stream, and read the data back to the Memo component:

```
S.Position := 0;
Memo1.Text := S.ReadText;
```

The contents of the stream can be saved to the file:

```
S.SaveToFile('c:\s.txt');
```

then reloaded from it:

```
S.LoadFromFile('c:\s.txt');
```

After we have finished with the stream, we should close it:

```
S.Close;
```

Above we have seen the set of basic operations that can be performed with the stand alone Stream object. By combining this with the ability to represent the data associated with the Record object, we get nearly endless opportunities to create new types of business applications.

Conclusion

In this chapter, we learned about the new features in the ADO 2.5. We have seen the properties and methods of the new Record and Stream objects and new and modified methods of the Fields collection. We also discussed some basic changes in OLE DB, as well as implementation details of the OLE DB Provider for Internet Publishing. After this introduction, we also saw some examples of the new Record and Stream objects that were used to open files and folders on the Web server.

BDE TO ADO MIGRATION ISSUES

This appendix contains information about using ADO and BDE data access to different databases, as well as some general recommendations for new and existing applications.

Paradox and dBase

The following two tables contain information on the data access mechanisms available for these databases, and what the specific requirements are for them.

dBase

Dbase Version	OLE DB Provider for ODBC Drivers		Native OLE DB Providers	Native BDE 5.1 Driver
	Read-only	Read/Write		
III	√	BDE 4.x or later required	-	√
III+	√	BDE 4.x or later required	-	√
IV	√	BDE 4.x or later required	-	√
5	√	BDE 4.x or later required	-	√
7	BDE 4.x or later required	BDE 4.x or later required	-	√
7.5	BDE 5.x or later required	BDE 5.x or later required	-	√

Paradox

Paradox Version	OLE DB Provider for ODBC Drivers		Native OLE DB Providers	Native BDE 5.1 Driver
	Read-only	Read/Write		
3	√	BDE 4.x or later required	-	√
4	√	BDE 4.x or later required	-	√
5	√	BDE 4.x or later required	-	√
7	BDE 4.x or later required	BDE 4.x or later required	-	√
8	BDE 4.x or later required	BDE 4.x or later required	-	√
9	BDE 5.x or later required	BDE 5.x or later required	-	√

Note: The Microsoft Jet 4.0 database engine, used with ODBC drivers for desktop databases, supports importing, exporting to, and linking to Paradox 3.x, 4.x, and 5.x and dBASE III, III+, IV, and 5 tables, and, when we link to these tables, the data in them will be read-only. Microsoft Jet 4.0 does not support Paradox 7 and 8 or dBASE 7 tables. For read/write access from Microsoft Jet to all versions of Paradox or dBASE tables, we must also have the Borland Database Engine (BDE) 4.x or later installed on our computer.

We have seen that these two DBMSs requires BDE for full access even using OLE DB and ADO. However, BDE is not required if we need only to move data from these DBMSs to another one.

Note that you may consider the CodeBase database engine as a replacement for dBase, FoxPro, and Clipper files access. For example, it contains ODBC drivers for the databases mentioned above, as well as xBASE-compatible OLE DB provider and a set of Delphi components. For more information, visit Sequiter Software's Web site at `http://www.codebase.com` or Sandage & Associates' Web site at `http://www.softsand.com/` for details about CodeBase Delphi components.

InterBase

The following table contains information on the data access mechanisms available for different versions of this server.

InterBase Server Version	Native OLE DB Provider for InterBase in MDAC	OLE DB Provider for ODBC Drivers	BDE 5.1 (InterBase SQL Link)
4.0	-	√	√
5.0	-	√	√
5.1	-	√	√
5.5	-	√	√
5.6	-	√	√

For this DBMS, no OLE DB providers are available at this time. We can use the OLE DB Provider for ODBC drivers to access the Interbase data through ADO. However, it is preferable to access InterBase databases through BDE or using native components for direct access to InterBase engine (for example, using the components included with Delphi 5 Enterprise, or IB Objects by Jason Wharton, `http://www.ibobjects.com/`).

Microsoft Access

For obvious reasons, it is recommended you use ADO and OLE DB with databases created with Microsoft tools (Access, FoxPro and Visual FoxPro, MSDE, SQL Server). All of them are accessible either through native OLE DB providers or ODBC drivers.

The following table contains information on the data access mechanisms available for different versions of this DBMS.

Access Version	Jet 3.5 and 4.0 OLE DB Provider	Native BDE 5.1 Driver
Access 95	√	√ (Microsoft Jet engine 3.0 required)
Access 97	√	√ (Microsoft Jet engine 3.5 required)
Access 2000	√	-

When considering migration of your existing BDE-based Access application, it is strongly recommended you use ADO, because it is the only data access mechanism that supports most of the Access features.

Microsoft FoxPro / Visual FoxPro

The following table contains information on the data access mechanisms available for different versions of this DBMS.

FoxPro Version	Native OLE DB Provider	ODBC Driver	Native BDE 5.1 Driver
2.0	-	√	√
2.5	-	√	√
2.6	-	√	√
Visual FoxPro (all versions)	-	√	-

Microsoft SQL Server and MSDE

The following table contains information on the data access mechanisms available for different versions of this server.

Microsoft SQL Server Version	OLE DB Provider for SQL Server	ODBC Driver	Native BDE 5.1 Driver (Microsoft SQL Server SQL Link)
4.0		√	√
6.0	√	√	√
6.5	√	√	√
7.0	√	√	√ (implements only the MS-SQL Server 6.5 feature set)

When upgrading your old BDE applications with this DBMS, it is strongly recommended you migrate to ADO.

Oracle

The following table contains information on the data access mechanisms available for different versions of this server.

Oracle Server Version	OLE DB Provider for Oracle in MDAC	ODBC Driver	Native BDE 5.1 Driver (Oracle SQL Link)
7.0	√	√	√ (7.3 or later)
8.0	√ (Oracle 8 specific data types not supported)	√	√ (8.0.4 or later)

When selecting the data access mechanism for this DBMS, you need to take into account what features necessary for your application are supported with the particular OLE DB provider, BDE driver, or ODBC driver. For example, it is better to use BDE driver or native third-party components for Oracle direct access if we need to use Oracle 8 specific data types, and Microsoft ODBC driver for Oracle along with OLE DB Provider for ODBC drivers (or use Oracle 8i), if we are writing MTS objects for implementing distributed transactions. You may also consider Oracle's own OLE DB Provider, which is currently in beta.

Note that there are some sets of native access VCL components to work with Oracle, for example, Oracle Data Access Components (ODAC) by CoRe Lab Co. For more information, visit the company site at http://www.crlab.com

Sybase

The following table contains information on the data access mechanisms available for different versions of this server.

Sybase Server Version	OLE DB Provider for Sybase in MDAC	ODBC Driver	Native BDE 5.1 Driver (Sybase SQL Link)
4.0 (with DB-Lib interface)	-	√	√
System 10 and later with CT-Lib interface	-	√	√ (10.0.4 EBF7264 or higher)

Informix

The following table contains information on the data access mechanisms available for different versions of this server.

Informix Server Version	OLE DB Provider for Informix in MDAC	ODBC Driver	BDE 5.1 (Informix SQL Link)
7.0	-	√	√
9.0	-	√	√

You may consider Informix's own OLE DB Provider that can be used with Informix Dynamic Server, Version 7.3 or later, Informix Dynamic Server with Advanced Decision Support and Extended Parallel Options, Version 8.2 or later and Informix Dynamic Server with Universal Data Option, Version 9.14.UC5 or 9.14.TC4 or later. Informix OLE DB Provider is distributed with Informix Connect and the Informix Client Software Developer's Kit (SDK).

Informix OLE DB Provider supports an apartment threading model and local transactions. (Refer to Microsoft's COMspecification, available at its Web site, for more information about apartment threading.) Informix OLE DB Provider works with MTS (Microsoft Transaction Server) packages; however, pooling and distributed transaction support are not implemented in Version 2.0.

DB2

The following table contains information on the data access mechanisms available for different versions of this server.

DB2 Version	Native OLE DB Provider in MDAC	OLE DB Provider for ODBC Drivers	BDE 5.1 (InterBase SQL Link)
DB2 for NT, OS/2, IBM MVS, or AS/400	- (available from vendor)	√	√

 Note: OLE DB Provider for DB2 (IBMDA400) is available at IBM Web site at the following address: `http://www.as400.ibm.com/ClientAccess/oledb`

General Recommendations for New Applications

In general, when creating a new application, the following issues should be taken into account.

- It is recommended you use BDE with databases created with DBMS by Inprise (or companies that now own these products), such as dBase, Paradox, or InterBase.

Please note that using dBase and Paradox with Jet database engine requires BDE installed if we need a read/write access. This produces a mix of two data access technologies resulting a non effective work.

■ It is recommended you use ADO and OLE DB with databases produced by Microsoft DBMS (Access, FoxPro and Visual FoxPro, MSDE, Microsoft SQL Server). All of them are accessible either through OLE DB providers or ODBC drivers; when upgrading old BDE-based applications that use such databases, it is strongly recommended you migrate to ADO.

■ When developing an application for the Windows 2000 operating system family, it is recommended you take into account that ADO 2.5 is installed as part of the operating system and there is no need to perform extra deployment steps.

■ For all server DBMS, ODBC drivers or OLE DB providers are available, so it is possible to use both BDE and ADO in applications with such databases. When selecting what to use, BDE driver or OLE DB provider, it is recommended you check whether the features necessary for your application are supported. See Chapter 3 and Appendix H (on the CD) for more details.

■ Native interfaces, implemented in third-party or DBMS vendor VCL components (e.g., for InterBase or Oracle), can be preferable in the case of using the specific DBMS.

Generally, when selecting the data access technology for a new application, we need to take into account the availability of BDE drivers and OLE DB providers (and their architecture) for the selected DBMS, as well as features required by the application and supported in these drivers.

Migrating Existing Applications

When we need to move from BDE to ADO, we need to take into account that the TADOTable, TADOQuery, and TADOStoredProc components were specially designed to replace its BDE counterparts, namely TTable, TQuery, and TStoredProc.

However, these components are not fully compatible because of their different implementations. For example, comparing source code for TTable and TADOTable components, we have found nearly 90 differences in methods, properties, and events that are available for one of these two components and absent for the other—this results from the architecture differences of these two data access technologies.

There is not a direct analogy in ADO components for TUpdateSQL component. Instead, use the TADOCommand or TADODataSet components with appropriate CommandText property. You can also use Dynamic Properties to tell ADO which tables or fields will be used in an update. To use cached updates, it is possible to use TADODataSet component with the LockType property equal to ltBatchOptimistic, and use the UpdateBatch method to update multiple records in a single operation.

Also, there is no direct analogy for the TBatchMove component; however, we can implement the same functionality manually if necessary. Note that there is no SQL Monitor, Decision Cube support, or Data Dictionary support for ADO applications.

In general, when moving your legacy application from BDE to ADO, it is recommended you rewrite its code in order to get the most from the ADO features.

Index

Wordware Delphi Library

Wordware Publishing, Inc., a rapidly growing publisher of intermediate to advanced level computer books in Plano, Texas, has established a strong presence in the Delphi developer book market with the Tomes of Delphi series. The majority of the books in this series are ideally suited for experienced Delphi programmers and developers and include CDs. Many of the authors are well-known in the Delphi community including John Ayres, Alan Moore, John Penman, Warren Rachele, and Julian Bucknall. The Wordware spring 2000 Delphi list is very robust with a number of new titles and revisions of best-sellers. If you have any questions about the Wordware computer book publishing program, please contact Jim Hill at jhill@wordware.com or 1-800-229-4949.

Tomes of Delphi: Win32 Graphics Programming
Larry Rutledge

This reference to the graphics file formats used in the Delphi development environment targets experienced programmers and developers.

1-55622-722-1 $49.95
Fall 2000   CD Included

Delphi Developer's Guide to Communications
Alan Moore, John Penman and Chad Hower

Focuses on the use of Win32 Delphi from a communications perspective for experienced Delphi programmers and developers.

1-55622-752-3 $54.95
Fall 2000   CD Included

Learn Object Pascal
Warren Rachele

This introduction to Object Pascal is organized in two parts: a step-by-step tutorial and a reference section for experienced programmers.

1-55622-719-1 $32.95
Summer 2000   CD Included

Advanced Delphi Developer's Guide to ADO
Alex Fedorov and Natalia Elmanova

Targets Delphi programmers and developers who are interested in database programming in Microsoft Universal Data Access architecture.

1-55622-758-2 $49.95
Summer 2000   CD Included

The Tomes of Delphi 3: Win32 Graphical API
John Ayres, et al.

Describes the graphical Win32 API functions used to display graphics and user interface elements.

1-55622-610-1 $54.95
Available Now   CD Included
Revision Due Summer 2000

The Tomes of Delphi 3: Win32 Core API
John Ayres, et al.

A concise, detailed reference manual for using 32-bit Windows API functions in the Delphi 3 development environment.

1-55622-556-3 $54.95
Available Now   CD Included
Revision Due Summer 2000

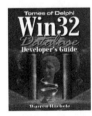

Tomes of Delphi: Win32 Database Developer's Guide
Warren Rachele

Describes the theory and nature of relational databases, including a full chapter on SQL.

1-55622-663-2 $39.95
Available Now   CD Included

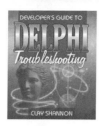

Developer's Guide to Delphi Troubleshooting
Clay Shannon

Focuses on design-time errors, compile-time errors, and run-time errors, providing concise and easy-to-locate solutions.

1-55622-647-0 $49.95
Available Now   CD Included
Revision Due Winter 2000

Nathan Wallace's Delphi 3 Example Book
Nathan Wallace

A well-organized programmer's reference that includes brief code examples for all language and component library items.

1-55622-490-7 $54.95
Available Now   CD Included

Delphi Graphics and Game Programming Exposed!
John Ayres

A tutorial and reference describing high-performance graphics and game programming techniques; covers DirectX 5.0 to 7.0

1-55622-637-3 $54.95
Available Now   CD Included

Learn Graphics File Programming with Delphi 3
Derek A. Benner

Details ObjectPascal source code for eleven of the most popular graphics file types and includes a sample viewer application to serve as a framework.

1-55622-558-X $49.95
Available Now   CD Included

Collaborative Computing with Delphi 3
James Callan

Provides practical examples, especially with SQL, to impart the concept of team-based software development.

1-55622-554-7 $59.95
Available Now   CD Included

Delphi Developer's Guide to OpenGL
Jon Q. Jacobs

A step-by-step review of OpenGL programming with any 32-bit version of Delphi, including Delphi 3 and 4 and future versions.

1-55622-657-8 $49.95
Available Now   CD Included

Tomes of Delphi: Algorithms and Data Structures
Julian Bucknall

Comprehensive coverage of such topics as arrays, binary trees, data compression, and other advanced topics.

1-55622-736-1 $59.95
Fall 2000   CD Included

Tomes of Delphi: Win32 Multimedia API
Alan C. Moore, Ph.D.

Provides information on using 32-bit Windows multimedia API functions to incorporate audio into Delphi applications.

1-55622-666-7 $59.95
Summer 2000   CD Included

ibooks.com offers you the best selection of on-line digital IT reference books.

ibooks•com
Changing the world one book at a time.™

A full-service e-book source that gives you:

- browsing capability
- full-text searching
- "try-before-you-buy" previews
- customizable personal library
- wide selection of free books

www.ibooks.com
512-478-2700

I don't have time for learning curves.

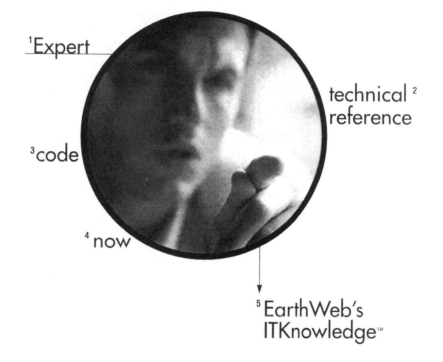

[1]Expert

technical [2]
reference

[3]code

[4] now

[5] EarthWeb's
ITKnowledge℠

They rely on you to be the **1** expert on tough development challenges. There's no time for learning curves, so you go online for **2** technical references from the experts who wrote the books. Find answers fast simply by clicking on our search engine. Access hundreds of online books, tutorials and even source **3** code samples **4** now. Go to **5** EarthWeb's ITKnowledge, get immediate answers, and get down to it.

Get your FREE ITKnowledge trial subscription today at itkgo.com.
Use code number 026.

©1999 EarthWeb Inc. All rights reserved. EarthWeb's ITKnowledge is a service mark of EarthWeb, Inc. EarthWeb and the EarthWeb logo are registered trademarks of EarthWeb Inc

EARTHWEB
Go further *faster*

About the CD

The companion CD-ROM contains all of the source code from the book, Appendices B through I in PDF format, the Adobe Acrobat reader, and a 60-day trial version of Delphi 5.0 Enterprise edition. The files are organized as follows:

- Appendices PDF—Appendices B through I in PDF format. See the introduction for more information about the appendices.
- Code—The source code used throughout the book.
- Delphi 5.0 Enterprise Demo—The 60-day trial version of Delphi 5.0 Enterprise edition; you will need to register with Borland in order to use this software.
- AReader—The Adobe Acrobat reader to read the PDF files.
- Links—A file containing links to various Web sites.

For more information, see the introduction and the following Web site: http://d5ado.homepage.com.

 Warning: Opening the CD package makes this book nonreturnable.